The Ballad Of Rock.

by

M. A. Sloane

This book is dedicated to Adapt and its CEO Eddie Cobb who gave me a chance when no one else would.

Prologue

Clean day number 5. Sunday morning. No sleep, par for the course with the methadone though. And the spice (mamba) to be fair. Last night I was close to cracking. Marcus absolutely fucked out his head and temptation came a knocking but I held my line and wake up today with another day under me belt. Marcus got the pages of chemically (mamba) infused paper and though I struggle at times to maintain my sobriety there are of course perks to living in a cell with a drug dealer. A never ending supply of vape capsules, protein powders, supplements for training and the cell is well stocked with tuna, noodles, beans, sweets, coffee, milk, sugar and myriad other things which make life in here a little easier. Anyway, the reprobate is already highly intoxicated and telling me a tale after I ask him why it was he stabbed a fella we know called G---- about four years ago.

"Well", says this mong, out his fuckin' head right now, "I didn't stab him for nothing Sloaney".

"Yeah, but you stabbed him so bad in the arse cheek and the actual arse hole that he had to sit on a rubber ring for twelve weeks, that's what I heard anyway".

"I did Sloaney", he says, "but what you don't know is that when I was his mate in Dover one day he hit me around the head with a champagne bottle and I didn't see the cunt for two years".

"Fuck me, I'll bet you held a grudge knowing you", I say.

"You're fuckin' right I did but I got my chance and I got the cunt".

"How did you get the slippery cunt"? I ask Marcus and indeed G---- is a bit of a snake it must be said.

"Well, on the day I went to my nan's funeral I was coming back from Gravesend with Lauren and dropped her off at home. But I went back out in the Audi. I was driving toward Dane Park (a park in Margate) and saw him going into the entrance and it's dark now Sloaney. So, I park the Audi and follow on foot. He was with C----, his bird. I followed him, waiting 'till he was in the centre of the park ya know"?

"Well dark in there at night too", I interject.

"Yeah, right, anyway, I creep up on the cunt right Sloaney and I've got the kitchen knife in my hand now right so I creep, creep, creep and he don't see me or hear me and soon as I'm close enough I plunge the nine inch blade straight into his arse, draw the blade back again and aim for the centre of his arse and plunge again into the actual arse hole ya know"?

"Savage", I say.

"Yeah", he goes on, "he dropped to one knee and he wouldn't of even known it was me if I hadn't of said to him 'I'm gonna kill you you cunt'".

"Thank fuck you got a not guilty", I say.

"Yeah, but two weeks later I got him again in a traphouse where these Somalians from Woolwich were shotting (selling drugs) from".

"What d'ya do to him"? I say, the hairs on my arms standing on end.

"In the traphouse I found two carving knives and opened the cunt's face up, slicing him proper and with the knife in my other hand I go to plunge the cunt in the chest but one of the Somalis grabbed my arm, stopping the kill".

"What happened next"? I ask.

"Well, obviously these dangerous Somalis put all their tools, like their own tools in a bin in the bathroom and make me do the same like in a gun and knife amnesty thing and told me if you just calm down we'll give you as many snowballs as you like. They fed me copious amounts of crack and heroin and offered me work as a hitman to take out all the other drug dealers in the area. They fuckin' loved me man". This story has moved me for I only know a nice side of Marcus, the lost soul that has suffered so much but there is a dark side in stark contrast juxtaposed to his character for sure. The description of such savage violence is chilling, even for me, a violent man myself when pushed but unlike Marcus I have, thankfully, never had to use a knife though I have pulled a few on drug dealers.

Anyway, lunchtime now and we are banged up until two pm. Marcus has flopped and is dribbling like a special person having consumed 4mg of subutex, 300mg of pregablin, 4mg of clonazepam and all this atop the many joints of spice paper he has smoked already this Sunday morning. I have to accept I cannot escape the drugs being around me. I have thought of moving off to another wing but that is pointless for this is supposed to be the drug free wing so if it's flooded on here then, well, you do the math. No matter where I go it's there, as it is in every prison across the country right about now.

Book One.

A Portrait Of A Prison

I never went to school and I've no formal education. I am 42 years old and the year is 2018. I stand five eleven and am told I'm pretty. Anyway, that's by the by. I wish to tell a tale. A tale of a modern man. A man named Andrew. Get through the first 100 pages of this and you may find you enjoy it.

My mother was one of seventeen in a family from Ballyfermot in Dublin fair city. I think the four foot fuck all tiny woman was about tenth through her mother Josephine's birth canal. I dare say my Irish nan would of cut off an arm for a bit of birth control but the Ireland of old, still steeped in catholic bullshit would hear nothing of the word contraception. My father, born of an Italian serviceman and a Londoner during the war years is somewhat more of a mystery. My grandad, who wasn't my real one by blood was a Welshman who took on the scandal clad woman with the strange half Italian baby whose patriarchal predecessor she absolutely refused to discuss. It wasn't until first my Welsh grandad then shortly after my nan died that we got a look at our real grandad, my siblings and I. My sister has the one photograph found beneath the carpet of my nan's bedroom which she had occupied with my Welsh grandad for the best part of sixty years. My father, a handsome well-built beauty who sadly took his own life at the end of the nineties was known locally, so says my mother, as the 'Italian Stallion' and was a man who enjoyed multitudinous women through his life, siring children all across the British isles and leaving me and my brothers and sister with newly discovered siblings in the Republic of Ireland too. Anyway, I am the eldest of four. A mixed bag we are too, each with his own story to tell. For now though let me regale you with my particular tale, a true tale of prison life.

Right now I sit in a cell, HMP Rochester. My cellmate Aidy is talking animatedly as usual in his rapid rattle style, sputtering like a machine gun. He's a slim and wiry well-muscled dude of 44 standing about five feet nine. Looking at him makes me think of Road Runner for some reason. Quick witted and shifty he has given nicknames to others on the landings which stick and proliferate until the unfortunate, sometimes, recipient finds the rest of the wing and prison population calling them by the new name.

"You know that cunt Stuart Little"? he said earlier and I'd told him:

"I've no idea who the fuck you're talking about bro".

"The downsy little cunt with the soppy hippy hairdo, proper looks like he's down syndrome, oh, what's his fuckin' name again", then Aidy scratches his chin for a while before I see the light bulb appear above his head, "Aron, that's it".

"Why do you call him Stuart Little"? I ask.

"'Cause his name is Aron Little", and of course I get that.

"What about him" ?

"Had a spice spliff (mamba) with the idiot earlier in his cell and the cunt had a proper spaz attack. He was smashing his head off of the floor and screaming 'get 'em off of me man help help' and all that palava. Last time I ever have a joint with the twat again".

"Did you help him though Aid"?

"Did I fuck", says Aidy contemptuously, "I just shot out the cell rapid, fuck that shit man".

"Did you check to see if he was alright"? I ask concerned for the poor fella.

"Last I saw the screws were all in there with the medical staff. Shouldn't be such a greedy little cunt should he"? and of course this is a rhetorical question. Another of the nicknames concerns a fella up the landing who continuously slashes his arms and even his face horrifically with razor blades for whatever reason and Aidy has named him 'Cutyoucutme'; and one must think of the eighties hit 'say you, say me' to understand the denotation. Me and Aidy have actually come to dislike the cunt for he takes up much staff time, sometimes to the detriment of the rest of us on the wing. For when they are having to deal with him they can't unlock us for work or showers or exercise or whatever else the regime is at the time. The blood round the cunt's cell is savage and being a bit queasy I try not to look at the open wounds on his face and arms. As I sit and write away Aidy is talking and I catch snippets:

.............."we went and took the safe Sloaney ya know"..........

"Yep", I mumble without looking up.

"Took it to the traphouse and busted it open; fuck all in the cunt boy ya know, one a them ones".

"Shit man", I say absent mindedly.

"Craig came here earlier", he says now referring to the next door neighbour.

"Oh", I say, "why?

2

"Wanted a vape battery" he says "there were about seven of us in here all smoking spice hard and I think the cunt thought I was lying".

"We don't fuckin' use 'em, he should know that by now".

"That's what I mean man", says Aidy putting a cup of tea together. The cell is claustrophobic and originally built for one. The windows do not open here in Rochester and the only air is that which trickles through a barely fit for purpose grid making summer here an ordeal. X Factor catch up is on TV and some black beauty belts out a song which causes the hair on my body to stand on end. Robbie Williams and Simon Cowell on the judge's panel tell her they both just had 'a moment'. Aidy turns the TV over and the Flintstones movie is on and I look at Wilma causing a stirring in my sex starved loins.

"Wanna cup a tea"? asks Aidy whilst passing me another spice spliff.

"Nice one bro", and as I look at the TV my mind starts doing sexual somersaults with Wilma which gets me to thinking of the young wench I'd been poking and had sort of fallen in love with just prior to my incarceration. Unfortunately for me the chances of a nutter like her being faithful are slim for she likes to sniff copious amounts of coke before engaging in filthy frolicky fun involving her getting stuffed with cock and I'm damn sure she shan't be waiting for my seven inches. Tanya is her name and she is of Turkish Cypriot extraction. She is one sexy little fucker and has the lovliest bum I have ever seen on a female in all my 42 years. And of course she is exceptionally pretty, mouthy and opinionated too.....exactly my fuckin' type. I've 'known' Tanya for some time. I use the inverteds because though she was my cousin's girlfriend once we had never met anywhere else but in the digital realm. When she was with T----, my cousin, some ten years ago I remember looking at her in pictures posted on Facebook or Fuckbook as another ex of mine used to call the venerable platform. Scrolling through these images I'd clocked Tan next to T---- and thought 'fuck me she's a sort' and pulled up her own page to see more of the mischievous eyed little darling with the olive skin and perfectly proportioned five foot five frame with bumps and bits all in the right places and pointing in the right directions. She'd've been but 21 then for this was exactly ten years prior to me meeting her in the flesh. After my comprehensive Facebook stalking of her profile I'd engaged with her briefly over the years with small talk, not, of course, cracking onto her whilst she was with T----, and with him she was for the best part of ten years as I say. I remember thinking how lucky my little cousin was. Anyway forward a decade and whilst sat in another ex's flat I'd stumbled across her once again on the same site, seeing her posing beside foreign pools, bikini clad and clearly knowing the effect she has on men for in the background some stalky geezers can be seen staring at this

3

stand out sultress. Anyway, whilst at the ex Charlotte's I'd decided, noticing she was now single to try to throw a bit of bait out in the hope of a bite from the sexy wench. So, just prior to receiving a sentence of 27 months in the Crown Court for a burglary I'd done with T---- I'd fired some elusive nonchalant language across the fibre at her along the lines of: 'he must be a right cunt letting you go Tan as I doubt he'll bag another beauty like you' and when the fit as fuck little bit of fluff got back to me almost instantly I knew I'd half a chance of banging this beauty.

"Long time no hear", she'd said, "where are you these days then"? You really must picture this luscious thing to understand my excitement. Pretty high cheekboned face with large expressive almond eyes and a full mouth sheathing straight white perfect teeth. As I've said, banging arse but recently before my incarceration she and I had had this discussion:

"I'm thinking of getting my tits done", she'd said one day.

"Don't you fuckin' dare", I had responded immediately.

"Why not"? she replied naughtily.

"You know damn well why Tan; they're perfect and you know it", as indeed they are, just right, not too big nor too small and with nipples that point up to the ceiling, unravaged by the trauma of children. "It'd be sacrilege to fuck about with them Tan", and I meant it for his design here was point perfect. "Anyway Tan they're mine too so leave 'em the fuck alone" I'd half joked. Anyway, let me return to trying to get her to bite, before such convos were possible. So remember I've never met the bird in any realm but the digital though I'd comprehensively stalked her profile over the years. Seasoned digital stalker that I am. So whilst my best mate and ex-girlfriend Charlotte is out our ninth floor tower block flat shotting (selling crack cocaine and heroin to addicts) to cats I'd messaged her and she'd replied rapid with 'where are ya these days' and I'd said:

"Back in Thanet worst luck".

"Where abouts"? came the retort via Facebook's messenger.

"Millmead estate", I say.

"Millmead", comes the quick reply, "I'm in Millmead myself", and my heart misses a beat as I think to myself that with a bit a luck I could find myself hanging out the back of her!

"Fuck off", I say, "I'm in Invicta House on the ninth floor; where are you"?

"I'm in Elham Close", she says and this is literally a couple hundred yards across from where I am and can be seen from our back window, "second floor maisonette, I can see Invicta".

4

"I can see Elham", I say, "come to ya back window and look to the tower block, tell me if you can see a light going on and off"? I go to the light switch and flick it back and forth about three times and hear my phone burst into life on the bed before the window.

"What the fuck you doing"? asks Charlotte, a handsome blonde beauty now more than a sister to me; she'd dispensed with anything other many moons ago but we are extremely close.

"Nothing babe, just borrowing the bedroom, ya don't mind do ya"?

"'Course not ya wierdo, just got a few more shots to do so I'll be back in a bit babe yeah"?

"Cool Char cheers man; love you ya know"?

"I know ya do; how couldn't ya"? she says before flicking her blonde locks and firing out the door to deal drugs to the cats hungry for the food of crack and heroin that they so desperately need, much the same as me when on my binges. I pick up the phone and see a message from Tan which reads 'send your digits' and I do so without delay. Again, the phone bursts into life:

"Hello", I say and the sexy gravelly voice at the other end says:

"I saw the light, go to your window", and I do, immediately seeing across the way a light flashing on and off in the window of one of the maisonettes not three hundred metres or so from where I stand, gazing, now horny for the hot woman I'm getting the measure of.

"Hahaha man I see it I see it".

"Who'd of thought it"? says Tan over the air.

"Hold the line, just a minute", and I run to the kitchen to get my telescope. I'd brought the fine instrument to make the most of the view here in Terrible Towers, being a bit of a stargazer rather than the pervert others deduced I was when I returned with it! I set it down and aim it toward the window where I'd seen the light flickering on and off. I pick up the phone, happy the wench still holds the line and say:

"Still there Tan"?

"Yeah, why, what ya doing"?

"Come to the back window", I say.

"Ok", she says.

"Pull the nets aside so I can see ya".

"Ya won't be able to see me from there", she says but does as I ask anyway.

"Wow, pink knickers black bra, thought you'd be a matching kinda girl"!

"What the fuck"? she says, pulling down the nets, "how the fuck can you see me from there ya weirdo"?

"Brought myself a telescope the other day", I tell her and this causes peels of sexy gravelly throated laughter to emanate down the phone line before she says, "no fuckin' way ya strange cunt", and we both descend into raucous mirth before she says "you're fucked mate", and still I hear the delight in her throaty chuckle.

"Look Tan, what's the chances of me fuckin' you"?

"Pretty good at the moment", and we talk some more before Char returns to the flat and I end the call, looking up into my ex-lovers amused boat race.

"What"? I ask, her not yet having said a word but shaking her head ruefully.

"Andrew", she says, "do you think you're normal"?

"Well, not far off it Char yeah, I s'pose so"!

"Looking through a telescope at a woman you've never met and talking filth over the phone like a raving sex case you funny cunt", and she's genuinely amused as well as bemused at my slightly admittedly odd behaviour. "You do make me laugh ya freak"!

"Well, when you put it like that"........

"I do love you you fuckin' oddball", she says and I'm overwhelmed with love for her.

"Got a stone for me Char"? I ask, hoping for a rock of crack for free.

"Got a tenner"?

"Nope".

"Unlucky then", she says walking away and closing the bedroom door, ever the business woman. I muse to myself that she'll give me one later as I lay on the bed, put my hand down my trousers and play with myself whilst scrolling through pics of bikini clad Tan. Couple days later I was slamming the granny out of this pretty young thing!

So that indeed is how we came to be. A few weeks later I was living with this wildcat wench.

"Tan", I say one day with serious note in my baritone.

"Yeah", she says, fuckin' about chopping shit up in the kitchen, wicked little cookress that she is, "what's up cunt"?

"You know we've only been living together a few weeks yeah"?

"Spit it out for fuck sake", she says wishing me to cease going round the houses.

"Well, I want you to know before I go to jail that I appreciate what you've done for me; my last relationship didn't end so well".

"Punched that pretty blonde cunt didn't ya"? she says this as she attacks onions and peppers and sweet potatoes she's preparing for a stew. The smell of the lamb simmering in the slow cooker has me salivating.

"You know about that then"?

"Yeah", she says nonchalantly whilst slicing and dicing away, "kinda turns me on a bit if I'm honest with you", not looking up from the task in hand.

"Are you for fuckin' real ya mug"? and now she does turn round and has a saucy smile on her lovely face.

"Yeah a little bit", and she sort of chuckles, a little coy and embarrassed I guess but the next sentence throws me, "I want you to strangle the fuck out of me as you fuck me Andrew", and I splutter on the smoke from my cigarette.

"What", I say "for real"?

"Come here you sexy little cunt", she says and pulls the man's shirt she's wearing over her wholesome hips, puts a finger into her lacy sexy underwear, pulling them to the side as my loins immediately burst into life. She puts a finger into herself as I now sit stroking my seven before pulling it out glistening and saying:

"Stick that in me now", and she needn't ask twice as I'm up in a beat bending her over the worktop and sliding up inside her with an 'ahhhhhh' and proceeding to pump the fuck out the cute little thing, thrusting and pumping and pulling out then pulling her open with my fingers before smashing myself into her again and again until finally spending myself all up inside her, leaning onto her and panting with pleasure as pulses of ecstasy run through round and about my person, powerful orgasm leaving me truly spent.

"Now fuck off mug, I'm tryna cook ya cunt", and bemused I go back to the front room, roll a joint and luxuriate in the aftermath of the amorous activity, not at all sure I've managed to satisfy this wondrous wench. Never met one like it and I've been about a bit meself!

As I sit in this cell this lunchtime musing on these moments I have to remember I've a cell mate for as I write the remembering causes me to get hard. Fuckin' painful to recall as my balls are needing a barrow to carry the cunts right now. The door opens and I go to my maths class where I not only learn but help Ade, the Nigerian born blinder of a teacher to instruct the reprobates up to level two. Truth be known I'd never done any maths prior to this spell in prison and was somewhat scared of the subject. Now I'm at level two, the highest point possible in prison unfortunately, rather rapid but can't emphasize enough the fear the subject used to instil in me. Very basic stuff and I'll never be Stephen Hawking but hey, I'm teachable! A fella called Duncan who likes to be called Alex and has been dubbed 'DuncansAlex' by wiry Aidy was the one who got me into the class where I now help teach this magnificent subject.

"Come down Andy", he'd said to me in a cell one day whilst we sat smoking the spice hard.

"The subject absolutely terrifies me", I'd said with sincerity, "and it was on the TV the other day that the only subject that causes an emotional response in adults is maths"!

"Come on Sloaney, you're smart", says blond tall and handsome DuncansAlex, "if the muppets who're down there can do it I'm sure you can".

"I know I sound smart Dunc but the Universe gifted me with linguistics but when it comes to maths I'm a fuckin' retard man", I say all atremble at that feeling of stupidity I used to get when a kid in the classroom. Yet when I did sign up and attend a lesson I was amazed. In just two days I'd discovered long multiplication and division and had the ability to do all of the four main simple disciplines with fractions in whatever form they took, proper, improper etc etc. Now you may think that's' simple and it is! But only once you know how. Percentages and volumes and areas and even a little trigonometry came easy to me very quickly with this competent and loving Nigerian who even had the humility, when we started a cheeky look at level three stuff to admit that he was learning too the quick witted brilliant cunt! Anyway, let me tell a tale of how much the subject terrified me.

Another of my ex-girlfriends, the model blonde whom I did do damage with a punch after a crack, smack and booze binge had a little eight year old boy by the name of R----. Now the little boy used to regularly return home with his mum with the title of his class' 'maths king' for the week so quick of wit is he. This alone used to put me through some feelings! One day A----, the beautiful blonde broad asked if I could help R---- with his maths homework.

"Well, R----".........I'd started before his fine mum interjected with:

"'Course he will, won't you Andrew"? leaving me no wriggle room to extricate myself from this awful dilemma.

"Yay", shouts this magical little boy joyously and I'm thinking 'I'm fucked'! Sweat was pissing from my pores by now. Being the slippery fucker that I am and in a state of terror an idea popped into my head so I said:

"Come on then R----", and taking his tiny hand we go to his room where I put my plan into place.

"Oh", I say seeing the big widescreen TV is still all afire from his preschool gaming "forgot to turn it off R----"?

"Naaa", says this canny little fucker, " I like to leave Plants versus Zombies loaded on the X Box so I don't have to wait before playing it after school", and the mischievous little tyke says this as though he's being exceptionally naughty and I've a wave of love for him sweep over me. A grin curling my own lips I look at him all conspiratorial like, and say:

"I always kick your arse on that game though R----; you're rubbish"!

Whaaaaaat", he says in the way kids do today, "no you don't Andrew, you're rubbish and I", he says pointing to his own tiny form, "aaaalwaaaays beat you"!

"No way", I say, "it must be at least equal now R----, don't talk shit bro", and my swearing makes him laugh out loud and it fills me with joy to hear, "and anyway", I continue, " I've been practicing whilst you're at school me ol' china"!

"Come on then", he says picking up a controller, "let's play now and see who's the best then".

"But what about your homework R----"? I say slyly working to my own ends " I know, we'll just do it later ay"? though I have absolutely no intention of doing so of course, "we've got ages man". And that, indeed dear reader is the lengths I'd go to to avoid any interaction with maths at that time in my life. And of course the boy kicked my butt on the X Box!

So, I'm now astounded at what I can do after just a few weeks in the fella's class and as I say it wasn't long before I was offered, when the other guy leaves for he is still there, 'maths orderly' and had fallen in love with the thinking involved in the subject and the light bulb moments one gets once a problem solves in the mind of a sudden. Unfortunately maths only run in the morning and in the afternoons I have horticulture classes involving some theory and thankfully some practical, allowing me to get great gulps of the fresh air that prisoners are so starved of behind the door. Learning of the wonders of nature was another fantastic enlightenment for me. On practical days I get to go into the gardens, surrounded by a fuck off wall of course but a place nonetheless where I tend a cacophony of colour built this summer into a previously bland, grey paved area approximately fifteen by nine metres. The prisoners here have planted a menagerie filled with eclectic species the variety I've not the vernacular to speak of for I have no experience whatsoever. But the colour! And the mahussive sunflowers reaching for the life giving light emanating from our star! The other day I sat and watched as this busy little bumble bee went about its business for about ten minutes and I swear the little fella was watching me as I watched him! In fact I thought he was trying to communicate with me! I could see the dusting of nectar

9

over his perfect cute form and the proboscis as it slipped in and out of the tulip like flowers he was busy pilfering. And what a peaceful, wonderful time I had just observing him before I got up to a little light work myself, removing dead parts of flowers, turning the soil and adding compost to enrich the beds from which these pretty marvels of nature spring.

Anyway, I'm a person who's had many strange and esoteric experiences over my four and a bit decades. Let me tell you of one such thing, and this tale I regale is the third time this experience has happened to me. I'm praying that you dear reader can relate though I've investigated and only a tiny fraction of respondents to my informal surveys have similar incidences having happened to them. So.......

It's glorious summer 2016. I'm once again living in the flat with the wench, the ex, the gangster who is Charlotte. We are but friends, she just feels sorry for my homeless arse and lets me doss on her couch. One day another of my ex girlfriends, the pretty blonde and rich modelesque A---- mother of maths whiz R----, calls me. A---- has had a boob job, has hair extensions and is the very replication of Barbie in flesh. She makes her money doing tarot readings for people and is therefore a proper like white witch. She is quite famous on the circuit and has plied her trade on the TV. So my phone goes;

"What's up A----"? I say surprised to get her call.

"Andrew, are you ok"? she says, "I've seen pictures of you on Facebook and I've been really worried about you. Do you want to come over and see me tomorrow"?

"Jesus A---- I ain't heard from you in fuckin ages, what's happening"?

"I know but I just wanna see you", says the weapon of a woman, "please"?

"Can I fuck you"? I say comedically but hoping of course that she'll acquiesce!

"Mmmmmm", comes the reply, "maybe, but probably not you dirty fucker"!

"Hahahaha", I laugh, "I was only joking A----, course I'll come over", I tell this mysterious woman.

"Course you were", she retorts to my amorous request, giving a lusty throaty chuckle, "so you're gonna come over then and say hello to me and R----"?

"Ahhh man yeah, course I am so long as you cook up something nice babe"?

"Deal", she says, "you need feeding up ya skinny little cunt".

"Well, that's fuckin' nice init"!

"You look sick Andrew", she says seriously now, "just get that bony arse over here and I'll send you away a bit fatter with some decent grub in ya belly at least".

"Ahh A----, look, I'm really grateful darlin' and I'll see you tomorrow, what time shall I come"?

"Get here about eleven if ya want, nice an early"?

"That's good for me babe, see ya then".

Now dear reader I couldn't really give a fuck whether or not you believe the following but you rob yourselves, not me. This is my experience on Earth, in this realm. As I sit and type now in a bedroom in Oxford going from the 1300 sheets of handwritten A4 I wrote in jail I'm aware you're probably hungry for the gritty prison stuff and plead with you wait for there's plenty of that to come. If you just hold tight I will immerse you in the machinations of a prison wing where war is commonplace, comedy always present and where drugs and strife are daily companions. I'll introduce and carve out some colourful characters whom you'll get to know intimately so please do bear with me. But I want to share this tale wrote in jail in the order in which I wrote it, have patience, there's plenty of violence and savagery and visions of the prison to come. I just wish to give a picture of me first.

So, the next morning and for the third time in my life I awoke with a start and the instant I do so I've a premonition telling me that this day I will find a five pound note. Now explaining this phenomena is difficult but I have had it twice before regarding fivers. As soon as my eyes open I know on a subatomic level it will come to pass, that that day I will find five pounds. I dress in shorts and T shirt and say my goodbyes to Char.

"Where ya going weirdo"?

"A---- wants to feed me I think, maybe the rich bitch will give me a few quid", I say, not wanting to upset Charlotte.

"Give her a kick in the cunt from me", she says.

"I will babe".

"I'll be here when you need me", says the wonderful wench. Ramsgate to Sandwich is quite some trek; at least seven miles I reckon so I bunk the train, hiding in the toilet to avoid the guard. Once off the train I've still a walk before me as she lives on a posh estate some distance from the station. The day is Homeric with shimmering sunshine and birds fling their souls upon the air in celebration of summertime. I walk down ancient medieval streets and then take a right onto a place called the Rope Walk which is a tarmacked track with a hill sloping down to the left with trees, foliage and bushes and to the right, also a sloped bank, is a stream. Now the stream is a water in which I used to fish with my father many moons ago and holds happy memories for me. I remember as I was walking, now not a quarter mile from A----'s house, thinking to myself that this would be the first time I had had the 'knowing' as I call it, the premonition of the five pound notes and it having not come to fruition in the finding. I take my foot from the beaten track and walk towards the gently slopping stretch of water. As I get ten foot or so from the stream I notice something blue and oblong floating and immediately a smile curls my lips and my tread quickens as my heart leaps that once again this thing has come to pass. The dirty fiver was floating Queen's head up so I got a stick and fished it from the surface of the gleaming stream. Once in my hand I turned it over and over whilst marvelling at the inexplicability of such phenomena. Three times this has happened. And many more strange things too. This is my truth, my human condition. I bought myself a can of Special Brew strong lager and a cake before walking somewhat more lightly to the white witch's house.

After food she had begged me to return to the rehab where I had gotten clean for the first time in my life and that for a period of about three and a half years. In that time I had gotten my first job ever aged 33, a driving licence, a flat in leafy Oxfordshire and had made a set of friends the likes I'd never known before for all previous relationships had been based around drugs and drink and what you had for me.

"Look at the state of you Andrew, you look so sick mate", said the tall blonde Barbie like beeyatch.

"Fuck me A----, I don't look that bad do I"? I had remonstrated, thinking, like all junkies, that I actually looked ok!

"What drugs are you using at the moment"? she says as she strokes my bearded boat race lovingly.

"Just a bit of heroin and crack cocaine", I say nonchalantly and now she takes a closer look at my arms and notices the track marks I have been trying to conceal from her.

"Oh my God", she says, "you're banging up again you fuckin' idiot; how long you been back on the pin for you stupid spoon burning cunt"?

"Oh, fuck sake A----, I don't know, few months or something, not that long".

"Can't we phone the Ley Community in Oxford, ya know, the rehab, and see if they'll take you back"?

"Really"? I say unenthusiastically, " Fuck me A---- I'd be well embarrassed going back up there"!

"Why"?

"I hurt a lot of people when I relapsed babe and I'm not sure if they'd have me anyway". Not to labour it dear reader she convinced me, we

12

called them and not but the very next day I was whisked away by her back to the dreaming spires and the place my recovery journey started. Alas, I went back, lasted two months and relapsed. But I still wish to tell of the day that I did so let me recall my fall back into debauchery.

After two months, once the green goblin of methadone had been eradicated from my body and I again was well, I fell. Thinking I was fixed I trotted up the driveway leaving the rehab yet no sooner had I entered Oxford City the demon pounced and a snowball, crack cocaine and heroin prepared for injection in a single syringe, was upon me. The first thing I did was buy a beer and sit on a bench trying to read Rousseau and I remember I couldn't focus on the short wearing revolutionary's words. Looking up from my book I spot a couple homeless dudes and amble on over, asking without precursor:

"Can you score mate"? to the one with the dog, a dog that sits in a pushchair in the place a baby would normally sit.

"What d'ya want pal"? he asks in a northern colloquial deriving from the Yorkshire area I'd guess.

"One and one and I'll get you one mate", I say meaning I want a ten pound rock of crack and the same in smack and that I'd get him one item of his choice.

"Ya coming pal? This geezer's gonna give us a tenner so with what we've got we can get two and two now", he says to the other half of the street dwelling duo. I look down at the scruffy little aged Jack Russel in the pushchair which has one of those doggy coats on saying 'bouncer' and I smile at the little thing and pet its matted fur. I can smell dog on my hand straight away and regret the action but the poor little thing looks up at me lovingly and I can't help but pet him again God love him. Now the three of us are in a circle outside Tescos on St Giles and the bums are picking up their blankets and pillows from the pavement and it seems to be taking an age so I say:

"How long 'till we actually score chaps"? and the southern one, a fat looking bloated fella clearly very sick says:

"Ten minutes tops mate I promise", and I'm relieved it'll not be long before I can roll up my sleeve and get one in me. The other fella, the skinny scrawny bearded dog owner finally positions himself behind the pushchair and starts to push the poor mutt along.

"Come on then lads, have you even phoned 'em yet"? I ask somewhat more sternly than I had intended. Northern Bum One says:

"Foock me pal you're impatient int ya"?

"I am when it comes to scoring mate yeah", I say, "Come on, how fuckin' long then"? Bum One says to Bum Two:

"Gis the fuckin' phone here man for fuck sake", and now having confirmation the gear wasn't yet ordered I say:

"See, see, I fuckin' knew it", and I'm blowing exasperated wind, "fuck sake boys is this even gonna happen"?

"Hold on man hold on", says Bum One and I can hear in his wheedling tones that my angst and aggressive manner are starting to panic him a little so I make a mental note to slow down lest I scare them off. Bum One has the phone in his hand now.

"Hello", he says into the ten pound burner after dialling a number, "It's me", and I can't remember his name but watch as the fella's face contorts in concentration, "yeah,, yeah, we want three and three mate is that cool"? then a short pause then, "where should I go"? then, "alright mate, see you there soon", and he hangs up the phone.

"Sweet", I say, "where we going then"?

"St Clements roundabout, just over the Magdalen Bridge to the Plain", says Bum Two.

"Coolio", I say, "not too far then". And we set off, the fat one the skinny one and middling me. It's September time and there's a chill on the air but I'm buzzing and warm at the thought of the coming snowball and enjoy the sight of Oriel College on the right with its statue of Cecil Rhodes, causing so much controversy at the moment with the Black Lives Matter lot, in pride of place near the top of the venerable building. I marvel at the churches and chapels and spires of this lovely city, enjoy the Magdalen bridge with its view over Christ Church meadow and marvel at the architecture of Magdalen College itself with its intricate stonework and ancient wooden gates. Students bustle past us busily and the smell of rain is on the air as dark clouds gather overhead but we are oblivious to anything other than the coming drug dealer plying his trade amongst the cobbles of this excellent old academic city.

"Getting foockin' cauld at night pal", says the Yorkshire man to me and his cockney sidekick, now pushing the aged Jack Russell says:

"You wouldn't want to be out in this at night bro, it's fuckin' Baltic".

"Well chaps I am gonna be out in it".

"What yer not homeless are ya"? this from Bum Two.

"I fuckin' am chaps, exactly the same as you, I'm fucked".

"Join the club pal", says Bum One.

"Where ya come from"? asks Bum Two.

"I just left the Ley Community today, I'm from Kent but have been in this city clean for a long time but I relapsed, went home, came back to the Ley and walked out today", I say trying to be concise for I really don't want to talk of me, I just want to get one up me arm.

"Foock me man, there's loads a lads here on the streets that come from that foockin' gaff". The slim Yorkshire man with the jutting jaw has taken the dog out the pushchair and has him in his arms now as we wait for the drug dealer at the end of Cowley Road by the Cape Of Good Hope pub on the Corner. Just round a bit and across the way on Iffley Road is the Magdalen School and a phonebox just outside the gates and I know that's where I'm gonna stick one in me soon as the dealer gets here.

"Why d'ya fuck up" ? asks the rather more eloquent one, Bum Two, who hails from somewhere in the south.

"Well, I'm not blaming anyone else".......... But before I finish he is already there with:

"Bet it was a woman"!

"Yep", I say slightly sheepish, "you guessed right".

"Yeah man, same here", says the northern of the duo, "got a wife and kid back home in Yorkshire", says this emaciated and sick looking man. Suddenly Bum Two says:

"I can see him, he's coming", and my heart misses a beat in my chest.

"Wait here", says One, "you go", he says to Two and it makes sense only one of us approach the shifty looking black guy. It isn't long before Two returns with the drugs and now I have them in my hand I feel like I'm gonna cum.

"Oh", I say to the two before they amble off, "have you got some kit for me"? and by this I mean the stuff I need to prepare and suffuse my injection.

"Sort him ooot", says the northern of the two.

"Sweet lads", I say before bolting to Sainsburys for water then swift footing it straight to the old phonebox of which I spoke earlier outside the venerable elite posh school for cunts. The excitement of the coming hit is turning my guts to jelly and I fear I may defecate as my bowels loosen in anticipation. Sweating now I remove the specially for junkies designed spoon from its packet and place it on the little ledge next to the phone. Next I open the packet of heroin, about 0.2g and sprinkle it into the bowl of the spoon. I then sprinkle citric acid atop the brownish heroin which is used to break down any of the many impurities sometimes found in UK smack. I open the water and stick the needle (or 'works' as hypodermic syringes are colloquially known by the drug using demographic) in to draw up water which I then squirt onto the gear. Taking a quick look out the phonebox to insure that I am still safe and unseen I pick up the spoon and place the flame from my lighter beneath the bowl to cook the savage substance, watching as it dissolves into a brown puddle emitting the notes of heroin I find so pleasant and assuring me the gear is good. Then I place the spoon down and open the rock of crack which I place into the liquid I've cooked up. Using the plunger end of the works I crush the crack cocaine into it until it, too, has disappeared causing the brown liquid to swirl with creamy whiteness before vanishing from sight altogether. Excited now I whip the belt from around my waist and wrap it round my arm rapid, holding and tightening it with my teeth. Even now as I sit in a cell writing after the fact I can feel the adrenalin which is precursor to the rush of the snowball. I mentally say 'yes' as I see blood rush back into the barrel of the works like a blooming red rose after I'd successfully stabbed the vein, letting go of the belt which drops from my mouth, easing the constriction on my arm as I then blast the snowball into my blood stream. A long drawn out 'aaaahhhhh' is let out as I go hot all over with the rush of the crack. Just before the coke gets too much the heroin takes off the edge and I go hazy with the ready brek glow. I clean up and pocket my shit as orgasmic sublime sexual waves wash through me over me and emanate from every pore. I walk back over the Magdalen Bridge in a haze, wondering what all the fuss is about, thinking all is well with the world. Of course it wasn't.

The next day I am freezing and can feel a gap in the cardboard 'bed' beneath me, exposing bare skin to the biting cold concrete below. The left side of my body on which I am positioned in this large shop doorway is aching painfully where I lay on it in stupor all night. I pull the slim sheet I'd stolen from a washing line more tightly about me in anticipation of more slumber but as dawn's rosy fingers bring light a lady comes to open the shop and in kindly tones tells me I must move. I get up miserably without remonstrating for I'm too beat to argue and she's decent besides. I walk toward Cornmarket Street wondering what the fuck I will do next. For I need to score and score I will or die or be arrested in the trying. I can't cope with all neurons snapping and must escape my reality at any cost. I remember feeling very ostracised from the rest of the madding crowd.

Let me tell you of how I got to Oxford, long before I found myself homeless on her streets and living in a tent in Christ Church Meadow. So I'd brought myself to my knees in Kent, Margate by the seaside what with my poly drug using. By the time I had decided I had had enough I was fixing four fat snowballs a day, usually with half a gram of crack and half gram of smack in each, drinking ten cans of Special Brew and taking tons of benzodiazapines and pregablin on top of my 90 ml of methadone. Daily for fuck sake. So I'd gone to my local drug agency and settled on a rehab called the Ley Community which is nestled in a tiny village

16

called Yarnton in Oxfordshire about four miles from the city centre. Pretty place it is too, the Ley, tucked away amongst green pastures and old trees with a lake and pool and paddocks where donkeys are kept. But before my admission I had to do a detox at a place called City Roads in central London. My body was drenched in drugs and the rehab insisted I do a comprehensive clean out prior to admission. So I suffered horrific but controlled withdrawels at the detox and the day my meds ceased the car from Oxford arrived to pick me up.

"Fuck me", I'd said upon seeing the faces of the two big blokes, one squat and hench, the other tall and rangy, who'd arrived to escort me, "You don't fuck about do ya"?

"Nope, we like to strike whilst the iron is hot", said the squat burly one of the two. I later learned his name was B----, a senior member of staff at the Ley.

"And I'm Hugh", said the slimmer grey haired guy whom I later dubbed 'Hugh Janus' and with whom I'm still friends to this very day. Hugh then asks me "how ya feeling mate" ?and I tell him that I am feeling fucked, absolutely fucked.

"You look like a bag of shit", says squat burly B---- who, it turns out I found out later, is an ex armed robber. He'd completed the Ley programme twenty years ago and worked there ever since.

"Don't worry mate, this is the easy bit", says Hugh and I retort:

"Easy for you to say, looking all fit and healthy".

"I've been there mate", says Hugh.

"What"? I say now incredulous, "you're staff though ain't ya"? And here he laughs out loud before saying:

"Is that what you think"?

"Well yeah".

"Did you hear that B----"? says Hugh, still guffawing.

"What's that"? says B---- the burly bastard signing papers with the detox staff.

"He thinks I'm staff", and now B----, too, laughs, clearly thinking this is fuckin' hilarious.

"This cunt"? says B----, pointing at Hugh, "staff? cor", he says in his still strong London cockney, "we'd be fucked if he was"!

"Cheeky cunt", replies Hugh in good humour before turning to me and saying "nope, I'm just the same as you mate, a resident".

"Really"? I say, my interest piqued for I'd never seen a drinker, like a true street alcoholic or junkie looking like this cunt, well fed and healthy.

"Yep", he says, "no different to you", and this is truly astonishing to me. The geezer is smart, handsome and well dressed, much the Mr

17

Normal and I am in stark contrast with my emaciated nine stone frame, shivering, skinny, sick and pale.

"How long you been there"? I ask wiping tears from my constantly streaming eyes and snot from my dribbling nose for I'm bang in the heart of horrific cold turkey.

"About seven months now and it's the best thing I ever did".

"What, you finished then"? I ask, rather warming to the lanky fucker.

"No, still got a few months yet before I get to stage five and go out to work".

"Fuck me I'm sick", I say. Sweat has broken all over my body and I shiver with goosebumps whilst I cough green phlegm and clench my sphincter to avoid shitting myself. I can hardly stand up and want to die. I have a sneezing fit and shake violently. "What do you mean by 'go out to work'"?

"Everyone leaves with a job", says Hugh Janus and I'm very impressed with this info even in my dilapidated state. "Fuck me I feel rough", I say again as a wave of savage sickly nausea runs through me. My feet and hands throb with pain though the swelling from all the injecting in them has abated somewhat due to cessation.

"When we going man, I'm getting itchy fuckin' feet here bro"? I say to Huge.

"B---- has to do the boring shit, ya know, we can't just walk in here and take bodies away without the formal bollox Andrew"! I'm starting to like the guy more and more.

"Right", says Brian, "we are all good to go; you fit Andrew"?

"Well, I wouldn't say he's fit"! says Hugh Janus smiling at me looking me over and I can see he, too, finds this rather amusing, "Probably seen better days ain't ya mate"?

"Don't worry mate, this is the easy bit", says B---- and I think to myself that that's easy for him to say, all fat, rotund and healthy as he is the cunt, "strong before ya know it", he says very unhelpfully. We leave City Roads and get into B----'s fat beamer. Soon as we're in the car I say to these cunts sitting in the front:

"Can we stop at an off license on the way chaps so I can get a Special Brew please"? B---- and Huge both turn to me, Huge sputters his can of coke and nearly chokes and B----, deadpan, asks:

"Are you fuckin' serious"?

"Well yeah", I say, incredulous he'd think otherwise.

"Ain't gonna happen mate", he says.

"Andrew, you're coming to us to start a new way of life ain't ya buddy"? says the inimitable Hugh Janus, for the tall lanky slightly sarcastic fuck is like no one I've ever met. I shiver all the fuckin' way with these couple of cunts seeming to enjoy my discomfort. Having had a little bit of recovery, some years in fact and seeing the poor wretches withdrawing when they first find a bit themselves I kinda get this dark humour now for we have to laugh or we'd fuckin' cry. I did eighteen months at the Ley and stayed clean for nearly four years before meeting a bird and relapsing due to the fact I could not deal with my feelings, returning to the comfort of heroin and crack and base amphetamine, oh, and, of course, Special Brew. I didn't know it then, but I needed Narcotics Anonymous in my life. I'd been doing meetings but had dropped NA out thinking I was fixed. Psychos like me need a daily programme for a daily reprieve. More on that later perhaps.

I sit here now in the maths class with the teacher nicknamed AddemupAde and we are looking at level three problems together and discussing theological matters. Thanks to this wonderful guy I have gotten myself up to GCSE level in this wonderful subject though I know it's applied mathematics and not at all that academic. Still, the wonder for me was in learning through this guy that I can learn this subject like any other. And this is revolutionary for me. I know these levels won't improve my comprehension when reading books like 'The Little Book of String Theory' of which I still took much or Hawkings 'A Brief History of Time' or 'The Universe In A Nutshell' or the recent work I read by brilliant Brian Cox but I'm content to know I could, given time, do rather well in this fascinating field. Makes me smile when the blurb on the back of one of Hawkings' books reads 'this is physics for the layperson'! Cheeky cunts! Take such titles to the fella just got off the scaffolding or the bricklayer down the road and see how they get on with your abstract theories and complex calculations you out of touch cunts! These leviathans of intellectualism are lucky to have had the gifts bestowed upon them allowing for insight into the seemingly impossibly small and incomprehensibly massive. Most of us, I dare say, wouldn't know an antiquark from Proxima Centauri or the Chandraheksar limit from the Large Hadron Collider!

I woke up this morning with depressing grey light streaming through the cell window. My cellmate Aidy was bustling about, rummaging through the bin at seven AM trying to find the little pill bottle containing the liquid pregablin he sells for spice after spitting it out at the meds hatch, secretly secreting the stuff which sells for £5 per 150ml, the price fluctuating depending on demand. He gets 600ml per day. I'd had a couple days off of the spice myself and felt strong but, after returning

19

from my Thinking Skills class I'd bumped into, back on the wing, my lanky black haired bespectacled fraudster mate Grinley and he'd asked:

"Got any mix Andy"? and by this he means have I got any tea bag leaves that have been rolled in the goo between the plastic layers of a nicotine patch. Firstly the patch is heated on a plastic mirror on top of a steaming kettle then pulled apart and the tea leaves then smeared with the substance inside. Smoking had by this time stopped, banned across the prison estate and real tobacco is a rarity on the wing and fuckin' expensive at £25 for an eighth of an ounce.

"No mate", I say, knowing he wants it to roll a spice spliff, "I'm giving up today anyway".

"Good on ya mate", says the fraudulent fuck I rather like before bustling up the landing to continue his mission. Ten minutes later I walk into a cell where he, Tony Giles, a skinny and drawn immensely talented artist and lifelong friend of mine and Dean Hoskins, a big burly gentle giant, sit smoking away. They proffer the joint in my direction. Instinctively I take it. I draw from it heavily, feeling first nothing but disappointment wash over me for failing to resist.

"Bang up boys", says Ms H, a fit young newbe screwess who winces at the smell of the acrid smoke permeating the cell.

"Ok Miss H", I say now feeling more than slightly stoned.

"You alright"? she says, "you look a bit spaced".

"I'm alright Ms H", I say, noticing that all of us look absolutely spangled.

"Come on then", says the wily wench and I go to my cell and bang the door. Aid, a hardcore spice smoker sits on his bed and it should be remembered that this fella has never had, so he claims, what is colloquially known as a 'spice attack', which is basically an overdose on the stuff.

"You alright Aidy"? I say nonchalantly but the cunt just looks at me so I repeat the question and get the same lack of response, "talk to me Aid for fuck sake", I say, but he just looks at me all dead eyed, scary and zombie like. Fuck I could do without this, I think, as I'm close to the panic stage and tripping myself. He says fuck all then, all of a sudden, he starts to projectile puke. And he pukes. And pukes and wretches and pukes some more. He is panic stricken and he can barely breathe so regular are the heaves and he seems to be asphyxiating. I am getting seriously worried but know how much he hates the staff being involved so am loathe to jump straight to the emergency button. He briefly looks up to me and points to his mouth. I realize I must focus on him and not my own panic.

"It's ok man", I say, touching his leg briefly and trying not to choke on the smell of the foul contents of his stomach. He is trying to suck air into his lungs between bouts of puking and pointing to himself in wide eyed terror.

"Breathe my friend, breathe", I say and he looks as if, sounds as if and undoubtedly believes he is going to die. I'm very close to calling the staff. I hold off. I hear him suck in a gasping lungful and thank God for it. He is still in panic and shock and there is blood in the growing pile of puke on the floor and walls and himself. "Ya gonna be alright my man", and as the vomiting abates it is replaced by fearful fraught hyperventilating. I do my best to clean up most of the sick for I know Aidy and that he'll be worried about this. I want him to know his safety is of the utmost concern right now. "I've got you", I say as he tries to normalise his breathing. He is coughing and spluttering with the last of the attack.

"Fuck me", he says, then, "wow", and as the thing begins to pass I notice I myself am sweating and still intoxicated from my own smoking of this dangerous substance. I sometimes have terrifying trips on this stuff. Just recently I went to a realm where I'm sat at a table with two beings and we are playing cards and the stipulation was that the loser of the game would have to die. After a hand was played and I had lost I'd looked up at these two strange beings and said:

"It's me", and these beings were as real as the prisoners sitting across from me now in the maths class in which I write this.

"It is", say the two in unison.

"I have to die", I say to them with terror mounting in my soul.

"Help me, please", I beg, "please help me".

"It has started", they say again in unison.

"Noooooo", I say, eyes wide with terror.

"When the voice inside your head stops you die", they say and I'm now petrified and certain, absolutely certain that the end is nigh.

"Please please help me oh please please don't let me die", I scream, "the voice is getting fainter".

"You are nearly there", they say and I now know I'm about to die. Truly. Deadly seriously, I'm dying. It's over.

"Oh God", I say, "Please God no", and the voice in my head is so faint I can barely hear it. Imminent death, terrifying panic. Fainter, fainter, fainter still then:

"Sloaney", Aidy had shouted "the fuck is up with you?".

"Help me help me help me", I'd begged.

"It's alright", said Aidy, "it's ok man calm down you're ok", and despite his kind words I see in his eyes he's getting tired of having to do

21

this with me for unlike him I'm a regular to these realms when tripping. I always have too much and find myself on the floor screaming and foaming at the mouth. See, thing is, he can't enjoy his own buzz when I'm consistently collapsing. Anyway, enough of this for now.

17/4/2018. Well this morning multitudinous people on all wings were collapsing with a new strain of spice paper that has gotten through. Spice attacks necessitating ambulances everywhere. On top of this, my friend Ben who I see each day in the maths class is relaying a tale of the other story of the day about the man who climbed onto the roof of a wing first thing, refusing to come down and clearly in debt to dealers of spice. The bouncy castle safety thing was inflated for him as screws tried to coax him down from the fifteen foot position he'd taken up above them. We were all held up this morning getting to classes what with this and the spice attacks so Ben, my bald brethren, has the hump.

"What happened"? asks the venerable Nigerian teacher, AddemupAde.

"Well", says bald Ben, "you'd've thought it was a full blown riot the amount of 'nationals' (the elite incident prison officers who police a sector of the south east prison estate) that they got in".

"Did he come down"? I say.

"Yeah", says Ben, "I think they threatened him with stun guns and pepper sprays".

"How long was he up there"? asks the worthy Nigerian.

"Well he got on the roof at half nine and he's only just got down now and it's three p.m", says the bald one called Ben.

"Wow, that's why we were all locked down then", I observe.

"Didn't you see the bouncy castle thing Andy"? asks Ben.

"Yeah I saw it briefly when they escorted me to the Thinking Skills class but we couldn't have a proper look 'cause the screws were proper tight on us, proper controlled movements", I say, then, "what did he do up there Ben 'cause you're right opposite where it happened being on B wing ain't ya"?

"Fuck all really mate, literally just standing on the roof telling anyone who would listen that this ain't fair and that ain't fair and the world ain't fair; soon as the mufti squad came he got straight down".

"What a clown", I say, "I wonder why"?

"He wanted to be shipped back to a B cat apparently".

"Well he's gone the right way about it that's for sure".

"Got a vape battery Sloaney"? asks Will, another prisoner here in my beloved maths class.

"Naa mate", I say, "what for"?

"I got some power rice", he says, meaning some strong pseudo cannabinoids or 'spice'.

"Fuck that", I say "last time I did that here I ended up being marched back to the wing absolutely out me canister"!

"Ha ha ha", laughs Ben, "I remember that"! I had smoked a pipe of spice at the back of the class one day and ended up on the floor fitting, necessitating medical assistance before, upon regaining consciousness, being taken back to the wing by a team of very pissed off staff!

"Hello", says Ade above the steady din of chatter, "hello people, right, today we may have an assessor coming in to observe me so we all need to be doing something".

"Have you got a mock paper for me to do Ade"? I ask for at this point I have not yet taken my final paper.

"Just let me settle everybody else and then I will come back to you".

"Is there anything I need to brush up on do you think"?

"Not really", says AdemupAde, "I'm confident that if you took the exam now you would pass".

"I am too, but I want to take the exam once you come back off holiday because they take us off the class once we pass level two".

"Yes but remember that soon as you do that you'll have the orderly job anyway so you'll still be here", Ben is orderly now but due for release soon. "But yes, we can wait 'till I get back off of holiday, no problem", then he bustles about the class putting people to work. Though of course what I am learning isn't the stuff of physicists, I really have developed a love for this subject and want to insure I can keep my foot in the door as it were.

18th October 2018. Ade starts the afternoon class with a lesson on volumetric weighting. All students get involved. I learn that Parcel Force are thieving cunts. It's now 15:15. We go back to the wing from class at four pm. Shahab, a handsome Iraqi is next to me on my right. Next to him on his right is Adrian, a newcomer to the class.

"How old are you"? I ask him.

"Thirty five", he says in a slight northern drawl.

"Have you done 'percentage decrease'" ? asks Ade of Shabab before turning to me saying "Andrew, give us an example please".

"Right", I say to Shabab but looking at Adrian too so he feels included, "ok, let's say we have a jumper and its new price is £46 but that is with 20% off, we want to work out what the old price would have been".

"Ok", say Adrian and Shabab who decide to do the sum together.

"How will you do it"? I ask and Adrian replies:

"Well 80% is £46 because they have told you the new price is £46 and that leaves"........

"20%", says Shabab in his lovely accented English.

"Right", says Ade, overhearing this.

"So all we have to do is find out what the 20% is", says Adrian and I pipe up, showing the simple method.

"Yes, we know that 80% is £46 so we divide it by eight then multiply the result by ten and that gives us £57.50. From there it's a simple case of calculating the difference".

"What does 'divide' mean"? says Shabab?

"Ahh", I say, "so it is the language you struggle with", and I get up and get a book to show him the sign for dividing. Once I have sat back down and we get into it he becomes quite animated once I explain the different functions of the various devices, explaining how they work. Telling him, for instance, that the 'divide' sign means to share out he sits back with a big grin and goes; "ahhhhhh I see I see" which makes me feel happy too! I turn round and see AddemupAde, this beautiful young guy and excellent teacher, smiling at me.

"The fuck you looking at"? I say, returning his beamer.

"I was just thinking, you put me on the spot with the assessors today Andrew".

"How"?

"You asked me how I got the divisor of 5000 for volumetric weighting and I thought 'wow, I'm on the spot here'"!

"Hahahaha well, I didn't mean to and besides, it went well"! I say.

"Thank God", says Ade who is a faithful guy by the way.

"You had to think on your feet", says Ben. I won't explain the maths, mostly as I can't remember but Ade had responded to my out the blue question excellently, showing his research.

"Thank God for DHL and Parcel Force" AddemupAde says, "and it was good because it made it all really authentic", and hearing him say this gives me a buzz. I love this guy. Next thing I know we are talking about Brexit.

"Very shit for some people", I say to Shabab, mimicking his accent and intonation as we all tend to do when speaking to foreigners. Ishmail, another young Iraqi with a thick head of lustrous black hair is telling bald Ben that he needs a haircut, which gets a laugh out the boys in the class and which Ben takes with good humour.

"Don't need cutting, it just fell out and never came back"! says poor old Ben.

"Thank God there's someone in the class balder than me", I say, instinctively rubbing my receding and thinning pate. My hair is hanging on for dear life.

"That's it Sloaney", says Ben, "use my misfortune to make yourself feel better bro"!

"Well, you know what they say about bald men don't ya mate"?

"No, what"?

"Solar panel for a sex machine. And they also reckon that bald fellas are more virulent"!

"I hope so", says Ben, "I need some action when I get out after two years in here"!

"Well, November is just around the corner bro; you must be starting to get a bit excited"?

"Not really", he says, "I don't even know where I'm going to live yet, and the worry of that outdoes any excitement I may sometimes feel".

"I understand that mate", I say, " I used to get all hyped prior to release during my early stints as a kid in jail but not so much now".

"Exactly, all it is is back to the real world with all its pressures and shit".

"Yep", I say, "bills, jobs, somewhere to live: it's like having to start all over again". And it is. The last weeks in prison are usually, for most of us in my experience, fraught with anxiety. Many people don't even want to be released and no sooner are they granted freedom they go committing crimes simply to return to the comfort of what they know and find easy. They may be miserable in jail, like me, though I make the best of it, but still there is relief to be found in the comfort of the necessities of life, basic needs being met by an agency that won't let you down. Anyway, 'Freeflow', the term coined for the flow of prisoners back and forth to places of work, is called and I return to the wing grateful that Ade's assessment went well and a little sad the worthy man is off to Nigeria for three weeks to see his family for I shall miss him.

1994 or 5:

It is a bright blue skied day and once again I am in Sandwich. (For some reason I wrote this crime up in the third person in prison so will replicate it faithfully from the written document from which I type this narrative.) Sol is almost at zenith whilst a man, about five feet eleven with dark greasy hair and white pasty countenance strolls, skulking the ancient paths of the village. The man is painfully thin and wears mid thigh shorts which do nothing for his stick like legs. He is well muscled despite the emaciated look but it is lack of sustenance which causes the cords and musculature and bones to protrude so sharply, almost breaking

25

the thin layer of skin, especially in the drawn face where the cheekbones sit. His eyes are sharp and fox like slivers in the hollowed out eye sockets as he searches his environment for any opportunity to steal to feed the beast at his back, hungry for the heroin he craves and which causes his body to ache and sweat and scream in withdrawel. He combs the streets looking for any unlocked car, an unattended till in a shop or the door open in a dwelling. He is desperate. His name is Andrew and he is close to defecating himself at times so severe is it becoming, so dire the desire to fix this shit with a couple points of creamy smack to get him back to normal. But he knows where he is going. He was kind of just hoping he didn't have to. He comes to a big old house he recognises as the one from the day before. He had been with Ben, his blond bespectacled drug using droog. Ben had tried to creep into the old ladies big house to rob her handbag whist she had been out pruning roses in her back garden.

"Ben", Andrew called out to him as the old lady, at least 75 years old, had turned and seen his friend. "Ben", he had called, this time a little louder, seeing that the clown is about to be caught. "Fuck sake" he says under his breath because Ben doesn't hear him. "Ben you prick", and this time Ben does hear, turning and mouthing:

"What"?

"Look", says Andrew, pointing to the old girl who had looked up from her secateurs to see Ben wandering into the back garden and approaching the back door. Andrew, knowing Ben to be not so good thinking on his feet, goes to his friends's aid.

"Hello", said the venerable ancient standing proudly amongst the preponderance of colour she'd created with her blooms in the massive space behind her large Tudor pile, "can I help you"? Her tones are pleasant and not suspicious at all.

"We were just marvelling at the colour and beauty of your back garden weren't we 'Steve'", Andrew says to Ben.

"Oh yes, beautiful isn't it? I love this time of year you see", says this archaic, this lovely old dinosaur from yesteryear.

"We do too, don't we 'Paul'", says Ben-Steve to Andrew now Paul before continuing that "we both work at the garden centre in Ramsgate and we love flowers, don't we 'Paul'"?

"Yeah but wow", says Andrew-Paul, "but your blooms are far more lovely than those at work", and all of this is complete shit of course as the two cunts before her had never worked a day in their lives in their 20 years each on Earth. Both were scallies, heroin addicts with one thing on their minds: getting that cunt monkey off their backs.

"Does your husband help you"? asks Andrew-Paul slyly whilst fingering something pink and pretty on top of a long green stalk.

26

"Oh no", says this lovely lady, the poor unsuspecting cow, "I'm all alone now dear".

"Bless you, do you still get about"? asks Andrew-Paul.

"Oh yes, I'm going up to the Chelsea flower show tomorrow", and as I type from this document, writing right now at the computer dear reader I feel a rush of shame wash over me and shake my head sadly, ruefully, feeling the guilt of what I did still poignantly to this very day. This never has quite left me. Oh my days Lord do forgive me for I knew not what I did. The old lady does not know that she has, there and then, just signed her house's burgle warrant. The skinny and sick, sly and fox like twenty year old scumbag heard something like cheers going up in his head. They both move away, waving and smiling kindly to this poor old lady.

"You better come get me", says Ben to Andrew.

"I will won't I ya cunt", says Andrew to Ben, "why wouldn't I man"? They find a hand bag which they swipe from the back room of a coffee shop then flake out in a crack house once they get back to Thanet. The next day Andrew wakes before Ben and heads, alone, to the train station where he promptly bunks a train to Sandwich and marches like a man on a mission to the big old house not far from the banks of the River Stour where they had encountered the ancient with the secateurs the day before. Andrew knocks loudly on the big, black, wide old front door with the metal studs in it of many years past. After a suitable amount of time waiting to insure the house is indeed bereft of its owner he heads round the back and stands before the back door now which leads, he can see, straight into the kitchen. He takes a deep breath as he looks at the sturdy barrier and strong locks, the thickness of the wood bothering him.

"Fuck", he says to himself in exasperation. He looks up the garden to the shed but he knows if he walks up there he will be exposing himself to the neighbours' view and he can hear faint voices floating on the wind. No, too risky. Shit.

"Fuck fuck fuck", he says to himself now getting anxious and starting to feel the monkey's grip tighten and his sphincter loosen as the heroin from yesterday starts to retreat from his system. Suddenly he notices a small screwdriver at his feet in a drain serving the downpipe from a bathroom. Though wrapped up in what he is doing he can hear the sounds of hammer and riveting in a boatyard by the lovely lapping water of the Stour. Andrew looks overhead as birds tweet and whistle for the glorious coming of midday. Hot himself he takes off his T-shirt and tucks it into the waistband of the shorts he's had on for as long as he can remember. His socks had not been changed in weeks either, they were the only thing holy about that man at that moment. This was a predator at work at the height of the heroin epidemic endemic in the British Isles at that point in time. He stands with his square chin in his hand looking as bright as a smackhead can when wondering how best to break into a building built before the age of cheap unsturdy prefabs. This fucking door. He drops the poxy screwdriver and thinks 'fuck it'.

"Bollox", he says out loud, "I'll kick the cunt off". And that, dear reader, is exactly what he does. He leans back and smashes a smelly, dirty trainer into the business area of this worthy door. It splits open and he boots and boots and boots some more until the hole in the ancient wood is big enough to allow his skinny frame through. Once inside he squats by the cooker for some minutes sweating, trying to prevent his opioid ravaged body projectile vomiting from the exertion and effort. He doesn't want to be spraying DNA all over the place. When he feels fit he runs straight through the front room in search of the bedroom where he knows his prize will be. It is locked so he smashes that through, too, with his foot. He takes many trinkets, gold and jewels and pockets about £2700 in used notes. "Yes yes yes", he says to himself gleefully. Prize pocketed he leaves the property the very same way he came and gets on a train back to Thanet and the crack house from whence he'd set off this very day but a few hours before. Ben is still sleeping in stupor and Andrew-Paul kicks him awake.

"'Ere you are", he says giving Ben £1000 and then from another pocket he pulls a gram of smack, gram of crack and a quarter of an ounce of pure stinky base amphetamine.

""'Where ya been"? asks Ben

"Done that old ladies house in Sandwich this morning; still got a load of gold and that to sell too. Come on, let's have a hit bro". They both go to the stinking kitchen and stick needles into their still young fat veins. Andrew not yet knowing how much this burglary would affect him throughout his life. And the reason it haunts him is because the old lady was made human by the interaction of the day before. Made real. A decent and feeling human being. And it has never left him. Savage.

At the Ley Community rehab and it wasn't long before I was getting into trouble. I am trying to doze on a settee in the living area.

"Get the fuck off of me man", I say as a hand shakes my shoulder to wake me. I look up and see Hugh Janus the lanky fuck. "Every fuckin' time I fall asleep some cunt wakes me".

"It's because we're trying to train your body to sleep at night", says Hugh.

"Yeah", pipes Chris, a senior resident, a good looking likable cunt I don't like very much in that moment, "you need to try to keep your eyes open during the day bro, I know it might not seem like it but we are just tryna help".

"You're all driving me fuckin' mad with your bollox. Please just fuck off and leave me alone".

"You caused a real scare yesterday", says Matt G, a bespectacled Notts lad with real rhythm who loves to dance every morning so happy is the soppy cunt. Great lad really but I hated everyone right then.

"Oh God", I say, "not again".

"The whole staff team were out searching the village for you", Huge says.

"And you were asleep in a tiny little wardrobe upstairs", says Chris P not able to stop himself laughing at the shenanigans.

"Don't laugh Chris, or you Matt, seriously mate, people leave here and die Andrew". And Hugh speaks true for many parents have left benches and plaques and other memorials to their sons and daughters who had the only clean time of their lives here before relapsing and dying of overdose.

"Tomorrow Andy", pipes Matt, "they're gonna let you sit in on a confrontation group 'cause you've been here a couple of weeks now. Have you put any slips in? Done any pull ups"? Now, dear reader, in the Ley we have two weekly confrontation groups. We sit in circles of 30 or so in two houses for there are 60 of us. Now there's a thing called a slip box. If you call me a cunt, I write out a slip and put it in the box. The top three, known as 'top of the pops' people who have the most slips written on them get group time where they are confronted and have the slips read out to them. They are challenged aggressively on their behaviour before then having the group probe to ascertain where the behaviour stems from. Being in the hot seat used to make me sweat and tremble with fear. Pull ups are also a tool we use to try highlight behaviour. So on the walls in all rooms in all buildings are 'pull up' sheets. If we get more than three a week for things like swearing, farting in front of others, smoking at work or not having a saucer with your cup then we get a consequence such as a solo wash up or solo cleaning duty or a seminar we have to deliver to the rest of the community.

"Alright Mel", we all say as a sexy mixed race chick walks in.

"So, you done any Andy"? From Matt.

"No slips, it seems like grassing but I did pull Mel up for farting in the smoking shed yesterday"!

"Did you let one rip then Mel"? asks Matt smiling at this lovely looking light skinned lady.

"It just slipped out", says Mel, incredulous.

"It's quite difficult asserting myself", I say to anyone listening.

"It gets easier and that's the whole point of it", says Hugh Janus the penis. "Please don't go disappearing any more Andrew will ya"?

"Promise", I say very insincerely. The next morning I see the head co-ord, (coordinator) a senior resident who runs the show, collect the slip box to count and work out who has the most slips and has been behaving like a twat of late. The harsh but growth inspiring groups run Monday and Thursday. I now know it was a gift to see how others really experienced me for how can I grow if I don't know? And, this day, the group was on me.

"Right, all those with slips on Andrew can now read them out", and each person with slips on me said their piece before the group was opened for elaboration.

"Andrew", says Matt, the sly fucker, "who the fuck do you think you are? Why the fuck", he says, raising his voice in anger now as I start to sweat profusely, " do you think it's ok to call me a cunt you little twat"?

"Andrew", says Huge now the fuckin' knob, "why are you going round the place constantly mugging people off, swearing at people and getting aggressive"?

"Do you think you're hard or special or different than the rest of us or something"? says Chris the good looking piece of shit.

"When Hugh when"? I say perspiring heavily now with all these eyes upon me but I can feel anger rising and dismissively say; " oh fuck the lot of you anyway driving me fuckin' mad all the time".

"Shut you're fuckin' mouth and listen" says the staff member, lovely Emma.

"And you", I say, turning to Matt G, "are a sanctimonious little prick ya stupid cunt". And no sooner has it left my lips than the rest of the group erupt into life with:

"Oi oi oi shut your fuckin' mouth", and, "who the fuck do you think you are"? etc etc.

"You're an obnoxious little shit with no gratitude whatsoever", says sexy Emma the staff facilitator.

"Don't fuckin' talk to me then", I say petulantly.

"Listen", says Emma, "we didn't drag you up the drive with a gun to your head; you came to us for help. What the fuck are you doing here anyway"?

"I came to get off the drugs and drink". I say.

"Unless you start to listen to what people are trying to tell you everyday you won't last, you won't learn", says Emma.

"Andrew", says Hugh, " I know it don't feel like it but everyone here actually wants to help you. Why don't you start by trying to tell us all a little bit about you"?

"Fuck that", I say.

"You an 'alf an arrogant cunt", says Chris P.

"And you have absolutely no humility or gratitude", says Mel.

"Is that really what you see"? I say.

"And you're so manipulative", says Matt now in more gentle tones though this makes me squirm, "after you called me a cunt in the kitchen the other day you came back to see me a couple hours later begging me not to stick a slip in on you".

"I was just tryna"...........

"Shut up Andrew", says Emma, "don't try and justify your behaviour".

"Ok", I say and I proceed, after a little prodding, to give an anecdotal account of what it is brought me to my knees and to the Ley. I have Emma and Mel the two ladies in tears with a few of the more in touch with their feelings lads. For the record, Emma was my keyworker. Model like I thought I'd fallen in love with her! She had my back the whole time and still does today.

3rd November 2018. Aidy is going home to Chatham after serving his time. He is escaping the seamless sameness of prison life but he will be back. Two months ago he and I had had a horrific fight at 5.30am. Let me tell of it.

We had banged up the evening before having both of us acquired a significant amount of the hallucinogenic powerful spice sprayed paper. Aidy had, being the greedy little cunt that he is, ploughed through his in a much shorter period than I had mine. The last joint I rolled he had asked me for some and I had given it to him but he hadn't smoked it; he'd got into his bed and put it under his pillow after putting it out of course. Anyway, at around 5.30 a.m I had awoken to a cough and looked down from the top bunk to see him smoking this dog end and I'd asked him for a puff. Seeing there was still enough for me to have a couple of drags and being a junkie I had watched him smoke it and throw the end on the floor and sat on my bunk fuckin' fuming at the greed of this nasty little fucker. 'Cause that's exactly what he was at times. Anyway, not able to keep my mouth shut I leaned down and said:

"You're a selfish little cunt do you know that"? And he had said..........nothing. So I continue, "you tight cunt, I can't fuckin' stand you at times do you know that"? And still the muggy little fucker had said fuck all and I was growing more and more infuriated as the seconds ticked by without a sound from the bunk below. "Fuck you you fuckin' spastic", I'd said and jumped onto the chair below beneath the window intending to wag my finger in his face and continue my diatribe of invidious hatred but the chair had other ideas, collapsing and causing me to fall onto Aidy who had immediately responded by putting his hands around my throat, proceeding to throttle me 'till my eyes felt like they'd pop from my head. We wrestle and find ourselves on the floor rolling about then we are standing and throwing each other round the cell but I have socks on, Aidy does not and I keep slipping over on the shiny floor. This allowed Aidy to twice have me down with both of his thumbs in my eyes which left them severely bruised and bloodshot for a week after. He also stabbed me in the head with the battery end, with sharp edges, of a vape pen and I have a small scar on my forehead that'll be there for life. He hit me round the head with a lump of wood we had for protection. He and I both know he did not land a single punch on me. Now, I am sitting on the floor and he on the bottom bunk both breathing heavily and choking for breath. I see my opportunity and strike like a snake, snapping his nose and he is on me again, me underneath him and the blood gushing from his face is going into my eyes my mouth and my nose and all over my bare chest. We wrestle some more until finally we are spent and find ourselves at opposite ends of the cell.

"We going again"? I say thinking fuck I'd rather not.

"Well, what you saying"?

"I'm happy to call it a day; you"?

"Shake on it"? says the wily wiry hard ass little fuck and we do exactly that. The reason me and Aidy were so tight after is because the staff tried to get both of us to move out for of course it couldn't be hidden; we'd woken the whole wing and the night screw was obviously aware. But Aidy refused to grass or move and I did the same after each one of us was called individually into the wing office. The staff made both of us sign papers saying if we were hurt or worse the jail wasn't liable for said injury and, like I say, we were inseparable. The next door neighbour, Craig, gave us 25 quids worth of spice in the morning so impressed was he with the length of time our pugilism lasted. Thinking of that night now makes me think what a lonely, frightening place jail could be at times. But at the time my mask of madness was well in place to protect me. Being vulnerable right then, whilst still using drugs heavily, was not an option. And now Aidy is leaving.

Anyway, I move in one of my friends, the afore mentioned Aron 'Stuart' Little. We have thoroughly scrubbed the cell finding lots of Aidy's oddities; empty capsules he used to fill with paracetamol and pretend to newbies were narcotics, little pill bottles full of washing up liquid tinged water which he would sell as methadone to the same demographic, new birds unwise to the ways of the system. We have both just been to the treatment hatch to get our methadone and mine is now down to 16ml, from an initial 50. I'm coming down two ml per week and the journey has been relatively smooth thus far. Stuart goes out the cell for a Saturday morning visit and I'm behind the door alone whilst on the in cell telly Christine and the Queens perform their excellent song 'Tilted' which is not only good on the ears but very visually stimulating too in the music video showing on the channel 4 Music. Down at the treatment hatch I had had a conversation with a fella from another wing who was buzzing he only got five years for chopping off a geezers hand with a machete. He had managed to have the charge lessened from a GBH Section 18 to a Section 20 on some sort of technicality. He had a touch!

For my first three months at the Ley I found myself being confronted in groups twice a week every week for my outrageous and childish and somewhat slippery behaviour. Finishing the Thinking Skills course here in the prison showed me just how much I did actually learn in that place. I was saying to Jason, the manager down the Programmes' Unit and someone who I still care about very much that:

"It's funny the fact that we really don't feel how cave man esq we are until we get an education in what it really is to be human ya know"?

"What do you mean"?

"Well", I say, "people during the sessions here sometimes say things like 'fuck me it's common sense' when you're teaching".

"Yeah", says my worthy interlocutor.

"And yet", I continue, "without the skills you teach of 'stop and evaluate' they would never realize they have been acting on compulsion , impulse, most of their lives".

"What d'ya mean"?

"For instance, in conflict situations, right, when we feel the adrenalin, before these skills are given we just act on the anger and fear whereas you help to equip us with a set of tools that offer other realistic options that can save us from a whole world of pain".

"I just wanted to ask", says Jason "do you think there is anything else we can do to help to improve the assimilation of these ideas to prisoners Sloaney"?

"Yeah", I say, "make the course longer". We both laugh.

"We have trouble keeping people focused for six weeks as it is". The Ley community had taught me much of the skills taught here and though I relapsed I must say that this may be due to the time it truly takes to imbibe such abstract ideas. As I said, I got nearly four years clean time but old thinking crept back in.

It had taken me, at the Ley, months to start listening to people in those terrifying circles of bodies. After some months I stopped reacting and screaming back 'bollox' and instead opened my ears to what people were saying they were seeing in me. So when I was being told I was rude, arrogant, manipulative, devious, unkind, selfish and uncaring I tried to take away these messages, mull them over and come up with ways to fix these defects of character.

"And you go around as if you think you're smarter than everyone else", I remember someone saying one day.

"Really"?

"Yes", echoed the group in unison.

"I can see that you're realizing that we are trying to help you now Andrew", said Emma after one such group. Always had my back this gorgeous girl and I truly did feel I was in love with her! Still do sometimes, along with a few others! Defect right there as I type from the written document ten years after the Ley and 2 years after this one was written!! Once I started listening and seeing myself as others saw me the work could really begin. I could start detracting the more unattractive aspects of my personality. My name slowly began to appear less frequently on slips. And I started to be able to point things out in my peers. And in doing this I would reinforce my own learning. I was on the pull up sheets less, those pieces of paper on the wall in every place in the establishment and found myself getting less 'TTs' or 'talking toos' as well. Now a TT was given to unfortunate recipients who'd transgressed the rules. The Head Co-ord and Assistant Co-ord would sit in the office and those on talking toos would have to sit in the front room in silence whilst everyone else went for a fag at lunchtime. The Assistant Co-ord would then call me in, just for instance and I'd have to stand before them with my hands behind my back whilst they read out the charge before me.

"Today you are receiving this TT because it was noticed you did not lock the chickens up last night before bed space", says the Head Co-ord and then the Assistant Co-ord takes up the narrative from the big book they read from in which TTs are written up.

"This shows an uncaring attitude and a shocking lack of awareness which could have led to all the chickens being eaten by Mr Fox", and then he passes the book back to his boss once more and he continues:

"Your Further Action is Sunday's cooker cleaning wash up solo; please write your TT on the board outside the office and log it in the book in silence. Then you can have a fag". These things are done to teach us addicts about consequences. Each evening those who had had TTs have to, after the evening meal, stand in front of the whole community and read out their TT and consequence with hands, once more, behind their back. Hand rather for one holds the card on which it is written. Consequences are not always punitive; for some it may be to deliver a seminar or state once a day at 'crew check' when all residents are accounted for that they are doing their issue work, meaning doing written work on some of the trauma experienced in their lives.

0800hrs. 6th November 2018. Stuart is pottering round the small cell, kettle is on and he suddenly turns to me with wide eyes:

"Oh my God, do you know what you did in your sleep last night"?

"No", I say, "what d'ya mean ya weirdo"?

"It was about three in the morning, you were shouting 'get out get out' and making these strangling noises for about two minutes and you sounded like you were like in pain and then,'cause I got out my bed to check you were ok, you suddenly sat bolt upright in your sleep and said 'I'm nefarious' and then laid down and started snoring"!

"Nefarious", I say, "I've never even heard that word, if it even is a word".

"Really"?

"I swear Stu", I say, "grab my dictionary bro". He does, I look the word up and it means 'criminally wicked'.

"Int that mad"! says Stu.

"Wow", I say absentmindedly. But I remember that this disturbed me greatly.

At 9am I go to horticulture class. We travel up to the north end of the jail and the greenhouses surrounded by allotment like spaces filled with flourishing veg and flowers. Despite the massive walls I feel free here. Thankfully none of the action that happened in the film Scum happens here though this is where it was filmed. However, two weeks or so ago there was a fella raped on one of the other wings. I can't categorically say it happened but it was all over the prison that it did. Anyway. Fuck that. It's a fine day. Chainsmokers are on the radio singing about Paris and it makes me nostalgic for my youth. In this greenhouse my workmates are cleaning the tables on which the Geraniums sit. Some of the flowers are being saved and some are off to compost. I find myself lovely examples of each colour and plan to take them back to my cell. A youngster called Jack, quick witted, tall and gangly with a mop of blonde hair and to whom I've taken a liking says:

"Fuck me Andrew, look at all this equipment", and he waves his arm across the feed systems and lights, "imagine all the weed you could grow here"!

"Worth a fuckin' fortune mate", I say. Whilst everyone else works I sit and write outside in the watery sunlight. AddemupAde is still away but I look forward to maths with Bev in the afternoon.

1400hrs.

"Hello Bev", I say walking into the classroom.

"Hi Andrew", says the worthy woman.

"I have a dentist appointment at three", I tell her.

"Ok", she says, "no problem" then she turns to our Kurdish Iraqi friend Shabab, "you have a dentist appointment too don't you"?

"It is at three o'clock also", he says in his deep tones.

"Right", says Bev to the class, "we are working on mean, median and mode today".

"What is this Andy", asks Shabab as an aged prisoner walks into the room.

"Basically these are different ways of finding the average or middle point using data", I say, not at all sure my explanation is sufficient or comprehensive enough.

"I don't understand", he says, predictably considering my concise inadequate answer.

"Ok", I say, "let's say we are using the 'mean' method. If ten people went to the swimming pool and each one logged how long they stayed in the water you would add up the time then divide that number by the ten people to find the average or, like, the middle amount of time that a person was in the water for. Not the shortest time, not the longest but like the middle, the average amount of time".

"I do not understand 'divide'", says Shabab.

"Fuckin' hell", my internal voice says whilst my outer voice actually says:

"Remember the other day when I showed you the little line in the book with the dot below and the dot above"?

"Oh yes, I remember now, on Friday you said this means 'shared' yes"?

"Yes bro", I say giving him a high five and feeling rather chuffed he'd remembered!

"Ok Andrew", he continues, " so if one man say he in the pool for 40 minute (he doesn't put the 's' on) and another man he say he in the water for 30 minute I would add the 30 and 40 and then divide this, like share this by two"?

36

"That is exactly it", I say feeling something akin to joy flowering within me.

"And if I have ten men I just add up the ten times and share by the ten men"?

"Yes bro"!

"So", says Bev now, "I want you to go around the room and find out how many children each of you have". There are seven of us in the class and we ascertain that the mean amount of kids here is 3.5.

"So that is the 'mean' method", she says and my sick mind is looking at this aging woman and thinking sexy thoughts. But I dispel them. I just think she's so lovely and in hindsight feel I can't separate recognition of loveliness from sex stuff. Anyway. "Most people would say that this is usually the most appropriate method of finding an average with most sets of data", she finishes. We go through the other two and also 'range' which the class grasp easily before me and Shabab go have our mouths poked around in by the proficient dentist. I have a wisdom tooth removed. All's well with the microcosm world today. Apart from the disturbing revelation this morning!

1210hrs 7-11-2018. Now that was yesterday. As you see dear reader it is now lunchtime on a Wednesday afternoon. Now yesterday, Tuesday, is the day that 'canteen' forms are given out. Now the canteen sheet day is an important day in the life of a prisoner. This is because this is the sheet on which we order our goods for the week which are listed on the thing. The list contains things from vape capsules for smokers (smoking now banned across the whole prison estate in Britain) to toiletries treats and sweets and greetings cards to send to loved ones. Atop this otherwise impersonal list of goods is the prisoner's name and the amount each individual has to spend that week. So me and Aron 'Stuart' Little return from our respective places of work on 'Freeflow' when everyone shuttles to and fro on the officer lined routes and we find our canteen sheets under our door.

"How much you got on yours Andy"? asks Stu.

"£34", I tell him "but it ain't no good seeing as I'm £130 in debt", and this is depressingly true. Spice debts. "So I've actually got fuck all".

"Same here man, £50 on the sheet but none of it mine", says Stu rubbing his twisted ankle which he snapped horrifically many years ago. It left the leg three inches shorter than the other. He got £65000 in compensation which he spunked on crack and heroin. And some bits and pieces for his kids it must be said. Anyway, back to the here and now or then as it may be as I type from the handwritten sheets here in 2021, on a bed in a house with Homeric light streaming through my window on a

37

lovely July day in Oxford England! So, do not be deceived, class divides do not stop at the prison gate. Some prisoners are rich and get richer selling drugs in jail and some are in poverty and addicted to those drugs. Some walk about spanked out in Armani whilst others wear prison issue clothes and shoes. Saying that, in prisons where there's work like here everyone can live relatively well but a common saying today is it's 'the spice life or the nice life' and I'm in the former category right about now along with my cellmate although we do have our own clothes and trainers! But the truth is that if you smoke spice you'll live in a dingy cell with no creature comforts for every penny goes on the shit. We both, Stu and I, look skinny, sick, drawn and pale! The rich ones who don't indulge look smart, well fed and healthy. Me and Stu have to run round the wing to our creditors letting them put what they want on our sheets. If I were to stop smoking now I would be able to negotiate paying half my debt but I just keep adding to it and my sheet is booked for the next fuck knows how many weeks. So on Friday, the day we get our goods, all mine will go out but I will be able to get more drugs. Not that I really ever go without. I always find a way. One more thing to add is that on Fridays many people all over the prison 'bounce' or leave the wing they are in debt on. Leaving their creditors fuming when they fuck off. Invariably the dealer will know someone on the wing onto which they go and they'll still get ironed out, smashed up. No escape here. Famously canteen day is called 'black eye Friday'.

I return to my cell after work to find a letter beneath the door from a friend called Cork Andy, an Irishman I've known, along with his lovely late wife Irish Angie, for twenty years or so. He is about 60 years old now. He and his wife fed me for many years along with Charlotte and Claire, girlfriends, the latter another lovely lady who was hopelessly addicted to hard drugs like me but who is now clean. Now next door to this couple (then just Andy when Ang died) there lives an old girl who, when I moved into the building (Invicta House) in 2001 must have been 75 so is truly ancient now. She has been leaving money and food outside Andy and Angie's for many, many years knowing that these two then pass on these blessings to the struggling disenfranchised and downright low like me. Anyway, Andy tells me in the letter that the venerable soul had gone missing for a week. She walks miles daily but always returns home. Now I have been in and out and had three flats in that building and nothing changes, including her. In all that time I have never known her talk to anyone but Andy. That's just the way she is. Lovely thing! I have earned nods from her but this took much time. But she actually loves Andy. And I know she has a soft spot for me. I have occasionally put loving notes through her door thanking her for the many, many kindnesses she has shown us all. Anyway, Andy tells me, the police found her. I pen her a letter, knowing her door number thanking her again and telling her I pray for her. I tell her there's hope for me yet and that all her kindness may yet bear fruit. It is imperative for me to let her know that one of the 'poor misfortunates' to use Andy's vernacular, that she has helped, may honour her efforts yet. Remember dear reader it took me two years to get a nod in my direction at my 'hello'. The only real dialogue had with her was when I was on the stairway of this tower block flaked out on heroin only to be woken by her tiny foot nudging me in the ribs. I opened my sticky eyes and gazed up to her and immediately removed any anger from my emaciated face upon seeing her grey haired bespectacled countenance looking down upon me.

"Errr, oh, hello", I'd said trying to sound soft and gentle. I have massive respect for this old girl.

"Must I phone an ambulance or are you ok"? she most definitely asked me.

"No, no, I'm ok but thank you so much for asking", I'd said, trying to sound as respectful as possible in my heroin drenched bedraggled state. She'd simply nodded serenely at me and gone along her way. This lady, though she lives on the sixth floor, never, ever says Andy, used a lift in the 35 years they've known her. I don't even know her name! But she is a remarkable soul. She leaves her front door open yet has never been robbed when out! What a woman! I pray I see her shuffling down the street upon release July next year.

0927hrs 8-11-2018. Yesterday's highlight was the discussion I had with the optometrist who tested my ailing vision for me. We discussed many and eclectic subjects. I remember he'd asked me:

"Do you feel any guilt for your crime"? and I'd thought but not said 'which one of the many hundreds or thousands I've committed' but stuck to the one I'm in custody for now.

"Not really, it was an empty house bro, just stripping fixtures and fittings".

"It was still somebodys' property", he says.

"I feel guilt for the people I have harmed who have loved me over the years", I say quite honestly.

"Ok", he'd said, "That's a start".

"Hahahaha", I laugh, genuinely amused, "listen mate, what good did Dostoevsky's protagonist's guilt do him over the old lady? What good does guilt ever do? Rolling around in the shit is not the best way of getting clean bro". He looks thoughtful at this.

39

"Hmmm", he says, "I like that".

"Look, the best way to make amends for all my mistakes is to do good for the rest of my days. That's the way I look at it".

"I like that even more", he says and tells me at the same time that my blurry vision when reading is a result of my advancing years.

"But I'm just 42"!

"Well, not exactly old but you're no spring chicken either"! Cheeky sod!

"Wow", I say smiling, "I've enjoyed my time with you. Any book ideas for me"?

"Have you any for me"?

"Novel wise I loved John Fowles, The Magus. Or Heinlein, Stranger in a Strange Land; both blinding books. But Fowles first for it's fantastic".

"And I can offer Gulag by Solzhenitsyn or Blueprint by Robert Plomin. Both excellent reads. I wish we had more time", he says.

"Me too", I say honestly, "I'd love to discourse more on Nicomachean ethics but alas I'm but a prisoner and must return to the cell I've been condemned to for the foreseeable future and mix with the many halfwits I share my living quarters with".

"We find diamonds in amongst the lumps of coal my friend", says this learned aged P. I ponder this truth as I walk back to the wing and regret my outburst of hubris and arrogance. I go back to the wing and my cell and soon as Stuart Little sees me he is in soliloquy:

"Breaking news, eleven people have been shot in a bar in California, fuckin' hell, and a paraplegic man is dropping his legal action after successfully petitioning for change at Luton airport". Aron has a gravely and scratchy voice to match his mad scientist one eye bigger than the other lop sided mouth physiognomy and personality. But I do kinda like him, slippery fucker though he be. "Can you lift your legs up Andy"? he says now as he manoeuvres a broom around me."Sweet mate", he says as I do what he asks and my pen scribbles along paper. As I write I marvel at the speed and diversity of the snapping of my synapses. I think of Tim Berners Lee writing HTTP or HyperText Transfer Protocol from the bowels of the supercolliding atom smashing particle accelerator at Cern, Switzerland. Or Vint Cerf and Bob Kahn who penned TCP/IP or Transmission Control Protocol/Internet Protocol allowing for the linking of systems under a uniform set of procedures. I did a bit of programming in Visual Basic 6 at college within the paradigms of a HND in computer engineering which I didn't finish, dropping out after the first year. But learning of the different layers from cable to application was fascinating.

Yet even the systems we have today are nothing in comparison to the power of the human brain.

"I'm a genius, a genius, a little bit of genius", I say out loud without even realising I'm doing it.

"And a rambler too", says Stu. I have picked up spice and smoked today and I am starting to notice I get irritable and angry each time I break and give in to the demon drug. Part of withdrawels from this drug are stomach pains which recede soon as one puts a pipe or joint of the spice into the body. I consider going to the NA meeting in the prison today. Intoxicated or not, there is always a welcome there. I miss Ade and his peaceful happy demeanour. His beaming face full of love. I think now that if I had one wish it would be for a thousand years of life. I would spend it in the rain forest. I'd get God to mark the poisonous plants and the others I would test and the best purify to get high on chemicals no one had before me. This seems a good idea now, smashed out my head as I am.

"You going to the meeting today"? I say to Stu now, looking up from the pages. I mean the NA meeting of course.

"No", he replies, "I'm on that Bridge programme ain't I, mornings and afternoons". Bridge is a stepping stone into the twelve step NA orientated recovery programme run here at Rochester.

"Quite intense then", I say.

"Not really", says Stu, "the only really intense one is the TRE".

"What's that"?

"Total Release Experience, it's well heavy man, it's like a sort of yoga but where you focus on areas of the body where trauma is stored. See people in there crying every week I do".

"Wow man, sounds good".

"Yeah", he says, "it's done on Bridge. We also do acupuncture, creative art and the gym on there". He's rolling a spice spliff as he talks.

"Two puff pass", I say, not wanting to wait before I suck on the thing.

"She's sexy as fuck", says Stu, referring to some bird on Coronation Street catch up now showing on the telly.

"Proper sort int she"? I say. "Do you find when you ain't got a joint you feel sick Stu"?

"Yeah, course I do. It's all in the gut this shit and I sweat like a rapist as well".

"Me too bro, me too".

1995: Someone is trying to shake me awake. The house I am in is owned by Trish, a large and lovely lady with long blonde hair and much mischief about her, and her husband, Craig, a drawn shifty but canny cunt with mousy hair and foul mouth and with whom I struggle at times. Both are twice my age, as is the handsome black man, Wayne, known as Waff to his friends, who lays prostrate on one of the sofas in the tiny front room. There are other bodies about the place in various states of intoxication. This house is where my heroin habit really reached fruition. Though I'd been using a while by now, everything, including my criminality, stepped up a gear here. All three of these people are dead now. Craig and Trish through drugs and Wayne was murdered. But, alas, these things were a long way off back then. Craig is saying:

"Wake up Sloaney ya cunt", but he is only coming through in waves, "the fuckin' filth are at the door you little prick". I open one eye and see his skinny boat race looking down with a fag hanging out his gob.

"Fuck off Craig for fuck sake".

"Tell this cunt Waff will ya"? he says to the black man, whom I loved much, on the sofa. "Fuckin' filth 'ere for 'im all the time ", he continues, pleading to Waff.

"Sloaney man", Waff is saying, "There's old bill at the door bro, wake up"!

"Fuck off Waff", I say and I hear Craig drawing deeply on his fag making a sucking sound as he used to when inhaling the smoke.

"You're taking the fuckin' piss Sloaney", says Craig.

"Ahhh Craig man he's alright", says Waff.

"They're pulling off now", says Craig, "but you're a liberty taker Sloaney bringing them here with all the drugs in this house". I open my eyes now, stuck hard with sleep.

"How the fuck do you know they're for me"? I ask.

"They came here looking for you yesterday Sloaney", says Craig. I look about the room and see many sleeping bodies peppered here and there on furniture and the floor. Upstairs there's doubtless more drug dependent dudes and dudessess flaked out on fuck knows what. Drugs and drink are consumed here 365 24/7. All sorts of crimes from robberies to burglaries and even murder are committed by frequenters to this property. I love it here. It is home pretty much.

"Wow, I'm wanted then", say I.

"Duh", says Craig, "fuck me Sloaney", he says in justified exasperation.

"They told us yesterday that they're gonna come back for ya", says Waff.

"Why the fuck didn't ya tell me last night"? I ask no one in particular, talking more rhetorically, to the ether.

"We did", say Craig and Waff in Unison and then Craig continues that, "you were so out ya fuckin' nut you weren't listening ya cheeky

42

little cunt", and as he finishes he sucks greedily with the hissing sound at his cigarette, "fuck sake", he mutters before trudging to the kitchen and calling out to me from there; "do ya fancy a livener"? Meaning an injection of amphetamine.

"You tryna get rid of me or what"? I say, smiling up at the Waffster who flashes his brilliant teeth, handsome sod. Looking up from the page I see Zara Larson now, in this cell, 23 years or so or maybe more later. I'd like to bite her bum. Anyway, I digress. Back to all those years back and off the sexy cunt on the telly. I go into the kitchen, wading through bodies and slam some 'phet. Craig fucks off upstairs and I trample people to find my spot back in the front room hemmed in by flesh all around me. Waff, smoking a fag looks to me and says:

"Got any tackle Sloaney"? By this he means heroin.

"You're talking to me"! I say to him, "come on, let's go in the kitchen". Craig comes back down. He sees me preparing a hit and pulls out some foil for Waff who rarely injects.

"Got some for me Sloaney"? asks Craig.

"Course man". A screw opens the door and I must leave this for now. More later. I have now smoked spice and am fucked. Tripping. I'm down to 14ml of methadone, so justify my use of spice for I cannot be properly clean 'till that has finished. Seven weeks at two ml a week. Then no sleep for weeks and weeks and weeks.

0925hrs Sat 10/11/2018. All the cells are open for association here on Alpha wing this morning. If we get out for association on the morning we are locked up in the afternoon. Tomorrow will be the other way around. Banged up morning out afternoon. Still I sit in the cell writing. Aron Little comes in.

"I need a shit Sloaney", and I fuck off to socialise with the reprobates I love. And smoke spice of course, not wanting to inhale the emanations from his turd.

1225hrs. Let's go back to yesteryear. I leave Craig's house and head for the train station, looking for police all the while. Although I have burgled up and down the lines in Whitstable, Faversham, Margate, Dover, Minster, Folkstone, Martin Mill, Deal, Walmer, Herne Bay and myriad other places whether of poor or plenty I again, this day, purely for its proximity, choose Sandwich. I get there and traipse about to no avail. I skulk and scuttle for hours and hours and realize too late I've missed my train. It's at least seven miles home and in my starting to withdraw state I'm not gonna walk it. I must find something. Money, I need money. I fuckin' need dough and quickly before I start to feel the

43

monkey loosening my bowels. The drugs I had this morning are wearing off fast and I'm starting to feel real panic set in. I must have heroin, speed, crack and beer. I cannot be straight, I can't live with being me. Even if I did go back, Craig, being a cunt and with the hump because I bring heat to the house, would not be inclined to let me in unless I have a prize. As I sit writing in the cell I think of Alan Turing, Edward Cod and Sir Tim Berners Lee again. My mind wants to wander from the tale I'm about to tell. But it must be told. Why I don't know, but here it is. After slipping through the tiny cobbled streets of this beautiful historic town I come to an old house with leaded windows and through the grime I can see the aged owner, an old lady, pottering about in what looks like nightwear. So, hoping that she might soon turn in I go around the back where I see an old fella also doddering; he has a brandy or whisky glass in his hand and I can see the light of an old black and white telly flickering on his face as he sits down and lights a cigarette. Soon the old lady, too, comes into the room and sits, picking up what looks like knitting as she does so. I sneak around in the overgrown garden till I find a spot where I can sit, myself, and observe their movements. It is still mild but a chill sweeps through me and sweat lines my skin as the insidious sickness starts to set in. It is 1am before the scene changes. Eventually, the two of them, like ancient elephants in the speed of their movements, take themselves off to bed. As soon as I see the light extinguished in the bedroom I'm out the long grass, off my now aching skinny bottom and onto my feet which are now freezing due to the temperature having dropped severely. And of course by now I am clucking, withdrawing and in desperate need of the heroin which whisks me away from the worries of the world. So, I creep around this archaic house with its ancient occupants until I find just what I'm looking for, a window slightly cracked, not quite open but one that soon will be. It has diamond lead shapes all over the glass like the rest on this pile and I know I can pull it hard without fear of breakage. I pull the bottom corner and use the screwdriver I nicked from the couples very own shed to push the old handle up, pinging the thing open and making, thankfully, little noise. Though barely a sound is made I still stand silently, stock still to insure nothing was heard by the old people upstairs. After what seems like an age but is actually but a few seconds I climb into the kitchen. Again I stand silently to make sure I am safe. Oh the irony. Thankfully, all the doors inside the property are open and I creep from room to room pocketing the few hundred pounds I find in the old ladies purse and the old fellas wallet which they've left downstairs in the very room in which they were knitting, smoking and watching t.v but an hour or so ago. I can smell the aroma of old people heavily here and my imagination is running wild in my drug deprived state. Clucking can sometimes bring with it vivid hallucinations. As I tread lightly on the first step of the staircase the probably imperceptible creak is massively magnified to my own ears and I stop, holding my breath inside my chest so I may hear anyone stirring or anything else in this old scary building. I stalk the stairs in this manner ceasing my movement to ascertain, every so often, that I haven't woken anyone. I know it may sound like the warblings of a madman but I truly fear ghosts and, worse, demons and constantly look about me to insure the devil isn't at my back. I'm always terrified when I do these types of burglary, or 'creepers' as they're known. It was a big ancient frightening house and what's more, old people are strange. Though the majority of the bedrooms are bare I still remember pocketing a chequebook and card, credit card and an old ring. As I approach the room in which they sleep I can hear the rhythmic breathing of the two old fuckers in the bed. One snores quietly and the other inhales noisily with a sort of hhhrrrrrmmmpphh followed by a ssscccccceeeewww which makes a whistling sound. The closer I get to their door the stronger the smell of old people and lavender, pungent perfume and tinned sweets. I step over the threshold of their room and am startled by the sudden noise of a cat bolting from beneath the bed. I freeze on the spot before, seeing no change in their slumber, moving toward them stealthily, tiptoeing and cat like myself. I walk around to the old boy's side of the bed and, for some reason I can't quite understand to this day, poke my hand slowly, slowly beneath the very mattress on which they lay. I use my hand like a snake, sniffing hither and dither until my fist finds something. I grasp the object with my fingers and slowly, slowly pull out a massive wad of banknotes, almost squealing in delight as I see what it is. There was the best part of £4000. 'Oh my God' I'm thinking as I pocket the massive parcel of paper whilst still standing over the old couple as they breathe, peacefully, blissfully unaware of the desperate drug addict who stands literally over them but a couple of feet away from their dreaming forms. I go now to the dressing table and marvel at the multitude of diamonds, emeralds, rubies and gold I see upon lifting the lid of the jewellery box sitting atop it. I fill my pockets with these treasured trinkets and get to the bedroom doorway before turning back, returning to the dressing table once again. I dig the jewellery out of my filthy trousers and return them from whence they came. With the wedge I have there's no need to cause real heartache. I had never done this before and didn't again but that night it felt right. I've enough. And besides I also have their credit cards and chequebook and card which at that time were very easy to use fraudulently. And the cheque book and card I'd sell for ten pounds per page. Now I'm leaving my tread isn't so soft and stealthy but neither is it too loud for I get clean out the property, though I left forensic evidence which would bite me some time later. Along with a few other burglaries for which I went to prison. So, once out the window I go to the first red phonebox I see and order a cab. Soon as he turns up I say:

"Staffordshire Street, Ramsgate please mucca", and hand the driver £30 saying, "keep the change bro".

"You sure mate"?

"Yeah man, step on it geez please and what's the time mate"?

"Twenty to two fella".

"Cool". Soon I'm getting out the car and banging on the door. Craig opens it, fag hanging out his gob.

"Fuck sake Sloaney", he says but he's smiling. He lets me in. The room is full of bodies and everyone greets me heartily. I pull out the wedge and there's a few 'fuckin hells' go up. Waff winks at me, handsome beautiful guy, always had my back man.

"Where the fuck d'ya get that"? asks Craig.

"You know me man", I smile, "any tackle for sale"?

"We just picked up tonight, got an ounce of crack as well".

"Let's get fuckin' crackin' then"! And the rest, my friends, is history.

14/11/2018. 1705hrs. I'm hitting 95% on my mock papers and I'm well pleased with this considering I couldn't do a simple sum until Ade showed me. I learnt wonderful things in the horticulture class this morning. Dull to some but magical to me. The units we done today were 'applying organic and inorganic mulch' and 'planting of previously potted subjects'. These units were written, along with the rest of the course, by our very erudite teacher Dave who is also the education manager here at Rochester. He was busy so the class was taken by another very learned fella called Tim who can teach anything from maths and English to mechanical engineering and who of course knows his shit on horticulture. I'm a lucky guy. Anyway, I'm now back in the cell and Aron 'Stuart' Little is talking about a ruffian friend of ours, currently on another wing called Jay.

"His bird got a not guilty on that murder Sloaney".

"Really"? I say, "I thought it was a cut and shut case".

"Some technicality or something apparently. I think she was just there when it happened anyway. I used to fuck her back in the day; she was proper fit".

"She's still a sort man, I've seen pictures of her on Jay's wall when he was in Elmley".

"She turned up at my door with a tin full of coke she'd stolen off her boyfriend", says Stu.

"Oh yeah", say I, "I forgot you're a Medway boy".

"I met her years ago when she was with Jamie P.....she was, oh my God, she was fuckin' tidy mate I swear".

"How d'ya end up fuckin' her if she was with him then"?

"Naaa she'd split up with him by then and soon after he got murdered".

"Yeah man she is pretty", I say again remembering Jay's pics.

"Proper tasty", Stu goes on, "she had all that coke and I said to her, like, what ya gonna say to the fella she took it from, like the new boyfriend and she said, like fuck him in it, I'll tell the cunt he shouldn't of left it there".

"What, and you served her up all night sniffing Charles"?

"Yeah, well, we washed a lot of it up to be honest", meaning they turned the coke to crack using a simple process known to most junkies.

"I asked David M---- if I could write about him in my book today", I say now.

"What did he say"?

"Yeah he's cool and anyway, even if I did write stuff and a court decided to try prosecute it'd never stand up 'cause at the end of the day I'm a lying thieving fuck"!

"I don't care what you write about me", says Stu, "no one can make me worse than people think of me already".

"Me too man", I say laughingly, "fuck me, I'm down as a burgling, thieving, violent, woman beating cunt though I dare say the press I get locally is a bit better nowadays". Still, I muse, I suspect there're some who'd happily assist me in shaking off this mortal coil.

1800hrs. Fuckin' Flog It is on the T.V. Stu is on his bed absolutely pickled after smoking a joint of spice. I've not broken yet myself. Stu flicks through the channels. He comes across something on E4 with a big black woman in soliloquy to the camera and says:

"You can fuck off ya fat slag, and you", as he finds the news on ITV. We have agreed that each day I get to watch one news programme. Channel 4 News. My favourite and it's an hour long.

"What about Emmerdale and that? Won't you be pissed me having the news on 7 till 8 mate"?

"Naa man", he says, "I can do the catch up thing at the weekends".

"Cool man, I only watch that one because I think it's more informative and objective. Usually I'm a BBC man but I do like a bit of Piers and Susanna Reid in the morning". It's true, I do, as these two have chemistry and I can't help but wondering if Piers is boning Susanna, beautiful brunette that she is. My one complaint is the table they use at

ITV studios disallows for views of her legs which she showed off so well on Strictly Come Dancing. My God she's hot. That's one fit bit of kit boy. She could only be more perfect if she had an off switch so we could turn her off when nagging. Maybe upon release I'll get a blow up doll version complete with movable limbs so I can sit her at the table for nice romantic dinners before boning her and putting her under the bed until our next date. Ahhh, the perfect woman indeed. I'm joking of course!

Anyway, today I've been in the gym. I came out of maths at three pm and had a great, sweaty and satisfying workout. Squats, clean and press and a bit of bench. Few miles on the treadmill and I'm done. Once finished I went to the showers but due to being so skint down to spice debt I've not even a shower gel to my name and wash on the wing with prison soap which isn't the same as the Queen's White Windsor just to set the record straight. Finding half a bottle of Nivea in one of the stalls I'm sorted then realize I brought no towel either so mosy down to the gym orderlies room and pick up a few prison vests to do the trick. I lather myself luxuriously then get out and appraise my skinny form in the full length mirror. The look of a spice head is much akin to that of a heroin addict. And I am both! Saying that, it's twenty hours since my last joint. I bared my struggles to the 20 or so bods at the NA meeting yesterday. I'm truly sick and tired of being a slave to addiction. Yet have not the power to stop. Anyway, more on prison life later. Let me take you to 2001 now, when I had just been released from a sentence for another burglary.

2001. This is when I first met Charlotte. I had been awarded a flat by Thanet Council who have, in all fairness, always been good to me. Invicta House, or Terrible Towers as I call it, was where my new abode would be. At the time I was still with my son's mum, E----, who I was and probably still am deeply in love with. Anyway, whilst in jail I'd met a man I won't name but will simply call 'S', an ex military and extremely dangerous guy. He had offered me work in the form of large consignments, well large for me, of drugs upon release. Kilos of base amphetamine and weed. So, loaded with a big parcel of drugs, a few kilo, I land on the estate where Invicta House is situated in an ill fitting Burton's suit thinking I'm the shit make no mistake. I really thought I was Pablo Escobar. I had myself a Sierra XR4x4 2.9 litre motor and felt like gangster number one. Gradually I started to build my empire on this deprived shithole, undercutting everyone and threatening smaller dealers, telling them if they didn't work for me they could expect to have their front doors booted off on a regular and acts of violence committed upon their persons. Another bonus was no one could match the quality of the drugs I was getting so business happily came my way. The speed would melt through plastic so potent was it. Local speed freaks were regularly having serious psychotic episodes on the shit. Proper perv powder. I used to get pretty little E---- to run much of it here and there, protecting her legal status by telling her that should she be stopped by police she should say I coerced her into running for me. For the record, E---- is a double of Scarlett Yohansen. I'd been supplying a fella, a youngster, called 'Bucktooth Billy'. He had had 100 ecstasy tablets off of me on top of the speed and weed for I'd got a foot in the door there too and was getting thousands at a time and the lovely little fucker I still have a soft spot for to this day had failed to pay me for the umpteenth time. I phoned Mel and Chris, the latter who I once hit with a hammer for the same transgression and who died of drugs some time later, to get an address of where the buck tooth brother might be hiding.

"Where the fuck will that little cunt Billy be"?

"What", says Mel, "Buck Tooth Bill"? I call Mel 'Smell',

"Yes, Billy Smell, where's he likely to be"?

"He's in a flat near Tivoli Park, number 18 Tivoli Gardens I think", she'd told me, grassing the little fucker straight up. I'd remember not to trust her too far in the future. I get in the whip in Burberry shorts and bare chest and press my Reebok Workout Plus to the pedal to motor down the other end of Margate. I find the flat the little fuck is hiding in and knock the door. Two minutes later and the shitbag is before me and his usually robust young face immediately loses its healthy flush as he turns ashen white.

"Upstairs you little cunt", I say.

"But Sloaney".......he stutters.

"Upstairs Billy", I say, "Don't want the neighbours looking do we", and he leads the way to the flat door inside the building, looking over his shoulder all the while and me being careful to close the door to the complex tight behind me. Upon entering I see it's but a room, a bedsit.

"You alright Sloaney man"? asks poor Bill and I can hear his voice shaking. My resolve is slipping. He owes me for not only pills but speed and weed too.

"Who the fuck are you"? I ask a gangly looking youth in the corner.

"I'm Paul", he says, "can I go"? I can see he's shitting himself and I'm sure he let out a fart of fear the savage. He stands.

"Sit the fuck down", I say. He does.

"Sloaney".......starts Bill.

"Shut up Bill", I rasp, "and who's this slut"? I ask, looking at the young girl of about eighteen or so who sits in a chair in the corner of the room.

"I'm Charlotte", says Char, no fear at all and actual defiance in her voice.

"Who the fuck asked you to speak"?

"Alright Geez, calm down", says the ballsy bitch and immediately her tone endears me to her.

"You're a mouthy cunt ain't ya? Please shut up". I turn to Billy.

"Bill man I came here to smash your cunt in but can't fuckin' do it you little worm".

"Ahhh thanks man", he says, letting out a sigh of relief. Charlotte tuts.

"What the fuck's up with you wench, proper game cunt you int ya"?

"Got a be these days mate", she says before unbelievably saying "and you're a proper gangster ain't ya"? in the most sarcastic tone of voice I'd ever heard in my life. I laugh out loud.

"I could smash your head in Billy and let me tell you if you ain't got my money in a couple days I'm gonna fuck you up nigga".

"But Sloaney, how can I get your money if you don't give me any work to work"?

"Are you taking the piss"? I ask incredulous, "how the fuck can I give you more work when you already owe me hundreds you little cunt"?

"Well he ain't got no income unless you give us something to work with", says the nutjob mouthy fearless fucker from her place in the corner of the room. I'm intrigued by this psycho for clearly she's batshit crazy.

"Us"? I say to Bill, "proper under manners I see Bill".

"You funny cunt", she says to me before continuing that, "I wouldn't touch that cunt with a bargepole", before looking me up and down and saying, "you either for that matter"! Unfuckinbelievable. I laugh from the pit of my belly.

"You are a prick", I tell the handsome wench, ballsy motherfucker.

"And you're a plastic gangster cardboard cut out if ever I saw one". I just smile at her, gobsmacked.

"Fuck sake Bill", I say to this buck tooth fuck, then I look to the geezer reclining on the bed, the gangly one, "and you Pump Up Paul, what's your game bro"?

"Me"? he says.

"Yes, you you skinny cunt", but seeing his fear I instantly pity him. I'm too soft for drug dealing. I throw him £20 and tell him to get the three of them something to eat. They all look like they need it.

"It's not food we want", says Charlotte once Paul fucks off out the room to the fish and chip shop, "it's a line geez".

"Wait there", I say and shoot down to the car to get some stinky base amphet, two ounces, and a bar of solid. (9oz of cannabis resin).

"Billy man", I say upon returning and throwing him the drugs, "you better start coming with some money for me bro and I want some off of the debt you already owe me each time you see me on top of the dough for this work I've given you now you get me mate"?

"Ahhh Sloaney mate I really appreciate this man I really do", and the worst thing is he actually is grateful the poor lovely fucker. And that, dear reader, is how I met Char who has been my on off lover for years and who now I count as one of my best friends ever. I would die and or kill for her the hard arse bitch.

0832hrs 17/11/2018. It's a Saturday. Last week we were out in the morning so we are banged up today and out afternoon. Staff are running up and down the landings attending the buzzers, emergency cell bells which continuously find fingers being pushed into them due to the fact everyone is behind their door. Right outside the door now I can hear an officer trying to reassure a prisoner that he will soon be out for his meds.

"What? What's that"? from the officer, then after she's heard more she says to the flap in the door she's talking at; "fuck sake, yes, you'll be out for your meds in a minute, Christ", before I hear the flap of the spyhole being closed in exasperation. Look, I have to say this, being a screw ain't fuckin' easy and to see a screw still optimistic about the job after years in it is rare. But this wing has a good staff team in general.

"Is 'Pocket Rocket' on today"? I ask Stu now, meaning the lovely fit little screwess Ms H who has all the prisoners salivating, including me. Stu is watching 'Over the Hedge' and spoiled my music channel fun this morning with his Emmerdale catch up. He doesn't hear me and I'm cool with that, smoking potent spice. One more thing to mention is that last night I had one of those strange sleep paralysis things happen where I'm panicking for some reason, trying to shout and move but simply cannot. Very strange phenomena that! Anyway, in the typed document there's a load of scrawled spiced up shit but the gist is this: I was fuckin' horrible to my friends this day. Moody and threatening and through the narrative I was clearly feeling guilty.

1200hrs 18/11/2018. Sunday lunchtime. I am in a cell with Bradley, a dark haired five foot ten handsome fuck I've known since a kid and grown up with and who is wildlife nuts, keeping a pet wolf spider in a little aquarium he made himself in his cell. Grin, the fraudster, is also in the cell. Brad is in for a burglary as usual. Upon me entering the cell and after yesterdays' behaviour Brad says:

"Oh, 'ere 'e is", with a slight smile on his pretty face. He doesn't avert his eyes from me as Grin pipes up:

"Feeling better t'day Sloaney are ya mate"? and he, too, keeps his gaze on me.

"Look lads I was horrible to you both yesterday. Please forgive me boys".

"You was Andy", says Grin and Brad, a talented artist and lover of nature and animals, an authority on any species of plant or bird or mammal or reptile the latter of which he's had lots of, also needs to say something.

"Sloaney man, I was even trying to tell ya because you described this exact behaviour the other day but you just wouldn't stop", and I'm feeling sheepish and embarrassed now.

"Rantin' and ravin' you was Andy, just lookin' for a fight with absolutely anyone mate", says Grin now.

"Then Andy", picks up Brad, "you deliberately went down to big Scouse's cell trying to pick a fight with him because YOU owe HIM money"!

"Pickin' and proddin' and pokin' you were Andy, tryin' to get anyone to argue with ya so you could have a fight mate", says Grin.

"Ahh man lads, I'm so sorry, really I am", I say plaintively.

"And ya know Andy", says Bradders in his carefully crafted speech, "that it's projection; you used spice, you hated yourself, then, like then you just cunt everyone else off like it's their fault".

"Yep", says Grin, "and we're ya mates Sloaney; fuck knows what you'd be like to your enemies or some cunt you didn't like".

"Well", I say, "at least something good came of it 'cause today I feel good about being good", and by this I mean I haven't smoked the spice.

"Anyway shut up Sloaney 'cause we're watching this", says McFradders. (Brad).

"Yeah Andy", says Grin, sucking on his vape, "sit down", he smiles, "ya lucky ya still welcome ya cunt".

"Cunts", I mutter.

"This old geezer(on TV) is 93 Andy", says Brad, "the poor cunt was in a Jap prisoner of war camp and Alan Titchmarsh has built him that beautiful new garden", and on TV Titchmarsh, bless him, is holding the old man's hand leading him round this piece of art crafted using nature. At the end of the picturesque garden is a newly built artists studio where this still fit and very lucid old boy can wield his brush and his pictures prove he does so with great competence.

"Ahhh in it lovely Brad"? says Grin.

"Look how happy he is man", says Brad, "and to think he spent three years seven months in those horrific conditions".

"And those Japs were fuckin' savage", says Grin.

"Yeah man" says Brad, "when they asked him how the Japs treated him d'ya know what he said Sloaney"?

"No", I say.

"He said that even though he holds no grudge the Japs were almost inhuman".

"There was no need for such barbarism", says Grin.

"How'd he get through it"? I ask the room.

"Do ya know what he said when they asked him that very question Sloaney"? asks Brad rhetorically, "he said this 'cause I wrote it down: 'two men looked out through prison bars one saw mud and one saw stars'" and he looks up and smiles at me, "the bollox in it"?

"Wow", I say, "wow, that is fuckin' beautiful bro for real",and I get up and grab a pen from a shelf in the cell, "give us it again Brad".

"Two men looked out through prison bars one saw mud and one saw stars", and I write it onto my hand so I could share it with you dear reader. I return to my cell and Stu is having spice convulsions on his bed but he's breathing ok. Anyway, I want to regale a tale of just before I got locked up this time.

2017/18 maybe. Just before I got collared I had been through a phase of robbing drug dealers. This particular morning I wasn't looking for anything. I was just hoping Charlotte would fuck off out so I could watch Sky News all day or whatever. She hates the news.

"You alright mug"? says Char coming into the front room from the bedroom.

"Yeah, you? What ya doing all tarted up; you want fuckin' or something"?

"Not by you ya fraggle", she says smiling as she applies a little mascara.

"Whaaaa", I say, mock incredulous, "you're not interested in this"? and here I make a sweeping gesture with an arm, encompassing my skinny naked emaciated frame laying horizontal on her sofa.

"Nope, not you Andrew", she says applying finishing touches to her high cheekboned handsome face in the mirror, "I've gone and got meself a 25 year old toy boy, no strings attached, winning", she finishes and this 'winning' has become a regular feature of her colloquial Margate mouth.

"Well I'm not fuckin' winning am I"? I say joking but a little slighted if I'm honest, "I thought we were getting married"? She guffaws at this.

"You wish mug", she says, "sort yourself out and I'll think about it. Much as I love you you're fucked mate. And you know I hate that shit", she finishes referring to the smack.

"I know I know. But you're gonna be safe though right"?

"Yeah mug. Anyway, the only man I'd marry would be Marshal Mathers. You know that. Right", she says, kisses me on the cheek, says her goodbyes and flies out the door. Gone. Not ten minutes after I hear the sound of the flat door next to Char's opening and then our letterbox being lifted followed by the voice of my friend being fired through it, Damien J, a blonde mountain of a man of 30 or so who terrorises these towns, putting the fear of God into drug dealers.

"Sloaney, Sloaney, you in"?

"Yep", I shout, running naked to the door and opening it wide so my pal of many years can see all my glory swinging free.

"Jesus Sloaney, you ain't fuckin' right ya cunt are ya"? but he's chuckling. Ahh, sitting here now in this cell I miss him. The flat next door belongs to Ian. He's been injecting heroin for years the old coot. So have his sons Gary and David the latter of whom just died from drugs. I went to school with these boys, one a year older and one a year or two younger. Rhona, his daughter, also uses hard food. (Class As). I have known the family literally all my life, like Brad, for we all grew up on the same street, Nixon Avenue in Ramsgate. Damo comes in and shuts the door.

"You alright Sloaney"? he asks. Now things are tough for Damo right now thus him dossing on kind Ian's sofa. He is one of the kindest, loveliest spirits I know and his favourite hobby is holding up drug dealers, the cunt just fuckin' loves it.

"Yeah man", I say, pulling on pants, jeans and T-shirt, "can I do anything for ya? Fag? Jack Daniels"?

"Nice one bro", and I pour him a shot or three whilst he rolls a cigarette. "I came to see ya 'cause I might have a bit of work for us".

"What sort of work? You know I'm on bail for a drum (burglary) as it is".

"No no nothing like that", says Damo who we all call 'D'. "Another drug dealer if ya fancy it"?

"Well I'm pretty skint", I tell him, "and I'd love to pay Charlotte's speed debt with Steve McColl ya know"?

"Come next door to Ian's 'cause he's in on it too". We go next door but I've misgivings

"Won't you just hold us up"? I say to Ian, "I mean you're sixty something for fuck sake".

"Ahhh let him come Sloaney", says D, I don't like it but we both love the old cunt so don't want to hurt his feelings and besides, the small bearded smurf like man is sprightly enough.

"Ok", I say, "so where is it"?

"Come into the kitchen Andy", says D and the three of us do.

"Ok", I say and we stand looking out the window of this ninth floor flat, "but what for"?

"Just keep looking", says D and we do for about ten minutes before from the back of the block we see someone emerge from the building; though we can't actually see him exit we know he's come out of a flat here for we know him; this fat fucker moved onto the third floor three years ago and he sometimes has dealers working from there and 'runs' for them, runs the shots of crack and smack to the junkies who phone the line. They man the phones, he does the running. Slowly I'm getting it.

"Look Sloaney", says Ian, who reminds me of the quick one from Mice and Men, Lenny's mate, George I think. His movements are rapid and his wit too. He, like me, has had two decades on amphetamine though I still bang the base and he partakes of only class As today. Ian is gnome like and Damo's six feet two is in such stark contrast I almost laugh as I think of the two of them from this cell. Anyway. Damo and I are getting excited and Ian continues that "he's been going back and forth to that alley all morning, at the back, next to the doctors".

"And ya know what that means", says Damo.

"He's got a couple people down there shotting"?

"Bingo", says D, "so you up for it or what then"?

"Course I am", I say, "when"?

"Well, like, I'm thinking now Sloaney", says D.

"Me too", says Ian, "you got any tools in there next door or what Sloaney"? Meaning have I any weapons next door.

"You know I've got that samurai sword on the wall boys", I say and promptly go to retrieve it, returning also with one of Charlottes' stockings which I like to use to smother my face to avoid recognition. Damo, who has robbed more dealers than anyone I know, absolutely refuses to wear any sort of covering for he loves the notoriety.

"Look D", I say, "don't you think you should smother up as we don't know who the cunt is working for mate"? 'Smother up' means use a balaclava or something like I'm using like a stocking.

"Naaa", he replies, "fuck that", then I turn to Ian who also refuses to wear any sort of mask. We wait and watch 'till the fat fuck downstairs on the third again exits the building to feed crack and smack to cats then quickly take the stair to that third landing, me masked with my stocking and holding the sword. Once there we stand, waiting anxiously for the cunt to come back. Damo knows, he says, that the fella never uses the lift so he waits by the door he must come through to his landing from the stairwell. The split second it is opened Damo, despite his massive stature, responds like a startled cat, grabs the fat cunt by what would be the lapels and smashes his forehead into the geezer's face which instantly spurts blood from its bulbous nose.

"Don't fuckin' fuck with me ya got it? Ya got it cunt"? says D to this now very, very frightened man. It has to be this way.

"What, what"? the geezer stammers and again, quick as a cobra, Damo smashes his head into the man's face.

"Did I ask you to speak cunt"? growls Damo more menacing than I ever saw him before.

"Ok ok", says the fella now, dripping blood in a steady stream all over his clothes and the floor.

"Right", says D as I draw in closer, pointing the sword toward the man, "now how many people in that flat and don't fuckin' lie to me ya fat cunt"?

"Four", says the fat man, "two black kids and two of my friends". We march him to the door. No sooner has he opened it D pushes him hard, propelling him to the front room where he falls flat on his face, Damo right behind him shouting:

"Robbery"! Ian points two weakling fellas into the kitchen, picking up a carving knife himself where he guards them, blade held at his side.

"On the balcony cunt and shut the door", D says to the fat fuck, "and shut the fuckin' door", and the geezer slides open that door and shuts himself out as ordered. I point my sword at the two black boys on the sofa, neither of them older than eighteen, poor cunts. Old enough to sell hard drugs though.

"You fuckin' move I swear on all I love I'll run this right through you you get me boys? Comprende"? Their eyes are wide with shock and terror. So, Ian has two junkies in the kitchen, one fat cunt is on the balcony and these two boys sit before me and Damo, shitting themselves at my sword and the beautiful monster of a man before them. I dare say the stocking is a bit off putting too, to say the least. Damo simply, very calmly, says:

"Is it fuckin' worth it lads"? and it's all over. When we get to Ian's I immediately spew puke all over the toilet, most missing the mark in my breathless psyched up state after running up the stairs and the violence of the robbery. We sit in the living room and laugh. We had a great days work, counting out £1390 and 45 £20 shots. We split it three ways. I have a quick snowball and go next door to clean my teeth and wash up. Wow, what a fuckin buzz.

19/11/2018. 1400hrs. I awoke last night with a start and then felt this feeling of inexplicable warmth that was very clearly saying to me not to worry, that everything would one day be ok. Three o'clock in the early hours. It was the same 'knowing' or premonition feeling I have when I know I am going to find a five pound note. And those premonitions always materialise. It really was the most profoundly peaceful and odd thing. It was immediate. I awoke then found myself awash with this gift, as if an angel had whispered in me ear just to say 'don't worry'. I have given my document, what I've written so far to a fella named 'Matchstick Model Maker Trevor' to peruse. He is an old, short, long time jail bird and an erudite fella to whom people turn on the wing for legal advice and stuff. Anyway. I learnt today in the maths class that the sine on a right triangle is simply the ratio of the opposite line on the triangle, the line opposite the hypotenuse to that hypotenuse. My maths are weak but learn I can! What a wonderful revelation.

Like George Orwell I have been down and out. Not Paris though a little in London but I have spent most homeless time on the streets of Canterbury, Cardiff, Essex and Oxford. I say down and out but that only came in time. Initially the freedom of no responsibility was exhilarating but, yes, eventually it nearly killed me with depression, dereliction and degradation. Though I broke my homeless virginity in Cardiff my first experience of how cold it can get in this country without a roof under which to shelter was in Grays in Essex. I remember this particular night where I was just so fuckin' cold it nearly killed me. I also learnt of the amazing power of chemicals and their ability to warm the body despite icy cold blasting barbarous winds. This night I was so cold that I was actually sobbing as the wind sent fingers beneath my inadequate clothing. In the daylight hours I had met this couple who'd taken pity on me and taken me home to dinner. As I was eating the female whose name eludes me must've clocked something in my face.
"What's the matter fella , you look like you're in pain"? I showed her the bunions on my punished feet and told her:
"They're absolutely fuckin' killing me", before putting the fresh pair of socks she provided me over my misshapen plates of meat.
"Thankyou so much", I said.
"Wait there", she said and she went away. Two minutes later she returned, taking my arm gently she said, "come with me, me mate wants to see you", and she took me across the road to this old ladies house. The lady, looking piteously upon my dishevelled appearance and the clear trouble I had in my shuffling gait pulled out a tray with a selection of pills and potions which would cause a skip in the heart of any junkie worth his salt.

"Wow", I said, "can I take a couple of these patches; I'll give you a tenner for five",as I pulled a solitary ten pound note from one of my filthy pockets.

"Oh, I don't want any money; please, take what you want", said the old dear whilst the other lady looked on, smiling. These Fentanyl patches are not only good for alleviating pain but also for keeping the monkey off of my back. And his fingers were starting to tighten their grip.

"Are you sure you don't want this"? I said, genuinely trying to push the paltry sum upon her.

"No dear, you need it more than me", said this magnificent matriarch, this lovely, kind old girl. Her and her magnanimous friend were full of charitable love.

"I am truly grateful; thankyou so very much".

"Are you coming back over for a bit"? asks the first lady from across the road who brought me here so thoughtfully.

"No, no", I say quickly, pocketing the patches from the tray now sitting on the table , five of them. Anyway, I chewed those patches but lost one inside the filthy bag of bollox I used to carry about with me; the bag was full of miscellaneous shit I'd accumulated, dirty needles and stinking clothes predominantly. Massive thing it was. When one night I was, as I say, freezing nearly to death with cold in some corner of a shop doorway in the early hours I dug around in the bag trying to find that lost patch. I was so cold and shivering so much I could hardly direct my limbs in any one direction. Then, by God, I found that patch and after chewing on the potent Fentanyl for fifteen minutes I was warm, content and snug as a bug in a rug. The homeless need the drugs and drink to keep them alive.

On the subject of Essex, let me tell another tale from those interesting towns. Upon waking up one day in a crack house with these two sons and their father, after sharing another hit, a snowball, the father said to me:

"What you doing today, to earn some dough"?

"Well, I'm going back to Grays (we were in Tilbury) because I've been battering the large Morrisons' supermarket there".

"Fuck me mate", says one of the brothers.

"Yeah", pipes up the other, "you don't wanna go there you'll get yourself well nicked".

"I've been smashing it for days, weeks even; it's fuckin' easy man".

"Well, that's probably because they don't know yer face", says one of the brothers.

"We been killing it there for years", says the other, "so can't go in there".

"Fuck that", says the dad, pulling a works out his arm, "I'm banned for life from there".

"I'll come back tonight if I make a few quid; don't have a bike I can use do ya"?

"Sorry mate", says the dad, "those out there are ours and we're all going out on the graft too",(shoplifting in this instance).

"Sweet lads", I say, resigning myself to the long walk up the main drag between the two towns. So I aim myself toward Grays at a rapid pace until I reach Paddy Power betting shop near the police station and realize that my rotten belt has broken. Across the road is a Childrens' Hospice Charity shop.

"Shit", I thought to myself and remember specifically thinking that: "if you steal from there Sloaney you'll be punished". I procrastinate, dither then think 'fuck it' and aim my tread toward the shop, promptly and determinedly picking up the first belt I find and walking out with it. Pulling it round through the hoops of my jeans I do an experimental few steps to ascertain its efficacy. Satisfied, I head toward Morrisons where I quickly dart to the alcohol isle and grab two bottles of Ceroc vodka and two bottles of Jack Daniels. I make my way, unmolested, out the shop without incident. I walk back to the High Street and to Paddy Power where I always have no problem finding a buyer and where I regularly bang up snowballs in the toilet.

"Alright mate", says this big burly fucker, "is that lot for sale or what"? He can see there's about £160 worth of booze and says; "I'll give ya twenty quid for it" and I promptly snatch the bag closed.

"You're having a bubble bath mate int ya"? I say, laughing out loud.

"Score mate, that's it", he repeats.

"Look fella, I'd rather take me eyeballs out with a spoon bro". I go to walk away. No sooner had I taken a step the fat steroid spastic makes a grab for the goods. Adrenalin immediately spurts through my skinny crack and smack ravaged body and I let go of the bag whilst almost simultaneously letting loose with a left jab which lands squarely , perfectly on the front of his chin. This big cunt falls like a felled tree straight to the penny, hitting the floor so hard all the betting shop's twenty or so customers go 'ooohh' and someone says 'good punch' and this is music to my ears. My elation, however, was short lived. The fella gets up and smashes me with a right then a left, one opening up an old wound over my left eye earned in a fight many years before. I am instantly aware upon regaining my senses on my back that a couple of people are pulling hither and dither on my lithe, not so young but still well sprung legs. Not to labour the point I was ejected but I was happy enough for the bag of booze was thrown out to me by the fella behind the jump, the shop steward geezer. Happy days. Still, I'm convinced that this would not have happened had I not stole that belt from the charity shop.

20/11/2018. 1040hrs. I became very agitated this morning. The reason I was raving is because the prison are trying to employ some shock tactics in order to lessen the load on emergency services being called to these walls. Ambulances of course. Daily we are draining resources for this wing alone sees at least two per day and whether it's because of spice attacks or people carving themselves up it is all, invariably, related directly to this mental drug. Ten wings. Four topside four newside two enhanced wings for good prisoners. But even on the latter two people are using this gear, this spice. Anyway, like any other day we expected to be unlocked for activities at 8am which didn't come to pass so after half an hour or so I pressed the buzzer I haven't pushed for my entire stay-I think.

"Ms Gilchrist", I say to the kind middle aged officer, a good one, who appears at the door, "Ms, I have waited since October for my doctors appointment today 'cause it's the twentieth isn't it"?

"Unfortunately Sloane that'll be cancelled because the whole prison is locked down today".

"Ms, but, like, what the fuck"?

"Look mate I'm sorry", says Ms and she continues that "I'm literally here on my own and Oscar One haven't given any details more than everyone is to remain behind the door", and here she pauses registering the storm brewing on my brow, "sorry", and she shuts the flap.

"But Ms", I say through the slit running the hinge side of the big steel door, "I've been having outbreaks of genital herpes Ms man, fuck sake", and I say to Stuart Little:

"Did you hear that Stu"? with incredulous tone.

"I know, the no good cunts, they're just lazy fuckers".

"Fuck it", I say and push the buzzer again.

"Sloane", says Ms G, appearing once again at the door and worst thing is I know it ain't her fault.

"Ms", I say, "I have never pushed that bell. Not even when losing in a fight with a madman I thought might actually kill me. Even when I'm spiced up fitting on the floor I tell my cellmates 'never push that bell'. I never fuckin' bother you. I even deliberately live with your most dangerous and difficult prisoners yes 'cause I like 'em but also to help you, Aidy was a fuckin' nightmare. Ms", and she lets me rant bless her, "Ms, I've waited a month and all I need is a prescription of Acyclivor to stop me having herpes flare ups as I detox. Please God get me to the quack at New Health Care today Ms", I finish, whiny like.

"Sloane, look", she says, "I really am on the wing on my own and I've been honest with you, you won't get there today 'cause everyone, absolutely everyone is on bang up", and the decent enough officer walks away. I shout shit I don't mean out the door like:

"I'm gonna slaughter this place for medical negligence and drain much needed resources in compensation: fuck sake Ms, you ever had genital fuckin herpes"? Anyway dear reader it took me some time to calm down, cold, without a coffee and hungry. I missed my meth yesterday too and thought it was on 8ml but is actually still on 10. Drops again tomorrow.

"D'ya hear that Stu"? I say to my mate on the bottom bunk who's reading.

"What"? he says.

"Listen", I say. We both hear it.

"What, the dogs barkin"? says Stu.

"Yeah", I say, "course the fuckin' dogs barkin man".

"What, that's inside the prison"?

"Stu", I say, "for a bright booky bloke you're not half thick at times; course they're in the fuckin' jail ya silly cunt"!

"What, d'ya reckon they're spinning"? (Searching cells).

"Well, listen, that's a few mutts mate in it"?

"Sounds like it", says Stu and the next thing we hear is Beany next door shouting with his mate from Echo wing through the grill in the window and his mate on the wing that parallels ours is telling him that there's indeed dogs on their wing and that cells are being spun. We are going to be fed at the door today. These cunts ain't fuckin' about and are clearly sick of the shit going on all around the jail right now.

"Wow", I say to Stu, "at least the poor cunts are tryna do something about the spice I suppose".

"Yeah, but all those dogs barking just advertises they're coming". He's right and we both laugh at this. "Stupid cunts" he continues, "by the time they get on the wings everyone would have bottled (stuck the drugs and phones up their arses) their shit soon as they 'ear the dogs". Don't forget dear reader the phones here are thumb sized mobiles.

"I know mate", I say, "truth is Stu they're never gonna stop it bro". Anyway, I'm calmer now after we smoke some spice. Lunch is slowly and laboriously brought to cell doors. More later.

Same day. I want to tackle A---- now, mother to maths whizz R---- ,and this is quite difficult seeing as I went to jail for punching her in the head shortly after the tale I'm about to regale. I guess the following was in about 2016. This wealthy, beautiful woman witches for a living. She is an extremely intelligent, interesting and intriguing girl to say the least. She has the longest lithe legs and pretty perfectly formed features and an hourglass figure to die for. But she's mental too in the nicest possible way, thus the attraction. She makes her dough doing 'readings' dear reader with two very specific sets of cards. She has thousands of followers, two salons and other business interests. Very clever and the single most wonderful mother I've met bar none. And she has the look of Conchis' statue in the cave, the self satisfied look of one who has had access to privileged information. Anyway, this gorgeous 32 year old has plotted me up in a bedsit, paying out her own pocket where her and R---- visit me daily, the little maths whizz I spoke of earlier in the book. I can't live with them as social services told her in my drug addled state and due to the police being called out to domestic incidents I had to go for R----'s sake, the lovely little fucker. That little boy loved me and I miss him right now. She was paying for my accommodation on the proviso that I clean up. One day she pulls up and bibs the hooter of her sexy little Merc and I go down to see them in the car.

"What ya doing weirdo; you alright"? I ask but A---- is just sitting in the whip, smiling, and it is R---- who pipes up.

"Andrew. Andrew", he squeaks in his absolutely delightful little high pitched voice with the hint of an endearing lisp, "look at all the bags in the car; can you guess where we're going"?

"No", I say, breaking into smile, "why're there so many bags in the car R----"? then looking to mum, "A----"?

"Mum, mum can I tell him paaaaallleeeaaase mum"?

"Oh go on then R----", says A---- then, turning to me she says; "look at his little face".

"I know man", I say, "killer"!

"Can ya guess Andrew, go on, try" he says and I stand, looking thoughtful like I'm tryna work out the spin, direction and location of some elusive subatomic particle.

"Erm", I say, finger to lip, "I know I know, you're going shopping"?

"Nope", R---- laughs, "try again", says the mischievous eight year old officially dubbed King of Maths in his class at school.

"Errrmm, let me see, I know, I've got it, you're going to the zoo"?

"hahahaha", laughs the little shite, "nope, come on Andrew, look at the clothes", he looks to his mum, "mummy mummy can I tell him mum"?

"For Gods' sake R----", smiles his mum, "if you don't we won't bloody get there"!

"Andrew, can you guess", he can't help teasing a little further, "Andrew we", and he draws it out, "are going", he says pausing for effect, "on holidaaaay yaaaayyyyy"!

"What"? I say smiling and a little taken aback, "wow, that's brilliant"!

"We're going to Egypt Andrew", he says absolutely brimming with excitement.

"Wow, A----, how long you gonna be gone for babe"? I ask, gutted to be losing them.

"Ahhh, look at his little face R----", says A----, regarding my sorry looking countenance.

"Can I tell him mum? Can I"? says R----.

"Go on then R----", says the lovely lady.

"You're coming with us too", and through the car window he throws his little arms around my neck. "We are gonna have so much fun", and it's too much for, like, I've never had a real holiday abroad in my whole life.

"Awww", says A----, "I bloody love you, you getting in the bloody car or what then come on come on"? and I'm so excited I could wet myself, I feel like a big kid.

"Where's my passport and driving license"?

"Just get in the bloody car will ya", so I shut the door to the property and get in and R---- squeals with joy. Gold. Priceless.

"I've got no bloody clothes A----",I say.

"Oh shut up, I've brought you loads of holiday bits and some smart stuff for when we're having meals and that. And I've got your I.D don't worry".

"I've not a penny A----, you know that".

"For fuck sake Andrew".….

"Mum, swearing", says R----.

"Sorry R----", she says, "I've got a grand, flights are paid for and we are all inclusive at a holiday resort, a water park for a week".

Dear reader I must take a break for Stu is having a hissy fit with two screws who stand outside the locked door over his meds. He is shouting at officer Fellows, known as 'Arge' to all on the wing due to his likeness to that fella from Made In Chelsea. Officer Broomfield, a young officer known as 'Broomy' is standing next to Arge who is also relatively young, late twenties perhaps. Stu missed his meds due to the bang up this morning.

"Stu, Stu", I say to him, "it ain't their fault bro, it's the medical staff mate".

"I know Sloaney",he says, turning back to the glass 120cm squared window in the door which has the flap on the outside, "I know man I know but they're cunts mate", and to Arge and Broomy he says "will I get it later though guv"?

"Yeah", says Arge, "they said you'll get it at about two o'clock".

"See, it's cool Stu and if they don't then you can rip into someone mate", I say.

"Medical services are shit though guv, nice one though", he says to the two overworked young officers at the door, then, turning to me he says: "they better fuckin' sort it out at two or else"! Truth is, dear reader, there's fuck all he could do if they didn't.

0915hrs 21/11/2018. Back to A---- and R----.

"A water park" I say to R---- now, "what, with rivers and streams and stuff"? I deliberately sound disingenuous as the car belts toward Gatwick Airport.

"No dummy", says R----, "haven't you been on a holiday before"?

"Well no R----", I say "I mean, I've been on a ferry and lived in Ireland once for a year when I was little but nothing like this bro".

"Whaaaaat", says R----, "like proper really never been on a holiday before? Is he lying mum, like is Andrew messing with me"?

"No R----", says the blonde beauty, "not everyone has been as lucky as you R----, that's why I always tell you to be grateful".

"Can I tell Andrew what a water park is mummy"?

"Course you can R----",and there is such happiness, such excitement in this car right now.

"Right ", says R----, very studiously, "have you ever seen, like, one of those swimming pools with like the massive slides, like the biggest slides you can actually get"?

"Like Fantasies in Dartford", interjects A----.

"Childrens' home took me there once , massive slides coming out the building, shut now", I say.

"Well", says R----, proper animated like, innocence incarnate, "well, it's like that but like a million times bigger and better isn't it mum"?

"It's amazing Andrew", says the lovely lady, "honestly, you're gonna love it"!

"It's just got, like, so much to do"! says the little man, "lots of different rides and, like, these massive slides and swimming pools just everywhere and like just lots of really fun stuff", and the little fucker throws his arms around me, "and mummy you'll be able to, like chill out and me and Andrew can play mummy"!

"That's exactly what I plan to do", says the wonderful wench in her pretty but decidedly witch like cackle. The drive for me was quite emotional. Never before had anyone showed me such kindness and without expectation of anything in return. That's the thing. After ninety minutes or so we arrive at Gatwick Airport. I'd been on a plane once to Ireland as a young boy but the only thing I can remember as that eight year old was the overwhelming sense of de ja vue I'd experienced. Anyway dear reader, what happened next you could not make up. Still all very excited we swipe our passports and go through the necessities inherent with travel. We are off to Sharm El Sheik. My nerves are playing havoc as I think of being cocooned in a steel tube for hours and hours as it flies miles above terra firma.

"You excited wierdo"? asks the wily witch and I know she can see my nerves and trepidation!

"Shittin' myself if I'm honest A----",and I'm not at all surprised to hear her hearty cackle.

"Andrew", says R----, "swearing"!

"He's just a little scared R---- because he hasn't really flown before", says mum.

"Are you really Andrew"? from R----.

"Do you want the hard man answer or the true answer R----"?

"The real one silly".

"I'm fuckin' shittin myself R----", his little face lights up in delight. He looks to his mum and seeing she smiles, signifying the swearing can be forgiven due to the innate honesty of my answer, relaxes. What do you think this bright bubbly boy does? He simply puts his arms out to hug me! I squeeze him hard as I can without popping him.

"Ladies and gentleman, you may now start to board your flight for".........goes the tannoy. Fifteen minutes later I find myself next to R---- who's by the window and his mum is on the other side of me. Eventually everyone is seated but no sooner was this the case, two uniformed police officers walk onto the plane.

"Wow", says A----, "must be a terrorist on here or something".

"Why are the police on the plane mummy"?

"Don't know R---- but don't worry, it's nothing to do with us"!

"Andrew Sloane", calls one of the officers, "is there an Andrew Sloane on the plane"? and A---- has gripped my arm, her perfectly manicured nails almost breaking my skin in her anxiety.

"Mummy", says R----, "they said Andrew's name mummy".

"Shhh a minute baby", says mum and now the police are beside us.

"That's me", I say, instantly defensive, "what do you want"?

"Could you step off the plane please we'd rather discuss this outside", one says.

"Are you going to arrest me"?

"Please, we'd rather not"..........

"Are you gonna fuckin' nick me"? and I can hear R---- saying to his mum:

"Are they going to take Andrew away mummy"?

"Yes or no"? I ask.

"Yes",says one of the burly uniformed fucks. As soon as they say this I turn to A---- and say:

"I'm so sorry babe", then turning to R----, "sorry bro, don't worry, I'll see you again soon little man", and I can see he is quite upset by the whole fiasco. I start walking off of the plane but before I am out of earshot I hear A---- say to R----:

"Don't move baby, I'll be back in a minute ok"?

"Ok mummy", he says being brave and wiping tears from his lovely little face. Once outside I'm hit with it.

"You are under arrest on suspicion of burglary, you don't have to say anything unless you wish to do so but what you do say may be given in evidence. If you don't say something now which you later rely on in court it may harm your defence", etc etc. A---- is now positively sobbing and through tears says:

"This is his first holiday; do you have to take him"?

"A----, babe, don't worry, I bloody love you".

"Promise me Andrew", she says handing me five brand new fifty pound notes, "promise me that soon as you get bail you'll meet us in Egypt, here", she says handing me my ticket, "you'll easy get over with that and there's more than enough dough there ok"?

"Oh A----", I say. I can't cuddle her as I'm cuffed to the back. After having heard reports of previous assaults on those trying to hold me and my propensity for absconding they're taking no chances. I had half been expecting a nicking for using fraudulent cheques which had come from a burglary recently but had not actually burgled myself. I knew who had done it but was at a loss to understand how they were holding me for such a charge. Should be handling really. We went to, I think, Crawley Police Station but this was merely a formality for I was waiting for Margate Police to come and pick me up. Crawley police treated me pretty well and thankfully Margate were quick in the coming. They cuff me and put me in their car, two coppers I'd never met for I'd been out of Thanet for a while.

"Lads", I say, once we are on our way with one of course driving and the other beside me in the back of the disappointing Vauxhall, "I really ain't got a clue what this is about because I ain't burgled anything for fuckin' years".

"Well Andrew", said the one next to me, "I can forensically place you at the scene of the crime", and now I turn to him, incredulous:

"That's fuckin' impossible boys because I haven't been fuckin' burgling"! And it was fuckin' true.

"Look Andrew, I'm not even supposed to have given you that information until interview so let's wait till we get to the nick ok"? says the fella in uniform next to me.

"Listen, when bang to rights I always 'fess up, but this is bollox".

"Relax mate", he says.

"Will I get a bit of James Whale"? (bail).

"I can't comment, that's for later, just wait and see". The rest of the ride is unremarkable apart from the amazing fact that these two old bill would not go over the speed limit! Whether for my benefit I do not know.

1500hrs and me and Stu have been banged up all day due to no activities being run. We will be let out for the evening meal at four. For an hour. Anyway, let me continue my tale. I don't want to procrastinate. Let me simply tell you how it all turned out. I'm not in the interview room for more than a minute when one of the two officers puts a bag on the desk containing a Swiss army knife. Immediately I see it the penny drops.

"I know where you found that; Trove Court in Ramsgate".

"No Andrew", says one of them, "we found it at the offices of a travel company that suffered a burglary in which a chequebook was stolen. Five of those cheques were cashed for large sums of money and one of the accounts where one of those was placed was an account under your name".

"I admit that I used one of those cheques and fraudulently wrote it out for a few grand but I didn't do the burglary man. I've been waiting for this to bite me on the bum".

"Well how do you account for this knife, found at the scene and covered in your DNA"?

"I was sat in a crack house in Trove Court out my nut on crack and smack and used it to carve myself up, scratching myself with it 'till I bled", and this, dear reader, is the truth. "When was the burglary commited"?

"19th Sept", says one of them.

"I was in Oxford at that time", and this is also true. And bright A---- got the exact dates when we returned from Egypt. The police later discovered that my cell phone was pinging off of Oxford masts and that the car I had at the time, a little Merc, was to be seen by ANPR cameras in that venerable city too. The burglary charge was dropped though I was charged with obtaining monies by deception. Thankfully I was bailed. Soon as they let me out I went straight to a crackhouse for a fuck off great snowball. Then I slept 'till the morning before getting a train to Gatwick Airport. I had to wait 24 hrs for a flight and was resigned to having to hang about in the airport due to the cost of the extra flight and train ticket and snowball having depleted my funds when turning away from the desk I find myself, amazingly, staring straight at a geezer who I was in rehab with. Grant S. He takes me to his mum's after we score and we snowball all night before setting me on my way to Sharm in the morning. We had a beautiful holiday with memories being made. No arguments just pure joy.

25/11/2018. 1030hrs. I haven't put pen to paper for a couple of days. There're probably a couple of reasons for this. My methadone is reducing and this is leaving me bereft of energy. Also, I have been smoking crack and spice and, worst of all, buscopan, which leaves my eyes unable to focus for some three days or so afterward. So, yes, I've been into the valley of the shadow of smashed.

1204 hrs. It's a Sunday and we have just had our weekly prison roast dinner. The doors are open and as I wash up my plastic plate a fella, a big blonde lunatic called Henry who is close to one of my surrogate brothers, a true knife wielding lunatic called Steve McColl whom I grew up with, opens my door.
"You alright Sloaney"?
"Not so bad, truth be told Henry".
"Fancy a joint"?
For a few seconds I consider this. I have gym this afternoon and don't wanna be wankered for that. However, like a turtle poking his head out his shell at the smell of a carrot I say:
"Go on then mate, why the fuck not"? He pulls from his pocket a piece of paper, A4 size. Now consider a credit card sized piece of this can sell for anything between £25 and £50. He tears me off a strip say 2cm long and a cm wide. This paper has been absolutely drenched in a spice solution before being sprayed with acetone to seal in the 'goodness'.
"Wow", I say, "that feels cardy".
"It's power Sloaney",says Henry, "look at the shine on it".
"I can see it", I say, "I'll be alright smoking this won't I"?

"Course ya will Sloaney, fuckin' hell, after all the drugs you've done over the years I'm surprised you're even asking me that"!

"I know", I say, "but this stuff's different".

"Why you shook at spice"?

"This stuff", I say, holding up the piece of paper in my hand, "this stuff is like acid and can leave permanent psychological scars. I've had trips on this stuff as strong as any of the acid I used to take as a kid".

"Naaa man you're right", says Henry, "have you ever had those, like, life or death trips 'cause I have and they're fuckin' mental"!

"Fuckin loads of em"! I say honestly, "terrifying. That's why when I make a joint I take a couple puffs first then put it down to get the measure of it before I pick it up again".

"As you know, I don't smoke it much Sloaney because not only does it shit the life out of me at times, in here, it's the nice life or the spice life"!

"Funny you say that Henry, me and me cell mate were just saying earlier that we can't even afford a bag of sugar or coffee each week we're so fuckin' in debt".

"Your cell mate is Arron Little ain't it"?

"Yeah", I say, "like me he owes hundreds. Well, I don't owe quite as much as him, his debts are ridiculous; about £500 I think".

"I saw him get a slap the other day over a debt", says Henry.

"I know", I say, "he owes so many people whereas I just stick to Phil The Face and that keeps me out of any shit". Phil The Face is a six foot blonde dealer on the wing dear reader.

"Have you had to stop people weighing your cell mate in"? asks Henry, meaning have I had to prevent Stu getting properly hurt.

"Well, I can only go so far when he's in the wrong. I can't stop him taking a punch but I would stop his head being stamped on or anyone pulling a shank on him if I could".

"It's hard man, and he is fuckin' disabled after all", says Henry.

"Exactly", I say, "but Henry bro, he does tell continuous fuckin' lies he needn't tell ya know? He always pays but not on the days he promises to".

"See me though Sloaney, if I'm in debt and someone wants to punch me then that's debt paid as far as I'm concerned".

"I agree mate, if I take a punch they ain't fuckin' getting paid and if they come back again I won't be taking that punch without landing a few back myself".

"Damn right", he says, the lanky gangster, "motherfucker smashes me up and still thinks he's getting paid, he's mad bro. Fuck that".

"You fuckin' know that" I concur, fist bumping Henry, "and if they come back again I'll be doing the smashing"!

"Yes geez", he says, we smoke and chat and that is that.

Anyway, if I was telling an anecdote forgive me. My stoned mind is barely managing to string sentences together. Aron is on his bed reading some crime book. I have been handwashing clothes just to keep myself busy. Know, dear reader, that as I sit in this house typing on a summers day in Oxford I ask myself whether I should put inane shit like this in but I shall at least give a little of my mind when smoking. I debated whether or not to insert my present existence into the text but wanted, and indeed want to give the manuscript as I wrote it in the prison. So. The regime here in Rochester is improving. The new influx of staff is creating a safer environment for all. For the record, I had a breakdown in jail myself once and slashed a wrist open, only ever once, being truly sick of it all. But, alas, I digress. From what I can see right now, levels of violence, on this wing, are dropping. So are incidents of self harm. Once all the new blood is trained up we may enter a brave new world in the way this establishment runs. Rochester seems to be imbibing an attitude of recovery and there is a drive from management to work on such values for perpetuity. And education both academic and emotional is the way forward if we are to slow the rate of reoffending. There is a good education dept here and there's an agency called PACT who specialise in finding secure employment for prisoners upon release. I can tell you now that many jailbirds feel unemployable yet give them a chance and in many cases the employer would find themselves pleasantly surprised with the dedication of such people who invariably have immense gratitude that they have a job when they thought this could never be so. A simple bedsit and a job upon departure from Her Maj's Hotel would see many never return to their previous ways of life.

26/11/2018. Just finished Hardy's Tess for the second time purely for the beautiful imagery. I often wonder what drove Hardy to his inherent pessimism; I'd've loved to have a happy ending in that book. Tess rising, like the tiger burning bright, a phoenix from the flames. But no, she is unjustly executed and the more emotional reader, like me, is brought to tears. And how my heart was touched to the quick when she was rejected by Angel, despite his own indiscretions. Anyway. I get my weekly nicotine patches today which I sell for a load of spice every time I get them. They are worth a fiver each, for the 21mg ones and I get seven of 'em. Another thing of note is that I have had my allotted 155 hrs on the Horticulture course so find myself banged up in the mornings now. So my door is currently locked and I'm behind it penning this for you. My flap opens and two faces I do not know appear at the glass slip in the heavy steel.

"I know you got patches today bro", and how they know this I do not know, "can you sell me one mate"? and dear reader remember what we use these patches for: for turning tea bags into pseudo tobacco.

"Sloaney", says the other one, and fuck knows how they know my name, "I know you don't know us but please can you sell us one geezer"?

"Mate", I say, "they're always gone soon as I get 'em man", I say truthfully, "I'm flat out on the spice".

"Who'd ya sell 'em to then"? asks one, "point us in the right direction bro".

"Behave boys", I say, "if I do that I'm no better than a grass who can't keep his mouth shut", I tell them frankly, "if I sold 'em to you or owed 'em to you I wouldn't throw your names up either".

"I like that", says one of them, "respect man", and they thankfully fuck off from my door, shutting the flap for my privacy. My door should be getting busted soon for I have a dentist appointment to remove a rotten wisdom tooth from my mouth. Despite being a junkie I've all my railings bar one I snapped in half opening a beer bottle. And my health doesn't stop at my teeth either; I've literally used dirty needles thousands of times yet am virus free thank fuck. I think anyway. Long time, to be fair, since I last had a blood test.

28/11/2018. 0525hrs. Stuart Little is asleep the poor suffering fuck. I feel for this wonky legged misfortunate and as I sit in my withdrawing sleepless state I'm aware my emotions are running wild. My dose is low and the monkey is starting to claw nastily at my back, willing me to bottle it and stay on this soul supressing script. Stu is in real debt on the wing to the tune of a monkey,(£500) and people are regularly in the cell threatening him though I have made it clear anything more than a slap won't go unretaliated. I'm not having him have his head stamped on. Or more than one person at a time attack him. Poor old Stu never complains that I'm up and down all night now my dose is diminishing and sleep elusive. Well, he does complain a little about the foul emanations from my arse and the smell of the liquid shit squirting out the back of me. The croaky crim is though on the whole quite understanding for he knows what is in store for me having no doubt done cold turkey himself. As for me, well, today I threw my dignity once again to the wind whinely begging dealers for spice. Yesterday rather for it is early hours the next day but the time slips by in a steady stream for I have been conscious all the while. I feel so weak, so sickly and would kill for heroin to whip me off to Xanadu. Or a big bottle of methadone. Why the fuck am I detoxing off of these opioids anyway? I pick up Pope's version of Homer's Odyssey but can't focus my mind. Besides, because one of my side effects in withdrawel is blurred vision even more pronounced than normal I have to shut one eye to read, even with reading glasses on. Savage.

0640hrs. Stu is awake. The news this morning, delivered by Piers and Susanna the sexy sort is on migrants crossing the channel and Stu has an opinion about this.

"It ain't fuckin' right Sloaney", he is saying, our Stu, "these fuckin' migrants mate, they come on a fuckin' dingy stuffed with untold bodies and instead of us turning them around and fuckin' 'em off out of it and sending 'em back to wherever the fuck they come from we say 'welcome'"!

"Yeah, but Stu", I say, devil's advocate, "don't believe the bollocks the media feed you and me mate, 'cause without immigration our NHS and our farmers would be fucked bro".

"I know we need some immigrants but it needs controlling, we can't just keep letting any cunt in, like terrorists and that", says Stu whilst making his bed. "And furthermore", he goes on, "didn't you hear that fella down education the other day saying how he'd been a carpenter, a craftsman for thirty years and how migrants or immigrants or whatever we're supposed to call the cunts keep, like, undercutting him"?

"No", I say, cocking an interested eye his way.

"Yeah, like, one minute him and his pals were earning £25 per hour and now they're, like, doing it for minimum wage, the immigrant scum and, what's more", he carries on, "is the fact the cunts lap up the work for that shit price and work like fuckin' dogs too"!

"Yeah man I get that for real. That isn't good for anyone in the long run", I say. We put on the music channel and Dave raps his brilliant smash rap 'Funky Friday' with Fredo.

"Can't believe my personal officer is coming in to support me with that presentation I have with the drug teams today on his day off"! says Stu.

"What", I say, "Mr Maddison is doing that for you"?

"Yeah man, he's a banging screw he is", and he is right, Maddison is, along with the rest of the staff team here to be fair. My favourite is the sexy little young screwess called Ms H, also known as 'Pocket Rocket'. She is flirty and fuckin' fit and has all the boys salivating! She's like one of the lads and I dare say there'll be more on her later as I spend a lot of time with her on association some days. She sometimes has a workout in the gym when we are there training and we all perv at her lycra clad bod and I'm sure she laps up the attention happily! Anyway!

0920hrs. OK. Been downstairs and got me meds. All six ml of it, the green goblin, the methadone. Just prior to that, at around a quarter past eight I return to my cell after having a chat with another old friend of mine, Paul Stone, who I once had a fight with and who packs a heavy punch for a slight guy, and, upon entering my cell after leaving Paul's I find Grin sitting waiting for the kettle to boil.

"Morning Grin; you alright mate"? I enquire of the bright, intelligent fraudulent fuck.

"Yeah mate, you"?

"Not too bad at all mate, no real complaints", I say. "Shut the door Andy" says Grin, he and Brad sometimes call me 'Andy'. I push the door to and he asks:

"You got a battery and an element Andy"? and by this he means do I have the battery end of a vape pen and a broken vape capsule with the element exposed on which spice paper is then placed and smoked by heating the element and burning the paper. It is also used as a lighter to light roll ups and joints since the smoking ban across the British prison estate came into force. Once the spice paper is being burnt the recipient of the toxic fumes sucks the smoke emitted through a rolled piece of paper. I pass Grin the requested items and watch as he prepares what we still call a 'pipe'.

"Where d'ya get the spice this fuckin' early Grin"?

"Saved it from last night", he says, inhaling smoke." I laugh at this. Grin looks up.

"Fuck off Grin", I say, "you can go to sleep with drugs in your pocket about as much as I can ya cunt"! Grin cuts his face with a smile.

"Naaa, honestly Andy", he says.

"Fuck off Grin".

"Naaa, someone just give me it; want one"?

"Naa mate, not yet" I say and Grin cocks a brow before me as if to say 'you sick or something'?.

"What, you honestly don't want one"? he asks, almost incredulous.

"Naa man, I feel alright this morning".

"Sweet man", says the warm lovely guy, "more for me".

"It'll cost ya half ya coffee though", I say and he pours half his luxurious coffee into my cup, for Grin has dough and never goes without despite his penchant for drugs of any kind. I am now alone in my cell an hour or so later and feel pretty good. French Montana's 'No Stylist' is pumping on 4Music T.V. Though I love gangster rap, Pachalbel's Canon In D moves me to tears every time. I do hope you are enjoying my mellifluous prose dear reader. As I sit in this back garden in leafy Oxford typing, self isolating after a member of the household tested positive for COVID 19 I want to tell you there are many mental tales to come in the handwritten document I now type from. And funny anecdotes of dark prison humour. I considered, as I said, interjecting with my current circumstances but decided against it for I wish to give a representative illustration of my thinking at the time of writing. This is the first book, there is another also waiting to be typed..........

0915hrs 29/11/2018.This morning has been uneventful on the whole bar a short minute of angst I experienced the minute the door was unlocked. I'd seen my mate Grin with the hunting drugs look whilst I was sweeping out my cell. He's with a short fella from Folkestone called Jake The Snake who's a slippery but not bad sort with long golden locks and shifty demeanour. He has a face shaped like a quaver crisp. Now on my wall written in graffiti is a silent cacophony of sound in the form of inspirational words penned crudely by me. 'Humility' 'Dignity' 'Respect' and 'Karmic Debt' and 'Karmic Scales' are some examples though there are many more expressions of my madness to be seen. Well, I don't even believe it is madness. Anyway.

"You alright Andy"? says Jake before Grin pipes up:

"You got a battery Andy"? Immediately I switched into junkie mode and I ask you to remember dear reader that this has been my default setting for many, many years. I start hunting about in my cell for the battery before suddenly seeing the word 'Dignity' on the cell's western facing wall. I stop in my tracks. I think. I turn to the boys and say:

"Do ya know what lads? I'm not being rude or anything but I have to clean the cell and don't want to smoke right now. Can't find the fuckin' thing anyway".

"Naa Andy, that's cool", says Jake.

"No worries man, more for me", says Grin. Jake reminds me of a character called Quilp from Dicken's Old Curiosity Shop which I read many moons ago. Although Jake isn't vicious or hateful he has the same bearing of this much reviled chap, hunched and short and shifty. I push the door to, not locking it and sit in my writing chair. Not to write, but to hold my head in my hands. This is a fuckin' battle. Coming down and off this meth is not easy and leaves me not only physically sick but emotionally unstable and prone to moments of depression and anger in fluctuations sometimes minute by minute. Though I love my friends on here they are not, most of 'em, on the same page. And Grin, much as I do enjoy his company, makes no bones about the fact he never plans on stopping using though he is in his 50s. And been a hardcore intravenous drug user since the early nineties, like me. I first used acid in 1990 and by 92, maybe 93 I was injecting heroin despite my tender years. And burgling houses daily to pay for my desperate desire to escape my reality, the torture at the time of being me. Lost. Now, after all the investment in me over the years I don't quite have the same desperate desire to escape my reality though I am still very much in a transitional period. And irony of ironies the drugs that once used to make me feel good no longer do so for no sooner have I used than my dignity and self respect leave me as I exhale or remove the needle from my arm. That word 'dignity' is a belter at the moment. Running around after dealers begging for scraps. Cunt drug dealers, though I've sold drugs myself. But in this microcosm we see people really up close. Me at one end of the spectrum, running to cells and pleading for more and the all powerful prick who holds my happiness in his hands and dispenses at will. I feel like I need to smash something, someone, any fuckin' thing. Cunt. Motherfucker. Bollox. I sit here wondering how I am going to satisfy that psycho side of me without the kick of sticking a needle in me not knowing whether or not I will wake up. Motorbikes, bungee jumps and other near death experiences will be needed. My drug use was always suicidal. Pushing in that plunger knowing not whether my eyes would gaze upon the world ever, ever again. Succeeding once in stopping the beating of my heart for a minute and a half. But that is a tale for later for, as I may have said, I learnt that day that we never, ever truly die.

1030am same day. My dad was still alive in about 1985. He had yet 13 years to live at this point. We had moved from our house in Nixon avenue because my poor paddy long suffering mum was too scared to continue living there due to the strange noises and demonic sounds we used to hear in the loft some nights in the early hours. In fairness, those scratching, banging and raspy breathing noises coming from what sounded like the attic were pretty fuckin' terrifying. When it happened on the nights my dad was working away my mum would come get me and my brother P---- from our room and put us in bed with her. We all used to cuddle up together, eyes wide with terror, trembling and wondering in my case what the fuck it might be. So, eventually, sometime after the birth of J----, my sister, but before the birth of J----, the youngest, we moved to St Peters' in Broadstairs where I had my first kiss with Natalie G and Natasha A and met my long term criminal mate now doing fifteen years, Darren G. That's' another story. So, joining a new school called St Peters' I learn that there was a sports' day coming up. Now, dear reader, I have always had the most awful, ugly bunions on my feet though I exacerbated their severity with shoes to small as I grew up. None of my other siblings got 'em, just me. Now this is relevant as you'll see. I have only ever been good at one sport, boxing, though I am fit and can cycle and run at a steady pace for miles. So, sports day is coming up. I was to be included in the hundred metres run and with the likes of athletic big dog Sam B against me no one expected me to get anywhere near the front of the pack, let alone me. But I fuckin' knew I was gonna win it. I had experienced 'the knowing' I've had throughout my life in the form of a dream though I was too young at the time to know what it was. I had dreamed the night before the race exactly how the thing would come to pass and upon waking on the day I knew, I just fuckin' knew that that was how it was gonna be, that I would win. I knew not academically, but intrinsically, I knew it had been ordained and had already come to pass when I woke. And guess what? I fuckin' ran it and won it in exactly the way I had seen it play out. Same people in the same places, same stewards and parents (though not my own) stood and with mannerisms the same as I'd seen. Same bird flying overhead I'd seen in the dream. The thing was the first experience of this strange phenomena for me but in my child state I simply assumed this was the normal of the whole human condition. That everyone would have these things happen to them. I still marvel at these things to this day and upon doing research I have learned these things are rare. Doubt me if you like, this stuff is my truth, my experience here on planet Earth. I am not sure if I told you dear reader but my brother P, Dr P, had a dream that I would write a bestseller. He dreamed this in 2014 and told me and my sister when they both visited Oxford to do the museums with me. He said in the dream he felt angry and resentful after all the academic achievements he has obtained. I still struggle in articulating this stuff, this for-knowing of things.

Anyway, a little more on dreams. And a concise history. The home I shared with my mum, dad and three siblings became so unbearable that I ended up being taken away by the police to a children's home when my dad simply had enough of me sniffing solvents and being unruly at school before I'd hit my teens. I used to run away from the kids' home despite the fact I experienced cuddles and love here for the first time in my life. I would run away to sleep in the woods or sheds or abandoned cars or the houses of my friends when permitted by their parents. For the record I broke my virginity at this kid's home to a big German girl. I remember I didn't have any pubic hair so poked my little willy out my jean zip with the button done up so she couldn't see this. It was not a magical experience for either of us me thinks! I was at this place a year though stayed there only six months for the other six I was missing, by now using pot, speed and acid, particularly the latter, heavily. I could not understand why my dad didn't like me or want me to live with them. He refused to communicate with social services in any way whatsoever. Writing this today hurts man. Still. I was but a boy. Nobody touched me in these kids places. Anyway, one day I return with the police to the kid's home and there are two burly blokes waiting for me. I am bundled in their car and driven to a secure unit, a prison for kids in County Durham. That was my first experience of lock up, prison gates and restriction on my movements. This just made me worse and upon release I soon found harder drugs and by '93 my heroin habit was such I was burgling houses literally daily and ended up on remand at Rochester Young Offenders Institution and was sentenced in 1995 to two years of which I served eighteen months and ten days for I was fighting throughout. Time was added on for bad behaviour so instead of serving the 12 I did 18. After release I reuptook my use of drugs, particularly smack, crack and amphetamine immediately. Again finding myself arrested for yet more burglaries I received another sentence of eighteen months, this time after writing the newly qualified judge a letter which convinced him to be lenient with me; I played on his heart strings. One day, during the run we used to be able to have around the football pitch of Elmley Prison first thing in the morning I met my mate Matt R, a gangster I know from Broadstairs and who was on another wing for all wings could do this together them days. He ran up beside me and said that he'd spoken to my aunty Cathy who used to run the Dolphin Pub with Dave B, a proper local legend, and that she had said something about my dad being dead. So Matt draws up to me and says:

"Sloaney man, look pal, I don't want to ruin your day mate but Cathy says your dad could be dead mucca".

"Naa man", I say, "no way, he's too young man there has to be some mistake", and the thought of his passing was preposterous to me.

"OK mate, I just thought I'd better tell you; you alright though"? and we continued on the circuit. Upon returning to the wing I go into the office and ask the screws to make a call. They do. My father took his own life in the early hours of May 1st 1998. Suicide by carbon monoxide poisoning from the exhaust fumes of his brand new Rover. I cannot remember much from the moment but being stupefied speechless, shocked. Hurt. Incredible loneliness descending upon me in great engulfing waves. Right. So. We are there. So, after finishing my sentence, again serving more than I should have losing remission for fighting I return to the outside world and rapidly reuptake my drug use, desperately needing to escape my reality with heroin predominantly for this drug wipes the psyche though of course but transiently. Once again I'm burgling houses for it is all I know and very quickly find myself in the clutches of the law, facing more porridge. How I got arrested I cannot recall but I remember being sick in withdrawel when they got me the cunts. When I was in the cell I remember the thin blue sheetless mattress and curling up for a restless sweaty sleep. And I dreamed. In the dream I was in the car with my dad, the poor fucker, but not in the garage in which he was found. We were driving. Though my dad was in the driving seat unconscious and I was pulling desperately on his arm. The unconscious piloting wasn't the issue, no, it was that from a green hose pipe which curled from the back window into the car was being emitted this noxious, rust coloured gas that had rendered him inert and on which I too was choking coughing and spluttering whilst pulling on my dad roughly, trying to get him out the moving vehicle. I was crying and being sick and the rust was coming out in my coughing.

"Please dad please", I was begging and my tears too were rusty globules of gas. I awoke in the cell on the blue mattress sobbing hard and noticed instantly that on the plastic was smeared the red, rusty stuff I'd been coughing. I remember, oh I swear this is true, I fuckin' remember weakly trying to wipe it off with my snotty sleeve and was so sick, broken and feverish but the rust was too much and I too weak and I couldn't be bothered to clean it so curled up again still sobbing all the while. After sleeping again I awoke and instantly jumped up, staring stupidly at the mattress. Nothing. I remember being confused and perplexed for I know I fuckin' know it had been there and that I had seen it with my very own eyes. I remember putting my hands to my head, utterly baffled. I know, may I die here in this cell in jail that I awoke and saw what I saw. Dear reader, writing this here now in leafy Oxford on a sunny July afternoon has brought me close to tears as I listen whilst typing to touching classical music through my I Phone. This is my truth. I know something is afoot around me. I have been watched all my life by forces of darkness and of light, the latter waiting for me to make the right choices. In my second book I will tell of the mental visions that took me from darkness. But, alas, we are not there yet.

Later this evening now. I am very very stoned on spice and Stu Little is having some sort of spastic attack after choking on his cup of tea. The crooked cunt is out his canister and not only is he innately crooked his leg is crooked and his mouth too, almost post stroke like, and he's spitting and coughing shit all over the gaff. This cunt. I'm laughing my cunt off at the cunt. Shit!

"Stu", I say through tears of mirth, "shit man", but I just guffaw some more. He's a mong if ever I saw one. A fuckin' mong I tell ya. I just nearly shat myself laughing.

2129hrs 29/11/2018. I pissed myself again laughing at Stu earlier for the miserable fucker just told me off for turning the light on in this cell so I could write for the urge just sometimes takes me to do so. Only ten mins or so and I'll turn it off for the acerbic little shit. He still hasn't paid £360 of what he owes and keeping him safe is not easy right now. He owes it to three separate Gs on the wing, all three of which are capable of extreme acts of violence. The £100 I owe is bothering me but I am safe. He isn't because he constantly tells lies to his creditors about the timing of payments. All I can do is jump in if it gets really nasty like his head being stamped on or tools being pulled. The cunt. Anyway, Sarah Harding, our C.M or Custody Manager, basically the boss on the wing here on Alpha is looking incredibly sexy of late. I mean, just a few months ago she looked dogged, down and depressed but of late her gait has transformed. She is near and we have a little look upon her loveliness, me and me mate.

"What's up with her lately"? I asked me pal J.T, a handsome, tall, blue eyed blond headed youth as she passed us chatting at the cell door earlier.

"Dunno", says J.T in his quick intelligent deep drawl, "but she's looking fuckin' fit int she"?

"Yeah man she is", I say, "fuckin' fit, proper hot bro int she"? Ms Harding turns to us, hand on sexy hip, head to the side and school mistress mode on her pretty and open face, blue eyes in comedy reproach and says:

"I heard that Andrew". I feel like a naughty little boy.

"I was just saying that you look well Ms is all", I say, and J.T, the cunt, sniggers like a reprobate child himself.

"Yeah Ms", he says, "nothing to hide here, we were just saying that you got a bit of colour in your face of late, that's all Ms", and I'm trying not to piss myself.

"I know I'm hot boys, don't worry", she says saucily the wonderful caring woman that she is. She is bloody alright her.

"Yep", says J.T, having to push the boat out, "you are hot"! Fuck sake J.T! Thankfully the blonde bombshell career climber cocks and wags a finger at us and we both fuck off out of her sight before our mouths and hormones get us in trouble.

30/11/2018. Morning. By banging up with Aidy Edwards I was doing Alpha wing a favour for he was batshit mental and is dangerous to boot. In a cell with Brad earlier I had said:

"I was thinking of Aidy this morning; I'm worried he'd be back living in a tent outside Chatham Magistrates Court", and of course this is exactly what happened to the poor cunt.

"I can't believe I miss him man", says Bradders.

"I fuckin' know! The 'orrible little cunt"!

"You must a got on in that cell being banged up so long together", says Brad, "I see loads of people move in with him one day only to be getting kicked out the next morning along with their kit and shit".

"Naa man that cunt was cool", I say, "I'd rather have him beside me in situations where I need help than the majority of the cunts you find today that'd sell you out for a rock of crack".

"Old school values", says McFradders, "don't grass and don't leave ya mate to get nicked or killed or beat".

"Hope he's alright", I say, "he's been shouting over the wall to Gibbo of a night time I think". (Gibbo is a short, very dangerous gangster with cropped blonde hair and cute face who's done serious time in serious jails; more on him later).

"He'll be back in here soon man I guarantee it bro; I'll bet he's hitting it hard out there", says Brad.

"Swifty told me he's been flat out on the light and dark out there", meaning Aidy is on the street using crack and smack.

"Don't surprise me", says Brad, "there ain't enough help on release Andy, you know that", and Brad is right of course; there isn't. Housing alone is sparse for homeless lags re entering the community. As it is for the normal bod on the street. Providing secure accommodation and work opportunities would, as I have said, drastically reduce re-offending rates but, alas, we are an economy in our own right and lots of state depts depend on us for their pay checks each month. Can't have too many of us changing our ways can we now for they'd all be out of a job! After this conversation with Brad I return to my cell to find that Stu has 'bounced' to another wing to flee his debtors. He said he would never do this but alas has gone. There will be a price on his head now the silly cunt. You can't run in here, no matter where you go.

Before I write this I want to let you know I was wrong about this fella I'm about to speak of. He is not a grass. But I want to write from the document exactly as I was feeling at the time and true to what I penned for you right when it was happening. So. Verbatim from the written text.

I let my dignity fly out the window with the spice I smoked yesterday and ended up having to threaten a big, fat, block headed fella named Terry who got my mate Alex seven days solitary confinement in the block after they'd had a fight in the cell, being cell mates as they were. My mate was dragged off of the wing yet Terry stayed here, the fat cunt. Then when Alex finished his CC (cellular confinement) and confronted Terry on the walkway Terry screamed for the screws, getting Alex dragged off. Just like me and Aidy who bit, punched and gouged one another Terry and Alex went at it hard in a cell one night and Terry, coming off worst got on the buzzer saying:

"Guv, guv, get me out this cell this cunt weighed me in". Alex told me exactly what the fat fucker did. Well, yesterday I'd humiliated myself by asking the fat fuck if I could have a puff of his spice spliff.

"No, it's not mine Andy. I'm just gonna smoke half of it and put it out for me mate". Now in begging this snakey cunt my dignity had gone and I felt anger well up like a terrible torrent to engulf me. I had a desperate desire to smoke though already highly intoxicated.

"Who you talking to, saying no you fat prick"?

"Why you talking to me like that"? asks the fat greedy grass.

"Because you're a horrible, mean, fat greedy grass", say I and he goes to get out the chair he's plotted on and I say, "if you get within arms reach I'm a let loose on you spastic I swear".

"Oh leave it out Andy".

"Leave it out? Leave it out you fat horrible grassing cunt I'd love for you to put your hands up to me you fat cunt ya know that? I'd smash the granny out of you you fat prick".

"Fuck sake Andy", he says, seeing that I am very serious and desiring to sink my teeth into his fat face.

"Don't ever talk to me again", I say, briefly thinking I may be going a little overboard as the poor cunt only told me 'no', "oh, and if you've any ideas about doing me from behind, make sure you kill me you fat cunt 'cause otherwise I'll make it my life's work to cripple you motherfucker", and I walk out the cell, come back to mine. No sooner had I sat down than a couple boys come up from the ones landing to ask about Stuart Little.

"Is he not back Sloaney"?

"Lads", I say, "he went on a visit so he says, and some of his bits are here but the slippery fuck has taken stuff that indicates to me he ain't coming back. Think he's bounced to be honest".

"Little cunt's bounced for sure", says Big Wes who along with his brother Martin aren't bad lads. Martin is short and thin and Wes about five ten and squat, barrel chested. Dark haired tough faced boys the both of 'em. Wes continues that, "if he ain't back now….what's the time Sloaney"?

"Quarter to five", I say.

"Yeah", goes Wes, "if he ain't back now then he ain't coming back, little cunt owes me £300".

"£300? He told me he only owes you a oner Wes"!

"Naaa mate, three hundred quid Sloaney; he owes me three, a oner to Martin and a oner to Dan"!

"And another oner to Nev", says Dan, a burly blonde gangster from Medway.

"And", I say, shaking my head ruefully, "another oner in vapes and shit on the wing; sorry lads, he's even been lying to me".

"I told ya he'd do it Sloaney, knew he'd bounce the little cunt", says Martin now. I am relieved these boys know this shit is nothing to do with me 'cause Arron moved into my cell already in a fuckload of debt. Thanks Stu you little fuck wit. And when you get your stuff Stu you will see, for bouncing, I have relieved you of a couple nice pairs of jeans and a T shirt or three. Hope you're alright though you silly cunt. And at least I get a night alone in the cell to wank myself to bits!

1/12/2018. 1015hrs. Oh, dear reader, I have literally just had a fight. My hand is still trembling even as I write for the fight took place not fifteen minutes ago. Now, I have to give Terry, yes, the same whom I wrote of not a chapter yore, his due. He walked past my cell earlier and said:

"Andy", and put out his hand for shaking.

"The fuck I wanna shake your slimy hand for ya fat cunt"? I'd said. Well, dear reader, he'd walked away only to come back with a steaming cup of coffee which he promptly dashed into my unexpecting face, scolding and shocking me into breathlessness. Then he disappears. Grin, who saw the whole thing says:

"Oh no, you gotta do him now Andy". And of course he is right; I can't let this go. I go toward his cell but he is already coming up the landing.

"In your cell", I say, "put the cup down".

"Got to have fair play", says little short stocky pikey Bill bless him.

"Yeah", says Big Pete from a couple cells down from ours and the block headed five ten fella continues, "you gotta have fair play Tel, no tools mate".

"Come on, in the cell", I say once one of the boys has removed the cup from his hand. But he ain't listening and comes toward me and I catch the big lump lovely, right across the nose which splits in a vertical

82

cut across the bridge. He catches me a beauty in return but my next, a right cross sends the fat fuck reeling but as he falls he has hold of my collar and pulls me to the floor with him where I split my head open on the hard cold linoleum covered concrete.

"Screws", shouts Grin and thank fuck Terry shoots toward the very cell he was loathe to enter with me but a few minutes before. I quickly bolt into the shower where I hide 'till the staff fuck off. Thankfully Brad cleaned up the blood before the officers reached the landing. So, thus far there are no 'legal' repercussions. I went to my cell, cleaned myself up a bit , patched the tooth cut on my right forefinger and cleaned my bloody head before going to get my meds once fit to do so. Now I'm back, alone in the cell waiting for the door to open at eleven a.m for lunch where, I must confess, I'm praying I do not have to go another round. As exhilarating as I find fighting at times I'm no spring chicken at 42 years old; too old to be biting punching kicking and gouging and too old to be being kicked punched gouged and bitten! Still on six ml of meth and after that I think I'll indulge in the spice today for sure. My ribs are broken I think.

3/12/2018 0930hrs and it did come on top. The staff had seen it on the cameras and Grindley like me and Tel has been nicked; me and Terry for fighting and Grin for putting his hand over one of the cameras the silly sod for there are multitudinous of these on the landings so he should have known better! Nice gesture though! So today, this Monday morning I am waiting for the staff to unlock the door so I can go to the seg with these two reprobates to be given our punishments by the prison Governor. Seg means segregation unit where everyone goes when they have been nicked. For the record, as I've said, Terry is no grass. Him and my mate Alex went, like me and Aidy, hard at it in a cell early hours of the morning. They were at it for about fifteen minutes until Terry opened Alexs' throat with a smashed cup, just missing the jugular vien. Not finished and Alex being a bit of a psycho Alex kept attacking and Terry slashed two further into the back of Alex's head which needed extensive stapling in hospital. Terry tells me that Alex simply would not stop coming so Tel got on the bell for staff to remove one of them before death visited one or other of them that night. Today, to be fair, they have a healthy respect for one another. And this is the nutter I chose to have a row with! Anyway, we both took blows, we both have scars and I have a broken rib to boot for I'm having trouble breathing right now. I'll tell you how I get on when I return from the block. So that's that. In other news there's no sign of Stu Little. I asked an officer what wing he went to but he would only confirm that he is still in the prison. When someone

83

finds out exactly where he is he will be in trouble for sure for spice can make people do things that aren't nice to others and Stu's creditors have plenty of that to give some desperate spicehead.

"Sloaney", I suddenly hear outside my door, "you getting your patches today Sloaney"? and it is Beany the beanpole from the cell next door, who lives with a squat stocky pal of mine from Medway called Craig D, "Sloaney, you get your patches today don't ya"?

"I do Beany but I owe 'em all out bro; Nobby at the end of the landing has some for sale though".

"Sweet mate", says Beany and he's off. Dave's Funky Friday is playing on 4music and I marvel that the number one track in the UK for many weeks is about knives and drug dealing amongst other things, At least art is representing what is reality for many in the country right now. Anyway, I have had J.T move in, the six foot tall youngster of 28 I spoke of earlier in the narrative. J.T has been 'trapping' (drug dealing) most of his life. He's a highly intelligent kid who was born in London but moved to Brighton. He got big in the game and used to send kids shotting drugs for him all over East Sussex and Kent, reaping massive rewards attested to by the way the handsome flash fucker dresses. I mean, the £400 Gucci shoes are worth more than my wardrobe in here put together. Anyway, Sigrid is now singing Sucker Punch to my left on T.V and cleaners are sweeping up and down the landing outside the locked door. When I went to collect my 6ml of methadone, due to drop to 4 tomorrow, the nurse said to me:

"How you feeling with the detox Andrew"?

"Well", I say, swigging the liquid which I mix with water, "I've not suffered much yet Ms if I'm honest".

"Really? No sweats or sickness yet"?

"Not really Ms, I won't really start feeling it till about 2ml Ms".

"Well", she says, "we are all a little impressed; you're doing really well".

"Thanks Ms, it's nice to know you care", and I mean it.

So, J.T. Now this fella made the fatal flaw of starting to take the drugs he was selling and has ended up with a habit. Now he, like me, smokes spice and sells his meds, Pregablin, to fund his spice habit. J.T has a wicked sense of humour and is also quite a dangerous guy who takes no bollox from anyone. Before he moved into the cell I'd clocked him at the meds hatch a few days ago when he'd been seen by an officer concealing his tablets. The screw went up to J.T asking him to empty his pockets which J.T absolutely refused to do, even when surrounded by more and more of the big burly uniformed fuckers. In the end he simply stuffed the pills in his mouth leaving the staff no other option than to simply walk away for they, like us, can't be bothered rolling about on the floor and besides, what's the point for a few pills anyway? Stopping J.T getting his meds back won't stop the saturation of spice in the jail or on 'A' wing. So it would be an unnecessary bothersome load of bollox to bend the bloke up when it achieves nothing at the end of the day. Though there are some staff, dog motherfuckers that would make a massive issue in the same situation to be fair.

1625hrs and I'm fucked on spice. Brad is in the cell with me and is due for release. He has been approved for a place in a hostel which has invigorated him. Brad, by the way, never smokes spice.

4/12/2018 0955hrs and yesterday I found myself being very sick with the spice, puking up my ring. Last night, once the puking was over me and J.T got very stoned with hysterical laughter permeating the cell. This morning I am already stoned having had three joints though it is barely ten a.m. Yesterday, on association, young Ben T, a 20 something year old pretty boy who looks like he should be singing in a choir came to the cell, flicking his dark lustrous hair from his face as he sat to roll a joint. Handsome square faced lad speaks at a rapid rate and I dare say thinks at speed also. He rattles off sentences on eclectic subjects and has changed course much of the time before his audience have grasped his previous proposition. He is another drug dealer who succumbed to the tune of the drugs he was selling, ending up with a raging crack cocaine and heroin habit. Anyway, me and young Ben are sharing a joint of spice when he says:
"What's that big pile of paper Sloaney"?
"Fuck me Ben, surely you know I'm writing a book? Most people on the wing do".
"Fuck off", he says, smiling, "what, like, writing a proper bonafide book? I had heard something".
"Yeah man", I say, smiling up at him.
"What", Ben goes, "can I have a look at it"?
"Course", I say, passing him some of the handwritten document, "eeeyaa"(here you are). Ben sits silently for five minutes or so, perusing the pages intently.
"You alright Ben"? But he doesn't lift his head from the work he's reading.
"Ben", I try again, "Ben, you in"?
"Oh shit sorry man was you talking to me"?
"Naaa man, s'alright" I say, "just wanted to know what you think is all mate".

"It's fuckin' sick Sloaney man; where the fuck did you learn to do this, it's actually fuckin' brilliant"!

"Really"? I say, smiling like a Cheshire cat.

"I swear Sloaney this is sick man I wanna read the whole lot now. I knew there was talk of you writing one but I didn't know you'd properly started and done so much". I think he is amazed that the talk was true for he seems genuinely surprised I've got 250 sides or so already written. I'm surprised myself to be fair.

"That'll sell Sloaney, I promise you that", he says.

"Someone else said that to me the other day too", I say truthfully.

"People love stuff about prisons Sloaney", says this bright young lad, "I was talking to my drug worker the other day about you".

"What was you saying"?

"I was telling her there's this really bright fella on the wing who says he's gonna write a book".

"Well, I wouldn't go so far as really bright but what did they say"?

"She said her and the rest of the team had already heard but I didn't know you'd already practically written one"!

"It's far away from a book right now but I have been on it for about six weeks I reckon and I still have seven months to serve so it could be interesting. I plan to document for an audience a realistic experience of a modern British prison".

"Well it's fuckin' brilliant mate", says Ben who goes downstairs and gets another joint of spice for me to smoke at will. I thank him and the sharp fuck goes on his way. As I write cleaners are arguing outside the door about who is meant to clean the showers today. Little Bill, the traveller, is also on the landing and is always the loudest voice to be heard. But he's fuckin' alright really the cunt. He just has a bit of small man syndrome and in fairness the fucker will fight anyone.

My cellmate, Jamie Taylor, gets meds which he sells, like I said, every day. J.T never takes his Pregabs (Pregablin) which is a strong end of life care drug also used to treat nerve damage and anxiety and which has what can only be described as a very strong and admittedly very pleasant narcotic effect on the user. I've taken many, ten at a time outside and rendered myself unconscious in conjunction with the heroin and methadone and speed and crack and benzodiazapines and antipsychotics I like to swig down with my cider or strong lager. On the black market in jail one Pregab will sell for £5 and there are those that would pay much more so coveted are they. Spice, say a quantity which would cost £25 outside, the green leafy gear, will sell here for £900, yes, nine hundred fuckin' quid! Heroin, crack, benzos and subutex, the latter a heroin

86

substitute like methadone also sell at vastly inflated prices. Now, regarding these revelations you may think, 'greedy drug dealing cunts' but one must consider that when it comes to drugs much money is lost in failed throws that the staff get, throws that don't reach a spot accessible to prisoners within the walls, all the captures on visits, the spice discovered in the mail and the stuff that gets found by staff and dogs during cell spins. All these factors increase the price. When there is little in the prison spice that would normally sell for a fiver will be inflated to a tenner or more when desperation drives greed further. And regarding the tiny thumb sized mobile phones well they, on the out, sell for £30 yet in here they'd cost you a twoer (£200) at least. As for a smart phone, even a cheap one, you're talking a straight grand for the privilege of being able to put posts from prison on your page! If one is caught with the tiny thumb sized phones a six month sentence is to be expected but get caught with a smarty and it's another two years on top of that you are already serving. They frown very much on crims organizing empires from the walls of the prison estate.

4/12/2018. 1105hrs. A screw opens the cell door and J.T comes in from his drug course.
"What you been up to"? he says to me.
"Not much mate, got a couple hours writing in, had a couple joints with Ben".
"Can't believe you passed me that joint first thing this morning", he says, "blew my fuckin' head off".
"Sorry man", I laugh, "I forgot you don't really smoke during the day", and it is true, he controls his intake better than me. Charli XCX, the sexy bikini clad beauty is bouncing around on 4music T.V in her song 1999. I'd love to bite her bum.

Anyway, I have in my pocket a 14g nicotine patch which I will soon heat and into the goo smear tea leaves that me and J.T, when the door is banged over the lunch period,will smoke along with some powerful spice which is all over the jail right about now. J.T, despite living all over did much of his growing up in West London. I ask him if all the boys he grew up with have ended up doing bird, ended up in a life of crime.
"Not all of 'em", he says, "one of my mates built his own company drilling holes in nuts and bolts and a few of the people I grew up with went legal but most of 'em ended up trapping". Trapping is modern vernacular for dealing hard drugs.
"I'll bet you know a few handy people then"?

"I have a lot of 'plugs'" (people to get large amounts of drugs off), he says, "I could get out now with no money and get an ounce of each (crack and heroin) if I wanted to start trapping again. Not many white boys have got the plugs I've got, I'm lucky". This man is the best example of hardcore, dangerous inner city youth I could have asked for as a study in my cell.

"What you gonna call your book"? he says to me now.

"Memoirs Of A Modern Man I've been thinking".

"That's quite catchy actually", he says.

"Where you from originally"? I ask him.

"We ended up in South Acton when my mum met this guy but I've lived all over; Bermondsey, Charlton, Essex, Battle and even Birmingham back in the day".

"How comes you been all over like that"? I say.

"Well, we used to move around a lot as kids but obviously I been trapping all over the gaff, ya know, living in 'cunch' (country) shotting anywhere and everywhere. Oh look", he says, looking at the T.V "the Kardashians are on, I love it, do you"?

"I don't mind it and think that that fuckin' Kourtney is hot"!

"This Donamatrix guy", says J.T, referring to the Kardashian's personal trainer, "he's fuckin' sick, he's like, he like never fuckin' stops, he's a fuckin machine mate trust me". Anyway people, he is making a joint now and trying to read a TRE brochure at the same time as watching the T.V. Remember I mentioned TRE or Total Release Experience recently?

"So what the fuck is TRE, like advanced yoga"? I ask.

"You only do a tiny bit of stretching, it's not really like yoga, we do all sorts of bits and pieces".

"What's the point, the idea behind it"?

"It's supposed to like help you release all the bad, residual energy from all the trauma we've had in our lives and that".

"Do you find it helpful"?

"Sometimes", says J.T, "I always find myself thinking of my dad"."

"Why"? I say, "is he not here anymore mate"?

"He died when I was six. Cancer", he tells me, "and I feel so lonely sometimes 'cause my mum never even bothers to write to me".

"It's hard out there at the moment bro", I remind him, "people are struggling to just get by, to make ends meet".

"I know man but it still hurts mate", and I remind myself that he is still but a young man.

"There's no manual on parenting mate". Anyway, in other news me and Terry get a slap on the wrist in front of the Governor. Couple days loss of earnings but Grin gets two weeks no canteen at all for covering the camera! Ironic. I'm very stoned now. Handwriting is skewing. J.T is talking but my mind wandered so I'll pick up the thread.

"This fella was next level shit Sloaney mate" he says now, "I met this geezer through my Scottish uncle, a bloke he knows. This fella was a proper like old biker, like a Hell's Angel sort ya know? When I first met him I had to get on the back of his Harley Davidson and we drove to this gaff, like a safehouse or something. And I'm telling ya, the geezer pulled out a box (a box is a kilo of drugs), a straight 36 ounces of raw, (raw is vernacular for very high grade pure cocaine) yeah and the cunt meat cleavered off what we wanted yeah and I'll tell ya something else Sloaney, this cunt had some hardware too mate. This cunt was mean bruv, handguns, machine guns and mental stun guns and that. The fella was proper dangerous man and the sniff! The sniff Sloaney, oh my God bro it was rocket fuel I tell ya. About eighty percent pure I swear. It was the bollox bruv".

"Sounds like a serious guy man! Wouldn't a minded washing a bit a gear up like that myself", I say, meaning I would of liked to have stuck it with a bit of bicarbonate of soda and a bit of heat to turn it to crack. Theresa May pops up on the telly, the robotic boring scripted stubborn cow.

"Just get rid of her", says J.T.

"I think we should back her on Brexit", I say.

"Oh yeah, for real, but I'm Jeremy Corbyn all the way me bro".

"Me too", I say. We put on some music, listening to Drake and Travis Scott, French Montana and Fredo. Gangster motherfuckers all.

5/12/2018. 0915hrs. I've been so out me nut since J.T moved in that I can't go to my maths class with AddemupAde. Ever tried doing maths on drugs? So been telling the staff I'm sick. And I guess there's some truth in that statement. Anyway, we have had an update on the eye incident on 'B' wing. Turns out the eye wasn't deliberately poked out; no, the punch crushed a cheekbone and part of the bone severed the optic nerve. Poor fucker. A young black fella no more than 22 or 23. Two staff were also assaulted during the incident. All over one of the tiny mobiles I educated you about. The 'eye' perps were intending to steal the mobile phone from the fella. Gives a new meaning to the term I Phone though doesn't it? Sorry! Just messing. Savage really.

1416hrs and once again today due to my intoxicated state I stayed away from the classroom. I've had a nap and am a little more compis mentis now so while I'm of reasonably sound mind let me talk of another fella I smoked with in Brads' cell earlier. Reece T is his name. Now in Bradders' cell over lunch but before bang up I found young Reece in the toilet for Brad has a single cell with a recess area where people fly in to smoke, Brad, the cunt, being popular and amicable as he is. Me and Grin toke on spliffs of spice in there regularly. Anyway, Reece is but a boy of 22. He has myriad deep gashes on his arms. He gets prescribed multitudinous potions which are dispensed to him daily. Though the pills are to be taken in front of the nurse he always manages to get them back onto the wing proper from the medical dispensing area. He brings back his Ritilin and Concerta XL meds which are for serious ADHD. I myself have used Concerta when I used to run out of amphetamine outside, swallowing handfuls of the stimulant tablets to mitigate the comedown. Anyway, he is a small, dark haired cute faced clearly very quick and intelligent boy who started going right off the rails when his father had sex with his young girlfriend which fried the poor fuckers napper. His father was charged and convicted of having sex with a minor; wasn't rape because she had consented. So at a critical developmental age young Reece had an awful lot of confusing and warring thoughts thanks to the very questionable behaviour of his dad. And these thoughts and feelings were of course manifested in unruly and unlawful behaviour the poor little cunt. Reece speaks at a fuckin' frenetic rate so imagine the thinking! I can only imagine it! My canister snaps at a rapid rate but the way this cunt spits his words he's miles ahead of me. The trick is in turning the dark thinking into positive self approving thoughts. I've a way to go myself with that. Still, I digress. Mobb Deep plays Shook Ones on the stereo as I write. Deep dark rap. As I say, Reece sells his meds every day in his desperate desire to smoke the zombie drug I too struggle with. He speaks so fast it is difficult for me to encapsulate him for you. Suffice to say it all comes out in a mad rush of just comprehensible, to me but not everyone, sound. No gaps between his words.

"YasmokingAndy"? asks Reece from the recess area of Brad's cell. I sit on the bed, Brad is on the landing somewhere.

"Yeah, fuck it", I say.

"So", says Reece, "whatyabeenuptothenSloaneyboy" he pauses to suck on the joint I pass back to him, "smokinghardbythelooksofitboy" he finishes with a mischievous Grin.

"Thanks Reece bro", I say, "you know how to make a man feel good", but I'm smiling, there's no malice in this kid.

"Corthat'sstrongboy", he says passing me back the joint.

"Do you mind me writing a little about you Reece"?

"Namanwriteaboutmemandowhatyouwant", he says all in one go.

"Can I come and ask you questions about your life sometimes-do you mind"?

"Naamancoolbro",hesays, "Sowhat'syourbookaboutthenSloaney"? he asks now.

"Well, I want it to be about other people rather than myself mate if I'm honest; my own stories could get a bit monotonous ya know"?

"Whatssoyouwanttogetstoriesaboutuslotandlikewriteaboutusandthat"? and dear reader this guy speaks more quickly than anyone I have ever met in my life for sure.

"Yeah man", I say, retrieving the joint from him and drawing deeply.

"GottagoSloaney", and the fucker shoots off on his just as quick as his thought and speaking feet.

6/12/2018. 1200hrs. I'm smashed. Again. Mr Saville, a former security screw I used to really dislike but with whom I've now built something of a rapport after coming to understand his cynical humour, is just back off of holiday and I have a convo with him at my cell door. He is clearly invigorated by his break. He is quick of wit today the cunt.

"Enjoy ya holiday Guv"? I enquire.

"Nope", he says, "I couldn't wait to get back to you lot". I look at him quizzically.

"What", I say, "really"?

"No Sloane you silly cunt.....and you're supposed to be intelligent"! I laugh, genuinely amused at my own stupidity!

"I know right", and think on the fact I'm genuinely astounded when new prisoners tell me I'm the 'really smart one' and I guess this is how people refer to me on the wing though I doubt the truth of such shit.

"How's it been here then Sloaney"? asks the sarcastic screw.

"Not too bad", I say, "Nothing major to tell ya really guv".

"Apart from you and Terry H fighting, Selby (a big wanna be bully geezer who no one likes) being booted off the wing, an eye being lost and a hundred or so ambulance call outs for spice attacks it's been pretty quiet then yeah"? and I have to laugh heartily at the funny fuckers' sarcasm; he's quality really this cunt. Smiling now I say:

"And that's just bits and pieces of it in all honesty guv. They shut the whole jail down the other day and spun lots of cells on all the wings. Bundles of phones and spice was found".

"Yeah, heard about that too in the brief this morning".

"What do you think about all this stuff on the T.V about kids coming home to their parents saying they've been born in the wrong body"? I ask this grey haired chap of about fifty eight or so, changing the subject to something bothering me of late.

"Well", he says, "all I've learnt, and I've got a few years on you, I have learnt to live and let live ya know; whatever floats your boat, why"? I must tell you that as I write my hand is skewed and the ink is barely legible dear reader.

"Well, have you seen that scene in Wolf of Wall Street when Di Caprio asks his business partner who is married to his own first cousin what he would do, if, like, they had a baby and it came out all fucked up and that"?

"Oh yeah", says Saville, "I remember, and he says that he'd take it to the woods"....

"And open the car door and tell it to 'run along, you are free now, go' well that is exactly what I would do if my little boy came home deciding he wanted to transition ya know"? I interject.

"Pack a bag and put some food in it son", says Saville, smiling.

"Call me Lucy now dad", I say.

"Ok Lucy, pack a nice bag, you're going somewhere special with the wolves", and in my stoned state I was and am even now chuckling in recollection of the conversation. I'm only joking of course. But I do question the idea of fuckin' about with the creators' design. Anyway, J.T has the hump at the inability of the jail to create a clean environment, even on this, the supposed to be drug free wing, in which addicts can stop using and where drugs aren't available. Anyway. Enough for now, I'm fucked.

7/12/2018. 1000hrs. I have spent time this morning with Jake (not the snake one) who is from Thanet, the same place from which I myself hail. He is a slight fella with a handsome snub nosed face and thick black quite long hair and always dresses very smartly. He is 25 years old and had avoided prison up until fairly recently despite the fact he has been trapping all his life. However, his world fell apart when he was convicted of death by dangerous driving after he and his best friend and blood cousin Jimmy were travelling in a car Jake crashed, killing Jimmy instantly. Jake has a massive family in Thanet but many have abandoned him and some, indeed, wish him harm. Though never having been to prison prior to his seven year sentence for this offence, he will now leave as a hardened and more educated in the ways of crime con. He has to live with the situation for the rest of his life the poor cunt. That incident could easily have been the other way around for Jake has told me they used to take turns driving, joyriders that they are and were. Ariana Grande is on telly singing Thankyou, Next and I wish I too was 25, looking at her banging body. More on Jake later. Henry is in my cell now talking with me and Noel, a six foot three beast of a man of 40 from Medway, about motorbikes, Henrys' passion.

"The R1 or the RR"? I ask Henry now.

"The BMW RR all day long Andy", he says, "I'm telling you they're just too powerful man. I was getting 97 mph in first gear", and he becomes animated, this young trapper, when he talks of bikes.

"What you bustin' round on out there now"? I say.

"Oh I've only got an R6 at the moment but that's still fuckin' rapid man believe me", and by this the bald man means the Suzuki R600 which is a savage racing machine worthy of respect from any rider.

"The biggest thing I ever rode was a 500cc and that scared the fuckin' shit outta me", I say.

"You get used to 'em though Sloaney, once you've got the feel for it, I mean, the R6 is like a little toy to me".

"Yeah but you still have to respect it, surely", I say.

"Oh yeah", he says, "don't get me wrong, I've had it down the motorway in the pissing rain".…….

"Wow" interjects Noel, "fuck that mate"!

"I'll bet you had some scary moments in weather like that, aquaplaning"? say I

"I'm telling ya mate, at a ton, ton twenty the thing in that weather felt like the tires were literally nowhere near the road man".

"Me"? I say, "I'm gonna get a bike license but I'd be a fair weather rider me bro, I mean, they're fuckin' dangerous, my grandad used to call 'em a coffin on wheels".

"That's the whole thrill of it though Sloaney", says Shane R now, a traveller from the Medway area, about 38, average height and beefily built, "knowing at any moment the elements could just snatch the bike away, leaving you to slide on your arse down the motorway"!

"I know and can understand the thrill of potential imminent death. But bikes scare the beJasus outta me; I know, I've got a banging idea"!

""What"? say Noel and Henry simultaneously.

"I'll get an R1 and put stabilisers on it"!

"Hahahahaha you crank", says Jake coming in the cell now, smoking a joint, "ya can't put fuckin' stabilisers on a fuckin' R1 mate".

"Dunno", says Noel, "could make some really strong ones I guess".

"I'm the next Valentino Rossi me lads", I say.

"Yeah, on a steppy 90 or fizzy 50 maybe ya cunt"! says Shane.

"We could create a new sport, superbikes with stabilisers", I say, thinking I'm getting stupid now.

"That fucker Dan bounced yesterday the little cunt", says Noel now.

"Who the fuck's that"? I say.

"Ya know, the little young kid with blonde hair and bright blue eyes", Noel helps.

"Oh, the little pretty boy with the big mouth", I say.

"That's him", says Noel.

"Yep, owes my cell mate bundles", says Jake now.

"Owes me too", says Noel, who despite being a smoker manages to sell too.

"I did try to help the little cunt out a few times, talking to bods for him", I say.

"He won't like it on 'B' wing", says Jake, "last time he was on there he refused to come out his cell for six weeks", and 'B' wing is notoriously feisty and violent to be fair.

"I remember the last time he was on there, he begged me and Brad from his window as we walked past to help him get back on here". And it is true, I still remember it today. He'd shouted out to us:

"Sloaney, Brad, Can you ask Ms Harding or Governor Green if they'll have me back on 'A' wing"? said the little cunt through the bars.

"Yeah", said Brad, "bet ya don't like it on there do ya mate"?

"I can't even come out the cell lads, if I do I'm gonna get shanked up", says the frightened fuck.

"Fuck sake Dan", I say, looking up at his scared sad face behind the bars of his window; 'B' wing still has old style windows that open, having not yet been refurbed.

"I'll try for you", I say, "I'll see Ms Harding and tell her you're struggling on there. Bet it's 'cause you owe money though in it you little cunt"?

"Yeah man, got myself in a pickle", he says.

"If we help you and you come over and start robbing cells again and behaving like a cunt I'll personally make sure you get weighed in ya little fucker", says Brad.

"Please Dan, if we help and you get back you need to be grateful and remember how you feel right now on that wing boy", I say.

"I will lads I swear, please help 'cause I'm shitting it on here at the moment".

"Alright mate, we'll try", says Bradders kindly.

"Cheers lads", says the little boy from behind the bars. "Shall we help him Brad"? I ask as we walk to the education block.

"Yeah, we can only try, I don't like seeing the poor cunt like that".

"Me either, and with me and you on side I reckon Ms Harding will have it".

So, with me and Brad pressing the kind hearted Ms Harding (now pressing her properly would be nice!), appealing to her softer side we did manage to get him back to our wing six or so weeks ago. And now the little fucker has bounced off again after accumulating debt for drugs he damn well knew he couldn't pay for. There's now a £500 contract on his head for anyone who smashes fuck out the little cunt on sight and I myself was offered it today. Fuck that. I couldn't, not to him anyway poor sod. He's just a hopeless junkie and I, of all people, know how it is to be that way. Anyway, I think, in my drugged up state of late I have mixed my dates up. I'm gonna go by the text though and continue. In this house, in Oxford, typing the document in 2021 and isolating from Covid I just checked the day it would have been on the seventh of December 2018 and the next page I write from has that date at the top, a Friday according to google which is right for a few pages further on I see I'm in a weekend. Forgive me, time is a funny thing in jail. Right, back to three years or so ago.

7/12/2018. 0930hrs. We were opened up at 8am. Got my now 4ml of methadone; thus far any symptoms have been minor and Catherine, my keyworker from the drug agency working here, the Forward Trust, asked me:

"How are you Andrew"? My handwriting is skewed on the written document so I know I'm out me nut here.

"Yeah, no real complaints Catherine, some restless nights, bit of a shiver and sweat and some flu like symptoms but hey, no biggy"!

"Well, if you need to talk, or want some symptomatic relief you will come and see us won't you"?

"Of course, thank you Catherine, I appreciate that". This lady is magnificent. So genuine. She actually cares! I go back to my cell which I give a quick sweep and mop and tidy. Once that is done I take some pain relief so breathing doesn't hurt my broken rib too much. If I turn to my left, at speed, forgetting it's broken I get the sharpest of pains. So, now I've 4Music to my left, outside the window it is pelting it down but despite this it is still very warm though we are already well into December. The tall light skinned sexy new lady screw just came in the cell and took our kettle when she did the daily rounds of 'bolts and bars' which is basically a security and integrity check of the cell. She'd seen the wires hanging out of the kettle and claimed it, being as it is unsafe. We expose the wires so that if either of our vapes are not charged we can still get a light for our joints. To do this we wrap and hold a piece of tissue over one wire and flick the other off it, creating sparks which ignite the paper. I have had some serious electric shocks doing this, as have many jailbirds over the years I guess. Certainly since the smoking ban, bastard that it is. Anyway, Peter Lanes, a friend of mine and Brad's since we were boys had bounced off of 'B' wing and is now here with us on 'A'. He is fairly rotund, five foot eight and has a fat head with a cute countenance I guess. I love this burgling fucker, prolific thieving cunt has spent most his adult life in jail; he is 44. He has banged up in a cell with Tony Giles, known to us who have known him all his life, for we are all lads who started drugs and burgling together, as Jewlsy. Tony 'Jewlsy' Giles. He is wiry yet muscly and has a handsome shifty face with slitted suspicious eyes. This cunt is an artist though and does murals of gangster rappers in the Banksy style for money to get his spice, selling them regularly and with lots of work booked up. He is a notoriously moody cunt this prick, but, having grown up in kids's homes with him I truly love the cunt intensely. All these lads, Bradders, me, Jewlsy and Peter started our criminal careers after falling for the lady who sways in fields under blazing Afghan suns: Lady Diamorphine Hydrochloride who sings such a sweet song to ensnare the unwary. I can picture the heads of those poppies swaying in the breeze in blazing hot heat as I write. For the record, Pete Lanes, known as 'Bundy' or 'Bunt' to his friends is in for the same burglary as Bradders. Nothing else to report today and, to be honest, with the insidious onset of real withdrawel I am struggling to write.

8/12/2018. 1200hrs. Not much to say but it was weird being in Brad's cell this morning where me, him, Jewlsy and Bundy were all together for the first time in about twenty years. We have reminisced on going out to big country houses booting screamers and alarm systems off of the rooves. Screamers are like bullhorns used on isolated country piles so someone may hear them if they're broken into. We used to drive miles to find these massive estates then steal all we could carry in the car.

"Wow man, this is mental; all together like this. Do you remember when we all took our first acid tabs round Rosy Georgio's all those years ago"? Brad says to the cell.

"Yeah man", I say, "with Trip (nickname for a dear friend of ours, a massive character called Tristan Wood who died of an overdose some five years ago), Justin Lane, Arron Jones, Gary James and you three cunts! Wow"! Justin, Arron and Gary are all still about but have never done any real porridge so we, who have grown up in jail, haven't spent much time with them over the years since we were kids.

"Ahhh", says Bundy, "I do love you lot".

"Feels fuckin' weird being all together", says the reticent and moody Jewlsy Giles.

"I love all you cunts", I say sincerely.

96

"Did we tell you about that burglary Sloaney"? says Brad to me but I can't go on dear reader, I am sick and suffering right now. More later.

A bit later. I am very stoned right now. I have seen two UFOs in my lifetime. One with my father who took me into the back garden to show me this star like point doing mental moves in the sky at phenomenal speeds before dead stopping and bolting off in another direction. It didn't gain speed. It just got there. Then literally it would dead stop. Again and again before bolting off into the black never to be seen by me until thirty years or so later. The second time I was with Charlotte and a gangster black bird called 'Black Sam' in Thanet. Very beautiful looking lady she is too. We were outside the local shop in Millmead Estate Margate when Sam said to me and Charlotte:

"Look at that, look", pointing up into the sky and I see this point of light travelling at a steady speed and say to her:

"Just a satellite Sam", and she goes:

"Keep watching", and me and Charlotte and she do just that. The next thing I do is put my hands up to my head and exclaim:

"No fuckin' way, no fuckin' way", as we watched this thing move in exactly the same way that one had all those years ago. It zipped at ridiculous velocity, literally like a speeding bullet, hither and dither, dead stopping and changing direction like nothing else on earth can in the current epoch. Then this strange man, now remember we have lived on this estate for years and know most faces, this tall overcoated thin faced guy comes up to us and gets us all a beer each, buys us cigarettes and says, mysteriously:

"Walk with me", now I can't remember the convo but it was on subjects concerning God and the afterlife and such. He walked with us a while then simply said:

"I must go now", and disappeared up a side street never to be seen again. We had stood, afterwards, us three, utterly flabbergasted! Never seen the guy again. Just saying, Char and Sam will corroborate this independently.

Anyway, they robbed a safe, Peter and Brad and the thing was filled with gold and jewels, some of which the police never retrieved. Rare and expensive pieces. They love a bit a tom (gold) these two cunts.

9/12/2018 0930hrs. Stoned already, me and J.T are having a conversation about weird shit.

"I was living at this sexy sort's house for about 2 years, at her mum's house in it", he says.

"What sort of strange stuff did you see"?

"Well, she had this big fluffy yellow eyed Persian cat called Mushi and it, like, all of a sudden started doing things it had never done before".

"Like what"? I say, thinking about the mysterious jet black cat that turned up at our house in Ramsgate when I was but ten years old; the cat stayed with us for six months before disappearing just as mysteriously as it had appeared. My dear mum was sure it was the devil's cat, just as surely as she does, at times, believe I am the devil's son. God, mum, I miss you right now and can't wait to see you again. Anyway, J.T continues that:

"Soon as we started having sex me and this bird, this cat would stand staring at itself in the mirror like, meowing really loud whenever we were at it".

"What, and it had never done anything like that before"?

"Nope, and other times it would watch us shagging and make these weird whining sounds".

"Any other phenomena"? I say

"Like we had two lightbulbs explode just out the blue and this bird said she was starting to feel bad vibes in her own bedroom"!

"Freaky", I say.

"So I asked her one day if, like, anyone had died in the room, she said no, but that her grannies ashes were under her bed".

"What, the bed you used to fuck on"?

"Yeah", says J.T, "so I explained to the bird that that was why all the strange shit was happening. We took the ashes to her grannies favourite spot and spread them over the water".

"Did the strange shit with the cat and that stop"?

"Straight away, and she said it no longer felt oppressive in her room anymore"!

"Not surprised man, gran's granddaughter being given a good seeing to right on top of the poor old cow"! I laugh, but inside I am reminded of an incident when my dead trendsetting cool mate Tristan 'Trip' Wood, who was such a cool dude and someone I knew all my life and for whom I spoke at his funeral, visited me from the other realm when I slept with his sister. Now she and I had gone to her house but soon as we walked in we tried to turn the lights on but every time we tried the trip switch went, and this happened again and again. We took out all appliances from sockets and still every time we tried to turn on a light it tripped the switch. Now, remember that he was never called Tristan, no, everyone, and this guy was popular, everyone called him 'Trip'! Anyway, we lay in the dark for ages then we tried to turn on lights again and it was fine until, suddenly, in the hallway, a lightbulb exploded, literally exploded for no reason at all. There were strange noises all night too and both of us knew it was Trip. So, Trip, I'm sorry for that but no harm was done mate, Kerry is ok.

11/12/2018 1200hrs. Midday and me and J.T are banged up. J.T has been off the wing running round the jail all day wheeling and dealing no doubt. He's singing Mabel's Finders Keepers now, happily intoxicated the lazy languid confident cunt. Ms H, not Harding but the other young fit sexy dark haired pretty one known as Pocket Rocket to us inmates has organized a quiz with prizes for everyone over the Xmas period. Me and J.T are talking of the fact suicide is the biggest killer of men in this country bar none.

"And guess what", says J.T, "when you hang yourself you end up with a hard on, like a proper bone on when you die".

"Really"? I say.

"Yeah, I've wanted to kill myself a few times but like I'm scared I'd, like, end up like a cabbage. Like fuck it up and that. But yeah, it's true, if you hang yourself and die you get found with a massive hard on".

"Hahahaha", I laugh, "well, it might be a massive hard on with you ya cunt with the fuckin' beast you're packin' but in my case it would be described as a slightly over average boner mate, I'm seven inches hard ya fucker, you've seven on a soft man"! And this fact is literally true. I have never seen anything like it! Everyone on the wing jokes about it. He calls the beast Cecil.

"It ain't as good as you think having a massive cock Sloaney", he tells me.

"Well, I wouldn't complain if I was packin' that fuckin' beast bro".

"I can never get it all in mate, I've never really pushed the whole thing in and the women who can take it are black women which is handy 'cause I prefer light skinned birds anyway", and he does indeed have a mixed race seven year old girl with a woman he tells me looks like Alex Scott.

"What", I asked on learning this, "she's that fit"?

"I swear bro, she's the spitting image of her, yeah, Alex Scott man".

"She is a fuckin' weapon though int she, that Alex", I say thinking of her luscious golden skin and pretty face and perfectly turned legs. Hot you are Alex. Anyway, I'm literally out of paper.

12/12/2018 0930. Headie One and Dave rap 18 Hunna on 4Music. Sick. Mr Maddison, one of the better screws on the wing, kindly got me a load of A4 paper from the office so I can continue writing for you dear reader, a narrative I do hope you are enjoying. Ok, the door opened at

8am this morning to a wing in what feels like a good mood. People are chatting at tables, converging in small groups and the volume isn't hurting my ears. Bradders is up and about no doubt buoyed by the fact his outside probation officer, who is also my officer, has agreed Brad for executive release. Now this happens when you have been recalled on license which both he and Pete are for that burglary with all the old and rare gold. He only awaits a bed in a hostel now and he is gone, maybe before Xmas.

"Morning Slicker", says Brad to me, using an old nickname of mine.

"Fuck me McFradders", I say, "why the fuck you so happy"?

"That probation report yesterday bro, come in me cell and have a look at it, I'll make you a coffee".

"For real"? I say, incredulous, "you're inviting me for a coffee in yours at eight bells"?

"Why does that surprise you Slicker"?

"You fuckin' with me"? I say, continuing, "you're not exactly normally a ray a fuckin' sunshine at this time a the day Brad"! Anyway, not to labour it, we had a chat read the report and I basked in his company for I love this thieving cunt to the bones. Now look here dear reader, there may be some polarisation between the way you and I feel about thieves, murderers, robbers and drug dealers but it is rare indeed to come across the innately evil and as a therapist once said to me and I have already said to you, it is very difficult to dislike someone up close. Despite popular beliefs and rhetoric about 'scumbag burglars' and headlines like 'thug gets 20 months for assaulting his girlfriend' prisons are populated by the lost and the destitute, people who have had little encouragement and difficult upbringings and next to nothing in the way of love and nurturing. Trauma. Anyway, enough of that. I'm hungry and cook up some noodles in our new kettle whilst J.T tells me a story about a prostitute he once saw cleaning her vagina in a puddle! He is telling me he used to shot (sell drugs) to her.

"Fuck me, really"? I say.

"Yeah man, she had her skirt up and was splashing water onto her cunt, rubbing it, then she took off a sock and wiped herself saying she had to get ready for the next punter"!

"Bet you had a go on her ya dirty fucker"!

"Fuck that bro: riddled that cunt I bet"! Now he is pulling hairs from his nose in the mirror.

"Always makes my eyes water doing that", I say. What is causing a leaking from my orifices is the fact I am now on but two ml of methadone and starting to feel the onset of the pain I must go through to rid my body of opioids. My nose runs, my eyes stream, my arse leaks and my pores secrete sticky sickly sweat that leaves a chill on my emaciated body. I look, and feel, ill.

"Don't ya love doing this Sloaney after having a shave look", says J.T now, putting a soft clean towel to his smooth face. He waffles on as my pen scrawls despite the fact most of my responses are in the form of grunts and 'er hems'. He's popping spots now and I reckon he loves the mirror the tall handsome charismatic cunt.

1700hrs. Door's shut. J.T is making a mix. He has boiled the kettle with a plastic plate atop and in the centre of the plate is a patch. Once hot he'll peel the patch apart exposing the sticky goo then smear a PG Tip teabags leaves' into the substance so we can place them in paper, Bible paper I might add for it's just like rizla, then put pieces of the paper spice into it before rolling it shut and sealing it with the glue from an envelope after licking it to make it wet. Savage using the Lords' word for this I know and to be completely honest I was reticent sharing that but, hey, I'm sharing my heart here and I want the world to see all of me. Oh, a new fella came on the wing today; about thirty, from Brighton and a bit of a boat race apparently. Many years ago I was on a wing with him somewhere. Stocky and strong and with a massive parcel of drugs on his person he is now walking round the wing a £1000 down and black and blue after being robbed by Noel whom I spoke of earlier.

"He said in the dinner que to Noel who was the first to go in on him that he, Noel, is a dead man Sloaney", says the drug dealing mofo J.T now.

"What, Mark told Noel he ain't gonna suffer it"? I say.

"Yeah", says J.T, "after that Mark had cleaned himself up a bit he told Noel by the servery that he's a dead man"!

"Yeah", I say, "I've seen that Mark somewhere in jail before and I reckon he ain't gonna suffer losing that sort of dough". I suspect we can expect some fireworks on the wing. Saying that Noel is scary so who knows, maybe not. In other news, Marcus T, a much loved and popular drug dealing cunt I have known both inside and outside prison for twenty years or so is coming to 'A' wing. Now I won't say too much now because I know you are gonna hear more about this truly remarkably good looking, funny, interesting and likable man. At 33 he's considerably younger than me. He has nicked two screws off of the landings of British prisons, two good looking women officers who fell for his blonde haired blue eyed baby faced youthful looks and musculature men envy. He went on to have long term relationships with them and still has one on the go on the out now. This cunt, when he comes, I promise will make for brilliant entertainment. And though he sells drugs both in here and outside, he loves taking them too and is the greediest yet most generous cunt I know. I owe him £25 myself for spice he sent from another wing to me ages ago and I haven't paid him. Watch this space.

0930hrs 20/12/2018. Good morning dear reader. Well, if you clock the date atop the page you may notice it's been some time since I put pen to paper. I am now completely free of opioids; methadone. I started my first day of a week of 2ml but due to the desperation and impatience of the other prisoners who line up for their meds each day my claustrophobia got the better of me.

"Fuck that", I said to the dispenser who stands behind a great wrought iron prison gate.

"What do you mean Andrew"? says my keyworker Catherine who stands behind the big bars next to the chemist.

"That's my last fuckin' dose today Catherine, I can't fuckin' stand being in this que each day and count myself lucky I've avoided violence 'cause these cunts", and here I wave a hand expansively in the general direction of the ramshackle line of agitated cons, "are fuckin' savage rude fuckers and have no manners". Catherine smiles knowingly at this; the poor woman sees the ungrateful fucks every day. It's been five days since then and therefore since my last dose of the green goblin. And, as I expected, the small reductions have made for a relatively soft landing. Yes, I do have cold like symptoms of snotty nose, running eyes, constant cold shiver and a feverish sweat but it is bearable and won't kill me. We become more sensitive to external and internal for that matter, stimuli, and I'm enjoying the way the tiny hairs all over my body stand on end when a good song comes on or when I hear something or read something or think something inspirational. And it is indeed this propensity of being so sensitive to feeling that drove me so desperately to heroin in the first place. Let's not forget dear reader that opioids and opiates sit squarely in their own field. No drugs are capable of giving the utter release, albeit temporary, from all pain, physical, spiritual, mental and emotional that heroin and its affiliates do. They numb from the soul outward. For those who struggle with being alive due to oversensitivity in myriad ways, heroin, when met, will become their lover brother sister and mother. Yes, the newcomer to crack and coke and Es and speed may enjoy their sojourn with these things but for the utterly suicidal, the destitute and the frightened to the core, like me, heroin is perhaps the only thing that will carry them through, keep them breathing until such a time they find some spiritual fulfilment, for addiction is a disease of the spirit. I have literally been trying to kill myself by lethal injection of opiates since the early nineties but alas the Universe has some other ideas it would seem for I fuckin' tried, succeeded once in stopping my heart only to go to Heaven and come back! A minute and a half I lay dead but where I went, well, I'll regale that tale later in the text. Anyway, J.T is talking:

"Oh my God Sloaney, I'm fuckin' telling you, that fit tall light skinned screw fancies the fuck outta me mate, there's no other fuckin' explanation for it"!

"What, you fuckin' wierdo"? I say.

"This morning mate I'm telling you, she stopped me on my way down the stairs by putting her hand on my arm, like proper stopped me in my tracks man".

"What", I say, "she put her hand on your arm as you tried to walk past her"?

"I swear Sloaney and then she went 'where you rushing off to with that cheeky little smile' I'm fuckin' tellin' ya mate", and he is wide eyed, animated and excited. He is talking again:

"Do ya reckon she likes me or what"? but this is a rhetorical question, "'cause I keep, like, proper catching her looking at me and that", and he is really starting to believe this young and personable fit Amazonian just in the job learning officer is cracking onto him. And she might well be. On the T.V U2's excellent track I Still Haven't Found What I'm Looking For plays. J.T is truly convinced this beautiful bird is bang into him.

"D,ya think she really does fancy me"?

"No you silly cunt give your head a wobble".

"But I thought you said".......

"Well", I laugh, "you know what thought did"!

"But I feel something from her though"!

"J.T bro, you're sex starved mate, she isn't".

"Did you hear about 'Fats'"? asks J.T now. Fats is a stocky dark haired very popular lad on the wing and has his fingers in many lucrative pies here in Rochester.

"No, why"?

"They've stopped his ROTLs" says J.T. A ROTL is Release On Temporary License which is in easier to understand parlance a home leave cons get, sometimes, when close to release date.

"Why"?

"Well, I think it's because he bought a smartphone back along with a massive parcel of drugs when he last went and the cunts have probably heard about it from some grass. Or just noticed the activity on the wing when he came back, everyone at his cell door".

"Or, they've been watching his Facebook feed miraculously being updated despite the fact he's here behind the door, in prison"!

"Yep, he's fucked now. All that money he's had from people who were banking on him picking up their Xmas parcels he'll have to give back". From J.T.

"Still," I say, "he's earned enough on here to buy a house already".

"There's been an atmosphere on here this morning, like everyone is depressed 'cause they don't know how they're gonna get their Xmas drugs now". And it's true, I myself felt an air of despondency about the wing this morning. In the cell now I'm thinking of Bradders who has suffered with horrific asthma all his life. I popped into his cell earlier where the cunt was doing a jigsaw puzzle the size and complexity of which I dare not speak. I poke my head in the cell and get:

"You alright Slicker"?"

"Yes Brad bro; how's your chest today"?

"It's getting better".

"Fuck me, I remember in the dump in Pullman Close when we were kids and you was always catching lizards and shit, you used to have all different inhalers that you were always sucking on".

"I've got even more now", he says, pointing to an array of pulmonary devices designed to make his breathing easier. In this cell now J.T is well out his canister. Our cell.

"J.T", I say now, looking at the retard laying on his bed clapping his hands together like a seriously deficient person with major learning difficulties, "what the fuck you doing ya fraggle"?

"Eeerrrr, arhhh, shit, where am I? I thought I was driving down the road then huh huh huh"! And I can't help cracking a smile at the way he laughs, like a true spastic!

"You're fucked J.T".

"Huh huh huh" , he sort of says, "I really thought I was driving down the street shotting to cats".

"You're in a bed in a prison in Kent ya silly cunt".

"I know, wicked in it"? he says lapsing into mongy mode before jumping up to roll another joint.

"You was laying there clapping your hands together like a seal you psycho"! I say.

"Yeah, I do that when I get excited", he says.

"What, clap your hands together like ya got downs ya cunt"?

"Yeah, just get excited, even do it when I'm not conscious".

"I know; hope ya don't drive like that"!

"Fucked in I"? he says, and I have to say this cunt is a great cellmate.

1325hrs 22/12/2018. In Brad's cell earlier with Gibbo and Seb, the latter a slight scrawny dangerous little fella who reminds me a bit of

104

Gollum and he, Seb, gives me a knowing nod so I go with him to his cell next door to Brad's; he too having a single. Long termers generally do.

"Didn't you see me trying to get your attention Andy"? says Seb.

"Well, I'm here now bro". Brad pokes his head in:

"Coming in for a coffee in a bit Andy"? for Brad wasn't there when we were, he was out doing his thing on the landing.

"Yeah, just gonna have a quick joint with Seb and I'll be in".

"I need you to keep an ear out for my cell door going whilst I go and get my meds", says Brad.

"No probs Brad", say me and Seb at the same time.

"No ones gonna nick anything out your cell bro", I reassure him. The reason he is concerned for the security of his cell is because Friday, canteen day he collected in £80 worth of vape capsules which he has to take down to his spice supplier at work in order to reload, get more. As I say, Brad doesn't smoke but he makes a buck and gets his pregabs, which he does like, by swapping them for spice. Anyway, Brad pulls the cell door to and Seb proceeds to roll a spice spliff, a rare bit of the green leafy stuff which smells extremely potent.

"Fuck that's strong", says Seb.

"Gis a go then", I say, taking it from him and inhaling deeply. No more than a minute later I am absolutely rocked by the potency of the product young Seb has managed to procure.

Prior to that, this morning I had been talking to a young, tall, dark haired half Jewish fella called Max, from Brighton.

"Have you ever tried DMT"? he asks me.

" No, but it is a product I've been looking out for for a while".

"Have you ever taken, like, LSD back in the day, ya know, like acid"? says the man at least 12 years my junior.

"Yeah", I say, "in my formative years me and me mates all fucked ourselves up with microdots, purple oms, penguins, supermans and strawberries".

"Did you ever have a life changing experience with it"?

"Well yeah", I say, "I mean, this may sound mad but during one of the more intense ones I found myself being shat out the arse end of a worm into hyperspace where I learnt that all is based on frequencies".

"Ahhhh", says Max, "so you had like a breakthrough epiphany moment then"?

"Well, I suppose you could call it that, yeah".

"I had the same thing with DMT and learnt all about the Annunaki and Nibiru", says Max.

"What the fuck", I say, "how do you know about planet X"?

"I was telling my cellmate about it the other day", says Max.

"So you know we were originally slaves of the Annunaki, meant to mine gold for them"?

"Yeah", says Max, "they took a liking to our females and mated with one, creating us and giving us our own intelligence then fucked off again on their 26000 year orbit". This subject has fascinated the fuck outta me for years and I am absolutely convinced of our cosmic origins. I don't know, but as I tell Max:

"I have an affinity with the constellation of Taurus being a May eleven baby ya know? I know that if we change our position in space the stars of constellations we see as bunched together would actually prove to be many light years from one another and that is it highly unlikely that they are gravitationally locked in but".......

"I know what you're gonna say", says Max, "you feel as though you are from the Pleiades star cluster"!

"Egg-fuckin-zactly", smiling as I talk to another blessed soul, a brother in being inquisitive. "And", I continue, "I like looking up there with a telescope or pair of binoculars".

"I know right! Don't they just jump out at ya"?

"Literally, like a fuckin' jewellery box full of diamonds", I say.

"I love looking up to the Heavens full stop", says this interesting bespectacled guy.

"Me too", I say, "but even more I like connecting with enlightened interesting people like you who make my hair stand on end".

23/12/2018 0830hrs.

"I can't believe Arg, (Officer Fellows) nearly got me taken off my pregablin yesterday the soppy cunt", J.T is saying.

"J.T", I say, my tone exasperated, "he didn't nearly fuck your meds up, you did bro".

"How the fuck do you work that out"? asks this miserable fuck this morning.

"Well", I say slowly, "if you weren't blatantly trying to bring your meds back to the landing Arg wouldn't be asking to search you mate".

"I know, but he lets everyone else get through".

"Because they're not so fuckin' blatant J.T, you mug him off right under his very nose bro and he has to be seen to be doing his job by challenging you ya know"?

"Well, I'll never talk to the cunt again".

"Wierdo, sort it out", I say, as I run out of paper in this cell right now. I go to the office and beg some from the staff team. J.T goes and gets his meds. Comes back. We are all banged up and despite the fact a screw followed him back to the cell to bang him up he still managed to somehow swap the pills for spice, how I don't fuckin' know. He is now preparing a fat spice spliff. We smoke and talk. My handwriting is skewed.

"I like these jeans", says J.T, "I wore 'em, these D and G ones when I was just gettin' with this bird and I pulled up outside a One Stop init". I smoke some spice and ask him to explain.

"This is nearly ten years ago now, 2008, 2009, I'm not sure, anyway", says J.T, "I'm in a car, a two litre Civic, she was in a Fiesta, outside the shop and I just got her number and fucked the life outta her that night".

"Fuck me, didn't take you long then".

"Don't fuck about me mate", says J.T. "Ms Gilchrest (a wonderful middle aged lady officer we all like) blatantly saw me like taking my meds out my mouth and putting 'em in my pocket earlier but she just looked away", he says now.

"It's horses for courses J.T", I say, "some of 'em give a fuck, some of 'em don't bro". A screw opens the cell door now, along with everyone elses' and Craig D, our next door neighbour, a feisty stocky quick tempered fucker with piercing blue eyes and deadpan countenance comes in, looking a little upset.

"What's up Craig, you alright"? I say.

"Just got a letter from my bird", he says, "we ain't been together and she's been seeing this other fella but she knows I'm getting out soon in it".

"How long you got left Craig"? I say.

"Six months, I just dunno what to do".

"Well", I say, "I've gone out and kicked a girlfriend in once in that situation, when she cheated on me. My beautiful baby mum, E----. But that never ends well and riddles ya with shame and guilt if you're anything like me. You could get out, tell her what a cheating cunt she is and live together in mutual hatred or you could say, like, it's just sex, she clearly loves me and accept the fact that you are perhaps a little to blame by sheer point of fact you wasn't and haven't been there for her. If you love her and want to be with her you'll have to forgive".

"It's burning me napper out Sloaney it really is", he says, walking solemnly out the cell with an "anyway, see ya later lads". J.T is wondering if he, when living in Bexhill some years ago, had bumped into me when I lived briefly on the streets there myself. He shot down there for years. (Sold drugs).

"Did you do pills (Es) when you was down there 'cause I swear I met you before 'cause I was shotting down there about the same time you was there ya know? No, I think it was a bit of gear (heroin) I might have sold ya I can't remember".

"I was in Bexhill for a while so it is entirely possible that I met you", I say

"Yeah, I remember, like, you were proper hard to get away from", he says, continuing, "yeah you were like proper quick, like a hundred miles an hour and me and my mate were saying when we left like 'he's proper nuts in he'", and I have to admit that this sounds very much like it may well have been me! I truly hope I'm capturing the essence of this guy for you and for posterity dear reader! And for God!

We are banged up now for a couple of hours over this Sunday lunch period. We are gonna smoke some spice when J.T can be bothered to roll a joint. He's telling me that I'm an ignorant cunt when I'm writing 'cause I don't seem to listen.

"What d'ya mean"? I say.

"Like when you're writing sometimes and I'm talking to you you just, like, grunt and that and it's proper rude"!

"You cheeky fucker"! I laugh, "even as I'm writing about you you're cunting me off! I'm literally sitting here trying to immortalise you bro"!

J.T laughs now, throwing his big square head back like a lion as he does so. He keeps pointing at the TV when different rappers come on:

"Look, look he's well cool in he", he says of Prof Green now.

"Yeah", I say, "Prof Green is a G still", I say trying to write and talk at the same time; the fact the fucker had to take one of his tablets today, a pregablin, means he hasn't shut up since as these pills notoriously make people chatty and jocular! I am very stoned and as I sit in Oxford now three years later I ask myself if I should include these really scrawled pages and decide I will share at least some of it. So the next paragraph in the written document reads:

I'm very stoned now and can barely see as my pen strokes the page. I'm right out my nut and can see Tan's butt but then I find myself back in Oxford. I'm out walking, beating the street as I make my way to Christ Church Meadow where my sleeping bag is, in a little copse. I use the down for a pillow. Now I'm flying past planets, gas giants and granites toward the gaping black hole at the centre of the galaxy. I need Tan, I need to fuck......now I'm thinking about God, wondering, wondering......I really hope that I have time left on Earth to alter the kilter on my Karmic Scales. I must spread love. I'm so grateful but must rest before they open my door in an hour. My brother dreamed I wrote a bestseller. P----, you and I are intricately linked and I love you brother.

1400hrs. If Chris Brown and Little Dicky ever hear my words I'll know I've made it. I love Chris Brown when he goes: 'no ones looking 'cause I'm black and my controversial past' in that Freaky Friday song. I love music. My stoned has worn off a little now which makes it a bit easier to put ink onto the page in a legible manner. Now it's Anne Marie and Marshmellow Man 'have you got no shame you've gone insane, I told you one two three four five six thousand times'. J.T is laying on his bed chonking away on his vape 'till clouds of swirling smoke are drifting round his big breezeblock bonce.

"Gis a little blast a that J.T", I say.

"Oh you wanna talk when you want something", he says, passing the nicotine delivery system for the 21st century. Anyway, I can hear gates swinging and doors being opened for the afternoon association period. I plan to drive me mate Bradders mad for a cup of coffee or three. I'm in full philosophising mode. The last I tried was Kiekergaard I think, oh, no it wasn't, it was the little one I stole from Waterstones in Oxford, Symposium or something and all I can recall is much talk on homoerotic subjects which left me thinking that it's no wonder half the aristocracy are kiddy fiddling noncy motherfuckers. Plato and Socrates and one of their mates, can't remember his name, who REALLY loved boys. Young ones at that. Though I am someone who doesn't judge gay men, for me, the idea of a hairy bum just repulses me, but each to their own. Now Tan's sexy cute bum on the other hand. I look up and see Ariana Grande then Miley Cyrus on TV and feel like a pedo myself lusting on them! Anyway, I'm taking my pad and paper to Brad's cell. I find him doing yet another mahussive puzzle and he says:

"I'm tryna get it done before Christmas 'cause I wanna have it done in time to put a little spread on this table", he says, continuing, "someone said to me earlier why do I do all these puzzles and I told him that it's good for the brain this sort of shit man", as his fingers work away at the finicky little pieces of puzzle he so quickly and expertly puts together. Our Thanet pal Jake, well dressed as always comes into the cell to discuss business with Brad.

"Can you sort us out a little something Brad? I've got a quarter of a page coming later", he says.

"What", says Brad, "so if I give you a little something to smoke now will you promise to give it back to me later"?

"Honestly Brad, got some coming later bro I swear". Brad sorts him. Remember, Jake got seven years for accidently killing his cousin and best mate in a car.

"How long you got left to serve Jake"? I say.

"Only nine months Sloaney".

"What ya gonna do when you get out"? I ask.

"Probably be trapping in Margate", he says, "get myself a zed pack (£1000 worth of drugs, half heroin, half crack) and start stacking some paper". Traveller Bill, nutjob small man who'll fight anyone, and behind him Frank, another pint sized lunatic poke their head now into popular Brads' cell.

"How d'ya make that like spider cube thing"? Frank asks, pointing to Brads' pet spider in the clear Perspex habitat cube Brad built for it.

"Easy mate, couple bits a plastic and some glue bro, then I just built the little stand for it out of matchsticks".

"What's the genus of the spider again Brad"?, I ask.

"Tegenaria Dulica", Brad says, continuing that, "it's actually called Tegenaria Dulica Domestica which means that genus plus the Latin for house, so it's a house spider when you break it down", Bradders finishes helpfully. Jake has just gone downstairs to get some tobacco, real tobacco, to make a joint.

"D'ya think he'll come back Brad"?

"Maybe" he says, "but you know what it's like, people will be on him and he won't get up here with it. You're better off going after him".

"To be honest, I've smoked enough today and am happy as I am at the minute".

"Fuck me Slicker, you sick or something"? Grin comes in. Jake comes up and Reece is here too and we all smoke spice, taking turns with the joint in the recess area of the cell.

"lookatthat" says Reece, pointing to a bird Grin is looking at in the paper, "that'sthatBiancaGascoigneshe'dpropergetitheryaknow" he rattles off. Say the words fast in your head dear reader and you've half an idea of how this young lunatic talks.

"Reece, have you got that cap you owe me"? asks Brad, meaning a single vape capsule that goes atop the vape battery for vapers. But Reece has already bolted out the cell the slippery little sod.

"Jake, you alright bro"? I say, seeing him holding up the door frame of the recess area; there's no door of course but he's hanging off the wall, dribbling, clearly very stoned. I can hardly see the page now, drifting............

"I've had to ask P---- (my Bro) a few questions over the years Brad" I say.

"What d'ya mean"? asks Bradders, playing with pieces of the puzzle.

"Well, when we lived in Ireland we both saw the woman next door dressed as a bonafide witch, stirring a big cauldron", I tell him, "and 'cause I needed to make sure in my own mind years later I hadn't dreamt it I asked him 'do you remember that P----'? and he said, yeah, course he did. And another time Brad", I go on.

"Yeah" says Brad.

"Another time our dad took us into the back garden and pointed our gaze toward the sky and we saw our first UFO and he also confirmed that too", I say, marvelling at the mentalness of the universe. I continue, rather stoned that "there's a lot of philosophising in this book of mine Brad, do you think I'm a pretender to philosophy"?

"You don't need to have a degree to be a philosopher Slicker", says Brad and I took some comfort from his words. I do marvel at my brother for he too was once homeless and injecting heroin after the dark period post my fathers' dispatching of himself. Well, his particular poison, like me, was a propensity for a snowball but he cleaned up rapid and achieved much. He has been clean at least seventeen years at the time of writing. Perhaps longer, significantly longer in fact. Twenty maybe. I myself also used much base amphetamine, for years and years and years. Perhaps for the same reasons kids are prescribed Ritalin today. To stem the mental psychotic side of me although after a week awake I would not be very sane to say the least. I reckon that gear opened a few neural pathways in my brain that would otherwise have gone unexplored. I used to tamp down the speed, like take the edge off with heroin and benzodiazapines like tamazepam, diazepam, Xanax, nitrazepam or best of all clonazepam when I could get them. Thinking of pills I also used to like MSTs or Morphine Sulphate Tablets, the purple ones. Or Dicanol, I used to love injecting those pink potents in particular. The MSTs were covered in a waxy plastic like coating that made them hard to get into and through a works (hypodermic syringe) so I'd simply crush ten or so in my mouth, luxuriating in the foul glorious chemical taste to the point of ecstacy. Yes, it could be said I was a weird kid. I tell Brad and he says he also loves the taste of chemicals, narcotic ones of course, in his mouth. Matchstick Model Maker old boy Trevor has just come in the cell and all three of us are reminiscing on the good old days when the drugs were good. Trev never looks on the bright side of life the miserable but nonetheless lovable old cunt. He is, though, an energy vampire at times, 'cause that's what depressives do, suck the life out of a room. Gifted cabinet maker this cunt too. Genius with anything requiring artisan skill actually. Stacey Dooley is dancing on the TV on BBC 1. J.T comes in the cell and swaps a 300ml pregab for spice with Brad. Me and Brad both make comments, appreciative ones, about the body and curves on sexy Stacey on telly.

"I think I'm actually falling in love with her Brad; she's fit and smart", I say.

111

"She does a lot of conservation stuff all over the world Sloaney ya know", says Brad, who cares deeply for the environment , "she was the one who started bringing things like the way the dumping of clothes and stuff in the ocean is affecting lots of marine species and that. She's proper got her fingers on the pulse man", he finishes.

"That Ms Terry (another lovely middle aged lady officer) is fuckin' lovely ya know Brad", I say.

"She is, but why you saying that today"? asks Brad.

"I ran out of paper again earlier and she went straight into the office and brought me out a whole brand new pad".

"Yeah, she's one a the best on here man, known her years and she's always been good to me". Grin comes in and gives me a fat pipe of spice. There is a lot of cocaine on the wing but the boys don't want raw, they want to turn it to crack but the problem is there is no bicarbonate of soda on the wing.

"If I had a gram of bicarb I could literally swap it for a gram of coke right now 'cause there is literally none, like none on the whole wing. Painful, loads of coke but no way to turn it to crack", as Brad was talking Grins' eyes lit up.

"What", he says to Brad, all wide eyed like a kid, "no one got any fuckin' bicarb"?

"No one", confirms Brad, "honestly Grin, if you had some I could swap it gram for gram right this minute".

"Shit", says Grin, "where the fuck can we get some from"?

"Wow man", I say, luxuriating in the thought of a great big fat cherry, a great lump of crack atop a pipe, poisonous fumes intoxicating me to ecstasy. Crack calls the user like no other drug. It's song is like that of the siren, irresistible initially until one has gone through so much pain in its pursuit it is simply to tiresome to chase in the end. Either that or it kills you. Or you go to an NA meeting and have a spiritual awakening which is the only thing more powerful than the allure of drugs to the addict in the end. Anyway, I am so skint and in debt I don't let the thought run away in my mind; prices are ridiculous for this, the daddy of drugs. Grin shares a joint with me. A screw comes in the cell we are in and does 'bolts and bars' to insure we are not trying to escape. As I sit here I wonder if I'll ever find a publisher brave enough to publish this, as it is, with the vernacular used by me and the people around me. I try to record faithfully. Brad stuck a centipede he found on the yard earlier into the cube with his spider; dinner! We watched as the arachnid sank its fangs into the many legged critter, paralyzing the ill fated thing.

"She's getting fuckin' massive man that spider of yours bro", I say.

"I know", he says, "she's been getting spoiled for a week so I won't feed her now for a few days at least".

"What, it can go days without feeding Fradders"?

"Oh yeah", he goes, "they can go weeks without feeding if they have to"! On the news now is a report about immigrants landing in Kent from Calais in rickety arse tens of thousands of pounds inflatable dingys the smugglers extortionately charge the poor cunts. Bang up is called after we have eaten. I think, in my stoned state, of Conchis showing Nicholas the statue with the look upon its face of one who has had access to privileged information. Makes my hair stand on end. Next I am thinking of Mr Craig, a teacher at school when I was about eleven. In a class of about 30 he had, one day, looked over to me, sitting in his wheelchair the likeable old cunt, and said, pointing at me with his finger:

"You Sloane, you're fucked, you are gonna learn the hard way son"! Never left me that. Now I think of my mum and look forward to seeing her when I get out. I miss her awfully, though I doubt she'll want to hear from me right now. No doubt the popular Irish fuck, the tiny woman with the massive personality, will be in The Crown, her favourite boozer, bending the ears of all those people who love her so much, with her infectious laugh, welcoming kind countenance and lilting Irish accent. She's so effortlessly the centre of attention my mum. She doesn't choose to be that way, she just is! God, I love her. Though I have treated her awfully.

24/12/2018 0700hrs. Xmas Eve, early morning and J.T the lanky long lazy motherfucker still lays prostate in his pit, snoring, soundly asleep. 'I would go for Presidencies and stop all these infantries.......wish I was home for Christmas' goes the Xmas song asking Mr Churchill to bring the troops home. It makes me think. I think and think, tormenting thoughts. I have pushed my tiny little drunken mum over before in her house when she wouldn't give me money for drugs. I used to, when we were all kids, kick the fuck out my younger siblings, particularly P----, but a year younger, until one day the poor fucker had had enough and broke my nose. I never did hurt him again. Anyway, I feel to share my ping pong thinking with you. I have spent years, when not in jail, speeding out my head, never sleeping, looking up at the Heavens on my back in fields. I reckon I have looked upon the sky for more hours than most people do in three lifetimes. Then I did a burglary and found me someone else's prized Celestron telescope which I aimed here and there comprehensively, arcing the sky with my now super enhanced eye to gaze upon the marvels therein. Always thinking the police were watching all I did in my paranoid sleep deprived states. I used to spend hours and hours on the internet also, looking at everything space related, like the Hubble telescope pictures. I remember I used to piggy back via someone else's Asynchronous Digital Subscriber Line or broadband as it's more popularly known. I'd discovered that if I dangled my wireless network adapter out the tower block flat window, this is back in 2001/2002 mind you, that I could detect and jump on insecure signals. Wonderful it was. I used to think that the police were allowing it and watching what I was looking at: if you were and you saw my preference for big black men serving small petite white women massive sausage then I hope you enjoyed it as much as me! Anyway, on the news there has been a massive tsunami, Charlotte Hawkins, sexy newsreader, alongside Piers and Susanna are reporting it on Good Morning Britain right now and I think back to the boxing day one that caused horrific loss of life all those years ago. Now I'm thinking back to the times I would be stabbing myself in my mum's bathroom with blunt needles in the winter, trying to get a vein for hours and hours and my mum would be saying from the front room:

"Aahhh son", think musical Dublin accent, "ahh son wud ya come out a dere now wud ya, what ya doing ta yaself son, I know ya hurtin' yaself in dere, ahhh son beJasus son wud ya come out now, please son, I can't stand da tought a ya hurtin' yaself son", oh God this is hard, remembering. I would invariably reply:

"For fuck sake mum, you ain't fuckin helping so shut the fuck up will ya", as blood dripped from various holes I'd punctured in me, unable to find a healthy vein for I'd ruined 'em all. And now in my minds' eye I can see her, hurting, her lovely open face so sad and in anguish. Let me just interject now, from here in Oxford years later, and tell you I am sobbing, sobbing thinking on this. Throwing my glasses down I wipe my eyes and tell myself to man up. Ok, interjection done. But now I am going to type from this next page in the document, and it is a tale I must tell, about my little mum.

Ok. One night, it must be at least twelve years or so ago now at the time of writing, perhaps a little more perhaps a little less, I had been very skint, very sick and desperately in need of money to get the heroin my system craved. These times I always had a front door key to me mum's little flat, over in Broadstairs, me being in Margate at the time. Anyway, I trudged my way over laboriously and painfully, taking a disproportionate amount of time to reach her gaff in my sick state. Eventually I get there and am gutted when I find she's not home; I hadn't bothered to phone, presuming she'd be in because it was at least 11pm. I wait for her for about an hour but in the end, after trying to ring her mobile phone from her own landline for I would a been so skint I'd've had no credit, I decide to fuck off. Anyway, the next day I get a call from the police, who are in her flat with her, and they ask me to come over; my mum had been raped. Now, it took many months until my mum could talk about it and out the blue, as I say, many months later I get a call.

"Come and have an ol' drink wid ya mudder would ya son"?

"Alright mum", I say, knowing she'd give me money to get some drugs as well God bless her, "I'll be over in ten", and I cycle over. We go to the Red Lion in Broadstairs and she says, suddenly, and remember this is a Catholic lady who only had three, and I doubt she let two of them touch her, men in her life and she hated talk of sex subjects, she says:

"Can I tell ya about dat night wit dat pig son", and I look at her lovingly and say softly:

"Course ya can mum, what happened then"?

"Well, I was in da Crown roight, it was really busy and I was wid me mates and dat son, ya know me roight, and t'rough da crowds of people I see dis pig, dis big ugly ting ya know and he kept looking at me son so he did and after a while he comes over and chats to me and me ol friends ya know. Anyway, I bought him a drink so I did, ya know what oim like, den he wen away and I tought no more of it ya know"?

"Go on mum".

"Anyway son so da pub now calls last orders and all me mates, they go dere ways ya know and oim waiting fer me taxi yer know. It doesn't come da fookin' ting and den I notice dis ugly shite and he comes up to me and he says 'ya waiting fer a taxi luv, mines just here now, ya can share it with me if ya want'? I tink nooting of it son and da taxi goes ta mine first and da ting says 'can I come into yours for a drink'? I say to him, as you know son, I don't drink at home ya know and den da ting says 'well a cup a tea den' and den I tought, ahh, what's the harm and ta be honest son I was a bit scared now dough ya know but I tought it would be ok", and here I'm thinking: if only I had waited that night, that cunt would a been fucked straight off out of it. She continues, "so we go in and I make a cup a tea and he's on a chair and oim on da sofa ya know and den da ting says to me 'get ya foockin' clothes off or oim gonna foockin' hurt ya. He comes over and starts stripping me and den he does his ting son so he did"........

"Jesus mum".....

"And when he was done he told me not ta foockin move and he sits den he does his ting again".....

"Mum, mum mum".....

"Anyway, once da pig had dun he pulls out a picture of him wid a woman and sum kiddies ya know and he says ta me, 'ya won't tell anyone wud you, I've got a wife and kids' and den he foocks off son and dats when I phoned da po-lice".....

"Oh mum, oh God I wish I'd've just waited a bit longer"......

"Ahhh don't worry son", says this most magnificent woman, "anyway, da police come and dey make me see dis doctor woman who takes some of da stuff from up dere, ya know son".

"I get it mum".

"And dats dat son, ya know da rest, I just needed to talk to someone ya know, tell someone". Now as you may understand dear reader, this is harrowing. Now they got the cunt. The police and my mum lied about the court date to me because they know I'd of killed him there and then in the courtroom. I had visions, as I looked forward to the fictional date they gave me, of jumping across the benches and grabbing the cunt round the neck, squeezing the life out of him before the very eyes of all in court. But no, to protect me, it was already done by the date I was given. The cunt went not guilty and my simple mum in her simple way told the court her simple truth and the motherfucker got ten years, the fucking horrible dirty sexcase scum cunt. After the hearing his ex wife came to my mum, for she was at court, and thanked my mum, saying thankyou for doing what she didn't have the courage to do and it turns out that when he raped her he had killed their Alsatian dog in the process, stabbing it, I guess as it tried to protect the woman from this monstrous, disgusting man. Anyway, believe it or not there is a happy ending to this tale. About eight months after, two months after the convo in the Red Lion described above, I get a call from me mum, same thing:

"Son, come and have a drink wid ya ol mudder wud ya"?

"But I ain't got no money mum".

"Ahhh son, don't worry about dat son, I got loads a money so I have".

"What? What the fuck you on about mum"?

"I got twenty t'ousand pound so I have son".

"Twenty fuckin' grand; really"?

"Come over son, oil get ya sum a ya shite as well don't worry, it's only blood money from dat filty ting, loike compensation ya know", and I peddle over there, nine stone dripping wet and when I get there I go in and she says:

"Ahhh son, don't be angry wid me now wud ya son".

"What the fuck you on about mum"?

"Well oi've only ten t'ousand now son".

"Well what the fuck you done with ten grand in less than half an hour mum"?

"I gave it ta da kiddies in Great Ormand (pronounced 'arrrrmand) Street Hospital son, ahh God bless 'em son", and the beautiful soul had,

116

over the phone, made an anonymous, yes, an anonymous donation to that worthy place. She didn't want people knowing, just quietly did it, wanting no recognition, no bells and whistles, that's what she did and it's hardly surprising God love her for she worked as a dinner lady for the schools for free for years as we all grew up, always gives money to charity and worked for many, many moons at the British Heart Foundation Charity shop in Ramsgate. She loves to give. This is just what she does.

"But don't worry son", she said, "We'll foock da rest up da wall in da pub son", and that, dear reader, is exactly what we did. Can't wait to see the woman. I've a lot of making up to do.

25/12/2018 1100hrs. Christmas day and sat before me in Bradder's cell are Seb, Gibbo and Grin and of course Brad who has put on a spread of crisps and chocolates and cake and fizzy drinks and mince pies and myriad other goodies all paid for by him. I fuckin' love this cunt. Brad talks of the terrifying trip he once had on spice which put him off ever smoking it again, and this thieving fuck did lots of acid with me as a kid and is pretty hardcore so that gives an idea of how hallucinogenic this gear really is.

1500hrs same Xmas day. We are locked up after being well looked after by the prison today. 'Body On My Innocence' ft 'Brando' is on 4music and I am mesmerized by the bird in the video. I have taken a multitude of drugs today and my pen scrawls diagonally across the page. I have had two Concerta XL tablets, a pint of hooch, 3000ml of Gabapentin and 100ml of Pregablin and of course I have smoked much of the zombie spice, all day long which continues now in the cell. Me and J.T are discussing the news we heard today that on 'F' wing two days ago a fella was beat so bad that he is now in intensive care. And today, despite it being Xmas, little blonde Frank punched a young scrawny chap called Nathan in the face for taking the piss paying the money he owes him. Every day the alarms ring, multiple times for violence and spice attacks across the jail. Ambulances daily frequenting the site. Staff being attacked often. Just the way it is.

26/12/2018 0830hrs and I have just gotten out me pit after hearing a screw open the flap on the door as he or she does the count to ascertain that no bodies are missing. The long, lanky J.T still lays languidly lazing on his bunk with one lithe arm hanging out, long tapering fingers occasionally twitching. Now he starts making grunting, whistling, exasperated sounds as he prepares to wake himself up. He is one

117

miserable, moody cunt in the mornings. Mind you, so was Aidy and we lasted six months although we did admittedly literally try to kill each other, which was why we were so close in the end I guess. I suspect the reason people in prison are moody in the mornings is because it is the start of the day where it has yet to be gotten through whereas when behind the door at night we know it's done, another day up the queen's bum and out the way. Aidy was the worst at the crack of day. I used to feel like killing the cunt at times. But by the end of each day I'd be like:

"Gis a cuddle Aidy".

"Nope", he'd say with a smile on his butter wouldn't melt mental face, "don't do cuddles Andy".

"Ahhh come on ya cunt, gis a cuddle bro, ya need one and anyway, I thought we were like proper pals after all we been through, smashing each other round the cell"?

"We are pals Andy mate", he'd say looking up from making a joint, "I just don't do cuddles yaknowwhaImean"? and the last would come out as all one word as he used to do, the poor fucker. Anyway, the door has just been opened, J.T is on the shitter having a pony and I'm gonna fly to the shower.

0930hrs now and I am sitting next to Grin on Brads's bed. Brad is standing over his table, tattoed arms out and is breaking open Gabapentin capsules and putting the powder from them into a pile on the surface. He doesn't have a blow out often but today, on this celebratory day in the Christian calender, he will do so along with me and Grin.

"You alright today Grin"? asks Brad.

"Yeah, got a go down the seg (segregation unit where adjudications or 'nickings' are heard) for a nickin' for them finding that bloody bong in the cell the other day".

"Fuck me", says Brad, "what, you're going down for a nicking today of all days"?

"Yep", says Grin, "and they came in and took our T.V off us last night putting me and Briggsy (a nutter Grin's banged up with from Sussex) both on basic regime as well". (Basic is when a con has continually been coming negatively to the attention of officers and means you get next to nothing. There are three tiers in British jails; basic, standard and enhanced-I'm sure you can do the math round those three reader), after a pause he adds "cunts", to the end of his sentence.

"Done a whole bag of coffee in here yesterday", says Brad, "so many people in here though, still , weren't a bad day for a prison Christmas and all that", and now he is putting a coffee together for us boys.

"Got no fuckin' sugar", says he now.

118

"No worries, I got a bag in me cell Brad", says Grin.

"Sweet Grin", says Brad, "get ya cup too mate rather than use this plastic one". Grin goes, comes back. Couple minutes later Grin's cellmate comes in. Now Grin and Briggsy are both on Subutex, a potent narcotic opiate and heroin substitute.

"I got mine back easy Grin, just been down there", says Briggsy, "the bird behind the bars ain't even bothering checking today".

"What", says Grin, "you got it all back"?

"Yeah", says Briggsy, "ya wan' a get down there now Grin it's easy bro".

"Sweet", says Grin, "back in a minute Brad", and he's gone. Peter 'Bundy' Lanes, my long term squat bald burgling friend has just walked in the cell.

"I didn't even phone home yesterday", Pete says to Brad.

"I did", says Brad, "I got on the phone at twenty past nine and my family all passed the phone around. Spoke to me sisters, me mum and all me nieces and nephews and that, it was great".

"Rick was right out his nut when I see him this morning at meds", says Pete now, talking of his brother Ricky who is on 'B' wing but comes to get his meds over here every day. Of course we know the bald brother as well as we all know each other; Rick is a spit of Pete but a little older, Pete at about 44 and Rick at 48 or so. "And the cunt took a load of MDMA a minute ago so he's gonna be gurning all day". J.T walks in the cell now just as me and Pete are talking about a friend of ours who has spent ten years out in Thailand. Darren McManus is his name; he had to come back as his life was in danger. I say to Pete:

"I asked him about that 'yabba' they all take out there and Darren told me it's just like crystal meth".

"What's 'yabba'"? asks J.T.

"Like I say, like crystal meth, like really pervy top a the range speed", I tell him.

"Yeah, that's what it is", confirms Pete, "instead of perv powder it's perv crystals".

"Why do they call speed 'perv powder'", says J.T.

"'Cause all amphetamine based products are extremely pervy", I tell him.

"It's true, all speed freaks are always proper pervy ain't they Sloaney"? says Peter, smiling the cunt.

"Hahahaha", I laugh, "well, yep, it's definitely true, but I ain't that fuckin' pervy Pete"!

"You fuckin' are mate, all those hookers you've lived with and the threesomes and that you've told me about. And I've seen you with some

119

right rotters too ya cunt". Anyway, as it's Xmas let me tell a very short tale I remember from an Xmas day not long ago in Oxford when the Universe once again blessed me, for they say finding money is a sign that angels value the recipient, and I have found lots and lots in my life. This was, in fact, just last year, 2017:

And I am asleep in one of the entrances to Oxford's famed Covered Market, arch like sheltered spaces that give many homeless relief from the worst of the elements. I open my eyes to a cold Christmas day, which wears the weather like a sodden grey blanket, slushy snow turned black by footfall and traffic not helping me feel any better about my dire circumstances. I have only fifteen quid in my pocket despite the fact my habit is at least a £100 per day and there is nowhere to thieve from and no one to beg off as all mankind that haunted nigh had sought their household fires. I get up and stash my sleeping bag and pillow and wrap my clothes around me tighter, trying to keep winters creeping claws from my skin.

"Who's on, where can I score"? I say to a black homeless guy I really don't like; he's ripped me off a few times, shorting me when I have trusted him to go get my product in the past. Cunt. I myself have done it to people but how dare someone do it to me!! Anyway, he says:

"Sergio's on", and I immediately, traipsing miserably, lend my step to a red phonebox, thankfully still in commission for I have no phone. I ring the guy, who isn't called 'Sergio', rather the line is just called that and any number of people can appear with the drugs, depending on who's manning the thing, the phone. He answers and tells me to meet him at Botley Road Community Centre down by the train station, under the bridge and just past Ferry Hinksey Road where I used to work at a butchers called Aldens who supply specialist meat products to all the colleges of Oxford and Cambridge along with many other franchises and establishments. Great place actually. Now I only have the money for one and one (one rock of crack and one of smack; dealers do deals of two ten pound bits for £15) and am extremely worried about how the fuck I am going to get through the day and worse the night for without the drugs to keep me warm I could literally freeze to death. So I cycle through the city streets on a bike that I stole a while ago, a mountain bike that now has no tire on the back wheel so makes a God awful noise as I make my way down past the old Oxford Prison, past the SAID (pronounced 'Sayeed') business school and the train station and under the bridge past the YHA Hostel backpacking kids use before turning in to the community centre to wait for the geezer to come with my drugs. I put the bike against a wall and before long see a young black youth coming toward me, he recognises me, I score and I go into the bushes on the park at the back of the centre and promptly put one in me, a poor snowball to be fair for I usually pump much more of the crack and smack up my arm, at least two and two. Anyway, I go to get on my decrepit bike when I see something shiny out the corner of my eye and see atop one of the three bins outside the entrance to the community centre a load of coins sitting there and my eyes go wide with glee. There are pound coins, fifty pees and twenty pence pieces piled in stacks, I guess, for the binmen. Well, there was fifty quid there near on. I promptly phoned Sergio again and pumped something more substantial and satisfactory into me, thanking the angels, God and the Universe for having my back all the while.

27/12/2018. 1000hrs. I'm in the cell alone, J.T out somewhere on the wing doing fuck knows what. I get on the toilet and have a dump when suddenly the cell door is opened and J.T and with him Ms Terry come in; he's on his way to his drug group and forgot something so the lovable lady screw is waiting for him at the door and the cunt, upon smelling the pong permeating the tiny pad exclaims:
"Fuck me Sloaney, that's disgusting bro".
"But".....I try to say, looking at the lovely Ms Terry, mortified, but the cunt is in full flow.
"Can you smell that Ms Terry"? the cunt says, "fuck me Sloaney boy you smell ill man, you should go see a doctor or something", says the well dressed smooth talking fuck as Ms Terry, bless her, trying to save my blushes just laughs and I take comfort in the fact the wily woman has seen it and, I dare say, smelt it all before! Her and Ms Gilchrest are on today and the pair together are like a couple a naughty schoolgirls. Little Ms Hulbert is also on, Pocket Rocket as she is known. She has only been in the job a short while but with her bubbly road girl personality and good looks she has made an impression on all and many talk about what they'd like to do to her! She is representative of the government recruitment drive at present, trying to make prisons safer and more decent places to live.
Every day I think to myself 'I'll tell this or that story' but end up getting so out me nut I can't. Last night I was remembering a book called Lark Rise to Candleford, a collection of tales of hamlet life in days of yore. I was laying thinking how nice to live in such simple times! I think her tales were from in and around Oxford at the end of the 19th century, well, let me give a tale from the 21st and not quite as idyllic.

I don't know if you've noticed but I like to talk to people, every people, any people. Picture me, out me nut recently in the city of Oxford.

I'm running around shoplifting aggressively these times but it is morning, early and the doors to my places of prey are still shut and I sit huddled on Cornmarket Street, sick with shivers and cold sweats, desperately in need of my first fix of the day which won't come 'till I have relieved Boots, Superdrug, Debenhams or John Lewis of some of their more expensive floral fragrances. So, huddled in a dirty blanket I sit, morose but amicable enough.

"Morning mate", I say to a fella who catches my eye as he bowls on by. I think he doesn't hear me but the possibility he is deliberately ignoring my skinny, trampy, drug addled self is too alluring.

"I said morning mate", and now the fella turns and gives me the look I am hoping for from suited, clearly upper class sheltered motherfuckers like him; the look was one you'd give a rabid dog before putting him down. I jump to my feet and give chase with frantic pace and psycho eyes and the geezer looks over his shoulder at me, obviously hearing my heavy step.

"Morning mate", I say again and as he looks back upon me once more I see the true depth of disgust in the cunt's eye and my heart misses a beat as I briefly think how nice it would be to simply kick the fuck out the cunt, smash the granny out of him, giving him an experience he's never had before.

"What's that look for"? I say, rhetorically and you have to picture now dear reader that I am literally, literally running rings around and around him, circling him incessantly, eyes wide with righteous fervour and fire burning bright with resent for his prosperity.

"What is it mate"? I ask, round and round and round I go.

"Please mate", he says, head swivelling this way and that as he tries to keep up with my manic circling, "I'm just trying to walk to work in peace".

"You", I say, still circling insidiously, "you are a cunt, ya know that"?

"Look young man".......he starts.

"Shut your fuckin' mouth and open your ears you ignorant cunt", I say, teeth bared and spitting so angry am I, "you look at me like I'm the worst of humanity but let me tell you something you slick thick cunt, you are lower than I could ever be in my homelessness and addiction you judgemental privileged prick with your self absorbed little life. How would you feel if I sank my teeth into your face for looking at me the way you did when a simple good morning would've saved all this? But no, you look at me like I am everything you hate about the world. Cunt", and I spit the last disdainfully, disgustedly.

"Mate"......he says now with real fear in his voice and I say to myself he's had enough.

"Shut up and listen", I say, still circling now, "next time a homeless person says hello to you from beneath a dirty blanket you be sure to say hello back bro because it might just be me and I ain't that well and unlike you have been physically fighting people all my life. Keep looking at people like that some cunt's gonna fuck you up. Be fuckin' nice to people cunt", and as soon as I spit the last 'cunt' at him I'm gone from his gaze, smiling and feeling like I'd helped the world. Could a perhaps gone about it a bit better but hey, it's where I was at at the time! In the run up to Xmas 2017 I don't think Oxford ever saw a shoplifter like me. For twelve weeks or so I stole Armani tracksuits, Superdry coats, tons of alcohol but most of all aftershave and perfume to the tune of tens of thousands of pounds. I had another chance one day to offend the sensibilities of an upper crust normal in Superdrug, now demolished, in the city centre. I'm in the store filling my tied at the bottom coat with Lacoste and Jean Paul Gultier fragrances when I notice a sweet looking rich little old lady looking down at me as I'm crouched in the isle 'working'.

"Do you work here"? she says.

"No", I say, immediately sensing an opportunity to seriously offend a bonafide member of the upper class establishment for the blinkered old cunt was dressed head to foot in Chanel.

"Well, that's stealing what you're doing then", she said in her clear, clipped, cultured English. I smile up sweetly to her and say:

"That's right you crusty old cunt", and I pause briefly, luxuriating in the way this powdery old fuckers jaw drops open exposing perfect white teeth inside the 'O' of her mouth. I nearly choke, trying not to laugh out loud.

"I".....she starts but I am well ahead of her, still smiling up at her sweetly. I stand up now, jacket bulging, look her in the eye and say this:

"If I thought I could get away with it I'd snatch your handbag too you wrinkly old fucker", and her eyes grow wide with the shock of meeting a madman like me on her sojourn to the city but I'm off now, like a weasel and the last the poor old fucker would of heard of me was the sound of the alarms going off as the bounty I had triggers them at the store door but I am rapid and this bothers me not. I take a left to the phonebox outside the Market Street entrance to the Covered Market and suck on a crack pipe in there, stifling laughter as I splutter thick creamy crack smoke from my lungs before rushing off to sell my goods and buy more. For the record reader, though I've crept many houses, I have never robbed anyone in the street, well, apart from the odd drug dealer with Damo and my mate Frank from Canterbury. Even I draw the line at swinging old ladies about.

1345hrs 27/12/2018. I've just perused the little I penned this morning on my Oxford escapades and find I'm shocked by my own behaviour. I've never met anyone quite like me really to be fair. I mean, I can be horrible at times!! I showed young Ben Taylor who popped in to share a spliff earlier and the young buck loved it so I take that as representative and decide to keep it in the narrative. Staff are about to open doors to let people out for work and I myself am supposed to be going down to Ade's to help him tutor in the maths class but alas I'm fucked, clucking, and feeling the bite of withdrawel. My guts are twisted in knots causing me just this morning to literally shit myself. My back is absolutely drenched in cold feverish sweat despite the fact it is two weeks I think since my last dose. I am a little worried at the watery discharge being constantly leaked from my sphincter and hope it's not indicative of anything more serious than the deprivation of an opioid to my system. Hepatitis C perhaps.......need another blood test. Anyway......

0706hrs 28/12/2018. I want to tell you about a gangster, a real clever criminal named Dave M. Now Dave, my lovely sister says, just has 'something about him'. About 5'11, very handsome aquiline face with quick, foxlike intelligent eyes and a medium build. He dresses in slim jeans and Lyle and Scott tight fitting jumpers and is always in a pair of expensive loafers. He must be 58 now but the tale I am about to tell is from 1994 stroke 1998, I can't quite remember but I was definitely very young myself. So he would have been in his prime and me but a baby, a baby who loved being round this guy, who I thought of as my best role model for the cunt has done numerous successful armed robberies, proper bits of work netting him tens of thousands and now he was the biggest crack and heroin dealer in Thanet. By the way, Dave originates from New Cross, London. He speaks with a broad cockney drawl. He is also someone who always has guns around him, handguns, pen guns and even an automatic rifle at one point. Oh, and the odd shotgun of course. Anyway, I'm down at Staffordshire Street, Craig's and Trish's gaff and my Nokia 3210 phone bursts into life, Dave's name coming up on this modern technological marvel I hold in my hand.

"Sloaney", I would go, trying to sound important.

"It's Dave M Sloaney", Dave came down the line.

"Yes Dave; what's up bro"? I ask this G who pulls off massive bits of work with aplomb.

"Fancy coming over to me in Margate Sloaney (Trish's is in Ramsgate) I'll come pick you up if ya want; might have a bit of work for ya"?

"Yeah man definitely", I say, always eager to spend time with this dark fuck.

"I presume you're at Trish and Craig's"?

"Yeah man".

"Keep an eye out the window I'll come pick you up".

"You got any drugs Dave"?

"What do you think Sloaney? You'll be well looked after today don't worry ya greedy little cunt"!

"Sweet Dave, see you soon". Dave, at the time, had people shotting crack and smack for him all over Thanet in Westgate, Margate, Ramsgate and Broadstairs. I used to envisage him like an octopus sitting there with his tentacles out, running his very lucrative empire.

"Sloaney", he says before I cut the line.

"What"?

"You ain't out ya nut already are ya"?

"Not really Dave, I mean, I've had a bit of breakfast".

"How much breakfast Sloaney"?

"Half a gram of smack and a couple hits of base".

"Alright, don't fuck yaself up 'cause I need you on the ball".

"Chill Dave man".

"Don't make me pop you in the leg again ya mouthy little cunt", and here he laughs along with me for I had wound him up once, quite deliberately, so much that in the end he poked a pair of scissors in me leg. Just the end of 'em. I was still laughing at him when he done it as he was so red in the head, infuriated by my mouth. I was a difficult kid! I mean, back then an incident that will give an idea of where I was at is in a fight outside a pub, after the scrap I lay on the floor begging a geezer to kick me in the head again for in my mental state the blinding flash as a penalty kick hit me head gave me pleasure. So did biting and smashing people to a pulp. I wanted Dave to hurt me that day and he didn't really come through with his little pin prick.

"Who was that Sloaney"? asks Trish, coming into the room. She sits opposite me and pulls out a roll of foil. She already has a piece rolled into a tube which now hangs out her mouth. She puts heroin on the square she has torn off and melts it into a brown blob by stroking the lighter underside of the silver slip. She places the tube above the blob as it runs down the foil, inhaling the pungent fumes of the priceless potion. She blows out through the tube sending acrid sweet smelling smoke curling into the ether. I tell her it was Dave.

"What's he want"?

"Says he's got a bit of work for me".

"Did he say what Sloaney"? asks Waff, who is also smoking and who would be murdered many years later outside a pub on Newington Estate, Ramsgate, where both his family and mine have lived for years.

"Naa, you know what he's like the secretive cunt". As I say this I pull the little coffee table toward me. On it is my dirty spoon I use for cooking the concoctions I like to poke into my arm. I place two bags of smack into it, add some vitamin C and cook it 'till it goes a translucent brown colour. Next I drop a couple of small rocks of crack in, crushing them 'till they disappear into the solution satisfyingly.

"Well", I say, continuing, "I don't know where I'm going but he did tell me not to use anymore drugs before he picks me up the cunt"! Both these fuckers in the room with me smile and chuckle at this.

"You never fuckin' learn Sloaney", says Waff, smiling, showing the white teeth in that coveted face.

"He'll be able to see you're out ya nut if you stick that in your arm before he gets here Sloaney", says Trish, shaking her head.

"Well", I say, aiming the point of the big two ml needle at one of the fat veins I had in my arm all those years ago, "it's a bit late for that", and I push the point in, puncturing the purple protrusion which carries the claret my heart pumps round my system. As soon as the vein is stabbed I draw back on the plunger and silently salute God as blood blossoms into the barrel. I now put my index finger to the top of the plunger and push hard on it, getting the solution into me as fast as is possible. "Wow", I say, eyes going wide as I pull the pin from my skinny arm.

"Ya fucked when he gets here......oh, he's here Sloaney; just pulled up outside", says Waff.

"Shit", I say, rolling down my sleeve, wiping blood with the fabric of the jumper.

"S'alright Sloaney", says Trish as I go to clean up my paraphernalia, "I'll do that mate, you go".

"Don't let him have you doing anything too stupid Sloaney", says Waffster as I kiss his bald black head before bending to peck Trish on the cheek.

"Love ya both", I say as I scoot out the door, "see ya when I get back". I run out the door to Dave's Audi.

"Alright Dave me ol mucca"? I say as I slam the door shut.

"Alright Sloaney"? he drawls, cockney as ever and looking cool in Ray Ban bins. He has a pair of Stone Island shorts and a Ralph Lauren T shirt on the smooth cunt.

"Yeah man", I say, "been waiting patiently for you ya cunt".

"Getting out ya nut more like ya lying little fucker", he says, smiling all the while. He's in good form, "you forget I know you Sloaney".

126

"Well, I had another little hit"….

"Of what though"?

"Well", I start, but he's at me.

"A snowball I bet", and I can't help but smile, "well you seem alright so we'll crack on. And don't worry, you can have a proper hit a bit later".

"What we up to then Dave"?

"We", he says, "are going to London but you Sloaney", he continues, lowering his specks and his voice simultaneously, "will be coming back with half a kg of tackle on the train and a little toy too", and now he puts the car in gear and we pull off.

"Ok", I say, unquestioning of the main part of the plan, "when"? I ask excitedly.

"When the fuck do you think Sloaney ya silly cunt"? he says sarcastically, briefly rolling his eyes and giving me an 'are you thick or what' look, "today ya silly fucker", and he shakes his head ruefully but with the love I know the cunt has for me. "We're gonna pop to mine and grab some crack for you to pipe on the way up ya greedy little cunt then we'll shoot straight off. Ya sweet with that"?

"Cool man", and I'm all excited like a kid going in the lorry with his dad to work for a day trip. I love basking in Dave's mysterious ways. Still do to this day, the cunt. It isn't long before we are on the Thanet way on route to the smoke. We make short work of the drive, me piping creamy crack washed up by Dave with ammonia as the tyres tear along the tarmacked motorway. Eventually we get to Deptford. We park up and find a preordained telephone box from which Dave places a call. He comes back to the car and we wait. Soon we watch as a tall black man goes to the same telephone box where he seems to drop something before leaving. Immediately he has gone Dave is out the car and back to the box. He returns a minute later.

"Get a bit of foil together Sloaney", he says which I quickly do. David pulls a small packet, a tester from his pocket and I do what Trish did earlier, chase the dragon to ascertain the quality of the work. It is potent, good quality heroin. The colour, smell and taste are perfect and the ready brek glow I get on inhalation is sublime. Dave has a little try too.

"What d'ya reckon Sloanester"?

"Fuck me, warmed me cockles I'll tell ya"!

"Good enough to buy half a kilo"?

"Defo"! I say.

"I think so too", and the cunt is out the car to the box where he places a call. He drops something. Soon he comes back. We wait. The same fella goes to the same box, bends and picks up what Dave left in a grassy knoll behind it and drops the small ruck sack from his back in the same spot. He goes, Dave's out the car and retrieves the ruck sack. Returns to the car.

"Right", says Dave, "where do you want me to drop ya Sloaney"?

"Well, I'd rather avoid the tubes Dave".

"Just say where mucca; anywhere".

"Victoria Dave, d'ya mind"?

"Nope, that's sensible as you won't have to fuck about changing".

"My thoughts exactly Mr M", I say, "so, what treats can I have for the journey"? and Dave smiles.

"There's an eighth of light and an eighth of dark there", he says, passing me 3.5 grams of crack and 3.5 of smack, "and when you get back I'll give ya an ounce of the tackle and another eighth of white", and when he sees my eyes go wide at the prospect of an ounce of top quality tackle and more he pulls the bag from the back seat, placing it on his lap.

"The reason", he says, unzipping it, "that I'm paying you so well is because of this Sloaney", and he pulls out the smaller of the two parcels in the bag. He removes what looks like a handkerchief and inside this is a snub nosed revolver.

"Fuck me Dave", I say, excited and feeling like I'm gangster number fuckin' one!

"You've got eighteen ounces of tackle on you Sloaney so it wouldn't make much difference if you got nicked with this as well anyway mate. And at your age you'd only get a five and you know you'd be well looked after if the worst did happen. If I got taken with this lot it's twelve at least. But that ain't gonna happen, the only two people who know are the two in this car, me and you. You're sweet me ol son, don't worry". And I trust this fucker anyway. I'm excited, exhilarated and in anticipation of consuming cunt loads of crack and smack on the journey home. Dave pushes the chambers out and everyone has a round in.

"Fuck me, it's fuckin' loaded"!

"Well fuck me Einstein, wouldn't be much use empty would it"? I laugh heartily.

"Can I shoot it"?

"Behave yourself Sloaney ya silly little cunt", and he puts it back in the backpack with the heroin. Two and a half hours or so later I am alighting at Margate train station where I get a taxi to Palmer Crescent in Millmead. I get a big cuddle and an ounce of excellent diamorphine hydrochloride along with a sizable lump of crack cocaine! Happy days.

It's funny dear reader for even as I write David is on the wing juxtaposed to ours; Echo or 'E' wing, serving a sentence of four years for stealing twelve thousand pounds from a commercial premises. Bit harsh the old judge on that day if you ask me!

The cell door has just opened though J.T is absolutely out his canister and oblivious to the fact we now have a couple of hours relative freedom on association. I'm already sitting in Brads' with Grin who's been a little off of late.

"I'm still clucking (withdrawing) me arse off Grin", I say.

"You will be mate", he replies, "that meth takes proper ages to come out ya system".

"Last night Grin man, I was in pieces, eventually trying to sleep on the floor for three hours; me limbs would just not stop that twitching, that horrible marrow thing ya know"?

"It's fuckin' awful in it mate, like ya just wanna cut ya arms off".

"It's like something at the centre, like in the very core of the bones in it", I say, grateful to be able to share the lingering longevity of the flu like symptoms I'm having.

"How's ya guts an that? You bin heaving"?

"Yep, and constantly sweating from every pore and shivering constantly man".

"I bet it's at the small of ya back in particular in it"?

"You know the one mate", and he is right, there is a pool puddled there 24/7 at the moment.

"And", says Bradders now, piping up, "the worst thing is is that the sicker you feel the better ya look as the colour starts coming back to ya face so then people think ya fannying them when ya tell 'em how sick you are"! And he is bang on here.

"You fuckin' know that right"! I say, "and another crap thing is it literally takes at least six months after stopping any opiate for the pituitary gland to start spitting any real endorphins again. Fuck me it's a protracted thing this shit"!

"Be a while before you feel a 100% again Andy", says Brad.

"Well, I wish it'd hurry up 'cause I'm fuckin' struggling with this no sleep thing as well lads".

"Ya doin' well mate", says Grin, "I couldn't fuckin' do it I tell ya".

"Me either", says Brad, who is also happy being on a methadone script. "Tell you what though Andy", he says now, "why the fuck you'd choose to do it now with six months left I don't know".

"Brad, there's never a good time for clucking bro".

"Yeah, but you could of slept the sentence away on fifty ml and got off it when you got out mate", he says.

"I fuckin' tried doing it out there Brad, even went back to the Ley 'till they kicked me out for locking meself in me room and refusing to come out". Brad, too, has been to the Ley Community.

"How many times you been back there since you completed"? he says.

"Three times".

"They're pretty good like that really".

"They saw my first relapse coming man, they were right. When I got with A---- (R----'s mum) they could see what was coming. Guy and Danny (staff at the Ley) told me 'she's not good for you, if you don't stay away from her you'll be relapsing in no time' but I wouldn't hear a bar of it".

"What", says Brad, "Did they think she was a cunt then"?

"Not a cunt, just a bit of a nutter I think they were more concerned about my abilitly to deal with intimacy at the time.". Now Grin says:

"But you told me she's been a positive influence in your life but it sounds like she drove you to relapse"?

"I drove me to relapse Grin. No one drives us to use. I used because I couldn't handle the way I was feeling. She did teach me bundles man, she's an inherently good woman".

"Like what"? asks Brad.

"She taught me the importance of gratitude. She is always on about gratitude man, what it is to be thankful. I wasn't ready to listen when she used to say 'where's your fuckin' gratitude' and she didn't mean for all she'd done for me, she meant for wider things such as the safety of the state here in Britain, the fact you can't starve to death here, the fact I'm free and for the love in my life".

"You have always been an ungrateful fucker Andy", says Brad helpfully.

"I know man. She also showed me that there is more at work in the world than what we can see. It's a shame there's a restraining order which prevents me picking her brains further on these subjects".

"Why's there a restraining order"? says Grin.

"Got twenty months for an ABH, punched her in the head in a jealous rage".

"She can't be that enlightened surely", says Grin, "what does she do for a living"?

"She has made her fortune doing like readings for people ya know, like tarot and that", I say.

"Do you believe that stuff then"?

"Well, I've had mad shit happen to me and seen her readings come to pass as she predicted in people. Then I found Paulo Coehlo too and his books have just reinforced what I was beginning to suspect already. There is magic at work in the world make no mistake. Man, that woman though, she knows shit, like she's had access to privileged information man I swear it. But gratitude is a central tenet in her life and it's served her well, she's stinking rich".

"Didn't you say you used to love her little boy too Andy"? says Brad.

"Yeah man he is so cute. And so loving and incredibly smart man. I miss them two sometimes still". And it's true dear reader, I do.

30/12/2018 0830. It is Sunday and J.T is laying in bed though he's awake and watching MOTD with me.

"Watch this save man, this keeper is proper on form, watch how the cunt saves this penalty".

"Fuck me, that was a good save though".

"I knew he was gonna save that; good at predicting things int I"?

"What, 'cause you guessed the cunt might save that penalty"?

"No, not just that, I said about that Piranha fish film last night and it just came on, don't ya think that's like proper weird"?

"You're weird ya cunt, I mean, you know I believe in stuff like that but that's hardly evidence you're a seer mate"!

"Naa man I swear Andy I do it outside all the time man".

"You're a fuckin' nut job, that much is true". Door's just opened, it is exactly 0900hrs now. Because J.T hears the soft tones of a female voice upon the opening of our cell door saying 'morning men' and he couldn't see who she was being in his pit, just as I'm about to leave the cell he says:

"Who's that Sloaney, quickly have a look which woman screw that was and tell me before you go".

"For real, you really want me to run down the landing and find out who she is"?

"Yeah please, just run back and let me know please man".

"You are un fuckin' real", but I do his bidding. I return.

"It's the fit little blonde from 'E' wing".

"What? Really? You're not bullshitting me are ya"?

"She's only about 21, behave yourself will ya", but I can't help laughing at the lazy languid lout who wears his amorousness like a creepy string vest.

"Fuck that mate, I'm a put me best garms on 'cause she's proper like into me; you mean the new little fit blonde one right? Works on 'E' wing"? He asks this as he springs excitedly from his bed, thrilled at the prospect of chatting up a bird he's zero chance of bagging.

"Yeah mate, the fit little young one, proper young", I say, emphasising the last.

"Sloaney", he says, now checking his face out in the mirror, "you forget that you're like 42 and I'm 28"....

"And".

I'm just saying that 'cause you might not have a chance I still might".

"J.T you fuckin' pest, you ain't got a chance of getting into a bird like her".

"You actually (draw out the aaaaacccctuuuaaaally) don't know that and anyway, I just like talking to the women screws 'cause I like the way they look and smell and that".

"You're an even more prolific pest than me and I didn't think that was possible".

"She's proper fit though int she"? he says, picking up his toothbrush.

"Did you see Fats yesterday, proper chirpsing Ms Slane and then at night he was all over Ms Hulbert"? I say.

"I know", says J.T, "thing is, Fats has so much dough he probably could pull one of 'em".

"And", I say, "the cunt is charismatic and charming too, although he does remind me a bit of Buddha".

"Watch the wing change when he goes home in three weeks", says J.T, "people will be jostling to take his place. You watch Sloaney", and he is right. Anyway, I take myself off to Brad's cell, leaving the pest to preen himself for his mission. He is watching nature programs which are always on on a Sunday morning.

"What a majestic looking bird Andy, look", he says to me soon as I enter the cell.

"But why does that woman want to like own it Brad, wouldn't it be nicer to set it free"?

"No different to keeping any other pet man and look", he says, pointing to an almost albino looking bird of prey on the TV, "that's called a Gyrfalcon, one of my favourite birds".

"Wow", I say, "never seen such a lovely looking animal", and it is true, what majesty these noble creatures possess. Reece enters the cell. He is calm today and I think to myself he must be taking his Ritalin properly. Now Grin walks in too.

"Morning Grin", I say, "and Reece, why are you cutting your arms up again", noting marks on his arms.

"These are only old ones Sloaney we've had this conversation already don't you remember"? and you dear reader should remember that this sentence is emitted at a rapid rate like all one word.

"Just checking", I tell him.

"You know you can always come to us if you need to talk", says Grin to this quick witted and mischievous fucker. Brad leaves the cell and I say to Reece:

"We may only be a couple of cunts but we are here for you if ever you don't feel too clever bro".

"Ahh, thanks lads", and he, too, shoots from the cell. Brad comes back holding a pillow, like a proper outside soft feather pillow in his hands.

"Lift ya back up Sloaney", he says to me, as I sit on his bed with my back against the wall. He places the pillow behind me and seeing I struggle with the writing pad on my lap he brings a board out from down the side of his cupboard saying:

"There ya go, proper writing board and proper comfy; wanna coffee lads"?

"Yes please Brad and thanks mate", and he smiles his lovely smile.

"Bless ya Brad, I'd love one", says Grin. Last night I had had a proper odd half an hour. Sitting in the cell after bang up I suddenly, after smoking spice had heard a mental loud screeching noise in my ears and everything about me seemed to vibrate. For half an hour I sat, scaring my cellmate as the cords in my arms stood out with the pressure with which I was gripping the side of J.Ts bed and the leg of the chair on which I sat. Full of fear I began hyperventilating and J.T had been frightened himself.

"You alright Sloaney or what? You want me to press the cell bell bro"?

"No", I say, wide eyed and still gripping the chair, "fuck that, no".

"Shit, you look scary though you sure you're alright"? It had passed. The thing I was musing on and which caused me to feel fear was the idea that this narrative might actually bear fruit some day. Mad I know.

1400hrs. Banged up. J.T is now out his nut after having smoked a buscopan tablet and smoking a big spice spliff. This is how fucked he is:

"Where've you put the goat"? Now buscopan and spice mixed take the traveller to other realms, "where's the fuckin' goat Sloaney"?

"What fuckin' goat J.T"?

"The cunt in the toilet, oi, get out the toilet and start spinning some silk", he says randomely.

"What the fuck you on about you wierdo"?

"It's the fuckin' goat Sloaney....ohh, shit" and I see recognition dawn on his face, I think, but this shows he's still away with the fairies: "shit, huhuhuhhuhuh, behind the bike shed where all the girls are getting fingered", and he briefly strokes my hair with a hair brush before literally, dear reader, doing the seal thing again, clapping his hands together like a retard and continuing, "huhuhuhuh funny in it"! We get out again for an hour when dinner is served at about four pm where I throw my dignity away begging for spice like the junkie I am. When I am told 'no' I want to fight the refuser so angry does it make me when the truth is the anger is with myself for being so pathetic. We are now banged up and J.T pulls out another joint which we are sharing. Soon he once more lapses into mong mode and I see the sharpness fall from his face:

"Bruv, whack the generator on I got a poo-ey bum".

"You are fucked", I say.

"I always wanted to fuck my teacher", and again he claps like a seal with the look of a special person plastered on his boat race.

"Jesus", I say. Before bang up, when we were out for an hour tonight for the evening meal J.T could be seen on the landing spending the whole time next to the long mixed race Amazonian beauty, Ms Slane. Despite the fact he was clearly out his nut he puked pony talk all over her and she, humouring him, smiled and nodded I dare say marvelling at the man before her and the transformation in him when inebriated for my days he turns into a retard.

"I can just feel it Sloaney, I know she wants to fuck me man I just know it", he had said upon entering the cell for lock up.

"What makes you think that"?

"She told me, like, that I shouldn't smoke spice and that I'm better than that".

"What, and you think she's cracking onto you"?

"I reckon if I put a bit of work in I'd get her to leave the job an that".

"My days"! Anyway, I feel my mind meandering and am tripping myself! Still, I'm gonna try tell you a tale.

Two years ago now and I am living on the streets of Canterbury in Kent, a majestic and historically important city I've burgled in prolifically throughout my misspent youth. One day walking down the High Street I come across a young handsome homeless fucker of about the same stamp as I: eleven stone at the time, (I'm 13.5 when well). Frank is a good looking guy with dark hair, slim roman nose above a strong lipped mouth and chiselled jaw. He has the same suspicious eyes as I, always narrowed and calculating. He was twenty at the time and though double his age I, when with him, too felt young! So, I have about £40 in my pocket and see this young guy but as I am about to approach him he gets up and I follow him round to the square before the Cathedral which was covered in scaffolding at the time. He is looking back at me, clearly concerned at my presence and distrustful. I speed my step and stop him:

"You alright fella"? I say.

"Yeah man, ya good? What's up"?

134

"I wanna score mate". His eyes narrow and his handsome head is pulled slightly back as he appraises me.

"You old bill or what mate? You know you have to tell me if you're old bill don't ya? Like, if I ask and I'm asking, you fuckin' filth or what bro"? This fella wears his suspicion like a hooded black cloak.

"I'm not old bill bro I swear", I say, thinking how funny it is people actually believe this falsehood to be true for I have heard it numerous times from the suspicious homeless when I have been endeavouring to score; there must be something about the way I look. I had recently been released from jail and had my prison papers on my person.

"Straight"? he says, "you're not fuckin' with me"?

"I'm not long outta jail mate; d'ya wanna see my prison papers"?

"Go on then mate, sorry, it's just like I've never seen you before ya know"? he says, looking at me through veils of suspicion. I pull out the papers and finally satisfy him that I'm not a predatory policeman.

"What d'ya want then mate"? says who I then learned was Frank, him even giving me his surname of B----. Frank B----.

"One and one for me and the same for you if you can get it for £30"? By this I am asking if he can get one bag of smack and rock of crack for me and the same for him at thirty quid. This would normally cost forty but enterprising dealers are offering 25% off in areas of the country right now. Frank pulls out an old school Nokia 8210 from his pocket with grimy been homeless for ages fingers. He rapidly passes the digits of these over the keypad and presses the button to send the text message. 30 seconds later the phone, still in his hand, lights up. Frank peruses the screen before quickly putting it into a pocket and saying to me:

"Let's go".

"Where we going"?

"Canterbury West train station", and we both aim ourselves in that direction.

"Where ya from then mate"? I say. Frank, despite the rapid way we walk has a lazy and unhurried way about his movements. His eyes are hooded as he turns to me:

"From here; Canterbury".

"Are you related to Dominic B----"? I ask this nonchalantly. He immediately stops and turns, opening his cynical slitted eyes as much, I guess, as he could through the haze of heroin in his blood stream for that is indeed his favourite.

"How the fuck"? he begins, before looking to the ground, slightly sheepish and embarrassed I guess, "that's my dad".

"Oh", I say, putting out my hand, "well, look Frank, my name is Andrew Sloane and I know your old man; have done for years", and we continue walking now.

"How d'ya know him"? And we are once more walking rapidly.

"Well", I say, "sadly I've spent many years in jail and I'll be guessing you'll know that he has too".

"Yeah, I know that", says young Frank, "but I don't even really know him to be honest", and instantly I gather that me having known his dad for many years clearly means I know him better than the son who stands before me. "What sort of man is he"? Poor cunt, I later learned that Frank's mum died of a heroin overdose.

"He's a big, handsome, kind hearted fucker", I say sort of truthfully.

"Bang on the gear though", says Frank, meaning he knows his dad is a heroin addict.

"Well, yes Frank, that's true", I say as we now draw close to the train station, "but we all bear our burdens and have our own problems mate".

"Yeah, I guess", he says, before spotting a black guy and saying to me, "gis the money and wait here", and I do both. He scoots off, does a quick carefully concealed transaction then returns to me.

"Let's go", he says.

"Where"?

"24hr toilets; I've got a disability key", and we walk right up the other end of Canterbury High Street up by McDonalds and CEX and Superdrug.

This is simply how I met the daring and mischievous lovely poor young fucker. Never had a chance. Anyway, he's so hardcore homeless he has a key which opens the disabled toilets which I quickly learn he uses as a safe place to inject and sleep. He keeps his stuff not far away; sleeping bag, clothes and some toiletries. There soon came a routine. Within a week I had already committed multiple offences around the city such as shoplifting and car theft and stealing handbags from staff only rooms in shops to feed my desperate desire to escape my reality and keep warm on the cold nights. We prowled together, birds of a feather, he and I. Anyway, Frank's favourite thing to do, like Damo, was robbing drug dealers. We wake one morning in the disabled toilet skint and desperate and he says to me:

"Fuck Andy, what we gonna do to score today"?

"We're alright for the minute; got a few beers ain't we"?

"Yeah, it's alright for you though, you've got a methadone script, I gotta score else I'm fucked".

"If you'd just come with me to get an appointment you'd be able to get a script too", I say for the umpteenth time.

"What, and get put on a waiting list for six weeks? Fuck that, I need a bit of gear (heroin) now".

"We'll sort something", I say, huddling down further into the sleeping bag and cracking open a lovely warm Skol Super 9% lager. But we struggled to get the money to score this particular day though I was ok with the methadone provided lovingly by the state and the beers we continuously steal as standard from any shop we pass. Anyway, it's later now, about eight bells on a cold evening in this lovely city:

"What we gonna do man"? says Frank.

"Fuck knows Frank; come to the Forward Trust with me in the morning so we can sort a script (methadone) out for you".

"Stop talking shit man, I need something now". And he sits moodily looking at the wall in the big open disabled toilet. Suddenly he pulls the phone from his pocket and exclaims:

"Fuck it".

"What ya doin' weirdo"? I say, thinking how much I am coming to love this sad and deeply disturbed boy. And no, pervert, I don't do boy love though I guess were I that way inclined Frank's handsome features were certainly not disagreeable. Anyway, knowing we have no money and that the phone is a batphone for drugs I look quizzically over to Frank.

"Sent a text to 'Reds'", he says, meaning he had texted the drug dealer we had been using.

"Why, we're fuckin' skint", I remind him.

"I know, I'm gonna rob him", says Frank.

"How much"? I say.

"Seven and seven", he says, meaning seven bags of smack and seven rocks of crack.

"Sweet, fuck it", I say.

"Come on then", says Frank, and we walk from the top where the taxis line up by the side of Superdrug to Canterbury East train station, by the homeless centre where we get fed along with the other down and outs every day. From there we walk through leafy lawns right next to the ancient city walls; I think the park we go through is Dame John's Gardens. We find the little bridge next to a tinkling stream. We'd been there no more than ten minutes when a kid comes up to us, Red's 'youngen' as the kids say today, the runner.

"Frank yeah"? asks the drug dealing kid of no more than eighteen.

"Yeah man Frank", says Frank, quickly pulling a carving knife, "gis the fuckin drugs cunt", he says in lazy and laconic but none the less menacing tones of clear unequivocal instruction. The geezer, the kid, looks to me and I see that he sees pity in my countenance but with my penchant for crack and smack I'm afraid today that he is looking in the wrong place though I'd not see Frank stab the boy.

"Don't look at me fella I'm just along for the ride; better hand it over though dude the cunt's a psycho"! And here I put out my hand, by his mouth where I know the drugs are.

"He yar", says the yute, "have the shit", and he spits the fourteen items into my hand and as soon as he does so I say:

"Fuck off then", and he turns on his heel and is gone in a second, probably relieved we didn't search him, strip him. Soon as he is gone me and Frank are jumping up and down like school children.

"Fuckin' yes Frank"! I say.

"Fuckin' sweet; is it all there"? I pass him the small haul of drugs and we count the seven and seven.

"Come on", he says, "let's go home", and we hop, skip and jump all the way back to the disabled toilet we've now next to completely commandeered. Once there we enjoy a snowball or three and bed down for the night. But this tale is not the end of my shananigans with this young fella; there's more to this yet. As I get up to turn out the light in this cell I think to myself that the English language is so meet for the utterings of the mutterings of a modern man's mind. And the writing as I type from the written document here in Oxford is skewed, so I know I was stoned in the telling of that tale. But it is truth nonetheless.

30th December 2018 0730hrs and J.T is sleeping whilst Dave and Fredo talk of cutting their way through the west end, their banger emanating softly through the speakers of the TV so as not to awaken the six foot dreaming psycho. This morning I feel to share with you some probably useless but nonetheless interesting information. When I first used the internet we used a thing called a 'modem' to get data from one computer to another. Now 'modem' is born of the bigger words modulate and demodulate which is essentially what a modem used to do. Now I've no recourse to tech to check my facts and I'm gonna keep to the written script from here in this house in Oxford; some of what I say may be erroneous. So, your computer needs to get a message to my computer so it sends the data to be transmitted to the modem which turned the digitised information into old school analogue sine waves before throwing the packets of data onto the then copper core infrastructure and the modem at the other end on my PC receives the data and turns it back into the digital that the computer can read. And you could not be using your telephone at the same time someone was using the modem. I think, if I remember correctly, that the modems of old received and transmitted at 9600 bits per second which is incredibly slow by todays standards.

Anyway the door is yet to open so let me talk more shit for you! Right, let's say in the old days you brought a PC and the processing speed was 3.6 gigahertz. Now 3.6 is fuckin' fast but anymore and the system would need ridiculous and expensive cooling capacity. Now that means, 3.6 gig, that your machine can process 3.6 billion machine instructions per second. Fuckin' impressive! This is a phenomenal feat of engineering but at this speed you would not be able to multitask, say, talk to ya mate on Skype at the same time as downloading a film and having a game running in the background. The system would freeze or crash. So, knowing the speed of processor power was an issue some bright spark came up with the idea of putting multiple processing cores onto a single piece of silicon and these are what we have in our systems and phones and such today: if you have a PC today with four cores working at 3.6 gigahertz that system processes 3.6 billion machine instructions per second times four! And that is why systems today are so powerful. That, along with the advent of major rollout fibre optic cabling allows for fucking unbelievably quick access to digital information. I find this stuff truly fascinating.

1/1/2019 1000hrs. So, it is New Years Day and I am in a packed Brad's cell. Yesterday he finished a massive Wasgij jigsaw puzzle only to almost immediately disassemble the cunt! I'm sitting at the top of Brad's bed by his pillow. He is before me on his chair by his writing desk. Next to me on my right is matchstick model maker master craftsman cabinet maker Trevor the glass half empty misery. As I have said, what this cunt can't do with a bit of wood and glue ain't worth doing. And that was his job on the out; cabinet making until the drugs took his ability to work away. Next to him is Grin. On the floor in the middle of the cell is that insufferable hyperactive psycho cellmate of mine, J.T. Jake has just walked into the cell and looks heavily hungover, looking at me now as I write with bleary and hooded eyes. Being young Jake still oozes anger at the hand he's been dealt as of yet unable to see that he could turn tragedy into a turning point in his life. He needs to truly imbibe and believe in the truth of what happened in that car: it was an accident. Once he lets go of the crippling guilt he'll be able to grow.

"What's this Sloaney look", says J.T, "my mate found these pills wrapped up in a bit of tissue paper", and I peruse the pills proffered to me, five tablets I look over with my unfortunately expert eye.

"That's a DF118" I say, pointing to a dihydrocodeine tablet, "that's a sericol, that's a Zomorph morphine sulphate tablet, that's a codeine phosphate and this last one is a Xanax".

"How the fuck do you know all that"? he says.

139

"If it's a benzo, barbiturate, opioid, opiate, antipsychotic or tranq of any kind I'm invariably likely to have fucked about with 'em though I much prefer the injectable examples". Jake is in the cell toilet talking quietly with Brad, doing some sort of deal no doubt, speaking in hushed tones. I look around at Bradley's cell walls which are covered in Banksy type shadow pictures of Snoop, Che, Tupac and Bob Marley amongst myriad others. On the designated picture board Brad has pinned legal documentation amongst his own drawings of heads, faces, Bauerhaus art and his intricate depictions of flowers and birds and other creatures representative of his deep lifetime love of nature. On the wall above his desk where he does most of his work are photos of spiders, jumping spiders, orb weavers and others the genus of which I've not a Scooby Do. On the ceiling Brad has paper chains fashioned from the wing application sheets which have carbon copies of pink and blue as well as the white which goes to the screw. The other two, one goes to the prisoner and another to the dept to which the app is directed. They now serve as pretty Xmas and New Year decorations. This is the most festive cell on the wing without a doubt. He has even managed to get some baubles from somewhere and I marvel at where the fuck from! They are made of glass and potentially extremely dangerous and I can't help but think that in order to get through there is something rotten in Rochester! Still, the jail is in transition and things are getting better. Security wise I mean. Anyway, Trevor is telling me now of the irony of him trying to sue Norfolk Social Services for suffering he endured but it is proving difficult as he burned the Social Services building down in the 1970s so they don't have his records! But, sitting in this cell I want to return to Frank B----.

2017 sometime I think. I'm with Frank at Canterbury East train station. Opposite here on the other side of the road just to the right if your back is at the station entrance is a lifesaving centre for the homeless run by a beautiful and dedicated staff team. We are waiting for it to open and once it does we are pulling on new clothes kindly donated by the public before sitting down for a sustaining meal, cooked by a caring handful of volunteers. After the meal Frank gets up and fucks off for a fag and suddenly, talking of fags, what looks like one pulls up a chair and sits opposite me, staring disconcertingly in my direction. I look up and cock a quizzical at him.

"What's up mate"? I ask this funny looking mousy haired little fucker of about forty or so.

"You like ya drugs don't ya mate", he says, not a question.

"Why", I say, "why the fuck d'ya come to me and say that"?

"Well, do ya or don't ya"?

"I do as it goes, yes", I say, only slightly exasperated. He sticks a paw out.

"My name's Nick", he says, "and I'm gay", and gay people always seem at pains to tell me their sexuality.

"I'm Andy and I'm"........I start, about to say: "heterosexual" but sensing immediately an opportunity to manipulate I change direction, saying instead, "I'm not sure what I am but a junkie", and he laughs at this, showing rotten teeth.

"Well", he says, "have you ever tried crystal meth"?

"No", I say, "missed that ship".

"Wanna try it"?

"Try anything me mate".

"Come on then", he says.

"Where"?

"My flat; I'm in supported housing so I'm allowed to eat here at the hub".

"Come on then; let me just find me mate Frank and let him know", but Frank is nowhere to be found. Leaving off looking for him I go with this weird, strange but decent enough guy to try this new potion. We walk to the roundabout by Canterbury Police station, up by the cinema complex to a building with a basement flat to the side and down a dark set of steps. The small bedsit like place is clean and functional.

"How d'ya do ya drugs mate"? he asks me.

"Bang 'em up of course", I tell him, as any self respecting junkie would.

"Good", he says, pulling a small plastic zip bag from a pocket, "cause look what I've got", and inside the bag is about a gram of what looks like tiny little shards of glass.

"What the fuck is that"?

"A gram of finest quality crystal meth", he informs me.

"And what's it worth"?

"Hundred and forty pound a gram at present", he says.

"Well, not being funny mate but I bang potent snowballs so I'm not really expecting much from this to be fair", I say.

"This would normally last me a week", and again I raise my brows, this time in surprise.

"Straight"? I say, "I'd stick the lot in me in one go"!

"You'd be in trouble if you did", says this actually quite personable little fella and he goes on that "you'd be in nowhere else but the hospital if ya did do that pal let me tell ya", and I hear the slight hint of a northern accent in his relatively quick speech. He is a 'phet head after all.

"So, how we gonna do this"? I say, intrigued now. I usually don't get excited over new drugs after having literally experienced them all but this has piqued my interest though I'm still sceptical.

"Watch", says this funny little fucker. He picks up a one ml works straight out the packet. He fills a glass with water.

"What about the spoon"? I ask. He doesn't look up but says:

"No spoon", and now he removes the white plastic plunger from the barrel of the hypodermic. Opening the zippy bag he carefully pulls out one, two, three, four of the tiny slivers of crystal from the bag and places them directly into the back of the barrel. I watch intently as he puts the plunger back into the works before drawing up water into it, immersing the tiny shards. At this point he says:

"Right, that's yours, hold it up and watch it as I prepare mine", and I do, marvelling at the way the glass disperses, disappearing into the water.

"Wow", I say, "that's genuinely impressive; can I stick it in me now"?

"Fill ya boots man", and I stick the solution through a slow vein in my right leg. He does his.

"Feel it yet"?

"Nahhh, not really mate", I say, nonchalantly, not expecting much, "like I say bro, I'm a seasoned"........but suddenly a liquid rushing pulsating warmth envelopes my whole being from head to foot and my synapses light up like a Christmas tree.

"What the fuck"! I say, gripping the kitchen side now, "wow", and I am a little frightened. He sees my fear as waves of wizardry pulsate and permeate my whole person.

"It's cool man you're alright man trust me", and his tones reassure me enough to let me enjoy this new phenomenon yet to become readily available on the streets of Britain, thus the high price. I have just smoked spice in this cell now and I read the skewed language on the page and wonder whether to type it as it is written. I will, madness though it is. So, to continue from the words 'high price'. And I don't mean phenomena in a good way for though there are undoubtably military applications for large fields of war this chemical could write me off in six months for it kept me awake for a week despite me only having three injections within three hours of each other. It is moreish but lack of sleep can be dangerous in the extreme. It breeds a violent demeanour in me only suited for secret psychotic soldiering. The heightened and hyperactive senses would be good in war zones. I get all excited when I think of creeping up on cunts in the jungle and slicing open throats with my motherfuckin' Rambo knife. My rib is still hurting where Terry caught me and he has a handsome scar on his nose. Aidy Edwards left a mark for life on my forehead and on his back are my teethmarks indelibly showing my undying love for him. Fighting is exhilarating and some men, like me, especially in my youth, need to fight. We are a war like species after all. This despite the fact that in a truly advanced society the edge of war, like an ill sheathed knife, no more shall cut its master; mankind.

Anyway, we are banged up in our cell now, J.T and I. The news is on the TV and an 'Allah Akbar' cunt has stabbed two fifty year olds and a policeman outside the Manchester arena where 22 died in the Islamic attack on the Ariana Grande concert some time ago. A Nasa spacecraft is getting pictures of a far off thirty kilometre wide deep frozen object that whips round the sun on a fuck knows how long orbital trajectory. Anyway, back to Frank.

So, say, like, after thirty six hours this fella realizes he ain't gonna get in me bum and kicks me out although in order to get more injections from him I'd initially told him I was bi curious and I might have, no I did, have a wank over babestation on the sofa in front of the telly in the tiny space; do remember the essence of amphetamine products is perversion. This gave the poor gullible fucker the promise of a penis that was never gonna happen. So, as I say, he kicks me out in a sulk and I re-enter the homeless habitat but can't find Frank. I see a homeless dude named 'Soldier Simon' on the streets, genuine papered ex military and lovely guy and ask him as to Franks' whereabouts. He tells me that he had fucked off with some bird. Now the crystal meth had me awake for a week after, literally not a wink the stuff was so strong so I stalk the streets day and night, treading the ancient stones to death in more and more delirium as the minutes hours and days ticked by. So, after six or seven days I finally find Frank and by now I am truly psychotic, wired to fuck.
"What you bin up to"? I ask.
"Fuck all but you're look fuckin' mental bro, what you bin doing"?
"Out me nut on crystal meth some queer geezer gave me who I met at the homeless hub. I literally haven't slept for a week Frank man, not a wink since the last time I see you bro". I can see that Frank is aware I am struggling with my sanity; the boy is perceptive and I can feel I must look absolutely shot to bits and I desperately need sleep that just won't come right now.
"You look like you need a big fuck off hit of heroin bro", says Frank, as I say, very perceptive for that is exactly what I need.

"Mmmm", I say dreamily, "got any money"?

"Nope", says Frank.

"Me either", say I sadly.

"I'm gonna text Reds again", says this nut job.

"Don't be fuckin' stupid Frank we robbed his runner last week". But Frank has pulled the phone from his pocket and his fingers have danced across the keypad, texting.

"I've done it", he says and not a minute later a confirming text is received, "no fuckin' way man, he's gonna meet us with ten and ten"!

"You take the piss, even ordering more than we took last time ya silly cunt. Fuck it Frank, I'm not coming bro".

"I'll do it on me own then".

"Really? For fuck sake! Really Frank"?

"I'm doing it bro whether you come or not man".

"Oh my fuckin' days, I don't fuckin' like it Frank man, this is dangerous".

"Comin' or what? You're not scared are ya"? and the young fuck is smiling, taunting me playfully.

"Scared of nothing me mate"!

"Let's go then", he says, and we go to a little bridge over a small river, not the same one but similarly sheltered where we wait not really expecting anyone to come. We wait underneath.

"No fuckin' way anyone's coming bro", I say.

"Who's that then"? says Frank from beneath his hoodie looking at a fella not 300 yards away.

"No fuckin way", I say, "it's only the same little young runner", and I feel a shot of adrenalin and excitement wash through me. Immediately he is beneath the bridge Frank presses him up against the ancient wall letting the poor cunt see his face and the runner's eyes grow wide with recognition, the silly fucker. Frank says nothing but I say, looking into his caught in the headlights eyes:

"Drugs or you're going in the drink battered and bruised; you're choice bro", and as before he shows me the shots and spits 'em into my hand whereupon I tell him to "fuck off", with an accompanying jerk of the head. Once he is out of earshot I look to Frank and say, barely able to contain myself:

"Yes yes fuckin' yes no fuckin' way! Where the fuck we going Frank"?

"Disabled toilets man", and we run like fans invading the pitch when their team have won a major trophy, exultant and jubilant in our excitement. We arrive 'home'.

"Got works and that Frank"?

144

"Yep, got a load of new kit today", says he, "I fuckin' love robbing drug dealers man".

"I've noticed ya cunt".

"It's the only thing that makes me happy man. I get a right buzz out of it".

"Me too, especially when we rob the same one twice"! I hand Frank the cap of an Evian bottle and get him to put some water in it for he is closest to the tap. I take it, placing it next to the spoon I've placed on the floor for my hit. "Citric", I say after putting two bags of heroin into the spoon. Frank hands me the small square packet of acid and I sprinkle it atop the heroin, "and while I cook this up will you open two of those rocks Frank"? I say, pointing to the crack cocaine.

"Yep, got it", he says, picking sellophane from the items.

"Fuck it, gis two more points of dark and open two more of those stones too bro", I say.

"Cool man", says Frank, eyes all afire, "let's have a proper hit"! Now, this decision is key. I cook the smack, crush the crack and pass Frank his hit telling him:

"Right Frank, you do yours first and once I know you're alright I'll do mine".

"Why you waiting"?

"'Cause I don't trust you not to go over ya cunt".

"Alright Andy, don't get angry".

"Just get on with it with ya big fat young veins ya cunt". He puts the needle into the purple without preamble and immediately upon pulling the pin out bursts into a crack induced sweat.

"You alright ya cunt? Look at me, eyes Frank give me your eyes man". He looks up at me, perspiring profusely and says:

"Fuck me that's lush man", and starts, slowly, sliding down the wall his back is against for he'd had the hit standing up. The heroin is clearly starting to kick in behind the crack cocaine.

"Look at me Frank, look at me you prick", and I use the expletive to get his attention.

"whaaaa man fuck off".

"You cool mate"?

"Yeah, fuck off will ya"?

"You ain't gonna go over on me"?

"Sweet man, do yours I'm cool", he whisper stroke mumbles to me. I sit on the toilet seat in the tiny space and take five minutes stabbing around till I find a fat vein at the joint of knee to thigh. I push in the probe and after seeing blood blossom into the barrel I press the head of the plunger down hard sending the extreme chemicals into my blood stream at velocity. I feel the rush of the crack envelop me and my ears ring as my body sings to the chemical cacophony overwhelming me. I look up from my knee to Frank to say something like 'fuck me' but the cunt is staring directly at me, eyes wide but with no light on. At all. Nothing. No dancing mischievous spirit and there is a purple hue round them and his mouth. Wider than I ever saw those eyes before and the jaw is slack. The cunt is gone, gone, nowhere to be seen. Dead. I jump up and punch him, connecting with the cold flesh of his face whilst screaming:

"Fraaaaaaannnnkkkkk, Frank, Frank, Frank you cunt" and I am slapping him with all my might, slap slap slap. I am in terror panic now and realizing he's in real trouble I open the door to the night and scream out to the ether:

"Help help fuckin' help there's a geezer dying here", and dragging him out the toilet I learn in an instant why the term 'dead weight' was coined. He feels thirty stone the skinny cunt. I drag him outside where I again assault him smashing him hard in the face over and over again. I pull him up by his hoodie and slap him so hard back down he cracks his head on the cold hard concrete. My own panic causes me to projectile vomit and I'm a fuckin' mess not having slept for a whole fuckin' week. Thankfully one of the taxi drivers has called for an ambulance and the dedicated fuckers, after some protracted frightening minutes had the soppy fucker breathing to my infinite relief. Now, think, no sleep for a week, I've just robbed a drug dealer, had a mental fat potent hit of crack and smack then saw me mate, a kid, literally dead in front of me. I wasn't very well to say the least. Whenever there's an overdose paramedics here in Britain are obliged to call the filth, the police. So an old bill saunters up to me and says:

"Look fella, the paramedics are very worried about your mate but they reckon that you are more of a concern at the moment".

"What d'ya mean"? I say, looking, I suspect, quite the psycho.

"You're clearly fucked", one of the other boys in blue says, "and let me be straight with you; you either go with them or come with us".

"Well then I'll go with them", preferring a hospital bed to a police cell. Fuck the latter! Both me and a prostrate and still heavily intoxicated but breathing Frank are taken to hospital. Please remember I am in extreme psychosis. Fucked. However, these details are correct for I returned to the hospital to thank the staff after and ascertain this shit actually happened. We were put onto a small ward of seven with the doctor in charge, a lovely Asian fella, introducing himself as 'Doctor Bob'! Doctor Bob and his camp six foot tall clearly gay medical assistant who I took the piss out of and who took it in good heart looked after us wonderfully. These two were the bollox.

"Come and get some of this", I would say to the six foot camp guy waving my manhood at him, swinging it like helicopter rotors from the bed in my white gown. But he just smiled. Anyway, Dr Bob clocks I'm fucked and I tell him what I've been up to so the switched on fuck gives me one, just one blue ten ml Valium and I'm out like a light to the blessed slumber my body and mind so desperately needed. His fuckin' name is really Dr Bob! And he and his team including the camp guy were so lovely to us junkies usually scorned in hospitals. Anyway, I wake up four hours later, shake Frank awake and we fuck off, return to the toilet and slam more gear. Frank emotionally tells me he's never had a friend like me. I've come to love him. I persuade him to come to Margate where he stays with me and Charlotte who also fell in love with him. He stayed for three days then left. I was happy being waited on by the lovely wily wench who always puts me up. On seeing him off we arranged to come and see Frank in Canterbury.

"But where will I find you"?

"Just phone me", he said. Me and Charlotte did, six or seven days after and got no response so we took a train and asked a homeless fella me and Frank both know where Frank might be.

"He died two days ago Sloaney; overdose bro", and as he said the words Charlotte's hand went to her mouth and I slumped against a wall, broken, both of us, for there was love and sadness and pain in that boy. He was beautiful. Typing this now has been hard for I truly loved him. I'm so sorry Frank.

Now let me tell you dear reader of the mysterious fact of me meeting up with Frank's dad, Dominic, after having not seen him for some twelve years or so, the last time being in Elmley prison in Kent. Now the reason it is a bit odd is because Dom, like me, is a Kent boy. So, Frank had been dead no more than six months and I am now myself homeless, once again on the streets of Oxford. Despite this I am managing to hold down a job at Mini in Cowley near Blackbird Leys estate. I was only briefly there with an agency , actually working from a pickface located directly above the factory floor where the cars are built, the line constantly running , fed with components from cunts like me driving little train car electric things with the parts needed for assembly. I used to be absolutely out me fuckin' nut and was a real danger in this busy work place, gouching out on heroin driving heavy machinery. So, Frank died, we later found out, of a heroin and fentanyl overdose in Canterbury somewhere, on the street the poor cunt. People were severely battered, some stabbed even so angry were some and so popular was he. Anyone who had used with him was in danger so I heard yet the truth is Frank needed no help in using heroin; he was flat out already by the time I met him. Anyway, like I say, not long after the event, some 6 months later I've got my wages from the car plant so decide to go to the City Arms pub where I proceed to get plastered on all manner of beers and spirits. Leaving the boozer I decide I want to score and walk toward the SS Church of Mary and John just down the road and there are myriad people, I notice, homeless druggy types I suspect, sitting round the monument that sits in the middle of that graveyard. So I enter the hallowed consecrated grounds and see about four women and six men. One girl, a pretty blonde, is hanging underwear, just washed I guess, from a tree. Why I do not know, but there you have it. She has a flimsy cotton white dress on and I look at her longingly for she is indeed lovely and it's been a while!

"What ya doing"? I ask her.

"What the fuck's it to you"? She is one of those hard faced but pretty predatory prostitutes I so love to fuck when I can convince them to sleep with me for free! Many of my girlfriends have been working girls, for obvious reasons, same 'interests' as it were.

"Nothing, I just wondered what you were doing hanging underwear from a tree is all".

"D'ya wanna fuck me or something"? and instantly I feel my loins burst into life as my old boy presses tight against my pants.

"Well, I certainly wouldn't mind", I say as she sexily tiptoes to hang more underwear from the makeshift dryer, the tree, causing her lovely buttocks to undulate beneath the thin cotton making me strain ever harder in my pants.

"I've just had two through me", she says, "but I'll go into the toilet in the pub and scrub me pussy out for ya if you pay me the money up front. It's £30 normal but if you wanna do me in the arse it'll cost ya a bullseye". I literally laugh out loud on hearing this, hard on forgotten in my mirth.

"I'd rather disembowel myself than pay for pussy but", I say, "I could really do with one and one and one and one for you if you can score for me".

"No probs man", she says, flicking her blonde hair and she puts something else on the tree and I keep watching the way the cotton rides up, revealing the bottom of naked creamy buttocks. She catches me staring. I feel sheepish under her gaze but she smiles and really is pretty though I can see the drug damage just starting to rear its ugly head in her.

"What ya looking at"?

"Your beautiful bum", I say.

"You're quite good looking you", she smiles, pirouetting, allowing me another flash of bare creamy flesh, "d'ya wanna kiss it"?

"What, really"?

"If ya want to", and now she turns around, pokes her bum up seductively not but twenty feet from the other homeless and pulls the cotton up to her back, allowing for a full view of her sex. I go over, drop to my knees, quite pissed remember and kneed and tug at her taught flesh, planting sloppy kisses here and there despite being able to smell spent sex which only turns this sick puppy on more, before she laughs, makes herself relatively decent and says:

"That's enough now", and she skips away from me, her prettily turned calves shining in the light of a lamp here in this churchyard.

"Please man let me fuck you", but she only laughs before taking me over to a fat fella flat out asleep on the ground. She nudges him, well kicks him.

"Dom", she says, "Dom, there's some geezer here wants some work ya lazy cunt, wake up", and she kicks him again, turning to me and saying, "don't worry, he's me boyfriend". He grunts and groans and turns over, slowly opening hooded eyes. As soon as I see this six foot machine of a man's face I burst into smile.

"Dominic B"!

"Andy Sloane"!

"What the fuck"...........say I.

"You doin' in Oxford"? he finishes.

"'Bout to ask you the same thing, ain't seen you since about 2006 or something".

"Years", he says.

"Wow man look, I'm so sorry about Frank", I say.

"What you on about Sloaney"?

"Frank", I say.

"What about Frank Sloaney, what you on about"? he asks, clearly clueless. Oh no. Oh no please God I think to myself.

"He's dead Dom", and now his eyes go wide and he climbs to his feet, poor cunt.

"How Sloaney and when"?

"About six months ago Dom, overdose bro, I'm so sorry mate".

"Who with"?

"That I don't know Dom but I do know he was found next to someone else who they managed to bring back round. Shit man look I'm so sorry bro but I had to say something; I just thought you'd've known", and I can see the fella is in shock.

"No", says my old friend, "it ain't your fault Sloaney", and Dom was so shocked, so hurt that he didn't even want the drugs I offered to buy him, instead arranging immediately for transport to take him to his mum's Franks' nan's, in Ramsgate. Needless to say I needed to escape the way I was feeling for this had had a very sobering effect upon me. I didn't want to be conscious as I lay in my tent in Christ Church Meadow that night and insured that I was barely breathing by the time I had crossed through the open plain and found my thin polyester place of solitude in the small copse that covered me.

Dear reader once more there is spiced up shit I just don't want to type from the written document because it is waffle I thought profound at the time. The gist is I smoked too much and thought I was gonna die, tripping. Officers give me more paper, Gilchrest and Terry, wonderful wenches.

11am. They ain't opened the door like they normally do though it's eleven o'clock. This is because the staff team are spinning, searching for the shit for as I have said, something is rotten in Rochester, spice everywhere causing real misery, mental breakdowns and pain. So they spin on a surprise basis. Mental Bill, little Bill I spoke of earlier and who lives in one of the cells just across the landing from me and J.T has taken umbrage at having been targeted for a search and is now on the floor with six staff atop him, the panic alarm ringing to bring more staff from other wings and he is going nowhere but the segregation unit. I shout out the door:
"Bill, stop resisting bro else they're gonna hurt you more", but he is trying to punch and bite and spit and gouge leaving staff no option but to strap him up with cable ties. Literally dear reader, cable ties. He has less than a week to serve but as I have said, as I myself know, the closer one gets to release the more one can act out as fear of the future and loss of the security prison offers sets fear ablaze in the heart. Uncertainty, see, is a fucker for the mindset. Anyway, one of my friends here, a stocky dark haired five ten block headed guy, Peter W has given me his prison diary from when he was recently in HMP ISIS in Thameside in London. I promised him I would write it up in this narrative verbatim so here goes, the next chapter is written in Pete's own words. Pete:

Day 1. First day in HMP ISIS not much going on. Gotta couple boys on the wing, Chang and Bobby Hope. It will be a week or two before I find my feet. This was a bad move but jail is jail. And I just see my old cellmate Dave King AKA Dave Perrett. He didn't recognize me with

150

wild hair and mad big beard. Tell ya one thing I must make a fresh start here, stop bashing TVs off screw's heads. It ain't done me no good.

0753 Day 2. Just woken up and I am waiting to see what kind of regime they run here on a weekend. So far this is the strangest prison I have ever been to all applications including canteen orders are done on a touchscreen computer. No paperwork. Put a code in and a thumbprint. Shit association today bang up till 1530. As now 1430 and Spurs just won three nil and that's us to the semi finals of the FA Cup. When we win it makes me think of my old dad. I just wish he was here to see it for himself. He'd be well chuffed. Day nearly done now, long day with not much happening. Met another geezer who is the pal of another geezer I know called Dizzy. This prison is mad since they stopped the smoking. I seen people smoking green tea bags and spice paper. It is a shocking sight. The government are just creating a different problem for themselves in the future. I hate to think of the effects on prisoners' health. It's gonna cost the NHS millions in the future. But I suppose us being criminals it is OK.

Day 4. Never wrote a word yesterday today is Monday been unlocked since half eight. It's now eleven been a long day so far can't wait till lunchtime bang up. Coming out of the block to here is a big change. And it will take a little time to get used to. But I'll get there after no time. Puffing on this vape is too much, it's not hitting the spot. Funniest thing is both my next door neighbours have had spice attacks this morning, one of them swimming up the landing and the other is in a puddle of sick screaming the monkey. I can't wait, I'm gonna write this all down then bring the house down with a book. They don't know what they have done, people are dropping like flies. All due to no burn. 17 months down, 13 to go and man do I have some stories to tell from the two jails I've already been in. Elmley is full of bent screws, Coldingly is flooded with drugs by mail now here at ISIS it's a security jail but it's flooded here too. I'm not so sure how it works here yet so give me time. 'Bird N Spice' will be a great read. Prison is too hard.

Day 5. Couldn't believe it this morning. Went into my next door and had a chat with Bobby about their spice attack yesterday. Then all of a sudden three screws came in and searched us and found nothing but they took a pipe from Bobby and 'cause he ain't owned up to it I've been put on basic regime, no TV or association, what a fuckin joke. I'm gonna punch up Bobby and his cellmate first chance I get. He should own up to it the two bob piece of shit. He will regret it for sure.

Day 6. Took me off basic before we banged up I caused em some hard work just by covering me flap up. They couldn't see me in the cell every hour they checked. So they have to get a firm of them to come open my door just to check I'm still in there cause I was ignoring them too. Wilmott 1 HMP ISIS 0. I tell any jail I go to you'll wish your prison never heard of me. So they better ship me to Rochester or Elmley to avoid any more upset. This little book that I'm writing in will bring the house down. We have had three more code blues this morning with spice attacks, boys are like the walking dead here.

Day 7. Up at 0730 unlock at 8. I done a cup of tea then I see the number 1 Governor and had a chat with her about me being fucked over and sent here. I explained to her that I can't get a visit here as my mum is old and unable to travel. She seems like a nice woman. I think I might be able to get somewhere with her, cut out all the bullshit. Then she had to run off because there was another code blue for a spice attack. And another assault. This wing has a bit of an atmosphere. No burn lighters or rizla but the boys still overcome it. Green tea, the Bible for rizla, spice, then pop the top off of a vape capsule and bam you have a lighter.

Day 8. The wing stinks badly of tea bags and they're fuckin scumbags for doing this to us. But fuck it what can you do I have been on the vape two months and the need to smoke has passed. All I'm doing is three capsules a week by the time I go home I won't even be doing the vape. March is nearly over now the time is moving along nicely the weeks seem to fly past here. We get our canteen today I 'm kind of looking forward to it. I can have a nice cup of coffee they don't give out any tea bags here. I have just been informed I can get the PTS (Personal Track Safety) ticket here and also the CSCS card I'll be winning! Bang up now and I've got a cup of coffee and The Chase is on TV I must admit that I am pretty damn good at it. If I never had a criminal record I would apply for it.

Day 9. It's eight o'clock waiting for the door to open so I can get meself a cup of tea. Not much happening today, association on the wing in the morning then bang up the rest of the day with cold food brought to the door for dinner. Still ain't got a kettle and it's been nine days now any other place you'd of got one straight away but this one is slow. I can hear bells going off out there, someone's been fucked up or had another code blue. They normally are code blues. Prison system is fucked badly these screws really ain't got a Danny what they are causing take away tobacco and caused a hazard to health to screws and inmates and set up another black market with people paying up to £400 for an ounce of burn which normally costs £12.50 but now it's a tenner for a single roll up. This is pushing people further into the shit i.e people getting smashed up over money or dying due to the spice being too strong cause they're smoking it pure. When people are dying on a regular basis they might have a change of heart. Seen the boys smoke a nicotine patch today with spice paper and a tea bag they was proper in a mess.

Day 11. Something big has just gone on in the jail I don't know what yet. There was about 30 screws on the wing and they banged us all up. A screw hit an inmate in the face, makes me laugh if we hit a screw we would get the shit kicked out of us and catch extra charges. Hopefully next week things start moving in here the induction in here lasts six weeks, education and all that bollox. Again told do it and we will log your score so you won't have to do it again but here we are.

Day 10. Do you know what pisses me off? These cunts come and wake you up for meds and I'm not on any fuckin meds, piss take. They come into my cell earlier and told me I have to move out my cell into a double with a Puma trackie (Paki) I told em it ain't gonna happen as I'm a high risk prisoner and can't guarantee another man's safety!

Day 14. Bang the door opened yesterday and they told me that me and the cell are going to be searched. So when they stripped me and told me to squat which I did without question I felt someone touch me balls. I can't believe what just happened I thought I was supposed to be kept safe. Now I feel like a victim. I have put in a comp 1 (complaint form) and told em I want police involvement. And the cunts over here have forced me into a double cell.

Day 15. Been banged up all morning got out for a quick shower for 30 mins then some lunch and bang up. Me and me pad mate's the only ones who ain't had canteen yet. What a fuckin liberty. We have no fuck all and I'm slowly getting the pox with it. I had the SO (Senior Officer) from G wing today to do my behaviour review. I told him straight you cunts take the piss. Spin my cell, touch me in an inappropriate way kick me off the wing with no property then send it over with no DAB radio, no vapes, no duvet cover, no coffee and then say it wasn't in the cell we left. So I have to lose out cause of these cunts. And now they've robbed me of me canteen. So I'm not ok. I told him I want the police involved to report the sexual assault. He went a white colour as if the life drained out of him. I think this may be my way out of here and back home to Elmley or Rochester. And surprise surprise they just came to the door and told me they found my canteen at the gate house after I told em I want the police involved. I'm going all the way with this they ain't getting away with it. I want their jobs if I laid hands on them I'd be in big trouble.

Day 16. Easter weekend is under way and April calls us just over a year and I'm done with this life. I can't believe how long I've wasted in these places. Been up all night with toothache and can't even get a couple of painkillers. I have got the hump and can feel a hunger strike coming on. Maybe I'll start that on Monday or Tuesday. I've decided I'm the wrong colour for this prison. I think that this prison might break me if I'm here for too long. I'd rather go over the road to Belmarsh. The screws keep calling me Peter but to them I am Mr Wilmott and that's what I want to be called or they are going to be ignored. I ain't wrote nothing for two days but this place will be the death of me the double standards in this place are not right I can't do anything but the little niggers can it's a fuckin joke. When I came to jail I told them I can't share a cell. And I don't get on with blacks pakis or any other ethnic group. Then they go and put me in a double cell with a coon. Just as well he ain't too bad cause I would smash him up.

Day 19. Just had a governor come and see me about my complaint. And he tried to scare me off by telling me the police will tell me to fuck off. But I'm still going to do it as a crime is a crime after all. The prison service has a duty of care to keep me safe and they haven't kept me safe. I've got screws trying to threaten me. If they just ship me back to Kent then we both win. If not the shit will hit the fan in a big way. 17 months is a long time to go without a visit from my family.

Day 20. The days are flying now. I've applied for a job working on the bins to get out the cell and off this wing cause the little niggers are doing my head in. And I'm still waiting for the police to report what happened.

9th April. Spoke to my outside Probation Officer today about being touched up by a staff member. She's going to find out what I can do about it. She didn't seem too happy about it. I have to call her back Friday afternoon. Hopefully they get me out of here ASAP.

10th April. I had a screw that I don't know come to the cell and threaten me. About my complaint. He said if I continue down this road it will only be me that is affected. Cos this is their jail and I don't have no back up. I told him to go away and bring it on. I'm gonna see what happens in the coming days and weeks. But I'm going to make myself a shiv (stabber) just in case I have to open someone up cause I won't be bullied into changing my mind.

11th April. Two little niggers had a bitch fight on the landing earlier the pair a cunts really ain't got a clue. Doing it right in front of a screw.

Still Peter W: Now this is Elmley 2017 on Houseblock 2 and with my pal Danny who I can't mention his full name. And Jack Stoker. One night at dinner time Danny got arguing with a couple of egg and spoons (coons) over a spice debt that my mate Wes owed. We was both on remand, me for robbery and Danny for attempted murder Danny being big in the game, a serious geezer. Anyway it's been arranged for a straightener out in the yard. Straight away I've got me mates back. You know how it is loyalty stands before anything. Even Jack said he was

154

coming, yeah right. So the morning came and off we went. As soon as we got on the yard I went off, Danny is like Rhino off Gladiators a bulldozer of a geezer. So I set pace on a black man called Arms and split his head with a wig splitter (lump of iron) and all hell broke loose but what we didn't realize is that they was all muslims and there was about 40 of the cunts it was a mass brawl. 2 of us against 40. We were well outnumbered before we knew it we were surrounded by more people than I can count. This went on for about 20 minutes I got knocked down four times but got up cause I'll stay down for no man. In the death the screws come and separate us all. Danny had a couple teeth missing but me on the other hand I had lumps and bumps all over me I'd been stabbed in the ear and had a Nike Air Force One shoe print on my forehead. I was placed in my cell and had about ten mad muslims at my door fuck them is what I told them. I fear no man accept my late father. I haven't seen Danny since, I was told he got a not guilty for the shooting. I been left with the agro it's 2 and a half years now non stop. Death to all muslims. (That's a bit strong Pete!).

Dear reader, whether you like it or not this is my friend's reality. This is real life shit. His world. Sorry snowflakes. That was the end of Pete's diary.

04/01/2019 0740hrs. J.T is still asleep and is talking as he snoozes, asking the ether if "you've cooked the burgers yet and did I put the salmon out". Guess the buscopan and the spice still work as he sleeps. It's actually amazing; before he gets out his head me and him can have really lively debates about many subjects, like the contentious immigration issues we are experiencing in the country at present with migrants from Iran in particular being launched from Calais in dinghies and coming to the Kent coast.
"Fuckin' pakis", J.T had said the other day, continuing, "look at 'em all on the beach there shivering", and on the BBC news there were indeed three miserable looking migrants sitting getting the once over from Border Force officials and J.T is still going, "I don't know why we don't just put 'em back on the boat or better still blow the dirty cunts out the water".
"J.T", I say, and, dear reader, I'm a little upset to hear J.T talk like this, "J.T man that's a bit deep bro; I mean, I know we have to protect our borders but they must be desperate to do that journey man 'cause it's fuckin' suicidal bro".
"I wish the fuckin' boat had turned over on the dirty cunts", he says.
"Really"? I say, aghast.

"Really mate", J.T had said in his cockney drawl looking disgustedly at the poor wretches on the TV screen as they sit forlornly on our own hallowed blessed silt, "if I had my way", he goes on, "honestly Sloaney I'd take 'em clean out with a bit of target practice given half a chance the dirty smelly Iranian paki cunts".

"Wow, you are hateful; did you vote remain"?

"Did I fuck, what, so we can let 'em all in to take our jobs the smelly cunts"?

"Fuck me J.T, for an intelligent guy and as a mixed race daughter siring father you ain't half a truly ignorant deceived guy at times".

"So you think we should let 'em all just come in then, to take our jobs and women"?

"Women as well"?

"Well they do don't they"?

"You have a mixed race daughter, told me you like mixed race and Indian women yet you spout such vitriol bro, hatred. Where's your compassion"?

"You can't say that just 'cause I like and mix with a lot of mixed race people I can't have opinions on immigration".

"Let me tell you J.T, if we completely stopped immigration the NHS would collapse and have you ever worked on the fields or in industrial greenhouses picking grown products"?

"Grown products"?

"Grown products J.T; don't play stupid bro; tomatoes, potatoes, cabbages and that".

"Oh", he says, "no, why"?

"'Cause all the people that do these jobs that British people don't want to do are foreign bro, invariably from the European Union".

"So what then", says J.T, "you think we should just, like, let 'em all in then do ya, sucking all our benefits and basically just ripping the arse out of us"?

"No man course I don't", I tell him, "but contrary to popular opinion which is wholly media driven the vast majority who come here are willing to work, benefiting Britain and grateful to be safe from savage persecution".

"Ok then", he says, and his tone tells me he ain't quite finished, "if they're so scared, those Iranians for example, why don't they claim asylum in France instead of continuously trying to reach our shores"?

"Well", I say, searching my head for a relevant and truthful answer where I don't really have one, "we'd need a little history lesson here but perhaps it's because they feel France is just a little bit too close to the Iranian regime which is persecuting them".

"But what pisses me off is that it's the rich ones coming over here 'cause they can afford to spend all that money with people traffickers and that".

"Wealth doesn't stop people being kidnapped, raped and murdered though bro. The poor ones left over there invariably suffer awful fates if they don't comply with the monstrous savage regimes they live under. Think about the Christian woman in Pakistan savagely persecuted because of her beliefs".

"I know and I admit that ain't right", and now I can sit back slightly satisfied that I may have put a cat amongst the pigeons of his murky mind.

0915hrs. The methadone withdrawal pains are still very much with me. I saw 'AddemupAde' that wonderful maths teaching Nigerian on the 2nd January for the first time in a while because I have been so sick. I have, I don't know if you remember dear reader, fallen in love with the subject though we can only do up to level two and it is functional maths as opposed to the academic stuff I'd like to be able to give a go here. But, alas, I'm happy I have learned that I can learn. And quicker than most it would seem.

"I thought I had lost you", Ade said upon seeing me, continuing that, "I was just saying to the other teachers that I think I have lost Andrew Sloane".

"Ade", I say with sincerity in my voice, "you'll never lose me after what you have done for me", and dear reader don't doubt the depth of feeling I have for this great guy. All these years I thought I was thick, stupid, dumb but bang, give me a good teacher and it would seem I am more capable than I thought. Because I had tried a few times to come to the class smashed and failed to work out even simple problems I had started to reinforce these misguided beliefs. But, as I was straight the other day we were able to recap a few things and surprise surprise I was fine. Ade got me to do some basics such as working out from three mortgage providers, purely academically of course, how much I could borrow from each company, how much I would need for a deposit and which company would thereafter prove more conducive to my needs. Then Ade gave me a load of data on modes of transport to and from a particular school and told me to visually represent the data with a pie chart using a protractor and a ruler after drawing up a table of my findings. Then a little work with mode median and mean before a little percentage work just to recap. Oh and some area stuff, a little work with decimals and fractions and a few other bits and pieces. I remember watching a Sherlock Holmes thing once where Sherlock worked out how

157

far he had travelled on a train, the speed he was travelling at and therefore how long it would take to reach his destination and I thought 'wow, wish I could do that' and alas, now I can! Nothing for Richard Feynman but magnificently enlightening for me. Ade is completely satisfied that within the parameters and paradigm of prison education I can't learn much more here. And I know that to try and monopolize his time to teach me some more in depth academic stuff would detract from the work he does for others more needy than I. But I tell Ade that:

"If I could I would greedily snatch all your time and suck you of anything numerically related you ever did learn Ade".

"I like teaching you Andrew because you enjoy it", he says, "but look", and he waves his hand over the class of students, foreign nationals, travellers and young reprobates all looking to him to help them. Well, some just want to get out the cell so sign themselves up but Ade wants to help them! These people need his academic expertise and also his wonderfully endearing people skills. Oh, and his patience which, after trying to teach the little I know on the subject I realize I don't really have. I tell Ade this a little worried he might think me an ungrateful so and so not wanting to work in the classroom but he is fine with it bless him. I'd only end up getting frustrated and calling someone thick or something, harming someone by potentially driving them away. No, I don't want to do that. The only teacher I would work for is the red headed sexy head of education here, one of the managers, Claudia who always has prisoners drooling lasciviously over her. Not deliberately like, she just has the dirty, sexy pretty look with the fittest arse you ever saw. But I digress. Forgive me. Ain't fucked for six months or so and even for one appalled by the sexual act and its baseness that is a long time. Appalled! Huh! I even make myself laugh. But dear reader, picture your own face in orgasm! Rather not wouldn't you? Rutting like rabbits, it's very uncivilized me sometimes thinks!

11am and Coldplay and the excellent music of the Chainsmokers completely envelop me, causing, in my withdrawing state with its heightened sensitivity to stimuli, all the tiny hairs on my body to stand on end. I'm loving being alive in this cell as I sweep, wipe walls and surfaces before 'mopping' the floor with a wet soapy towel. I initially started cleaning to keep J.T off my back who says the only things I do when awake are smoke spice and write. I have as of yet smoked no spice and this by choice for there've been offers this morning but I feel high on life alone. Now Jax Jones and Raye sing 'Don't Act Like You Know Me' and I'm positively bouncing as I clean, enjoying the feel of life coming back into me as my body starts the process of eradicating the meth from my very marrow. I feel naturally high on life and have smoked no spice of yet.

1423 hrs Fri 4th Jan 2018. Brad's cell. Canteen day. No black eye's as of yet. I sit as people come in and out whilst I look upon the shadow pictures and my mind wanders as I clock Andy Jackson popping his breakthrough gangster moves which inspired the likes of Justin Trouser Snake Timberlake who after such a gay but glorious start went on to become a legend the good looking smooth talking slick moving cunt, he's pure quality and not a bad actor either. The tosser. There's also Snoop on the wall who's album Doggy Style was a key milestone in gangster funk. Dr Dre is beside him, from the streets of Compton to superstardom. Anyway, as I sit writing here in this cell I'm feeling pretty switched on as I listen to voices around me inside and outside the cell arguing and jostling for payment. Young Reece is arguing with Briggsy and now big Phil The Face, the 16 stone quaver headed lump is shouting at big Scouse from a few cells down from Brad's.

"Fuck it, keep it", Phil is saying, "and don't ever come to me for anything again".

"Phil, honestly, they fucked me over on me canteen mate", the Scouser is saying.

"Yeah fuck off", says Phil, "pulling strokes ya cunt", and now I can hear another Scouse, Steve 'Fiddler' who does a bit of dealing on the wing, saying:

"Well, if ya don't pay me this week ya know I want two packs of vapes next week instead of one today so it's your choice". Now dear reader one pack of vapes, the capsules containing e-liquid is £4. Standard unit of currency in here right now. Brad has just returned to the cell:

"Trev ain't paid me", he says referring to the cabinet maker, "I've still got 22 boxes to collect in and", he goes on, "my man at work wants a minimum of seventeen boxes this week", so Brad has his work cut out. Now Grindley is getting stick from someone and my senses go hyper 'cause I can't have anyone fuck with Grin though the cunt's been known to be dangerous enough himself. I can hear him telling Fiddler, who's a big lump, that he will:

"Honestly have 'em for ya Fiddler just hold ya 'orses". He comes in the cell now.

"Alright Bradders"? he still finds it in him to ask, "and you Sloaney you ignorant cunt"? and he says this because I seem to ignore people when actively writing. The problem here is that I can receive and record information as events play out around me but trying to listen and write

159

and speak all at the same time is testing, even for me, the most articulate man you will ever meet. Trying to do so all at once causes some sort of overheating in my frontal lobe. I can hear Fats now, that little legend so popular on the wing saying to someone in near vicinity of this cell "don't take me for a mug ya know", and I hope the recipient of his reprimand takes note 'cause the money man Fats can always pay nutters to come serve up on your arse without the need to get his hands dirty. He's plenty of pals would do it for fuck all. Now I can hear little blonde cute faced dangerous been to Parkhurst back in the day Gibbo's voice saying "cunt I want my vapes". Now Little Manchester fast talking hyperactive Ritalin Reece comes in the cell and out the blue says to me:

"Don't give these pisstaking cunts fuck all Sloaney fuck 'em all none of 'em 'ave paid me", but before I can inquire as to what he refers he is back out on the landing the little psycho. Not such a bad one him, always makes sure he pays Bradders. Craig D, angry little bulldog from next door to me and J.T comes in the cell and sits down.

"Hey ya Brad", he says, paying Brad the vapes he owes him. When I first got here Craig had bundles of spice around him and was making real money but his love of the spice put paid to that. I like Craig, warlike little fucker that he is.

"Cheers Craig", says he before he too leaves to go hustle, "I need to go and see Terry", he says in parting, referring to my pugilistic pal, the lovely lump who bust my rib. Brad gets up as well saying:

"I need to go see Terry too", but returns seconds later saying, "we couldn't find him and his door is banged shut", before bending over to put stacks of packs of vapes into the locker beneath his bed.

"You gonna stay about to watch the fort Andy while I do some running about"? he says to me.

"Course man", then Brad walks out the cell shouting:

"Reece, Reece", and the one he is calling is another Reece, also hyperactive, dark haired and bespectacled who's so alike the other I may well have confused them in the narrative. Both are small, young and fuckin' mental and Brad continues to him "you got my vapes or what"? And glasses Reece rapidly replies that:

"As soon as Phil The Face gets his vapes in I'll have 'em for ya Brad". This means he's gonna borrow off Phil once Phil has got his hoard in.

"Alright but don't let me down though", says Brad and his footsteps recede, unmistakeable for his step is heavy due to the bunions on his feet that I too suffer with. He's back two minutes later with Grin and whilst we sit chatting shit a fat fella I've not seen before comes to the door.

"D'ya want them things Brad for a pack of vapes I'll give you 'em for a whole week"?

"If I get the vapes I'm owed in then I will", says Brad.

"Alright mate", says the fat fucker and he's gone.

"What's that mate"? Grin asks.

"Wants to sell me a weeks worth of Concerta Xl (speed like tablets for hyperactive nut jobs) tablets", says Brad.

"Ya like them don't ya Brad"? I say.

"I like 'em with a pregab and a cup of coffee in the morning Andy; proper sets me up for the day on top of the old juice", (methadone) says Brad.

"I never really understood pregabs", I say, "but they're alright when ya take like nine or ten 300s then they proper fuck you up", and this is true, I used to drive Charlotte mad when I would be out and about with her and collapsing like a spastic all over the gaff. Shops, in the street, round friends' houses, everywhere. I know no moderation, and therein lay the problem. Grin is talking to Brad now:

"Has Peter paid ya Brad"? Remember Pete is a childhood friend of me and Brad.

"Nope", says Brad, "he ain't even come to see me but I've known him all me life so it's hard when it comes to him".

"And it's true we all take advantage of our friend's kindnesses at times. I mean think about it boys", I say, "if you owe a pal who loves you and also have to pay the big cunt downstairs who likes to bash people and you can only afford to pay one of 'em who ya gonna pay"?

"I know Andy but it don't fuckin' help me", says Brad.

"I think it's a liberty Brad", says Grin. They both leave the cell and I sit here with pad upon me lap and in the quiet I notice that the volume on the wing has reduced somewhat. I guess it is because after an hour and a half people are cooling off after either being paid or being paid bullshit. Either way people have an idea of where they stand so the energetic urgency disperses to be replaced by a plodding tread as some try to round up stragglers.

1530hrs and of course we are still unlocked this Friday afternoon. Now the reason for all this manic activity is, fundamentally, an economy driven by spice which is really hurting people. Before, when I first came to prison many, many moons ago you'd be lucky if there was a bit of solid cannabis on the wing occasionally. You could truly come into jail and proper clean yourself up in a relatively safe, drug free most of the time environment. They have to get a handle on this shit man. Mr Rory Stewart, Prisons Minister, to achieve your goals of reducing profiteering by organised crime, reducing the prevalence and availability of drugs on these landings and lowering the levels of violence that come with all this you'll have to take draconian, drastic and ballsy action. Unprecedented change is needed and though a Remainer at heart, (not sure that is true now) some of the stupid laws of the ECHR preventing the proper policing of prisons and prisoners by the Crown will hopefully be rescinded leaving room to sort this issue. Young people can come into jail without a drug problem and leave with a raging spice Roger Rabbit, a habit they take with them into the community. Anyway, Brad comes back in and we are talking of Tony Giles, Jewelsy as we know him. Tony came, as he always does, and paid Brad the packs of vapes he owed immediately. Remember, Tony is another childhood friend of ours and I myself grew up in kids' homes with the cunt; fuckin' love him despite the fact he is one moody motherfucker.

"Can't fault that cunt Brad", I say, "he's so fuckin' staunch man".

"yeah he is", says Brad, "thing is with him he's just so fuckin' honest (this of a thieving burgling fuck but he IS honest) and true to his word and if he's got ya back he's got ya back".

"But my God Brad he is you have to admit one moody motherfucker at times mate".

"I know", laughs Brad and I can't help but guffaw with him at this and as Brad stands and starts to prepare a coffee he continues, "have you ever tried to talk to the cunt in the mornings Andy"?

"No Brad, I'm too scared of the skinny cunt's moods at the best of times bro, let alone early doors; I steer well clear of him before sort of midday at least", and me and Brad chuckle some more at the image of the miserable fuck. We are both very fond of him. Anyway Grin comes in and him, me and Brad talk of the etymology of the word 'cunt'.

"It's a thousand years old", says Grin.

"One of my favourite words", I say, also continuing that, "the oldest place I found the word was in Chaucer in Canterbury Tales when someone 'promptly grabs her by the cunt', who the lady in question was I can't recall, or the grabber but I gather it could be Donald Trump 'cause he likes to grab 'em by the pussy don't he"? During Trump's presidential campaign the other side found an old recording of him saying that if you were famous women didn't mind if you just straight grabbed 'em by the pussy and this of course outraged the hashtag Me Too movement and the wokies of the world. Naughty naughty Donald you old pervert you! Still won though and though I dislike some of the more outrageous parts of his presidency there's much to admire in what he has done for the economy in America. Populism is marching across the Western world at the moment evidenced in the Brexit vote. What does piss me off is the fact the Remainer side won't just accept defeat, calling for another referendum. We lost motherfuckers, accept it. In one of the biggest democratic exercises ever carried out on our hallowed soil. Get over it. Stop calling for a 'People's Vote', we lost lost lost and to have another vote would damage the democratic process so please kindly just fuck off for it is tiring now. Let's sort this shit out together and be done with the hateful thing. As for Trump, some of the rhetoric he uses is questionable at times and plays right into the likes of the KKK and other extreme right wing groups. He said of the Mexicans he is trying to keep out by building a massive border wall that they are all criminals and rapists which though funny is wholly unbecoming of the leader of the free world. What else is worrying is that before Trump I had never heard journalists say the words World War Three. Trump has severely angered China by imposing trade restrictions and embargos on imported steel from that country. We can only hope he is kept in check by the Senate and the House of Representatives. Checks and balances. I really fear for Trump for some nut job may put a bullet in his skull so controversial is he.

In the cell this evening and we are both smashed. I throw my dignity on the floor daily with this stuff and the posters around the wing on the walls stating 'you can keep many things in your addiction but not your dignity' are hitting me hard, so hard I want to tear them down.

10pm and as you can clearly gather I am still awake despite consuming lots of spice and the reason for this lack of sleep is opiate withdrawel. Jason Gould, the manager at the Attitudes, Thinking and Behaviour unit continues to help me and I am particularly grateful for the fact that despite it being late on a Friday evening a large A4 envelope just came under the door with some work and inspirational quotes and the invite of a coffee down the unit where he has a book for me to look at. I have been avoiding the unit for shame due to the fact I am still smoking spice. Still, I shall take up the offer and see him next week. Jason has been here for thirty years. I am also learning that all the power through the prison emanates from the Programmes Unit. And that because some of the old school staff, veterans of Rochester are situated there. Jason was an officer here for many years before going over to the therapeutic side, liberal lover that he is. Also there as the principal officer is a mean looking like proper dark gangster geezer screw who has clout within the nick, and though mean looking he is a gent. Never has a prison made such an effort to help me. Another officer frequently in the unit is a small grey haired thirty year vet security screw who came over one day when I was banged up with Aidy Edwards to do spins on A wing. A knife was missing from the kitchens and they'd narrowed it down to our wing. Anyway, upon entering mine and Aidy's cell he had during the search found some spice and paraphernalia. He took his boys out the cell briefly, like the less senior screws before coming back in and saying, waving his hand toward the drugs:

"We haven't seen this; comprende"?

"No problem man", I'd said whilst Aidy just stood open mouthed. When they had gone and banged the door Aidy turned to me and said:

"Did that just fuckin' happen Andy"?

"What the fuck was that about"? was all I could reply. And on the subject of old school screws I went to the chapel to watch a band the other day. Upon leaving I passed a big square headed bulk of a screw standing manning the flow of prisoners coming out and he said:

"And where do you think you're going Andrew"?

"How the fuck do you know my first name"? I had said, slightly taken aback and instantly paranoid I was on a security watchlist.

"Oh, I remember you here back in 1993", he says.

"Fuck me, how the fuck can you remember that"?!

"Don't you worry about that Sloaney, you just behave yourself son, you ain't a bad lad you".

"Ahhh man, thanks Guv", I'd said, quite touched to be fair. We'd continued chatting briefly. He told me that:

"We could deal with you lot twenty years ago but this lot", he said, indicating the rowdy, entitled thinking, ungrateful and sometimes damn right hateful youth passing us and still sat on chairs in the chapel, "it's a different ball game today. People used to come in and get off drugs in jail, now they sue us and spit at us and cut themselves if they don't have their drugs. You lot used to just get on with it. It's a fuckin' shame but hey, I'll be retiring soon so happy days". He's right! You can't put a cunt like me in a cell today and bang the door telling me my opiate withdrawels are my problem and to get on with it. You can't discipline these youngsters today, instead the prison panders to their every whim. Look, when I first done bird there were not plug sockets in cells. Now I wouldn't take away peoples' TVs and Playstations but it should not be a right. I learned to read in jail and would perhaps never have picked up a book were there a TV before me to numb my mind. I am grateful for all the system has done for me though it has been painful at times. I'm glad I did numerous, many, many agonising opiate withdrawels because had I been given the cushion of methadone at an early age in jail I'd never have had the courage for consensus around this stuff is fear inspiring. Yes, it is very uncomfortable but it won't kill you. It is a brave new world indeed today. I love the way these dinosaurs and the new staff respond to me, it warms me from the core. Though I have committed quite appalling crimes from assaults on both men and women, burglaries and blackmail and fraud and multiple misdemeanours people in general seem to see I am not bad, but that drink and drugs rather make me do bad things. Just prior to coming to prison for this burglary I had met my new probation officer and soon as I lay my pesty eyes upon her I'd thought: what a sort! So fuckin' beautiful she is, and goes by the name of Ellie S. I sat chatting the breeze with her and after a while she had looked up with her sexy secretary look, glasses perched on the end of a cute nose and said:

"I was expecting to meet the worst man I had ever met in my life today after seeing your lengthy criminal record". Rather perplexed at this but nonchalantly uncaring what those involved in law enforcement really thought to be fair, I'd cocked a quizzical and said:

"And"?

"And then I met you", and ever since that day she went out of her way to help me, not breaching my probation when she could have, realizing that I was on bail, on my way to prison anyway and to be fair I was not committing offences, and she believed me when I told her that. She could have breached me because I was still using but she chose to take a risk. I did not offend. I was plotted at Charlotte's, then Tan's, being looked after as I anticipated the sentence I was facing in my approaching middle age years. I liked her modernist, progressive approach to her job. I can still see her in my minds' eye now, glorious bum she has! Some officers, probation officers will breach you despite the fact you pose no risk to the public. Through fear for their own arses.

Sat 5ᵗʰ January 2019 1010hrs. Doors been open since 0900 hrs when I promptly went to the shower to sluice the last of the sticky remnants of the opioids in my body from my skin. I'm in Brad's cell now. The cunt is shushing me as he tries to watch a programme in peace about snakes. Now people I have to remind you that me and Bradders have both got the ugliest feet complete with the biggest bunions you ever did see. Brad believes his to be less hysterically funny than mine but I ask him:

"How's ya feet Brad"?

"They're alright ya cunt; why d'ya ask"?

"Just interested is all. Let me have a look Brad, come on Toebocop, show us ya plates", and the cunt throws his head back and laughs!

"How can you, you of all people", he says, mirth written all across his handsome face, "how the fuck can you say anything with those fuckers at the end of your legs"?

"They ain't that bad"!

"They ain't that good though either, old Tobywankanobie", and I find this fantastically fuckin' funny, both of us creasing at our fucked up feet.

"Did ya watch Last Of The Toehicans last night"? I say to him now and both of us are holding our bellies with laughter and I think how much I love this cunt.

"No fuckin' way, you cunt", says Brad, "Last Of The Toehicans! Seriously though, did you watch that half Filipino half Australian bird on that nature programme yesterday"?

"No", I say, "why d'ya ask"?

"Well", he says, "not only was she the most sexy woman but she's also a nature nut like me but I fell even more in love with her when she took her shoes off to get in the water and she had bigger bunions than you and me and I thought, wow, fuckin' hell, that's like literally my perfect bird"!

"No fuckin' way", I laugh, "you're telling me that you saw her bunions and thought 'wow, my type of bird"?

"Well, it's not just the bunions mate! You gotta see this bird bro, she's a right sort mate honestly Sloaney you clown footed fuck"!

"You're mental"! I say.

"What I actually said is that she's proper gorgeous and seeing her big arse bunions made her even more perfect"!

"Anyway", I say, once my laughter has subsided, "ya know, like, Nike let people design their own trainers now right"?

"Yeah", he says, looking at me suspiciously.

"Well, I've designed a new pair for you, I, and your future half Filipino bride with a new built in bunion bubble"!

"You're fucked ya cunt", he says, chuckling, "could actually be an idea though really"! Lee 'Gibbo' Gibson from next door comes into the cell now. He is one of the nicest and most dangerous fuckers on the wing with a love of holding up drug dealers outside.

"Did you watch that snake programme Brad"? he says to McFradders now.

"Tried to, but I had this cunt next to me", he says, smiling toward me.

"The bollox weren't it"? says Gibbo who then goes on to ask Brad if everyone paid him yesterday.

"No", says Brad, "I'm still owed twelve packs", and it is true that many people haven't paid him, coming up with colourful excuses as to why they couldn't and invariably promising to cough up next week.

1700hrs. Went to the gym, came back, now I am very stoned, using against my will. I can barely see the page and am riddled with self loathing. Me and J.T argue, may be time for a new cellmate.

166

0900hrs 6/01/2019. Before I get back to the boring tale of me I want to let my mate, a big blonde beast of a Scot, say a few words. He has written something and wants me to put it in the book. So, over to you Craig:

My name is Craig McNicol and I am a recovering alcoholic addict. I'm 33 years old and so grateful to say I am in recovery here at HMP Rochester. This would not have been possible had I not signed up to the Bridge Programme here on 'A' wing. I have been an alcoholic really since the first time I encountered alcohol when I was 14. I was never in control in addiction and so for 18 years my life was chaotic and desperate and I was just drinking and taking drugs and committing crime. They say in addiction that what to expect is jails, institutions and death. Well, if I had continued my life death was certainly in the post. As for jails and institutions they were my only spells of abstinence. From 19 I tried AA and never thought it was for me. I was not looking at the similarities but the differences. Not identifying with the similarities because I didn't want to fully give up. I did want to stop but never gave it enough. So when I began the bridge programme in September I wasn't sure what to expect. What it did right form the off was to get me to accept that I was powerless over my addiction and that my life had become unmanageable. I could definitely identify with this and realized I wasn't alone for the first time and I felt a real sense of belonging. I built up an understanding of my Higher Power and learned how to hand over my feelings and emotions that I'd been supressing all my life. I was taught on Bridge that it would only work if I was honest, open minded and willing. This was hard as I was set in my old ways, a compulsive liar and that I had no will power or that's what I thought. My desire to stay clean became more than my desire to use. I started to really look at myself in depth and recovery became the single most important thing in my life even ahead of my family and girlfriend for without recovery there was none of this anyway. I began to be honest, always. I became happy to try any ways to stay clean and realized I have will power. A tremendous determination to succeed. I learned to give and receive feedback both positive and negative. Self care, hygiene which I'd lacked so much in addiction became an important aspect of my life. I basically completely had an awakening of some sort when I started the Bridge Programme. It's the single most important thing I've ever done in my life. My mum has her boy back. My fiancé has her man back. I've found myself and as each day goes by I thank God for giving me my life back and for giving me the strength to remain clean and sober. One day at a time. Oh, in finishing I recommend the programme to anyone with a desire to stay clean to sign up. It can and will change your life if you want it enough. Forward Trust here at Rochester thank you for referring me and Steve, Jan and Arron thanks for giving me my life back and I'll be forever grateful. Many thanks, Craig McNicol.

Now, the door has just opened. As I dare say I have stipulated, we get out one day afternoon one day morning on a rolling basis on the weekends but if we are out in the afternoon we still get out between the hours of 11am and 12pm for lunch and when it's a morning unlock we still get out in the evening from 1600 to 1700 for tea. So it has just gone 11a.m and I am plotted up in Brad's cell though I know not where the spider loving jigsaw puzzling nature knowing nut is though I am helping myself to his coffee 'cause I ain't yet had one this morning. Oh, he has just walked in the cell.

"That little Reece", he says, "promised me he'd have my three packs of vapes today but there are three other people outside his cell"......

"I thought he paid you"?

"He paid me half what he owed but said he'd be able to clear it today 'cause he had some coming".

"Is he locked behind his door"? I ask.

"Yep", says Brad, "and there's people screaming for vapes off him so all that fanny he gave me about 'oh, I'll have 'em for you Brad I promise' was a load of shit".

"So you lost two with the other hyper little fucker and now three with him"?

"Yep", says Brad, running his hands over his thick head of hair in consternation. Now, remember Brad only took on a spice parcel to sell so he could make our Xmas memorable. Anyway, we have dinner and bang up.

Right, we are now banged up. J.T is just about to blow his brains away with a Buscopan. He's talking about the fact that upon his imprisonment his sister burgled his flat. I'm not really listening. I have something else to share with you. Now downstairs there is a lifer called Stephen Bennett who's been in on this sentence since 2006. It's now, as you know, 2019. Now me and he have become quite close; like Rob 'Fats' Whiting Steve too is a little stand offish but, again, like Fats I've built a friendship with the guy after proving my credentials though it has taken six months. These types of people need to know one can keep one's mouth shut. Now Steve is tall and skinny with a thin face and cropped grey hair and is in his fifties. It's worth noting too that this cunt is a comedic genius. Anyway, Steve came up to me today and said:

168

"Andy, I've been thinking about what you asked me, ya know, to write something for ya but 'cause I ain't that good at writing and that I thought I'd give you this".

"What is it Steve"? I say, taking the proffered paperwork.

"It's the judge's summing up when he sentenced me", and he can see my excitement as my eyes light up and smiles.

"What", I say, eagerly, "can I write this up"?

"Yeah man, that's why I'm giving them to ya ya silly cunt". I'm scanning the sheets already.

"Oh my God", I say, "my fuckin' God, this is priceless"! I will let you make up your own mind dear reader. The following is the summing up by Judge Van Der Werff as he sentenced Stephen Bennett for murder on the 14th December 2006

.

Judge: "Stephen Bennett, stand up. You pleaded guilty on the 10th of November this year to the murder of Trevor Moriarty, and this, as you well know, means that there is only one sentence which the court can impose for such a crime; that is one of life imprisonment and that therefore is the sentence on count one of this indictment. I have, however, to determine how long you must serve before the parole board can consider your case and decide whether or not to release you on license. It may never happen. If it does, you will remain on license for the rest of your life and you will be liable to recall to prison at any time if you breach the terms of your license. Trevor Moriarty had in fact done you no harm. Your girlfriend, Natasha Davies, rang you up and said that he had struck her. It is clear from the evidence that that was an accident, when she had intervened between him and another man. She suffered no injury. Instead of looking into the matter and, if necessary informing the police like a proper citizen, you immediately went out, called upon your friend Parker, stole a sharp knife from him , found Moriarty almost immediately, got hold of him with one hand and bent him back over a wall and struck him once in the chest with the blade with such accuracy that the blade entered his heart and killed him. You have a bad record for violence in the past. At the age of 41 you have 65 crimes on your record, 3 for actual bodily harm and, in one court appearance, for three robberies, attempted robbery, carrying a firearm and wounding with intent when you received 12 years. Since your release you seem to have not only lived by shoplifting, but funded your drug habit in this way also. On this occasion today, instead of behaving sensibly, you determined immediately to exact your revenge upon Moriarty whom you treated with horrendous violence without giving him any real opportunity to explain what had happened. You had decided, in what evidence of Parker made thoroughly clear to this court, was a cold blooded way, to attack Moriarty for daring to raise his hand to your girlfriend Natasha. I take as a starting point a period of twelve years for punishment and deterrence. I increase that by two years because I am quite satisfied that this was a premeditated act. I reduce the total by one year for your guilty plea. It was entered at a late stage after the first trial, several months thereafter. I find it difficult to understand how you can have been so badly represented at the first trial that you did not understand the legal position in which you stood. However that is why you changed your plea when you received direction from a different counsel. I also bear in mind that you are now remorseful and have sought to apologise to Mr Moriarty's widow. I also understand you did act as you did because of what you thought had happened to your girlfriend. So that period of 13 years will start from the date you were arrested and I therefore deduct the 464 days during which you have been in custody pending this hearing. The parole board may therefore start to consider whether it is safe to release you on license in 11 years and 266 days from today. I shall make no other order of any kind. You may go down.

The rest of the day people is spent smashed on spice. I am not, from here in Oxford now, going to type up the scrawl of shit I wrote throughout the day for not only is it barely legible it is pony, poo, and would only confuse you. Let's just say this; I throw my dignity out the pram, incur more debt, behave like a mong with J.T then lament my financial and spiritual situation, desperate to stop using but unable to do so. The methadone still sticks to me very slightly but it is getting easier, though sleep is still elusive. Goodbye for now.

11am 7-1-2019 and I'm in a cell with Lee 'Gibbo' Gibson. He is telling me a tale:
"Yeah, I was in Parkhurst", he says, puffing deeply on the vape he is always to be seen with.
"How the fuck you been there; you're too young"?
"I was, honestly, 2008, I swear, two eight to two ten I was there. Doing a ten stretch", he says.
"What"? I say, incredulously, "what was it like there"?
"It was a good jail but even though I'm white and it didn't directly affect me, I couldn't believe how racist they were there".
"What d'ya mean man"?
"Went from Swaleside so it was a proper contrast; they don't follow none of that black shit there like they do in Swaleside bro".
"What d'ya mean"? I again ask this dangerous baby faced lunatic.

"When we got shipped out of Swaleside, me and a few others including this black fella called Little Leon, we got to reception at Parkhurst and he was the first to come out the holding cell to get searched and that. When he was coming back from being strip searched he was muttering under his breath sort of thing, saying 'racist cunts, fuckin' racist cunts' and then", continues Gibbo, "within five seconds of him saying it every officer within earshot suddenly surrounded him and told him that 'this is the Isle of WHITE mate, Isle Of WHITE, WHITE, WHITE' and these cunts let him know rapid like that he was in white mans' territory". Gibbo goes on to tell me that every person of ethnicity, non-white, were put on a foreign national wing despite the fact that most of them were British. Gibbo even went on to tell me that on 'G' wing there a black fella, little bit posh, loved his clothes and bits called Eddie, old school Cockney fella was victim to a fire in his cell for refusing to move to that foreigners' wing; screws paid another inmate to burn him out, destroying all his cherished garments, photos and personal effects so hated were the blacks in that place at the time. Savage.

J.T and I are banged up now and I regale him with the tale I just heard from Gibbo and he too is horrified as I was. I mean, 2008 ain't that fuckin' long ago right? It baffles and bewilders and concerns me that there could still be places so awfully prejudiced in the system just a short while ago. And I dare say are still. Gibbo's tones still trill in my ears now as he said about the black fella 'this is the Isle Of White mate, the Isle of WHITE, WHITE, WHITE'. Wow. Poor fucker to be subjected to that. Going to a prison of such repute would be scary enough without that sort of shit to contend with. Just before I got banged up I talked to 'Fats' and he too has seen some horrors at the hands of screws.

"Yeah man", he'd said, "I've seen a screw deliberately slam a fella's fingers in the cell door and I'm tellin' ya Sloaney his fingers just fuckin' fell off"! Right, forgive me dear reader for I've been given a book written by an ex con now CEO of a prisoners' trust thing named Bobby Cummins. Jason Gould down at the Programmes Unit gave it to me when I spent some time with him and his beautiful in every way colleague Lucy early this morning.

In a class now, 1500hrs, with the lovely AddemupAde. We are rehashing a bit of time over distance stuff. Elementary I know but to me it's exciting and fresh and new and I get a buzz from doing these exercises. So, for instance, we have a world class runner who won an 800 metre race in a time of 1 minute and 45 seconds. OK? Right. Now we've to work out his average running speed. First I turn my minutes into seconds which translates, one minute forty five into 105 seconds. Then I work out how many seconds in an hour which is 3600. Then I take my 105 and divide it by my 3600 giving me 0.03. Now my 800 metres is 0.8km. So I now take this 0.8km and divide this now by my 0.03 giving me 26.666km per hour or 26.67kmh. Boom! Now, like I say, to most this is very basic stuff but to me it is magic, learning the processes by which these things are worked out! I get great joy from this stuff. And it has a wonderful stimulating effect on the mind, playing about with numbers in this way. And this calm Nigerian radiating such loving and patient energy never gets tired of me, even when I am petulant and childlike or sitting monged on drugs in his class! He only ever shows concern when seeing me in such states, sadness even. And he has made learning this stuff so easy for me!

Ok, sitting in Oxford typing the manuscript on a warm day in September of 2021 I say to myself 'do I type the next' for I am clearly very stoned on spice when the following was written. But I am going to, for I want to give a true reflection of my condition at the time. It may not make much sense and be disjointed and fragmentary but here goes.

1720hrs 7-1-2019. So it's Monday. Good maths. Now I'm stoned. I loved capturing Gibbo today. Today I am grateful for the prison, they gave me two pairs of lovely glasses which were prescribed by an erudite optician who tested my eyes and with whom I discussed on various academic and current affairs subjects. Anyway, there were a pair for sunlight and a pair for inside reading but both of the same optic specification. So I gave one pair to Tony Giles. Now I can see the lines of the page when I am stoned and therefore put more on the sheet and not scribble too incomprehensibly. I burgled many houses with Tony Giles through my teens and early twenties. And Brad. And Peter Lanes. We were all so taken with drugs once we'd plucked the fruit from the tree. Pop ya can't stop. And now I'm very very lucky. And grateful. Both Buck Tooth Billy and David M I passed on route round the prison today. I loved seeing both of them. I feel that the Judge's summing up in the case of Stephen Bennet was so dark and so powerful. Marcus's cell was spun today. Don't know why. I saw the lovely Bev today. She is magnificent. I told her she'll be shocked how I lusted over her in the classroom one day when she reads my book. She has something about her. We discussed gratitude. We talked of drugs and being thankful for the lives we have and to see the positives and not the negatives. We spoke on the modern God. The personal God free of religious doctrine and constraints. Tony Giles was so grateful for those glasses bless him.

He was in childrens' homes with me as a kid. Lucy looked luscious at the Attitudes Thinking and Behaviour Programmes Unit today. I do love the lovely looking ladies. Me and J.T and all the guys know all the girls that work here, all the screws and civilians, sexy nurses, psychologists and creamy dispensing staff.

"Have you seen that Ms P"? asks J.T.

"Fit as fuck", I say.

"Do you know her real name? asks he.

"How the fuck would I know that"?

"Ellie P-fit in't she? And the lesbian one with the beauty spot on her nose and my personal officer, Miss Meehan, proper sexy ain't they"?

"Yeah, the one with the beauty spot has defo got something about her and yeah your mate, the little dark haired screw the other day with the Scarlett Yohanson lips and perfect teeth is cute".

"And Ms Butler, I'd fuck her too", says J.T.

"I'd smash the life out of that too you know that but that Lucy, smart as well as sexy at the ATB Unit-cor", and I feel I must shut up on the subject. J.T is now smoking Buscopan, hitting himself with the idiot stick. I'm gonna read. There were two alarm bells on here today. Manchester hyperactive Reece bounced. So both the hyper Reece's have gone now owing absolutely everybody. I've glasses now. Sometimes I think I am a genius. Sometimes I think I'm a pretentious egotistical and slightly psychotic twat.

9th January 2019 0900hrs. J.T is really quite sick and has just thanked me for looking after him last night.

"Hardly looked after you mate", I say, "I just wanted to know you was still breathing, that's why I kept calling your name".

"I know, but most people just wouldn't give a fuck, d'ya know what I mean"?

"Well, I hope that's not the case but, J.T, bro, I gotta tell ya mate, you've lost some fuckin' weight of late for sure geezer".

"I know, I collapsed in the shower half hour ago as well".

"What"? I say, "really"?

"Yeah, came over like proper nauseous", he confirms, "so I just like curled up in a ball under the shower; I've never been sick, like never felt this bad before".

"Mate", I say, concerned and feeling a lot of love for this usually obnoxious fuck, "don't you think you should like tell the staff and get yourself looked at"?

"Let me get me meds first", he says, "and if I still feel the same then I'll go see health care".

"Send them to me and I can tell them truthfully how sick you've been all night".

"Cool mate", and the cunt is defo not himself right now.

Anyway, last night as I broke through to deep space after smoking a pipe of very, very strong spice. My mate came to see me on a pushbike dressed as a clown and I was in terror whilst the cunt creased up in laughter at me. His laughter comes from his eyes and creased Buddha face telepathically to me.

"Andy", he then said seriously, "I've been to you in premonitions, dreams, long before you were on drugs, I'm always with you".

"I know I know but I love to see you here", I say.

"Fuck sake", he says through his eyes, feigning fakely anger for he is a funny fuck, "Andy, there is nothing else for you to see here, let it go now, let it go, let it go", and I smile, the peace with which he says this sends shivers through me and my hair standing on end as a massive smile creased my face and I say to him:

"Oh thankyou, thankyou, thankyou", and I just know that sometime soon I am going to be A ok.

Anyway, enough of the spiritual dear reader for I don't want to scare you off. Now, downstairs this morning whilst I shared a breakfast of beans on toast with the pretty boy soon to be my cellmate Marcus T (for we both start the NA orientated Bridge programme together) a rugged handsome dark haired gangster called Mark from Sussex sat with us. He kindly proffered his vape to me for a puff after my morning meal. Now, sometimes people come onto wings and there is an instant wariness, an appraisal period where we weigh each other up, unsure each of the other and this is what Mark and I experienced around one another. This fucker is six foot, well built and has the most piercing blue eyes I ever saw. So us two have sort of skirted one another but after a couple of months we have built rapport when we realized we aren't the horrible cunts we judged each other to be. Anyway, I haven't time to write more on him now but this morning I had said to him:

"I heard you talking about running into a Post Office and sticking it up", and as soon as I say it his eyes light up and I see the madness within, the joy he gets in armed robbery.

"It's my favourite hobby Sloaney: I just love running in and taking control, calmly giving orders with a shooter in my hand"! More on Mark, perhaps, later.

Anyway, a bit later now and J.T has gotten some anti sickness stuff and seems to be back on form. Now our window in the cell has been broken for like ever. The window is outswung and through the grill from which we get the little ventilation these shit systems allow for we can't close it because the mechanism is broken, the turny knob thing with the lever and arm. So Longshanks, J.T, has found from fuck knows where a spare arial lead and stripped it to the brightwire core and fashioned a tool before poking it through the grill and hooking the window and pulling it in. The windows are designed to stop filthy prisoners throwing rubbish out and swinging lines of contraband to each other. Anyway, he hooks and shuts the window against the odds and I have to admit to the prick that:

"That was fuckin' amazing"! If you saw what he had to do you'd realize this was no mean feat.

"I know", he says, smiling from ear to ear, "proper clever in I"?

"I like the thinking", and it is true, I do. The holes are tiny and the widow has nothing to grab onto but he did it despite me saying that he was wasting his time.

"I'm feeling much better now", he says. And we pass a joint between us this cold brisk Wednesday afternoon in January.

"You looked well pervy looking at Ms H earlier", says J.T now.

"What d'ya mean ya wierdo"?

"In ya new glasses as well; all you needed was a plaster in the middle of 'em and you'd've looked like a proper seed"!

"What, did I look proper pesty"?

"You did mate, but when she was bent over in them tight trousers everyone was looking so you weren't on your own mate don't worry".

Fri 11-1-2019 1630hrs and I come back from the education dept and upon walking onto the 'twos' landing I see my pals from boyhood Peter 'Bundy' Lanes and the staunch miserable cunt that is Tony Giles. They are at the back of their cell and as I walk in through the open door I marvel at their stupidity having it open for Pete is rolling the biggest bazooka of a spice spliff though the pair of cunts can hardly hold their headlamps open so clearly inebriated are they. They are both doing the nodding, bopping spice shuffle but being hardcore seasoned smokers they can both hold it. I creep up behind Tony Piles who's standing over Peter who's sitting doing the rolling as I say. They haven't heard me enter the cell so I tiptoe to Tony whose back is to me and run my index finger along his throat playfully whilst whispering in his ear:

"I'll cut you you cunt", and I am so pleased when the normally morose fuck turns and says:

"You couldn't cut cardboard ya cunt. Fuck me, smell the joint from the education dept did ya"?

"You mug", I smile.

"Eeee yah", says Pete, "shut the door Sloaney and smoke this with us" and I do just that. Pete puts the banger in his mouth and lights it up. "This is proper power mate".

"Ain't you had a joint yet today"? asks Tony Piles.

"Nope", I say.

"Go easy then Andy", says Pete who usually calls me Sloaney so I know him using my first name is in caution for the power of the spice. I smoke some as the bat of a blunt is passed between us, round and round it goes. Immediately I hit it the strength becomes apparent as the ringing in my ears, always present, increases in intensity and frequency.

"Fuckin' hell", I say, "Wow". Tony is now beside me with a fuck off grin and Pete's eyes are bloodshot as fuck. I feel love and Pete is shaking my arm with a stupid smile on his cute bald headed countenance.

"Do you remember", he is saying, "when we was gonna have a fight, I dunno, we were about ten or something, just up the road from your mum and dad's house and I threw a lump of dog shit at you"? and now the silly lovable fucker I've known since forever is chuckling and I note how shiny his bald pate is as he goes on after I mutter:

"Cunt"!

"Yeah right Tone, Sloaney started giving it"……….

"He's always giving it", smiles Tony.

"Yeah, yeah", continues Pete, "but I just couldn't be bothered to fight the cunt Tone so I picked up this proper old"……..

"Grey Pete you cunt", I interject.

"Yeah, proper grey bit of old dog shit weren't it and threw it in ya face didn't I Sloaney"?! and the Buddha is now bent in mirth and Tony too is smiling from ear to ear as he tries to stop his eyes rolling up into his head.

"Did he Sloaney"? drawls Tony.

"He did", I say and can't help but laugh at the foul way he dispensed with me that day many moons of yore. Pete is talking again:

"Do you remember when we were all at the synagogue, smoking weed and Clarkey (our boyhood pal Alan Clarke) broke both his arms on the rope swing"?

"Hahahahaha, shit man", I say, feeling kinda guilty, "that was too fuckin' funny".

"Not for him it weren't I bet", says Tony.

"Tony", says Pete, "do you remember that swing though it was on top of a like cliff d'ya remember"?

"Course I fuckin' do Peter d'ya think I'm thick or something"? says Tony in mock incredulity.

"Anyway right", says Peter through chuckles, "this day right, I had a go, Sloaney had a go then Alan got on Sloaney d'ya remember"?

"Yep", I say, "soon as the cunt kicked himself off the cliff I knew the grip he had on that bit of wood at the end of the rope wouldn't hold him", I say, and Peter continues that:

"The silly cunt swung right out didn't he Sloaney"?

"He did", I say, playing the scene from thirty years ago through my synapses. Pete goes on:

"And he let go mid-air and flew and Sloaney goes 'oh shit he looks like superman' and Alan must have fell from at least forty feet up in the air weren't it Sloaney"? and I'm laughing even at the recollection of our beloved pal flying through the air with terror on his face.

"Ahh mate", I say, crying now with the remembering, "and all those stinging nettles the silly cunt landed in; broke both his arms didn't he"?

"The cunt didn't move for about ten minutes Tony and what do you think me and Sloaney done"?

"Well, I'd've hoped you'd've helped him you pair of cunts", says Tony.

"We did, but not for ages 'cause we was in proper stitches. Once we'd stopped crying though we went down there and when we see his arms were snapped we phoned him an ambulance the poor cunt. But it was so fuckin' funny Tony".

"Fuck me", says Tony, "right pair of pricks to have around in an emergency you two ain't ya"?

"Savage", I say.

"Shit man, that was fuckin' funny though. It was the way he, like, soared through the air for time, like proper ages and the fuckin' stinging nettles, like they were waist high and evil fuckers and he went right in the middle the poor cunt", says Pete and now it is bang up for lunch so I bid you adieu for now dear reader. I return to my cell and find that Marcus T is now my cellmate for we are both on the Bridge Narcotics Anonymous orientated programme next week so he swapped with J.T.

12th January 2019 0930hrs. My cellmate, Marcus is laying prostrate on his bottom bunk. He is in withdrawel for though the last I spoke of him he was fit and clean he has been slipping. The worst thing is that it would have been half alright if he'd have stuck to the spice but the cunt has been using subutex, an opioid analgesic.

"I can't believe you been on the 'tex mate", I say to him

"I know man I know", he says, trying to lift eyelids already leaded with spice though it be but 0930hrs on a Saturday morning where we are locked up 'till eleven when we get out for an hour for lunch. "D'ya wanna bit"? he says, offering me the spice spliff.

"Fuck that mate; too early and if we carry on smoking hard like last night we'll end up like a couple of crackheads"!

"We are crackheads Sloaney", he reminds me, as if I need to be told.

"Not gonna be in active addiction forever me mate I tell ya", I say.

"Couple of days clucking I'll be ok", he says.

"I hope so", and I do dear reader. Now let me describe this cunt again for you. Firstly he always has lots of money and even when the cunt is flat out on the drugs he looks well, is impeccably dressed and lives well. We have a DVD player, DAB radio, lots of lovely toiletries and if I wanted to the generous fuck would let me wear any of the untold designer garms he has with him here in Rochester. He truly is a pal of mine. And remember I have known him many years in and out these walls. Let me remind you of his physicality too. Anyone would tell you he is the sort of fuck you wouldn't want your woman around for too long ya know? Five foot ten or eleven with a shock of blonde hair above bright blue eyes. He has the build of an Olympic athlete and is 13 or 14 stone of pure muscle. I wouldn't wanna stand next to the fucker in a pub for I'd not get a look in with the birds believe me. He is kind and generous though he is no one's cunt either and isn't frightened to get aggressive should the need arise. I look up now from my pen and pad and notice the heavy bags beneath his eyes, the two day shadow on his usually clean shaven pretty boy face. The poor fucker is hanging right off for opiates. I am acutely aware that I may have jumped out the frying pan into the fire for the whole reason I changed from J.T to Marcus was because of Bridge and the fact J.T makes no bones of the fact he does not want to stop using. Marcus assures me he wants to stay clean but the cunt is fucked already and dawn has barely broken. Thing is, the spice alleviates the withdrawel a little but not for long. I just can't understand him picking up opiates again. He crashed off of methadone at 35ml and suffered horrifically so to come back to this wing and pick up illicit subutex again is madness. It will take him backwards. I myself haven't taken any opioids for nearly four weeks I think and I still suffer aching limbs, sweats, little proper sleep, cold and flu like symptoms and sickness. Fuck putting subutex in me for it would take me back to day one. The spice has helped me get through but that must go soon too. I'm very nearly there. It is residual now, the withdrawing, and I can't believe it is to be a year before my body functions like someone who never took methadone, according to addiction specialists. Anyway, maybe me being ten years Marcus's senior and being in the middle of an active spiritual awakening just maybe, maybe, I will be able to help him. I hope so for he

178

desires to be clean. I think. Unlike me Marcus has never experienced real recovery. No rehab, no rooms of Narcotics Anonymous. The criminal justice system and drug agencies have invested lots in me and I am hoping that once again I can bring all this investment to fruition. The only intervention Marcus has had has been in the form of prison bars. Marcus, by the way, is serving a five year sentence for robbery.

We have just been let out. Unlocked. I'm in Brad's cell with Brad, Grin and Pete Lanes. Marcus is still in his bed. Pete and Brad are 'codees' or co-defendants, as I say, in for the same burglary. Pete is talking about the time me, him, his aunty Jackie and the late David Gardner, who took his own life and was found dead by my son's mum, went out burgling many moons ago.

"D'ya remember that day Andy"? Pete is saying, "when me aunt Jackie took us all out, David was with us and we went right out into the sticks but didn't find nothing"?

"I know what you're gonna say ya cunt", I say, "when Dave got shot"!

"With a salt pellet by that little old man", and here we all have a little chuckle, Pete's cute face and bald pate reddening as mirth crinkles his features. Jackie had been our driver that day whilst us three were the burglers.

"I fuckin' remember that I told you and David that we should leave farmhouses the fuck alone for exactly that reason. Do you remember me saying to you two that I wasn't comfortable doing that gaff"? I say.

"I just remember us three trying to break in", he begins, before I take it up.

"And the little old man came through the back garden gate with his shotgun", I say.

"And you shouted 'oh shit' and the little old cunt shot Dave straight up the arse and Dave was proper screaming in agony d'ya remember"? says Pete, proper laughing like me at the recall of the almighty yelp Dave emitted as the salt penetrated his shorts. After the discharge we ran through fields and bogs and nettles trying to find Jackie and the car, quite lost, all the while Dave was pissing blood from the wound on his bumcheek. Anyway, moving on, Brad bought a mouse yesterday for a bit of spice off of some spicehead who'd trapped it on the wing knowing Bradders would not be able to resist. Well, Brad has only gone and built like a proper cool habitat for the cute little rodent which now sits on the table on which he usually does his fuck off big jigsaws. The 'lair' consists of three plastic 'Celebrations' sweet 'tins' like the Roses chocolate things ya know? Only in plastic? Ok. Instead of the lids Brad

179

has put Perspex over the top so we can all see the little fella, the mouse and into the plastic he has drilled airholes. He has used shredded J cloth for bedding and all three 'tins' are connected via plastic plumbing pipes which he 'borrowed' from the workshop where he works. He has created this thing in a matter of hours so inspired by nature is he. Absolutely amazing.

"How does the mouse breathe Brad"? asks Lee 'Gibbo' Gibson who has just come into the cell with Seb to have a look at the new pet which sits close to his other ward, the fuck off black spider he has in the Perspex plinthed cube so all can see the savage beast sinking fangs into prey when Brad feeds it.

"I just put a few airholes in the plastic", says Brad, "I love the way he can just run around the different compartments man, like one for his food, one with a couple of ping pong balls and one with bedding so he can snuggle himself down and that".

"It is cool", I say, "where's the mouse"?

"See the little box in the corner of the first one"? says Brad, meaning the 'house' closest to the wall.

"Yeah", I say, leaning in and looking.

"She's in there, snug after eating all the lettuce and oats I put in there for her last night". And indeed in one of the nodes there are bits of apple, rice crispies, oats and a tiny trough for water.

"Spider's getting fat too Sloaney", says Brad now and indeed the creepy critter is getting very fat and hairy, massive scary thing. Now, and please don't ask for I cannot keep up, Manchester hyperactive Reece has come back to 'A' wing after bouncing from whatever wing he ended up on and now after having paid Brad, Brad allows him in the cell and they are both marvelling over the creature whilst Gibbo says to me:

"I've got some stories for ya; have you ever heard of Crusher and Mary"? and as he asks he takes a big fat pull of his vape, sending creamy swirls of vapour into the air as he exhales the nicotine infused substance.

"No", I say, "who the fuck are Crusher and Mary"?

"They're like proper famous in the 'A' cat dispersal (high security) prisons", says he, and dear reader do try to remember this baby faced assassin has spent most of his long sentences, all violence and armed robbery related, in these dreadful dark jails like Parkhurst, Albany and Long Lartin.

"Why, what'd'ya mean"? I ask, taking the coffee Brad passes to me.

"Crusher is a six foot massive black geezer, like, proper, proper dangerous", he says, continuing that, "Mary is his 'girlfriend', a fifty something year old fella with long grey hair and he wears like make up and that".

180

"What, were they cellmates? On normal location"? I ask.

"Yeah course", says Gibbo, "Mary shaves 'her' legs and I'm telling ya, if Crusher finds anyone, and I mean anyone", and here he emphasises his point by waving his vape in an arc before him and widening his eyes, "even looking at 'her' he'd proper kill 'em and I see Crusher smash someone up just because Mary shouted 'he touched me he touched me' 'cause Mary is a proper bitch and Crusher is a seriously jealous man"!

"Fuck me", I say, "I'd love to meet 'em"!

"Sick cunt", says Gibbo, "you'd probably fuck Mary"!

"You're sick even thinking that", I laugh, "that's your mind ya sick fuck, not mine"!

"Naaa, only messing", he says, rubbing me leg lasciviously!

"You're fucked Gibbo"! Don't get any ideas, Gibbo is hetero and this is pure banter prison style. Anyway, moving on, to give a little recap I can't remember if I told you but Phil The Face has been kicked off the wing for drug dealing or suspicion of I think. Along with Fats he's been running things on here for some time. Now people like Phil and Fats are the types that keep wings in check, sort of creating balance so powerful are their personalities. Fats is leaving in a couple of weeks and will be sorely missed. He is so kind and though he sells drugs here the irony is that he has gotten himself clean and sober and for those looking for recovery he's the most supportive go to guy and has helped several people clean up. He is also as pesty as the rest of us round the female staff and unlike most of us he seems to be getting somewhere with one particularly pretty young thing who I won't name. Anyway, the point I am trying laboriously to make here is that there is going to be a bit of a vacuum and potential for a power struggle as the wing takes different shape with the loss of these two characters.

Now I couldn't be bothered to write this earlier but me and Marcus moved to a big, massive cell on the wing that he 'brought' for spice but no sooner have we moved in the cunt sold it for double the money he purchased it for so we are moving again back to the cell I was originally in. Drain but he now has two full A4 sheets of power spice paper. Remember a credit card sized bit goes on average for £25. And can at times inflate to £50. Or another way to measure is £25 for a line. Marcus is no longer in a state of withdrawel having gotten some subutex and the semi synthetic opioid is putting some wind in his sails. It is 1330hrs and we are waiting for the door to open at 1400hrs. Gangster rap, Headie One and then Skepta emanates from the DAB. The door opens. We move back. I go to Brad's with pen and paper. The mouse thing he built is amazing and I was wrong about the lids for they are not Perspex but acetate he tells me, stolen from overhead projectors round the prison. Now, dear reader, as I type here in Oxfordshire three years or so later I say to myself as I look at the next pages to be typed, 'really' for I am clearly stoned and it fucks me up reading the disjointed fractured bollox but I want to be true to you in case there is something I don't see there so feel it right I give it the way I wrote it there and then in the jail so forgive and skip if need be. Some may not make sense, I talk pony sometimes when tripping out. However, sometimes I saw things otherwise hidden! So, to continue faithfully.

"Sloaney, you staying here to guard the fort I've got a few bits to do"? ask Brad.

"Yeah man course can I have a pipe though"? I ask, hankering after spice.

"When I get back, I'll be five minutes Sloaney", and remember dear reader that yesterday was black eye Friday so Brad has about eighteen packs of vapes stashed away in the peter. (cell). He will take these to Flowplast, the workshop where he labours and where his supplier is on Monday. We had Jay Nevin in here earlier and this cockney gangster is, no denying it, a fuckin' fruit loop but fuckin' funny with it at times. More on him later I am sure.

Marcus has gone to gym (he goes on drugs or not) but my body is too broken from the savage circuit I tackled yesterday for me to join him. Tony Giles is at a table on the 'twos' landing doing one of his Banksy style art things on a prison sheet which he will then sell for a good price and which he does to keep him in spice. Brad has just returned with beans on toast which we share with a coffee and after we have a roll up between us, like a proper Golden Virginia bonafide tobacco roll up, rare as rocking horse shit on the wing at the moment. Me and Brad regularly talk about our old boyhood friend, Tristan 'Trip' Wood who could well have been here with us were it not for his untimely death through overdose on pregablin and heroin. This Baurhause art on the back of Brads' door which he did trips me the fuck out when I look at it straight let alone when tripping on spice. I drive Brad mad for spice after driving Marcus mad for the same and I am fucked , fucked, fucked. Gibbo is at Brad's table and he and Brad are talking of a prisoner they both know who's:

"An encyclopedia of knowledge but I see him get proper weighed in", Brad is prattling, "I had to tell him myself once that he can't expect me to pay for his spice habit. Anyway Lee, I forgot I owe you a cap". (Vape capsule).

"Oh yeah; only if ya got it", says Gibbo.

182

"Yeah, I've got one for ya", says Brad. And now they are discussing the likelihood of Gibbo getting out and his chances for being as Lee is doing an EPP or Extended Public Protection sentence he has to go before a parole board to be considered for release on licence. Someone shouts "Gibbo" on the landing and he shoots off. I am very stoned and me and Brad talk about Steve M, brother of Dave who has just been released after serving a life sentence. I wrote of Dave earlier, when we went to London and I came back on the train. I am close with both these bad boys. Jake comes in the cell now, Jake who had the fatal car crash. He's also from the manor and one of us Thanet boys. There's lots of Thanet in the prison system in the south east of England. I feel so drained of energy. It is still the lingering of the methadone in my system which is reluctant to leave. This environment that if you are reading this I dare say you find quite interesting is a fuckin' drain to me. Boring. And as I type I think how much I'd love a dictaphone for so many conversations go amiss, interesting ones I dare say for you dear reader though standard for me. The thing is with just good old pen and paper I have to hone in on particular things and accept the fact I miss other things. Still, I try my best for you. Oh, and I know I am run down for I have had an outbreak of herpes. Just saying.

0830hrs 12-1-2019. Morning campers. So I explained recently, me and Marcus T now occupy a cell together as we both have the same objective of leaving the prison clean and sober. And we start the Bridge NA orientated programme today. So, I sit in the group room now with the facilitators as we await the arrival of the rest of our members; this will be a day of getting to know each other. Trust has to be built so that we can all open up to try to work round some of our issues for the next six weeks. Marcus has just turned up. Then Terry Winters, a staunch dark haired doesn't say a lot type who's just moved on from another wing to do the course. Now Terry Hughes comes through the door, my former buddy in pugilism. Next through the door is Ricky Lanes, Peter's brother who looks much like Pete and has the same shining bald pate. Done many a burglary with this chap, a few years older than me. Now the warlike Craig D enters. And finally Craig Mc, the big blonde Scot, six foot six or so but gentle with it and a leader of recovery on this wing at the moment. Groups open, more later.

1700hrs. More stoned stuff I was gonna skip because typing it here in Oxford today nearly three years after the fact is draining. But I wish to give the full picture and also know that I stopped using soon, back then in 2019. So, same day, 1700hrs in January 2019, Monday. Banged up for

183

the evening with Marcus. I am stoned and after three days I have succumbed to the seductive tones of the subutex myself. So, the move with Marcus is good 'cause I am banged up with me mate but bad as I am now bang at it. I am right out me canister this minute. Listening to the sounds of small planes going overhead and the rattle of trains in the distance. Bradley Walsh is on the T.V beside me. Prisoners are shouting to one another out the grilled windows on Echo wing across the way from us here on Alpha. Marcus is lying on his bed as I scribe away on our soft comfy chair. Looking at him now, as he breathes deeply, eyes rolling and profoundly out his nut on 'tex' and spice and pregablin I wonder the cunt's still here the amount of drugs he uses on the whole. I am the most greedy, prolific drug user I know except for the lunatic here in this cell with me right here right now. His top is off showing his ink and muscles. It's hardly any wonder his girlfriend is an extremely attractive sexy as fuck prison officer he plucked from HMP Elmley seven years ago. And she was not the first screw he'd seduced and stolen from the prison service either. He manged to literally charm the knickers off of another one before her also. I tap Marcus' foot and he groggily opens very stoned eyes. I actually do believe that I deserve the drugs today. (How erroneous is that as I now look back from Oxford as I type). I am enjoying the warm enveloping effect of the opiate. The sublime itching is orgasmic. So I am well high right now. When one has not indulged in any form of narcotic for some time the poppie's embrace is so seductive. I think of the song by the Stranglers, Golden Brown, as my mind runs through poppy fields under a blazing sun. Oh, Brad's mouse chewed through the plastic and escaped.

So, it is nearly six PM this mild Monday in the year of our Lord 2019. Today a screw was punched in the face on one of the wings down the other end of the nick. I heard this in an NA meeting here today; prisoners from the wing in question were marvelling at the two punches the fella landed on the screw's boat race.

"Didn't you hear the alarm bell Sloaney just before they called freeflow"?

"Yeah", I say, "but it rarely even registers with me bro there are so many of them every day".

"We had another geezer on Saturday", continues me mate from G wing, "got proper sliced up with a razor blade melted into a toothbrush, savage man, face was fucked and he needed about fifty stitches".

"Yeah, it's fuckin' mental here at the moment", I tell him, "Martin and Wes Davidson took tools out to Darren Selby the other day and got nicked; both of 'em got carted off 'A' wing mob handed. And on Friday they come and got Phil The Face. They're proper shaking 'A' wing up. Do you know Curtis Cooper on your wing"?

"Yeah", he says, and goes on to confirm that my friend of old got weighed in for the drugs he had brought back from his home leave the other day. I saw Curtis when I walked to the education block Friday and noticed the big black eye he sported.

8pm and me and 33 year old Marcus 'Money Team' T as he self styles himself are absolutely pickled. He is awake and I feel to ask the heavy lidded gouching geezer a question or two.

"Smarcus, when did you come to Margate"?

"Bin there all me life, same as you", and I can hear in his voice he wishes I'd leave him alone.

"Where are your parents"?

"Found my dad on the bathroom floor dead one morning".

"Why? How"? I ask.

"Drinking", he says, not opening his eyes.

"What about ya mum"? I ask.

"She died of cirrhosis of the liver same as me dad; drunk herself to death".

"Did you love 'em both bro"?

"Yeah, seems all I've ever known is pain", he says. And it is true. I've always been able to see the pain in him, even when he was a whipper snapper when I first met him in about 2001. After his mum died Marcus went to stay with his dad but only for a little while as the old man used to get drunk then kick fuck out young Marcus. He tells me that after eight weeks or so Social Services come and got him and that he went into care with two different sets of foster parents where, he says, he was treated better than he ever had been.

"They were really nice, like proper middle class, both sets of foster parents".

"Where"? I ask him.

"Both in Westgate, they were both fuckin' lovely, I was lucky".

"What'd'ya mean"?

"Well, you hear some proper horror stories about what happens to some kids in care so I'm just really grateful that I was treated so nice".

"Me too Marcus, I was exactly the same bro, I loved it in care. I think my first proper cuddle was from these old ladies when I went to a kid's home in Deal when I was about twelve".

"You used to get clothing grants and that d'ya remember"?

"Yeah man", I say, "couldn't fuckin' believe it; before long I was head to foot in designer clothes as the state saw to it I had everything I needed. I just remember feeling that all the staff there really loved me man". Dear reader you need to know my mum and dad did love me but my dad was such a man's man of his generation that cuddles and outward displays of affection were not tolerated. But he worked his arse off to feed and clothe us and worked two allotments to insure we had wholesome fruit and veg all year round. I just couldn't stand the oppressive atmosphere of fear permeating the house all the time. Once my dad busted his back at work I just couldn't cope with him at home 24/7. He terrified me.

15-1-2019 0830hrs. We are now back in the group room Tuesday morning and I realize I got the date very wrong yesterday. We are now halfway through the first month of the new year and today is the day that Theresa May's Brexit deal will get voted down in Parliament, throwing the country into more uncertainty. Anyway, still in the group room and there are visitors from the Forward Trust drug treatment services agency here to ask questions about the services being offered by them here at Rochy. Marcus is telling these five execs that Rochester prison and the services herein have saved his life and the cunt ain't lying for he nearly died of drugs here not that long ago and a lot of effort was put in to help him.

"I'm so grateful to Rochester for saving my life", he says now and Craig D my warlike friend says:

"Me too Marcus", and turns his attention to the visitors, "if it wasn't for Rochester I'd be dead by now". Craig Mc my big Scottish pal is telling the people, the important looking visitors, that the Forward Trust has saved his life, that he has his family and fiancé back in his world and that he has hope again.

1200hrs. Me and Marcus are banged up, along with the rest of the jail, for lunch. Marcus is, as per usual, absolutely mangled. Opiates, spice, pregablin. He offers me a joint of spice.

"No thanks bro; I meant what I said yesterday mate, it has to stop somewhere".

"I've got a plan", he tells me.

"Oh", I say, "what's the plan of action bro"?

"Honestly", says he, "I'm not taking any more opiates, I'm just gonna use the pregablin to get over the withdrawel and a little bit of spice to help me sleep".

"You are a blind fool Marcus".

"Why d'ya say that"? he asks.

"Behave man".

186

"I know what I'm doing honestly Sloaney", and to avoid any more conversation on the topic Marcus starts doing inane unimportant things like tidying the already immaculate cell and asking bollox questions like:

"Did you get your washing Sloaney"?

"Oh Marcus, you came off that meth mate, crashed off, went through hell and now you're rowing backwards again".

"Sloaney man I want to get clean but it's a fact that people get there in their own way man".

"Yes", I say, "that's true but you just went through such a savage detox, pissing, shitting and puking only now to be retoxing yourself, preparing yourself for one day having to go through that awful depressing process again".

"I know, it don't look good does it".

"No mate, it doesn't", I concur but realize that this conversation isn't for now and that all I can do is have compassion for the fact he has the desire to get clean.

16-11-2019 0900hrs. In the group room but before group starts I want to tell of a conversation in Brad's cell with Grin this morning.

"Got a story for ya", says Grin.

"Oh", I say, my ears pricking because I always need stories for me book.

"Yeah", says Grin, "about ten years ago I was sitting in a pub and this old geezer who I knew, to, like, nod to and that comes up to me, like pulls a chair up to the table I'm sitting at".

"What did he want"?

"Well Sloaney, he sits down and asks me if I smoke weed"......

"Why"?

"When I tell him 'yes'", Grin continues, "he says to me he's got something to show me".

"Like what"? I ask.

"Well, I took him back to my flat and this old boy sits and has a drink before pulling out about four ounces of pukka, and I mean pukka weed".

"So, why did he want to show you it"?

"Well, this is the thing Andy", Grin continues, "I asked the geezer, like, 'what's this' and he says 'this is for you and I want you to call me and give me an opinion on it' and then he left".

"Ok", I say, "what was the weed like and did he leave you the lot"?

"It was the bollox and he left me with the whole four ounces so I phone the geezer up and tell him I can sell the gear all day long and guess what he says to me Sloaney"?

"What"?

"He said to me 'I've got four kilos of that, how much do you reckon you can get me for each unit'? and I told him I can get at least four thousand pounds a kilo knowing I could get at least £6000 for this weed 'cause I swear to you mate it was banging. So I started selling kilos and the geezer kept getting more and more but one day he calls me and tells me he's got a load of amphetamine which really ain't my thing but I told him to bring a tester round and he does. The geezer clearly wasn't a drug user 'cause soon as I saw the stuff I knew it wasn't speed".

"Fuckin' hell", I say, getting excited, "what the fuck was it"?

"I snorted a line and I swear to ya I burst out in a sweat and the side of my face went numb with the twang of pure cocaine mate".

"Jesus", say I, "tell me you washed some of it up"?

"I'm telling you mate", says my tall business man esq friend, "it was the best coke I've ever had in my life and I swear to you it washed up cold".

"What, no heat"?

"Nope. It was the best crack I've ever had in my life and soon as I told the geezer he went 'right, good, I've got ten kilos of that'"!

"Fuck me, where the fuck did he get all this shit from"?

"I'll get to that", Grin responds, "so I go and see these yardies and they were taking two 'key' (kilograms) a week mate. At one point I was driving round with a quarter 'key' of personal in the footwell of me car with a Glock handgun for protection", and I don't doubt Grin for a minute and he continues that "at one point Andy my wardrobe had £108,000 stuffed in shoeboxes and I just didn't know what the fuck to do with all the money and coke I had round me".

"What happened"?

"Well, this is the bit", he says, "it turned out the reason this fella was getting all these drugs was because the incinerator used to burn the drugs found by the police at Sheppey docks was broken".

"What, they destroy the drugs at an incinerator located at the docks"?

"Yeah, but it was busted and the next nearest one is at the hospital in Medway where the geezer works".

"Wow", I say.

"So this incinerator was manned by just one man-this fella-and what he used to do was when the police would bring the drugs to be destroyed he had two incinerators. Now one you could just go down this little walkway bit, lift a flap and see the drugs burning but the other side was a real squeeze to get to the flap so because it's all done by computer what he did was just run a test programme which to all intents and purposes would look as if it was firing but actually it wouldn't be. The police would just sit in the office with him watching the programme running thinking all was well the silly cunts"!

"Wow", I say, suitably impressed, "genius. Did he ever get nicked"?

"He did in the end", says Grin, "'cause the cunt started turning up to work on a Ducatti dressed head to foot in Armani. Even though the cunt must have been sixty he used to pull it off as he was a dapper sprightly fucker. Anyway, he got an eight year stretch but that ain't the end of it. It took me twelve weeks to kill off all the money I'd made. So, one day I'm sitting in Medway magistrates court waiting to go up before the beak for something silly when suddenly two old bill plot up either side of me in the waiting area and told me they knew I'd sold all the drugs and that by hook or by crook they were going to get me".

"Did they"?

"Never heard another thing about it Sloaney", says Grin, grinning!

"Fuckin' lucky", I say.

"You know that don't ya", says he, "tell ya what though mucca, the state of me after all the drugs and money had gone-I was fucked mate"!

"Ever see the fella again"?

"Nope, never seen him since, mad in it"?

"Fuck me Grin, I need to go put this on paper".

"I'm going to work now anyway you old cunt so I'll see you later".

"Less of the old"! I say, smiling.

"Well you're no spring chicken Sloaney", says Brad, "ya bunions don't look so out of place now you're going grey"! and the fucker laughs like he's the funniest fucker ever. I too can't help but chuckle though 'cause the cunt also has flippers for feet.

"You pair a cunts", I say, loving my mates and the banter, "see ya when you get back".

1300 16-1-2019. Me and Marcus are banged up for lunch now and watching Piers and Susanna doing an interview on Loose Women. We both agree that Susanna is the sexiest woman alive with the best banter! We lament the fact that the chairman of Crystal Palace football club has turned her head. Anyway, I shan't bore you with our pesty conversations. Marcus is actually coherent and has not yet used any drugs. We are back in the group room for Bridge two 'till three then at the gym which we are both looking forward to. News is on and Brexit forefront. What a mess! Does the sovereignty of the people and the vote not matter? It is clear the remainer majority commons is not doing the will of the people. The House has been decimated and parties divided by the whole shoddy affair. And the dithering is allowing for a proliferation of racist isolationism exacerbated by the fury people are feeling as we hesitate in

189

navigating these dark choppy waters. We must have some cross party consensus that whether we like it or not we are leaving Europe. It is done. The people spoke. Anyway, enough of that. I sometimes wonder at the loving way we prisoners and old friends interact with each other, like the way me and Brad greeted each other upon returning from work just before the bang up period for lunch.

"Slicker ya mug", says Brad to me, "ya coming round for a coffee before bang up ya pedo"?

"Who the fuck ya talking to bro? I'll smash the fuck outta ya"!

"You couldn't smash yaself up ya soppy cunt", he returns.

"Right guv", I say, hailing a screw, "open this mug's door so I can carve the cunt up please".

"Hahaha", Brad replies, "don't worry guv, he's got mental health problems", and even the officer finds our banter amusing. On the way back to my cell for bang up I see Peter Lanes, whom I love, the fat fuck, sitting at the dining table and when he looks up I'm like:

"Who you looking at ya fat fuck"?

"You ya cunt, come on, get in the cell and I'll smash the fuck out of ya ya skinny little prick".

"Right", I say, "that's it", then I turn to the screw who's tryna get everyone behind their doors, "guv, turn ya back please whilst I smash the granny outta this plank a wood".

"Ok", says the screw, "but be quick", and me and Pete just laugh! This sort of talk is a regular part of daily life here, especially with us boys who hail from the same plot. Anyway, I'm gonna have a look at a Richard Gross psychology book and perhaps have a nap if God be willing.

Door's just opened and I am sitting in the group room alone loving the sunlight streaming through the window. Fine filaments of dust dance and swirl in the fingers of light and I get up and switch off the strip lighting to enjoy the effect. Outside the open door I can hear someone shouting out the corner of a cell door:

"Oi, guv, open my fuckin' door I've got education", and the cute Ms H goes and opens the disgruntled con up. Steve, one of the facilitators of Bridge here employed by the Forward Trust has just walked in carrying a stereo and I am guessing we are gonna be doing some sort of meditation session. Jan his colleague now comes in too and she is arguing with Marcus, who follows her, about the fact that here on Bridge using drugs is not tolerated past one warning. Marcus is saying:

"It just feels like if people are honest and admit to a slip up they get punished".

"Yes Marcus", Jan tells him, "but this is an abstinence based programme and we need to have some boundaries in place". I myself am going to get a warning for I should have been clean when I started the group process on Monday but I have now been clean nearly 48hrs. I can't believe I have gotten nearly two days beneath my belt. Anyway, we are not meditating but having an art hour with music, relaxation music. I am writing, seven other prisoners are painting or drawing pictures and I feel profoundly peaceful, like this room is a regular Xanadu right now. And I marvel that if I can feel this way here in jail then it shouldn't be so hard to have gratitude outside. There is an ambience in this room here right here right now. Even the psycho Craig D and Terry Hughes the fight loving fucks are sitting silently scribbling away. Hyper Manchester little long haired Reece, still alive on here and having cleared his debts is also actually quiet as he plods away at a mock English exam paper. Even the idea of having a bunch of can't usually sit still for a minute fucked up lunatics silently absorbed in art or study in a room together is difficult to believe.

0500hrs 18-1-2019. Me and Marcus have just woken up. It is five a.m and the DAB is making some awful strange noises and I get the raving hump and throw my pen and paper down and turn the cunt of a thing off when Marcus tells me too.

"Fuck sake Sloaney no need to get angry".

"Well why didn't you get the fuck up and turn the poxy thing off yourself instead of laying there and giving me orders"?

"Well, you don't have to start writing first thing in the fuckin' morning do ya"? he says.

"Actually, I do mate; I like to write all day if I can ya miserable moody cunt".

"Alright Sloaney", he says, smiling now the fucker, "don't blow a fuckin' fuse will ya"? Anyway, I, dear reader, have had another day without using. Can you Adam and Eve it? And know this: when I say I haven't used I mean I have not used anything bar coffee and the occasional sneaky roll up when it is available. So, today I won't be on Bridge for I have my final maths exam this morning, at level 2. It is kind of sad for I won't be in the class with AddemupAde anymore but I will never forget him that is for sure.

1345hrs and Fats was released today. He left me with his phone number and gave me a warm hug prior to prancing out the gate. It was lovely to have a hug for it's not something prisoners tend to do that much though I'm not short on love in here right now. It is lovely to be popular but if I pick up and start using spice again I dare say it wouldn't be long before I really do push people away for even those closest to me were getting tired of my mood swings, sulking and aggression. Anyway, I did my exam and it took me the whole of the allotted two hours as I was careful to check and recheck my calculations. Some of my working out wasn't pretty but I'm quite sure I've done enough to pass though seeing some fails from a couple other students the other day has left me concerned that maybe I'll have failed. However, on the whole, I think I did enough. So, it is Black Eye Friday and me and Marcus are arguing. Now, people, as you know, I am on my third day of abstinence. As I reported, Marcus has been to hell and back recently; he was polydrug using so many substances simultaneously: methadone, heroin, crack, buscopan, valium, pregablin, spice and anything else the cunt could get his hands on on the wing. The breakdown he had when his wits left him fucked him up big time. Not only was he in extreme psychosis, he was physically fucked too, shitting and pissing himself and puking whilst trying to bite through the steel chains with which he was tethered to the metal prison bed. For two months the poor cunt lay like that in fevered delirium yet today he is not only continuing to smoke the spice, taking subutex and copious amounts of pregablin and gabapentin, he has just ordered two A4 sheets of power paper spice. He is telling me now that:

"I just love drug dealing Sloaney and there's so much money in it".

"Not for you there ain't ya silly cunt", I tell him gently, "you're a junkie Marcus, don't you get it"?

"I'm just gonna use some of it to get over this rattle (withdrawel from opioids) Sloaney and anyway, I thought you was gonna support me bro"?

"Marcus", I say slowly, "recovery is selfish and I'm trying to get better bro. I could suffer you having a few joints for a few days but arranging pages and coveting pregabs and gabbis and subutex whenever the door is open you're just going back to square one bro".

"Drop me out Sloaney, please man", and I do, I love the cunt and enjoy being banged up with him. In other news, canteen day and as of yet I know of no punches or assaults having come to pass. Some moody faces and plenty of spice on the wing though. I just went into the office and Mr Mads, Ms Nixon and my fave Ms Gilchrest were sitting chatting; looking at the latters face makes me smile. I walk in, call 'em all lazy fuckers then seeing her looking at me and smiling as if to say 'fuck off' I smile back, stick my fingers up at her and walk out the office. Great banter that one. I make my way to Brad's cell. I sit. Gibbo comes in fuming 'cause cunts, as usual, don't fuckin' fly straight but believe me Gibbo will get paid as he really won't stand for anything less than those that owe him doing so. I wouldn't want the genuinely good hearted little psycho coming after me. Terry Hughes comes in and shares a roll up with me and Brad just brought a litre of hooch for some spice and offers me a cup which I politely decline. Now there is an alarm going off on the wing but I can't be fucked to go and investigate. The inevitable sounds of heavy boots on the landing now as the mufty squad come to deal with whatever it is that is going down: spice attack, fight, self harming, who fuckin' knows?! Paul Stone, a former partner in pugilism with me who surprised me with his hefty punch which rocked my jaw one day just poked his head in looking for Brad but Brad has left the cell, guarded by me in order that he can go do the rounds to collect his vapes in. A lot of people are pissed up on the wing as is usual as all the hooch people have been brewing comes out on pay day. I myself am somewhat richer now Phil The Face is no longer on the wing but he is my mate so I will at least trickle him a pack of vapes every week for I owe him hundreds and he is being very kind about it. Grin comes in and sits in Brad's recessed toilet area where he lights a joint of spice.

"D'ya wanna puff of this or what Sloaney"? he asks and I again respectfully decline the invitation but am sorely, sorely tempted to be truthful. I remind myself that no sooner I put my lips to the thing I enter into a whole world of pain and will hunt and hunt and hunt, demoralising myself and throwing my dignity to the floor, stamping all over my self respect as Brad, now back in the cell, politely reminds me as he rolls a proper rollup for he and I to share. I love these couple a cunts, him and Grin. J.T has just come in the cell and tells us that he can't raise the vapes he owes Marcus and I tell him not to worry too much.

"It's like Marcus thinks he can bully me", he is saying, "expecting me to pull the vapes out me arse".

"Just do what you can J.T", I reassure him.

"Furthermore", he continues, "the long haired lifer down the gym has asked Marcus to punch me as hard as he can over a £25 debt I had with him on 'B' wing like fuckin' ages ago but I told the long haired lifer bully cunt I ain't paying him 'cause the spice was shit", and I can see J.T has the hump as he goes on that, "if anyone punches me over that we'll be rolling about then I'll go down the gym with a shank and poke the cunt up", and let me tell you dear reader I don't doubt him at all. There are many irate people on the wing as this canteen day plays out and there is a fella I don't know behind his door downstairs with a smashed up face which must account for the fracas I heard earlier. Oh, also, in other news, we were stuck down education for half an hour after the usual allotted coming back to the wing time due to a debtor who didn't want to return to his wing being on a roof. Standard way of avoiding having to pay it would seem at present.

1730hrs. Ok. So, that's canteen day done. Banged up for the evening. Marcus is sitting smoking spice out his fuckin' nut but I am ok thank the good Lord. He has the desire, our Marcus, to get clean but I simply feel he is not quite ready yet. Anyway, before bang up my Jewish mate Max had come up to me and said, eyes all asparkle:

"Sloaney man, Sloaney, I've got a book you just have to read bro".

"Oh yeah, what"?

"The Secret", he says, excitedly.

"No fuckin' way", I say, "read it from cover to cover twice two years ago: fuckin' amazing read man, all we need to do is ask".......

"And the universe will see to it you get it", he says.

"But you need to believe", I say.

"Yes you do", and we both laugh like we are indeed sharing a secret. In more news, Tony Giles or Piles as I call him, my long term friend of old has been kicked off the wing for refusing to cooperate and submit to regular testing to keep him on this, what is supposed to be, the drug free wing! I don't know why he doesn't comply the silly cunt for spice doesn't show up on the tests anyway for as soon as a test is developed which does work the spice makers simply change a molecule causing the detection of the drug to once more be made obsolete. As fast as the tests are developed the structure of the drug is also changed to beat the system thus it being the prisoners drug of choice. He has gone to 'B' wing I believe. Anyway, in this cell now I peruse the Gita, enjoying the tale of Arjuna and Krishna. Edifying myself I hope.

Saturday 19th Jan 2019 1007hrs. Morning people. It is out in the morning and banged up this arvo for us on Alpha wing though we get out for the gym for an hour at three o'clock, those of us that are partial to pumping our muscles up. As usual, I am in Frad's cell surrounded by only my Thanet friends and Grin. So, in the cell are Marcus and Jake and Ricky Lanes brother of Peter, Brad, Gibbo and of course me. On the telly of course a nature programme is playing but Brad is busy peeling apart a nicotine patch and adding PG Tips to the solution to smoke. Steve Kemp, another Thanet boy, long haired, tall and handsome and a funny pisstaking fucker who has just landed on the wing has just come into the cell and we can barely breathe in here. J.T is now regaling tales of his nicking, his arrest:

"Yeah", he is saying, "Arge and Broomy (officers) just looked me up on google and it came up in Kent On Line and my mugshot came up and it says how the police followed me on a pushbike and how I tried to throw the drugs I was selling and how when I tried to get away the other

194

old bill in a car threw his baton at my legs on my bike and I crashed and got nicked but it's the comments from the people below saying 'I've never done anything good for society and should be given the lethal injection' man, wow", he continues, "people are fuckin ruthless man". J.T is reasonably compis mentis right about now it would seem. He makes me read his vernacular back to him and seems pleased at the possibility of preservation. Now Jake is talking about his offence where he killed the fella sitting in the passenger seat of the car next to him in which he was driving, earning his poor young butt a stiff seven years in prison. This compounded by the fact he has to live with the consequences of what was essentially an accident for the rest of his life, poor cunt. The inimical feeling that pervaded the wing yesterday has thankfully dissipated it would seem. Brad has put 4Music on now and Stormzy is rapping 'you're never too big for the boot'. Legend. Art is reflecting the reality of the country right now, unsavoury and difficult to accept as that reality might be: drug dealing, stabbings, shootings and a disenfranchised youth causing chaos. Some of the youth escaping gangs and poverty by showcasing talent, just like Stormzy is. I dare say some of the values and attitudes replicated for you in this book will make for difficult reading but one fucking fact remains dear reader and that fact is that they are conversations and situations that have happened, that are real, and fact has no opinion on sentiment. Fact is fuckin' fact. So sorry you of the woke brigade. If you find this difficult reading, unfortunately the values and attitudes herein reflect reality for some. Simple. Gibbo and Brad both look a little hungover after a day on the hooch yesterday. As for me, the nasty horrible feeling that the spice, in withdrawel from that, leaves in the tummy has gone thank God. I am managing to abstain despite Smarcus smoking copious amounts right before my very eyes. Brad treats Kempy to two two centimetre long pieces of spice paper for just coming on the wing and being from Thanet. Jake has just told me a story about a pal of his who smoked spice flat out in jail for three years, ended up with a piss and shit bag only to be released and die two weeks later as the nasty spice had already done its damage. This is the gear that is all over the British prison estate right now. Jake himself is holding his belly even as I write, knowing he has to get the spice to alleviate the symptoms.

20-01-2019 0830hrs. Clean day number 5. Sunday morning. No sleep, par for the course with the methadone though. And the spice to be fair. Last night I was close to cracking. Marcus absolutely fucked out his head and temptation came a knocking but I held my line and wake up today with another day under me belt. Marcus got the pages of chemically infused paper and though I struggle at times to maintain my sobriety there are of course perks to living in a cell with a drug dealer. A never ending supply of vape capsules, protein powders and supplements for training and the cell is well stocked with tuna and noodles and beans and sweets and coffee and milk and sugar and myriad other things which make life in here a little easier. Anyway, the reprobate is already highly intoxicated and telling me a tale after I ask him why it was he stabbed a fella we know called G---- about four years ago.

"Well", says this mong right now, "I didn't stab him for nothing Sloaney".

"Yeah, but you stabbed him so bad in the arse cheek and the actual arse hole that he had to sit on a rubber ring for twelve weeks; that's what I heard anyway".

"I did Sloaney", he says, "but what you don't know is that when I was his mate in Dover one day the cunt hit me around the head with a champagne bottle and I didn't see the cunt for two years".

"Fuck me, I'll bet you held a grudge knowing you", I say.

"You're fuckin' right I did but I got my chance and I got the cunt".

"How did you get the slippery slag"? I ask Marcus and indeed G---- is a bit of a snake it must be said.

"Well, on the day I went to my nan's funeral I was coming back from Gravesend with Lauren (screwess) and dropped her off at home. But I went back out in the Audi. I was driving toward Dane Park (a park in Margate) and saw him going into the entrance of the park and it's dark now Sloaney. So I park the Audi and follow on foot. He was with C----, his bird. I followed him, waiting 'till he was in the centre of the park ya know"?

"Well dark in there at night too", I interject.

"Yeah, right, anyway, I creep up on the cunt right Sloaney and I've got the kitchen knife in my hand now right so I creep, creep, creep and he don't see me or hear me and soon as I'm close enough I plunge the nine inch blade straight into his arse, draw the blade back again and aim for the centre of his arse and plunge again into the actual arsehole ya know"?

"Savage", I say.

"Yeah", he goes on, "he dropped to one knee and he wouldn't of even known it was me if I hadn't of said to him 'I'm gonna kill you you cunt".

"Thank fuck you got a not guilty", I say.

"Yeah, but two weeks later I got him again in a traphouse where these Somalians from Woolwich were shotting from".

"What d'ya do to him"? I say, the hairs on my arms standing on end.

"In the traphouse I found two carving knives and opened the cunts' face up, slicing him proper and with the knife in my other hand I go to

196

plunge the cunt in the chest but one of the Somalis grabbed my arm, stopping the kill".

"What happened next"? I ask.

"Well obviously these dangerous Somalis put all their tools, like their own tools in a bin in the bathroom and make me do the same like in a gun and knife amnesty thing and told me if you just calm down we'll give you as many snowballs as you like. They fed me copious amounts of crack and heroin and offered me work as a hitman to take out all the other drug dealers in the area. They fuckin' loved me man". This story has moved me for I only know a nice side of Marcus, the lost soul that has suffered so much but there is a dark side in stark contrast juxtaposed to this character for sure. The description of such savage violence is chilling, even for me, a violent man myself when pushed but unlike Marcus I have, thankfully, never had to use a knife though I have pulled a few on drug dealers.

Anyway, lunchtime now and we are banged up until two PM. Marcus has flopped and is dribbling like a special person having consumed 4mg of subutex, 300mg of pregablin, 4mg of clonazepam and all this atop the myriad joints of spice he has smoked already this Sunday morning. I have to accept I cannot escape the drugs being around me, their spectre always present. I have thought of moving off to another wing but that is pointless for this is supposed to be the drug free wing so if it's flooded on here then, well, you do the math. No matter where I go it's there, as it is in every prison across the country right about now.

1400hrs and we have just been let out. As per I'm in Brad's cell with Max Potter, my Jewish gangster The Secret loving Nibiru curious pal. Ms Terry, wonderful lady screw just gave me a couple brand new pens. These officers on here really are not such a bad bunch and make us feel human. Yes, I stripped metal from an empty house and because of the fact I have forty two previous convictions, many for burglary, thefts, impersonating a police officer, assaults on men trying to arrest me and punching and breaking a fellas nose and also two domestic violence related offences the judge gave me, for this drum, 27 months. Thankfully most of the staff here see past the offence to the person. Right, to summarize the cell right now. Jake is talking to Brad and Ricky Lanes about Peter, Ricky's brother, and his propensity to be extremely slippery in his searching and acquisition of drugs and now Steve Kemp is talking about burgling a house where he managed to get away with thousands of pounds but was caught inside the house by a lady who hit him over the head with a metal bar. I am reminded of the time my mum was working

197

in a charity shop across the road from Boots in Ramsgate High Street and my sister was with her, like, having just popped in to say hello. I came out of Boots after having stolen a lot of perfume and aftershave and a store detective tapped me on the shoulder from behind and not knowing it was a she I turned and punched her clean in the face. Another time in a shop in Whitstable I was caught red handed in the staff only room with my hand in a handbag, pilfering the purse and a lady came in and slapped me round the face. I tried to get out the shop but the fella behind the counter locked the door and I smashed fuck out the shop trying to escape and sunk my teeth into his face but being as I was so young I avoided prison. Exactly, well nearly, the same thing happened on Grange Road in Ramsgate another time where the proprietor caught me in his storeroom stealing cigarettes and though I initially got away he and his son caught up with me in a car and I took a big chunk out the son's arm, again using my teeth in a bid to escape justice. However I was caught in a bin, actually inside a bin by police though to this day I have no fuckin' idea how the fuck they could've known I was in it. You may not like me dear reader but I hope you are enjoying the narrative!! One more thing today: I have been praying a lot lately. Though I am of no religion I feel there is a Higher Power and am reminded of Tennyson's words: 'more things are wrought by prayer than the world dreams of'. And, dear reader, I'm banking on it.

21-01-2019. 0900hrs. In the group room this morning and I can't write much as I must participate. Jan and Steve are here, the facilitators, but no Woody, their colleague, for he is currently off sick and I remember that I had looked at him last week and thought he looked a little off. I'm so proud of me. Six days clean. No chemicals. None. Nada. Just came out of a relaxation exercise which took me off to faraway places. The shoreline alone with the dog and the dark blanket above and I was looking up through it at the constellations in the heavens. I could feel the shapes in the sand beneath my feet. I could hear the gentle lapping of the waves. Hear the occasional squawk of a solitary seagull and the dog's breathing as it pelts up and down the beach excitedly beside me with not a care in the world. Just had a break, cup of coffee and a quick vape. Back in the room now. Ricky Lanes is using the group to share his concerns around his son Steven who has started using crack cocaine. Hearing his worry the first thought that goes through my head on hearing this is 'futility' for when someone first picks up drugs of this nature they have a journey before them and there's no words in the world that will convince them to stop until the drug has brought them to their knees. I'm a little restless right now sitting here hearing this. Very sad

198

that a young man who's watched his father go in and out of jail for crimes born of his need to get money for drugs should think it a good idea to follow in such flawed footsteps. And poor Ricky is powerless and in pain.

1745hrs and we are banged up. Mong time for Marcus as I sit on the comfy cloth chair in the cell scribing away for you with my pen. He is truly pickled as per usual and is currently smoking his spice in a camomile tea bag roll up having run out of the ridiculously inflated of price real tobacco he buys. Wu Tang Clan on the radio rapping 'cash moves everything around me cream get the money, dollar dollar bill yall' and now it's Biggy the legend with 'if ya don't know, now ya know, nigga'. These guys kept me alive in aggression for many years. Next Marcus puts on a little Tupac who is saying 'I ain't a killer but don't push me, revenge is like the sweetest thing next to getting pussy'. I love these bangers but my music of choice when selling drugs from Invicta House on Millmead estate for many years was the sound of Mobb Deep with the album 'Infamous' which has those epic tracks '41st Side' with the lyrics in one of the verses saying 'if I don't know your face then don't come close to me I got too much beef for that, it's drama in the first degree and to the kids you don't wanna be me I'm up in the mix of action and niggas wanna kill me, but it's the start of their ending'......and their other bangers 'Survival Of The Fittest' and 'Shook Ones'. I had this album pretty much on loop through my Technics amp and the neighbours fuckin' hated me. I used to drive the fourteen floors mental with my antics. Junkies from far and wide partying twentyfour seven at my gaff. Of course Eminem had a place on my playlist too and even his newer stuff is fantastic with the likes of 'Bagpipes From Bagdad' having the hair on my carcass standing on end. My descriptions of music remind me of Brett Easton Ellis and his protagonist in American Psycho. Wonderful, brutal reading. Anyway, Marcus is looking decidedly downsy right now, just like J.T and I guess I too look when out me nut on the spice. I think of the book Dune now where the spice is the life blood of the planet.

"You're fucked Marcus", I say to the benny on the bottom bunk who is literally, literally dribbling big globules of spittle from his mouth which runs down his chin and drips in a steady stream onto his bare and hairless having been shaved chest. He opens heavy eyes:

"Errr, why you takin' the pishhhh outta me Shhhhloaney man ur ha ur ha ur ha", and he is smiling like a demented and very brain dead zombie and I think to myself that I shouldn't laugh as the lovely silly cunt looks at me through his bright baby blue eyes. Now he manages, just, to relight his joint but the fuck can't, truly can't find his mouth, instead putting the end of the thing to his cheeks, chin, eyeball before finally hitting the mark and I tell him:

"You look like a proper spastic man", and realize from here in Oxford as I type such language that I, too, though I did not know it then, was still very spiritually unwell at the time.

"Urrrrhhhh", he says, "you're bang out of order Shhhloaney man", but I am just happy, in the cell back then, that it ain't me. Before we had banged up me, Marcus, Steve Kemp, Peter Lanes, Ricky Lanes and Jake were all in Brad's cell, packed in like sardines, absolutely laughing our nuts off as we remember some antics from many moons before. First we reminisced about the time me, Brad and Peter all took 'purple om' acid tabs with a friend of ours from old called Justin L who was clearly terrified of the trip he found himself experiencing. Before mine had started working on me Justin had turned to me sitting beside him on the sofa and said solemnly that he had:

"Just shattered into a million pieces", and he continued that he thought he was going to die but for some reason this was the catalyst for the coming on of my tab and I turned to him and started laughing hysterically, lost for seven hours in that realm, creasing up for the whole time to the point of splitting sides and tears and tears of pure unadulterated mirth. Some months later around the same house, Rosie Georgio's in Ramsgate me, Pete and Brad were again with Justin and this time the tabs were called 'strawberries' and were known for causing hilarity but Justin was too scared to take one, happy instead to sit and smoke weed but Brad having none of it stuck one in a cheeseburger and fed it to Justin who sat in petrified silence for hours thinking, I guess, that the weed was strong 'till Brad couldn't help enlightening him to the truth of his situation but I was gone anyway, again in mirth of deepest design. Don't worry dear reader for Karma bit me in the arse when I took a 'penguin' tab with Tony Beumont, David Gardner God rest him, Channon Hughes who is now due to have a leg amputated through injecting heroin, Brad and Tristan 'Trip' Woods bless the latter soul, some months later and just as I was coming up on the acid a Chinese man shut my fingers in the door of the twenty four hour garage which sent me spiralling into a trip of terror which lasted many hours and profoundly affected my psyche and still does even to this day. I visited Hades that night for sure. I still have recurring dreams of that trip where I am on an ancient black bark cutting through inky black seas in which the backs of unspeakable beasts breach the surface of the foul brackish waters and rise up like the Craken to consume me. The boat goes through piers which are either side of the ship and there are lamp poles and hanging off of these are human sized bird cages and skeletal remains grip the bars in silent screams of mortal terror. And though not in prison, I know, in the trip and the recurring dreams that I am in jail, hopeless, helpless and terrified. Anyway. The spice has finally finished Marcus for the night and the handsome knob I have much love for is laying with food all round his full mouth and up his face and there's grease on his designer jeans. I wish I had a camera so I could film him for you. And him. Maybe that would shock him into relative sanity. I've not the power of description to comprehensively capture how comical the cunt looks in his tragedy. Kempy was telling me a tale of when Marcus and he were banged up together some time last year and they both could've died of smoke inhalation in the cell. Marcus had turned Steve on to Buscopan tablets and their intoxicating qualities when crushed on foil and smoked. Both of them were also smoking much spice and Steve said that in his trip he thought he was an athlete and that he had been honoured having been asked to light and carry the Olympic torch. So, out his fuckin' nut Steve had rolled up newspaper and lit it and was running around and around in circles in the cell holding the 'torch' aloft celebrating and smiling I dare say idiotically believing he was parading past throngs of jubilant people until he realized through the haze of drugs that he had set fire to the jumper he was wearing and he had tried to put the now flaming garment out the window with the burning newspaper 'torch' but of course the windows do not open, grilled as they are and now there is fire all around the cell floor and whilst Marcus sat smiling his big toothy smile Steve in now sobering terror had put out the blaze and they'd both laughed their heads off but oh the situation could've, had the bedding and other fabrics and books and magazines in the tiny space caught alight, been so much worse. They had both, said Kempy, laughed their nuts off at this afterward and it is funny but also quite frightening too I reckon. Death by smoke inhalation or burning I guess ain't quite so comical.

Same day, 2030 hrs and Marcus is snoring like a dirty old diesel engine, like a tractor and the Secret Life of the Zoo is on TV. I feel I want to talk to you about Bruce Jenner of Kardashian fame. He is challenging my thinking see. He is currently transitioning into a trans woman. Firstly, to me, a tranny isn't a woman for they can never be internally female and have babies and periods and PMS. And I get angry when I see tranny women competing in normal women sports and winning all the accolades. Savage. But, I used to be scathing about trans people period. But, well, I like Bruce I think. Now, I just don't feel I can come to accept that it is a good idea to fuck around with God's design you see. But I can't help but have a bit of a soft spot for the long haired and loving sporting legend. Look, I'm willing to take advice on this gender fluidity thing and I dare say that if Piers Morgan can get his head around it then so can I. There is one saving grace as far as old Brucey bonus is concerned and that is the fact that he will be using his own money to turn his todger inside out. So if he wants a surgeon to savage his sausage and sort him a pair of tits I guess it is up to him but I can't help but feel an innate dis-ease about the whole issue for kids are coming home aged nine and ten telling their parents they are born in the wrong body and this is anathema to me; not the kids but the response from society and medical infrastructure which panders to such shite to the point of assisting kids not yet in puberty with the transition which to me is criminal. Anyway, I do like Bruce but prefer to gaze upon his progeny and step progeny though they are all compounding this problem endemic in the modern era of obsession with appearance, pumped up lips and tit and bum implants and botox and fillers and fuck knows what other shite has cunts making millions from the collective insecurity borne of addiction to misguiding media. But Brucey Brucey, don't you like your willy anymore? Are you sick of sinking it? If not, why not just go gay and have your arse pumped like the rest of the homo population? Marcus has opened an eye and is trying to talk to me now but it comes out like a load of blubbering idiotic mumbo jumbo and I'm trying to avoid using vernacular like 'spastic' 'mong' 'retard' 'downsy' etc but in response to his nonsensical noises I respond with:

"Marcus, I don't speak mong mate sorry bro", but he is once again gone and hears me not but snores and blows snot from his nostrils. From Marcus' pointing I think he was asking me to do him a cup of tea but that ain't gonna happen as it'd no doubt end up all over him for the cunt can't find his mouth with a joint let alone a scolding cup of cha. Marcus is the first ever junkie I have met greedier than me. And I'm a hardcore glutten greedy fucker make no mistake. Just ask those who grew up with me who was the glutton and they would tell you me. But Marcus is next level shit in his consuming of poisons. Anyway reader I have had enough now and am gonna lay down my pen to peruse more of the Gita. Bye for now.

23-01-2019. 0830hrs. By the Universe I feel good today. Day eight with no Persian rugs and the obsession to use has been lifted. Marcus is up, out his nut and trying to tell me how to open sugar sachets.

"Marcus", I begin.

"No Sloaney, I'm just showing you the best way to open them is all".

"Marcus mate, I'm a reasonably intelligent bloke and know how to open a paper packet", and now the cunt is having a wash in the sink, stark bollock naked and as per usual, despite the fact he knows I'm

202

heterosexual, is waving his manhood like a kid discovering his cock for the first time.

"Get dressed for fuck sake you iron".

"I know you want it really Sloaney", he says, advancing toward me menacingly. I know the cunt is joking but the other day whilst I washed he pressed the thing up against my boxer shorted butt giving me the raving hump.

"Marcus, for fuck sake man", I say, genuinely disconcerted and disturbed.

"huh huh huh huh", he laughs already very inebriated despite the early hour.

"Get dressed you fuckin' faggot", I say, dismissing him with a wave of me hand. Anyway, I'm now wondering if my blasphemy throughout this narrative will earn me the same as it did Salman Rushdie for his excellent book The Satanic Verses. Have I blasphemed in this work? When I read the work just mentioned I was expecting a diatribe against Islam but found instead a comedic novel that started with a couple of fellas falling from the sky; can't remember much for I read it years ago but it wasn't what I expected. I do remember that the book I read after was Philosophy In The Boudoir by the Marquis De Sade. And that did indeed shock me. Depictions of the sewing up of vaginas and smashing pregnant women together if I remember correctly. Monstrous descriptions of sexual violence. Found it in the prison library. Anyway, door is about to open and I already have the beans and tuna and bread ready to cook on the facilities downstairs soon as it does.

0855hrs and I am sitting in the group room with 'Woody' the facilitator and awaiting the arrival of the rest of the gathering. Ricky Lanes is with us and complaining about the fact his window in his cell is broken and that it is leaving him freezing cold all through the night. Mine and Marcus window is also hanging off and I don't have the tool J.T made. Ricky is saying right now that he is:

"Not fuckin' happy I tell ya".

"Ours is the same Rick", says Marcus.

"Chris Brown just got nicked for rape", says Craige D now.

"I'm not a racist but it's always them fuckin' darkies", says Terry Hughes now and there are murmurs of assent from some and denial of this erroneous statement from others. Hyperactive Manchester Reece just joined us and Pete Harlow, a slim five foot eight fair headed fella comes in shortly after, sitting in the circle of chairs alongside us. Craige just shared an excellent poem he wrote with us and I ask him if I can have a copy for my book and he says:

"Course ya can". Woody is alone facilitating today. He is a rotund, tattoed, barrel chested bear of a guy who looks like he could be a competitor on Worlds' Strongest Man. He is in stark contrast to the demure Jan with whom he works! These worthy people are passionate about recovery and helping people get better. Anyway, Terry Winters, a slim grey headed fella of about forty, quite morose to be fair and whom I've seen on many of my previous sentences is opening up in the group and just said that:

"Though I'm close to my family I still feel like a stranger and like I don't belong", and I myself can relate to this. I had to put my pen and paper down but I can tell you that we explored jealousy, anger, sadness and frustration at length.

Ok, lunchtime bang up and Marcus is hard at it though he says he is still gonna come gym today. I can't wait for that sweaty hour and feel myself getting stronger as the methadone and spice are well out me system though sleep is still sketchy. Just before bang up Peter Lanes and Kempy were in the cell telling Marcus and Jake of the time in Canterbury prison on 'B' wing when I shat myself whilst playing pool many years ago. I had stood after taking a shot and squeezed a reluctant withdrawel driven fart out at velocity and felt something warm and wet roll down my trouser leg. Shaking the leg I was horrified when a small round pellet fell from the bottom of my slacks. An old schoolfriend and superb fraudster pal of mine saw the thing and said to me:

"What's that Sloaney, a lump of puff"?

"No mate, I just shat meself bro", and I'd run up to my cell hoping the incident would be confined to me and Scott but no, it was out the bag or out me arse so to speak. Scott, in hysterics, the cunt couldn't contain himself and shouted to the whole wing that:

"Oi, oi, everyone, Sloaney just shat himself", and I had all the incarcerated firm, including that cunt Peter Lanes the slag and Just For Men Kempy laughing their fuckin' heads off along with the rest of the wing. Of course I took it in good humour, no other way really, embarrassing though it was. Then Marcus was telling the assembled that in the here and now at night in the cell I keep looking at the photos of his sexy blonde bird, Lauren, who is up in pictures all over the wall and asking him if I might get the chance to fuck the life outta her.

"Honestly, no, listen", he tells Kempy, (Steve Kemp) Peter and Jake, "he keeps saying that if I let him fuck me missus he'll let me have a go on his sister"!

"What", asks Kempy, "is your sister fit Sloaney"?

"Well", I say, "I suppose she's a bit of a tool yeah", and the cell erupts into laughter.

"No way Sloaney", says Pete.

"Sloaney man", says Jake.

"You're fucked Andy", says Steve Kemp.

"No", I say now, trying to backtrack on my misinterpreted words, "I just mean she's a handsome enough woman ya know"?

"No fuckin' way"! says the cunt Pete Lanes.

"Oh fuck off you lot", I say, "I just mean that she ain't ugly lads for fuck sake".

"Would you do her though Andy"? asks Kempy.

"Fuckin' behave will ya", I say, "but I did used to watch my auntie shagging through the keyhole of her bedroom door when I was a kid"!

"Noooooo", says Jake as the cell descends into mirth.

"Look", I say, "everyone's curious as kids boys that's all ya know"?

"Is she fit though, your auntie"? asks Just For Men Kempy the cunt.

"Well, yeah, actually she is proper hot though of course she's a bit older now", and I regret it instantly as the room once again descends into raucous laughter.

"Sloaney man you really are fucked", says Marcus now, getting his two pence worth in.

"Well travellers marry cousins so the odd impure thought about an auntie can surely be forgiven lads for fuck sake", I say.

"Would you fuck her though Sloaney"? and this of course comes from Kempy the good looking Just For Men loving cunt of a comedian.

"Only if I had to to save the human race", I say, "I mean, I'd rather fresh genetics but necessity is the mother of all invention as they say"!

24-01-2019 Lunchtime bang up and I want to just check in with you. Just to confirm, man has not had any mind altering substances for nine days now. Marcus, this morning with spice paper, brought me a Ralph Lauren T shirt, a pair of tracky bottoms and a Superdry jumper the kind ass cunt. Last night whilst the poor misfortunate was monged out on his own paper product I drove him mad with such facts as the 2.5 million light year distance to the Andromeda galaxy and its capacity and density of suns being twice that of our own Milky Way, the speed at which light travels (186,282 miles per second), the size of CY Canis Majoris and the 1100 years it would take to do one orbit of that massive star at transatlantic speed, the 93 million mile distance to our sun, the 72 times more massive than every other planet in the solar system put together giant that is Jupiter, the marvel of its Great Red Spot storm and the eight and a half minutes it takes the light of the sun to reach us here on earth.

Then I bored him with the Gita, marvelling at the use of terms like antimatter and atoms and Cosmic Lord being used so long ago. Then I proceeded to recite my favourite poem ever to him, Hardy's Darkling Thrush which I've driven my erudite brother P---- mad with over the years. I then gave him Anthem For Doomed Youth and excitedly told him that Owen penned such prettiness whilst being under fire on the front line where he then lost his life. Then it was Kubla Khan from worthy naturally brilliant Coleridge then Tyger Tyger before I bored the poor sod further by quoting the first twenty lines or so of Henry The Forth Part 2: "So shaken as we are, so wan with care, find we a time for frighted peace to pant"...........In the end the poor cunt, Marcus's head was not only battered with the drugs but also with my warblings and hyperactive tones. Anyway, today, in anticipation of Black Eye Friday tomorrow a little cunt called Elliot who was banged up with Just For Men Kemp our Thanet pal bounced when Steve was at work owing Brad two packs of vapes and Marcus three and a blonde tall cunt called Tom who owed Marcus £30 by bank transfer also slipped off to another wing to hide the cunt. Marcus is now monged on the bed. I rowed, on the rowing machine, 10,000 metres yesterday and Marcus repped out on his rocks and boulders. (shoulders). Bye for now.

25-01-2019 0639hrs Morning dear reader; I have had but three hours sleep but can't be anything but grateful for those blessed moments given to me by God above. Also, I am making a conscious effort not to masturbate for the preservation of my prana in the physical form of seminal fluid gives my synapses something of a sharper edge. So though each night I consistently toss and turn in my bed I do not rip the head off my purple tipped warrior and this is no mean feat for abstaining from playing with the poker can leave a fella damn uncomfortable at times. Saying that, my technique of distracting myself when the urge comes on of picking up a book or penning this for you is reasonably effective. When we stop using and it is now ten days chem free, our libido is one of the first things to rear its head. Remember we have hot staff on here like the lovely Ms H who has pricks standing all over the wing but I do try to avoid fawning all over the female officers as watching others do so is an uncouth sight indeed! I spent an hour yesterday at the ATB (Programmes Unit) where I did wonderful work with the facilitators Jason Gould whom I've built something of a warm relationship with and Naomi the peach faced lovely long distance all year round freezing cold water swimmer. And of course present was Lucy K who is not only truly absolutely stunning but also extremely bright compounding that beauty further for intelligence on a sexy chick is surely the most alluring asset of all! Anyway, sorry for the boring stuff but I want you to get a comprehensive overview of a modern prison estate. Smarcus still snores to my right as I write, re knocked out at 5am with another pipe of nasty spice. I am trying to be more understanding and it would do well for me to remember that the obsession to use has lifted for me but I can't expect others to follow my lead for they have their own personal journeys to traverse.

Just came out of our Friday morning NA meeting and I feel hopeful that the likes of me and Craig Mc can inspire others in the room to see that there is hope through twelve step fellowship. Now in me and Marcus's cell are Peter and Ricky Lanes and Beany from next door all talking to Marcus trying to get spice out the poor cunt who put everything he had out onto the wing yesterday and has nothing left. 4Music is on the box with a song singing 'body on my innocence' and a sexy young chick dances alluringly and we all watch lasciviously. Next a song from Little Mix comes on and Pete Lanes goes of the light skinned beauty:

"She's got the fittest arse".

"I like Perry best", I say.

"Yeah", Pete says again of the mixed race one, "even though she's a shit skin she's fit", and I turn to him aghast and dear publisher this is simply the truth of what I hear. Offensive, yes, but what I am experiencing in real time right now.

"What'd'ya mean"? I say.

"Well for a nigger she's fit and I like fuckin' black bird's pink fannies 'cause the old lips are like rose petals"! says Peter.

"I'd fuck any one of 'em", says Marcus.

"Pete", I say, "you know what you just said is savagely offensive don't ya mate? I mean, that's a brutal point of view you have there bro"?

"Yeah yeah", he says, completely oblivious, "let me tell you about Paddy G----", he continues, "you know Gina P---- right"?

"Yeah", I say and we are all listening to him.

"Well", he says, "Paddy pulled her and took her back to Bleak House in Broadstairs, ya know, the one Charles Dickens used to live in or something and Gina's old man"..........

"Todd P the entrepeneur", I say.

"Yeah, right, anyway, Paddy took her back there and the reason he had to leave Thanet was because he hated her for some reason right so she thinks she's going to get fucked but he handcuffs her to the bed in Bleak House and puts a cucumber up her arse and a dildo in her cunt and left her there for Todd P and his wife to find".

"No fuckin' way", Marcus says, "I wondered why he ain't been about for years".

"Savage", I say.

"Yep", continues Pete, "that's the reason he fucked off 'cause the old man woulda had him killed. Proper handcuffed her then stuffed both holes with things, left 'em hanging out of her for her parents. Imagine seeing ya little girl stuffed with a dildo and a cucumber and gagged and that"! And, dear reader, I merely recall these tales faithfully for you! Must I make them more pretty? Lie and twist the reality? I think fuckin' not! Distasteful as these tales may be they are what I hear and what I see. And art need be faithful or it ain't fuckin' art at all. Now Mabel the sexy songstress is on the telly singing one of her bangers and I go to the room:

"She ain't half fit this one if a little sketty", and Rick Lanes says:

"Yeah she's sexy but, I dunno, there's something just a bit down syndromy about her ya know? Don't get me wrong, I'd still do her but she looks like she ain't quite right if you ask me"! And Marcus says:

"Have you got shit in your eyes or something Rick"? Meghan Trainor comes on next with 'It's All About The Bass' and Rick has something to say on her too:

"Bet she's got a burger cunt, like, bit a lettuce hanging out ya know", and wow dear reader he continues that, "I bet it's like a fuckin' axe wound down there man".

"I think she's fuckin' gorgeous Rick man". You could not make this shit up. And, I confess, with shame, that being so small minded I find some of these conversations hilarious at times. Don't shoot me.

"Can't believe you're laughing at that racist stuff Sloaney", says Just For Men Kempy.

"So was you you cunt", I say.

"Yeah, but I don't care. You go on as if you're not racist and that but by laughing as well you show that you are".

"Fuck off Kempy you prick"!

"Alright, chill out, I'm only joking ya cunt, wow".

"Kempster, only stupid people are bigoted and I like to think I'm not stupid".

"I ain't racist really", says Peter.

"Coulda fooled me", says Kempy.

"Just 'cause I use words don't mean I'm actually a racist. I like black people", and here everyone laughs at the common response to a charge of racism! 'Some of my friends are black' being another example commonly heard.

So, Black Eye Friday and our cell door has just been opened for the afternoon of dealing and debt settling. The rest of the wing are flying past my open cell door in hurry to get in the que for their victuals and vapes and toiletries and coffee and tea and sauces and matchstick model making kits etc etc. I am gonna get on the telephone, something I rarely do since Tan stopped visiting some time ago.

Ten minutes later and I am off the phone and fuming. I phoned Andy Moynihan and he informs me that someone has stolen my passport from his flat. My Irish friend, the one who lives next door to the old lady who kicked me on the stairs when I'd overdosed that time in the stairwell, has an open door policy for all the reprobates and alcoholics and addicts for he is a big drinker himself and since his wife died, the lovely Angie, he has gone to pot the poor misfortunate. Still, I am so angry I immediately write Charlotte a letter asking her to put the word out that upon my release I will be kicking off front doors if I find out who had it, carving cunts up. Anyway, I haven't been recording today's events which are relatively unremarkable though a prisoner on 'B' wing apparently tried to drag a female officer into a cell for some unknown reason but was promptly savaged by other inmates, one with a sock filled with pool balls and absolutely smashed to bits for his transgression so the story goes. Staff need to feel safe in this inherently dangerous environment. It is enough that they are exposed to spice fumes all day every day along with the abuse and occasional assault and bucket of shit being thrown over them by disgruntled inmates.

Anyway, there are currently two people on the wing I wish to paint a picture of for you. Let me describe the first fella. Adam W is on Alpha with us but is not an addict like the majority on here. No, he sniffs a line of coke now and then and likes a tipple but let's get to the point: this young man was importing kilos and kilos of heroin and cocaine and having meets with contacts all over Europe, arranging for copious amounts of drugs to be flown into Britain via helicopter. His cell is a regular shop of goodies, he has a massive Panasonic music system which, fuck knows how, he has managed to hook up to his TV and the fuckin' internet enabling him access to all sorts but of course he can only use it when the door is locked at night. This cute faced five foot ten blonde banged fucker is also feared and respected and considered dangerous and has the money in here to have people hurt should the desire so take him. He dresses head to foot in Armani and Gucci though these garments are understated as are the Gucci and Patrick Cox loafers he wears when he has a break from the expensive Nikes he usually parades in. And the only reason he is on 'A' wing is to swerve the consequences of a positive cocaine piss test which could affect his parole if he is not seen to be doing something about his 'problem' which isn't really a problem at all. Anyway, the point is that tomorrow he is going to give me some of his time to do a bit of 'journalism' with him, to tell me some stories basically. I have had to, over time, gain this man's trust for people like him are not want to give up their secrets easily; I promised him I would only write what he wanted me too and not other stuff I have learned from him which could cause him harm through the criminal justice system.

Anyway, whilst I scribe I feel I must mention a couple of people I have grown up with. Just briefly. Many years ago (1993/4 perhaps) whilst at Craig and Trish's house described earlier in the narrative, a muscle bound young boy of about 13 or so had knocked on the door bearing a gift of a cauliflower for Trish, who opened the door to him. This is the stuff of legend in Thanet now.

"You're my mum", Steve Mcoll had said to Trish. Trish last saw this beefy beautiful young boy some twelve years before when she had had to give him up for one reason or other. This fella, now nearly forty I guess, is now one of my closest friends and is also one of the most feared fuckers in Thanet. He and his older brother Michael grew up in that mad house with me and both always had my back despite the stigma attached to heroin addicts at that time; neither of these two lads have used hard class A drugs though both have had their problems with other drugs and drinking. They never called me 'scaghead' or 'junkie' but some years later I was sitting in a house in Ramsgate using heroin when suddenly the front door was kicked off and these pair of cunts dragged me out kicking and screaming.

"What the fuck you doing man? Get off me you pair of cunts", I had screamed.

"Calm down ya silly cunt", Steve had said, "we ain't gonna hurt ya Sloaney but you are gonna be locked up bro".

"What the fuck"? I remonstrate.

"Sloaney", says Michael Mcoll, "can't keep seeing you like this man", he says as they manhandle me into the back of a stolen Subaru Imprezza rally spec, "you're just gonna do a detox mate, we're tryna fuckin' help ya".

"Who the fuck told you I was here? I'm gonna fuckin' kill 'em whoever it is".

"Oh shut up Sloaney", says Steve, "what the fuck could you do anyway; look at the state of you ya silly cunt".

"I'm gonna fuck you two up too", and this gets a laugh out the pair of pricks as Michael gets behind the wheel and Steve in beside me in the back of the car.

"Shitting meself Sloaney", says Michael, the handsome womanizing prick from the front of the car.

"Yeah man, I won't be able to sleep at night mate", says the brother beside me bearing teeth in a big stupid grin.

"Just let me get one more in me you proper pair of cunts, one more hit before we go".

"Ain't happening mate", says Steve.

"You're fucked ya cunts", I say, "you can't do this to me man you're bang out of order".

"We're actually tryna help ya Sloaney", says Michael from the front of the car.

"Well, it don't fuckin' feel like it".

"You'll thank us for it soon man", says Steve.

"I'm gonna fuck you up you pair a cunts I promise you", and I sit sulking in the back of the car, considering the horror of cold turkey before me. Anyway, thankfully, something else got in the way and I managed to escape because whilst in the flat a day later whilst Michael was out Steve found out that his best mate, Dibbsy real name Dwayne Olive, now dead from an overdose, had fucked his bird whilst Steve had been in prison. So Steve had grabbed a carving knife and found his friend and promptly plunged the business end of the knife straight into Dibbsy's throat, very nearly killing him and leaving a scar like that on Frankenstein's monster's neck. So, soon as Steve had left the flat, no longer there to guard me, I had promptly made my escape. Anyway, just wanted to mention that pair of pricks whom I love so very much, as I did their mental mum when she was alive. Back to this cell now, where me and Marcus are banged up for the evening. Marcus is on his bed dribbling and every time I say this I must emphasise that this is a literal statement, so, dribbling, mouth hanging open and laying in the cup of hot chocolate I made for him which now resides in the fabric of his bedding, down his jumper and basically all over the silly fucker.

"Knew I shouldn't a fuckin' made you that you soppy cunt", I say to him now. He hears me not through his dribble and snot but snores oblivious to the fact just mentioned. Today he pulled in £175 in bank transfers and 47 packs of £4 a pop vapes. Then, slippery as he is, he managed to blag a screw to open a gate on spurious reasoning allowing him to run down to 'F' wing at the other end of the prison where he met with a pal who passed him a page of power paper spice through the bars of the gate at the front of that wing before returning victorious and distributing to the cats here on 'A' wing. He's hailed as a hero on here today and making money hand over fist the crafty cunt. Good on him I say!

26-01-2019 0730hrs. Chemical free and eleven days clean. However, last night, I literally did not sleep a wink. Anyway, I took some notes from Adam W as he regaled a tale to me yesterday so am gonna try put something from him together for you.

Adam's dad was a big player in the smuggling game many years ago and though Adam described his old man as 'being a bit of a cunt to me mum' he said that nonetheless he looked up to him as a bit of a hero. He told me that when his mum and dad split his father went a bit off the rails along with Adam's two older brothers, Darren and Wayne. The splitting of the mum and dad was a little traumatic for mum ran off with their father's business partner. Two years later Adam's dad stabbed his old friend seventeen times for the betrayal, necessitating the removal of the wife thiefs spleen amongst other quite serious injuries. By now Adams's oldest brother Darren was working with the old man importing ecstasy from Holland through the 1990s. Darren is a live wire so Adam tells me. Anyway, this activity went on for some time and the operation grew and grew with many other participants; however, within the cell of people organising and running these activities was a woman called Eve Fletney who was sleeping with one of the men involved in what was now a very sizable operation. This woman is a famous supergrass; google her. Anyway, eventually the lad's dad, Adam's dad, got a 7 year sentence, she got 23 years but served just 3 months before being released. However, Darren and his co conspirators were still on remand and whilst being held the lads would play cards and the loser, as a joke, each time they went to court had to tell the judge he had important information then when asked what it was he would hold up a monopoly 'get out of jail free' card. I love the fact that people like us can find humour even in the most dire of circumstances. Eventually the lads got large sentences ranging between 12 and 16 years however, before this happened, one particular day the judge had fucked up and had no other choice than to release the boys, all involved in the case, on bail for one, yes one, day! Adam and Darren's dad tell Darren that he needs to get out of the country. He leaves for Spain, but in prison he had gone and gotten himself a heroin habit and by now was in the grip of raging addiction. Whilst he is away the others in the case get the terms mentioned above. Now police officers also got bird for when Fletney grassed on one bust, involving hundreds of thousands of pounds worth of product, the police returned the drugs to her which were then redistributed to the streets. After Adam's father is released he sadly died in a car crash and his scummy girlfriend cleared off with all he ever owned, robbing the lads of all their rightful inheritance. Darren's place in Spain is raided and 3 ton of cannabis is found but he swerves the charges but has to return to the UK where of course he is still desperately wanted by police. However the Spanish police put him on a plane, seeing him off but having not liaised with British police he got home free, walking from the plane at the airport astonished at his good fortune. He still has a heroin habit and starts dealing drugs at mid range level to live and feed his habit. The fella he was working with was a Tony G who once escaped Wandsworth jail. It's the first Xmas without their dad and Wayne and Adam are with their 72 year old nan at home waiting for the still wanted Darren to turn up for Xmas dinner. Darren had borrowed the straight going bother Wayne's car but he had smashed the blue Escort and the only door to fix the fucked one was red so you must picture what Adam says is an old jalopy blue Escort with a red door which he is flying around in on Xmas day trying to score before his intended return to his nan and his brother's for dinner. So, he is driving up Stretham High Street in the car tryna score when that worst of things happens: blue lights in the rear view. Darren stops and gives his brother's name. The police, though, know who he is but thankfully the thick cunts hadn't taken the keys from the car and in one swift movement Darren gets in the car and motors off but one of the filth is hanging from the red door and falls off at some considerable speed and the other officer is behind now ramming the top speed of 80 mph Escort. Darren runs a red and dumps the car and jumps the fence of a random family home, pulls open the back door and runs through the house whilst this family, having Xmas dinner, look on at this nutcase, open mouthed. He gets to a friend's house but his mate is in the sun in Spain so he smashes a window and hides out. He finds himself a ridiculous outfit, phones nan and the boys saying he won't be home, describing the events. He tells them to expect police and Adam tells me that no sooner had he got off the phone there's a knock upon the door and nan has the hump telling the two clean cut filth to fuck off. The police clock Wayne, Darren's double and erroneously thinks it is Darren, cuffing him before excitedly calling on the radio to the officers who'd given chase and Adam says the state of the police car that had taken the chase-and the smashed up beat up officer was a scene of comic genius. So now the old bill who'd originally turned up at the house are excited but the filth from the chase, dirty, battered and bruised quickly dispel their joy. Suckers! The old lady, the nan, is now going nuts and Wayne is released and Adam sarcastically wishes the cops a 'merry Christmas lads'! The filth are fuming but they fuck off with Adam mocking them saying 'what, my bro did that to you'? Darren does, of course, eventually get nicked to face his justice but the police were clearly so embarrassed they never charged him with events relating to that Xmas day, smashing their car, escaping and dragging an old bill up the road and near on killing him! He never heard anything about it but did get a hefty double figure sentence for his part in the massive importation operation. Anyway, I'd thoroughly enjoyed taking notes with Adam for this yesterday whilst listening to Biggy pumping from the Panasonic!

Sunday morning 0130hrs. 27th January 2019. It is 36hrs since I last slept and as I sit in this cell now with Marcus monged out before me I feel nothing but gratitude for the fact the obsession to use is lifted. Coming into my 12th day chemical free.

0900hrs. Got three hours sleep in the end. In Brad's cell now.
"My nan had a pig called Ethel", he is saying, "my nan's Alsatian used to run from it with his tail between his legs, it was terrified of it, the pig used to terrorise the dog as if it was saying, 'I run the show'. Honestly Andy, it was so big, the pig, I used to ride on its back when I was about eight . This thing was as big as my nan's farm gate". We are watching Countryfile and reliving, through the programme, the horrors of swine flu and foot and mouth disease. Apparently African swine flu is close to our shores and Brad is saying:
"We have lots of wild boar here so if it did get here it would devastate our pig population", and clearly Brad knows his stuff. Now he goes on to tell me that malaria isn't far from these shores either. Grin comes in the cell saying:
"I'm not giving Ricky (Lanes) any subutex today", meaning that when he secretes his opioid at the meds hatch and brings it back to the wing he won't sell it to Rick.
"Have you got some for me though Grin"? asks Smarcus.
"Of course mate, so long as I get it back, depends who's on down there at the hatch as you know". Brad tells me a story about when he shot a couple of pals of ours with an air rifle in the dump where we used to ride stolen motorbikes and where he used to catch lizards and spiders. The cell is packed now. Just For Men Kempy, Smarcus, Ricky Lanes, Grin, me and Jake. Kempster is telling us a story about his cellmate Paul Stone, a pal of ours, mentioned him before I think, I had a fight with him here a while ago. Paul got a nicking for a positive piss test last night. Now this will cost him an extra three weeks in jail but he had a chance to get away with it because the new screw who issued the nicking sheet had

214

forgotten to sign and date the paperwork and this completely invalidates the thing. So he and Kempy are behind the door and the screw puts it under. Kempy, being smart, immediately spots the blunder. The screw returns and says through the door which can't be opened because it is patrol state time:

"Poke it back through, I've made a mistake", and Stoney goes to do it but Kempy screams at him:

"No no don't do it you'll get off mate I've seen it happen before and there's fuck all they can do about it", but the screw, brand new wet behind the ears says:

"Please mate, please put it through", and Kempster goes:

"Don't you dare Stoney", and Stoney goes to the screw:

"Hahahahahaha, you fucked up"!

"Please mate", says the screw, "I'll get in trouble".

"Oh eeeeyaah", and Stoney, says Kempster, only went and passed the fuckin' thing through the door.

"Why the fuck you do that"? asked the absolutely incredulous Just For Men.

"I felt sorry for him man", says the soft fucker Stoney.

"I couldn't fuckin' believe it", says Kempy now.

"What a plank", I say.

Evening now. Got to the gym with Craig Mc and Smarcus and had a savage workout. Marcus, two minutes prior to the end of the session turned fuckin' comedian. Now, there were twenty people from 'A' wing in the gym plus two staff and three lifer orderlies and Marcus says:

"Sloaney, you want to straighten your back you was saying"?

"Yeah", I say.

"Come here and I'll show ya something", and he takes me to a set of bars from which people hang and do chin ups and such.

"Right", says he, "hang up there and just let your spine stretch out", and, of course, I do as asked and no sooner was I hanging, suspended, he promptly rips down my shorts to the delight of the whole gym which erupts into raucous laughter; 'A' wing, orderlies and staff alike and I was just grateful that it was at the end of the session after I'd gotten warm and had a bit of weight on me old boy down there. I too cried with mirth to be fair for it was fuckin' funny the way he set me up! The prick. Even when we got back to the wing it wasn't long before everyone knew. It is moments like this that relieve the monotony of prison life. Anyway, Marcus said today that I use the word 'grateful' more than any other. Interesting!

215

30-01-2019. 0800hrs. Door's just opened. Day 15 clean. Haven't written for days as sleep deprivation has left me drained and down. Also, as the days drew on and boredom set in I ended up ripping the head off the purple headed warrior multiple times two nights ago but seminal stocks are once again replenished and after a little shut eye last night I feel somewhat more invigorated. Marcus is swearing he ain't gonna be using any subutex today. Like me, he is planning on using the spice to help him get off the opioid. After that, he says, he will reduce the pregablin then come off the spice. He had me in stitches last night; his subutex yesterday, illicit of course, came in the form of a transdermal body patch bought off another inmate. He was out his fuckin' nut as usual after mixing it with gabapentin and spice. When he found that he'd done all his spice and had no more in the cell he was scratching and scuttling around for scraps of paper like a rat, sniffing round every corner of the cell.

"That's it mate", I'd said helpfully, "scuttle about like a crab! Still got the sliver in ya mouth? The patch"?

"Shit man, I swallowed it", he says and reader know these patches are left in the mouth and work all day when used this way. Meant to be stuck on the upper arm but more narcotic when used like this.

"Best scuttle after Ricky tomorrow, get some more", now this might confuse you as Ricky was in Grin's bad books for not paying him for a subutex tablet but Ricky gets patches and uses them the same way as Marcus and sells half of them for spice leaving he himself withdrawing and having to buy off of other people at times.

"I told ya", says Marcus looking in the business brush end of the broom for scraps of paper spice he may have swept up, "I ain't doin' it no more".

"If only I had a camera", I say.

"Stop hating man". Anyway, as I said, we have just been opened but now staff have rapidly locked us all up; something is clearly going on. Yesterday an officer working down the new side of the jail had a bucket of shit thrown over him. And in other news, a notorious nutter name of Dale Pearson has just moved onto Alpha wing after assaulting staff on 'B' wing. Been on here a week now. He is truly, this lunatic of 24 years of age, extremely handsome. He is six foot two with mousy hair and a square chiselled face with an athletic perfectly proportioned build. He has a fresh slash wound running from the top of his right eye down to his lower cheek bone, inflicted by himself. His crystal blue bright eyes are mesmerizing and harbour the madness which definitely resides within. Marcus and Dale are very close and Dale has been Marcus's muscle when the latter is selling drugs all over the jail. Dale would wait 'till

216

mass movement when all wings go to work and get the debtor, invariably scaring the poor fucker to death and obtaining the errant funds. You wouldn't want this cunt on ya case and make no mistake. I'm glad I've gotten to know him as I'd bustled round the jail for even David M said to me, who was with him on 'B' wing that he, Dale, is one of the most psychotic fuckers he has ever met after watching him slash a fella down the face with a blade in a toothbrush in order to get a debt paid. The first time I set eyes on him he was surrounded by four screws and a governor on mass movement saying:

"Don't fuckin' come near me, I swear I'll let loose on you cunts if ya do".

"Just calm down", Kirky, officer Kirk, a great screw from our wing, Alpha, had said after some stalemate and Kirky had persevered and calmed the loon down with his caring tones where none of the other brute screws and cunt governor could. People skills are needed and in this job it is these that get results. Now Dale has, in a week, come to be loved by us Thanet lot and the little firm we have around us. He spends his time in Brad's cell with the rest of us when the doors are open. People other than Marcus have been offering him money to collect debts for them but we have put a stop to people using him this way.

"Fuck that Dale", Brad had said, "we have rather come to enjoy your company and if you start all that shit they'll soon kick you off here bro". You should of seen the effect these words had on Dale, who craves love.

"Yeah man", I'd piped up, "fuck them cunts Dale, why risk getting kicked off here when you've found a little niche on here with us lot"?

"Ahhh man you boys", he says all abashed and embarrassed, "you lot are lovely", and he smiled showing perfect, straight white teeth.

"It's right man", said Marcus, "we like having you about", and Just For Men had echoed the sentiment. We wanna keep the cunt about for we not only like him but he is handy; his mere presence around us will insure Brad and Marcus get their debts in easier and Dale won't have to get violent for the mere possibility of this loon flying into your cell with evil intent is enough to motivate those who owe money. Anyway, it's now 0830hrs and clearly we ain't gonna be getting out this morning for group as the whole jail is locked down by the looks of it. Oh, before I forget, Dave M is down the block in an 'E' or 'Escape' suit after being found in possession of a screwdriver and a hacksaw. The attire is a jumpsuit, blue with fuck off great yellow high vis stripes on. He was due out in four weeks and on the way to work yesterday Brad had called him from the back of the segregation unit or 'block' as it is colloquially called and Dave had shouted out the window that he knew nothing of these tools which were apparently secreted inside the metal bed somewhere and with such a short period left to serve why would he? It's all a bit weird and we only have thin, sketchy information about the whole thing. Oh, fuck me, the door has just opened! I ask a screw who tells me there was an emergency staff meeting. On the wing is the beautiful Ellie P, the pretty screwess who usually works D wing and I'm not sure if I told you but she is now with the officer who used to be with the ex screw who is now Marcus's girlfriend! Just thought I'd share that with you in case I haven't already!

Ok, it is 1930hrs and Marcus, whilst we were down the gym today, scored another two pages of power spice soaked paper. At this very moment he has a joint in his hand which has burnt a hole in his duvet, he is naked bar a pair of boxer shorts and is halfway up the wall, half on the bed and snoring like a tractor. The cunt is fifteen stone of muscle at the moment and we had a wicked session today where we used predominantly dumbells and cables and, after, I finished off with ten intense minutes on the running machine whilst kick ass energy inspiring house music pumped from the sound system. On the way back from the gym I stopped in at the ATB unit where I spoke with Jason Gould and Lucy K with whom I have grown quite close. Lucy suffered a family loss lately and told me she got her first nights sleep for five days. During the Thinking Skills Programme I came to really respect these two for all they wish to see is those like me making something of themselves and not being driven back through the gates in a sweat box. During TSP, though I wasn't clean I had the respect not to turn up in the morning out me nut: it was just when I returned to the wing I couldn't, at the time, curb my spice use. I would come back all afire with the new information I was learning then throw my dignity on the floor hunting the drug, selling my soul and mugging myself off. Make no mistake, when I use I am a fraggle on the wing. A nothing, just another cat, another zombie, skinny sick and in pain. At the whim of drug dealers who hold me in the palm of their hands. I would treat my friends like Bradders and Marcus awfully, knowing I could rip them off without fear of reprisals for the cunts love me. Look, ethical questions about what they do do bug me but the other side of the coin is that they both just do it to get by, Brad on a small level to get creature comforts and Marcus selling perhaps £700 or £800 worth of spice a week to keep his myriad habits going, to feed the monkey on his own back. And of course Marcus makes some added extras from which I too profit for my life is comfortable here right now. I have proteins and creatine with which to train in the gym more aggressively, luxury foods and nice toiletries with which to wash. There's also the fact my friend of many years, full of steroids he also buys on the black market here which are giving him a bit of a belly, keeps me in fits of hilarity with his antics the funny fucker. And he's harmless the cunt, well, to me anyway. Unless I snidely wrap a bottle round his head like the fella he stabbed which was, admittedly, a bit of an extreme reaction but in that world we have to show people that we won't stand for shit for if one does then one gets eaten alive. Anyway. Me, Marcus, Just For Men Steve Kemp, Dale, Craig McNicol and 'H' whose real name I still don't know due to such not being necessity for all call him 'H', little Martin, a quiet lad who's now on the Bridge Programme with us and even skinny Beany from the cell next door to me and Marcus came along to the gym with many other reprobates from A wing. Again, on the way back, after speaking to Lucy and Jason I bumped into Tony Giles my lifelong pal who got kicked off of 'A' wing for not complying with piss tests and such. He told me and Just For Men that on 'B' wing where he now lives he and his cellmate had their cell spun and the screws found a tiny thumb sized CZ mobile phone and two shanks (knives). He says they were his cellmate's but of course he ain't gonna grass him up so they'll both take the charges I guess. I'd love to see Tony get clean for then he'd stay out of jail as of course he burgles houses, as I do, in order to feed the habit. I do love the morose and miserable cunt.

1-02-2019 0712hrs clean day 17. Smarcus is in his pit after another night flying far from here and from his fears in a temporary fix of drug induced fog. Last night for the first time in months I rang Tan, the sexy lass pulled via facebook and telescope many moons ago now it seems. She really looked after me prior to my imprisonment, feeding and clothing and loving me when I was very fucked on hard drugs. Her gravelly hot tones emanated to my ear down the receiver:
"Andy".
"Tan".
"Oh Tan, ya cunt, I ain't half been worried about you; you ok? I fuckin' miss you ya know".
"I think about you all the time Andy".
"Likewise, not a day goes by without thoughts of you flowing through my head".
"What you been doing in there"?
"Well, I'm a different man from the last time you came up and saw me".
"I should hope so: you were fucked, out ya fuckin' nut", she says honestly.
"I know man, I'm sorry about that and suitably embarrassed".
"So", she says, "when ya getting out"?

219

"Well, my tag date is February 22nd but I don't think I'll get it 'cause I've no address". A tag is a tracking ankle bracelet which allows for the early release of prisoners with specified conditions. "Without the tag", I continue, "it'll be July".

"Well", she says, "I've just got a new flat in Broadstairs and I'd have you here if you promise you'll behave".

"Wow", I say, "getting excited here Tan; you for real"?

"Well, yeah", she replies, "we're just friends though but if I tell you to fuck me you have to fuck me and I want massages on tap too"!

"Well, err, yes, I'd be honoured to be able to fill those duties Tan, like, I'd love too", I say, thrown off as per usual by the crazy sexy wench.

"And you have to look after my dogs and just do as you're told", and I love the mischief in her voice.

"Well, Tan, I'll get me a receiver transmitter stuck to me back and give you the remote control for it with buttons for 'sex' 'rubs' 'walk dogs' and 'clean' how's that sound"? She laughs heartily at this along with me and we talk some small talk before ending a lovely call. God bless her.

2-02-2019 0100hrs. Sleep is still very elusive but this is to be expected. Marcus has been snoring smashed for hours but I can see him stirring on his bed. He puts a pipe to his mouth and blasts more spice then dribbling and eyes rolling says something barely intelligible to me:

"Can ya Plllaassshhh shemm ahhhh Crispssshhhhh Shhhhloaney Pleashhh man".

"What crisps wierdo"?

"Da, da, da, dem things, erm, da thing, pleashhh Shloaney man, pleash bro".

"You're hungry"?

"Yeah man pashhh food pleashhh".

"Penguin? Biscuits"?

"Yeah prrreash mate". I pass him some grub and look lovingly upon him. His eyes are completely bloodshot and seem to be on elastic which keeps pulling them into the back of his head. He's been out his nut for hours and has already spilled a whole can of coke all over himself and his bed the poor cunt.

"Love you Shloaney man", he says when he has the food in his hands.

"I love you too bro", and, indeed, I do, it's true. And sitting here in Oxford typing today I can tell you I spoke to him via facetime yesterday and he is ok right now, bless him.

220

So, door's open now this Saturday morning and me, Dale and Smarcus just had a big fuck off breakfast of eggs, tuna, beans and toast with hot chilli sauce. Dale, the handsome six foot psycho with the piercing blue eyes and high cheekboned and crafted bearded face is turning out to be a belter of a guy.

"Dale", I said, as we sat eating and Marcus was in conversation with Pete Lanes who sat beside him, "please, as we said the other day, don't go bashing people for debts, even for Marcus and Bradders bro. You've got it really good on here at the moment mate".

"I'm not gonna do it for others but for me friends I don't mind man and Sloaney debt collecting is what I do bro".

"I get that, but don't you like being on here with us? Me, Marcus, Bradders and that"?

"Course I do".

"How long you got left"?

"Same time as Marcus, December this year I get out".

"Well, you've got a spot with us on here and there's worse wings to do your bird on as we both know. And the way you lose it they'd have you back in Elmley bro and let's have it right, that's the biggest shithole as you know. I always end up rolling about with cunts in those filthy three man cells. Did this time, fuckin' hate the gaff. Shouldn't be allowed, three fellas in one a those tiny cells".

"Fuckin' shit in it mate. I'm the same, always end up fighting there. Didn't you smash that horrible skinny cunt up, that 'Fingers'"?

"I did, proper bullied me for two weeks before I snapped though. I'd just come off the street Dale, I was so depressed and he kept getting the hump 'cause I talk in my sleep. And when Ricky Stocker, the other fella in the cell, would go to pass me the spice spliff he'd snatch it and say 'I'm having that first'. He made my life hell for those couple weeks and one night I was talking in my sleep and woke up to him telling me if I didn't stop he was gonna smash me up. I'd had enough by then and jumped out the bed and dragged him off his bunk. For someone with so much mouth he screamed, literally screamed like a baby when I let loose on him. Ricky had to drag me off 'cause I was so angry I couldn't stop smashing his fuckin' face the skinny cunt. Makes me angry even remembering it".

"I know the cunt, proper thinks he's something. He was here a little while ago".

"Yeah, he was on here. Apparently he's been nicked again and is meant to be coming back here the soppy cunt. I just ignored him when he was on here, though he did try to say hello and that".

"I'll smash him up for you if he comes back".

"No you fuckin' won't man. Listen, let that shit go and mate, you don't need to actually weigh people in to collect debts ya weirdo; all you have to do is be around Marcus and Brad and they're benefitting d'ya get what I mean? Your presence is enough to put the fear of God into people".

"Well, we'll see but I'm not gonna let anyone mug the boys off. Anyway, you seen my bird Sloaney"?

"No, why, is she fit"? Marcus turns round at the word 'bird'.

"Come have a look".

"I'm coming"! says Marcus, "wait 'till you see this Sloaney she's a fuckin weapon bro", and he chuckles such a pesty laugh I can't help but smile myself. We go to Dale's cell and upon the picture board on the wall are myriad photos of a dark haired smooth skinned luscious looking young stunner.

"God, I can't look", I say, pulling on my glasses nonetheless, "wow man d'ya mind"?

"Naaa man have a good look", says Dale and I do, knicker and bra shots and all but I don't indulge for too long lest I get too pesty myself and end up with the horn. God, though, crafted in the upper echelons of heaven that one. We all leave the cell and me and Smarcus go to Brad's where J.T and Grin are reclining sharing a joint of spice. Grin is in the recess bit and rocking back and forth doing the spice palsy shuffle though it be but 0930hrs. He is smiling at us all like a big goofy kid and I have a wave of love wash through me for I like this cunt, so generous of spirit is he. Ms Terry pokes her head in the cell just after Brad returns from running around calling in debts.

"Morning Ms Terry", I say and everyone else does the same for she's sound. She winds her head round and clocks Grin and says to him:

"Fuck sake Grinley, don't you go out on the landing like that", and Grin just smiles back like an idiot and Ms Terry shakes her head forlornly but smiling before pulling the door to.

"Sound her", says Brad.

"She is", echoes Smarcus. Marcus, sitting beside me on the bed as I write keeps poking and prodding me and is now inebriated and slurring after caning a spliff.

"Fuck off Marcus man I'm tryna write ya cunt", and now he is tapping me and pointing to Grin who's sitting on the toilet in the recess rocking back and forth. We are watching Komodo Dragons on the TV and it should be known that reptiles are Brads' specialist subject.

"Fuck me they're mahussive", I say now and a Komodo is taking a buffalo and Brad tells me that the dragon bit it weeks ago, following it

222

until the poison takes full effect. Fuckin' fascinating and Fradders loves it.

"Is the Komodo the governor Brad"? I ask.

"Yeah man", he says, "they grow like three metres long and weigh 100 kilos Andy", and I love the way he calls me 'Andy' for some inexplicable reason. Now a monitor lizard is tryna take a baby possum whilst the possum's mother looks on and it savagely succeeds in its barbarism. Smarcus and Dale are snorting subutex now and Ricky comes in and goes:

"Got a bit for me"? and Smarcus goes:

You're too late Rick mate but I've got a bit coming off of Grin if he gets his back so I'll give you some then".

"Please mate, I'm bang in it", says Rick.

"Look, Grin is gonna give me a bit in a minute if he gets it back and I promise I'll sort you out then".

"Please do mate 'cause I'm bang in trouble bro". Pete, Rick's brother, has been employed by Marcus to do some graffiti, like proper arty graffiti on our cell wall. He is stencilling the words 'gratitude' 'humility' and 'respect' for us. Pete has a piece of art at the Turner Centre in Margate right at this very moment. Terry Hughes, who has pinged money to Marcus for spice has just come into the cell asking Marcus to get on the phone to get his missus to check the account to see if it has landed so Terry can then have the other half of the spice he paid for. Now dear reader from here in Oxford I can tell you now that I remember this next little thing. I had briefly left Brad's to get something, leaving my paperwork on the bed and when I return Marcus the comedian had written after the words 'spice he paid for' 'TERRY SUCK MARCUS COCK SO HARD HE CUMS INTO BRADS MOUTH WHY DALE WANKING COCK OFF'! It is written exactly like that in the manuscript and I remember returning to the cell and picking up the page to write and laughing me nut off as I read it to the assembled. I chuckle here now as watery late September sunlight streams through the window behind me. If you knew Marcus and his sick humour and character you'd get why I and the rest of us found it so funny! And watching his boyish face crease up in mirth is priceless. Anyway, Marcus gets on the little mobile and Terry's money is indeed in so my pugilistic pal gets the rest of his spice.

Last night, whilst Smarcus slept I listened to Heart 80s and was dancing round the cell early hours to Prince and Purple Rain, Fleetwood Mac's Wanna Be With You Everywhere and Joy Division Love Will Tear Us Apart. We have gym this afternoon and bundles of new whey protein to bring out the best in us. In other innocuous prison bollox I walked past the office earlier and saw Ms Gilchrest and Ms Terry talking away conspiratorially and stuck my finger up at Gilchrest who smiled and promptly gave me two back. I love this decadent pair. Then we return to the wing, feed, and are banged up at 1700 as always on the weekends. Adios for now.

3-02-2019. Little sleep last night as per usual. I have struggled this weekend to be fair. Everyone is using around me, and, since Tan has offered me a lifeline with the tag I am ever more anxious to leave this place. Despite the fact Rochester HMP has helped me so much I am finding my peers lack of initiative, drive and gratitude draining at times. Also, with the younger ones needing constant reassurance and validation I am getting worn out. For instance, Dale, this morning came out his cell so fuckin' angry and we were all in Brad's cell once the door was open for the lunch hour and he comes in:

"I'm gonna kill that cunt in cell 201, he's fuckin' pissing me off" he says, face twisted in fury.

"Who's that"? asks Brad.

"Mark or Adam", says Smarcus.

"Yeah, that Mark", says Dale menacingly, "he keeps fuckin' looking at me, like proper staring at me every time I walk past him and that".

"He probably don't mean to", ventures Brad.

"Fuck it", says Dale, "I'm going down there", and that, dear reader, is exactly what he did. Upon returning he told us that he told him, Mark, a poor quiet fucker, that 'if you keep looking at me I'm gonna smash you up you cunt' and I dear reader stay silent through it all, I simply can't be bothered tryna educate today. Drain drain fuckin' drain. I'm so tired, but still clean and sober thank God.

4-02-2019 1520hrs. Just got back from our weekly Narcotics Anonymous (NA) meeting and today I actually opened my mouth and shared some of the wonderful stuff that is happening with me at the moment. Firstly I gratefully listened to the fella who came in to tell his tale of experience strength and hope with the ramshackle group of prisoners. He was six years clean and had that serene rosy cheeked comfy in his own skin look of one who had come to be at ease with himself. His experience, his trajectory through different mind altering substances was pretty much the same as mine. And the feelings he felt he just couldn't sit with resonated with me too. Like me he started sitting at the back of the class with tipex thinner and went through butane gas, petrol etc before discovering more orthodox drugs. I remember myself sniffing gas and thinners then finding weed and Es and speed and acid then crack and heroin and benzos and spice and any fuckin' thing that changed the way I felt. On a fundamental level addicts medicate themselves because they've, we've, not the tools to cope until we are shown another way and that way for me is the NA way. I, as a kid, felt an overwhelming sense of being less than, more stupid than, more unlovable than anyone else on Earth. And later unemployable and unsavable also, to compound the rest. Yet all along I'm starting to feel that there was a plan because I should be dead many times over the way I have used but maybe the Universe wants to use me for something as of yet elusive to my senses. I feel, however, I may be here to help people. Who knows? Life was once a living nightmare for me but I sit in this cell right now feeling freer than ever despite the bars and doors and screws and limitations on my physical liberty. Jay Nevin and Steve Kemp are in the cell now.

"I fuckin' hate tiling", says Nev.

"Me too", says Just For Men Kempy, "my real speciality is plastering".

"He's a jack of all trades this cunt", says Nev, in his broad cockney drawl, to me sarcastically.

"I'm a multi house building engineer", says Kempy.

"I've never been any good with my hands", say I.

"I love roofing", says Nev, "'cause I could create other jobs by fuckin' up the next door neighbour's roof too".

"And you can sit looking at the scenery having a beer and a sniff", says Kempster.

"Especially in the summer", says Nev.

"Not only would I sometimes fuck up other rooves", says Kempy, "sometimes I'd burgle the next door neighbours. I just couldn't help it, especially when I've got a raging Roger Rabbit on crack and smack and you're looking at all their lovely bits and pieces through like a skylight window ya know"? They both leave and I'm not even sure they were aware I was penning but I know they're both happy to be immortalised. Now Marcus is in the cell, our cell, trying to find his spice, forgetting that he left it in Brad's cell whilst Brad is at work so he will have to wait 'till Brad gets back and Ricky and Peter Lanes and 'Pony Tail Paul' and little Jake and Kev are in our cell asking Marcus, desperately, for spice for, it would seem, the wing has gone dry and people are panicking. Everyone leaves when Marcus explains they'll have to wait 'till Brad gets back but Peter stays for he is painting on the wall, designs around the words I told you he'd been graffiti stencilling for us, earning daily spice from Smarcus. He is deliberately taking his time about it in order to milk as much spice as possible from him. He's been at it a good few days and it is nowhere near finished by the looks of it. Jason from the ATB Unit sent me over a lovely letter today telling me that they really believe in me and that I need to remember that getting clean here makes me really strong for it is all around me, the drugs. His lovely words brought a tear to my eye. Then Ms Nixon, another fine officer on A wing, brought a brand new pad of paper into my cell so that I can pen this for me and you dear reader. I feel insecure and naked if I haven't the means to write. I am eternally grateful for the support I am getting from across this prison estate.

So, it is 1600hrs now. Marcus is playing at being Pablo Escobar shotting what spice he has to the cats but insuring he leaves enough for himself for there's fuck all bar what he has on the wing. Oh, and, his subutex habit now dear reader is absolutely through the roof along with his daily intake of illicit pregablin and quetiapine and concerta and spice and any fuckin' thing else the fucker can get his greedy drug loving hands on bless him. Still, he tells me this is easy to stop and he can do it if he wants. And will soon, he says. J.T has just come into our cell now to update us on his health situation for he has been out at the hospital today. Remember, he is still smoking buscopan and spice, selling his pregablin daily to get the latter and prescribed the former for his guts.

"Sloaney", he is telling me now, "they didn't stick any needles or anything in me today but I've got to go back next week, like, and they're gonna stick a tube down me neck and one up me arse to try find out what's wrong with me insides and that".

"But, J.T", I reply, looking up from this piece of paper, "I can tell you what it is from personal experience: it's the fuckin' tablets, the buscopan, and the spice alloy wheel cleaner and cockroach killer you're smoking bro".

"It ain't though Sloaney", replies the moron, "'cause I've been smoking these buscies and spice in prison on and off for years and it ain't ever done this to me before mate. Honestly, I'm being sick all the time and shit just comes outta me like water and it's scaring me Sloaney".

"Jamie mate", I say solemnly, removing my glasses so he knows I'm serious, "you're young ya silly fucker; you've gotten away with it for years because you're strong and fit but now your body is simply asking you to give it a break mate", but he ain't listening and changes the subject.

"I asked that fuckin' Colin on the servery for some extra food but the prick wouldn't give me any the tight cunt and worst thing is I know that the cunt sells anything left over for spice the mug".

"Does he smoke spice then"? I ask, "I thought he wasn't a smoker".

"He fuckin' does the cunt he's just proper, like, undercover with it. Fuckin' hate the prick I do", and with that J.T ups and leaves, bless him. Peter Lanes, standing on a chair still painting the wall says:

"D'ya like what I've done on the wall Sloaney"?

"I do actually", I tell him.

"Starting to look proper alright now init"? he says, continuing, "do you remember Mobb Deep 'Shook Ones' Andy"?

"Gangster shit kept me alive", and now I sing from the track: "'while my mac runs double, I'll cut you, and leave you with not much to go home with, my skin is thick and I'll be up in the mix of action'" and we both laugh, remembering the genius of this duo. Pointing at the wall and his art now he says:

"He can't fuckin' moan now Sloaney can he, it's starting to look proper good ain't it"?

"Why", I ask, "is he whinging"?

"Naaa", he says, "but he complains about what he's paying me mate".

"Don't worry about that", I say, "when he picks up again I'll make sure he looks right after you".

"Don't get me wrong", he says, "he has give me loads but he expects me to rush it and if I do that it's gonna look shit man".

"Fuck that", I say, "it's starting to proper take shape, just plod along as you are mate and milk it I say"!

"I ain't got fuck all to smoke tonight Sloaney man".

"Pete mate", I say, "half the wing hasn't bro 'cause as you know it's proper dried up on here today", and it is true, there are some proper stressed out heads on here tonight and I can only thank God that I'm not one of them. It will be exactly three weeks chemical free tomorrow. Marcus has just come in:

"Fuckin' Craig D just spat his dummy right out because I told him I ain't got no spice left. And fuck me, as you know Sloaney, I ain't fuckin' lying to the stupid cunt. I've sold it all and what I have left I need myself".

"No one's got any on here man it's mental", I say, "and everyone seems to have the raving hump on here tonight man".

"There's little bits here and there", says Marcus, "but people just don't want to let it off. I've got a couple of joints for me and that's it: fuck 'em and fuck him anyway". Now dear reader I must start doing my NA Step One for group tomorrow. Perhaps I will get back to you later.

Later. So, Drake pumping on the radio and Marcus is in the curtained off toilet cubicle trying to wank himself off with a porn mag. He's been there the best part of an hour.

"Too much 'tex' today mate", I say, referring to his intake of the semi synthetic opioid, "you know it stops you coming".

"Fuck off talking to me Sloaney man you're putting me off", but he comes out from behind the curtain proper lathered in sweat, declaring failure.

"Told ya", I say.

"It's the mag", he says, "all the best pictures have got sticky where Dale's wanked all over 'em".

"Weirdo you are; it's the fuckin' drugs stopping you getting there man. How the fuck do you expect to cum when you're out your canister on so many different spunk stopping drugs ya cunt"?

"I know it takes fuckin' ages but I can usually get there".

"But not after the concoction you've had today. Concerta, pregablin, clonazepam, subutex and spice oh and quetiapine too"!

"Yeah, s'pose you're right".

"Shit man you've got no chance. And get that toilet paper from over the peep hole else the night screw will think we're up to sick shit in here bro. And put some fuckin' boxer shorts on for fuck sake ya sick puppy"!

"Oh, but it's alright for you to walk round naked"!

"Only late at night if I jump off the bed briefly; and I don't fuckin' wave the thing around tryna slap you round the face with it like you ya cunt"!

"Hahaha", laughs this twat, "funny though init"! and I can't help but laugh to be fair.

"You ain't fuckin right you"!

5-01-2019 1700hrs. So, today we have had an intense day of group therapy. Little Martin and young hyperactive Reece, both in their early 20s, have really started to come out their shells, sharing stuff and taking risks they've never taken before. Some of the stuff they spoke about is pretty dark God bless them and these two boys have been victims of trauma for sure the poor fuckers. I can't share their personal shit but suffice to say that they have suffered what no child should have to suffer when young. It's hardly surprising that these two have gone well off the rails: you fuckin' would too. I feel humbled and privileged to be a part of their journey and witnessing them experiencing what recovery looks like. Even should they relapse they have seen another way and a seed is sown. Some get it first time where others, like me, have to relapse and realize what I had. Anyway, today I have been thinking about the place I went to when my heart stopped for a minute and a half in overdose, the UFOs I have seen, the dreams I have had that came true, the £5 note 'knowing' premonitions, the night 'Stuart' Little told me I sat up in my sleep and

228

said 'I'm nefarious' despite never knowing the word and that feeling I had when once I woke on my bunk here in the middle of the night with the all enveloping feeling that one day all would be well with me. Earlier, anyway, J.T had pulled me for a chat.

"I tried to phone my mum earlier Sloaney", he said, "but I ended up in tears because when I asked her if we could start to build a relationship again she said 'no, you're a junkie and I don't trust you' and she straight put the phone down on me".

"Oh bro", I say.

"I was proper in tears".

"Look mate, sometimes, when we've hurt people we love over and over it just takes a little while of them actually seeing us get better, seeing us do well before they're willing to trust us again mate".

"It was the crack and smack that made me behave that way though mate, not me".

"But they can't understand that as we do. We know that we could never behave in such savage ways without drugs, that we are driven by demons when in the grip of active addiction. But to them, they just see a complete disregard for anyone and anything. And we cause them real heartache and pain man. I'm the same J.T. I would never have burgled houses, held up kids at knifepoint for drugs, assaulted numerous people tryna nick me or lashed out violently at girlfriends and friends when in my right mind. Drugs truly make us insane. NA taught me that".

"D'ya reckon then", says J.T, "that if I get out and stay clean she'd, like, come around"?

"Mate, I can fuckin' promise you mate, you sort ya shit out and she'd be overjoyed to have her son back. She's just in pain bro is all. I know it may be hard to believe right now bro but she loves you man".

"I get it Sloaney man I do", he says solemnly, "actions speak louder than words". Anyway, I'm now tired dear reader. I'm a read a little, suck me vape, marvel at Marcus as he mongs out and hopefully get some sleep as the last few nights have seen very little shut eye. Headie One is rapping '18 hunna' on the radio and Marcus is fucked on cockroach killer. Bye for now.

2300hrs. Still the same day. I simply never sleep and am doing 24hr bird at the moment. I lay on my bed and try to focus my mind on spiritual things but my mind keeps wandering to Tan. To sitting cuddled up next to her. I miss her sexy banter and foul mouth. She is very smart and has a degree in psychology or something along those lines. I miss her naked form and pert bum too. She is, though, undoubtably a cocaine addict for sure. On the phone the other day I had said to her:

229

"Have you ever thought about going to NA meetings Tan 'cause I'll be going to loads when I get out".

"Andrew, my drug use isn't like yours; I don't stick needles in my arms like you you sick cunt".

"Tan, the definition of a drug addict is not restricted to someone who bangs up. When I was clean for some years in Oxford I saw students who were in the rooms, like in NA, because they simply could not stop smoking weed and their lives had become unmanageable just through that ya know? Anything that becomes all consuming, anything we put before all else is addiction, especially if it destroys relationships, stops us functioning at work or whatever and in your case causes you to sleep with cunts you'd never entertain were it not for the fact they had lots of coke".

"I'm alright Sloaney honestly and I know what I'm doing, trust me", and I hadn't wanted to push it. She's still relatively young. Anyway, the reason I got up and picked up the pen is because me and Marcus have had an argument. So, I have not been going round to Brad's so much of late because the common denominator has been removed and the only thing I crave is the space to write in my own cell. To pen this and my Step Work. I am really trying to fix myself against the odds here. I still, of course, get cravings. Anyway, so, by the time we bang up each night Marcus is of course out his fuckin' nut. Now earlier I am writing Step Work puffing away on my vape, happily immersed in growth inspiring activity. Marcus has two vape batteries but has run them both out smoking the alloy wheel cleaner. The spice.

"Can I have your battery whilst I put one a these on charge Sloaney"?

"No Marcus, you've got two, just wait while one charges 'cause I'm doing step work here bro".

"I ask you for one fuckin' thing", he says.

"D'ya know what"? I say, "fuckin' have it ya selfish cunt".

"Selfish", he says, "you wouldn't have a vape if it weren't for me".

"You stupid small minded cunt", I say, "I've put so much energy into you. You came into my cell promising you were clean, a blatant fuckin' lie. I sit watching you get out ya fuckin' nut day and night. I pick you up off the floor every fuckin' night, babysit you you fuckin' retard 'cause you throw food and drink all over yourself. Constantly on guard you don't scold yourself, don't set fire to something. You're a fuckin' drain. Then, after throwing coffee all over the floor or puking your ring up everywhere you've the cheek to get the fuckin' hump with me when I leave paperwork on the side once you've woken up with a bit of clarity in the morning ya cheeky fucker".

"What d'ya mean"?

"Look man, you might well help me but don't be blind to the fact I help you too. The thing is you're so out your fuckin' nut you don't see it mate. You've even got me doing your fuckin' Step Work for fuck sake. And lying for you on Bridge! I hate fuckin' lying when I'm clean Marcus! Remember that question in the green and gold NA Step Working Guide where it asks 'what did you do in active addiction that went against all your core values and principles'? Well. I'm going against them now, clean and sober and I fuckin' hate it but do it out of loyalty, to fuckin' protect you you cunt".

"No I know man but I am gonna get off the drugs man watch me bro".

"Oh Marcus, turn it fuckin' in".

"What, you don't believe me"?

"No mate". And here he sulks. I give him my vape battery and he smokes more spice and then none of this matters to him anyway for he is dribbling and snoring and spluttering once more. I tell myself I need to remember that I too struggled to get clean, that it isn't easy and that I must simply accept the fact he is as of yet not quite ready.

6-02-2019 1130hrs and we just got out of group. Kempy and Ricky Lanes are in the cell.

"Any spice Kempy"? asks Ricky.

"Naaa mate", says Kempy to Rick, "you got any mix for me though bro"? meaning the tea bag rubbed in a nicotine patch described through the narrative.

"I have got patches", says Ricky, "but I can't get a PG Tip anywhere".

"Give me half a patch then", says Kempster to Rick.

"I will, just let me sort something out", says Rick.

"Fuck it, keep it", says Just For Men who, once Rick has gone, tells me:

"See him Sloaney he'll get fuck all off me mate, he's such a tight cunt", and now Pete, Rick's brother, has just walked in the cell.

"How much was that coat Kempy"? he asks of Just For Men.

"One fifty", says Kempy.

"Where d'ya get it"?

"At the garden centre in Ramsgate", replies Just For Men.

"Got some fuckin' nice clobber up there ain't they"? says Pete.

"Yeah man I've had some lovely bits from there over the years", says Just For Men Kempy. Anyway, I popped into the wing office earlier this morning only to find Ms Slane, the tall Amazonian beauty and the sexy little Ms H, otherwise known as Pocket Rocket, bent over the computer studiously. My days, those two beautiful bums stuck out pertly for my

231

perusal. Needless to say I fucked off pronto before my mind got too pesty deciding rather to return later when they weren't busy.

"Still writing that book Sloaney"? says Gibbo, who's just come into the cell, "you must have a thousand pages by now".

"Not quite", I say, "707 is the number atop this page".

"Fuck me", he says, "you won't be able to carry the cunt by the time you get out".

"You gonna do that graffiti for me? 'Cause if you do, I'll use it for the cover of the book when I publish it".

"Yeah, you'll have to give me the book title though".

"Memoirs Of A Modern Man", I say, "but I'm also thinking 'Cellmates' now too. Fuck knows, one or the other".

"Cool man", he says, "I'll get it done for ya at some point bro", and he's gone, on whatever mission he has this morning for the baby faced loon is always wheeling and dealing and up to something.

1600hrs. Okay, now, even the great gangster above can't help me with the tag, for I, not He, have already done the damage which disallows for my early release by breaching every bit of trust I have ever been granted. I.e: being recalled on licence, breaching bail, committing offences on bail over the years etc. So the tag people have decided I can't be trusted to adhere to the tag stipulations. So I will be released on the tenth of July, not in February. No biggy. It is sad for Tan for I know she was getting her hopes up but, hey, it's life.

2045hrs. Great workout earlier. And for the record, J Huss the rapper lives on the wing opposite ours, E wing. Just turned up. People are scuttling over to get the admittedly talented fellas autograph on their prison ID cards. Anyway, remember Tony Giles moved off the wing leaving Peter the task of finding another cellmate? Well, Lanesy got a fella called Alex Black and I have to confess I became very aggressive with him yesterday which is unbecoming of me today. He owes everyone on the wing money, this Alex, including of course Smarcus, or El Chubbo, reminiscent of El Chappo, as he is being called by all us Thanet lot of late. So yesterday as I write away my cell door opens and this fella comes in, sits down and says to me:

"Sloaney, Marcus won't mind if I don't pay him the £20 I owe him this week will he"?

"What d'ya mean? You put it off last week didn't you"? I say.

"I know, but I'm right in trouble and Marcus has got loads of money anyway mate".

"Why can't you pay this week then"?

"'Cause big Scouse Fiddler is on my case so I'm gonna pay him this week and Marcus next week if that's ok"?

"So you think it's alright to mug Marcus off to pay someone else you pisstaking cunt"?

"'Sloaney man I just thought"..........

"Get the fuck out this cell you muggy little cunt. You take the fuckin' piss mate".

"But Sloaney, I'm tryna talk to you mate".

"And I don't want to talk, please just fuck off".

"Sloaney man".......

"FUCK OFF CUNT", and the slippery snakey slag rapidly reverses out the cell. Dear reader I haven't been out the cell for days though of course my door is open and I receive a stream of visitors such as Brad, Just For Men, Dale Pearson the big good looking psycho, Beany and Craig D from next door, Pete Harlow, a skinny fair gangster from Milton Keynes, Pete W whose diary I wrote out for you earlier in the narrative, Lifer Steve who's summing up by the judge at his murder trial you have perused if you've gotten this far, Mark Tattnell the armed robber with the piercing blue eyes, Pete and Ricky Lanes, Terry Hughes who rolled around the floor fighting with me and with whom I now get on with really well, kinda got love for him actually, J.T, Jake, Fiddler, Hyper Reece, Little Martin, H, Craig Mc and of course Grin amongst many others who poke their heads in now and then to shoot the breeze and talk shite. Oh, and Terry Winters. This last is the fella in his perhaps middle to late forties whom I told you is on the Bridge Programme with us but, being inherently honest he couldn't lie and owned up to the fact he is still using which of course meant he could no longer attend. Anyway, he came to me today:

"I've sorted out a move to HMP Brixton", said the ruddy faced softly spoken Tel.

"Oh", I say, "why"?

"Remember I told you I just can't do it here? Well, they run another course in Brixton and apparently there ain't nearly as much spice there as there is here know what I mean"?

"So you're happy then Tel me ol' mate"?

"Buzzing Sloaney, it's just too much here mate with the spice, I've never known anything like it bro".

"I get it mate I do and all power to you man. I reckon though that soon as you get a couple days proper clean time under your belt you'll be off and flying like me".

"Ahhh Sloaney man, I've honestly got nothing but admiration for you, you've done so well to come off all the shit mate and you're a different man from the fella running round like a lunatic on here a while ago. You've put on loads of weight and look really healthy man. You've given me hope bro", and this last makes me feel quite emotional man!

"Terry man that's lovely mate; I don't know what to say bro", and I really don't. He sticks out his hand. We shake warmly and he says:

"You just keep it up 'cause you're a real inspiration mate".

"Fuck me Tel, thankyou so much bro", and I am a touched this staunch man of few words came to tell me this.

7-02-19 1400hrs. Often I think and ponder that had I not been such a little fucker as a kid I mightn't be in this situation now, at forty two years of age. Anyway, before I forget, let me tell you that the exam I sat, the level 2 maths paper, well, the results came back and AddemupAde, who came to tell me said that I literally got 100% of the paper correct. It was, it seems, worth spending the full allotted two hours checking and rechecking my calculations! I can remember the paper hurt my brain in the satisfying way only maths can! I find the subject so stimulating and really wish I'd more time on earth to learn a little more about this magnificent discipline. As I say, I'll never be Newton but there's still exciting stuff for the average man to discover. So, this pleased me and, it must be said, AddemupAde greatly. Anyway, we are all now in the Bridge group room doing our creative art session thus me penning this whilst others colour and draw and doodle. Relaxing music plays in the background and the sun illuminates swirling eddies of dust with watery fingers.

"What we got next week"? asks Terry Hughes my boxing buddy of Aron 'Woody' Wood, the facilitator.

"Next week", says he, "we have peer evaluations".

"What happens on them then"? asks Marcus.

"Well", says Woody, "it's paperwork based and what we do is stick names in a hat and the name you pick out you'll be writing one positive thing and one negative thing about that person".

"Shit man", says Hyper Reece, "that sounds daunting".

"Bit like when I was in the Ley Community", I say, "we used to have this game called 'back to back'. So, basically, at first, someone from the co-ords (house management) office would choose two people from the multitude of us in the room. These two people stand back to back in the middle in front of the thirty or so of us watching and the senior, the one who'd been there longest would start with 'one thing I don't like about you' before letting the fella he's back to back with have it with the flaw he has for him. Then the other person would do the same, the 'don't like' thing first. Then, once the harsh bit is done, the two walk to opposite

234

ends of the room and face one another before telling each other something they do like about one another, then the room would applaud and two more people get a go. And so on. There were loads of mad games in that place which used to help us understand ourselves better, warts and all".

"Yeah", says Woody, "it's much the same thing really; it's not about attacking each other guys so don't worry". Anyway, in the room right now young Martin, (Little Martin) Terry Hughes and Paul Mitchell are colouring stuff in. Marcus 'El Chubbo Money Man' T is writing a letter to his sexy screwess chick, I am writing this of course and Ricky Lanes the fat fuck whom I love is sitting perusing a book in the corner of the room.

"What's that fucker Alex's name your brother was banged up with 'till he got banged in the mouth this morning"? I ask Ricky. Ricky furrows his brow above his reading specs.

"I dunno ya know" he says, "shitcunt"?

"They've nicked Peter", says Ricky, meaning Pete will have to go in front of the governor and perhaps have days added to his sentence for banging the ballbag in the face.

"What's the charge"? I ask, "fighting or assault"?

"Well", says Rick, "because they've only seen Pete smash the cunt in the face on the cameras and not what came before it it's assault".

"That could cost him his D cat", I say.

"You know that don't ya Sloaney", says Rick, "and if that happens I'm gonna go kick the cunt out the prick meself ya know what I mean"?

"But Rick", I say, thinking I need to be the voice of reason here, "if you do that then that's two of you fucked 'cause I've no doubt the cunt would grass you straight up".

"I know Sloaney but I can't have that cunt fuckin' my brother's sentence up ya get me"?

"But Rick, you'd be kicked off of Bridge, kicked off the wing and no doubt lose days yourself mate".

"I'm just fuckin' fumin' mate, ya get me Sloaney? That cunt, who owes absolutely everyone on the wing is just walking about whilst Pete is stuck behind his door waiting to go down the block for his nicking".

"You've got to let go of it Rick", says Marcus in a rare burst of common sense, "you've been fuming over it all morning".

"I know Marcus but that cunt deserved a dig", says Rick.

"He is a fuckin' nause", says Terry Hughes, "all the cunt ever comes to me saying is 'have you got have you got' and I've felt like weighing the cunt in myself".

"Me too", I say, "I told him yesterday to get the fuck out of my cell then felt bad for getting aggressive with the soppy cunt".

"Don't feel bad mate, the geezer's a cunt", says Rick.

"Yeah", says Terry, "fuck 'im Sloaney", and of course they're right. It's lovely in this room right now to see Reece and Martin smiling and laughing together the young fuckers. As I said earlier, I am not at liberty to disclose their stuff but they really are starting to open up in what are becoming intense, honest therapy sessions in this room during the mornings, week days. Both these boys have broken in here, as I first did when I felt safe in the Ley Community many moons ago, realizing I could do so without fear of ridicule. I dare say both these lads have never before talked about how they felt growing up in extremely dysfunctional environments, and that's a euphemistic way to describe their respective upbringings. The stuff they are talking of is the stuff that they have been using drugs on for years. Feelings of isolation, being different, not fitting in, being less than, low self-esteem, believing they are stupid, unlovable, not worthwhile, unemployable, ugly and myriad other erroneous beliefs about themselves brought about by trauma they suffered whilst very young and things they were told during formative years.

"Size a ya fuckin' arms Martin", I say now.

"What", he says, "d'ya think they're getting big"?

"Behave mate, you fuckin' know they are bro", I say, smiling.

"I know right", says Marcus, "you on 'roids or what bro"?

"Naaa man", says young Martin, "since I stopped smoking I reckon it's like helped with my blood flow and that".

"It does", I say.

"And I've been using creatine and whey protein as well", says Martin.

"I'm gonna start getting down the gym", says Reece.

"Yeah yeah", says Marcus to Reece, "heard it all before mate".

"Yep", I concur, "talk's cheap mucca".

"I know I keep saying it but I am gonna get down there I'm just workin' myself up to it" and now the session is nearly finished and we are about to say the serenity prayer in closing as we always do: God, grant me the serenity, to accept the things I cannot change, courage to change the things I can, and the wisdom to know the difference.

We come out the group room and immediately we are on the landing Marcus talks to a fella who reloads him with pages of spice paper worth £1300. Yes, thirteen hundred quids worth 'wing' value. Peter Lanes, let out his cell despite having not yet been down the block for his nicking by one of the decent officers on this wing, is in the cell completing the art on the wall now he knows that Marcus has 'got' again!

"Marcus", I say, "I don't feel comfortable leaving this cell with all the spice in it so one of us should hang about in here if the other is out the pad".

"Yeah, you're right", and he goes out to do a bit of running about. Pete W comes in and gives me a fist bump before shooting out to go about his business shaking cunts up in anticipation of Black Eye Friday tomorrow.

"You alright Sloaney"? says Steve Fiddler, popping in to say hello.

"Yeah bro, you sweet"?

"Yeah bro, same shit, different day", before he, too, goes out and about his business.

"Do you think I was in the wrong this morning Sloaney"? asks Pete Lanes who stands on a chair with a paintbrush in his hand, "bashing that cunt I mean"?

"No", I say, "can't fuckin' stand the cunt: you should of hit him a couple more times man".

"At least one good thing came out of it 'cause now I've got Kempy moving in my cell", he says.

"Yeah", I say, "Kempy is a fuckin' blinder man", and dear reader the handsome Just For Men using cunt really is. I have known the fella thirty years and he has always been an absolute gent with me. I'm slowly wearing the cunt down though with conversations like this:

"Steve", I'd say, "you know that to have any chance of changing your life and staying out of places like this you have to stop all drugs don't ya mate"?

"Naaaa man", he'd reply, "I'm always gonna have a drink and a joint and maybe a line of coke and that".

"But Steve, a drink and a joint and a sniff have never been enough for you mucca, you're a hardcore user like me".

"But I can handle the drink and the weed though".

"Ok then, when was the last time you were just having the occasional drink and joint out there then mate"? I say.

"Errr", he says, "err, it, well"...............

"Egfuckinzactly", I say, "when you and I were kids right"?

"Well", he mumbles, "well, I suppose, but I reckon if I can get off the methadone and get out clean I could stick to a joint and a beer".

"We are binary people", I say, "we are either in active addiction or not: it's on off, one or zero, yes or no".

"I don't like the idea Sloaney", he says, "of having nothing in my life ya know? I mean, how fuckin' boring would life be without something to look forward to after work and that"?

"Steve man, look where you are. This is where using any type of drug eventually gets the likes of you and I bro".

"I know Sloaney man, it's just fuckin' hard in it mate"? Anyway, Gibbo has just walked in the cell to admire Pete's handy work on the wall:

"Coming along nicely that in it Sloaney; how long has it taken you Pete"?

"A little while", says the brush wielding Bundy, "I know you could do better Gibbo but it ain't bad is it"?

"Naaa man it's cool", says Gibbo, looking over the big fat graffiti words surrounded by bubbles and love hearts and stars and stuff. Oh, and some admittedly ingeniously drawn flowers. The words so far are 'Gratitude' 'Love' 'Hope' and the cell is looking great considering that when I was in here with Aidy we were living in a spice shit pit which stunk of our rarely washed drug addled bodies and rarely ever got cleaned. Savage, but just the truth. When one has a raging habit needing feeding any free time is spent searching or smoking with little time for anything else in between. Gibbo shoots off and Jake comes in.

"You alright Jake"? I say as he too looks at Pete 'Bundy' Lanes work upon the wall.

"Yeah man, just slowing down a bit with the spice ya know, tryna get off it Sloaney".

"You should man", I say, "get out nice and clean and fresh and healthy".

"I've been doing proper nice cook ups with Russ, me cellmate ya know, got a proper food boat going where we all chip in, me, Russ, Noel and J.T. I ain't eat a prison meal in weeks Sloaney; got a frying pan as well and 'cause the toaster heats from the top and bottom (it's a rolling toaster thing where we put the bread in the top, it goes through the heat then comes out the bottom) we whack the pan in there with chicken we buy from the canteen, peppers, onions, garlic the lot. I made a banging curry the other day; chopped tomatoes, jerk seasoning, egg fried rice, bit of cheese and bundles of other seasoning", and he clearly enjoys and gets excited by cooking.

"You sound like you proper enjoy doing it Jake mate", I say.

"Just something new to do in it", he says, "maybe I could do something with it when I get out. Anyway, has Marcus picked up yet"?

"He has mate yeah; fuck knows where he is though".

"Sweet mate", and he is gone. I had said to Marcus earlier, after he picked up:

"You'd be foolish to start pumping that out today seeing as it's Friday tomorrow".

"I know man", he said, "I've already thought of that 'cause I'm already owed in like 60 packs of vapes tomorrow so there's no point strapping people up until they've already paid me what they owe me. I ain't stupid Sloaney"!

"I know that. Well, you are a bit stupid but I just wanted to make sure we were on the same page"! Anyway, dinner was actually fuckin' lovely tonight: curried chicken leg, I love it on the bone as I enjoy sucking out the meaty marrow afterward which some find distasteful but hey, I never purported to be fuckin' royalty. Now the new handsome young officer Mr Russell is in the cell doing bolts and bars to check the cells' integrity security wise, also insuring that the toilet, sink and cell bell are all in working order. I was gonna go round to Fradders cell but can't be arsed and besides I know El Fat One Marcus is laying all over Brad's bed and will be, against advice, playing El Chappo, distributing drugs and enjoying being king of the wing with all attention on him at present due to the massive amounts of drugs he is holding. That's the new names we have all been calling him of late though; El Fat One and El Chubbo. He loves the steady stream of desperados coming in and out of the cell to him, pleading and begging for what they need. I'm gonna put my pen down for now.

8-02-2019 0719hrs. Each night I get a little shuteye, I find myself mired in using dreams. Last night's dream reminded me of how things could feel if I relapsed for in the dream I found myself street homeless at Kings Cross St Pancras scuttling and scratching around trying to make money to score. I could feel my desperation and loneliness and that feeling I get when I put a fat snowball into my arm of wishing and hoping it is enough to see that I don't wake up. In the dream I remember walking around trying to find, as I have in waking reality, a suitable place on the pavement to bed down for the night, wondering if I'm far enough from rowdy pubs to insure some pissed up prick doesn't decide to set fire to me for fun. In the God sent dream I was truly suicidal and upon waking from this terror I initially struggled distinguishing from the dream and reality, panicking until I realized I was safe and warm in this cell, with the reassuring rhythmic breathing of El Fat One on the bunk below me. I feel God is warning me of what awaits should I pick up. Anyway, canteen day today. I'll report if there are any fireworks.

9-02-2019 0930hrs. Saturday morning and it is lock up 'till eleven, lunch, bang up midday 'till two then out till five. El Chubbo, as I told you, picked up a load of power paper spice the other day and though it is very strong so the boys are saying, Marcus still manged, last night, to plough through £75 worth before eating piles and piles of chocolates and crisps and drinking five cans of coke the last of which the bed drank, all over himself and his duvet. Seeing as I get little sleep I was alerted at 3am by the sound of him coughing and spluttering and he has come over very sick due to his drug use but predominantly his opioid use which, despite massive doses, is failing to 'hold' him, or keep him well, right through the night. He is needing ever larger doses to keep him well and his pregablin habit is also massive. Even now, at this very minute as I write, despite the fact there is an icy breeze, nay, wind whooshing through our broken window, El Chubbo is lathered in sweat and shivering sickly. All night, whenever I hear a lull in his laboured breathing I bang the side of my bunk and go:

"Marcus, Marcus mate you're worrying me man".

"Eeerrrddrrrphlew Shhhloaney man", he would go, or something else just as unintelligible.

"That's enough bro, just want to know you're breathing mate". Anyway, throughout the long night the DAB kept me company as I smiled and sang along to Fleetwood Mac and Seven Wonders, Madonna and Like A Virgin, U2 and Still Haven't Found and that banger Fade To Grey by fuck knows who, can't remember. Oh, and Stone Roses Wanna Be Adored with the wonderfully dark guitar rift in the background accompanying the worryingly just as foreboding lyrics of Ian Brown. Anyway, today I have promised Billy Banks and Jay Nevin, nutcase psycho cockney boys both, that I would spend half hour with each of them at some point during the weekend. With me pad and paper. I can't do 'em both at the same time as it would just get confusing as both these fuckers can rabbit for England. Nev gave me a brief synopsis of what he plans to share with me and I promise it sounds amusing if, like me, you can find humour in violence and people doing funny things with sawn off body parts. I'm sure you can, for we humans are good at laughing at the misfortune of others; tell me you haven't seen someone trip and fall but despite the fact they're clearly in pain you, you savage, find nothing but hilarity in the situation!

Marcus reminds me of Sisyphus and his boulder in Hades. I mean, El Fat One did a savage detox, getting to the top of the hill but now he has tumbled right back to square one again the poor cunt. For fleeting moments during the nights I find myself envious that he can sleep and sleep and sleep but then I remind me that I'd rather be clean and be clockwatching, awake 24/7 than be in that place again for sleep, if I just hold on, will eventually normalize. I have to remind myself when

240

lamenting my insomnia that I am just 25 days clean. El Fatto is stirring on the bed beside me as I sit with my pen and paper.

"Ahhh man", stretches he, "I feel like shit man. Not sure I'll make it to the gym today", but I can tell from the lack of tremor or laboured breathing he is a bit better at least.

"You sound better bro and I must say I'm relieved you seem more lucid".

"Last night I felt fucked: did you hear me struggling to breathe and coughing and that"?

"You cheeky cunt", I say, "don't you remember me babysitting you"?

"Naaa man", he says, "I couldn't even move and it felt like I'd had a dirty hit Sloaney 'cause I was like proper sweating but shivering and freezing at the same time", and reader a dirty hit is when we prepare an injection but pull some foreign particle into the syringe before blasting it into the blood stream causing horrific symptoms where the recipient wishes he or she were dead so dreadful are they.

"I know mate, don't you remember me getting up at 3am and making you a cup of tea"?

"Oh yeah, honestly Sloaney I felt fucked man".

"Marcus man, you and me both know that the majority of the NPS (New Psychoactive Substances or Spice) you are smoking is either alloy wheel cleaner or cockroach killer? And you smoke literally more than anyone else on the whole wing. Can you imagine what that is doing to your insides mate"?

"I wish God could just come down and take all these drugs out of me with no withdrawels ya know"?

"He could", I say, "but then there'd be no sense of consequences and we'd never learn that way. Pain is a way of showing us what not to do".

"I suppose so", he says, El Fat Stuff, forlornly.

"Have you got a like high pitched ringing, like constantly, in your ears El Chubbo"?

"No, why"? he says.

"It's God's personal song to me then", I conclude, happily. It's midday, banged up. Just before that when the door was still open I was on the phone to Tan:

"You alright wench"?

"Yeah, just getting ready for work; can't wait to get back to my dementia patients", and she laughs out loud.

"Fuck me I'm missing you Tan".

"I am you too. You know I got this nice new little flat and a job for you don't ya"?

"Ahhh babe, really"?

"Course. I did listen to some of the things you said to me ya know, I already knew I had to start making some changes".

"God Tan I wish I was there with you now, snuggled up beside you in bed. I'm fuckin' surrounded by people here babe but still fuckin' lonely at times ya know"?

"Bless you. You're making me sad".

"What ya wearing", I can't help but ask.

"A pair of old PJs".

"No knickers"?

"No knickers"!

"I'd love to be sliding those PJs over your creamy bum man".

"Don't fuckin' wind me up Andrew, I love your cock in me".

"Sliding up inside you"………and dear reader I must stop. It's too much. I'm horny as a goat in season. Painful. Anyway, yesterday's circuit has written me off and now El Chubbo, who's now had his spinach in the form of subutex, is telling me I need to be doing this and that in the gym and I tell him that:

"That fuckin' circuit slaughtered me yesterday Fat Boy so I'm just gonna plod along on the running machine today bro".

"You can't pick and choose Sloaney; it's leg day today".

"Smarcus", I say, patiently, "there's no fuckin' point in me doing legs if the muscle is already ripped to shreds man".

"You gotta push through that Sloaney".

"Naaa mate, cardio today bro". Oh, while I'm at it, let me tell you how very devious this good looking drug dealing fuckin' sick puppy really is. Now, dear reader, remember I told you that his last two girlfriends, including his current, were officers he pulled whilst serving sentences, literally he having charmed the knickers and uniforms off of them? Well, he has his eye on the sexy sultress Amazonian screwess, Ms Slane. El Chubbo employs Steve the lifer, by paying him spice, to go up to Ms Slane with little messages.

"Steve, right, just go up to her and say 'Marcus has got real feelings for you Ms Slane and he actually told me that he'd leave his girlfriend for you' but make sure you tell her not to tell me you told her ya get me", then the deviant laughs at his own ingenuity! Steve comes back and reports to El Chubbo that Ms Slane said 'ahhh bless him, did he really say that'? and then Marcus deliberately, he tells me, each time he passes her, puts his head down as if he is all shy! I'm laughing now as I type here in Oxford! He is truly incorrigible! A deviant of the highest order, he has spent the whole of the lunch period in the toilet with a porn mag and comes out sweating profusely after beating himself half to death! Regarding Ms Slane he tells me that he is waiting for any indication that she is interested and if she takes the bait he's gonna go to work on her properly.

"Sloaney", says Brad, poking his head through the now open cell door, "I'm just gonna catch some food for the spider", and he has a thin stick in his hand. He will go onto the high fenced yard which is open on association periods and use the stick to tickle creatures from crevices and then he will put the live usually tube web spiders into his pet's lair. I go round to his cell and he returns with two of the little spiders, well one is quite big really, and he opens the door to the Perspex box containing his beast and puts both the doomed little critters in before closing the door on them.

"Wow", I say, as his beast immediately pounces on one of the prey presented, sinking savage fangs through it.

"No fuckin' way"! says Just For Men.

"What if you fed it spunk"? says sick boy El Fat One.

"What sort of cunt says that"? says Steve Just For Men Kemp, continuing, "it's still alive in her mouth man"!

"It's pumping necrotic venom into it now", says Brad, helpfully.

"Yeah, but Brad, would it eat spunk though"? asks the sick puppy again.

"Marcus man you're fucked bruv", says Kempy. I can't help but snigger though, which says a lot about me I suppose!

"No Marcus man", says Brad patiently, "she won't eat anything unless it's alive". Now Ms Slane comes in doing bolts and bars and we are all looking at her banging arse and smelling her perfume as she walks into the cell, bangs the bars and window, checks the fittings before turning and sauntering sexily out again, knowing we are all pervertedly perusing her profile.

"I fuckin' hate spiders", says Chubbo.

"Me too", says Kempy.

"I think she's fuckin' fit", say I.

"She's got the best arse on here", says Marcus.

"Look at the colours on the spider Sloaney", says Brad, "proper brindle she is".

"I know man, I was looking at her yesterday. She's a gorgeous beast". She is but a bit smaller, only slightly mind you, with all her legs splayed, than a regular beer mat. She is extremely happy, it would seem, in the ingeniously designed box on its clever plinth that Brad made. We now have Beany, Craige D, Matchstick Model Maker Moody Trevor and Jake all looking in as the spider sucks the innards out of its prey and there are noises like:

"Errrr".

"Wow man".

"Shit".

"Savage", and it really is an interesting thing to behold. She is manoeuvring it now, doing fuck knows what with the poor thing doomed to be food. Steve Kemp is now using a magnifying glass to get a closer look.

"Wow man", he says, "she's proper like chewing on it now".

"Can you see her eyes sparkling back at ya"? asks Brad.

"Yeah man".

"Did you see her fangs Steve"? asks Brad then.

"Yeah man, they're like sheathed in a sort of housing".

"They're called 'chelicerae'", says Brad, "most people actually think they're the fangs but they ain't".

"Wow man, she's made short work of that", I say.

"The other spider you put in there Brad, the one she ain't eat yet, ain't she, like, a bit big for her"? asks Kempster, "couldn't she hurt her"?

"Naaa man", Brad says, "d'ya like the way she stands on tip toes when she's eating Sloaney"?

"Yeah man", I say, "why does she do that"?

"So she doesn't contaminate her food with her web or detritus from her web".

"Have you named her"? I ask.

"Monster", says Brad.

"Apt", say I. Trust me people if you don't like spiders then this cunt in your house would scare the shit outta you. Anyway, I'm off to the gym. Later.

1600hrs. I stuck to my guns and ran 9 kilometres on the treadmill, plodding along slowly. Upon returning to the wing a little while ago there were four sexy female screws on the ones landing, Ms H, (Pocket Rocket), Ms Slane and two I've never met. I left but Pete Lanes and El Chubbo loitered and Marcus tells me that one of the ones I don't know asked Marcus if he would fill in an 'officer of the year' form and Pete Lanes piped up to all four of 'em and said:

"I'll do it for a blow job".

"No fuckin' way", I say, "did they bollock him for it or what"?

"Nope"!

"What did they say then"?

"Nothing", says El Fat One, "they just laughed"!

"So what was you doing earlier, talking to Ms Slane on your own"?

"Tryna put some more groundwork in", he says.

"Did you get anywhere"?

244

"Well, I asked her if she was doing anything for Valentine's Day and she said she doesn't do Valentine's Day anymore".

"Oh yeah"?

"Yeah", he continues," and I asked her if she's ever, like, been hurt and that and at first she was a bit, like, scared to open up and that but when I told her I'd never repeat anything she said and that she should treat it like a counselling session she started talking and I was getting somewhere until you came along and spoiled it"!

"Spoiled what"?

"Well, I think I'm like getting somewhere 'cause she like told me she ain't had a relationship since 2016 and I said, 'what, you been celibate'? and she like laughed and I said, 'ahh, you've had a seeing too then' and she proper laughed again".

"You are incorrigible you know that"?

"What the fuck does that mean"?

"In this context it means you are a pesty fucker unlikely to change me old mucca"!

"Naaaa man it ain't like that, I'm just tryna like help her out and that Sloaney".

"Behave mate you're talking to me you fuckin' deviant"!

"I just really like her man", says this lecherous lunatic.

"Fuck off Marcus: would you leave Lauren for her"?

"No way man"!

"Then what you tryna get out of Ms Slane"?

"Just tryna pull her Sloaney man".

"Why though? If you ain't got serious designs on her then what you gonna get out of it"?

"It's just like a challenge in it"?

"You'd just like to fuck her you mean mate, come on"!

"Well you never know, she might be quite happy just to fuck me even though she knows I've got a girlfriend".

"Do you reckon you could fuck her here"?

"Fuck knows. I'd like to though. I'm thinking about writing her a letter. Today I asked her what she does when prisoners say sexual things to her and she says she deals with it herself. I asked if she tells the other screws and she said no, she can deal with it on her own and I thought 'boom' I can push the boat right out now but then you come along and start talking about the speed of light and that".

"You were proper giving me evils ya cunt", I say.

"Well naa but I was proper getting somewhere and you coulda just fucked off know what I mean"?

"How the fuck was I to know you was proper firing into her you pesty fucker"?

"I was proper getting a boner when you come along Sloaney and I just wanted you to fuck off"!

"My God", I say, hilarity written all over me, "you truly are a savage! What would Lauren think"?

"She'd be proper devastated 'cause she thinks I've never cheated"!

"Have you cheated on her though"?

"Course I have! Loads, but she'll never know that"!

"She fuckin' will now"!" I say!

"You can't write that"! he says.

"Yeah I can. It'll be alright. You just tell her I'm a lying burgling criminal scumbag and that I tell lies all the time"!

"I'll sue you Sloaney", says El Fatto and I can't help but guffaw at this.

"So sue me"! We are banged up and the cunt has been perusing a porn mag for two hours.

"This mag is shit, I just can't seem to get hard or excited over it".

"Cause you're out ya nut ya silly cunt", I say.

"I just need to have a good wank and get all this spunk out of me man".

"You're one sick puppy ya know that"?

"Right", he says, getting up and going behind the curtain to the toilet, "I'm gonna see if I can have a rub".

"You are a rub ya cunt", I say, "you never leave yourself alone. Don't it like sap your strength and that"?

"Shut up Sloaney man I'm getting hard now".

"Fuck me", I say after a couple of minutes, "I can proper like hear you heavy breathing and that".

"Fuck sake man please", he says from behind the curtain.

"The Queen Mother", I say.

"Shut up man please", and I can hear the turning of pages and spanking of flesh, "Please man Sloaney I never do it to you"!

"I never do what you do. If I have to to let off the valve occasionally I do it when you're out the cell and it's a minute tops, straight into the toilet and done"! He doesn't respond. He's in there over an hour usually. I'm gonna pick up Paulo Coehlo and try to wind down.

10-02-2019. 1017hrs. In Brad's cell this Sunday morning with Brad, Grin, Dale and Just For Men Kemp. Now dear reader I know this is repetitive boring stuff this book but hey that matches the circumstances. It is repeat, repeat, repeat and more of the same in jail with the odd bit of savage entertainment thrown in, sometimes and at its most amusing when at another's expense. I still haven't gotten Jay Nevin and Bill but I can't quite do it just now for they do drain the life out a me the mental pair a cunts. Dale is waxing lyrical right now on multitudinous and varied subjects which change so quickly I can't keep up. Needless to say there is talk of prior drug use, extreme acts of violence and 'I smashed the life out of her' sex talk between him and Grinley who hail from round about the same ends and know the same people. Brad is sitting, like me, no doubt, thinking 'fuck the volume is high in here this morning'.

"I used to tie her up and that and slap her with my dick my ex", says Dale, continuing that, "these female screws in here couldn't deal with me in the bedroom I'd rag the life out of 'em".

"I'd love to smash that Sarah again", Grin says.

"Yeah", says Dale, "I'm gonna tear through her again when I get out, have a pipe (smoke crack) and that then smash the slag 'round the bedroom". Now he is saying:

"I'd've been good in the army me; I'd've loved it, going out to Afghanistan and cutting terrorists up", and he continues, "yeah I'd've loved it but I'm fucked in the head now I'd've definitely come out with like PTSD and that and proper twisted up".

"Yeah", says Brad, "David Bowie was on a documentary saying he found a brother he didn't know he had and Bowie said his brother was a massive inspiration for him but he went in the navy and when he came back he went in a mental institution and never got out again". But this is lost on Dale.

"I'd've been lethal in the army man, a proper weapon, I would have fuckin' loved it". And now dear reader Gibbo and Brad are making rice crispie cakes with marshmallow and chocolate inside a washing up bowl, you know the big tub things, something prisoners often use to prepare food. Now me and Jake are discussing El Chubbo who doesn't leave the cell until he's had a line of subutex. Outside Brad's door I can hear J.T running up and down the landing going 'Sloaney, Sloaney, Sloaney' but I cannot be bothered to move. He told me earlier he wants me to help him with something but I've not the energy. The cell empties as people go about their business leaving just me and Grin who is telling me a tale of a fella in Swaleside high security prison. Grin is saying that there was this horrible bully prisoner on the wing that no one liked who nicked an ounce of heroin off of someone who had trusted him with the parcel. Now this horrible bully guy had a budgie and the geezer he nicked the heroin off, not paying him, was a fuckin' loon himself. Now, knowing that the bully non paying thief loved his budgie he waited for a moment when he could slip in and steal the cage which he did, taking the bird back to his own cell on the twos landing and being careful to always keep his door locked or guarded when they were out on association so the thieving fucker couldn't steal his bird back.

"You can have ya fuckin' bird back when you pay me my money", he told the debtor. Anyway, after some time, and realizing he wasn't gonna get his money he ripped the birds head off, wrapped it up in cling film like a parcel of drugs and, one night, being above the geezer who owes him he bangs the ceiling telling him, out the window, that he had one more chance.

"I'm gonna send you down something on a line and I want you to bottle it (put it up your arse) and keep it 'till the weekend. Don't open it", and he sends a line (torn bit of sheet) down with the 'parcel' on the end of it.

"Now Sloaney, the geezer thinks the cling film wrap is a parcel of smack, that he has got another chance the silly cunt. He thinks the budgie is just kidnapped due to the debt and he is contrite 'cause he knows he's done wrong man. He thinks when he eventually pays the debt he'll get the bird back".

"Go on Grin, what happened"?

"Couple days later there's no drugs on the wing. The drug thief is begging the fella to let him open the parcel in his arse but the fella tells him no, you've gotta wait. That night, an hour after bang up, you heard a wail from a bloke serving eighteen years that sounded like the scream of a five year old girl Sloaney. 'Nooooo, noooo, nooo', the geezer was going and obviously he hadn't waited and had opened up the parcel, expecting to find heroin but instead he found the head of his beloved budgie which sent him over the edge and he was never seen again".

"People get proper attached to their birds in those long term nicks I guess".

"He fuckin' loved that bird man. I bet it slaughtered him knowing he'd been walking about with his beloved birds head up his own arse"!

"Wow man, that is fuckin' brutal bro"! Not much shocks me, but I kind of feel for bird man!

"Yeah man, to hear a man doing eighteen years, a big bloke too, screaming like that, like a baby, was something. Big, hairy arsed gym nut too"! Bradley Cooper and Lady Gaga are singing their sonorous duet on 4music and my heart longs and hair stands on end. I realize I feel lonely. Yet think I probably deserve it as my karmic debt is massive.

"Got any spice"? J.T now asks Brad, "my fuckin' toilet is blocked up again".

"Stick some bleach and a bucket a water on it", says Brad.

"Honestly", says J.T, "I've proper had me hand down there but the shit is proper compressed and the water keeps overflowing every time I try to flush the fuckin' thing. I don't know what to do man".

"Ee'ya", says Brad, giving J.T a sliver of spice, "that'll fix it", he goes on with a sarcastic grin and talking of Grins he comes in the cell and smokes a fat spice pipe rendering him moronic and Travis Scott raps on the TV as I write.

1500hrs. I didn't go to the gym today. Smarcus has after calling me a pussy etc. No sooner has he left the cell I'm on my knees and praying to the Cosmic Lord. As I do so the singing in my ear rises and falls, fluctuating in frequency and confirming my prayers are heard.

1550hrs and Mr Saville opens my door as he goes about letting us out for the final period for feeding. He smiles at me.

"Sloaney", he says.

"Saville", I say and the jocular fella moves on. The wing is strangely quiet.

1730hrs. As soon as El Chubbo returned from the gym and noticed Ms Slane on duty he again paid Steve Bennett the lifer spice to relay a message to her that 'Marcus is a little bit worried that you'll talk to other staff members ' and she sent back the message that he needn't worry. Then, when Marcus hears this he scuttles up to her and spends the remaining minutes of unlock perving and pesting her up. I don't know what you think dear reader but from here it would seem his deviant masterplan may well bear fruit. Peachy, taut, firm fruit at that. Still, Ms Slane will never know the devious lengths the reprobate El Fat One went to in order to achieve his ends should it do so. Saying this, she's very professional and probably, like the rest of the staff team, just wants to help the silly cunt.

"Third time lucky", Marcus now says to me.

"So you would leave Lauren then"?

"Well", he says, "you just don't know do ya"?

"Savage"!

"I'd leave Lauren at the weekends and go to Ms Slane to see if it could work out and if it didn't then I know Lauren would always be there for me anyway like safe, tucked away waiting". Needless to say he has already told Ms Slane the genuinely sad facts of his family: mum and dad both dead, no aunties or uncles and he told me that she stood fluttering her eyelids, put her hand over hear heart and said:

249

"Oh sweetie, that's so sad". Anyway, I have decided I'm not doing Billy and Nev. The thought of spending time with them has me feeling faint let alone being in their company for extended periods of time. Good mental lads but too much for me right about now. Marcus is now out his nut after having picked up another fuck off parcel of spice down the gym from his lifer pal and though I said I'd avoid words like spastic and retard, as the cunt lays dribbling trying to articulate himself they are the words that come to mind as I say to him that:

"I'm sorry mate, but I don't speak mong".

Valentine's Day 2019. 2010hrs. Banged up of course. I had a real go at Brad today. He asked me why I had the number of my clean days written on my hand.

"So I can see easily how much time I have under me belt".

"It's like you want to show off your clean time Sloaney, like so all of us can see it".

"What"?

"It's like you're doing it, like getting clean, for us"! he says.

"Oh my fuckin days", I say, anger fuming within me, "you honestly think that I would get clean to show off to the likes of you you silly cunt when I couldn't get clean for my mum, my son, my partners or other people I love in my life? You're a fuckin' moron mate", and I had left the cell thinking if I don't get away and he says something I don't like I'd end up banging him in the boat race. That's how angry I felt. I must remind you that I would never hurt Brad but he is jealous for he will never get off methadone, never stop using drugs. He'll likely be navigating the choppy channels of addiction and incarceration for the rest of his days the poor cunt. Marcus is dribbling to my right on his bunk, barely able to speak.

"Shhhloaney man, Shloaney, I'm not giving anyone anything anymore 'cause they're all taking the fuckin' pissshhh outta me man", and he has the hump because Brad, who has been looking after his 30pks of vapes has been helping himself. Chubbo is talking again.

"pisshhhtaker", he says, "Shhloaney man pass me the tissue quick I've pisshed myself accidently", and I do as requested. He cleans himself up then throws a whole bowl of cereal down himself and his bed. "Fucksshh shake Shhloaney man help me man", and I clean the mong up as if he were a baby, putting tissue in his hand so he can try deal with downstairs himself.

"Kempy takeshh ja pisshhh man", he says, "nickin' my fuckin' protein powder earlier and helping himself", and indeed Kempster, the

250

lovable smiling deceitful fuck, after having asked me yesterday and me telling him:

"I'll give you one shake but you ain't willing to work in the nick so it's the one and only bro 'cause the shit is expensive man".

"Sweet man", said Just For Men but today he came in after gym saying:

"I've just seen El Chubbo downstairs and he said I could have some of his protein for a shake".

"Straight"? I'd asked, "I knew he'd fold with you even though he says that's the one thing he won't share with anyone".

"Yeah man, just seen him by the servery and he said I could have one".

"Ok cool", and I let him prepare one of El Fat Boy's shakes in the cell. When me and Marcus are banged up I say:

"I knew you'd cave in and give Just For Men a shake", but he looks at me baffled.

"What you on about"?

"He came in", I say, "helped himself to a shake saying he'd just seen you and you said 'sweet, help yourself or see Sloaney'".

"What", says El Fatto, "and you let him"?

"Well yeah, he's never lied to me before".

"He's a slippery cunt Sloaney man. Right, I'm gonna see him in the fuckin' morning man".

"He'll only make a joke of it Marcus, you know what he's like bro".

"Pisstakin' cunt mate and you shoulda known better man".

"Fuck me, it ain't my fault", I say.

"I know man sorry, it's just no matter what or how much I give to people they still take the piss".

"I get that mate, I do". Anyway, tomorrow morning at ten bells I have an appointment down the ATB unit with Jason, Lucy, Naomi and co. I must get the officer's names who work down there as they're good lads too. You have to remember, these lot are happiest when they are seeing prisoners making real change that would enable them to break the cycle which constantly returns them to these places. The majority of the British prison estate is peopled by the same souls who return time and time again. I always see the same lads in jail, year in year out. This is what's known as a 'C' cat training prison with work and courses to try break those patterns. Though many of the cons here are serving long periods, including many doing life, they are toward the end of their tenures and are here to prepare themselves for the outside world awaiting them. The officers I talk about on Alpha and down the ATB Unit and, generally barring a few idiots, the jail in general, are good people, not like the bully cunts one can frequently find in the 'B' cat establishments I have been attending for prolonged periods over the 27 years I have been holidaying at Her Maj's Pleasure. Although, like I say, if one looks hard enough it wouldn't be difficult to find a few arseholes who think they're hard but here they are really few and far between. Anyway, I'm invited down the unit for tea and cake tomorrow. I don't know what it is about Jason; I just fuckin' really like the guy. And Lucy's shining bright burning intelligence tempered with kindness. She is a fuckin' babe too. And the mental Naomi who, no doubt, despite it being February will be swimming in the freezing waters like a special person. So, I am looking forward to a pleasant morning.

15-02-2019. 1150hrs. I'd never hurt Brad, just for the record. Anyway. I spent an hour and a half down the ATB unit this morning as a sort of tester if you like to see if I was a lazy loafer or enthusiastic when it came to one half of my job: cleaning. They were wowed when I ripped through the toilet area, cleaning every nook and cranny then the sinks and surfaces and pipes and all I could in an hour before Jason called me:
"Come here mate you need to be in this staff meeting".
"Ok", I say, "just wipe off the suds and stuff", and when I've done we all go to a room at the end of the unit. In the room are Mr Hind (head honcho of the ATB Unit with three stripes on his lapels), Naomi the cold water nutty swimmer, Lucy the intelligent witty and occasionally moody babe and Jason of course, the manager of therapeutic programmes. As soon as the door shuts we all burst into 'happy birthday' for lovely Lucy who is 24 years old today. She blushes and looks emotional as we all sit down to a spread and she gets some lovely gifts from her colleagues and I love the way she smiles saying:
"Oh, I can't believe you've done this, thankyou all so much I don't know what to say", and when she clocks the Zara gift card included in her presents she goes:
"Oh wow, I can get that black coat I've seen in there now", and she really is beaming like a Cheshire cat. We are all seated around the table eating cake and the talk is of comedy.
"Just love the old Carry On films", says Naomi, "you just don't get that sort of slapstick humour anymore".
"I do too", says Mr Hind who says I can call him Paul, "at Christmas", he continues, "I watch 'em one after the other on loop".
"And you can't beat old Monty Python Life Of Brian", I say.
"Old 'Bigus Dickus'", says Jason, looking fondly up to the ceiling as he remembers the hilarious film.

"I tell you who I love now", I say, "8 Out Of Ten Cats and Sean Locke; that is one funny fucker".

"He's brilliant, so dry", says Lucy.

"I know right", I say, "he gives his humour in such a lazy disinterested way and has me in stitches regularly". It's great being here right now. Talk inevitably turns to Brexit. It came about when I'd read a passage of my book to the assembled which showed some of the racist views inherent in some prisoners, prisoners close to me. Jason had asked if I see a lot of it on the wing.

"You'd be shocked by the levels on the wing right now. I reckon Brexit and the rise of the right here, in Europe and across the pond with Trump may have a little to do with the fact people are more willing to espouse these views freely right now", I say.

"Which way would you have voted Andy"? from Jason.

"Well, I was originally a Remainer but I've kinda got to be honest and say it was only because I was scared of upsetting the status quo ya know"?

"I voted leave", says Jason and Mr Hind echoes this.

"Well", I say, through mouthfuls of madeira cake, "the reason I'm turning is because when we joined it was economic union, not fuckin' political union and I think we do need our sovereignty back". By the way, in case I didn't mention it, today was to see if I was up for being the orderly down here at the unit, a great job with perks such as many extra gym sessions and much time to sit and write. I would also be helping prepare for new groups and such.

"That's exactly it", says Mr Hind, "having our decisions made in Europe isn't why we were in in the first place".

"I agree", I say, "it was insidious the way the Eurozone impinged the political ideals they hold onto us; fuck me, we just about kept the pound"!

"I think the whole thing's gonna fall apart", says Jason, "it's very shaky at the moment"!

"And there's a massive increase in right wing political parties taking advantage of all the fear at the moment due to all this uncertainty across Europe and it seems to be sweeping the States too. Populist I think these parties call themselves today. I quite like some of them but it's a shame morons can't see that these are still pretty mainstream, I think, and not an excuse to espouse hatred", I say, thinking I'm a little confused by everything right now.

"Anyway", says Lucy, "how's the cake"?

"It's the bollox"! I say, "thanks for including me today people".

"You're welcome Andrew", says Jason, "and I think we're all pretty impressed with you so we look forward to having you down here".

"So", says Lucy, "you're gonna be a member of the team"! I say my good byes as the time comes for mass movement or 'freeflow' and head back to the wing. It is canteen day, Black Eye Friday. I'm back in my call with Marcus and Ricky Lanes comes in.

"It's all a bit mental, but I will get the vapes I owe you Marcus I promise", he says to Marcus. I can hear people frantically running about outside the ajar cell door, names being called, people looking for other people. Mayhem.

"You owe me five packs", Marcus says to Rick.

"I know but I owe Bradders as well so please just give me a little time", and Rick shoots off. Now 'Pony Tail Paul', a tall geezer with, surprisingly, a pony tail, comes into the cell. Marcus is stacking goodies he's accumulating today atop the piles of stock he already has.

"You got my vapes"? asks El Fatto of Pony Tail.

"Yeah, but can I borrow one pack back please"? and remember dear reader that when people borrow the return is known as 'double bubble' so Marcus lends one pack for two packs back.

"When I've collected everything in come and see me. Just want to know what I've got first bro".

"Sweet", says the Pony Tail, shooting off to hustle.

"Ricky's a fuckin' messer", says El Chubbo now but another fella called Briggsy comes in and says to him:

"I ain't got ya vapes Marcus but I've got 4ml of subutex if you'll take that instead"?

"Ok, that's sweet", says El Chubbo who takes little time in crushing the semi synthetic opioid up on a mirror before snorting the lot, and that is a reasonable amount to snort in one go, straight up his hooter.

1610hrs. The ballad of canteen day still plays out on the landings. Little Martyn comes into the cell and we play a few hands of cards. He too, like me, is clean and sober. Now, the story he tells I am gonna write verbatim, as he tells it. He tells me of a fella on C wing in this prison 5 years ago who tried to collect a debt for someone else, got involved trying to make a few packs of vapes as the creditor, his friend, had left.

"And the next day", says Martyn, "he was minding his own business, walking around the wing looking for spice and out of nowhere came a black fella who punched him. He didn't see it coming so he was shocked by the punch, lost balance and hit the deck".

"Go on", I say, prompting him when he pauses.

"So he hit the deck where his skull was shattered and blood was coming out his mouth and ears and he was moaning with the pain he was going through".

"Fuck me", I say, cringing, "go on".

"Yeah, at this point, my cellmate who was with me, stepped over him and asked someone for a rizla so he could smoke spice not paying any attention to what had gone on and where the man was put into a coma for two weeks and was on life support and they brung him out where they realized he was brain dead and had to turn off the machine, Fraser Black was the geezer's name".

"Shit man, that's savage", I say honestly.

"He was twenty-six", says Martyn, continuing, "I was watching the news a year later where the boy who done it, Bruce, he ended up with a manslaughter charge and got 6 years. It just goes to show that if we are put in the wrong predicament anything can happen". Wow. I thank Martyn for sharing this with me and he tells me he has another savage tale of similar nature but it will have to wait for dinner has been called.

1900hrs. Of course Marcus is literally, right now, snoring like an old fuck off fat fella. I really enjoyed today, what with my sojourn to the ATB Unit. Jason, Lucy and co were great company. Then I played cards with young Martyn Perry, drinking coffee and smoking on my vape. Martyn, like me, told me that he rarely masturbates. He believes that saving the old seminal fluid is beneficial to one when going about one's everyday business. Especially concerning using the grey matter and muscles in the gym.

"The ancient scriptures of India speak of this exact same thing", I told him.

"What d'ya mean"? Mart had asked.

"Well, they reckon that when we, like, cum, we are literally shooting out our life force, like our life energy".

"Shit man I knew it"! says this cute faced, brown haired brown eyed high cheekboned youngen of 24, "I always feel like when I shoot my load, like, the next day I feel sort of drained".

"Me too", I'd told him, "in fact, it fucks me up for two days and I don't function as well, ya know, like, my brain can't string sentences together as quickly and I get proper lethargic and depressed too".

"You're the first person ever to say that to me and that's exactly how I get too", replies Martyn.

"Mad in it"! I said.

"Yeah man", and I'm really warming to this humble little fucker with the stocky build and massive arms. Anyway, not only is Marcus right at this minute farting but he is blasting pure protein pong from his arse which necessitates me spraying each emanation down with fabreeze lest I choke on them. Now, despite being wholly unconscious, he is scratching away at his gonnads as if he has a severe infestation of crabs. He is wearing the spice like a hammer blow. I've never met a guy who can be even more uncouth whilst under than when he is when he is conscious. Oh, wait, he's just come around and I read this last paragraph to him as he prepares another massive pipe of spice and I have a brief window to talk to him.

"huh huh huh huh", he goes now, "you're so poetic ain't ya Sloaney, so poetic with your words", and we both laugh at his sarcasm, he mumbles 'uncouth' to himself after sucking the poison into his lungs then promptly loses consciousness.

"Smarcus, Smarcus", I say and he manages to give me a brief look through heavy hooded bloodshot eyes but his head is too heavy to hold and his hand is shaking like a person with palsy before it finds firmament on the bed and he is once again at rest. I watch his bare massive hairless chest rise and fall and hope he is in a peaceful place. Marcus rarely gets the hallucinogenic effect from the spice that I used to get because he puts so many central nervous system depressants on top of it which creates a heavy narcotic buzz rather than a trip. Today, Marcus has had rivotril, xanax, pregablin and bundles of subutex. He manages to sniff out anything of hedonistic value that finds itself on the wing. If Marcus could put the energy he does into his addiction into something productive, with his business skills I have no doubt whatsoever the cunt could be highly successful. Anyway, I have been clean 31 days today, so one whole month. Fleetwood Mac and Dreams emanates from the DAB. Oh, and on the news at the moment is the slut terrorist bride Beghum who, now the cunt caliphate is defeated suddenly wants to return to Britain. The government, however, in a rare show of common sense recognise this cunt has serious ISIS connections and could be only wanting to bring her unborn baby over so that when it is old enough she can dress it in a nice suicide vest and commit another horror like the recent one at the Ariana Grande concert in Manchester. This evil cunt told The Times that she was 'unfazed' by the sight of decapitated heads the savage slut. My God I hate this piece of shit. I'd be quite happy to have her back here but only after the government had sent her to a country where torture is legal and then send me on a plane after to spend a little quality time with her. I'd show her how it feels to be barbarised and hurt the way her people hurt people. I'd pull out her toenails with pliers, pluck out an eye, electric shock her and snap and saw off fingers for information about this savage cult. Fuck Al Baghdadi. And bless the brave Kurds driving last pockets of ISIS resistance from Syria. Make no mistake, this Jihadi whore is one dangerous fuck, even at the tender age of nineteen. We must protect ourselves from such scum. Not only is she what she is she still blatantly shows no remorse and holds true to DAESH ideals. There are certain situations where I could commit evil acts, put me in a room with any of these ISIS monsters tied to a chair and I swear by God I could commit savagery beyond belief. Revenging slaughter of innocents done so brutally by these savages. I would not only get sick satisfaction, but gather vital info for our forces too in the process. So, MI5, come get me, grab the slut, tie her up, make sure I've some sharp implements and electricity and fuck off for forty eight hours shutting the door behind you. Rip the burka from the cunt first. Allow her her underwear so the shit sticks to her when I slash and whip shock and saw at her but I leave the nipples for my electrodes. And some instruction on drug dosages which'll insure she's conscious the whole time. Oh, and info on voltages etc. Oh, and get me a gang of rapists from the local jail and I'd open the door then call 'release the rapists' so they can show her exactly what her people do to other people and how it feels to be so treated. How about it Shamima? Up for it love? I think, now, that the rape bit is a bit strong as I sit in this cell but then I think of all the rape and torture ISIS do and did and all the bombings and maiming and 7/7 and 9/11 and I think 'naaa, fuck it. Run with it'. Once the beastly rapists are done I could have fun gunning those noncy cunts down afterward anyway. Sitting in Oxford now this October afternoon I muse all this is a bit strong and not where I'm at today but, as I said, I want to give an account of me at the time and be true to the manuscript I wrote in jail in real time. So, it stays, for people like me exist, clearly. (Continuing from manuscript) Am I no different from her? Bollox! She is not fuckin' innocent. It's not like she went over at 15 took a look thought 'fuck that' and came back. No. She is nineteen now and only wanting to return because ISIS forces, of which her and her cunt of a husband were some of the hardcore last on the small land they still hold and control, are ousted, him being in Kurdish custody and her being in a refugee camp full of other dangerous cunts just like her now expecting the humanity them and their cunt pals no doubt never showed to the poor cunts in their custody as they begged and pleaded for mercy that would never come. Innocent men, women and children. No. No. No. Fuck her man. Bollox. So much for your caliphate cunt. Islamic sodomites of interbred shitcunts. You've no land. Defeated by the mighty west. I thought you said your flag would fly over Downing Street? Anyway, I must stop this for I am making myself sick.

Wow, shit man that was a rant! I hope you don't find my, my, my, my what? Barbarism? Anger? Disgust? Too fuckin' disturbing. I'm just a modern man. And she a jihadi decapitating murderous slut of the highest order. Anyway, The Stranglers Golden Brown are on her ship, tied to a mast and I'm transported, without heroin, to her distant shores through the melody of the drifting distant music which speaks of smack like no other track on Earth. 'Golden brown, fine a temptress, through the ages she's heading west'! Wow. What willowy words. Lady Poppy, what with your wanton whispers and smoky seductive tendrils and oh! Your warmth and comfort and easing of pain and angst. Your self cuddling cure all ills quality. Only recently divorced and yet still I long for your embrace. Anyway, I am to put down the pen for now but let me tell you that as I recall me writing 'release the rapists' I chuckle to myself at my own savage ingenuity. Ultravox and Vienna play followed by Joy Division and I'm gonna try and sleep.

0542hrs 16-012-2019. Sitting here in Oxford I again peruse the pages I'm about to type and consider, briefly, removing them from the narrative. More through laziness than the fact they swerve from the prison narrative. But I shall stay true to the manuscript. So, at 0542 hrs in this cell I can report that sleep is once more elusive. Just twenty minutes ago I'd woken from fitful slumber to the sound of the blob beneath me, El Chubbo, scratching and scuttling about before I'd smelt the familiar acrid stench of spice. After the sucking sound of the smoking I hear more activity and after some time eventually poke my head over the side of my bunk and see he has filled a bowl with granola then put a whole tin of rice pudding atop it and, when I looked, it was all over him and his bed so I jump off and clean the cunt up; he lifts heavy lids a couple of times and manages a:

"Thankshh Shloaney man", but I have no doubt that he'll remember not a thing when he wakes. He hears me laughing out loud and says slobberingly:

"You takin' the pisshhh out me Shhhlloaney"? and I go:

"Of course I am you fuckin' mongrel; look at the fuckin' state a ya". Dear reader be in no doubt, were it me throwing food all over the shop and generally being a dirtbag, and Marcus sober watching on, with his OCD he would have the right hump. Actually, I'm gonna put that very point to him when his head has cleared. Writing about Shamima Begum earlier took it out of me. I simply should not watch the news. It gets me in sick states like I worked myself into earlier on. News contaminates any semblance of serenity I might sometimes attain. Re her, I don't really know what should be done. Her family here say she should be allowed to return and to be fair there is probably an argument for that. I mean, she was fifteen when she left and is still but a baby at nineteen. Also, growing in her womb is an innocent child. Our government is saying that if she can get to Turkey we may consider helping her. Should she return, we should of course first of all ascertain what offences she has committed and potentially prosecute and secondly she of course needs to be monitored very carefully. Don't get me wrong, I can understand the sentiment of those who would wish her ill but, truly, hatred only ever beget more hatred. Furthermore, remember she was interviewed in a refugee camp full of other Jihadi women and her lack of contrition and comments regarding decapitated heads is perhaps said through fear of prying ears. I really do astound myself for one minute I am murderous and the next considering compassion for the poor foolish girl. I mean, I myself was full of hatred at her age, feeling there was no place for me in this world. I would happily have opened up on police and politicians with automatic weapons had I access to them and enough fury bubbling to spur me on. But would I really? Fantasy! I once asked a psychiatrist in jail if it was normal or uncommon for someone to tell him exactly that, that I fantasized about gunning down people in public and he said it was something he heard more regularly than people would think. Full of anger and vitriol, I gave the same out to the world which I anaesthetised myself against with chemicals. The people I hurt the most were usually those closest to me. Anyway, young hyper Manchester Reece got banged in the face by Beany earlier for a debt he has owed for weeks. I could protect him no longer. Reece also owes money to Craig D, Brad and Marcus but these boys know that he has opened up about some savage shit on the Bridge Programme group and all have such compassion for him they simply can't find it in them to take violence to the poor misfortunate fucker. Beany is in debt himself so panicking let Reece have it. See, Reece is still flat out on the spice. No sooner has he picked up his canteen for the week than the first of the many creditors to see him takes it, swipes it straight out the poor sod's hands. He took massive risks in the group, crying hysterically as he described horrors he went through that no child on Earth should have to endure.

17-02-2019 1330hrs. It is a Sunday afternoon. Marcus has just had his subutex and is asleep. The wing is still in a state of panic as no one has spice: angry bods running about everywhere. All looking depressed and saying 'what sort of drug dealers on here when no one's got nothing'! I used to get the hump myself. I tell you, it amazes me that it is 33 days since I last used anything. It is 8 weeks since I last had a dose of methadone and my back, though, is still lathered, daily, in sweat and sleep is, as is to be expected, elusive. I mean, I know I can expect to not sleep properly for at least six months but to still be sweating! Anyway. Talking to Kempster in Brad's cell earlier the subject was Hepatitis C.

"I'm lucky", I say, "not only me, but my brother P--- cleared it naturally", and it is true P---- did but I lie here, assuming that my genes would also do the same as my brother's and clear it without treatment if I had it for I don't know as of yet. I don't know why I lie but I do.

"That's impossible", says Kempy, "everyone says that".

"How the fuck is it impossible"? says Brad, "I did too".

"Kempy", I say patiently, "why the fuck would I lie", and indeed, why would I?

"Naa, I know 25% of people clear it on their own; I'm just jealous 'cause I had to have the treatment and it was brutal back then, that interferon stuff man it was awful".

"So I've been told but for those infected today it can be cleared with eight weeks on three tablets a day with no side effects", I say.

"I know", says Just For Men indignantly, "today they can clear any genotype too and you don't have to have all the injections and depression I went through. It was fuckin' gruelling mate I tell ya".

"Most of the research and development of the new treatment for it was done in Oxford", I say proudly.

"I thought it was 25% clear it naturally Sloaney"? says Brad.

"It is, one in five", repeats Just For Men.

"No", I say, "it's twenty percent, one in five".

"Still, though the treatment was shit I consider myself lucky", says Kempy.

"I just think it's amazing the breakthroughs in viral research and treatment 'cause not long ago serious viruses were a death sentence but even people with HIV can now live normal lives", I say.

"Just need to sort cancer out now", says Brad.

"But Brad", says Kemps, "if they keep curing all this shit then what the fuck will people die of"?

"I know man", says Brad, "ageing population and all that".

"I've always said", say I, "that if the doc says that I'm riddled with tumors I'd simply say 'no chemo, no scalpels, no treatment' and I'd hand him a list with 'diamorphine hydrochloride, morphine sulphate, diazepam, mogadon, pregablin, peach palfium' but now I reckon I'd assess the situation from the point of view of my loved ones. They may want me to stick about I guess and it ain't all about me. My thinking is changing all the time".

"You're just growing up Slicker", says Fradders.

"I'm having some sort of spiritual awakening right now", I say, not realizing at that time that though I thought I was, and had had, as described, many 'experiences' I still yet had not come to understand. But I interfere in the narrative here: forgive me.

"You really do believe in God don't ya"? says Kempy.

"You'll be going to church and preaching the bible next", says Brad.

"I fuckin' won't", I say, "that is not the way I worship God. My God is exactly that; mine. I don't need pervy priests, dictatorial threats of hellfire. Fuck organised religion. But, yes, I certainly believe in God".

"I'm an atheist", says Kempy, "what has God ever done for me"?

"What the fuck you ever done for Him"? I ask.

"Well", says Just For Men smiling, "when you put it like that".

"And anyway boys, you won't find Him in the drugs; we have to clean up to hear His voice more clearly".

"I won't hold me breath", says Brad, popping a pregablin tablet.

"He's very real Bradders", I say, "He is inside us all. Forget the shit religion we had rammed down our throats at school: it's all bollox. It's a personal thing, the relationship with God. The realization that we are all individual parts of Him", and I want to go into physics facts like the never changing amount of energy in the universe, the same since the start of creation and how it is but borrowed by us. "Anyway lads, before we bang up know this: you were created at the heart of a massive star that exploded in supernova seeding and peppering the cosmos with the prerequisites necessary for life. You are 100% exploded star matter".

"Really"? asks Just For Men Kemp.

"Really man, I promise you", I say, before walking back to my cell to bang up for lunch.

1854hrs. Banged up. So, today in the gym I did squats, hamstring curls and calf raises and the last twenty mins of the session on the treadmill. Marcus, unlike him in the gym, sat on a bench and did fuck all which gives good measure for his mood right now. But he did do what he set out to do down there which was to reload with a couple pages power spice paper to alleviate current angst and stress levels on the wing and of course line his pockets and provide purchasing power for the drugs he likes and the spice which of course he partakes of himself. Soon as he got back to the wing he started selling it off in ID card sized amounts at inflated prices due to the current drought on the wing. Where normally it would be £25 it is now £30 and this could go up yet more if things don't change. Those buying the ID cards will themselves be selling to punters and doubling their money on the outlay. Marcus is paying £100 per A4 page so as you may gather the cunt is raking it in. The cell is literally, as

261

I say, stocked like a shop. Though much money flows through him he makes little for he consumes what profit he makes but, to be fair, he always pays what he owes himself. It's just that the more he makes the more drugs he himself consumes. As I write, right now, the cunt is on his bed as usual in a state of extreme inebriation. He's hailed as a hero on the wing today for scoring and providing for those desperate for the spice which has been elusive on here these last couple days. Anyway, I'm listening to Heart 80s again. On the muted TV Cathy Newman and Hellier Ebrahimi are on channel 4 news and I think I'm in love with both of them. In other prison news Brad fed his spider today and I watched through a magnifying glass as the beast sank fangs into a smaller spider, a tubeweb, tickled and tricked from a crevice in the wall by wily Brad earlier. Ricky Lanes, brother of Buddha like Pete spent the afternoon on E wing with his son who lives on there, Steven Lanes. E wing has even more Thanet people on its landings right now; couple proper boys from the manner in the form of Shai O'brien and Josh Chambers. We are all over this jail right now, on every wing you'll find a firm from Thanet. Says a lot for the place really!

20-02-2019. 1930hrs. Smashed the gym today. Shamima Begum, the cunt ISIS bride who was 'unfazed' by severed heads and the torture of Azidis feels it's 'unjust' her British citizenship has been revoked. Quite frankly I think all jihadis should be kept well away from our shores. Especially her and her murderous cunt husband. I hope they die tortuous deaths. Today I do anyway.

Ok. A man I have spent much time, many years using drugs with has just been found stabbed to death in Medway, Wesley Adinyinka is his name. His girlfriend, a mixed race sexy Thanet lass I once had the pleasure of bedding, was also injured in the attack. Also, last weekend, a fella me and Marcus knew well called Ben Seed was found murdered in a flat in Margate. Must be murder month; savage.
Passing Ms Nixon earlier I'd said in truth:
"You've got the loveliest hair in the nick Ms ya know that"?
"Ahh thanks Sloaney, you always cheer me up"!
"That doesn't mean you can crack onto me Ms"!
"Oh fuck off Sloaney, you wish"!
"What", I say, mock hurt, "no chance at all Ms"?
"None ya wierdo"! she laughs.
"But Ms", I say, "out of like 0 to 100, 100 being certain and 0 being no chance where would you say I am on that scale? About 50"?
"Sorry mate, you're at 0 I'm afraid"!

262

"Wounded", I say, holding my heart forlornly.

"Plenty of fish in the sea Sloaney, you'll be fine when ya get out".

"Thanks a lot", I say smiling, "you're cool you Ms Nixon. Can you open my door please Ms"? and she does, the blinder. In the last week we have had another sexy young new officer start on the wing by the name of Ms Stevens and of course all the boys are trying to chat her up. But she seems resilient, politely rebuking the clumsy compliments coming her way if they get a bit too much. The other day, now bear in mind Ms Stevens has a sort of bowl, she walks with a sort of strutting gangster like gait and little Manc Reece, after complimenting her newly dyed hair says to this exceptionally pretty and shapely young officer of no more than 24 that:

"I love the little sassy bowl you've got going on Ms, it's proper attitudy"! in his cheeky Manchester hyperactive staccato rapid rattle vernacular and she shockingly says:

"No, that's 'cause I had a stroke as a kid", and she's smiling her lovely smile but Manc Reece withers and says:

"Oh Ms, I'm I'm I'm like really so sorry I didn't mean"........but the young officer quickly puts him at ease, putting a hand on the poor little fuckers arm in kindness:

"It's ok, hey, chill out", and she says this with the confidence of one totally at ease in her own skin and I think to myself 'she's fuckin' lovely'. Anyway, in this cell right here right now George Ezra is at the Brits where he has just won an award for his admittedly brilliant and catchy music. I look to a dribbling El Chubbo on the bed beside me and say:

"You're missing the Brits gay boy", but get but a snore in return. Copious amounts of spice, pregablin and subutex have him zonked right out. He has, this week, made £800 already though it be just Wednesday: this cunt seems to thrive on the pressure of drug dealing. He is so comical at times and was on form earlier winding a seemingly genuinely disturbed J.T up in Brad's cell. Present were me, Marcus, Brad and Kempy, all chatting away when J.T walks in with a towel round his modesty and Marcus, in full wind up mode goes:

"Looking sexy J.T".

"Wierdo", smiles J.T, looking a little scared at El Chubbo's leering looks. Marcus stands and reaches for J.Ts notoriously massive manhood, nicknamed 'Cecil'.

"What the fuck", exclaims J.T, eyes wide with genuinely shocked horror, "get off Cecil man! Did you see that Sloaney"? but me, Fradders and Kempster are chuckling.

"Don't be shy J.T", says Marcus, again grabbing a hold of 'Cecil', "come on, just let me wank you off a bit", and now J.T is smiling, red faced, uncomfortable and clearly nervous as he backs away from the smiling El Fat One who goes now:

"Come on, just a couple of strokes, no one will know, it'll be our little secret", and now Kempster has his head down, shoulders rising and falling in mirth and Brad has his head back unable to contain himself and I am in bits, knowing Marcus's sense of humour and barely able to breathe at 'our little secret'!

"What the fuck"! goes J.T, "Marcus man, you're fucked! Does he do this to you in the cell Sloaney"?

"No fuckin' way man but I reckon people think me and him are up to savage shit but let me get this straight right here right now I'm heterosexual and think Marcus is too, most of the time anyway"!

"Marcus man you're fucked bro", says J.T, laughing none the less, "like a proper pervert".

"Your loss", says El Chubbo, "you'd probably like it"!

"No way", says J.T, laughing but looking uneasy, he mumbles again, "Marcus you're fucked bro", and goes out the cell.

"'Our little secret' Marcus", I quote to him and again Brad, me and Kempy descend into raucous laughter recalling the scenario! Even as I write in the cell now I laugh and as I type it up here in Oxford years later I'm once more chuckling again at the memories. I photograph this page and send it to Marcus in Margate who facetimes me and we both laugh more as we recall the jokes we shared on that sentence nearly three years ago. He is a fuckin' legend. But back to the cell and he is flaked out on the bed. He's a mong right now and I'll get none of the cunt's charisma tonight that's for fuckin' sure. I do smile as I look at him dribbling and twitching though. Wrong, but funny nonetheless.

Right, I'm gonna share with you a brief anecdote. One day, when homeless in Canterbury sleeping on the streets with Frank B who I spoke of earlier, the young boy who overdosed, we'd been begging and were huddled up in a shop doorway just outside the cathedral main gates in our sleeping bags. It must have been about six a.m because footfall was slim on the ground and the sun just poking his head over the rooves of the buildings around us, slowly throwing his blanket down. I love that time of the morning and though Frank was snoring away as only the young do I awake at the crack of dawn. After lighting myself a roll up made from Kerbside Virginia (dog ends picked from the pavement) I start to survey the area properly and notice, squinting my eyes against the ever brighter burgeoning sun, a pigeon which looks injured about 20 yards away, trying to scuttle about, in search of crumbs I guess but clearly unable to fly and hobbling on one leg. One wing was hanging weakly down and a wave of pity washed through me. I hadn't had my eyes on it for more than thirty seconds when another pigeon comes down and immediately mounts the damaged bird, pecking viciously as it does so. It does it's thing and fucks off only to be replaced by another, then another and then another.

"Frank", I say, "Frank man".

"What? Fuck off bro I'm sleeping".

"Please Frank, look at this man", I say, unable to bear what I'm seeing.

"What the fuck you on about"? he says, poking his head out the sleeping bag.

"Look", I say, pointing at the pigeon, "just keep watching", and as we do so one after another pigeon comes down to savagely rape the injured bird.

"That's nasty man", he says, preparing to go back to sleep.

"Frank man we can't just leave it", I say.

"What the fuck man, let me sleep please bro", and I do leave the poor fucker to his slumber. Realizing Frank is fucked from a night of drink and drugs and ain't moving to do what needs to be done here anytime soon I get up and promptly pick up the broken bird and break its neck, trying to be strong enough to do it quickly and painlessly but not so hard I pull the head off. I walk round to Best Lane where the Chaucer statue stands where there is a grassy area with benches for the public and I dig a small hole with my hands and bury the poor bird. As I put it in the ground I say 'sorry bird, hope you're in a better place' and feel incredibly sad as I do so. I go back and snuggle in my own sleeping bag next to the kid.

"Where the fuck you go"? he says in his lazy drawl, head inside the bag still mind you, muffling his question.

"Snapped that poor pigeon's neck man then buried it where the red phonebox is in that little garden place near the statue up the road. Couldn't stand what was happening to it man".

"Soppy cunt really underneath ain't ya"? he says.

"Felt like crying", I say honestly.

"Give your fuckin' head a wobble"! says Frank.

"Honestly man", I say.

"I wanna give you a cuddle ya cunt", says Frank warmly, "but I can't be bothered"! Cheers Frank! God rest you bro. I will never forget you.

21-02-2019 1400hrs. Last full day with Bridge today. However, it isn't internal, prison stuff I wish to regale you with but a tale from a couple years ago when I was living at Invicta House in Margate with Claire Sharp, long term ex and very close friend today. Across the road in a flat was a drug dealer, a long term pal of mine called 'Sharky' real name Stuart who is, I must add, a good guy at heart. Anyway, one morning I wake up at 0730 hrs and I'm proper clucking, sick as a pig in withdrawel from heroin.

"Fuck me babe", I say to Claire, "I'm fuckin' bang in it here man".

"Should stop taking that fuckin' shit then shouldn't ya", she says scathingly.

"That's not fuckin' helpful babe".

"Nor the fuck are you", she says exasperated, "look at the fuckin' state of ya; you're driving me mental with your smack habit".

"Bear with me babe", I say, "I'm gonna get off it soon I swear".

"Don't even bother mate", she replies, "I've heard all your shit before".

"I mean it babe, I've fuckin' had enough of it I swear".

"We'll see about that", she says, "anyway, I can only give you £15 this morning 'cause I ain't got a lot".

"Ahhh man", I say in massive relief, "thanks babe; can I use your phone"?

"Fuck me, don't want a lot do ya"? she says, "who you gonna phone"?

"Sharky across the road", I tell her.

"What"? she says, "at half past seven in the morning? You got no chance"!

"He wants to sort it else I'll go kick the cunt's door off babe to be frank with you". I punch Sharky's digits into the phone and am irked when I quite expectedly get no answer at this un Godly hour. "Fuck sake", I say, shaking and sweating now with cold turkey.

"Fuckin' hell Andy at least wait 'till eight bells and then try again; you can't expect him to be at your beck and call", says sassy savvy Claire.

"Alright babe, I will", I say, "but what sort of dealer don't answer his phone 24/7"?

"Not many do unless they're speed freaks".

"Your lot then"! I say.

"Well", she retorts, "better than your smack head bunch"! and she has a point. Many heroin and crack dealers (for if you sell one you sell the other these days: light and dark in one place or the addict goes where he can get both if you haven't) today sell these drugs just to support their own habits. Sharky is one such dealer. Anyway, eight o'clock comes around and I try the phone again to no avail.

"Fuck it Claire, I'm going over there".

"Please Andy, you're being unreasonable and he is your mate after all", she says but I'm pulling my shoes on and at the front door.

"Exactly", I say, "back in a minute", and I run over to Sharky's flat and start banging the door despite the fact he has a girlfriend and young baby in there.

"Who the fuck's that"?

"It's Sloaney Sharky", I shout above the din of the dogs, two female Staffordshire Bull Terriers.

"Sloaney man for fuck, come back at nine o'clock".

"Sharky man I'm proper clucking bro can't you just sort me one and one"?

"Fuck off, please Sloaney, I have to go get it so just come back in an hour for fuck sake".

"Sharky, open the fuckin' door or I'm gonna kick it in", but there's no answer and I immediately go about trying to smash the door in with my foot until it is suddenly opened from the inside and all I hear is Sharky say 'geeert him' and before I know it two white Staffies are ripping and tearing at me.

"Sharky", I say, panic stricken, "Sharky man, not me Armanis", but it is too late. One dog is hanging off of me arm and the other, after puncturing my leg severely, which I'm not too bothered about, has ripped my jeans, my best ones and I'm low on designer clothing and prize this pair above all else. "You cunt", I scream through struggles and gritted teeth, "my fuckin' jeans you cunt, I'm a fuck you up Stuart, wait and see", and at last the cunt calls the dogs off and leaves me on the landing outside his flat door forlorn and sick and with blood dripping from limbs and clothes torn to shreds. Funnily enough, the next time I see him was on this wing, downstairs when he was banged up with Phil The Face. No grudges held though and we laughed at it. Saying that I would have fucked him up but was arrested a few days later and remanded in custody. Anyway, Bridge has just finished and I'm sitting at the back of our cell writing at 1540hrs this Thursday afternoon and Marcus is running around playing Pablo Escobar with pages of spice . Now he runs in the cell:

"Just bought an eighth (of an ounce) of MDMA Sloaney man", he says, all excited, like a big kid.

"Oh no, so you're gonna be proper gurning tonight then"?

"Nope, I'm gonna save it 'till the weekend", says this joker, living in dreamland.

"Behave you knob, you ain't gonna sit there with that in your pocket and not do it"!

"I will", he says, "but only because I ain't paid for it yet and you know what I'm like", and what he means by this is that it's in his pocket but he has to phone his girl, Lauren, to transfer money from his account to the recipient's who sold the shit to him. He is quite disciplined like this and I suppose that's why he can always get laid on drugs. Now a small, slightly greying 40 year old or so dude called Kyle comes in the cell and upon seeing me writing asks:

"How many pages you up to now"? and it is worth noting that this is Aidy E's co-defendant.

"800", I say, "804 to be precise".

"What you been writing about today"? he asks and I describe the tale of Sharky and the dogs and tell him how all I could think about was my jeans.

"Weird in it", he says, "I remember having a fight in Highdown prison years ago and all I was worried about were the Rosary beads around me neck".

"Yeah man, despite being in proper, like, danger, all we care about are things that don't really matter".

"I know man it's fuckin' mental", says the slight middle aged fella, "I'd like to read your book one day Sloaney".

"I'm planning on publishing so hope that one day you will".

"Yeah man, I bet it's interesting".

"I fuckin' hope so mate 'cause I've put some effort into it to be fair".

"Alright Sloaney", he says, putting out his fist for a bump which I reciprocate, "gonna go try get some drugs".

"Alright Kyle, later man", and he's gone as quickly as he appeared. Now Kempster walks in, absolutely plastered on prison hooch.

"When you gonna write my C.V for me Sloaney"?

"When you are compis mentis enough to sit and help me do it", I say.

"Fuck sake man I need it done Sloaney", and he walks out the cell moodily. Now Steve Bennet, Lifer Steve, comes in the cell and tells me of a time he was sick and clucking.

"Yeah", he is saying, "I was proper bang in it ya know"?

"Yeah", I say in a tone which lets him know I'm interested, "go on".

"So, on last leggings, with no money, I go around to me pals house to see if he can help me out but he's not in".

"Go on", I say.

"So I'm at his, like outside his front door with me head in me hands thinking 'I'm fucked' and all of a sudden I've heard this proper loud bang".

"Go on", I say, as my pen catches up.

"I look up and notice that someone was parking and had hit the car next to where he was tryna park".

"Yeah", I prompt.

"So I walk up to the geezer and go 'fuck sake mate what ya done'"?

"What", I say, "did you know whose car it was"?

"No", says Steve, "but I'm clucking and feel a few quid coming on; life saver".

"Go on", I say, intrigued.

"'It's me old man's motor' I tell the fella", says Steve, "I notice then", continues he, "that he was clearly pissed and the fella says 'I'm a mechanic mate, I'll take your details and fix it for ya tomorrow but", Steve goes on, "I go 'na na na I'm not having that, you're pissed mate so I'll tell ya what I'll do, I can't stand my old man so give me a oner and I'll say no more", and Steve then goes on to tell me that the fella said:

"Don't fuck me about then mate if I give you a ton".

"Don't worry about that", Steve told the sorry fella, "just give me the oner and it's finished".

"What, and he give you it"? I ask.

"Yep, and I was off to score like Linford Christie"! and no sooner has he said this than he goes, "where's Marcus, 'cause I need to do the same now"? and he's off out the cell like a greyhound, the skinny lovable cunt. It seems I've a stream of steady visitors today for now young Martyn strides in, bowling with his bulky arms out for all to see in his tight vest.

"You alright bro"? I ask, "fancy giving me a quick story"?

"Yeah man", he says, "I'll tell you a story about a friend I grew up with".

"Go on then Smartyn", I say to me big gunned pal.

"A boy I grew up with, went to school with and who I found myself in jail with was a boy called Ricky Coombes", he says, and I quote him verbatim.

"What", I say, "this is ya pal"?

"Yeah", says Smartyn, "he was 23 and I know him 'cause he lives around my area and we grew up together. But when I see him when I got to jail this time he was having a couple problems with his missus outside".

"What jail"? I ask.

"Lewis", says Mart, "on C wing".

"Go on", I say.

"He found out that his missus had been cheating on him in the short time he'd been there-I know her too", he says.

"Go on", I again prompt.

269

"So she'd been cheating on him with another boy who we grew up with so I could see Ricky was going through some pain and he just didn't seem like himself".

"Yep", I go.

"So, the next time association was on, I went round to play some cards with him, we played cards for a while and, err, finished and then it was dinnertime".

"Go on", I say.

"I went back to my cell to get my plate and bowl for dinner and so I went downstairs to line up in the que and err, well, I see all the guvs, the screws, rush up to the cell where I'd been playing cards".

"Yeah, go on mate", I say.

"There were three guvs around somebody on the floor where they had the defibrillator heart thing and were pumping somebody's chest but at this point I didn't know who was on the floor".

"Go on mate".

"It was just then a guy in the que went 'is that Ricky' and then I realized it was. So, I rushed over", continues Mart, "to see what had happened and realized he was in a bad way, that it was serious. The guvs were pushing us back going 'give us some space' and all we could do was stand back and watch and me and my pal was shouting 'Ricky, Ricky wake up' which he didn't do, and he didn't come back from it and we could hear the guvs saying 'we had to cut him down' and that 'they didn't get to him in time' which made us mad at the screws saying 'you should be keeping an eye on vulnerable people and doing ya job properly and this wouldn't happen".

"Wow man, Martyn, that's really fuckin' sad man-what, he never came around"?

"Naa", says Martyn, "a couple weeks later his family had to come in the prison and see how he was living", and J.T now comes in the cell and on being brought up to speed on the topic asks:

"How old was he"?

"23", says Martyn.

"Wow", says J.T, "barely a man". And now the lovely Ms Nixon and Ms Terry are at the door and sexy Nixon goes:

"Come on lads, bang up time".

"Hate to break up the party", says pukka Ms Terry.

"Gis some sugar quick lads", says Kempy, poking his head in as Marcus walks in and the others leave, Marcus sorts him and the door is banged closed for the night and I'm left with imagery of a broken hearted young man stringing himself up in despair over the loss of his lover. Fuckin' tragic.

270

Ok. It's 1905hrs. News on. We've now the New Independent Group, seven MPs who've defected from Labour, not happy with the leadership line on Brexit. And now we've had another three Conservative party defect saying that the party has been hijacked from the far right. One of the MPs defecting from the Tories is Heidi Allen, a sexy sultress with lustrous black hair and, it would seem, a conscience. Brexit has decimated traditional partisan lines.

2030hrs still the same day and I wish to share with you a brief moment of terror I just had. So, Smarcus, as always, is absolutely spangled but had been lucid enough to briefly address me earlier.

"Sloaney, look, d'ya like the new pipe I just made man"?

"Marcus mate", I say, "do you really think I give a fuck about the vessels you use to smoke your cockroach killer with bro"?

"Ohhhh Sloaney, always moaning", he says, "check this out though", and the idiot puts a massive pile of paper spice atop the tin foil he's put on top of the bottle where the cap would normally be. There're holes in the foil and a hole half way down the bottle he's poked and put a gutted pen in in order to suck through. He lights a screwed up piece of toilet tissue or 'wick' and after placing the flame on the spice paper begins to suck greedily and I watch as thick creamy poisonous smoke is drawn into the bottle then up the pen into his mouth before settling on the alveoli of his lungs where it will be picked up and absorbed into his blood stream. Now, what with the amount of narcotics in Marcus even with this amount of spice he is safe from a terrifying trip though he has experienced many of these before. On top of myriad other drugs the spice just knocks him out. Anyway, after watching the moron I get up on my bed for a bit then, not hearing him breathing, jump down to insure he is ok. His eyes are open and he doesn't seem to be alive. I bash his leg, saying:

"Marcus Marcus Marcus", but get nothing and I burst into sweat, "Marcus", and now I slap the cunt around the face and I thank God when I see the lights come on and his chest start to move.

"You fuckin prick", I tell him, "thought you was dead ya cunt; I don't fuckin' need the image of a dead you haunting me for the rest of my natural", the fuckers lids just slide down his eyeballs but his breathing at least seems to have normalised. This is literally happening in real time, right now. I need to keep an eye on the fucker tonight, what with his new bong contraption thing which allows him to consume much more spice in one go than is possible on the vape battery with element. Anyway, I'm watching Secret Life Of The Zoo and after that there's another good programme on though I can't remember what it is. So, I'm gonna put pen to bed for the day, quickly pray then go my way to my pit with the remote control, keeping one eye on this retard-forgive me Lord for that word-it simply serves to best describe the fella who's pretty smart when lucid. He looks like a pile of pale blubber right about now, dribbling, half on half off the bed.

22-02-2019 0153hrs and as you can see dear reader it is early hours of the morning. So, five or ten minutes ago I lay awake on the top bunk, in the dark, ruminating on life listening, yes, you got it, to Absolute 80s. Suddenly:

"Sloaney, Sloaney you awake Sloaney"? from Marcus in the bunk below.

"Yeah man, chill Chubbo, what's up bro"?

"I need, erm, I need that, erm, that thing man where's that thing"?

"What thing you fuckin' wierdo"? but my voice is kindly: I do love the knob after all. His heart is too big for one not to.

"That thing, that bottle and my paper, where's my paper man the spice Sloaney man I need it", and I can hear the panic in his voice, the desperate desire to escape a world that gets ever more stark and real as the drugs recede from his blood stream. I know this feeling myself, waking up after being blathered and the walls and people and matter around me seems closer and more frightening. Reality bites.

"Hold up ya fuckin' knob", and I get up and turn the light on in the tiny cell. He's been asleep for some hours now so is relatively compis mentis; relative the operative term for he is still only at about 20% of his normal cognitive ability. I pull the bong bottle contraption thing he's been using from out the bin and put it on the side next to the TV. Then I get his spice from behind one of his photos on the picture board, one of his normal hiding places. I put it next to the bong, get up on my bed and tell him:

"It's all there for you bro, next to the telly", for he's still in and out of consciousness you must understand.

"Thanks Sloaney, I love you man", and I feel so sad he's so intent on not being in the real world, constantly needing to change the way he feels. He gets off his bed and sits in the chair I do my writing in. He tears fuck off big bits of paper from the sheet of spice and loads up his contraption, once more lighting a wick and putting fire to it, sucking deeply on the poisonous fumes.

"Right, quickly get on your bed", I say, "'cause you've got about thirty seconds before you flop", but he's already putting more on.

"Marcus man, please, I won't be able to get you off the floor bro", but it's too late, he's fired it up again and now, already, as he puts the pipe down the palsy wobble, the spice shuffle, is on him.

"You're a cunt d'ya know that"? but he only looks, or tries to look up at me with bloodshot eyes and now he falls face forward off of the chair, smacking his head sickeningly with a thud to make the hardest of men wince.

"You fuckin' prick", I say as I jump off the bed, "shit", I say to myself, "Marcus you cunt", and I pull him up by beneath his armpits, "Marcus man, you've got to help me here bro, use your legs if you can hear me mate for fuck sake", and he must hear me from whatever realm he inhabits because I manage to get him onto his bunk, it's a struggle but his big arse is on the edge so I put my hand on the top of his head like a police officer putting a suspect in a car, to prevent him banging it on the steel of the bunk beds then push him backwards before quickly grabbing his legs and swinging them too onto the bed so he's now laying on his back, on the bunk and snoring, oblivious the cunt to the struggle I've just had and the sweat lining my skin from the exertion. His eyes stare up at me but they're bloody and red and there's absolutely no one home, the lights are out. His mouth hangs open and spittle dribbles down his chin and the hand hanging over the edge of the bed is shaking, twitching so I know he is definitely alive, barely, but breathing. Reader, as I write, right now, I'm reading the tattoo on the side of his abdomen which says: 'Angels Walk Among Us You Only Notice Them When They're Gone RIP Mum' and a wave of compassion for the cunt washes through me. He is so kind so loving to everyone on the wing, not just me. And boy this poor fucker has suffered. Addiction killed both his parents. He has been alone for many, many years and yearns to be loved. As I write dear reader I'm thinking about a coffee 'cause the cunt on the bunk below is snoring loudly and my synapses are snapping wildly and such brain activity isn't usually conducive with sleep. Annie Lenox is singing 'love love love is a dangerous drug' and I turn up the volume and now she is saying 'and I want you, and I want you' and all the hairs on my body stand on end and I smile drowning in the beautiful sublime she evokes in me and now I think to myself that this book is gonna be a fuckin' smash man! A magical mix of madness, mayhem, badness and brilliance and I ask God, please don't kill me off once I've self actualized for I'd love to see the response to this. Love to be alive for the publishing. Anyway, despite the above, I'm gonna try lay down again, calm my frenetic thinking and get some shut eye if possible. We shall see. Good night dear reader.

273

1530hrs. Afternoon. Marcus has left me with a debt list-he gave instructions for me to do some collecting but that just ain't me. I've spent an hour with Bradders, Grin and Kyle who I introduced you to yesterday but now I'm at the back of my own cell this black eye Friday which has only seen one person bounce, Mark Mall, and no violence as of yet but Adam W has the hump because Mark said something about him bullying him for a debt or something. I guess Mark needed a reason to give staff for his move and threw up the first name to come to mind the cunt. Anyway, people are consistently coming in and out of the cell asking 'where's Marcus, where's Marcus' and I truthfully tell them he's playing volleyball down the gym. Another development is Ricky Lanes son Stephen has come onto our wing to be with his dad and uncle Pete. No one has a bad word to say about Steve by all accounts but Ricky has already pissed us off by acting the geezer in front of his boy by trying to get a page of spice off of Marcus for a oner when Marcus is paying that himself for a page lately. Marcus told Rick, who was proper huffing and puffing for he has his own interests at heart, as we all do on drugs, that if Steve wanted a page it would cost him £150. And rightly so. The truth is Rick wanted Steve to get a page so Steve could pay all Rick's many debts off for his own situation on the wing is becoming untenable. Oh, as I write, thank the Lord, Marcus has just walked into the cell. I did a hectic circuit this morning, for the record. 880 reps of step ups, burpees and sit ups between laps of the sports hall. I fuckin' love it. And the creatine and whey protein I feed my muscles with afterwards. Marcus has, just now, brought an eighth of an ounce of tobacco, Golden Virginia, for £25 so that'll be a treat for tonight. Kempster comes into the cell and buys a couple ID cards of spice off of Marcus to graft with on the wing and, I dare say, smoke a little of himself. Now J.T comes in the cell camp as fuck and out his nut talking absolute pony. Now Craig Mc comes in, and I love the big Scot who did the circuit with me earlier.

"Thit wis thee bullox earlier Sloaney mate I really appreciate it, you pooshin' me", he says.

"I fuckin' loved it too", I say, honestly.

"Did ya knaw thit wis 880 reps we did"?

"Killer weren't it, but at least we know we did every single bit and completed 'cause there were plenty of cheats down there today", I say.

"I've git me mom coomin dun fre Scotland tomorrow; her and me missus are coomin tae see me ahh canni fookin wait man".

"How long since you last see them Craig"?

"I've bin in nine months and haveni sin thum once", he says.

"Wow, well, after the photos you showed me of when you were bang at it out there they're gonna be pleasantly shocked in the change in the way you look".

"Ahhh know man right", and as he says this he splits his face in a boyish smile and I spud him and he goes on his way.

1730hrs now and we are banged up. Just before that time when the doors are locked for the night Jay 'Nev' Nevin came up to me and started talking what I thought was drunken waffle for he was, is, clearly inebriated. Now, remember, I love the mental cunt but he don't half go round the houses before getting to his points.

"Sloaney, let's talk".

"Go on", I say.

"It's like this right, the fella is talking about seventy quid, now, right, I'm not saying anything but he's out there, in the meds que, going".......but here I interrupt him.

"Nev mate, I don't get involved in Marcus's business unless I need to and honestly don't know what you're talking about bro".

"No, what you on about"? says Nev, "not Marcus, Phil", and immediately, at that name, I flash anger.

"What, he's sent you to come see me"? and of course this is Phil The Face of whom we speak.

"He just said that you owe him £70", and this dear reader is exactly what I said:

"Nev mate, no offence, I don't give a fuck what he said; he's had over £500 out of me for muggy £5 shots of spice and buscopan tablets so, when I can, every two weeks or so I'll chuck him a pack of vapes if he's lucky".

"Sloaney, I'm not his jackhammer, I'm just passing on a message, there's no need to get like that".

"I'm just saying Nev I couldn't care less. Occasionally he'll get a few quid outta me if I have it; me protein and bits come first, he's way down the list", and then Ms Stephens and Mr Maddison call Nev out the cell for bang up.

"That cheeky cunt, that fuckin' Phil", I say to Marcus.

"Don't worry about it man, let it go", he says.

"I'm not worried but if the cunt even thinks about firing people into me they need to make sure they stop me breathing 'cause I'll fuck 'em up, and him, the cheeky cunt".

"Oh shut up Sloaney man, it ain't gonna come to that ya silly cunt", and now he's fucked from hooch, pregabs, clonazepam, subutex and the big bong of spice which immediately rendered him unconscious. Fuck,

Phil has really pissed me off, firing Nev into me for money the cheeky fucker. Still, I'm probably over reacting but when I see him out on freeflow I will have to tell him exactly where it's at. I need to remember, he's not such a bad fella when it comes down to it.

Back in Oxford in about 2014 I was still clean and sober after my time in the Ley Community. Living in Littlemore with my lovely landlady Angela with my old banger outside and a good job working at Aldens Specialist Catering Butchers I became aware through one of the boys at work one day of a site, a savage dating site called Plenty Of Fish. I found I could fulfil my propensity for promiscuous partaking hassle free simply saying sexy shit to willing wenches hungry for cock as I was hungry for cunt at that time. I met multiple willing females on there but a couple stick out. One was a sexy little 32 year old mother of two from Milton Keynes. So, I drove up there and all is going well; pleased with what I found at the front door once I'd driven to her house from Oxford I immediately set about smashing her about her rather sumptuous bedroom and all was going well as I pumped away behind her until she suddenly says breathlessly:

"Fist me, fist me, please please please fist me", and this is said to the rhythm of the pump until I, on assimilating this, stop and go:

"What did you say"?

"Please, I'm so wet, can you fist me please I love it"?!

"You telling me you want me to ram my arm up you"?

"Would you"?

"Well, I'm not sure"……and I'm pleased to say that my cock is still hard, seven inches which clearly isn't enough for her, inside her snatch!

"Ok, maybe not yet", she says, "but can you put it in my arse then"?

"That I can do", I say and promptly pull out the honey hole and slide on up through her brown eye, aiming my tool toward her bowels, hammering and rubbing her clit at the same time, marvelling at how sopping wet this bird can get thinking that this slut fuckin' loves it!

"I'm gonna cum, I'm gonna cum ohhh I love that cock in my arse", and her filth has my orgasm rising:

"So am I", I say, and let loose spurt after spurt of jism deep into her shitter.

"Oh thankyou, thankyou thankyou", she says as she quivers all over and I'm impressed I got her there so easily for let's have it right, some women are hard work and getting them to cum requires a workout on our part but this woman was easy! We sit smoking in the bed afterwards.

"Did ya like that"? she asks.

"Not bad at all; thankyou", I say, smiling.

276

"You never fisted anyone before then"? she asks, saucy like.

"No man", I say, sheepish now, "that's something I haven't done and I thought I'd done most everything".

"Maybe we can try"?

"I've got to go because I've got work tomorrow but next time we can have a go if you want".

"You promise to come back"?

"Course I do", I say, puffing away on me Benson, "next weekend man", and even as I say it I know I won't be coming back for any arm fucking.

"Thankyou", she says, kissing me and soon as she's snoring I'm off out the door feeling........unsatisfied as always with cheap meaningless sex! Yes, I love the pervy filth of it but my soul yearns for something more. And casual sex doesn't quite cut it. I use women much as I use drugs; trying to fill a spiritual void that can never be wholly filled with substances or flesh. Or material. Anyway, Meridian news is on, Marcus is snoring and I'm gonna put down the pen for a bit. Adios.

2020hrs. Ok, just watched Channel 4 News. More defectors from the Labour Party though not over Brexit but antisemitism and the perception Jeremy Corbyn's Labour is now nothing more than a hard left sect. Then the 16 year old animal who raped and killed a 16 year old girl in Scotland, the noncy cunt. Then Aduro, the Venezuelan president's intransigence regarding admitting American humanitarian aid lorries into his country which is in crisis, saying that it is just a ploy for yank military intervention. Then some stories from local Kent people on Brexit. But this wasn't what kept me watching; no, it is the beautiful, very clever sexily dressed high heeled perfectly turned calved Cathy Newman which holds me. The perfect woman. Marcus has just arisen and heads straight for the restocked shelves of food to satiate his spice fuelled hunger: this is the munchies on weed times 100. By the way dear reader, I am now weighing in at near on thirteen stone of muscle and still growing. Tomorrow I will be 39 days chemical free by the grace of God. Ok, so Smarcus has fuelled himself with cake and biscuits, borrowed the charged vape battery from me, lit a bong and the cunt's now gone. There's bits of cake and biscuits all over him, the bed and the floor.

"That's it you prick", I say to his snoring fat form, "Sloaney'll clean it up don't worry", and I think about cleaning him and the area but reason I may as well wait for the culmination of the night's rubbish spreading and clean up after he's down for the night which I reason will be about two or three am. I myself am feeling fat, but in reality there ain't an ounce on me as I'm close to the best shape of my life which is amazing considering just a couple of months, less than that, back, I was on my knees looking like the walking dead. I need to interrupt the narrative against my better judgement here as I type in my bedroom in Oxford. I just want to tell you that one of my best mates, Dougy Dance, just died of an overdose two days ago and the date is October 21st 2021. I am gutted. He was a legend. Addicts are dying everywhere presently due to fentanyl contaminated heroin and I thank the Lord I'm not in active addiction. Anyway, back to prison. The next I wrote in that cell that night is controversial but I'm gonna be true to what I penned for you at the time. So: God did a good job when engineering the human form; he didn't, just whilst on the subject of biology, make me male with my middle leg tail just to have me tell him I'm in the wrong form and turn me ting inside out. I've only just got my head around men 'loving' men-which I'm fine with by the way, each to their own and all that. Thing is with man to man love so long as it's two adults in privacy and they're happy then who am I to judge? Live and let live but I think 'gender fluidity', well, I can't accept any messing with the Chief Engineer's, God's, design. Sorry liberal lefties. It's just a stretch too far for me. Especially when the NHS is paying for such savage surgery and worse, the knife is being wielded on kids! Kids who barely understand the world at 8 and 10 yet whose crazy parents are indulging whims which the child could well later regret! What happened to the good old days when a willy meant male and a fanny female? Men, you can never be truly female anyway, you know this right? Never! You will never be a true woman, never bear children, never have a period, period! To be woman requires two X chromosomes. Sorry! Hard, factual truth. Trans women are not women, they are transsexual women. A distinct sub category but biologically you will always be what God made you. On this subject now I'm considering Sodom in the bible. God didn't particularly like the old Sodomites and I'm now wondering if me slipping me ol boy into the odd woman's batty over the years makes me a sodomite or was the term reserved for man love? I don't know, not read much of the bible and never been a church goer as me old man was a virulent atheist. Anyway, mongy boy is again silent apart from the odd snore, grunt and groan and tonight I've absolute 90s for a change and Kurt Cobain is belting out Smells Like Teen Spirit, inspired genius. Let me, once again, take you back to Oxford. Circa 2013.

I'm again in my bedroom in Littlemore and my fingers flick over the I-Phone keypad as I try to catch fish. Getting a bite from a sexy looking bespectacled dark haired Lithuanian I learn that she works and lives above the Head Of The River pub at the city centre end of the Abingdon

Road, just up a bit from the police station and on the banks of the River Thames as it makes its way through the Thames Valley here in Oxford. We chat via the app for a bit then exchange phone numbers pretty promptly, giving me hope of a mind on the same thing as mine. So, I phone her:

"Where're you", she asks straight away, without preamble as soon as she answers her blower.

"Not far from you", I say, "Littlemore".

"Do you have a the car"? her roots clearly heard here in her dialect.

"I have the car", I tell her.

"Would you like to come see me when I finish the work"?

"I'm working myself tomorrow so it can't be too late; what time do you finish the work"? I ask, mimicking her for some inexplicable reason.

"Ok, I finish at the 10.30 tonight so you meet me then at my pub where I work"?

"Ok", I say, excited at the prospect of a bunk up, "I shall see you then"!

"Ok then Andrew, I look forward to be seeing you and I will have on the red dress like the Little Red Riding Hood".

"Ok Little Red Riding Hood I shall see you then", and being it's about eight o'clock I chill for an hour surfing for more sluts-that's language I'd've used back then, sorry-before getting ready to see this young lady in red. 28 years old she says she is. At about 2220hrs I aim the banger toward the city centre and thankfully manage to park behind the beautiful pub itself. I walk through the lovely gardens by the river to the entrance and spot her immediately and in all fairness she takes my breath away in a figure hugging dress.

"You are Andrew"?

"Red Riding Hood"? and she puts out a pretty hand like a landed learned member of the gentry.

"Very nice to be seeing you", she says.

"You look very pretty".

"And you look very smart and very handsome too", and I think 'I should hope so, the Armani jeans cost £180 and the Stone Island jumper £130.

"Why thankyou", I say, "can I buy you a drink"? I say, noticing she already has a large white wine in hand. I'm thinking 'bingo'. Giggidy giggidy.

"This is very nice of you; you don't mind"?

"Of course not", I say, and at the bar where we now stand I call the fella behind the jump, "large white wine please", I turn to her, "Pinot"? and at her nod I tell the barman and order a coke for me.

279

"You are drinking the coke"?

"Yeah, I don't drink".

"Oh, why not"? she says, looking at me inquisitively.

"Well", I say, "I've had some problems with it in the past shall we say"!

"Ok", she says, "so you are the alcoholic then"?

"Errr, well, fuck, yes! Not shy are you"?

"My father, he say never to trust the man who does not drink"! and as she says this I realize I have forgotten her name. Tania I think.

"Well, I don't quite know what to say to that"!

"But your eyes, I see kindness in them and the naughty boy also", and as she says this she necks the first large white wine and I'm thinking 'fuckin' jackpot! She immediately starts on the second and says: "do you do the dating often"?

"Well, I mean, I've dated a few ladies in the past, yes"!

"But", she presses, "from the Plenty Of Fish"?

"Nope", and the lie comes easy, "this is the first so I'm a bit nervous", and I'm happy she's attacking her drink voraciously.

"You are very handsome you know", she says now.

"That's the wine", I say, "do you want another"? and I call the barman again.

"Are you sure? Thank you".

"No problem", I say, "are you studying here"?

"No", she says, again, not wasting time on the wine and starting to sound tipsy, "I am just trying to make some money before I decide what I want to do".

"What would you like to do"? I say, thinking, 'keep her talking about herself and look interested.

"I would like to do the nurse you know"?

"I'd like to do the nurse too", I say.

"Really", she says, wide eyed, "you want to do the nurse too"?

"Sorry", I say, "it was just an English joke"! She looks briefly confused but soon gets over it before asking me:

"You want to fuck me tonight"? and I nearly spit the coke out my mouth in surprise.

"Pardon"?

"You want I like you put your cock inside me", and she says this in such husky seductive tones I feel my old boy twitch as he cocks an interested ear at what he's hearing, the little fucker. "I want you to put your cock in me now"!

"What, now"?

"Yes", she says, standing and holding out her hand, "come with me now", and I do, dreamlike, in a trance. "Do not be frightened little baby", she says, pursing her lips seductively.

"Errr", I attempt.

"I will suck your cock good for you I promise; you like I suck your cock for you"?

"Well, yeah, I like it, but are you sure, I mean, we've just met"!?

"Do not be pussy, you must fuck me now", and she leads me upstairs dear reader and she fucks me. I'm always shy if I don't know the person properly-not shy until the bedroom bit but if I don't know 'em properly I'm not as assertive as I'd otherwise be: I like to manhandle my women into positions and tell them exactly how I want them, not usually possible until familiarity. However, this bird is very clear on what she wants and half pissed for sure. As soon as she closes the door of the little room above the pub she says:

"You take clothes off now yes", but it's not a request!

"You really gonna just let me fuck you"? and I'm feeling my nerves disperse as she slips out the dress revealing sexy lacy matching red underwear, "fuck me, you're fuckin' hot", I say.

"Take off your clothes", she says and I waste no more time, my eyes fixed on her all the while, mesmerised. I'm grateful for the sexy Calvin's I've got on and the hard on looking impressive under the tight fabric. Perhaps I will smash her round the room after all but I think this party is completely at her whim and me just her plaything.

"Ahhh, you are getting the hard on", she says, smiling saucily.

"You're fuckin' fit man", I say, almost breathless and panting like a dehydrated dog in amorous anticipation.

"You like this", and she turns around and I love the way the cheeks of her perfect posterior poke out the bottom of the lacy knickers and now she bends over, head looking at me from over her shoulder and says: "you like this too"?

"Fuck me", is all I can say, taking off my boxer shorts causing my handsome seven to spring up, standing proudly to attention.

"Ahhh", she says, sauntering toward me, "you have beautiful cock", and she puts out a pretty hand, grabs the shaft and starts wanking me slowly then pulling me, leading me to the bed as if my cock is some kind of lead. She points now, telling me to lay down and she frees perfect pert point to the ceiling nippled tits and removes her knickers revealing a neat Brazilian and tidy pink pussy into which she pushes a finger, pulling it out glistening and she says:

"Look , I am very wet now for you to fuck me hard", and I'm fuckin' speechless. She sucks the golden honey coated finger now and I'm wanking myself in a trance like state, she the charmer me the snake and I say to her:

"Please, please, sit on me Tania", gagging to feel her snatch envelop me. But she only throws her head back, lustrous curls and all, and says: "no no naughty boy, first the 69"?

"Yeah man yes, just come here for fuck sake", and I grab her roughly now and in a second her mouth is round my meat and her wet perfect paper cut cunt is on my face into which I bury my tongue before going in hard on the clit whilst finger blasting this hot piece of wench. I struggle to keep rhythm with hands and mouth for my body is arching at what she is doing to me for she takes me deep down into her throat time and time again, moving her head from side to side to get me halfway down her windpipe.

"Stop", I say suddenly, "or I'll come"! and she springs around, facing me now, atop me and she is smiling down at my breathless face. "You're so pretty"!

"We wait a little while so you keep the cum".

"Yes, we wait", but I grab the back of her head, pulling her down roughly and kiss her hard, tongues searching, entwining before I grab my cock, find the spot and drill deep up into her causing us both to arch our heads in 'aahhhs' and she rides me and I grab her buttocks when I can take no more, holding her still strongly so she can't move and I smash myself up into her hard time and time again and she suddenly peels:

"I'm fuckin' coming", but I am lost, barely registering ramming ramming orgasm building to a crescendo and it breaks, the dam bust and I'm saying:

"I'm coming", then, "ahhh fuck ahhh man", and I'm spurting gallons of thick gloopy cum deep into her pretty pussy whilst she, too, is lost in convulsions as waves of passion break inside her and it slows and we are rocking, rocking, rocking together as the intensity subsides and we are both finally satiated and spent and she collapses on top of me and I'm thinking 'fuck man wow' and her breathing is at my ear and I descend to a dreamless sleep still inside this woman I do not know. This remembrance, dear reader, in this cell on a Friday night is fuckin' frustrating to say the least. And not just the sex factor, no, I am fuckin' lonely. Human contact is a gift, and only those blessed with a penchant for penis get that in here!

23-02-2019. 0920hrs Ok, forgetting Tania of the Little Red Riding hood who I smashed a few times over the following months, just to give an idea of my promiscuity at this time, basically how I was fixing myself with women, using them like a drug, I'll regale another brief tale. So, around the same sort of time, or perhaps a little while before, I'm surfing the web hunting pussy once more when upon opening my facebook page I notice on my friend Bev's post a pretty young Indian girl at the front of one with some other girls and Bev in a pub. The sassy looking pint sized Asian stands at the front of a bunch of pissed up ladies, hands on hips, almost challenging the camera. My interest is immediately piqued. I comment on the picture saying: 'who's the sexy little thing at the front Bev'? Bev comes back, commenting on the picture herself with: 'you're terrible Andrew'. I go to private messages and text:

"I know I'm bad but who is she? Is she single"?

"She's my friend from work and I doubt she'd be interested in a dog like you"!

"Bev! That's a little unfair", I type.

"You're an awful womanizer Andy", she says.

"Well I'm not that good 'cause I didn't get you in bed did I"?

"Hold up and I'll get back to you", she says. Three or four minutes go by before my phone bursts into life with an unknown number, one I've not seen before.

"Hello", I say, suspicious tone to my baritone.

"Hello, is that Andy"?

"Yes, who is this? I don't recognise your voice".

"You wouldn't, you've never heard it before"!

"Oh, ok, well, what's up"? I go because the voice is female and sounds quite young.

"My name is G", she says, "and I'm the 'sexy little thing at the front' of the photo"!

"Ahhhh", I say, "and you're phoning to tell me off"?

"Well, not really, I'm phoning to find out a bit about you", and immediately I think 'fuckin' jackpot'!

"Ok, well, what would you like to know"?

"Bev says that you're a good looking guy but that you are a bit of a womaniser; is that true"?

"Errr, well, I wouldn't say that"!

"That's a yes then"!

"Well, I think the truth is that I'd like to be but maybe haven't hit the heady heights allowing me to use such a term as womaniser just yet"!

"Where do you work"? says this Indian delight with the husky voice giving me a hard on as it emanates down the line.

"I work for a specialist catering company called Aldens in Botley", I say.

"Ok, what do you do there"?

"Well, I do lots of things really; prepare orders, organise deliveries, take in incoming stock, check the law is being adhered to regarding traceability, clean, laugh, take the piss, you know, normal stuff. Money is ok too", and I don't want to tell her we are a specialist catering butchers because she might think someone who works chopping carcasses with savage knives is a bit of a potential psycho though I rarely cut meat anyway due to the fact I was only slowly learning what I soon came to realise is an actual art. I continue, "what do you do"?

"I'm an accountant with a firm in Headington".

"Oh, so you're smart then"?

"I wouldn't exactly say that, but it pays the bills ya know"?

"How old are you"? I ask her.

"Twenty one", she tells me.

"Twenty fuckin' one", I say, aghast, "well, that rules me out then, I'm thirty eight", I was maybe a year older or a year younger, can't remember.

"What's age got to do with anything", and again I'm thinking 'fuckin jackpot', "you don't look old in your facebook photos".

"Well, erm, cool"!

"So", she says, "you taking me out for dinner tomorrow or what then"?

"Sounds good to me", I say, "where shall I pick you up"? and she gives me an address on the Blackbird Leys estate. "What time do you finish work"?

"Five o'clock", she says, "what time can you pick me up"?

"I finish at four so whenever you like really".

"Ok", she says, "how about six thirty"?

"Perfect", I say, "see you then", and we ring off. Ten minutes later my phone rings and it's Bev.

"Andrew, you're fuckin' unbelievable", she says.

"You musta given her my number Bev", I say.

"I did", she says, "but only so she could tell you off"!

"Hahahahaha", I laugh, "and I got a date instead"!

"She won't let you get her in bed", says Bev confidently.

"I'll have a fuckin' good go though Bev"!

"Be nice to her please; she's only a kid".

"I'm not the fuckin' big bad wolf Bev", I say, "I can't believe I never managed to get in your knickers", I tell Bev honestly.

"Weren't for want of you trying mate".

"I know you wanted to before you got with Ian".

"You'll never know you male slag", she says, and we both laugh, "please be nice to her, promise me".

"Fuck Bev, I'm always nice man".

"You fuckin' better be", she says.

"I promise man, course I will", and I mean it. We say goodbye.

The next evening I do as asked and pick her up from her pretty little semi detached house just outside Blackbird Leys. I am again pleasantly surprised upon seeing the sexy little fucker in the flesh.

"Nice to meet you, I'm Andrew", I say, "and I have to say that you look lovely", and she has on a slinky black number hugging her figure and black heels. I've black shiny Armani jeans, a Lyle and Scott jumper with a black pair of Patrick Cox loafers crushing my bunions.

"Not looking too shabby yourself", she says, "right, where're we going"?

"You're the indigenous Oxfordite so I thought you could think of somewhere nice. Come on, your shout".

"I know this lovely little restaurant on Cowley Road, little Italian. Do you like Italian food"?

"Well, I like pasta if that's what you mean".

"There's more to Italian than pasta", she says.

"Well, I'm more than willing to give it a go", and I park the gold Rover I had at the time, awful colour, and we get a table inside the place she has brought us to. I can't remember what we ordered but I do remember having to have the drinks conversation again:

"Wanna drink"? I ask her.

""Yeah, white wine spritzer please and thankyou". When the waiter comes over I order her her wine and me a coke.

"Coke? Really"? she says, "you know you can have a pint and still drive don't you"?

"Truth is I never drink", I tell her.

"Why? How the fuck can a man never have a drink"?

"Well", I go again, "it's caused me some problems in the past so to avoid any more such I simply don't do it anymore".

"I've been told never to"………….but I beat her to it:

"Trust a man that doesn't drink, I know".

"Exactly", she says, "but I guess it's ok"!

"Well thankyou", I go, as our meal arrives. We eat and drink in quiet for a while before I say:

"Why did you not do as Bev asked and reprimand me for commenting about you on that photo"?

"Well", she replies, "I did a bit of the old lookee see on facebook and thought that you were a bit good looking so thought that maybe, instead of bollocking you, I'd ask you out on a date instead".

"I'm always up for a date with pretty little things, no brainer really but the fact you're so young makes me wonder why we're here; I mean, apart from the fact it's pleasant to have dinner with someone young and vibrant, there's like 16 years between us".

"Yeah, so, what the fuck has that got to do with it"?

"Can I talk frankly"? I ask her.

"Go on", she says, resting her chin on her hands and looking me in the eye.

"Usually I'm after 'that thing, that thing, that theeeeiiiing' ya know but with the age gap I'm sort of under the proviso that I'm not gonna be getting into your knickers ya know"? and she laughs out loud at this.

"So, do you do a lot of dating then"?

"Not really", I lie, sort of lie, "I mean, yeah, I'm not a virgin but, ya know, I'm not particularly promiscuous ", and again she laughs out loud.

"You lying fucker", she says, "Bev told me you're always out shagging something or other".

"Well, it's not quite like that"! I say, "it's more that I have a few women that are friends and occasionally they might let me, ya know"..........

"Fuck them"?

"Yeah, I guess, though I'd've said 'make love to them' myself".

"Stop talking shit", G says to me, "I know for a fact you're a womanising fucker"!

"I'd like to be", I say truthfully.

"Well", says she, looking deep into my eyes with her almond shaped brown beauties, "I need a fuck buddy", and again I nearly choke.

"Waiter", I say to one passing our table, "could you bring a bottle of wine and a spritzer and another coke for me please sir"?

"Yes sir; finished with your meals"?

"Yes, thank you".

"Were they good? You enjoy"? and we both truthfully reply that indeed we had. We decline desert but I'm eager for G to drink more wine to loosen her tongue and, perhaps, her knickers, though I don't want her too drunk for fucking a dribbling mess sober is not good at all. Half cut is cool though!

"Are you trying to get me drunk Andrew"?

"No", I say, smiling sheepishly, "I just know that it loosens the lips and I wanna know what you're really thinking", and she's plowing into the bottle already. We laugh and joke and talk on myriad subjects; academics, the museums in Oxford like Pitt Rivers and the Ashmolean and the Bodleian Library and fashion and once again this worthy young wench is looking deeply into my beady eyes.

"I'm wondering if"………..but she stops.

"If what"?

"Naaaa", she says, "I can't say that"!

"Please do; you can't do that, I must know what you were going to say now"!

"Well", she says, and now I feel her high heeled shoe running up and down my leg and my middle stump is twitching, awakening, "I was kinda thinking you could be my new fuck buddy"! I feel my lips curl in mirth for she truly has been oiled into looseness by the wine it would seem.

"Don't fuckin' wind me up woman", I say, laughing, "you're joking right? I mean, I'm old enough to be you're dad"!

"So what", she replies, "you look young, you're good looking and I just really really want to fuck you"!

"Wow", I say, I'm fuckin' flattered". And I am.

"Come on", she says, "you're taking me to yours and fucking me tonight", and unlike me I notice she actually articulates the 'g' when she says 'fucking'.

"I can't tonight", I say.

"Why the fuck not", comes the curt reply.

"Well, in truth, it's because you are quite drunk now and I don't want to take advantage of someone I have just met when they are not completely sober to be honest. Well, if you weren't quite as pissed I would fuck you but no, I'm happy to wait"!

"You're fucking me tonight and that's that", she says and as we stand to leave the gaff she pulls me toward her and I kiss her deeply, grabbing her pert arse in the process and generally copping a feel!

"Look", I say, once we've disentangled, "did you feel the wood up against you"? and as I say it she grabs the wood, outlined through my Armanis.

"Come on, take me to yours and fuck me please", and I can here the wheedling of a youngster in her now, someone used to getting what she wants when she wants it.

"Look, you've felt the effect you have on me but I am stone cold sober and I just wouldn't feel right fuckin' you when you are quite as drunk as you are".

"Ohhhhh", she says, "you're no fun and it's not fair", but she's smiling and says now, "but I think it's quite sweet really".

"Really"?

"Really", and she gives me a kiss. I drive her home and we smoke outside in the car before our goodbyes where we arrange to meet the following day. I pick her up from work, take her home and smash her all round my bedroom. Still, I have to tell you, as I sit here in Oxford typing away now, she is still very much my friend and we have great banter but she tells me, and I hate admitting this, that I never gave her an orgasm! Ohhh! Wounder! But, to take the edge off, she tells me it is very difficult for her to get there! Anyway, not to labour the point, we fucked for a year, her and I, and built a friendship that's thus far lasted ten years. She doesn't, despite me asking, let me in her bed today though! But we do spend time together regularly. Anyway, I can't talk of sexual escapades any longer for I'll inevitably end up thrashing myself to within an inch of me life in this cell should I not cease to do so. And Marcus, after having had a load of horny MDMA might get the wrong idea! Naaa, just messin' Marcus is camp, but I'm not sure he's gay. He told me to write that! What he doesn't realize is, is that no one cares if he is bi. He wouldn't be completely gay for he loves the ladies, evidenced by his past conquests and pesty behaviour round the women here and on other sentences where it bore fruit. I tell these sexy stories just to give you an idea of how I behaved when I first ever got clean for a few years after the Ley Community. I had never, ever worked until then, and I was 34 when I started work. I had never had relationships straight, never fucked without drugs, never had friends who weren't drug users. I got my driving license and a passport for the first time ever. A---- sorted the passport for me and driving was mental: I'd been driving all my life, illegally. Now I was road legal! But I was not happy and constantly tried to fix myself with transient things of the flesh. Or gym. Or shopping. I could not just be. I had to be doing. Work and gym and fucking and shopping and doing I was ok. But to be still, well, the thought terrified me. I needed a spiritual awakening and that was not to come for some time yet. My womanising was such that my landlady told me, upon my leaving the property we shared, that she'd never known anyone more promiscuous in her life! The women I have described are a fraction of what I got up to. There were more in Oxford and in the Thames Valley and every time I went home to my sister's to visit she, my lovely sister J----, would get the hump, one day saying to me:

"You're supposed to be coming down to see your family and all you do is run around shagging slags; it's not right", and looking back, she had a point. Always looking to fix the way I feel, one way or another.

Ok dear reader, it is now 2330 hrs and Bono is singing One Love and El Chubbo is of course absolutely spangled as per usual. Because he had all this MDMA earlier the first thing he did upon entering the cell for evening bang up was show me a load of magazines. He was already well fucked when the door was closed and said to me:

"Look Shloaney man Shlook what I've got gonna wank all night man you should see the bitches man Shloaney honestly man", and no sooner was this said he sat himself on the toilet behind the curtain with a bottle of baby lotion and his vibrating Gillette razor.

"What the fuck you want the fuckin' razor for man"?

"Pokey bum wank Shloany man", and he laughs like an imbecile and I can't help but laugh with him. He came out lathered in sweat an hour later.

"Shloaney, you wanna have a look"? And he is holding out the multiple wank mags to me.

"No mate, you're alright bro, I'll just do with this", and I hold up my copy of the Narcotics Anonymous Basic Text that I am reading.

"There's like proper cocks going into cunts though Sloaney man honestly bro you should have a look"!

"Marcus", I say, patiently, "I try to keep my mind off pussy bro 'cause it's just fuckin' frustrating in here man. I've enough to deal with smelling Pocket Rocket's sexy smell when she's on duty (Ms H) and watching the fuckin' Kardashians bro. Fuck looking at spread-eagled gash in those rags of yours 'cause I'll end up firing all my life force down the toilet".

"Your loss mate", he says before getting onto his bunk, smoking a bong and passing out. Earlier in the afternoon me, Smarcus and Just For Men Kempster went to the gym where we did 5 times ten reps clean and press with 45kg, then deadlifts with heavy weight then we went to the lat pull down machine doing three different grips and five sets with each hold and I finished by sprinting on the treadmill for the last ten minutes of the session. I am stacking creatine, eating tons of tuna, noodles and granola sprinkled with whey protein and having multiple weight gain shakes daily. I literally graze all day between fuck off fat meals because the servery in staffed by lads I'm close to: Craig Mc, little Frank and Jeff 'H' McCarthy so we get right looked after. Tomorrow me, Kempy and Smarcus plan to do legs and biceps-I'd set my bed up in that gym if I could. Anyway dear reader that's me for the day. Night.

23-2-2019 0530hrs. The Cranberries sing 'oh my life, is changing every day, in every possible way' on the radio in Delores's lovely lilting Irish accent. I know all about the lovely Irish for as I told you my mum is a Dublin Jackeen, whatever that term means. Andy Moynihan taught me it and I know it is a disparaging word used by those from other parts of the Emerald Isle for those hailing from Ireland's capital city. Anyway, I nearly got to sleep about half four but the selfish El Fat One, despite the fact the radio and TV were off and it was dark in the cell suddenly goes:

"Sloaney turn the telly on", which snaps me straight from my sleep.

"What the fuck", I go, "you're a fuckin liberty man; why don't you get up and turn the fuckin' thing on yourself"?

"You've got the remote"!

"How d'ya know that"?

"You've always got it"!

"I told you where it is if I'm ever asleep, you simply can't be bothered to move and you know it".

"I need a pipe man", and he begins to load his milk carton, yes, he is now piping spice through a foil lined milk carton people! This is his pattern: wake up and immediately escape being conscious by smoking Nippon Alloy Wheel Cleaner or K2 Cockroach Killer.

"Fat Boy", I say as he starts to get up to prepare this fuckin' great load of spice which, I promise, and it did, will knock him the fuck out, "Marcus, please pipe it on your bed bro".

"I will, just gonna get it ready before I use the toilet", and once again he turns on the light, grabs the mags, spanks the life out himself before sitting on his bunk lathered in sweat and picking up the pipe he'd prepared.

"Right", I say, "from the moment you suck that", and he's got the business end to his mouth and he's putting flame to the paper spice sitting on holes poked into the foil lined carton at the other end, "you've got 45 seconds tops so please lay on the bed", I say as he's sitting on it currently.

"Relax Shloaney man", and he does as asked, pulling his feet up onto the bunk and laying back. I observe him closely.

"Right, you've got 15, 14 13, 12, 11, and right now the blood is picking the poison from your lungs and the molecules are now spreading through you and 10, 9, 8, 7, 6"………

"Plesh Shhloaney man shluuu"……….

"5, 4, and you're palsy shaking and you're fuckin' gone you mong and now you can't even hear me as you twitch and now in case you can you normally handsome cunt you're mouth hangs open and you're already dribbling and you look like a proper retard starved severely of oxygen at birth you fuckin' absolute pickle", and he is now well and truly gone and despite the fact he looks like a fuckin' cabbage I briefly think how nice it would be to be able to escape the walls and steel and bars and stuff so easily with the pull of a pipe. I put the kettle on for my first coffee of the day. I think on yesterday. Many here on Alpha were out their heads on MDMA. In Brad's there were Jay Nevin, Billy Banks, J.T, Brad and Marcus oh and Kempy and more all gurning like ravers. I got the fuck out the cell for all were predisposed to talking absolute shit.

Nev came in the shower and was tryna talk to me whilst I washed but he could not articulate himself, eyes rolling and jaw hanging slackly. When I got out J.T was outside Brad's cell door looking proper pesty, rubbing himself unconsciously as the drug played havoc with his hormones.

"Phhroar", he goes to me, "I'd love to lick Ms Steven's bumhole I bet it's proper tasty", and though I call him pesty and have had no drugs I have to concur with him that he is probably right and that her bumhole would indeed be a delectable delight, though a bit gamey. The reason he is thinking on her is she is on duty, up the landing. She looks over and spots J.T looking at her and smiles sweetly and I go to J.T:

"You're making her nervous standing there rubbing your cock bro".

"Was I rubbing it? D'ya reckon that she's really nervous"? and he is a little worried, I see that I have got him so I go:

"Course mate", I say, "she just clocked you proper staring at her and stroking your cock man. Didn't you see her face? She looked well worried man, I felt sorry for her"!

"Was I really Sloaney? Oh shit, that's the MDMA and she'll think I'm proper rapey now, like a proper pervert"!

"That's what I mean J.T, you're out ya fuckin' nut and rubbing your cock whilst looking at a slight and pretty new screw bro. I'll bet she's gonna put a savage write up into your NOMS now bro", and NOMS is the National Offender Management System.

"Oh no man, she's gonna proper nonce me off man, oh fuck man what am I gonna do Sloaney bro? You ain't winding me up are ya 'cause I've had the MDMA"?

"No bro, I wouldn't mess around with things like that man. Rather you than me bro"!

"Shit man, I always get proper noncey on MD man, like a right pervert"! he says, "d'ya think I should go up to her Sloaney"?

"Yeah man", I say, "I would. Go up to her and say 'Ms Stevens I wasn't rubbing myself and perving over you when I was looking at you I was just daydreaming Miss that's all' that's what I would do J.T".

"Oh shit man, I dunno what to do mate. If she writes on my NOMS that I was looking at her and rubbing myself I'll get proper pedo'd off Sloaney".

"Just tell her you got carried away; your face looked all screwed up when you was doing it too bro, like proper deep perving you was like a noncey old man and you was proper wanking yourself mate". J.T is looking really worried now and it's all I can do to not laugh!

"What the fuck am I gonna do Sloaney"?

"Go say sorry and that you wasn't actually wanking over her man".

"What can I say I was doing though"?

"Say you was just scratching an itch but that you know how it musta looked to her. Say that that's why your face was all screwed up like a weirdo, 'cause it was the relief from the scratching, like the enjoyment of scratching the itch".

"Will you back me up though Sloaney"?

"How the fuck can I do that"?

"Just say, like, I wasn't talking about her when I was rubbing Cecil"?

"I thought you was gonna cum, standing there gurning, chin right out, eyes like slits and proper tugging and rubbing yourself"! Oh, I was having fun here!

"It's that fuckin' MD man I'm telling you Sloaney it always turns me into a raving sex pest"!

"Me too J.T but you've proper scared her bro, look, she's coming over"!

"Oh no", says J.T looking horrified, "she's gonna pull me up int she"? and Ms Stevens walks by us and only says:

"Alright Sloaney, alright Jamie, hope you're behaving yourselves", and I can hold my laughter no more!

"You cunt", I say, "I proper had you then man", and I am holding my belly I amused myself so much! J.Ts long handsome face cracks in smile.

"Sloaney, I fuckin' love you you prick", and the drug dealing fuck hugs me in relief, "what, that was all a wind up? I was shitting myself man"!

"Course it was you silly cunt"! He throws his head back, laughs and fucks off! One of the best on here old J.T.

1030hrs and I'm sitting outside in the wing yard. It is late February but the sun is beautiful, shining right on me and all I have on are shorts and T-shirt. I can hear the full hearted song of the birds in the twigs of the trees overhead; I wish I'd the knowledge to identify the many species from the sounds my ears are picking up but I don't yet nevertheless I marvel at the wondrous cacophony these tiny miracles produce from their even tinier lungs. To my left I can hear the voices of prisoners playing pool and the sweet sing song of Rosa Hulbert, Ms H, otherwise known as Pocket Rocket as she, too, plays with a cue; she's a wicked little officer to be fair. The tweets and warbles surrounding me and the glorious golden eye in the sky remind me that The Chief is in everything, everywhere, even under my bottom on the few strands of grass on which my pale arse sits. Oh! The sky is so lovely and blue dear reader and if this is global warming's produce then bring it on say I! In the grey grip of winter the hard lines of the walls, punctuated with windows with big bars look ominous, but, today, bathed in this Homeric glow these structures, the big fence topped with razor wire even have a certain beauty in and of themselves. I am literally alone on this yard right now. Just outside the enclosure is a camera pole whose eye sees all around and now a security screw walks with two dogs along the inside perimeter checking for parcels that may have been thrown over and I think how nice it would be two pet those smart arse hounds. I look toward the heavens and see the trails of an aeroplane as it climbs high into the sky and I think of the joy of being so free to soar across the firmament below. Now a small prop powered plane piloted by some free lucky fuck flies over and immediately after that a flock of birds, starling like small black ones soar in that magical swirling way, happily chirping and tweeting away. Then there are throaty warbles from specimens unseen and unknown and I think to myself that birds cheep happily away simply grateful to be alive and I wonder of what blessed hope they know but of which most of us are unaware. Still, I too am grateful to be breathing on this yard today, caged though I may be. This cloudless warm crisp sunny day has me feeling like flinging my own soul upon the ether. Though it be but February it feels like spring and I dare say that were I free to ramble country lanes I'd see the odd daf poking its head and blessing us with its beauty. Wow, I only came down to check on Smartyn, didn't have a thought of coming out here but oh I'm glad I did.

2130hrs. Marcus is out of it on MDMA and preparing a pipe on a milk carton right now. It is Sunday night and Top Gear is on. I had a good time at the gym working my legs and finishing with a trundle on the treadmill. Marcus has a new tiny mobile phone coming tomorrow, one capable of getting a better signal for the other one struggles. Comes with a sim, costing him a two-er and is ready to go, to use. The cunt has just lost consciousness now, one foot on the floor, one on the bed, propped on his pillow, head back mouth open and waterfall of spittle already cascading down his chiselled chin the knob. Swears to me he's gonna get clean tomorrow. Thing is, I need to remember that I, too, was terrified of detoxing and it took four years from relapse to gain the courage to go through it again and you dear reader have been walking it with me if you've gotten this far through this, my first book, if it can be called a book! I think it's good and interesting enough, really I do........most of the time! I'm praying a publisher will think so too! Again, today, all have been out their heads on MDMA which permeates the prison at present! I was unlucky enough earlier to get collared by Billy Banks the long winded drain the life out of ya go right round the houses lovable rogue who took twenty minutes to tell me this: One day in a jail in London a long time ago one prisoner asked another prisoner if he could sort him out a quarter of an ounce of burn (tobacco). So, the fella he asks says 'yeah, give me five' but in the five the would be recipient gets what he wants from someone else. When the 'give me five' fella returns the would be receiver says to him 'no thanks, I've got it now' and the other fella, the would be seller goes to his cell and searching himself can't find the item he was going to sell to the chap, the quarter of tobacco. Thinking, inexplicably, that the fella who asked him must somehow of nicked it he literally sticks a pen in his eye only to find the item on the route back to his cell after committing the dastardly deed. Fuck me I had to drag the details out of Billy who wanted to talk drugged bollox all the while bless him. Him and Nev are nuts for sure, there's no two ways about it.

25-02-2019 1700hrs. In the cell right now are a multitude of people all driving Marcus mad for spice paper he doesn't have until tomorrow. He is due to pick up three pages in the morning. Upon hearing El Chubbo telling this truth the desperate drug addicts retreat from our cell forlornly. El Fat One did get the new mobile today though. Amazing such tech in a thing the size of one's thumb. Anyway, the highlight of my day today was the time I spent at the ATB Unit with the team down there. I must confess that though I love Jason very much, for he is such a nice and erudite guy whose primary concern is the rehabilitation of prisoners, it was Lucy today who captivated me and then Officer Ellie P when she came into the unit to do some photocopying! Hormones are driving me mad today. It is graduation day from Bridge tomorrow so I'll report on how that goes. Feeling flat and not very eloquent right now.

26-2-2019 The graduation went very well. All eight of us who finished the programme gave a good account of our journey of change. In the room for the ceremony were a multitude of different people from the prison including Forward Trust big wigs like Head of Treatment Anita, a brown skinned intelligent beauty with big boobs, a prison Governor, health care staff and of course the facilitators Jan, Woody and Steve who sadly have now to leave this jail for twelve weeks to deliver the same programme at another institution, Elmley on the Isle Of Sheppey. These people have been positively inspirational to me. Anyway, last night things got heated with me and Smarcus. The fuckin' mong was, as usual at about eight p.m, spilling milk and cereal all over the cell, palsy wobbling in front of the TV whilst I was trying to watch stuff and throwing bowls, spoons and burnt bits of toilet roll he uses to light his spice into the sink and on the floor which I find, at times, infuriating. He was standing by the sink with his head actually in it, inside the bowl and he bent in half though standing up.

"Shloaney man pleashe help me man I've just spilt cereal all over the floor man", and I look up to see he has done just that, for the third time tonight. Every time he feeds I have to watch as he throws it everywhere due to dropping into an unconscious stupor in the process of eating.

"What the fuck d'ya want me to do"?

"Pleash man Shloaney", and his head, as I say, is actually in the sink, holding him up. Usually pity pervades me but it is anger now, fury at having to constantly be on guard in case this cunt hurts himself.

"Marcus, I'm not babysitting you anymore man".

"Plesh man".

"You're a fuckin' drain. I'm not doing this anymore bro, I fuckin' can't Marcus. I'm sick of cleaning the fuck up after you mate". He tries to straighten and manages to turn though he can't quite stand upright, still bent at the waist and he says, spittle hanging down as he drawls from his spastic mouth:

"Well, fuck your mum then", and immediately I sit up on my bunk.

"What the fuck did you just say to me you fuckin' mongrel"?

"Ahhhh, errr, I didn't mean that man", but I jump from my bed and yank the fat fucks' head up by his hair and whisper menacingly in his ear:

"You ever talk to me like that again, you ever mention my mum, that noun ever escapes your lips and I'll bite your fuckin' nose off man d'ya get me"?

"Shloaney man I"……..

"Shut your fuckin' mouth", I say, fuming, "you're a liberty takin' cunt mate. If you ever talk to me that way again Marcus I swear by almighty God I'll make you prove just how dangerous you think you are you rotten cunt. I've never ever spoken to you like that. I fuckin' dare you to do it again", and dear reader I half wanted him to just so I can let go my fury. He says nothing. I get on my bed and it takes an hour talking to God for me to be released from my anger. It wasn't really until the fat fuck who's monged in much the same way this morning apologised at the start of the new day that I began to feel better.

"I'm really sorry Sloaney man that was out of order bro", and don't forget that Marcus is a genuinely kind hearted lovely fella despite his mental and emotional immaturity.

"Marcus, I have never talked to you like that bro. And my little mum mate, well, she's had a horrific time of it man. All the shit with me and my brothers and being raped and mate she's still so kind as to donate 10,000 pounds to Great Ormand Street bro. She has fuck all to do with what goes on here man. Talking to anyone that way is savage, keep families out of it".

"I know", he says, contrite, "honestly man I'm sorry".

"I know you didn't mean it", I tell him, "but anyone else I'd've bitten bits off of 'em but look, it's done, let's move on", and we have done so. So, he scored a load of spice today, he is owed £800, pulled in £750 off of the last lot and has the new better quality mobile to make transactions easier. Marcus said earlier on that the numbers are even causing him some concern so big are they getting at present; he's feeling the pressure. He of course has to make sure he pays the man who lays him on the drugs. If Marcus wasn't using so much himself he'd always pay up front but such are his own habits that is becoming more and more difficult. Anyway, he is monged out right now and peace is upon me in this cell.

28-2-2019 0940hrs and I am down the ATB Unit this morning. Lucy is in her office, Mr Paul Highm, the CM head honcho is in his and Naomi and Jason are delivering the Resolve course to prisoners who are in for crimes that involved a violent element. Me? Well, I'm currently sitting in one of the staff rooms writing to you but prior to that I have been hoovering, polishing and cleaning which suits me fine.

"What date is it Lucy"? I shout from this room adjacent to her office.

"28th", she says, "last day of February".

"I thought it was the 27th today", I say to her.

"Nope", comes back the musical sexy sing song voice, "first of march tomorrow".

"How fuckin' quickly time passes", I say to her, "so you must have Ricky Lanes down for an Inclusion interview today then"?

"No, he's tomorrow I think", and I hear her checking some paperwork on her cluttered desk, "nope, he's in tomorrow Sloaney".

"Well, I'll have the hump if he don't get here", I tell her, "'cause I've reminded him and he promised me that he's gonna turn up".

"He's had a letter from me too", says she, "so he definitely knows he's due down here". The smell of lint where I've just mopped the floor is lovely in my nostrils. As I sit here now I am running a few things from last night through my cluttered head. Dale Pearson, the handsome psycho, is losing the plot lately due to having gotten back on the psychosis inducing spice without the resources of Marcus to alleviate such with large doses of narcotics. Sat-Nam, our Indian friend who does all the washing for the wing, the laundry orderly, was in Bradder's cell last night and Dale was proper bullying him, 'play' punching him with punches which weren't very playful at all.

296

"Leave him alone man", says Brad, "you'll leave bruises all over him man".

"So, I don't care", says Dale, whom I do like very much but there's no escaping it, he frightens many people on the wing and behaves like a nasty piece of work at times. If he punched me like that, playing or not I'd bite bits out of him no matter how hard he thinks he is.

"Come on Dale man, you're always punching people lately", says Little Frank, "it's not fuckin' nice Dale, it's bullying bro", and my admiration for Frank goes up ten fold.

"Sat-Nam", I say, "fuck off for fuck sake, just go", because I can't stand seeing this any longer. All I say to Dale, giving him a withering look as I exit is:

"Dale man", and shake my head before leaving the cell and heading to my own where I briefly feel sad for Sat-Nam but soon get over it.

2130. Marcus, Just For Men Kempy and Peter Lanes were plastered on prison hooch and when I returned from work to the wing mine and Marcus's cell stank of it. Marcus is very much still alcohol inebriated now and in all fairness has been very funny in his drunken state. Earlier on he and Just For Men had come into the shower whilst I stood happily washing away and they had bundled me to the floor and tickled the fuck outta me. Torment as I am extremely sensitive to tickles. I ended up threatening violence!! Anyway, Air and Sexy Boy emanate from the DAB and 8 Out Of 10 Cats is due on soon which I love, Jimmy Carr and Sean Locke crease me up. And the other fella, quite cute, on the other table, can't remember his name but he's good too. My chest is hurting from yesterday's workout and I look at unconscious Marcus now and feel helpless. Bye for now.

01-03-2019. Afternoon. So, it's Black Eye Friday. Marcus is absolutely out his canister as per. On the circuit this morning, just for the record, I beat Jeff 'H' McCarthy and Adam W, happily coming first out of about fifteen participants. It was the brutal dirty dozen, so twelve different exercises and twelve reps at each station in between laps of the gym hall between each exercise. I beat Adam, who came second, by a clear minute. At the end of the circuit I had that dry, gammy metal taste in my mouth and the moment I completed I collapsed to the floor but the gym screw, a great guy called Kev said:

"Sloaney, get up, let your heart rate slow down gradually", so I had to get up and walk round the gym whilst the beast in my chest returned to normal rhythm. I love the pump after such circuits, and the ruddy look of the blood in my face as my head turns red with the exertion. So, I'm now sat in Brad's cell with Brad, Marcus, Kempy and Gibbo who're all running in and out the cell and round the wing trying to pull in what they are owed. Outside the cell I can hear Jay Nevin draining the life out some poor fuck; Nev is plastered, pissed out his head. Seb from next door has just come in and is now telling Brad:

"I will have 'em for you mate, I've just got to try pull a few boxes (of vapes) in".

"Fuck me Seb", says Brad, "I'm owed in 36 packs and I've pulled in 3 so far and a cap", (single vape cartridge).

"Bear with me Brad", says Seb who then walks out the cell and Brad goes on:

"Ricky Lanes just come to me saying 'bear with me bear with me' but the cunt ain't paid me for three weeks Sloaney".

"Well, I wouldn't hold your breath for those packs Bradders".

"His brother Peter is a cunt too", says Brad, "and I know we all grew up together but they take the piss man".

"I don't know why the fuck you'd even try with them two; I mean, I love 'em but if I were getting up to what you do I wouldn't be trusting those couple a cunts for sure".

"Brad, one minute mate", says a fella I don't know and Brad goes out the cell to converse with him briefly before coming back and when he does another fella, Stuart, dark haired bloke who bounced from B wing comes in and hands Brad a pack saying:

"Owe you one more box bro".

"I need the other box though Stuart", says Brad.

"I'm struggling a bit", says the fella.

"If you get 'em in I'll show you a bit of love", says Brad meaning that if the fella manages to pull up the other pack Brad will give him a bit of spice paper and when Stuart leaves the cell Brad turns to me and says:

"Always good to give a bit of encouragement and the promise of a few spliffs for free always oils the wheels Sloaney", and the handsome fuck smiles and winks conspiratorially.

"Shouldn't have to though", I reply and I'm happy to be alone in the cell with me mate, enjoying a little peace and tranquillity. After some minutes Mr Russell, relatively new to the job, pokes his head in the cell and says to me:

"So you smashed the circuit today then Sloaney"?

"I did guv", I gloat, "can't believe I actually beat 'H' and Adam".

"I know", says this affable young officer, "Adam's proper fit too"!

"Well guv, not as fit as me"!

"So, what is the 'dirty dozen' then"? asks the officer now.

"Well", I say, "we each have a station with an aerobic matt and a bar weighing 25kg and there are twelve exercises. We start with five laps of the gym and finish with five and between each exercise we do a lap and we go through the whole thing three times doing twelve reps of each of the twelve exercises.

"So what sort of exercises are there"? asks this officer who is so handsome he has all the female members of staff tryna date him.

"Well, like, press from chest, press behind the neck, bent over row, upright row, burpees, sit ups, press ups, squat thrusts, dorsal raises, curls, power cleans and squats so there's a lot of bar work".

"Sounds fuckin' brutal", says Mr Russell, "you must be pretty fit to come first".

"Well, if you'd seen me six months ago you'd of never thought I'd be doing circuits".

"I've heard", says Mr Russell, who's becoming a very decent and competent officer, "Mr Broomfield was telling me that when you first got here you was using so much you looked like you was ready to drop down dead".

"I've been on here nine and a half months now Mr Russell", I say, "and I thought I actually was gonna die here".

"Was it that bad"?

"It was that fuckin' bad", I say, "living in a filthy cell with a filthy cell mate, smoking buscopan and spice and on gallons of methadone I actually wanted to die to be fair".

"Didn't you have a particularly brutal fight too"?

"Yeah man", I say, quite proud of the notoriety amongst the staff team, "the whole wing heard me and Aidy biting gouging and smashing fuck out each other at five bells in the morning one day Mr Russell. It was brutal to be fair"!

"What, was he hard then"?

"Not that he was particularly hard, I just think the both of us have a lot of heart and he doesn't care if he spends the rest of his life in jail! Little cunt hit me with a lump of wood, stabbed me with a vape battery and gouged me eyes but I did bite him badly all over his back and break his nose to be fair. I could taste him on my teeth afterwards but I think the little cunt had the best of it though it pains me to admit that"!

"Sounds savage", says the this charismatic screw, "clearly you're a different guy now then"?

"45 days clean today guv", I say, proudly.

"What, absolutely clean, like, literally nothing"?

"Mr Russell, I can tell you in all good faith that I have had nothing more than an ibuprofen for 45 days man".

"Well, you look really well", says this officer, sticking out his paw for a shake, "well done mate"!

"Cunt never stops shouting about it", pipes up Brad now, smiling.

"Well, I'd be the same", says Mr Russell before taking his leave and Brad says:

"You know I'm well proud of you and love you Sloaney", and I'm touched and we hug it out. Kyle Tyler, a pint sized pleasant fella with mousy hair and a big nose comes into the cell and sells Brad a 300mg pregablin or 'pregab' tablet. One of Bradders' favourite poisons.

"Can I nick a bit of spice off of ya Brad"? asks Kyle and Brad goes:

"Course ya can man", and opens his little stash bag and pulls out half a page of power paper, tears off a strip and gives it to Kyle.

"How you getting on in that cell"? I ask Kyle who is now banged up with Craig D, Beany having been booted off to another wing for something or other. People are moved from wing to wing here like musical chairs. Marcus won't last much longer on here if he keeps dealing like he does, but then he was kicked onto here for dealing so, well, what the fuck do you do! Anyway, Kyle says:

"I'm constantly on edge Sloaney and I thought I was moving out today but Groggsy (a gruff fella from Medway on the ones landing) moved into the cell I was supposed to move into so I've got to wait 'till a new cell comes up".

"It'll be alright, just hang on in there bro".

"Craig's alright", he says, "but he has the TV on like literally all night man".

"Fuck that", says Bradders. Kyle fucks off to go smoke spice and Paul Stone walks into the cell now looking ill, half dead and weighing in at no more than eight stone dripping wet and says to Bradders:

"Don't worry Brad I am gonna pay you I'm just waiting for someone to get back from a visit".

"I'll give you some love (spice) when you pay me", and now big Noel the nutter comes in and says to Brad:

"That spider's fuckin' massive man", and he comes closer to look at the thing in the Perspex cube behind my head, where I sit writing away in real time.

"She's still getting bigger yet", says Brad and now Manc hyper Reece comes in and clocks the page number atop the sheet on which my pen scratches and says:

"872isthathowmanypagesyou'vedone", and continues before I can answer and I'll separate the words for easy readings sake that: "Pete Harlow (a skinny likeable fella from Milton Keynes) just had a Code Blue and there's an ambulance crew dealing with him now".

"What, has he gone over"? asks Brad, meaning has he overdosed on spice.

"Well I presume so 'cause what else do you ever see ambulances on here for"? and the hyper little shitbag darts off and Marcus comes into the cell now saying to me:

"Don't hate me, but I've just got a better job than you".

"What job", I ask.

"Just got a gym orderly job", he says.

"What"! I say, "that's fuckin' brilliant man", I enthuse, genuinely happy, "this could be the fuckin' makin' of ya, help you clean yourself up and that man I'm fuckin buzzin' for ya"!

"I know man", he says, "but they're proper on me 'cause Kev said if they even think I'm under the influence they won't think twice about sacking me".

"Ahhh Marcus bro", I say, "this is proper meant to be man and I believe that God is working in you right now".

"I know I know but I've got to like, proper start cleaning myself up now, I just hope I can get off the subutex and that".

"Marcus man don't worry too much", I tell him, "don't start projecting into the future 'cause I'm positive you're gonna get there brother; good things are happenng for a reason bro".

"D'ya reckon I can do it Sloaney"?

"I fuckin' know so", I tell him, "think about it", I continue, "what's the one thing in the world you love more than drugs man"?

"Gym", says Chubbo.

"Well then".

"I'm just worried about".........starts Marcus.

"Stop it", I say, "that's the best way to make yourself sick, worrying about what might or might not happen days, weeks or months down the line; just think of today, enjoy the fact of your new job and give yourself a break for God is working for you Marcus man", and I am hopeful and full of joy for him. Scouse Steve Fiddler comes into the cell.

"Still writing your book Sloaney"?

"Yeah man"! I say.

"What page are you on"?

"873", I tell him.

"I hope you've written me up as the biggest gangster on the wing"!

"I have mate; regular El Chappo moving kilos"!

"The only kilos I move are the ones I shit out after eating myself sick on canteen day", says the big friendly scouse before shooting out the door and now Grin comes in. Marcus is talking with Brad in the recess and Grin asks me:

301

"Has Marcus slowed himself down yet"?

"No, but he's just got a gym orderly job and I reckon this could be the making of him".

"Has he really"? asks Grin.

"Yeah man, for real".

"I reckon that's the best possible thing that could've happened for him", and now Kyle comes in and offers Marcus a pregab which Marcus buys for a fat joint of spice.

"Sloaney man don't judge me", says El Chubbo.

"I didn't say a word Marcus", I say.

2115hrs same day. European championships athletics are on and Katerina Johnson Thompson or KJT, the current poster girl of British athletics is headed for a gold in the pentathlon. She is the most exciting Brit in the sport right now after the retirement of Jessica Ennis. Marcus is of course monged out and I of course have been taking the piss out of him. I have not masturbated for two days and have been literally praying to God to remove my lust as I have felt like I have been in heat of late, pulling and ripping the head off of my old boy, leaving me drained of energy. I can feel my prana returning to optimal levels. My synapses snap faster and I am more articulate both verbally and in the written. Right, on the TV is the final race with KJT, fit as fuck by the way, mixed race beauty and sexy blonde Emerson, also a Brit, running the 800 meters. Underway. Sexy bums everywhere. KJT right out in front. Sexy Emerson second. No, Emerson fell at the line and grabbed fifth! Stumbled right at the end! But fit as fuck KJT smashed it and won the pentathlon overall, getting gold and Emerson still got silver despite the stumble in this, the final event. Emerson is but a teenager at nineteen but boy she's a hottie and I don't care, bit pedo like but who doesn't look? Proper little sort, and not the sort that Fredo says you 'pitch in the foreigns and ditch in a cab'! Anyway, in other news Craig Mc, my big Scottish pal, left HMP Rochester today for an open jail, HMP Ford. If I put the music on the bums on the TV will stop distracting me, hold on. Ok. TV is off. So, Craig has gone. I gave the mahussive Scot a big hug and he said:

"Stay in touch Sloaney, and when we are out we will have to meet up".

"As long as we both remain clean and sober we will be ok bro and undoubtably meet again my friend".

"One day at a time man", says the big highlander.

"Write to me bro".

"I will", he says, we fist bump and he's gone from Alpha. Since stopping using I feel like I don't see as much of what goes on on the wing these days. I don't get to see, apart from with my own tight knit crowd, who owes what, who's getting slapped, who's new on the wing etc because most everyone on here is concerned with drugs and for the most part I'm wrapped around gym bods like Adam W, little Martyn, Craig Mc who's just left, Max Potter though he relapsed a few days ago on MDMA and 'H' who I'm growing ever closer to. Max is in bits right now as he has just found out that one of his best friends is fucking the love of his life outside and he has all but given up, saying when he gets out he's going flat out back at it again with the drink and the drugs. Anyway, earlier on I was around Brad's talking of my night time troubles with El Fat One AKA El Chubbo AKA Marcus, telling Brad of Marcus' mongy behaviour and Kempy comes in the Just For Men vain cunt, overhears me and Brad then not a minute later disappears back out the door again without a word. Now, dear reader, Kempy is the biggest stirrer! Born with a big wooden spoon! So, five minutes after Kempy left Brad's I go to my cell where El Chubbo reclines on the bottom bunk, his bed, and Kempy sits in the chair in which I do my writing. Marcus, as usual, is inebriated though only half way to complete retard mode. As soon as I walk in the cell Marcus goes:

"Been cunting me off round Brad's have ya"? but by his tone I can hear the smile and jocular manner and know it's but a bit of banter. Just For Men immediately pipes up:

"Yeah, proper out of order you are Sloaney, sitting around there cunting your pal off".

"I wasn't Marcus, don't listen to that cunt, I was just having a private discussion with Brad is all".

"Don't lie though Sloaney", says this devil I've known all me life, Steve Kemp, "admit you was proper slagging him off though", and now he turns to Marcus and says, "honestly mate, I wouldn't have it", then back to me, "Sloaney man you're bang out of order mate"!

"Fuck off Steve man don't wind the cunt up for fuck sake".

"You should apologise though Sloaney", says Steve the stirrer.

"What the fuck for"? I say.

"For saying Marcus is a proper mong and that when you talk to him at night it's like talking to a backward person", and you have to know the mannerisms of this cunt, Just For Men, to appreciate how funny he really is; he is right in his element here.

"Sloaney man, I can't believe you man", says Marcus monged already.

"Really"? I say to Kempy.

303

"Yeah Sloaney", and he turns to Marcus, "honestly mate, proper mugging you off", and he turns back to me, "and you do it all the time Sloaney"!

"Kempy man you're a proper shit stirrer", I smile, turning to Marcus, then back to Kempy, "look at him", and Marcus eyes are proper bloodshot, heavy and his mouth is ever so slightly open, "he ain't far from mong mode now Kempy to be fair"!

"See what I mean Marcus", says Kempy as Marcus draws on a spice spliff, "Sloaney man he's supposed to be your pal".

"Yeah Shhloaney man I thought we were mates man", and spittle dribbles from his mouth but being half, no, a quarter with it he manages to wipe it away, maintaining a little of his dignity. I turn to Kempy and ask:

"What the fuck has the cunt taken tonight"?

"Don't you worry about that", says Smarcus smiling like a silly kid who's been naughty, "don't tell him Steve".

"A zopiclone, two pregabs, a rivotril and six ml of 'tex", says Just For Men.

"Six ml of subutex"! I say aghast.

"I know", says Kempy, "I told him to save some for tomorrow but you know what the greedy cunt's like"!

"Yeah", I say, "proper junkie".

"So was you though Sloaney, proper greedy fucker you ya cunt"! says Steve.

"I know man but in here I could never quite afford to use the way Marcus does".

"'Cause I'm El Chappo, Pablo Escobar, money team Marcus don't ya know boys", dribbles the retarded reprobate laughing and chuckling slobberingly at his own hilarity.

"I'll give you your due though Marcus ya fat fuck, I couldn't deal with the pressure of all those pages you take on", I tell him honestly.

"Me either", says Kempster, "I couldn't sleep at night knowing I had to get all that money into my account and collect all the shit every Friday. It would fry my fuckin' head man. Fuck that".

"Init"! I say, "but he does get it in, fuck knows how, £750 this week and 60 packs of caps on top of that"!

"I know", says Kempy, "me and Peter were talking about it today saying we don't know how the fuck he does it"!

"And", I say, "he uses so much himself, gets his man paid and still manages to turn a tidy profit for himself"!

"'Cause I'm fuckin' Pablo", drawls the barely conscious clown once again, "people know they fuck with me and I'll fuck 'em up huh huh

huh", he dribbles and though I laugh there's some truth in this for he is a fuckin' tool merchant!

"And the fact you've got us lot behind you", says Kempy!

"I'll tell you why you're doing so well", I say to Marcus, "you ain't got a rat cell mate like your last one robbing you every time you're out ya fuckin' nut"!

"And", says Kemps, "you don't smoke or take drugs Sloaney so that fact alone leaves him with more profit"!

"Imagine if I was using"! I say.

"You two woulda been murder 'cause you're a greedy cunt as well Sloaney", says Kempster.

"You know that", I say, concurring, "anyway Kempster, what's happening with your bird bro"?

"Didn't I tell ya"? he asks, "just before I got put away my bank card went missing and the pin number was written on the back of it and the cunt has cleared me out"!

"What", I say, "that Donna bird"?

"Yeah man".

"How much money did you have in there"?

"Just under £2000".

"Two grand"! I exclaim.

"About that yeah", says Just For Men.

"Fuckin' hell, what a cunt", I say, "have you been able to get through to her"?

"Naaa man", he says, "the phone just goes straight through to voicemail after a couple of rings".

"Bless ya", I say seriously, "how're you feeling bro"?

"Fuck all I can do about it and it's hardly suprising really. She loves a fuckin' pipe. I am wounded but you know what women are like around crack cocaine: they're ten times worse than us"! And he is, indeed, in my experience, right!

"I know right"! I say.

"I mean, think about it", says Kempster, "if you want a blow job from a crack or coke whore all you have to have for 'em is a pipe or a line"!

"I know", I say, "that's exactly why I just can't trust Tan 'cause she'll do anything for a line of coke but at least she's honest about it"!

"Yeah, that's the problem, when they ain't honest and when the cunts're sneaky about it", says Kemps.

"And those cunts are the worst", I say, "sell their soul for a fuckin' pipe and fuck the likes of us over too as you yourself have just experienced. Will you still get with her when you get out though"?

"I do love the bird", he says, "so probably". Anyway, on my canteen today I brought another bag of Elite Protein rich in amino acids and another tub of creatine both of which me and Chubbo dosed up on immediately. I imagine in my mind's eye these chemicals fizzing around my muscles after the insane chest workout on Monday and the psycho circuit in which I blew away the best bodies on the wing today suprising myself I must admit. As I said earlier, it was nice for the second placed Adam to simply say:

"You was just too quick for me today".

"Yeah, but you smashed me on last weeks one and so did 'H'" and this is indeed true.

"Yep", said Adam, "king for this week".

"You know that nasty metal taste you get when running from the old bill? That's what I had in my mouth today", I tell him.

"You're getting fitter 'cause you don't even smoke now do ya"?

"Nope", I say, "but I did have a roll up last week".

"Yeah, but fuck me", he says, "one fag is fuck all considering all the drugs you was doing, smoking those patches and tea bags".

"Don't", I say, "fuckin' embarrassing looking back at it".

"Don't be embarrassed man, you should be fuckin' proud of yourself", he says and he's so fuckin' genuine this cunt. What a lovely, humble guy.

"Bless you Adam man".

"How many days clean are ya"?

"Trying not to count but 45"!

"Fuck me", he says, "that's fuckin' flown by; you've smashed it bro", and he sticks out a fist for a bump and goes along his way.

Sat 02-03-2019 1145hrs. So we've been out our cells this Saturday morning and me and Martyn not long ago were playing cards on the dining room table when Brad walks past with a bag.

"Feeding the spider Sloaney", he says, "got a catepillar and a little Orb Weaver here".

"Come on Mart", I say, "come and watch this boy", and we go round to Brad's where a group quickly descends to see this brutal big house spider savage these poor smaller critters. In the cell are Kempy, Gibbo and mad Pete W of the diary I included earlier in this book along with Martyn and me and Marcus and Brad throws first the spider in but his baby just misses it; she will have it later so now he puts in the hairy caterpillar and immediately the beast sinks fangs in before pumping necrotic venom into the critter which immobilises the back end of the

306

long insect but the front still struggles as she starts to suck the innards out and Pete W is standing watching going:

"Fuckin' hell man she's a beast boy", and then the door goes and Jay 'Nev' Nevin grabs Pete and pushes him out the way saying:

"Out the way, let me see", and Pete goes:

"Who the fuck you pushing"?

"Who you talking to"? goes Nev and now they're outside the cell arguing and Pete simply says;

"Get in the shower you bully cunt", and Nev is going:

"I'm not a mug ya know", and we are all listening from Brad's cell intently when suddenly we hear 'whack' and we all come out the cell and it's pretty evenly matched and we are all secretely hoping Pete smashes fuck out of this piece of shit bully cunt when suddenly Pete pulls back and snaps a jab which rocks Nev before pulling Nev's head down and smashing two brutal uppercuts into his face which carve a gouge of a cut over one eye and causes the cunt's nose to explode spraying and dripping blood everywhere and Pete again smashes him with a beauty and one of Nev's henchmen comes and pulls Nev away for he is well and truly beat as all bullies when it comes to it usually, in my experience, are. I'm standing watching thinking to myself 'fuck me those two uppercuts were gorgeous beautiful brutal punches' and after it seems like the whole wing comes to fist bump and congratulate Pete because he only done what everyone else wanted to do 'cause the energy vampire Nev has upset a lot of people of late and I learn afterward that Nev and J.T were very nearly at it last night and make no mistake, camp as fuck but living legend J.T doesn't give a fuck and is a lunatic himself. As for Pete W, gangster motherfucker, that was a polished performance of the highest order and I'm glad we're pals-quality! On the radio in Brad's Mick Mill and Drake rap 'back home smoking legal' and I am content with the world right now and thank God for letting me live.

1420hrs. So Pete absolutely smashed the granny out of Jay Nevin this morning and the whole wing was buzzing that this drain got his come uppance. J.T came up to me after and said that had that not happened it would of gone off with him and Nev anyway as J.T has had enough of his rude obnoxious ways. Don't be deceived, I genuinely like Nev sometimes but he can be a cock, especially when pissed on prison hooch. Anyway, Marcus has just transferred another £400 from his account to the fella he gets his drugs off and despite this and all the drugs he himself uses he is still left with a tidy £600 profit plus all the shit we have in the cell. I sometimes feel a bit guilty that I live so well off of misery. I mean, I want for nothing and have many creature comforts provided by my cellmate, my pal of many years who I really do love, the fat cunt. He's not really fat people it's just he's so big 'cause of the roids he does and, well, he does have a bit of a belly I suppose! Marcus buys me nice clothes, haircuts, gets our washing pushed up the que by paying with spice and even employs junkies to clean the cell for the spice! I used to be that nitty, cleaning cells for spice! Anyway, the point is this: even though I profit, clearly, from his activity, I refuse to involve myself in the headache of dealing or collecting debts. Canteen day yesterday and it being Saturday he wants me to chase stragglers.

"Please Sloaney do a bit of running around today when we get out for dinner. Chase some vapes and stuff up from the debt list".

"Smarcus", I tell him for the umpteenth time, "I told you mate I ain't doing that shit man it's too fuckin' stressful bro".

"You like to live good though don't ya"!

"Well", I reply, "I can't dictate what my cellmate does can I"? And it's true, I don't get involved in any of it. Were I to start, what with my job down the ATB Unit, I'd be getting asked to traffic drugs all round the jail and though to be honest I've no moral discomfort around drug dealing per se, I do have morals around abusing the trust placed in me by Jason Gould at the unit for I've come to love him and don't want to deceive him. For me to use the position he entrusts me with for spreading misery would be a liberty. As I say, I could do it, traffic drugs no problem were it not for this fact. I want to be able to look him in the eye with a clear conscience. I have what is known as a 'red band' which allows me to rove the prison freely and this is a much coveted and trusted position. I am the ATB Red Band Orderly. And I want the team to know they made a good decision placing trust in me. As you may see, intelligent dear reader, my morals are a bit fucked but basically it simply wouldn't feel right to take the piss for some reason and I'm going with my gut. Anyway, El Chubbo is buzzing he has sorted telephone banking out from the tiny mobile we have in the cell so he no longer needs to drive his sexy arse missus mad to continuously check, transfer and deal with the constant flow of monies into and out of his account 'cause I think she was getting a little pissed off with it all. We were all talking about birds this morning as we watched Bebe Rexha prance around sexily on the TV.

"You gonna see Tan when you get out Sloaney"? asked Kempy.

"Course he will", says El Fatto, "he tries to make out like he don't care but he loves her".

"I know she'll be getting fucked hard every weekend lads, that's the problem. She loves cock man", I say.

"What you gonna do then Sloaney? Go out on the pull when you get out? What's your, like main method"?

"Pestiness", says Marcus.

"Well", I say, "first thing I'm gonna get is a transit van; soon as I've got that I'll get me some chloroform and straps and tea towels and that".

"Hahahahaha", laughs Gibbo, "you're fuckin' brutal man"!

"Never fails", I say.

"Sloaney man, you can't go around kidnapping people", says Kempy.

"What's 'chloroform'"? asks Marcus.

"Fuck me", I say, looking at him, "what, you really don't know"?

"It's a liquid that if you put it on a cloth and put it over someone's mouth it knocks 'em straight out", says Kempy.

"Gonna get myself some of that then", says El Chubbo, "that sounds fuckin' brilliant".

"Kempy", I say, "I can't believe you the other day running round to Marcus telling him about me and Brad talking".

"What ya saying"? asks Brad.

"When I was confiding in you", I reply, "Kempy came in, heard us then ran straight round to Marcus and told him me and you were cunting him off"!

"Well, that's what pals do for each other", says the shit stirrer Kempy, spudding Marcus.

"Has Lanesy (Peter Lanes, Kempy's cellmate) paid you for that tracksuit yet"? I ask Marcus.

"Nope, liberty taking cunt", says Marcus.

"And Kempy", I say gloatingly, "Peter's sold the tracksuit ain't he even though he ain't even paid Marcus for it yet"?

"Errrr"........says Kempy.

"What", says Marcus, "and you didn't even tell me"?

"Well", goes Kempy, decidedly uncomfortable, "what it is"........but we all go 'oohhhhhh' and he doesn't know what to say.

"Proper pals look after each other yeah", says Brad laughing.

"Well Peter paid me to keep me mouth shut and I never break a contract"! says Just For Men Kempy. We all guffaw at his flimsy moral compass and logic.

"You're a proper fuckin' dog Kempy ya know that"? I say. I'm off to the gym people so more later perhaps.

1945hrs. Went to the gym three 'till four and me and El Chubbo absolutely smashed it. We started with 'bastards' which are extremely hard and work muscle and cardio. We do five sets of ten of each exercise. So, the 'bastard' starts with a 40kg bar which we first of all power clean from the floor then press from the chest before dropping it behind the neck, doing a squat then pressing up and reversing the exercise before repeating, five times ten times as I say. Next we did 5x10 power cleans with the same weight. Then we upped the weight to 100kg and did the same amount of reps with deadlifts. After that we did 5x10 wide grip lat pulldowns before finishing with rowing the whole stack of weights on the multigym, 5x10 again. The bastards alone had me feeling sick and pissing sweat, let alone the rest of the workout. I love these power exercises for they give me the strength I need to throw cunts about should the need arise and with my temperament it is entirely possible it will though my developing spiritual principles may preclude me from violence having to enter my life again with a bit of luck. Marcus, bless him, managed to purchase at the price of £40 for quarter of an ounce, some good old fashioned Golden Virginia tobacco and proper Rizla papers and I of course allowed myself the pleasure of partaking , puffing away happily not but minutes ago. Also, I used the small mobile phone, not to call Tan but to call Charlotte who was happy to hear me and Marcus and is doing alright outside where, we learn, nothing really changes, in Margate anyway!

"Move out the way of the TV Sloaney", says Marcus, tryna look at Dafne Schippers the sexy Dutch athlete on track right now.

"Why"? I ask.

"Tryna look at this bird, the blonde one look".

"What", I say seeing Dina Asher-Smith on the screen, "Asher-Smith"?

"No, the Dutch one".

"The black bird is sexy too", I say of Dina.

"I know", says Marcus, "my dad was black when I found him".

"Ahhh man, what the fuck d'ya mean bro? Talk".

"Right, my sister called me one day", he says, and he has never talked in depth of this so despite the sudden subject change I'm with him and he continues, "and my sister said 'Marcus I've been trying to get hold of dad all day and there's no response and I'm getting worried".

"Where were you"? I ask.

"Dover", he says.

"Doing what"?

"Living with the screw, the first one, Kelly, Ms G".

"So, what did you do"?

"Jumped in the car, drove with Ms G at 90mph to Margate and went straight to my dad's house".

"Ok", I say, "go on bro".

"Get to the address, meet me sister, kick off the door, my sister goes flying upstairs, I check downstairs and go into the downstairs bathroom and there he was, on the floor, face down. I turned his body over and he was black, black as the ace of spades".

"Go on", I say, "what did you do then"?

"My sister comes down the stairs screaming and my bird Kelly is also screaming and then obviously the police and the ambulance and all that come".

"What did he die of"? I ask my big hearted pal, the poor cunt.

"I don't know, like, the correct terminology of what actually killed him but basically it was alcohol, booze killed him man", and a wave of sadness washes through me for all that this poor fucker has suffered and I ruminate that it's hardly suprising the cunt has issues.

"How do you feel about it now Marcus"?

"Well, it's a mixture of emotions ya know".

"Like what"? I prompt, knowing there is some therapeutic value in the discussion, "what emotions though"?

"Anger, sadness, loss, guilt and loneliness thinking he died on his own. I imagine him trying to crawl up the bath and that and it makes me want to cry Sloaney the poor cunt ya know? On his own on that cold floor with his boxers on". Ahh dear reader, I needn't comment. So sad. I give Marcus a hug, lost for words. I know I rip the piss out of him and he me but we are very close at heart. You may be wondering how the fuck he is compis mentis enough to relate this to me tonight and I'll tell you he has had a fraction of what he normally smokes though he has plenty around him. I'm enjoying the cunts company tonight, rare as it is.

"Fuck me Sloaney", he says now, "spray some lenor for fuck sake man that fuckin' stinks man wow"!

"Protein farts", I say, smiling and now as I try to write, remembering the TV is right beside me Marcus turns comedian and turns the volume up to 90 and when I look up to him and scowl he grins like a kid and knows exactly what he's doing and I feel real love for me old mate El Chubbo right about now.

"Ahhhh you", he says, pointing at me in hilarity!

"You prick"! I say laughing. Goodnight dear reader.

03-03-2019 1204hrs. Marcus hasn't been able to eat his Sunday roast due to feeling sick because he's only just acquired subutex, which is scarce on the wing right now. Soon as it infuses his system he'll be able to function. Today, when we go to the gym he will pick up another £500 of pages (five pages) and I have no doubt he will then go around buying as many meds as possible and smoke and drug himself into a stupor tonight. He sold the last of the last lot first thing this morning.

1725hrs Went to the gym. Did squats, lunges, an ab workout, leg press and other horrific leg exercises with Adam W who took me to absolute exhaustion after I beat him on the circuit the other day.

"Fuck me", I'd said, "what you tryna do to me Adam"?

"Getting you back for beating me the other day mate", smiled the baby faced assassin. Also working out with us was little Martyn and Jeff 'H' McCarthy and by the time Adam had finished with us we were all quite sick with exertion. The lunges at the end were the crowning glory. When I returned to the wing Nev pulled me into his cell to apologise. Now I must first relate why he was feeling the need to do so. By the way, his face is fucked after the fight yesterday but to give him his due he's game and had a go. It just happens that Pete W is a fuckin' monster in a fight. Anyway, before that scrap yesterday Nev was walking past my cell and I was putting together a protein shake.

"Sloaney", he'd said, clearly already half pissed, "can I have a word"?

"What is it Nev 'cause I'm just about to run around to Brad's mate"?

"What"? he'd said, indignantly, "ain't you got no time for me anymore then"?

"Nev", I'd said patiently, "mate, I just don't want some draining story where you go right round the houses and, well, drain the life out of me bro", and immediately I can see this has affected him for he draws his shoulders up and a look of righteous indignation lights up his face.

"I can't fuckin' believe you can say that to me", he says in his Eltham drawl, "did I ever look down on you when you were bang at it did I? No, but, like, now you're all fit and clean and healthy you don't wanna talk to me anymore".

"Nev, don't take offence mate, it's just Bradders is waiting for me with a cup of coffee and I don't wanna be hanging about bruv".

"Naaa man, I know how it is, you ain't got no time for us lot now you've sorted yourself out"!

"It ain't like that at all Nev", I'd said, thinking that it was, in fact, exactly like that. A little disingenuous of me I suppose.

"Nope, Sloaney, don't worry about it", and he'd walked out the cell. However, like I say, upon returning to the wing from gym he grabbed me and I'll give him his due he was humble.

"Sloaney, look, I just wanna say I've been a bit mad lately and wanna apologise for yesterday morning bruvver".

"Ahhhh Nev man", I said, "no big deal mate, I never hold a grudge fella", and we'd had a hug. At least he has the decency to acknowledge his pissed up manic behaviour of late. Anyway, in other matters Marcus has been pretty low in himself today. We managed to drag him to the gym but he didn't do anything accept collect a page of spice; he is getting the other four pages tomorrow. I give him his due though for it is 1800hrs and the cunt has yet to smoke any spice. Other news: Arge, Officer Fellows has now got another stripe on his shoulder denoting the fact he is now a Senior Officer and only answerable to the sexy C.M, the A wing Custody Manager, Claire Harding whom me and J.T found ourselves sheepishly explaining ourselves to that time. Gorgeous she is! Fine woman in every respect to be fair! And Arge is a good screw too so why not! Gibbo has had his hair cut and doesn't look so scruffy, Kyle is struggling with anxiety being banged up with the bully Craig, sorry Craig but you are and I'd love to see you get a beating though I like you at times. Beany, now back on A wing in anticipation of starting a drug course had half a page off of Marcus and was out his fuckin' nut at bang up. Reece the hyper Manc was proper dripping with sweat withdrawing off of spice earlier saying he ain't doing it no more but at bang up he was back to his old tricks and out his canister. Little Jake Pendrick Harvey looks a little more alive of late and seems to be smoking less poison. I miss Craig Mc. Dancing On Ice is on. I watched Brad's spider cleaning its legs tonight after it devoured a meal provided by daddy Brad. Kempy is depressed because although Kempy does smoke spice he only does so at night but our lifelong friend Peter 'Bundy' Lanes, his cellmate, smokes it all day every day and Kempy the cunt is also suffering because due to the fact he refuses to work the wing staff have said, like, ok, you won't work we won't let you go to the gym so he is thinking that me and Marcus will be pulling ahead of him in strength and stamina. Little Martyn is buzzing because he has just been given a servery job so he will get any extra food allowing him to pile more muscle onto his already burgeoning body. The little big man's arms are massive. Marcus pipes up now:

"I'm tryna go as long as I can without nothing", he says as we both keep one eye on the aesthetically pleasing movements of the dancers on ice on the TV.

"What d'ya mean"?

"I just don't want to be like a mong and I feel quite happy today".

"Look at you, you look so much better", I say truthfully.

"Shane down the gym said the same thing to me today".

"What did he say"?

"He just said I didn't look out me nut today and I said to him 'what can you notice when I've had something then' and he said 'yeah, sometimes you look right out ya nut' and I said 'what, do you think everyone else can notice too' and he said 'well I know what to look for but yeah, sometimes you're clearly out ya nut man' and I said 'I know I've got to give my head a wobble'".

"So, what's happening with you're gym job then"?

"Well, it's not gonna happen yet", he says.

"What the fuck"? I say, "what d'ya mean"?

"I spoke to Ryan the gym screw and he said that someone told him that I've been using".

"What the fuck, you fuckin' jokin' or what"? I say.

"Nope", he says now, "the screw said 'do you think it's really a good idea Marcus because I've been told you are fuckin' up quite bad at the moment' and I said 'are you for fuckin' real' and he said 'don't get the hump, we can re-eveluate it again in a little while Marcus' that's exactly what he said".

"Wow man, sorry bro, I'm gutted for ya".

"I know man, it's given me the right hump if I'm honest but I'm just gonna like try and sort myself out so that I can go down there look 'em in the eye and tell 'em honestly that I'm clean and sober".

"That's the best thing I've heard you say in ages bro and the fact you're not right out ya nut now is proof you're starting to think about what you're doing", I say, hopefully.

"I've only had a ml of 'tex today", he says, "same as I had last night so I'm trying to cut down on the amount of opioids so when it comes to stopping I won't have to suffer too much". Dancing on ice has both of us with the hairs on our arms and at the nape of the neck standing on end: James Gardiner just smashed it with his professional partner Alexandra. The routine earned them tens across the board. Jane Torvil says she was mesmerised. Now Marcus is pulling me up on some of the ways I have treated women. I tell him I have been violent with men, fighting many over my lifetime. I tell him this so he knows I am no coward. He tells me this is no excuse, and he is right. I tell him I'm not the man who, in control of his senses, clean and sober, returns home to find the chicken not grilled the way he likes it and then leathers his girl. I tell him on drink and drugs I lose the plot, and it is true I have never been aggressive to a woman in sobriety. Crack and heroin and alcohol turn me into somebody I am not. Little did I know at that moment that I had more pain to come and that I would fall in love and hurt someone else, a high class hooker with whom I ended up using crack and heroin with in a hotel room before, after a year in the relationship, I assaulted her, resulting in me spending ten months of a twenty month sentence in jail where I would write another book. And don't let the high class hooker bit deceive you; this girl is a queen, a magnificent, bright human being who

314

is now clean. You'll know her name someday for she is destined for great things. This was the catalyst for me getting clean and returning to sanity and lead to me sitting typing this today for you in a lovely house and in recovery in Oxford. However, I digress.

2045hrs. Me and Marcus just turned the TV down because we heard a door being opened then the sound of a woman asking 'can you hear me can you hear me' and Marcus is standing at the door and reckons it's Nev 'cause he can, he says, hear Billy Banks his cellmate.

"Yeah, I reckon Nevin's had a code blue", he says.

"He smokes so much spice and buscopan I wouldn't be surprised".

"Fuck me", says Marcus, now half way monged himself, "there's an ambulance crew out here Sloaney I can see them through the crack in the door have a look".

"Oh", I say, "so it's 100% code blue then"!

"They're still trying to revive somebody by the sounds of it".

"So it might not be Nev then"?

"Dunno, but I thought I could hear Billy Bank's voice", he says and now I go to the crack and I think I can hear gorgeous Ms Ellie P saying:

"Can you stay awake Billy can you hear me"? and then there's a pause and she says, "ok, try to stay with me", and dear reader I will find out more for you tomorrow.

05-03-2019. 'It is not things which disturb men, but the way men view things that disturbs them'. Can't remember where I read this but it is extremely relevant to my recovery. The way in which I used to view the world, the thoughts I had about it led to shit feelings which led to destructive and harmful behaviours such as me killing myself with dirty needles and drugs and drink and causing harm and chaos, burgling, robbing beating and terrorising anyone and everyone in my desperate desire to get the drugs to escape the way I felt about myself. Drugs alleviated all those feelings of being less than, all the shame I feel, the low self esteem and feelings of worthlessness. Yet the irony is I exacerbated my shame and worthlessness by compounding these things with more shameful acts and behaving in ways not esteemable. Our self esteem grows when we do esteemable things see? I don't blame my mum and dad for they suffered too when young but there's something in the famous Larkin lines of 'they fuck you up your mum and dad, they might not mean to but they do, they fill you with the faults they had, and add some extra just for you'. Anyway. Marcus, having only just picked up more drugs today, has already pulled in £600. A fella called Scott, another drug dealer on the wing, got smashed up and robbed by Dale

315

Pearson our handsome lunatic friend. Forgive me for not wishing to write much today; Marcus is drinking hooch and in full mong mode smoking spice and pregabed and 'texed out his tree. I'm gonna wrestle with Brian Cox's book: Universal: A Guide To The Cosmos. I know the maths are well beyond me but I'll glean wonders from the text nonetheless. First I'm gonna fill some apps in to see about a move to 'H' wing, the enhanced wing down the new end of the prison.

06-03-2019 morning and I am currently in the ATB Programmes Unit where Jason Gould and Naomi are both going into interview for the Head Honcho position down here. Jason is manager in all but name and it is likely he will get the job. I hope so anyway, much as I like Naomi. Lucy, looking remarkably lovely today has told me that should Jason not get the job after 30 years of service he is planning on leaving. Hopefully it won't come to that. Lucy herself is planning on leaving for though she loves delivering the programmes to jailbirds, trying to help people, it is the mundane stuff in between courses that she struggles with. At 24 her eternal summer is in full bloom and I feel like the aged P next to her. The vigour of youth but I digress. The governor conducting the interview here today is an absolute cougar, fit as fuck at 50, maybe 55 years old and has the jail slobbering over her as she struts about in short skirted power suits showing mind bogling legs and beautifully turned calf muscles. Amazing how aging women can look so good today. Sharon Stone of the famous Basic Instinct cross uncross is testament to the fact ladies keep us lusting longer today. Anyway, I love playing devil's advocate with Lucy as I have been doing just now. She's a bit of a feminist see.

"So Lucy, if World War Three breaks out I think that us men should get a break from the carnage and send you lot, ya know, like the feminist generation out to the front lines, conscription strictly for women ya know"?

"Yeah? I'd be fine with that".

"Really? We'd lose the war though Lucy 'cause women just haven't got the element of psychosis, the killer instinct men have ya know", and as I say it I watch as Lucy pulls her shoulders back indignantly.

"Why d'ya think that? What makes you think I couldn't do just the same as you in a war situation"?

"Well", I say, "have you seen Band Of Brothers? And the particular sergeant who reputedly gunned down a load of German prisoners of war but was praised as an excellent soldier and killer by his superior after the war? His was loved by the men under him for his daring, his bravery and his savagery Lucy: he was a fuckin' animal in the field ripping out throats and gunning people down and I'd be the same, smothered in blood, always first in and I just don't imagine women being able to behave in the same way Luce that's all".

"How dare you put limitations on what I can and can't do"! she says wide eyed.

"Yeah", I say, "but I couldn't multitask the way women do, ya know, going to work, organising nannies, pick up the kids, wash up and talk on the phone and make a cup of tea all at the same time".

"But that's only because you have never had to do it".

"So you reckon you could be brutal, savage, ripping out throats with your teeth if necessary"?

"Well, I think I can do anything a man can do and if the circumtances necessitated me doing those things then yeah".

"So", I say, "if war broke out you'd have no problem with women going to the front line dying in droves this time whilst we men stayed back to look after the kids and stuff"?

"I'd be fine with that", she says.

"We'd lose the war though", I say.

"Oh my God Sloaney", she says, "you are actually infuriating", but she is smiling.

"I'm just playing Lucy", I say, "but the world is a confusing place today. Changing the subject a bit Lucy I have to say that if you're born white with a willy today you're immediately at a disadvantage. You have to prove you're like no bigot. Men are committing suicide in astonishing numbers today due to changing roles too. We don't know our place anymore. Then you've got all this other stuff going on with gender fluidity, ya know, like people wanting to call their new born little boys or little girls 'theybes' because they don't want to assign sex descriptive nouns like 'girl' or 'boy' to their child because they want them to be gender neutral until they themselves are old enough to decide whether they are male or female. What the fuck is happening with the world Luce"?

"But why have you got a problem with the theybe thing"?

"Because if you're born with a willy you're a boy and if not you're a girl Lucy; it's fuckin' insanity"!

"But it's all about inclusivity and acceptance today and people bring their kids up how they choose to ya know"?

"I've just got my head around same sex couples having kids man, ya know, I'm all for it but I have wrestled with this stuff".

"But why? As long as the child has a loving home and loving carers where's the problem"?

317

"Well", I say, "let me tell you this: if a kid goes to school and gets picked up by dad and dad that poor fucker is gonna get terrorised at school Lucy I promise you".

"I think you're wrong there, I think kids are more accepting today of such things".

"Lucy", I say, "let me tell you now, if I was at school, being the little bastard that I was, I'd've made the poor little fucker's life hell I promise you".

"But things have moved on since then Andrew, people are educated about this sort of stuff and you'll find that kids today are knowledgable about same sex couples".

"Lucy", I say, "you're living in a dream world. Do you really think we've come that far that they wouldn't get terrorised? There'd be kids like me, ignorant and uneducated and full of fear saying shit like 'you're faggot father picking you up today queer boy, which dad is it today'? and shit like that".

"My mum works in education Sloaney, honestly, times have changed".

"Wow man, well, we must agree to disagree here for I am not convinced bullies no longer exist".

"Well, I like to think you're wrong", says the worthy woman.

"I hope Jason gets the job today", I say, wishing to change the subject.

"So do I", she says, "fingers crossed". It is lunchtime and I say my goodbyes and set off for the wing where I find Marcus monged on his bed in the cell where he says, unable to walk and hardly able to talk:

"Plesh get dinner me Shhloaney plesh", and I do so, grabbing both our meals. Besides, if staff saw him like this he'd be in the shit for sure.

So we have to wait 'till tomorrow to see if Jason gets the job. I've been reading Prof Cox's book and get a little peeved when he says 'we will now do some simple maths' before then going on to describe the way in which we radio carbon date rocks using Rubidium and Strontium atoms and looking at decay rates, the half life of these. Dr Cox, simple maths to you with your $86Sr/87Sr$ $86Rb/87Rb$ and the creation of one as another decays but to the layman like me it takes a little time to get my head around. I must simply submit to the fact all I can do is enjoy your descriptions and conclusions without understanding the mathematical machinations at the heart of these matters. Alas, I love your work nonetheless. I'm not berating you Brian but the word 'simple' could leave the likes of me feeling a little simple! You yourself are gifted sir and what is simple to you is a veritable mountain to me.

07-03-2019 morning and again I'm at work at the unit. Lucy earlier, looking lovely like always:

"I took my friend's little dog out for a walk last night, I bloody love dogs they're so cuddly and sometimes I feel like Lenny out of Mice And Men d'ya know what I mean"?

"Yeah", I say, "beautiful book, so sad".

"Yeah", continues luscious Luce, "you know like Lenny just cuddles things to death, like loves 'em to death"?

"And that is the absolute tragedy of the book man; and also the genius of Stienbeck, challenging us in such a way".

"The other day two security officers, like dog handlers, brought in this eight week old puppy and I'm like 'oh, he's so cute can I hold him'? and I cuddle this cute little dog and I didn't want to let go of him he was so lovely".

"It's like dogs were sent just for us" , I say, "with those soppy loving eyes and teddy bear features and, what's more, no matter how big or small they'd actually die to protect you".

"I know right"! says she, "oh I've just got to get one; mine died a few years ago and I wanna get another one but 'cause I live at my parents they won't let me which is fair enough".

"I can't wait to get out and walk my friend Jan's dog", I say, "I fuckin' miss that dog more than I do people"!

"What sort of dog is it"?

"One of those ones, Japanese I think, with the tiny ears and wrinkly face. She's so gorgeous and when I take her down the beach she sees the sand and goes all stupid like running around in mad circles and that all happy just to go for a walk".

"What's her name"? asks Lucy.

"Bow", I tell her, "she's ten and so well trained and so well behaved unless she sees a cat. When she goes after one and I get her back to me I actually lecture her, like: 'Bow, you're ten years old and how many cats have you caught? You're ten years old and you've never caught one so behave will ya'? and she looks all sheepish before bounding off again searching for feline victims"!

"What, you take the dog out, someone else's? Why don't you get your own"?

"I plan too but Jan is sick so I just help out", I say and it's freeflow so I head back to the wing for lunch.

08-03-2019. Morning people, it is 0830hrs on a Black Eye Friday here at HMP Rochester and I'm feeling fuckin' Coolio! Beany, Jay Beany has just walked into our cell with his usual repertoire:

"You know I'm a gangster don't ya Sloaney"?

"I do Beany, you're a regular bad boy bro"!

"Do you know if Marcus is seeing his man today"?

"Honestly bro I ain't got a clue".

"Where is he d'ya know"?

"Scuttling about by the meds que tryna buy drugs I reckon if I know him at all"! He leaves and I go to the cell across the landing where Pete Lanes and Kempy are and Daisy and AJ from Trending Live on 4Music are on TV and Kempy goes:

"I'd fuck that black bird ya know, that AJ, proper fit man".

"She ain't bad for a nigger", says Pete.

"Do you remember that black bird Paul Grant used to go out with years ago"? says Kempy but first I have to tell Peter:

"Pete man, wow bro, you're unreal mate! You ain't really a proper rascist are ya"?

"No", says Pete, "I just think everyone should have two black people in their households; one for beating and one for putting under the stairs"! Look, dear reader, though I find these views abhorrent I'd be a liar to say I don't laugh but this is more in shock than anything else. Kempy too is beside himself.

"I shouldn't laugh man but Pete you're fucked bro", says Just For Men, his cellmate.

"You don't really believe these things you say surely Pete"?

"I fuckin' do", he says, "fuckin' shitskins. Fuck that, anyway, I had some proper power spice yesterday Sloaney. It was so strong I kept having, like, blackouts all day; it was well strong, weren't it Kempy"?

"What did you think of it Steve"? I ask Kempster.

"It was lethal man, spun me right out, I had to lay me head on the bed for a bit after two puffs on a joint".

"This cunt's a proper moody fucker in the morning Sloaney", says Pete, "this morning I woke up to him walking round and round the cell going 'fuckin' liberties man, fuckin' liberties'".

"I do wake up with the hump every morning but today all my paperwork was just thrown under the bed and I thought Pete had done it as a joke".

"Who was it then"? I ask.

"Fuck knows", says Kempy who's putting his shoes on now.

"Where you goin'"? asks Pete.

"This fuckin' education thing, I don't know".

"Induction", says Pete helpfully, "maths and English".

"Oh", I say, "like the assessment thing"?

"Yeah", says Kempy, "so they know your levels and that init".

"You should be alright shouldn't ya"?

"I hope so", he says.

"Sloaney", says Pete now, "remember I said this: I'm gonna be rich next year".

"How"? I ask.

"Don't matter", he says, "just remember I said it", wierdo! And now I leave the cell and go to the group room where we have a wing NA meeting and I'm sitting beside little Martyn P who asks:

"You coming to the circuit this morning Sloaney"?

"Naa man I can't, got to go to work 'cause they've got like visitors coming in and that and they want me to do a little talk for them".

"That Lucy is fit down there ain't she"? he says now.

"Ahhh mate", I say dreamily, "she's fuckin' something else Martyn man".

"You said she's proper smart as well didn't ya"?

"She is mate", I say, "that's what attracts me most", and it is indeed true! The meeting starts so I'll put down my pen dear reader.

And now the meeting is over and I skipped the circuit and I'm down at work with Lucy, Jason and Naomi and I can't help but wonder about my friend Peter Lanes. But, let's examine this: to be completely honest it isn't him that disturbs me, no, what is irking me is that I want to include the truth of my environment and the people around me at the same time as letting you know that the views some espouse are not my views. This has to be true to reality this document else what the fuck is the point? Shall I soften it? What or who the fuck for? For fact is fact and that is that! I would rather not publish than have these disturbing and uncomfortable things removed. So, if you're reading this thank fuck for the publisher who had the balls to stick their name to it! I myself was brought up in an environment fraught with bigoted views but I don't blame my grandad and father for these things for the vernacular of the time was standard, normal and unremarkable. Words like wog, nigger, faggot and paki and such were very much the norm. It has taken life experience and education to change my thinking, to alter my values and beliefs. My dad told me that all gay people fuck little boys and until I learned differently I believed it. He used to say Marc Almond was a kiddy fiddler because he was gay. On that subject, last night I watched the documentary 'Leaving Neverland; Michael Jackson and Me' and I am struggling for these men were convincing in their portrayal of M.J as a pedo. I don't want to believe it but it was compelling stuff. I feel sad as this could preclude me from ever again enjoying the sound of this master musician. I grew up on M.J, my mum would wet herself to Billy Jean or Thriller or Bad and I too know every word from these songs and would use my mum's hairbrush as a pseudo mic as I belted his ballads out tunelessly in my pre-pubescent voice. These men, last night, would have you believe that the King Of Pop was a deviant of the highest order. Anyway. The sun is shining and now Lucy has returned from picking visitors from the probation service from out in the community from the gate and she is now making drinks for them and tells me quickly that she bumped into Marcus and Kempy on the way.

"Hello Louise", said Marcus to her and Lucy says she said:

"That's not impressive Marcus, that's not my name", and Marcus said:

"I know, I'm just tryna get your attention; it's Lucy in it"?

"You got it", Lucy says she said and then she tells me Kempster piped up:

"Lucy Lucy I got a letter yesterday for an Inclusion interview".

"I know", said Lucy, "I sent it out to you".

"So, it's with you then Ms"? from Kemp.

"What did it say in the letter I sent"?

"Well, it said it was with you".

"Then it's with me then".

"Does this mean I'm gonna get on TSP (Thinking Skills Programme) then Ms"? Kempy had asked.

"Maybe", she had said. Anyway, I'm back on the wing now but before I left I was called into a room by Lucy who is entertaining five probation officers who sit round a table and who would like to hear from me so I give a soliloquy from the heart, then take questions on the good things that are happening here in HMP Rochy. Now I'm back with Marcus, banged up and El Chubbs says now:

"I'm gonna turn into a mong, can you build a pipe from a carton for me"?

"No Marcus", I say, "if you die in here it'd fuck me up enough; but if I play a part in you killing yourself by making an instrument for you to pull your drugs through then I'd struggle to get over it".

"Oh", he says, "so you don't care if I die then"?

"Of course I care if you die", I say, "but I'd get over it, unless I played a part in it".

"What d'ya mean 'you'd get over it'"?

"I mean that regardless of what you do to yourself I plan to live ya know? Even should you kill yourself I'm choosing recovery".

"You're ruthless man", he says, preparing the pipe now which he has absolutely loaded with spice.

"That's too much Marcus man", I say, referring to the amount of paper he has placed on the vessel.

"It's not", he says, "trust me", and now he has lit the wick and the carton he made is at his lips and he has sucked it in and now he collapses on his bed, his face white as a sheet and he is chuckling dementedly doing the palsy shaking and now he seems to be not breathing and he is going fuckin' purple and I go:

"Marcus Marcus you cunt I'll press that fuckin' bell so you better breathe you silly cunt", and now there's copious amounts of puke dribbling from his hanging drooping mouth and I go:

"Fuck you cunt I'm pressing the bell", and I do but in the time it takes for Mr Maddison to get to us I agonize and from the door Mads the screw can't see Marcus's face and I take a risk and upon Mr Mads enquiring as to my reason for calling him I say:

"It's alright it's alright", and I can see from Mr Mads face, looking at Marcus' arm hanging over the side of the bed that he knows what's going on and Mads ain't stupid but trusts me.

"Are you sure it's alright Sloaney"? and I go:

"Yeah Mr Mads it's cool man", and he goes away and I know he won't say anything bless him and I hope I made the right call tryna keep this cunt outta trouble. I pull the fuckin' retard onto his side, into the recovery position and he has soaked himself and his bed with yellowy biley dribble and his breath is coming, intermittently, in rasping noisy gulps and his fuckin' head is so red with his massively increased blood pressure now but I feel despite all this that the cunt will be ok thus the risk with the screw. He struggles to breath and is completely unconscious but he'll pull through. If the staff got involved, code blue, then Marcus could end up in trouble, be kicked off the wing, lose loads of money etc but the other side of it is he could lose his life if I make the wrong call. Marcus has said to me before:

"Never, ever press that bell Sloaney whatever happens", and I get this for I have been exactly the same. His breathing is normalising now so relief washes over me. Now it is 45 minutes on and he has stabilised and I get on my knees, literally, and thank God.

1430hrs. I'm sitting in Brad's cell describing the events of the lunchtime bang up and Marcus walks in as me and Brad chat and he is still looking decidedly dodgy like a fuckin' zombie and I say to Brad:

"See, look, look how fucked he is and this is two fuckin' hours later", and Brad says:

323

"Fuck me Marcus, you wanna stay out the way of the screws man", and now Kempy comes in and says to Marcus:

"You coming to the gym or what El Chubbo"? and I say:

"You takin' the piss or what man look at the cunt", and Kempster gets a proper look at the mong and goes:

"Oh my God Chubbo you look fucked ya cunt", and now El Chubbs starts spastic punching Kempy's bum saying:

"I'm toughening you up man I can feel your glutes they're getting bigger".

"I know", says Kempy the vain fuck, "I've been looking in the mirror and I'm getting proper hench", and Marcus says to him:

"I need ten packs of vapes off of you today Kempy", and Just For Men goes:

"You're having a fuckin' laugh int ya"?

"I'll fuckin' do ya", says Marcus.

"I've got four for you", says Kempy, "and you couldn't do me ya fat fuck, you look like a big fat water buffalo or a grumbling geezer on a park bench".

"What, you ain't got at least eight for me Steve? You fuckin' wanna have", and now Ms Slane the Amazonian walks in and takes one look at Marcus and goes:

"You wanna sort yourself out Marcus", and Marcus the mong says:

"What d'ya mean Ms"? and she goes:

"Go have a look in the fuckin' mirror Marcus", then she goes away disgustedly and Marcus says to me, Kempy and Bradders:

"Oh no man, I can't believe she's just seen me like that! How can I go to the gym? I've got to pick up from my man too! Can you go for me Kempy"?

"Yeah, I'll go down there; what do you want me to say to him"?

"Just tell him I want as much as he can give me".

"Cool man", and now Gibbo comes in the cell and Brad says:

"What's happening mate"?

"Nothing", Gibbo goes, "just tryna get my vapes in man. I've just had some tamoxifen and I feel well alright man", and I have to confess I've never heard of these tablets.

"That's what I had yesterday", Marcus says to me.

"Fuck me", I reply, "you've found another pill to add to your arsenal, that's fuckin' clever in it"?

"I've got some coming tonight too", he says gleefully.

"Proper plank you ya know that"? I say to him. Nev pokes his head in the cell.

"What drugs you got for sale Marcus"? he says.

"Nothing yet mate", Marcus tells him, "just got to wait 'till Kempy gets back from the gym".

"Alright mate, I'll see you in an hour or so", and all the time all this is going on around me I record for you dear reader. Literally with pad on lap and pen in hand as it happens. I get my own canteen and stack up neatly my new toiletries and protein and tuna next to Marcus's piles of stuff and Ms Hulbert comes in and checks the integrity of the security and fills the cell with her lovely flowery smell. Now I go back to Brad's and Jake is sitting on the bed next to Marcus and Chubbo says to him:

"Come on Jake, I need my vapes man".

"I'll get them for you in a bit, don't sweat it man I promise you, I'm just waiting for a couple of people", and now Marcus turns to Brad:

"Brad, where's the rest of the vapes you owe me man"?

"Marcus", says Brad, "you're not listening to me man. I've been let down by Dale, Peter, Kempy and Ricky who're all tryna make excuses and I'm getting fucked off always chasing the same people".

"Alright Brad, I'm only joking", says Marcus and I point out to him that he has only pulled in eight packs and now Reece walks in and both Brad and Marcus enquire of him where their vapes are.

"Just hold on lads I promise you I've got you both", and I say to both of them once he shoots off.

"You'll be lucky to get them in lads", and Marcus is half out his head so don't really take it in but Brad has got the raving hump and now tall ginger Paul who's banged up with Pony Tail Paul has come in and says:

"Marcus I owe you £45 can you give me a pack of vapes and round it off to fifty quid mate"? and this fella pays cash via transfers and Marcus regularly sells vapes as well as drugs for he has bundles and bundles of them always and makes a good profit on them.

"No", says Marcus, "but what I will do is give you three packs and call it £65", and Paul goes:

"No, I'll take three and round it off to sixty", and Marcus does it for him. Now little blonde Frank, proper hustler comes in and pays Chubbo the final two packs he owes Marcus and Chubbo says:

"Cheers bro always a pleasure", and Frank smiles, shoots off. Marcus the mong is barely conscious and his hooded heavy eyes are bloodshot as fuck and I say to him:

"Marcus, Ms Slane and Pocket Rocket have seen you mate and both have noticed you're out ya canister. You're lucky it's them two".

"They won't say anything, they both love me", and now, literally as I write, Chubbo's eyes close and his hand starts to twitch and I'm amazed he's still out his skull from that poxy pipe he had at midday but I remember the tablets he stuffs too. Steve Lanes, Ricky's son and Peter's nephew comes in, honourable fella, and pays Marcus the four packs of vapes he owes him and a pack of Haribos on top and Marcus perks up and starts stuffing his fat face with sweets and asks me to make him a coffee which I will do but I have to shoot out the cell myself quickly first. Now I'm back to do the coffee and Brad brings back a spider for his spider and we and Ms Hulbert watch the beast devour the smaller critter, gleefully revelling in the savagery of the assault. Life!

1745hrs. Banged up for the night. Kempy returned from the gym with two pages of power paper for El Chubbo and he has a few strips of the potent poison on the pipe already, on the same dirty carton he overdosed on earlier. I have on a dust mask to try protect myself from the foul fumes. He has also had two 300mg pregabs, a clonazepam and some of those tamoxifen things whatever they are. And of course the subutex, lets not forget the opioid he has to have every day bless him. Oh and the two litres of hooch he shared with Brad and Kempy have helped him along the way today for sure! Literally, now, at 1749hrs he is unconscious and I swear that despite the dust mask I myself feel high and though this could be my imagination I have seen officers collapse after walking into a cell and inhaling second hand fumes. Terry Hughes, clean for a while, has relapsed on pregabs by the way. Just saying, I'm rather gutted as he's my mate.

1950hrs and I can hear real screaming coming from another cell somewhere on this, the 2s landing. Maybe someone is having a spice attack or being beaten.

09-03-2019 1426hrs and my energy levels are low today. I've a headache and am sick to death of the same shit every day and the people on this wing, including my cellmate who're out their tiny minds day in day out. We have had two code blues this morning requiring health care staff attendance in order to revive Paul Stone first who was 'testing' some new green herbal spice which hit the wing. Then the pikey 'MarkwhoisJohn' from across the landing was fitting and convulsing on the floor in the cell directly opposite the one me and Chubbo inhabit. Last night, after a spell of two weeks where my sleeping pattern has somewhat normalised Marcus, being so inebriated, kept me up all night snoring like a fuckin' diesel engine with a dodgy big end. And talking of ends, due to my inablility to drop off I ripped the end off of myself which I relate directly to my lethargy today. I'm in Brad's now and he's about the wing somewhere and it comes over the tannoy that there'll be no gym today and I'm kinda relieved because though I don't feel like going I would of gone through the motions and this takes the decision from me. Little Kyle Tyler is now sitting on Brad's bed with me and Brad comes in himself, sits down on his chair.

"Yard's not open yet", he says, "but their gonna open it soon so I'll get the spider some food when they do".

"You alright though Brad", Kyle asks.

"Yeah", says Brad, "why d'ya ask"?

"You just seemed a bit moody this morning that's all".

"I hate being being asked if I'm alright man that's all it is bro, didn't mean to be rude if I was", and now Kevin W, that's his fuckin' name, the mug bully cunt I smashed up in the cell in Elmley has just landed back on Alpha again after bouncing from here before and now he's bounced back, accruing, no doubt, debts on other wings. Anyway, he's at the door and Brad immediately pounces on the piece of shit:

"You owe me a pack of vapes".

"How d'ya work that out"? Kev goes.

"You fuckin do", says Brad, "when you bounced last time you owed me a pack of vapes", and the would be bully skinny cunt Kev who I really did go to town on back in Elmley slinks off like the shitcunt rat he is and Brad goes now with his stick and box to tickle spiders for his pet. Gibbo plots up next to me on the bed.

"Alright Gibbo"? I go.

"Yeah man, I'm cool", he goes, looking, nonetheless, a little despondent as he draws heavily on his vape like always.

"Anything going on bro"? I ask this as Springsteen and Born In The USA comes on the radio. What a track.

"Naaa", he says, blowing clouds of vapour through his nose. He told me he gets through two caps a day and remember there are three in a box which costs £4. He also told me his tramadol habit, 200ml a day and not prescribed, costs him three packs a week and now as I write he says:

"I need a pregab man that's what I want", and he gets up and leaves the cell and remember a pregab costs £4 or £5 or a fat joint of spice. On the subject of pregablin Bradders has a massive habit on these and tells me when he doesn't have them he feels sick, achy, insecure, nervous and introverted. Little Reece just walked past the door looking zombiefied and is clearly on the green gear spice which is flopping people all over the wing, and prison for that matter. Brad returns.

"Got a tiny caterpillar, a lace wing and an orb weaver spider", and now Terry Hughes and Ms Hulbert come in to watch the carnage.

"Did that fella go to hospital this morning"? asks Brad of Ms H Pocket Rocket concerning the MarkwhoisJohn code blue earlier.

"Yeah, he's back now though", she says.

"Oh", I say, "so he did go to hospital then".

"Yeah, he was in a right bad way so we had to take him", says Pocket Rocket.

"Why was the gym cancelled this afternoon Ms"? I ask.

"There's an offender on the roof of the seg unit Sloaney who won't come down".

"Oh", I say, "how long has he been up there"?

"All morning", she says, "went to see the governor for a nicking but shot onto the roof instead".

"Selfish fucker", I say, "ruining everyone else's day", and now Paul Stone comes in to watch the carnage and the spider has first disabled the caterpillar then the lace wing which she's munching whilst keeping her front legs on the caterpillar to keep an eye on it and I say to Paul:

"That fucked you up this morning boy"!

"Only 'cause I smoked a neat joint of it Sloaney".

"What", asks Brad, "is it proper strong 'cause you looked fucked mate"?

"Have you been nicked"? I ask Paul.

"Think so yeah and yeah it is strong Brad", and he goes out the cell and Kempy comes in and says:

"Here they are, my favourite two boys in the world", before turning to the spider box Brad stares into and going, "what, is it eating again"?

"Yeah", says Brad, "she's got two bugs on the go at the moment", says Brad and Kempy has a good old look as the mammoth spider moves the lap wing about in its jaws before deciding that's enough of that and returning to the caterpillar which she then picks up and begins to munch upon. My Lord the thing is getting very very big now. Marcus walks in absolutely out his nut, lays on the bed, pulls out his cock in front of me, Kempy, Brad and Ginger Paul who's just come in and says:

"Ya don't mind if I get my cock out do ya"? and he's waving his fat member about the fuckin' fiend!

"You're fucked ya cunt", says Brad and Chubbo puts chubby away and Reece, hyper little fuck comes in the cell and he like Marcus is very bloodshot of eye. Kourtney Kardashian is on the TV and El Chubbo says:

"Kourtney KarGASHian she's so fuckin' sexy", and I must go and find myself an ibuprofen from somewhere. Brad is telling me the doctor gave him some new pain meds and the cell is filling up now and I'm feeling fuckin' claustrophobic.

"D'ya need a tablet"? asks Bradders of me, seeing I'm in a little discomfort.

"Yeah Bradders, but non narcotic".

"I ain't got no ibuprofen, but I've got some naproxen".

328

"There a non steroidal anti inflammatory ain't they"? I ask.

"Yeah, no opioids or nothing so they won't break your fast, don't worry".

"Cheers Brad", I say, "53 days clean today", and now Ms H comes back with a foreign screwess to show her the big spider eating and the foreign lady isn't scared of spiders and is fascinated by the process, asking Brad myriad questions about the beast and now Dale Pearson comes in to have a look at the greedy gorging spider. Dale wasn't smoking spice when he first landed on A wing but now is flat out stoned every day, morning 'till night which isn't good for his fragile mental health. Little Frank comes in.

"Got a paintbrush I can borrow Brad"? and Brad starts looking around for one.

"I'll come get it once I've got the food trolley from the kitchen", says Frank, who works on the servery.

"I'll put it in ya cell for ya", says Brad.

"Nice one brother", says Frank and now Dale asks Brad for a Kiwi fruit.

"Yeah man, they're really ripe though".

"That's how I like 'em", and Dale polishes off two in rapid succession before going on his way to get more drugs no doubt. Dale, in my opinion, is probably the most dangerous fucker on the wing. Kyle comes in now.

"Where's Brad"? he says as Brad has shot out to collect something and I tell him I don't know as I record for you in real time.

"The spider's still munching then", comments Kyle before he too fucks off and now Brad returns and says:

"Everyone always wants something for nothing", and he sits down and joins me watching the spider.

2000hrs and of course the shuffler is out his nut as we spend our Saturday night here in cell 208, Alpha wing in HMP Rochester year of our Lord 2019. I'm getting sick of sucking in the cockroach killer spice fumes and doubt the efficacy of the dust mask in preventing the poison permeating my person. My fat swollen friend is now on his bed snoring soundly asleep. Just before his last dose when he was a little conscious I was really annoying him, driving him mad with a Dua Lipa inspired rap I'd created called the 'Mong Song'. So, I'll give you a few bars I was spitting:

"Pregabs, gabys and rivotril", I sang then I beat box like 'boom boom chit, boom boom chit'.

"Cockroach killer alloy wheel cleaner, boom boom chit, boom boom chit, a little hooch and he's looking meaner, boom boom chit, boom

boom chit, this is my song and it's just for him, boom boom chit, boom boom chit, oh look there's puke running down his chin, it's the mong song, mong song, Marcus's mong song, mong song", and I guess you get the idea but he got the raving hump saying:

"Can you give it a rest Sloaney for fuck sake man".

"You asked me to rap yesterday though".

"Yeah but you ain't stopped since and it ain't very nice Sloaney man"!

"I'm tryna help mate", I say, holding back laughter.

"Well it ain't fuckin' helping", he says sulkily!

"Alright, I'll stop then", I say, "but Marcus man look at the size of your hands bro, they're proper swollen like two balloons. Aren't you worried at all"?

"I dunno man I dunno I'm alright man", and today I hate seeing him struggling like this. Anyway, I know the cunt will now be out for at least two hours. Before he lost consciousness he eat so much he is definitely gonna be sick some time soon. Two sleeves of Jaffa Cakes, a whole double bourbon biscuit pack, a whole sleeve of Gold Bars, two slices of lemon cake, a bowl of rice pudding, cereal and all this after a hefty meal from the servery. The spice gives pot munchies times 1000. I turn the radio on to Capital Extra hoping for some inspiration for some more rap to drive the poor fifteen stone beached whale mad with upon him regaining consciousness. He had hit it hard today and after doing a couple of litres of hooch with Kempy he'd gotten the hump with me for as we sat in the cell, him, me and Kempy, meds had been called over the tannoy and I'd watched as El Fatto's face had lit up.

"Look at ya", I'd said, "getting all excited and preparing to scuttle down there, scuttle scuttle scuttle like a skanky little junkie crab taking pills out people's mouths with your pincers", and he'd gone to me, even over Kempy's laughter:

"You ain't fuckin' funny Sloaney".

"I think it's funny", said Just For Men Kemp, "it's just the way he says that word and does the crab action with his hands", and the crab action I got from my mate Grant Smith in the Ley Community.

"What", I say, "scuttling"? and Kempy laughs more in his deep sonorous tone.

"Weren't that long ago you was scuttling about Sloaney", says Marcus.

"True dat", I say, "53 days ago in fact and I was scuttling here and scuttling there", and I bring both hands to the side of my face, screw my eyes up and do pincer movements feeding scraps to my mouth like a crab does and Marcus gets up to go and Kempy goes:

"Go on scuttle down there", and Marcus goes:

"You can fuck off too Kempy", and I truly laugh out loud! Scuttle. I love that word. Scuttling about! Sitting here recalling right now, chuckling as I do so I nonetheless feel frustrated, like the linnet born within the cage that never knew the summer woods. I forget what freedom looks like and am captive of the state, trapped, restricted and my sanity rests upon a thin foundation indeed.

10-03-2019 1915hrs. Just cooked tinned tuna and noodles for me and Smarcus using the kettle. He's now of course snoring out his nut on his bed. Madonna is doing Vogue on Absolute 80s. Because I've been a bit anxious and fearful lately I asked Cosmic Cathy, God, to send me a dream last night and dream indeed I did. In my dream I woke up under a bush all confused at the side of a country lane. It was a glorious sunny morning but I was lost and didn't know where to go and rubbing sleep from my dream form eyes I see a black sheep, a large black sheep in the road. I marvel at his thick black curls but then my dream eyes alight upon his face and eyes and I immediately deduce the blazing intelligence therein. My dream form communicates telepathically with him and I hold his gaze. My question was 'which way do I go'? and he inclined his eyes and head in the direction of the field behind me and I looked over my shoulder into fearful emptiness then back to this big well witted beautiful beast and his handsome head and eyes which he once again inclines in the same direction. I set out, upon my way and walk and walk and walk some more until I found a large hall where I went in and sat down amongst what seemed to be hundreds of other people dressed in biblical robes and I felt really insecure and thought my dream form smelt but no-one said anything bad to me and a man was talking animatedly and all including me were listening though I know not on what he spoke. I knew to just listen though and felt safe and woke up, only remembering my dream an hour after regaining consciousness whereupon I got up and got down on my knees and thanked Cosmic Keith for loving me and sending me signs.

2000hrs. Put the pad down picked it straight back up again. I've a compulsion to write. As I've said before, when I write it's like something works through me, an energy and force not quite my own. I've lived as Larkin's louts but suspect that writing for a living will indeed be the pitchfork driving the dreaded monkey from my back, the monkey that necessitates loutishness. And I must confess to liking the idea of preservation for perpetuity, posterity on this earthly plane. Anyway, the cunt in the bed is snoring loudly. Me, he and Kempy had a wicked

331

workout earlier, all power exercises like deadlifts and squats amongst others of that ilk. I'm now gonna read some of my own work.

2200hrs. After perusing some pages penned by me I must say I'm not wholly dissatisfied. Could be better, but one day I'll have to type and can clean the cunt then. Night dear reader.

12-03-2019 2020hrs. Hello people. Don't think I put a single word down yesterday. In fact I didn't. Still, I'm feeling fine today. I was on the landing this morning when Arge, Officer Fellows came up to me and said:

"You got a minute Sloaney"?

"'Course guv, why, what's up"?

"Oh", he said, "nothing bad. Just wanted to let you know that you've got your enhanced".

"Really"? I say, "you fuckin' with me or what"?

"Nope", he says, "you've got it and in all fairness", he continues, "you fuckin' deserve it mate; you've done so well", and here I stick my fist out to this worthy screw for a bump.

"Fuck me", I'd said, "cheers Arge, can't believe I'm an enhanced prisoner"! The prison estate across Britain, as I told you, runs a tier system, a band system and where you are in this system correlates to your behaviour. The scheme is called the IEP or Incentives and Earned Privileges scheme and those on basic get fuck all, losing their TVs, getting no gym, less visits than a prisoner on standard. So, Basic, Standard, Enhanced. Enhanced prisoners get paid more wages, more visits if they want them, more gym and I can now get on H wing if I want to, the enhanced wing. I wanted the status for this reason. My wages will now be £34 a week which is bloody good in jail. Things seem to be slotting nicely into place. Another conversation yesterday buoyed my spirits and this one was with Jason at work.

"I've been thinking Andrew", he'd said, "we need a new employee down here as you know to facilitate and teach the TSP and Resolve programmes and I've been thinking that instead of outsourcing and advertising the job, I've been thinking", and he rubs his bearded handsome chin, "I know it's outlandish but I've been thinking I'm gonna go see the governor and ask him if I can send you out on ROTLs (Release On Temporary License) for the training for a week and then employ you to deliver the courses 'cause what better advertisement of rehabilitation than an ex-prisoner coming back into the jail to deliver courses which helped him get better"? and he can see my shock but continues, "and anyway if we could get you out for the training my wife, who's a director at CGL (Change Grow Live) said that if the governor was too scared she'd give you a job anyway", and I am absolutely speechless and bamboozled by this most magnificent of mans words.

"Are you for real"?

"Well, yeah, look", he says, "it's so out there I don't hold out too much hope on it but why not? And, like I say, my wife is in a position to employ people and we think you'd be bloody good at it".

"Wow J", I say, "I just don't know what to say", and it is this dear reader, this life affirming trust from this worthy fella and his like that warm me to the quick today. And yet, I can tell you, as I type here in Oxford that I would let him down and though I am clean now and living as virtuously as I ever have, I hold shame for the way I was yet to behave, lost again and mired in active addiction, my sanity stolen by dark forces contained in drink and drugs. But, alas, that was a way off. Back to then. So. On Good Morning Britain with Piers and Susanna this morning on the news, they showed a video of a man who yesterday was walking past a store when, literally the second he passed by it, tons of bricks were broken off the top of the building, blown down in the strong winds and missing him by mere inches. This led to a conversation with Jason where he regaled this tale to me:

"I had a mate once", says the worthy man, "and him and his mate were in a work van one day and it's blowin' a fuckin' gale and they're having their lunch and one of 'em, my mate, goes to light a fag but drops his lighter so bends down in the van to get it and a tree was blown down, smashed through the cab and my mate said dropping that lighter saved his life 'cause his pal was killed instantly but he honestly said if he hadn't of dropped that lighter he'd've been a goner too, no two ways about it".

"There's something else at play J there fuckin' is, spiritual shit we know little of", I say.

"That's it", he says, "there's a thing bigger than us in control", and Lucy, hearing our conversation, comes out her office and tells us another tale which has the hairs all over my body standing on end at the final part.

"So", she says, "my mate told me that years ago he was meant to go to this business meeting in Europe and was due to get the train to the airport the next day but the morning of the meeting he got a call from a woman named Wendy. This Wendy told him that the meeting had been cancelled so he didn't go and the train he was gonna get on, the specific carriage where he would have been sitting was destroyed; it was one of those train crashes like years ago in London but this is the weird bit", she continues, "so he's at home and his boss phones him and asks why he wasn't at the meeting and my mate tells him that it was because a woman named Wendy had called telling him it was cancelled and the boss tells him it wasn't cancelled at all and that he'd no idea who this Wendy woman was either. My mate says to this day it is still a mystery but that if he hadn't of had the call he'd definitely have been dead".

"Wow", I say, "what the fuck! My hair is standing on end Luce"!

"Honestly", Lucy says, "my mate and his boss still don't know what the fuck went on".

13-03-2019 Right now, in the House Of Commons Theresa May is, after yesterday's second rejection by the legislature of her Brexit deal, trying to seek an extension with the EU over article 50 in order to try for a third time to get her definitely doomed to failure deal through the house. I have no doubt the deal will be voted down for a third time when the time comes. Surely reader, though I've some sympathy for her, she must go. I am so tired of the whole thing. We voted leave and leave we must. The problem really seems to be that the House on the whole is peopled with remainers so we have the majority of the public wanting to leave but an executive and legislature reticent to see the thing through. A sorry mess indeed. I'm confused to fuck by the sorry charade and don't pretend to know anything about it. But I can guess that all the time taken with this mess our sovereign problems are being neglected. Social care, the NHS, schooling, police and crime and unemployment and myriad other pressing issues that urgently need the attention of our inter warring MPs. Anyway.

"Marcus man look at you", and I hold up a mirror so he can see his face, stroke like, for himself though I'm unsure his bloodshot rheumy eyes allow for true introspection of the condition he gets himself into every fuckin' night. It's become so normal I'm fearful I'm boring the fuck out of you with repetition but prison is like that, very samey on a day to day basis with a highlight or two like a fight or hospitalisation thrown in now and then for a bit of entertainment, savage though that sounds. Marcus still sternly denies the drugs wish to hasten him to his tomb. You see, I'm an NA addict who believes addiction to be a dis-ease. I have something psycho in me that wants to kill me. The Basic Text, the bible of Narcotics Anonymous, tells us that the disease of addiction is cunning baffling and powerful, an insidious malady that wants us dead. The primary purpose of my disease is the desire to see me shuffle off this mortal coil before my time. But, NA promises, though there is no known cure, it can be arrested and recovery is then possible.

"Can you see moron"? I say, still holding up the mirror, but he's hardly here, barely conscious.

"Errr, yep, err, shit man, food, are ya doin' food plesh, plesh me plesh Shhloaney man need food plesh", and like I've told you like one two three four thousand times spice gives mental munchies and this causes regular bouts of severe gastroenteritis as users pile shit upon shit into damaged intestinal tracts, "oh yeah", he realizes, "parsh that plesh man", and he points at a bowl of rice pudding prepared and forgotten about earlier.

"You've literally just eaten two bowls of that", I say, "with piles of sugar you put on top too. No wonder you're getting fat Marcus".

"I know", he says, mongy like and unable to move his bloated carcass the four feet himself", but plesh Shloaney man plesh pash man".

"Ok glutton", I say and do as asked.

"And the shhugar Shloaney plesh man".

"That's full of sugar Marcus man you'll get sick bro".

"Plesh Shloaney Plesh pash man", and I do and he tips, from the bag, tons of sugar onto the stodgy thick double serving from our servery. So, he's had two tins of the same from the canteen which he brought, there are at least two tins worth in this bowl, he's eaten a sleeve of custard creams, a sleeve of bourbons, two packs of noodles with tuna and four Weetabix smothered in sugar after his dinner which was served at 1630hrs and it is now just past 2000hrs so you can bet your bottom dollar he's yet to eat more. The other night, because he'd eaten all his stocks before canteen day, he was so spice starving he was once again eating bread with margarine and sugar and coffee whitener sprinkled onto it. I, too, when on spice have partook of this particular delicacy. Fuckin' nasty man.

"Fuck me", I say to El Chubbo now, "you're a fuckin' animal bro".

"Shut up Shhhloaney Plesh man I'm shhick you takin' pish out me man".

"Don't go gentle into that good night", I say to him now and his mong features crease in confusion.

"What ya shhaying Shhlooaney man"?

"Nothing mate", I say.

"No, Plesh, tell me man".

"Rage Marcus, Rage against the dying of the light", I say having a bit of fun but at the same time well aware of the relevance of the words.

"Fuck shhhhhake Shhloaney man, I'm having another pipe".

"It's so sad watching you mate", I say.

"I'm gonna shhtop shooon Shloaney you'll see man I'm a gangster you'll see Shaloaney man", and the cunt has the pipe to his lips and is fading, fading, fading fast and all I can do is hope it's a temporary stupor into which he slips. Though symapathetic I myself am weary of him and this wing. As I told you yesterday, I got my enhanced status so could well be off to Headcorn or 'H' wing soon. Down the ATB Unit today I was talking to a fella called Greg who is an inmate on that wing.

"Nothing ever happens", he said, "it's great; you have a single cell with your own shower and there ain't no fights, no spice down there".

"So you don't get scenarios like my next door neighbour last night, screaming and on the bell after smoking spice and believing there are spiders all over him"?

"Naaa man fuck that bro, none of that shit", he says, "what happened to the guy"?

"They had to get Oscar One and a nurse to come calm him down and reassure him there were no spiders".

"That stuff man, it's fuckin' dangerous", he says, "I've seen people proper lose the plot and not come back and others tripping out and screaming for help and that".

"That was me once too", I say.

"Really"? he says, looking me over, "you'd never fuckin' think it".

"Honestly", I say, "go back just a few months , I was not in a good place but go back to May, June last year I was positively fucked and suicidal mate".

"You'd honestly never be able to tell you've been on drugs man", and I present my fist for a fist bump.

"That's music to my ears man", I tell him, "cheers mate", and it reminds me of the fella down the gym I told you about who said that all junkies, even those who've stopped using, can still be spotted as such and he used the analogy of people with downs who 'all look the same', his words, not mine. The gym fella said the same as Greg, that I was blessed, that you'd never know. Still, I know different to be fair for in the rooms of NA I have seen lots of people who were heavy hardcore heroin and crack users for many years yet you'd never ever guess it. Successful, affluent, productive people with more of an understanding of the human condition than most, believe me. Addiction is the malady of obsession and compulsion to the death in drugs. Our addiction manifests in other ways once clean, women, gym, academia or whatever. We know not how to moderate. But when we use we are insane, literally.

14-03-2019 1725hrs. Evening people. Russell downstairs, Jake's cellmate, got spun today and they found his debt list though no drugs. Marcus refused to provide a specimen of urine for a drugs test today earning himself a negative entry in his NOMS. Beany got caught with a crack pipe today and is feeling the pressure of the establishment upon him. And El Chubbs, our Marcus, due to the search activity on the wing has the heeby jeebies as he has got, of course, a tiny mobile which he keeps in a pocket in his boxers along with the folded pages of power paper. He is drinking hooch right now atop his usual concoctions. When he starts on the spice he'll leave this realm as usual. Me? Well, I have had a wonderful day. Resolve, the current course run at the unit where I work, has just ended and I have been able to get into the group room and thoroughly clean all the trunking which runs around it which had tons of sticky tape, labels and gunk attached to it, making the room look tatty. Love the company of Jason down there. I feel as though I escape the walls here, standing somewhere in between, a palace and a prison on each hand. Here, I sometimes feel, though my love of life was once buried, it is now being raked from the earth, invigorating me anew.

Marcus just received a text from his missus on the mobile and she has, obviously, looked via an online app at his account which up until today had £1800 in saved money but he has just transferred the whole lot to his man at the gym. He is getting bigger and bigger consignments and taking on immense pressure the likes of which would give me nightmares. He is owed in, right now, £900. Anyway, he says to me now:

"Listen to this text Sloaney", and reads from the tiny Zanco screen, "Marcus, you take the piss; where the fuck is all that money? You promised you'd start paying back the £15,000 debt you racked up in my name and this is where me and you are different. You don't give a fuck Marcus, you've never been able to save and I'm getting sick to death of it to be honest".

"Wow", I say, "she's clearly fuckin' fumin'; what you gonna text her back"?

"I've just written 'please babe, have faith in me, I will give you your money back I promise'. I hope she believes me man".

"You can't see it can ya"? I say.

"What"? he says, looking up from the tiny keypad his fingers are punching on.

"She is sick to death of the same shit and your relationship is crumbling brother".

"Naaa", he says nonchalantly, "she'll never leave me man".

"My God you're so naïve mate; she hasn't visited you for how long"?

"Four months but that don't mean nothing".

"Has she got one booked"?

"She says she's been trying to book one".

"Wake up man", I say, "if you don't stop lying and using and dealing and drugging you're gonna lose her mate, trust me".

"Sloaney man, believe me bro, she'll never leave me she just ain't like that".

"Ok, ok, whatever you say man". In other news Brad had a telephone interview with a hostel in Folkstone which provides accomadation for those leaving prisons in the south east.

"How'd it go Brad"? I asked earlier.

"Well, I had to give a mini PP", says Brad and PP, people, is a term used at the Ley Community where Brad also did a programme which saw him clean ten years and means Personal Profile and is basically a mini life story, "I was on the phone for an hour Andy".

"Yeah", I press, "but what, like, was their tone and are you hopeful"?

"They said that I am exactly what they are looking for and that I would hear from them in a couple of weeks max so yeah, I feel good about it man".

"Hopefully this place will see the back of you soon then McFradders".

"I hope so mate", he says, sweeping a hand over his thick lustrous head of hair, "I'm fuckin' sick to death of the place and my biggest fear has been being released homeless again so fingers crossed", and dear reader the reason for the ambiguity in Brad's release dates is because he is on recall so in order to be released before his SED or Sentence Expiry Date his probation officer has to approve and she will only do this if he has an address to go to. Should Brad not get early release he'll be out just before me, in July. The brilliant Sasha with Xpander is on the radio and I trance out to this classic anthem. El Chubbo wants me to record a few words from him verbatim dear reader.

"Go on then", I tell him, pen poised.

"I'm gonna make sure I give back to Margate I promise you this", he says, "I will make sure before I die that there is a detox unit and rehab built with my money next to the QEQM hospital. I'd like to prove a point to all the people who hate me and cunt me off and who think I won't amount to nothing by becoming the mayor of Margate".

"But you're out ya nut right now, how you gonna turn it around"?

"I will say to that, readers", he says, "please listen to me. All I wanna do is make things right. Yes, I'm fucked out my head right now but I'm gonna smash it and get better, mark my words".

"How you gonna get clean"? I ask, "what's gonna change"?

"I just wanna get clean Sloaney man and I was really honest in the NA meeting today", he says.

"I shoulda gone man", I say, lamenting my missing it.

"It's so fuckin' frustrating", says El Fatto, "I can't believe I've got myself another habit"!

"You'll get there", I say. Anyway dear reader there is good TV on, a series called 60 Days On The Streets.

15-03-2019 lunchtime and this morning I went to work for an hour before getting a sneaky gym session in, quick circuit to blow away the cobwebs. The only thing note worthy is the fact Marcus has stretched a piece of dental floss from the corner of our cell door, locked now, to the corner of Pete W's two cells down and after Pete has added bicarbonate of soda to the cocaine he has and turned it into crack he will shout Marcus out the door and Marcus will pull in the floss with some crack cocaine attached, a nice hissing spitting yellow rock of lovely crack cocaine, my favourite drug along with heroin. Two ounces of coke have just landed on here and the wing is like New Jack City right about now. I thank God the desire to use has been lifted for this is a test and no mistake!

18-03-2019 Marcus is cracked out his nut and getting paranoid about the money he is owed in. 49 people gunned down in two mosques by a madman in New Zealand. Marcus uses 'tex, pregabs and spice to bring him down and now snores soundly.

16-03-2019. Morning. I am sixty days clean today and even in the face of the king of drugs, crack, I've no desire to use, though of course it's not an ideal situation being in such close proximity to temptation. It is 0830hrs on a Saturday morning and I want to share last nights dream with you. So, in the dream I'm with Stacey Dooley and we live in an untidy flat together, not dirty, but clothes everywhere. She keeps asking me to make love to her but I'm too insecure about the fuck off great bunions on my plates of meat so won't get naked though in the dream I want to, in real life too, with her, for that matter! Anyway, in the dream I go out and the streets are so dark, so frightening and inexplicably I am loitering around a police station for ages before I go to a shop and get caught stealing a chocolate bar but I beg the proprietor 'please don't call the police' and he doesn't and I get on my pushbike outside the shop and Dr P---- my brother jumps on the back and at a T junction a big American car driver rolls down his window and says to me 'you're Andrew Sloane aren't you'? and I say 'yeah' and I cycle us through mad killer traffic and amazingly we aren't mown down. Then I woke up and now Marcus is giving me a quick history lesson on Cardi B and Bruno Mars and I tell him I don't give a fuck about them for I know them not! Both talented and she's fit to be fair.

0922hrs and we're out this morning and soon as I walk into Brad's cell after putting mine and Marcus's name on the gym list in the office I notice the spider box open on the desk and Paul Stone has a spider half our pets size in a container in his hand.

"Come to see her have some breakfast Sloaney", he says to me, "I caught this in my cell and brought it up for Brad".

"Fuck me", I say, looking at the size of 'breakfast', "ain't that too big for her though"?

"Naaa", says Stoney, "watch".

"Brad"? I say, looking toward my mucca.

"Naa man, he's right, she'll take it easily", and he takes the container from Stoney, lets the smaller spider crawl onto his hand then flicks it into the beast's lair and I kid you not she is on it in a heartbeat, impaling fangs into the smaller critter and the chase and savaging makes me, Stoney, Brad, Kempy and little Kyle go 'ooohhhh'and it's mesmerising.

"What's happening Gibbo", I ask as he walks in the cell now. He sees the pad on me lap and pen in me hand and says:

"I see what you're tryna do writing 'what's happening Gibbo' like you're tryna interview me for your book-here's a word for ya", he says, "cunt, how about that"! and he bursts out laughing at his own humour before saying to Brad, "you got a razor blade Brad"? and Brad passes him one and I say:

"What d'ya want a blade for"?

"Just got a four hundred ml tramadol but I gotta cut it up as I have to ration them man".

"Gis one a them Kyle", I say, pointing to his big bag of wine gums.

"Take two", he says, and I do.

"They're spinning (searching) Adam's cell", I say, meaning my mate Adam of whom I spoke. He returned from a ROTL yesterday.

"I hope he's got it banked", says Brad, meaning he hopes Adam has any drugs he may have stuffed up his arse.

"Did you see everyone all happy and smiling when he got back yesterday"? says little Kyle, "That little Pete Harlow who's never happy was shadow boxing and jumping around as soon as he heard Adam was back".

"Yeah", I say, "Marcus was cracked out his nut last night".

"Have you seen 'em all out there this morning"? says Gibbo.

"No", says Brad.

"People wired on crack everywhere man proper wide eyed, pale and sweating and running around looking all paranoid and that", says Gibbo.

"J.T is getting some and has promised me a pipe", says Brad, then he says, pointing to the spider, "look how big she is Sloaney, look, she's spread herself right out", and I do and indeed the bitch is big boy!

"Where's my coffee Kyle"? I say.

"On the side there look", he says.

"Cheers bro".

"What ya doing"? I ask Brad as he empties powder onto a placemat, "what's that"?

"The inside of a pregab", and now he rolls paper into a tube and snorts it up his nose. And now Gibbo who just shot out returns with more tablets and I ask:

"What are those you fuckin' lunatic"?

"Just another trammy, 150ml this time, a mirtazapine and a sericol", (quetiapine). Ricky Lanes comes into the cell looking well shifty and a little wired and says:

"I just nicked a DAB radio CD player thing, out the office, a fuckin' big expensive one, where's El Chubbo"? Just as he asks the question El Fat One walks into the cell, "Marcus", says Rick, "you know that stereo they took when they spun Hallsy the other day? Well, the screws left the office door unlocked and empty and I just nicked it, went in and nicked it; wanna buy it"?

"What d'ya want for it"? goes El Fatto.

"Give me half a card for it and it's yours", and Marcus tears off half a credit card sized piece of power paper for him.

"Sweet", says Ricky, clearly elated at his little tickle, "I'll go get it then", and he shoots off whilst Marcus turns to Gibbo and says:

"'Do you want to go halves on a point three (0.3g) of coke Gibbo; I've got some bicarb so if you do it's £25 each"?

"How we gonna do it"? asks Gibbo.

"I've got Adam's bank details so just transfer the dough".

"I'll go phone my people now".

"Got a phone here", says Marcus pulling the tiny thumb sized Zanco from his boxer shorts, "use this", and Gibbo does in Brad's recess, organizing transfers and Marcus goes away to let Adam know to check his bank. Soon as the money has landed and Adam confirms, Gibbo and Marcus will wash up the coke and be smoking creamy crack. It's crazy these prison prices, what would cost you £15 outside will cost £50 in here but, as I said before, it is all about the risk. Outside, drugs, at least class A drugs, are getting cheaper. On the street, when one buys 'one and one' one gets 0.2g of heroin and 0.2g of crack for £20 but dealers, to attract custom, do two for fifteen today, either two items as described above or two heroin or two crack, any combination.

"You staying in here Sloaney", asks Brad of me now and I look up from this pad and paper:

"Why"?

"Just wanna go get my methadone", then Brad turns to Gibbo, "is there a que down there"?

"Naaa man", says Gibbo the clown who now digs his finger fouly into his nose as Brad exits the cell, pulls it out and shows me the product, "smell that Sloaney", putting the foul green looking thing beneath my own nose as I write.

"Fuck off Gibbo man you're disgusting bruv".

"No, honestly", says the sick cunt, "it smells like beef look smell it it really does".

"Fuck off man for fuck sake bro that's sick bruv", and the fucker laughs out loud, "you ain't right ya cunt", I say screwing my face up in disbelief.

"I know I'm fuckin' about but honestly my bogies smell like beef", and when I regale the tale to Brad he throws his head and thick mane of hair back, guffawing heartily.

"That was quick", I say.

"No one down there", he says, referring to the meds que, "I was literally the last on the wing to go down there".

"Best way", says Gibbo, "I hate standing down there but I have to to get my trammys off of people and that". Sasha's Xpander plays on Brad's stereo again and I feel the hair on my body stand on end at the mesmerising space age trance. What a track.

"I feel grainy this morning", I say, "need to drink some water", and now little Kyle walks in and Gibbo goes to him:

"What ya bin' doin', smokin' buskies (buscopan) again ya wierdo"? and Kyle looks affronted and says indignantly:

"No I ain't actually". Brad laughs heartily again the stirrer, relishing such shenanigans and says to Kyle:

"You took that well seriously man"!

"I'm only joking", says Gibbo and now Sat-Nam the washer man comes in and asks Brad:

"You got any bicarb Brad please mate"?

"I ain't mate", and when Sat-Nam leaves Brad goes, "not for you anyway", and you must remember dear reader that the bicarb is literally as precious and expensive as the cocaine on the wing right now for without it there can be no crack, well ,there can but one would have to leave urine standing for a couple days so the ammonia settles and pissy crack just ain't as creamy! I turn to Kyle.

"When's the last time you had a buskie then"?

"Errr", he says, scratching his head, "yesterday"!

"You ever done one Gibbo"? I ask

342

"Fuck that mate, never", he says, "I don't like doing drugs that make me not know what I'm doing, I like drugs that, like, enhance the way I feel ya know"?

"That's the thing", I say, "drugs simply stopped doing that for me in the end".

"How long you been clean for now"? asks Gibbo of me.

"Exactly sixty days today", I say.

"What", says Gibbo, "like, not even a sleeping tablet"?

"Not even a sleeper Gibbo, I'm on or off, all or nothing, yes or no, one or zero ya know? It's binary for me"!

"You're a fuckin' weirdo"! says Brad, smiling.

"Well, I don't deny that", I say.

"You've done fuckin' well man", says Gibbo, "I remember when you got here, you was fucked and about ten stone".

"I know", I say, "I was in a bad way".

"What d'ya weigh now"? asks Brad.

"Twelve stone nine", I say proudly, "I got on the scales at the gym yesterday, got the whole print out thing and my body fat is 15%, muscle mass 56% and my visceral fat was really low too. My metabolic age is 32 and I'm 43 in May".

"I hate to admit it but you don't half look good right now Andy to be fair bro", and I'm quite touched by this if I'm honest. I love this cunt.

"You do", says Gibbo, "I couldn't get clean in here".

"Why not"? I say.

"It's just so fuckin' borin' I need something to take the edge off of it".

"Brad man I can't believe you're gonna come off your meth", I say, "I'm buzzing for you".

"I'm sick and tired of it like you mate", and now Craig D pokes his head in the cell:

"Where's Marcus"? he says.

"Fuck knows", says Brad and the little man syndromed admittedly quite hard but nonetheless bully cunt fucks off, scuttling about for a scrap of spice. Kyle comes back in:

"It's unusually quiet on the landing out there today lads", he says and Brad goes:

"Everybody probably tucked away piping crack then".

"Probably", says Kyle drawing on his vape, "too expensive for me", he finishes.

"Me too", says Brad, "I'm still waiting for J.T to put me on a pipe".

"I think he will", says Kyle, "he's usually quite good in he"?

"Yeah", says Brad, I dare say a little sceptical, for when it comes to crack people change, "I ain't gonna chase him or crack 'round the

343

landing". And now Marcus comes into the cell and goes into Brad's recessed toilet and talks on the mobile to his lovely lady, the ex screwess Lauren and they're arguing about the debt Marcus left her in when he went to prison. I feel the relationship can't last much longer. She has waited for two and a half years for him and yet he hasn't changed at all and when he gets out she'll see he's still not clean. The relationship is untenable. He drove her to a breakdown before his incarceration and I'm not for a minute criticising him for this for that is what addicts do, destroy relationships and hurt those closest to us though we do this against our will for we are ill ill ill! Sick people. I have caused a great many harms to those that love me: I have broken the hearts of my family, robbed and stole and lied and cheated and begged and threatened and whined and manipulated. I have been violent with friends and family and lovers in my depravity of drugs. In Step One of the Step Working Guide of Narcotics Anonymous there is a question and it asks: what did we do in our active addiction that went against all our core values and principles?! What a question! I've done things I would never, ever do under any other circumstances. Ever. But when I use I am literally insane!!! All I can do today is thank God that the obsession to use is gone, for today, one day at a time.

1750hrs and I've literally, with some difficulty, had to pick Fatto off of the floor because if a screw looks through and sees him outcold he'd be put through the rigours of the door being busted and medical teams ete etc. He's now on his bed, snoring, so he's not in any immediate danger of death. Earlier he smoked copious amounts of crack and Kempy and I had a little fun with the mong. After the gym I had returned to my cell and Kempy had come in:

"Where's El Chubbo"?

"Round Brad's piping I think".

"What's this shit"? he asks, pointing to a muggy gold coloured metal watch Marcus brought recently for spice, "and this", pointing to a stainless steel again rather muggy bracelet, "and this", pointing to some shiny plastic Rosary Beads.

"You know what he's like", I say, "loves paying out vapes and spice for a bit of old tat but the worst thing is Kempy, he puts all his best clothes on then wears all that shit outside his garments like it's bling"!

"I know", says Kempy, "proper mug in 'e"? but we are smiling at the antics of El Fat One and Kempy starts putting on the 'jewellery'.

"What ya doin'"? I ask, as he puts the massive Rosary Beads over his head.

"Come on", he says.

"Where"?

"Brad's cell to wind the prick up, come on", says Just For Men.

"Kempy, he gets funny when he's smoking crack".

"Fuck that, come on", says the long haired comic leviathan and we walk to Brad's where Kempy promptly kicks open the door. Brad's in his chair and a pale beached whale looking Chubbo reclines on the bed.

"Check out my bling man", and I see Brad start to chuckle and I too can't help it and I'm thinking, dear reader, you really have to see and know this cunt Kempy to appreciate why it is as I type here in Oxford from the handwritten manuscript that I chuckle in mirth years after the fact. The lazy, languid, six foot plus long haired handsome and sarcastic fucker is comedy gold. "Yeah man", continues Kempy, "gold watch, platinum necklace man and check out me beads bro, these are moonrocks ya know"! And as he says these things he's pulling poses and posturing like a rapper.

"You're a mug Kempy", says Marcus but Kempy just goes:

"Yaaaa maaaaann, check the bling bro, man's made it bro ya get me", and he struts and preens and prances and says this in what I guess he thinks is a road man dialect.

"You're a proper cunt Kempy ya know that", says Marcus with one side of his mouth drooping again, like a stroke victim. Brad is almost crying as Kempy struts like a cock, up and down the cell, mugging off the bits of metal Marcus purchases for drugs.

"Kempy man, leave him be bro", but I too can't help but laugh. Ruthless Kempster.

17-03-2019. 1045hrs. Morning people. Outside the Perspex between the bars of the window I can see the weather is changeable. Between clouds I can see bolts of blue but the air coming through the vent has chilly fingers stroking the back of my neck. The staff just let Marcus out to get his meds and whilst the door was open I shot across the landing to Pete Lanes and Steve Kemp's cell and said to Kempster:

"Who won the pools this week"? meaning the competition many of us, about thirty of us in fact, put a quid on weekly concerning the football. Kempy, the cunt, has won it three times in six weeks.

"I did", he says, "well, depending on one game today on whether I have to share it or not".

"No fuckin' way", I say, "three times in recent weeks ya cunt. You must have that almanac thing from Back To The Future"!

"Don't be hating on me man".

"Don't know how you do it ya cunt", I say before quietly slipping down to Brad's cell where he is sitting pulling shoes on getting ready to go get his methadone.

"Can I borrow your vape battery Brad"?

"Yeah man", he says, unscrewing his vape capsule from the top of it. I put on the cherry one I have in my pocket and draw from it deeply. Last night, and I really can't be bothered going into it so bored with this shit am I, but last night Marcus collapsed on the floor three times. Three fuckin' times I struggled lifting his dead weight onto the bed. After smoking crack all day, taking downers all afternoon and smoking spice hard all night the cunt has had me up and down like a yo yo and I'm furious, having slept not a wink. He's so selfish and I'm bored shitless with this. What's worse, the cell was a tip after he spilled food, milk and water and sugar all over the floor. At 4am he woke, jumped up, tripped and ripped the curtain from the window along with all the toiletries and condoments from the shelf.

"Sorry", he'd said.

"You're a fuckin' spastic", I'd retorted. I was so angry I launched the remote control at the wall, smashing it. Then, to compound my rage further, Chubbo loaded another pipe and promptly fell to the floor necessitating me climbing down and dragging the fat fuck up and onto his bed as he dribbled and drooled and droned on like a fuckin' severely handicapped clown with downs. Upon waking this morning the mong actually sounds indignant that I broke the remote control. Obviously, being completely unconscious, the cunt has no idea that I've been dragging him off the floor all night long, that he filthied up the cell and that he has been rude and obnoxious to me at times. No, he picks up the remote and smashes it off the floor but I say not a word because if I do we will be fighting and that achieves nothing. I simply need to get away from the prick and pronto, much as I do truly love the cunt. So, it's now eleven a.m and Marcus has just returned to the cell after going to collect his and other people's meds. Even as I sit, at this very minute, writing for you dear reader, he is over the toilet heaving due to the fact he has no opioids in him as of yet. Once the heaving stops and they've opened everyone up Marcus scuttles off to find his fix. I'm sure he'll do well for the wing is drenched in drugs.

1205hrs and though cocaine is copious on here right now, bicarb is not but, alas, the ingenuity of J.T saved the day for he, in foresight I've just learned from a wired Marcus, saved some piss from two days ago, scooped off the ammonia from the stinking stuff and washed up the crack him, Marcus and Kempy have been smoking using that. I've heard over

346

the years that this can be done but not been witness to it! The state of Marcus attests to the viability of the method though for the cunt is over the toilet spewing his ring and crack shitting. I only have to think of the stuff for my bowels to loosen in anticipation. I dare say that the opioids which will take the edge off the crack wired-ness are yet to kick in properly. I thank God for protecting me from active addiction right now. Just before bang up, round Brad's, me, Gibbo, Brad and Kyle were sitting chatting when Matchstick Model and Cabinet Maker Old Boy Trevor came in and Gibbo, on full rip the piss mode today goes:

"Look at the state of you you dirty old man ya need to go and have a wash mate".

"Oh fuck off Gibbo" says Trev, "ya got any of that spice left from the other day? That proper powerful stuff"? Gibbo, too, sells a bit to make a few quid sometimes.

"Not for you, look at ya you old pervert, I bet you're a pedo ain't ya, come on, you can tell us", and we all laugh out loud!

"Fuck you Gibbo", the indignant Trev says, "you shouldn't joke about things like that man".

"But you do look like a pedo though", then he turns to me, Brad and Kyle, "don't he look like a pervert though lads, come on, be honest"!

"Gibbo man", laughs Brad, throwing his head back nonetheless and Gibbo is fuckin' funny to be fair.

"Don't look at me", says Kyle.

"Gibbo man", I say, "ya can't say that bro".

"Dirty ol' bastard", says Gibbo, but, of course, he's laughing too for we know Trev is cool man, though he could do with a shower to be fair, "sorry Trev, I'm just messing man; anyway, tell Sloaney about the doors you built, the ones you fucked up for Saddam Hussien".

"It wasn't Saddam Hussien and I didn't fuck 'em up: it was King Hussien of Jordan".

"You told me you fucked 'em up", says Gibbo.

"No", says Trev, "right Sloaney, the fella who done these massive chapel doors before me didn't take into account the water content of the wood so when the wood dried they expanded so wouldn't open and shut properly so I had to redo them".

"For real"? I say, "you tellin' the truth here or what"?

"I fuckin' swear man they were nine foot tall four feet wide and bullet proof with steel going through the middle of 'em, weighed a fuckin' ton they did too".

"Did you get 'em right though"? I ask him.

347

"Course I fuckin' did man, what'd'ya take me for"? he says, again, indignant before turning once more to Gibbo, "so, you got any a that gear or what"?

"Yeah", says Gibbo, "come on, come to me cell you dirty old cunt", and again we all have a little chuckle at the on form Gibbo and his banter. Marcus is piping spice right now, in our cell whilst we are banged up. Probably in an attempt to dispel the wired feeling of the crack. He is complaining about having to pay Nev to fuck off earlier. Nev was loitering around for some crack and Marcus had to pay him spice to entice him to fuck off and leave 'em alone with the cocaine.

"The cunt just wouldn't leave the cell Sloaney", he says, "I had to pay the cunt to fuck off, he drives me fuckin' mad man".

"Well, we know what he's like. Marcus, what you gonna do man? You're in a fuckin' bad place, your missus is on the verge of leaving you and you've got a ravin' habit bro".

"I don't know what to do Sloaney man I know I've got to do something. I'm seriously thinking about rehab when I get out".

"You've got to do something 'cause you're getting worse and worse bro".

"I'm just scared Sloaney. If I went to rehab, where do you think I should go"?

"Not the Ley", I say, "you don't need that type of programme, you wouldn't stay there' cause it's brutal mate".

"You did it though Sloaney, so why couldn't I"?

"I needed that type of programme Marcus. I was a horrible, aggressive, nasty piece of work and needed a nasty rehab that wasn't frightened of me and wouldn't take my shit. The head honcho up there, Steve Walker, proper old London gangster, took none of my bollox and nor did the rest of the staff to be fair".

"But if I went to rehab I'd want to go there", he says.

"Well, it's one of the best things I ever did to be fair. You would get a lot out of it if you could stick it".

"Have they got, like, a detox thing up there"?

"Yeah man".

"I'd definitely want that one if I went".

"You need to do something man. But Marcus mate to be honest I think it's gonna take something drastic like another breakdown 'cause I can't see you getting clean off your own back".

"How have you done it"?

"With God's help Marcus man and don't forget I've had some years in recovery before bro. Mate, we have to reach rock bottom before we are truly ready to change".

348

"You're lucky man".

"I'm just tired of it all mate and want to find another way. I'm stubborn too bro and refuse to give up". Charli XCX and Troy Sivan are wishing they were back in 1999 and I'm gonna try nap for ten…….

1407. Brad's and Jake just come in and he is raving Quilp like because his people drove all the way up from Thanet for a visit only to be turned away at the gate by security for some reason.

"Fuckin' can't believe it", he is saying, "I get myself all spruced up for a visit only for these cunt screws to come to me five minutes before visiting time and tell me they've turned my people away. Fuckin' liberty man".

"Why though"? asks Brad.

"That's what I mean though", says Jake, "they won't fuckin' tell me Bradders; I'm gonna proper kick of I swear it, watch if I don't", and he fucks off, fuming. I think on something I read once: keep your temper. A decision made in anger is never sound.

"I been having her (the spider) out lately Sloaney watch", says Brad and he gets the girl out the box and she walks on my leg then Brad's arm then up his neck and face.

"Fuck me", I say again, "she's mahussive bro".

"Gorgeous int she"? says he and Jake walks back in.

"They come all the way up here and get turned away at the fuckin' gate the poor cunts. It's them I'm upset for", and he has a point the poor cunt and I can't imagine why they've been turned back but have heard of people in the past refused entry for being inebriated amongst other things. Tan was visiting me last summer and she was warned that if she didn't wear more appropriate less revealing clothes next time, she wouldn't get in the sexy wench! God, I miss her. Now El Chubbo walks in the door.

"Sloaney", he says, "can you do me a favour 'cause I don't think I'm gonna go gym today"?

"What"?

"Can you see my man down there for me"?

"I will if I have to but I'd rather Kempy did it if he can", and Just For Men comes in right then and Marcus asks him the same.

"Yeah, if I have to", replies Kemps.

"Between the two of us we'll sort it Marcus man", I say.

"Course I will", says Kemps, "why don't you wanna do it Sloaney"?

"I would if I had to Steve but come on lads, I don't smoke the shit. Like I say, if I would have had to I'd've done it no probs".

"Cool man, I'll do it anyway I get it Sloaney". Me and Marcus both thank him and he shoots off to fuck knows where. Ricky Lanes comes in and tells Brad:

"I know I still owe you Brad but I get my subutex patch tomorrow if you can do anything with that"?

"Well, I owe Marcus so if you could give me a couple of strips of that so I could pay him that'd be pukka Rick".

"Alright Brad no worries man, we'll do it like that then mate".

"No worries Rick", says Brad.

"I appreciate you bearing with me man", says Ricky before shooting off to hunt and hustle some drugs no doubt. Brad picks up a stick and a pot.

"Wait here Sloaney, gonna go on the yard and tickle me baby some food".

"Hurry up then Brad 'cause I'm off to the gym in twenty".

"I'll be two minutes", he says, firing out the door. I'm alone in the cell thinking how lucky I am to have this erudite kindly friend who I've been so horrible to in active addiction. I was so aggressive even in my younger days, fighting and attacking all my friends. I'm not sure I've ever been physical with Brad, but the poor cunt has tolerated my nasty tongue and greed. He returns with a fly funnily enough and promptly throws it in with the beast who wastes no time soon as the bluebottle is trapped in her sticky web.

2155. Ok. So I went to the gym and worked out with Smartyn and 'H' who insured I will not be able to walk normally for the next three days after a horrific leg workout. However, that's not what I got out my bed and away from Rude Tube to tell you. I couldn't turn in this evening without telling you that the reason Marcus didn't go to gym today is because there has been a hypodermic syringe doing the rounds on the wing and despite the fact the foul thing, for I demanded to see it, was clearly aged and not brand new as he claimed, he stabbed himself with it anyway, injecting cocaine and subutex. Yet Marcus is down, depressed and despondent despite having indulged in much mind meddling mayhem which begs the question I continually put to him:

"If you ain't fuckin' enjoying it, why keep it up"?

"I just can't stop Sloaney", and I, too, know what it is like to be using against my will. Don't want to use but don't know what the fuck to do to stop. I wish I could do what he is frightened of for him: the opioid withdrawel for that is at the fundament of it. A subutex detox isn't nearly as bad as heroin and methadone, the latter is the worst by far with no sleep for many, many weeks. Then again, if I did it for him he would not

350

learn the consequences of picking up again. Anyway, bye for now dear reader.

18-03-2019 1925hrs. I'm becoming lazy with my writing of late because I'm sick of this dull, droll, boring and repetitive environment. I mean, yes, a man from B wing was on a roof today. There's been a serious assault on E wing. Adam has been ripped off by those he trusted to look after his coke. Marcus has not been able to reload because he simply owes too much money. He has, thank God, gotten rid of the filthy dirty needle. The reason he is struggling is simple: crack is every junkies favourite drug and he has spent much money he'd usually use to score with buying the stuff for the wing has been flooded with coke of late. Anyway, re the syringe he says to me now:

"I just couldn't get a vein Sloaney, it was horrible man, took me ages and reminded me that I can't go back out to that".

"Couldn't get a vein but it was also undoubtably blunt as fuck you silly cunt".

"Na na it was new Sloaney"!

"Fuck off Marcus, you're talkin' to me mate. I once used one in a cell after five other people used it before me. I'm not judging you bro, been there man".

"Fair enough, I respect that man". I could tell you Adam had a sunbed on his ROTL (temporary release) and because an officer noticed he looked a little darker he got nicked for changing his appearance but the governor threw the charge out today. I could tell you Max, my Nibiru loving pal got swagged off by a security team for a strip search today on suspicion of drug dealing. I could tell you Paul Stone resembles a nazi concentration camp victim and gets sicker and skinnier with the spice every day. I could tell you the fat scouse downstairs, not Fiddler, the one who lives in the cell next to Martyn my mate, sells every meal every day for spice, not eating himself. I could tell you I used to do this too. I could tell you that over the weekend there were two fights in the meds que over people owing out their tablets. I could tell you that even now, as I write, this minute Marcus is searching the cell for scraps of spice, behind his photos, in his clothing pockets, in his bed, under it and I of course systematically rip the piss out of him.

"That's it, scuttle about looking for scraps, look at ya", and it would be true, I am ripping him but in all seriousness he is in real panic for due to him depleting stocks of vapes for crack along with myriad bank transfers he's had but a fraction of the normal dosages of the many different poisons he takes daily. He is fearful and the onset of a semblance of normal consciousness frightens the fuck outta him. I could tell you Nev has quietened significantly since old hammer fists Pete W got the better of him that day. I could tell you also though that Nev ain't no cunt and can fight! We all lose sometimes people. I could tell you Pete Lane is still as bigoted as ever and continues to use archaic discriminatory language most every day. I could tell you that despite this I love the silly cunt, and I do. Doesn't mean I like his views. I could tell you 'Arge' Officer Fellows is desperately trying to clean the wing up. I could tell you Beany owes Marcus a monkey (£500), Craig D is flat out on spice and got taken for a piss test yesterday. I could tell you Kempy the cunt refuses to work out of pure laziness but is the funniest fucker I know. I could tell you J.T beat up his old cellmate 'MarkwhoisJohn' yesterday too. I could tell you that Marcus and Brad told J.T that my cousin once got convicted for killing many, many cats, twenty years ago after coming out the army, lots of poor pussies.

"Didn't he Sloaney"? went Brad.

"Yeah", I said, "people had stickers up in shops and on lampposts all over the estate (Newington, Ramsgate) for missing cats but it turned out Joe had been murdering them all".

"Why"? asked J.T.

"Dunno", I said, "but I guess when he was in the army cats had upset him. He came out fucked is the truth J.T. He's actually not a bad guy".

"What"? says J.T looking horrified.

"Fuck knows J.T, but I've got a brother in Broadmoor too", and this is very true dear reader.

"Fuck me", says J.T, "I fuckin' knew you ain't all there Sloaney; I can see it in your eyes sometimes".

"Oh, he's certainly not the full ticket", says Brad. I could tell you Briggsy and Kyle both look as sick as Stoney what with the spice but these two also smoke buscopan. Kyle, after being banged up with bully Craig for a month feels like slitting his own throat again like he did on his last sentence after having a breakdown. I could tell you an officer today described the meds que as the most dangerous part of the prison. I could tell you I think about Claire Sharp, Charlotte, A---- and my son's mum E---- on a daily basis. Tan and Terri too. I could tell you Marcus hasn't, oh, no wait, he has! Literally right this second he has found some spice, a quarter of an I.D card and it prompted an ejaculation of 'hallelujah' from his crusty lungs.

"Oh thankyou", he says, looking toward the heavens. He found it in a pair of shorts in his dirty laundry bag.

"Oooohhh", I say, smiling for him though, "proper happy now ya scuttlin' about paid off ain't ya"?

"Thank fuck", he says, and he sets up his little pipe and sucks it in and now he's already chuckling like a retard and I'm thinking I shouldn't use that word but I'm also thinking that it is wholly appropriate and I'd not let a publisher push me, preventing you from seeing my thinking as it really is. I'm thinking what fuckin' publisher will have the bollox to take a risk with this? Then I think it's too good not to sell, not to create a storm and I also think come now, I can fuckin' write, no?!! Then a wave of insecurity engulfs me and I think 'what if this is a load of shit'? As the mong laughs like a backward boy I too chuckle along gleefully thinking I may just be self actualising. And as I sit typing form this lovely house, clean and sober in Oxford, I think, wow, I had more pain to come yet. More insanity. More madness. And I look to the other manuscript on the side, waiting to be typed after this one, also written in jail, a 'B' cat, more serious establishment this time. It's gonna be called 'Lucy' after the high class £400 an hour call girl who I still love to this day but with whom I spent a year on crack and smack, both of us, culminating in me assaulting her in a hotel room. I am sane today, with NA, one day at a time. I could tell you I want to do good for the rest of my days to rebalance my karmic scales. I could tell you Lucy is clean, only using hard drugs for one year before cessation. I could tell you I've had a spiritual awakening. I could tell you I'll give to domestic abuse and drugs charities if ever I'm in a position to do so, if my books sell, for I've many ideas for works in the future. But I shan't bore you with all this. I shall say goodnight, and continue loyaly from the handwritten manuscript in the morn.

20-03-2019. 11am. I'm currently at work in the Attitudes, Thinking and Behaviour Unit, ATB for short. I have been working making preparations for the next TSP or Thinking Skills Programme group which starts on the 01-04-2019. Me and Lucy have been flat out printing off paperwork, sorting out filing cabinets and creating folders with all the separate modules for the influx of the new students. Jason is doggedly writing reports from the last programme, the Resolve that's just been completed. Naomi is doing interviews with TSPers and Lucy has one coming down soon too. In other news, I no longer need to think of moving to 'H' wing because the problem has been resolved by me moving out of the cell with Marcus and in with clean and sober Martyn P, my little mate. I felt a little guilty leaving Marcus but it is necessary for my sanity and recovery. Each and every night without fail Marcus, who is a close personal friend of many years don't forget, has been absolutely smashed to the point of spasticification and this has been an ordeal for me, painful and soul searing. I'm also only 64 days clean and though I feel strong, constant close proximity, like in the same cell, to crack and opioid analgesics will soon wear me down and indeed I have been tempted on many occasions. Anyway, I must work, more later.

1710hrs. The Chase is on TV and I am now in cell 120, on the 'ones' as opposed to 208 on the 'twos' landing. Martyn currently sits reading the NA Basic Text and I marvel at the disparity between this behaviour and that of Marcus.

"How long you been clean and sober now Martyn"? and he tells me with a cheeky smile on his cute young face:

"One hundred and eight days", and his look and tone tell me he is proud of this and so, indeed, should he be.

"Where did you go for your shower, I didn't see you in there"?

"I know man, didn't get a chance, there was loads of washing up at the servery tonight so none of us got a chance to get in there. Oh", he says, "I called my ex today".

"Oh", I say, "what, on Marcus's mobile"?

"Yeah man, we had a good laugh and I asked her to write a letter to me and she said she will and the only reason she hasn't is 'cause she didn't know what to say".

"D'ya miss her mate"?

"Yeah man, she only left me 'cause of the crack, me caring about the drugs more than her; I lost myself before I lost her".

"Was she happy to hear from you then"?

"At first she didn't recognise my voice but when she realised it was me she was like 'oh Martyn I've missed you, how are you' and I just told her how far I've come, that I'm staying clean and doing really well and 'cause she knows Reece I told her that Reece (hyper) has moved out and that I've got a clean cellmate that ain't smoking tea bags and spice around me", and now I read what I've just written to Martyn and he loves it. He continues that, "when I get out, I told her, I'm gonna come find you and get you back. I can't see myself with anyone else, she's like my soulmate".

"What's her name"?

"Amber".

"Do you think about her every day"?

"Yeah", he says nostalgically, "it hurts though sometimes so I try not to think about her too much".

"Why, does it do your head in"?

"Yeah 'cause I don't like to think about what she might or might not be doing man 'cause she's not my girl anymore but it still hurts".

"Is she good looking"?

"Well, in my eyes she is", he says, getting up off the chair, "I'll show you a picture", and I look at her and say sincerely:

"Wow, those eyes, she's a little sort mate", and Martyn, five foot five remember, goes:

"She ain't that little".

"What d'ya mean"?

"Well, she's about five eleven" and I go:

"Sorry for smiling mate".

"It's cool man I think it's funny too"!

"Don't it bother you"?

"Not at all", he says, "her old man is fuckin' massive too".

"Did you used to get on with her family then"?

"Yeah, I lived with her at her mum and dad's for two and a half years".

"Nice people"?

"Yeah, and they're millionaires. They have a self storage company and they like store stolen cars and motorbikes for the police, you know, when the police confiscate them and the stolen vehicles get stripped and broken down for parts and sold abroad". This is confusing but I merely repeat what he says.

"Wow", I say, "and you're living with 'em you criminal fucker"!

"They didn't care, they knew, well her mum did, that I'd been to prison and she knew I was shotting too". (selling class A drugs, crack and heroin in this case). Now Martyn shows me the Mother's Day card he's brought his mum and I feel bad I forgot but ruminate my mum probably wouldn't want one from me right now; I miss her terribly but she is sick of me bless her. I have a lot of making up to do and talk won't cut it. Man, I love her so much. I have to prove to her I have changed.

"Wanna play cards"? says Mart.

"Go on then, what we playing? Black Jack"?

"Yeah man, best of five if ya fancy it"? and as we talk, on the TV Meridian News reports on an unprecedented swarm of flies in Uckwood the like never before witnessed in the UK. In other news the police are cracking down on knife crimes due to increased numbers of stabbings in the Kent and Sussex areas.

"Seen this poem from my mate in Inside Time"? (national prison newspaper), asks Mart.

"No, show me", and let me tell you that the little fucker is four one up at cards. He also says casually that:

"Me and my ex had two abortions and a miscarriage, it just wasn't the right time".

"Man, that's heavy shit boy, sorry bro".

"Na man it's cool, honestly". On the international news now we watch a report on a savage cyclone that has ripped through Mozambique and then one on New Zealand who have banned assault rifles after the horrific killing of now 50 worshippers in two mosques by a right wing lunatic. Another report off the back of this tells how five UK mosques in Birmingham have had their windows put through and me and Mart briefly discuss the Islamaphobia problem endemic in Britain and conclude that not all Muslims are bad people or terrorists as many on this wing would have you believe. It's still 4-1 to Mart and I say:

"You cheating somehow Mart"?

"Naaa man, positive I ain't"!

"You always fuckin' beat me though", I say despondently. The cards fall well for me and I win this game. "Yes"! I say, elated to beat the slippery little fucker. I win another game, 4-3.

"Catching ya bro"!

"I was gonna put down"..........Martyn starts.

"Don't matter what you was gonna do bro, shoulda woulda coulda and all that", and I'm buzzing I'm coming up the rear and on the news now a sexy, fit blonde school teacher has been noncing off her boyfriend's 15 year old son and he I bet was loving it the lucky little bastard but imagine if it wasn't a 38 year old woman shagging a fifteen year old boy but a 38 year old man on a fifteen year old girl! She avoids prison but in the latter situation HE would not! Saying that, I was always rather hopeful one of my teachers would want to play with me! Particularly Ms Borley at Hereson, she was fit and I and all my mates were always talking of what we'd like to do to her! Mart gets to five first and I say to him:

"Can't believe you beat me, one more hand"?

"Cool", he says, and we both briefly perv at Pria on Emmerdale Farm; by far the most gorgeous girl in soap! Let me though give you the poem in the prison paper by Martyn's friend, Harry Brackpool. It's about spice.

I came across a drug called spice
I first smoked it in jail, we would call it rice
My mind went mad and I was lost
Used to ring family and friends to cover the cost.
Sold all my stuff to get my green crack
Because that's what it is, it's worse than smack.
I developed a habit when I was in jail
So when I got out it's no wonder I failed
Went straight to the shop to get some Black Mamba
A pack of king skins and half ounce of Amber.

This all started in 2016
I would wake up, straight to the shop, my daily routine.
Then I'd be off my nut for all to see
Slumped over is how you would find me.
It's caused me problems I'm not gonna lie
Looking back at the past makes me wanna cry.
I lost my daughter and the ones I love to this drug
You might be reading this thinking 'what a mug'.
I wish I never smoked it that first time
But I thought it was like skunk, thought it would be fine.
Now I know that's far from the truth
Because I'm sitting under HMPs' roof.
It's been two years since it all began.
Now I hate spice because I know the pain.
2019 is gonna be my year
My mind's all clear and I'm off the gear.
I will never touch it it's awful stuff
You couldn't tempt me not even a puff.
Time's gone on and I've missed a lot
But this time round I'll give it my best shot.
I'm worth more than a life of drugs and jail
Where my mind's at now I just cannot fail.
So take my advice and stay away from spice
Because it's the devils drug and will ruin your lives.

And there you have it people, spice in a nutshell. Gonna chill. Peace out.

21-03-2021 1200hrs

"What's the date today"? I ask Martyn as we bang up for the lunchtime period on a Black Eye Friday.

"Twenty-first", he says, "me uncles birthday is the twentieth so that's how I know it's the twenty-first".

"What did those two screws drag Reece off of the wing for today"?

"Piss test", says Mart, "just a matter of time though weren't it"?

"Why d'ya say that"?

"Well, he brings it upon himself walking 'round the wing out his nut all the time. He makes a fuckin' fool of himself and now he's gonna lose days".

"He'll light the drug test up that cunt, how many days will he lose for a positive"?

"About 14", says Martyn meaning Reece will have 14 days added to his sentence.

"They got Beany as well didn't they"? I say.

"Yep, another one who's always walking 'round out his fuckin' nut all the time".

"Maybe it'll be a wake up call for 'em both", I say, "d'ya like Brooklyn 99 Mart"? Martyn has flicked through the channels and alighted upon the comedy.

"Yeah man, I think it's well funny do you"?

"I love it"! I say truthfully. Anyway dear reader, in other news, Marcus, who is now banged up with Pete W was last night woken by screws banging on his door asking if he was ok because he was monged out on the floor and Pete, also inebriated, unlike me, would be in no position to pick him up and put him onto his bed. I myself slept like a baby here in my new cell with my new cellmate. Oh, Kyle has moved out of bully Craig's cell and the moron, the poor blind fool Reece, has moved in with him now. Won't be long before Craig is terrorising him. I might be bad but I'd love to see that cunt get smashed up. If he gave me any excuse at all I'd bite his face in a heartbeat. Bully cunt. Yet, disturbingly, I like him at times. I'm fucked! This morning me, Adam W, Martyn and 'H' along with sexy dressed in spandex Ms Hulbert did an SAS circuit. Forgive me dear reader but I only tell the truth; I came first. I think I needed to be ahead of everyone throughout for being behind Ms H would have been extremely distracting to say the least. She has a banging body this lovely little bird. Seriously though, we all put in a good shift and afterward, to warm down, we all did squats to Moby's 'Sally Up' song where on him saying 'sally up' we stand and on 'sally down' we squat, holding the posture whilst clutching a fuckin' kettlebell which was excruciatingly painful but oh so satisfying. My muscles were screaming out with the burn of the lactic acid. Anyway, in other bollox, Brexit is in meltdown, article 50 is extended and I really can't be fucked to talk any more of the whole bullshit scenario. Martyn says now that:

"Reece owes bundles out this week, he could end up with a black eye today".

"How much does he owe"? I ask.

"Fuck knows, but quite a lot and he don't get no money sent in so he's gonna struggle. He used to smoke so much spice in here even though he's skint. Every week he somehow dodges a punch but it's gonna happen sooner or later", says Martyn.

"I know he owes Brad and Marcus", I say, "and obviously he owes other people".

"He owes loads more than them two", says Martyn, picking up the in cell landline phone, "just gonna call me mum quick", he says.

1704hrs and I was in the gym playing volleyball; us against the staff, me, 'H', Marcus, Kempy, Ricky Lines and Gibbo and fifteen or twenty minutes in a chaplain, one of the religious team here at Rochester comes into the sports hall, never a good sign. I see him talk to a gym screw who points at me and my guts do a flip. No, no, no I think. Not fuckin' me, please. We all stop playing and he walks over to me.

"Can you come with me Andrew, we need to speak to you", and I go, quite sternly:

"I'm playing volleyball man, can't it wait father"?

"No", he says, "you really need to come with me", and his tone sends a shiver of dread through me and, dear reader, I knew I knew I fuckin' knew.

"Ok", I say, now somewhat zombiefied by what I suspect is coming. We walk out the gym to the prison chapel and I press him, "can you tell me what this is about please"? but he tells me I need to wait and we get to the church and go up the stairs to the small chapel and to the left sitting at a small table is my sister, my beautiful sister J---- with a cup of coffee before her and a seat across the small table for me, I guess. Her youthful face lights up upon seeing me and we hold each other tightly before we both sit.

"Hello Andy", she says in her always measured tones and I love her so much, "I can't believe you look so well, I was expecting to see you in a state and dreading it".

"I can't believe you're here and man you look so well, so young", and now I see the tears well in her eyes and my belly has a greasy fear for her next words.

"Oh Andy, it's mum".

"Oh J----, don't say it please don't fuckin' say it I beg you, please God no".

"Oh Andy I'm so sorry but she's gone she's gone", and oh my sister is suffering God love her.

"When J---- when and how oh God fuck no".

"Oh Andy I'm sorry, but I had to come up straight away and tell you though".

"How though", I ask, "was she ill"?

"No, she was fine", says my sister, clearly broken hearted, "she was out drinking last night, and when she got home, V---- went to bed and when he got up in the morning he found her: she's had a fall in the front room".

"Oh fukin' 'ell J----", I say, "oh J---- I so wanted to make amends to her, to say sorry and make up for all I've put her through", and now I realize that I was making this about me. But I felt lost, broken and tormented with guilt and shame.

"She loved you, you know that don't you? When you were sent to prison you was in the paper and she cut it out to show me and was laughing her head off 'cause it said you was sent to prison for trying to steal a boiler", and as J---- talks I see the truth and can imagine me mum showing her the article going:

"A feckin' boiler bejasus", In her thick Dublin dialect and I find myself a little relieved, relieved she still loved me, even through my heavy heart and the shocking, smothering and all enveloping sadness.

"Oh mum, oh J----", I say, "how are you holding up and when did you find out"?

"I've been crying all day and I found out at seven o'clock this morning", and oh I love her for having thought of me straight away, oh God love my sister, "she's been out on the piss since St Paddies day, you know how she loved it every year Andy", and it's true and as I recall this for you I am so crippled with grief, so suffocated with sadness.

"Andy", said J----, "she was dressed up as a leprechaun since St Patrick's day, I'll send the photos in, you should've seen her, honestly she looked so little and lovely".

"Are you sure she still loved me J----"?

"Andrew", says J---- solemnly, and J---- does not lie for anyone, "she said when she showed me that clip from the paper 'look at the fookin' eejit going ta prison for nickin' a foockin boiler bejasus' and she was laughing her head off at you", and as I say I can see her, in my mind's eye, saying this and chuckling at my idiocy. I feel reassured.

"She always loved you Andrew, you know that", and it's true, I do, but oh I'm broken. My mum 'was', can't believe I'm using the past tense, my mum was such a binge drinker and always the life and soul of the party. I must put away my pen for now.

Anyway, when I got back to the wing everyone already knew, well, they knew something had happened and Martyn, Marcus, Kempy, Bradley, Peter, Ricky, Steve Lanes, Pete W, 'H', Kyle, Officer Fellows, (Arge) Officer Maddison, (Mads) Ms Slane, Ms H and many more were extremely supportive and all had kind words coming from the heart which warmed me greatly, just knowing people cared. The most dishonourable thing I could do now would be to pick up a pipe on the back of this, to use on it. I need to remember, I am my mother's legacy and can bring honour from ashes yet. But oh I wish I'd not forgotten that mother's day card......truth, shameful truth is that I could still have gotten one one way or another but I assumed I'd many more to go! Sitting in Oxford, typing now, I am gutted, gutted, gutted. I'm so sorry mum, really I am. My dear mum loved Jesus and her heart was so pure I know she'll be before Him, in heaven.

23-03-2019 0800hrs. Saturday morning and the doors will open at 9. I am crushingly conscious of the fact it is but 25 hours since my tiny long suffering mum took her last breath. A drunken fall it would seem. Poor V---- The Prod having to wake up and find the poor misfortunate lifeless on the floor where she fell God love her. I don't quite know how I feel right now. I can list some of them though: sadness, guilt, shame, regret but over all of this is an overarching love for the kind soul from whom I was birthed. I also have something of the disbelief within me for I haven't quite fully taken in the magnitude of this, I am indeed in shock. I think it will be some time before I can fully accept I'll never see her again and some part of me preposterously believes it isn't true, that it's a mistake, that she'll yet wake up, that I'll get a call to say there's been a mistake, we're sorry, she's still here after all. I can't believe that I've been under lock and key for the deaths of both my parents. On the subject of falls though let me briefly regale a quick tale of my mum. Nine, maybe ten years ago I had used my key to let myself into her flat only to find the tiny cute little fucker on the floor of the living room with blood leaking from her head. I had shaken her, shitting meself.

"Mum, mum, for fuck sake, wake up you idiot".

"Ahhh son", she'd said, "ahhh son, are ya aaaallllroight son, ahhh it's good ta see ya son, what ya doin' here son"?

"For fuck sake mum, what the fuck ya doin' on the floor man? Why's there blood all in ya hair and that ya fuckin' wierdo"?

"It's aaaalllroight son sure it's not; have an ol' drink wid ya mudder wuld ya son"?

"Are you fuckin' mad or what woman"? and I pull her onto the sofa, "I'm phoning you an ambulance mum".

"Ahhh feck off wit ya foockin' ambulance ya eejit; I'm aaaalllroight son".

"I'm phoning one mum".

"Ya will in me shite", she says happily, "ambulance me balls, have an ol' drink son and sit down wid ya mudder".

"Mum, whether you like it or not ya goin' mate", I say, "'cause if you've done yourself a mischief and don't wake up in the morning 'cause I didn't get you there I'd not be able to live with myself".

"Feck off son wud ya now, ambulance me shite".

"It's happenin' mate so ya might as well just accept it weirdo".

"Ahhhh fuck off son wit ya bollix wud ya son I won't go so I won't so get us both an ol' beer out the fridge son wud ya son? It's not much ta ask is it son"? She was clearly flat out for she rarely drank at home.

"Oh mum oh mum", and I cuddle the tiny thing, claret caked in her hair God love her, "you're comin' ya cunt".

"Don't use dat filty word round me son".

"Sorry, but ya comin' mate and that's that. You're fuckin' infuriating sometimes mum".

"Did ya really phone an ambulance son"?

"Yes".

"Ahhhh feck off son. Cud we have an ol' drink first son"?

"No ya mug, you're fucked already. Behave for fuck sake mum".

"Ambulance me shite", she mutters moodily.

"That's the door", and I go and let the ambulance crew in and as soon as the highly inebriated little woman with the massive heart sees the them she's like a kid:

"Ahhhh, hello dere, wud ya like an ol' drink dere wud ya? Sit down me loves and me son'll get ya an ol' drink from the fridge", and the lady and gent paramedics smile indulgently and I say:

"Don't listen to her she's abslolutely plastered. Obviously you can see the blood but when I came in fifteen minutes ago she was on the floor passed out". I tell them her name.

"L----", says the lady of the two and me gorgeous mum with her innocent eyes and loving open face looks up and says to the young lady:

"Ahhhh, are ya aaaaaallllroight love"?

"L----", says the paramedic, "we think you should come with us because it looks like you've had a fall and we need to make sure you're ok".

"Ahhh bejasus love I'm o.k sure I am; get us an ol' beer an' a fag and oii'll be fine sure I won't now".

"Get up ya mug", I say and I gently pull the pissed up paddy to her feet.

"Feck off wud ya son, get us an ol' fag wud ya at least son"?

"Will ya get in the ambulance if I do"?

"Aaaalllroight then son". I get her a fag, she smokes it and away we go. We get to A&E at the Queen Elizabeth Queen Mother hospital Margate and as it's early hours it doesn't take long for the old girl to be checked out and be given the all clear.

"Can we go home and have an ol' drink now son"? says the incorrigible alcoholic lovely little lady.

"Yes of course, have you got some money for a taxi mum? I'm literally skint", and of course I am dear reader.

"Ahhh son, I've not got me ol' purse wit me", and I ask the reception if they can help but they tell us there's fuck all they can do, and of course they're not a taxi service. I've jumped so many taxis I can't be arsed tryna find one that will not make us pay up front and don't want the embarrassment in front of me mum so decide to walk the mile and a half home.

"We're walkin' mum come on", I say and the poor little thing gets up, taking me hand. We start our trek but the misfortunate is riddled with rheumatoid arthritis and we make slow painful progress so I get her to climb onto me back but she keeps jumping, well ,deliberately sliding off the mug.

"Ahhh son let me walk wud ya"? but she keeps sliding and falling and stumbling and I'm shitting meself that she's gonna fuck herself up:

"Fuck sake mum, let me carry ya".

"Ahhh feck off son wud ya, what d'ya think I am, an eejit"? and I can only hold her hand but when we get to the shortcut we must use, an ancient, potholed, spooky dark alleyway with woods one side and fields the other she keeps stumbling and stopping saying shit like:

"Ahh son the cliffs, cud ya help me over the cliff son", and I'm trying to pull her along, like to keep her upright and she won't budge, "we'll fall of da cliffs dere son".

"Mother", I say now, turning to face her, making sure I'm close enough that she can see my eyes in the dark, "mum, now you need to listen".....

"Ahhh feck off son wid ya serious shite wud ya now".

"Mum", I say, patience completely depleted, "you're gonna get back on my back now 'cause you're fuckin' driving me mad. You're gonna break ya neck on this shit ground mum. No more bollox, get on me back or only one of us might be getting out the alley mum 'cause I'll fuckin' do ya meself".

"Ahh son, what ya talking about son"?

"I'll fuckin' bury you here myself mum".

"Ya feckin' eejit, foock off wud ya son"?

"Get-on-my-fuckin'-back"!

"Foock off ya big dopey t'ing", but I crouch down and the tiny t'ing does as it's told! I piggy back the foul mouthed pissed paddy, who never, ever swears when sober, all the way home which was no mean feat and me and her have laughed over this many times since. And we had an ol' fag and a beer upon reaching her little palace too; she was incredibly houseproud me mum. Was. Can't quite believe I'm using that word re her. Both parents gone, I'm an orphan. I'm worried about J----, me sister. J----, me brother in Broadmoor. And P---- the professor, me other brother. Martyn is out cleaning the servery. I was mistaken too, it is afternoon unlock for us today. I am alone in this cell and feel quite sick. I'm fuckin' gutted. I've been a shit son and done fuck all but 'cause the little love pain. My mind is in turmoil with 'I might as well use drugs 'till I die' and 'honour your mother Andrew' and I'm oh so confused. Mum, mum, mum.

1443hrs. I'm forgoing the gym today. I'm in Brad's cell but was in Kempy and Pete Lanes' just five minutes ago. I described, upon their enquires, the circumstances, the little I know, surrounding me mum's passing. I then related the story I just told you so they could get an idea of her lifestyle though both these boys have met me mum anyway. She was always in the boozers and anyone who's anyone knew me mum. I have had so much support from staff but it is my peers who've surrounded and astounded me. Max, Adam, Brad, Marcus, Kyle, Pete, Ricky and Steve Lanes, Kempy, Pete W, J.T, Terry Hughes, Noel, Pony Tail Paul, Ginger Paul, 'H', Dale, Reece, Beany, Fiddler and Matchstick Model Maker Cabinet Maker Trev, Craig D and of course my little cell mate Martyn. My mind is manic. Rhianna is on the TV in the empty but for me cell now, singing about being the only girl in the world and I'm thinking, for some weird reason, that the same songs that used to play when she was alive are still playing now she's dead. I don't know why I think such ridiculous thoughts but I do. Now I'm thinking that writing such horrible stuff about Shamima Begum makes me not worthy of grief. Though I didn't go to the gym today I know I must keep going through the motions. I need to eat and drink and stay healthy. I need NA and prayer. I can't wait to get down work, the ATB Unit Monday where I can talk with Jason Gould who is unbelievably central to my keeping a semblance of sanity here in this insane place. I now muse on the fact I felt, I just felt me mum may not be there upon my release. I wish I'd've brought that fuckin' mother's day card and got it to her early. I feel floored, gutted, bereft of joy and empty, oh so empty. Smothered in grief. Oh mum. When I lay on my bed in the cell and doze off, that, dear reader, is the worst time for it is like an oppressive smothering cloud of grief upon me opening my eyes and realizing she is truly gone from here, fuckin' gone man. Oh, one more thing, Brad's spider also died, yesterday it was I think. But me, right now, midway upon the journey of my life, I find myself in a forest dark and the straightforward way, dear reader, seems lost to me right now. Life is but a walking shadow.

1810hrs and me and Smartyn have just had a couple of hands of blackjack. In the shower, praying to God whilst I washed, I said to Him 'fuck you' then quickly apologised for my blasphemy. I need to remember I am not the only one suffering in the world and that others are experiencing real horror. Floods in Mozambique, the monstrous ISIS murdering and maiming and terrorising across Iraq and the Levant. We sit, Martyn and I, and watch Despicable Me which even manages to elicit a laugh from my morose soul.

24-03-2019 1210hrs. Last night Craig D smashed up and robbed the fella next door to me and Mart. Russ is the fella's name and he is banged up with Jake from my manor. Craig robbed him for the spice he, Russ, sells. I lay in bed last night again cursing God for taking my mum. I feel fuckin' empty.

1730hrs. I went to the gym, going through the motions. Had a good workout to be fair.

25-03-2019 1200hrs and after going to the ATB Unit this morning I came back and talked to a drugs worker named Claire who runs a thing called Goals Group. I talked of my guilt and loss and shame and came out feeling better than when I went in. I am grateful that the obsession to use isn't on me right now and I continue to read the Basic Text of NA which has tales of people in recovery who've experienced loss like me and not picked up.

26-03-2019 and last night me and Martyn watched England beat Montenegro 5-1 and though the victory is great the small minded racism of the Montenegrans was offensive and needs to be stamped out in football somehow. Me and Martyn were marvelling that the names of the players on the Montenegrans' team always ends in 'ic' or 'vic'; 'Savic' and 'Stonovic' etc and we take the piss.
  "Here comes Dickovic", I would say.
  "To Domybitch", says Mart.
  "To Bumovic".
  "To Spottybitch".
  "Knobovic", I say, then "great pass to Fuckmybumovic", and then Martyn clocks a strange looking plaster on the back of one of our opponents player's necks and says:
  "Did you see that? Looked like a screwed in metal plate or something"! and indeed it did look odd.

"Maybe he's like not a real man", I reply, "ya know, like he's a robot or something, Frankensteinovic or Remotecontrolovic", and Martyn goes:

"Yeah, like a drone, like Dronavic", and for some reason me and him crease up at this and Martyn goes on, "oh no, the Montenegrans are making a substitution, are they, is it going to be, oh, yes, they have, they've only gone and brought on Dronavic"!

"And", I continue, taking up the baton, "who knows who has the remote control? Dronovic is excellent up front".

"It's Dronovic to Fuckmybitchovic to Grabmytitsovic", says Martyn and he I are chuckling away despite myself and he goes on, "now it's Platemyclitovic to Bigdickbetweenmytitsovic", and I take it up:

"And now it's Suckmydickovic to Pissflapsic and Massiveclitlikeadickovic but Dronavic fucks it up"! And, dear reader, it feels good to laugh. I guess I'm overcompensating a little but hey, it's forgivable. Anyway, today the staff at the ATB Unit, Jason, Rodd, Naomi, Lucy and Mr Highm got me a lovely card to say they're all thinking of me. I was so touched and felt overwhelmed that staff could care so much to see to it to do this. I can't express my gratitude despite my mastery with the pen. Last night, upon nearly dropping off I had a real moment of panic as I realized at a molecular level that I would never see my mum again here on Earth. It's like I felt something drop into my stomach, something savage that caused me to screw up my face in grief and experience an all encompassing smothering feeling, a gutted broken this can't be real minute of excruciating pain and loss like nothing I've ever known. I'm fuckin' wounded and this is so hard.

"I swear that creatine is making my hair fall out Martyn", I say now, noticing my thinning pate in the mirror.

"It's making me come out in spots", replies Mart, "and I reckon we get stronger without it anyway".

"No", I say, "it's proven to increase gains in bodybuilders and I've noticed big improvements in me Mart to be fair", and as I chat Martyn is putting clean bedding on his bunk bless him, "have a bit of the news won't we"? I say.

"Yeah", he says, "catch up with the old Meridian", meaning the local news of that name.

"I love seeing the local stories and many times I've seen someone I know on there after they've been weighed off (sentenced) in court".

"I've seen loads of my mates on the news and been on there myself for loads of burglaries man", says the little big man.

"For real"?

"Yeah man".

"Fuck me, I bet you were a right little fucker out there; a one man crime wave bro"!

"No comment", he says, smiling.

"No wonder you got so fuckin' long; when did you come away"?

"June 2018", he says.

"And when you out"?

"2022 August".

"So, pretty much, in total, you got eight years serve half"?

"Yep".

"Does it seem long to you"?

"Not really, it could be worse, I could be dead in a ditch somewhere the way I was moving out there man for drugs and shit", and he says this as he gets up from doing 50 press ups. He opens a tin of tuna, protein for his admittedly massive muscles.

"You gonna fill your menu sheet in"? says Mart who works on the servery of course.

"I'm actually gonna do it because I'm sick of getting noodles for lunch where I never fill it in man". If we don't we get standard veggie shit and I'm always lazy round this.

"Don't forget then".

"I'll do it now", I say. In other news, my lovable rogue of a pal, Tony Giles, who was kicked off the wing some time ago is coming back. I had pleaded with Ms Harding to let him return here with us lot whom he has grown up with and the lovely lady, it would seem, has acquiesced to my request. Although Tony is staunch as fuck and had no trouble on B wing, notoriously the most violent in the jail, he knows he's far better off over here with us lot. Me, Marcus, Rick, Steve and Pete Lanes, Kempy and Brad have known the cunt forever and despite Tony's miserable demeanour and moody countenance a smile from the lovable prick makes my day. But he is a grouchy cunt of the highest order. Although, saying that, we all, us Thanet lot, have massive character defects but I love each and every one of those boys. The care and kindness I have received from this clutch of cunts is humbling and remarkable. Bless them all; I've probably cunted each and every one of them off throughout the narrative somewhere but that's more a reflection of my defects than theirs. Anyway, Tony told us today that a geezer on 'B' wing got stabbed four times and yesterday on the same wing someone burnt a cell out. Another one of our lot, on here yesterday, Kirk H, a lunatic six foot guy from Margate has succumbed to serious spice psychosis and has been taken from Rochester to Elmley Prison and the hospital unit there. His mental health deteriorated drastically and he was shouting obscenities aggressively to himslf whilst self harming and babbling bollocks basically.

"What ya writing"? says Mart now and I read the last page or two and he loves it.

"How the fuck d'ya write like that"? he says.

"We all have gifts Martyn, it is just a matter of finding them out. I always knew how to write man, no one taught me".

"Mine's operating cars and motorbikes", he says.

"Yeah", I say, "even though I have a driving license I'm a shit driver to be honest. As for bikes, my ex bird had an Aprillia Shiver 750 V-Twin on a 15 plate but when she offered me a go I shat meself and went out on her KTM 350 Freeride instead. It was road legal though it was a tracker".

"Fuck that", says Mart, "I'd've had the Aprillia up on the back wheel man, I love that shit".

"What, like, could you really throw a bike like that around Mart"?

"Yeah man, love that shit; the biggest bike I rode is a GSXR 1000".

"Could you sling it about"?

"More like it threw me around 'till I got used to it but once I did get used to it I had it up on the back wheel a few times but it had so much power I had to respect it".

"Coffin on wheels me grandad used to say", I say.

"I had a KTM 450 EXC when I was thirteen and kick starting it was well hard when I was that young".

"Did you used to throw that about"?

"Yeah, even with two mates on the back", he says, "it was so big I couldn't even touch the floor and it was well powerful. I could get 110, 120 out of it"! Martyn turns to the telly and says: "I love these war films", and on the TV a load of Americans are blowing the fuck out of something, looking all sexy in army fatigues.

"Me too", I say, "this is about the Bosnian Serb war".

"When was this"? asks Smartyn.

"End of the nineties", I tell him, "it was horrific, I nearly had a nervous breakdown because I couldn't believe we were seeing ethnic cleansing in Europe in the modern era. It really fucked me up Mart".

"What d'ya mean"?

"Well", I say, not that sure of the facts but just aware of the mass murder of civilians at the period in that place, "the Serbians were killing men, women and children in the former Yugoslavia, like Albanian people, trying to completely wipe them out and putting them in like mass great big graves where thousands and thousands of 'em were just buried together. It was awful man".

"No way, what, like, in the 1990s"? says Mart.

368

"Yeah man it was brutal bro", I tell him, "some of the stories on the news nearly tipped me over the edge man", and it is indeed true. Then, dear reader, after the 9/11 attacks I was watching the assault on Fallujah by the Allies in Iraq where James Wood, a British journalist, was bedded in to broadcast the campaign for media. He was telling a tale on the news of an American Marine Sargeant whose boys were under sniper fire where they were on a roof and and the Sarg got all his boys off of it but upon pulling the last of them to safety he himself was shot through the head, being killed instantly and for some reason this has stuck with me, this gallant heroism. It, too, fucked me up. So much for my ability to rip out throats in secret psychotic soldiering. Still, as I say, most Brits are a bag of contradictions. Undoubtably there is a fuckin' lunatic imbedded within me; however, there is also a kind loving soul fighting to get the sustanence he needs. The one who wins will be the one I choose to feed.

27-03-2019 0800hrs and I'm in Brad's and he himself is singing happily but complaining at the same time that:

"I put ten pairs of socks in with my washing and that fuckin' Sat-Nam brought my washing back with not one fuckin' pair in the bag the twat. And I fuckin' paid him a shot of spice to do it", and he bustles about the cell, sprucing here and tidying there before putting on the kettle for a cuppa. Brad's cell, despite the madness and drama that goes on here, is a sanctuary for me. He himself has such serenity about his energy that I enjoy his company very much; he rarely gets angry and is always quick to laughter. On the subject of me, well, I have come out in some sort of fuckin' coldsore on me face. My gums feel like they're rotting and I can now feel a protrusion on the underside of my top lip which worries me. The recent savage loss in my life is ravaging me. Brad's back in the cell after a sojourn:

"When I went down there Sat said 'oh, you forgot something last night' and I said 'no, you forgot to put my socks in Sat' but no worries man, he's alright and I've got me socks back", and he's smiling as he pulls on a fresh pair. Brad now looks at the whatever it is in my mouth, smiles, pouts tryna look intelligent then laughs and says:

"Do you know what they call a person who keeps and breeds lizards"?

"No", I say, picking up on the cunt's infectious smile and doing the same despite myself.

"A 'herpetologist'", and he continues, "and it's also the word for people that collect herpes spores on various parts of the body", and I laugh at the smiling assassin.

"Cunt", I say, "I'm falling apart Brad".

"It's just stress man, the shock of the loss of ya mum me ol' mate".

"I was laying there last night thinking I've got some sort of flesh eating cancer or something".

"Naaa, you'd know about it if that was the case Sloaney", says Brad, continuing, "I have a hard lump by the side of my left nipple but it's so fuckin' painful even though it's tiny. I'm frightened of showing the doctor so I just think, fuck it, I'll wait and see how it develops".

"You should go really Brad, just in case", and now we are watching Mary Berry scout around Rome for delicacies the posh old cow. Brad loves anything to do with cooking. Oh, Brad's mouse escaped, his new one, chewed right through the plastic tubing to freedom.

0938hrs. At work where I quickly mop and hoover and tidy and dust and clean in effort of eradicating, briefly, the darkness that pervades me right now, the bleak clouds that follow me can be forgotten transiently when I'm engaged in activity, no matter how mundane. After I blitz the already spotless toilets I go into Lucy's office and she's up on her chair, on her kness, talking at the window and I look at her lovely bum angled out doggy style but avert my eyes and fuck off lest I lech lasciviously at this lady I've come to respect. Doesn't feel right for me to be spying behind her like a voyeur, and that, dear reader, is a euphemism indeed! I wait 'till I hear her say her goodbyes to the screw she was chatting with at the window and return to ask:

"Could you google the word 'herpetologist' please Lucy 'cause Brad, noticing the scales on my face told me that a herpetologist is a person who collects lizards and reptiles but that it's also a term for those showing visible signs of the herpes virus. I can't believe he's right about the lizard thing".

"'herpetologist'", Lucy mouths aloud as she types the word into the king of search engines before continuing that, "yep", and she quotes, "'a herpetologist is someone involved in the care of reptiles and lizards' so yeah, he's right it would seem".

"Can't believe he's right! There's nothing that knob don't know about the natural world man", and now there's a knock at the unit door and it's another prisoner come to inquire about the next resolve course.

"We haven't got another resolve course running 'till January", says Lucy.

"January"! says the guy in exasperation, "that's no bloody good, I'm out in December".

"Sorry mate", says the worthy woman.

"Ok", says the guy going away amicably but clearly disappointed. And herein lay a real issue. If the programmes team here had more staff and resources to run more courses much more could be done to reduce reoffending rates. This course is specifically designed for perpetrators of violent crimes and addresses many prisoners in for dometic abuse offending. Many, many on the landings today are in for such offences as I myself have been. This course, run alongside addiction programmes helps break the cycles by changing attitudes and beliefs and resolve is a proven to produce results course. Two women a week are killed in domestic incidents in this country so austerity measures removing resources and reducing the number of courses available per annum is ridiculous, counter intuitive and downright dangerous. A little spending in these areas not only saves misery, pain and lives but also, in the long term, money that would be otherwise spent on putting people before the courts and all the enforcement that comes before that stage. Let alone the healthcare costs of patching the 'lucky', i.e, those that survive domestic abuse, up.

1700hrs. This morning I was down the ATB Unit as you know and whilst there two lads, identical twins by the name of Jamie and Kevin O'Niel came in for programme related interviews. Casually dressed, bearded in the modern style, handsome and amicable I thought to myself 'here's a couple of interesting fuckers' and because Lucy can only interview one at a time I was left with Kevin whilst his twin was processed. Now Kevin described to me the journey they'd had on their sentence for GBH (Grievous Bodily Harm) starting in Elmley, like me, before coming to Rochester. Kevin told me a tale about scum cunt prisoners stealing his and Jamie's clothes whilst they were out their cell one day in Elmley. Even whilst Kevin was talking I was thinking that I wish I had a Dictaphone but all I can do is try to relate the tale best I can from the scrappy notes I took as he talked. You may, dear reader, enjoy it and also get an idea what normally decent mild mannered not looking for trouble people have to go through upon entering our penal estate. Don't get me wrong, these boys are no cunts; they'll fight if they have to but only when forced. So, one day these two boys are at work at the tea bag packing shop in Elmley and whilst there some spice head wrongen tricks a screw into opening their cell door where the cell thieving slags promptly steal all the chaps lovely designer garms. These twins are quite close to two brothers on the wing, Jay and Jack. Anyway, with support from these and more friends they go about the wing, upon their return and discovery of the theft, tooled up, investigating suspect cells with suspect junkie occupants. They have no luck but the screws clock them and perceive the violent intent probably via some grass cunt and the twins find themselves subject to violence reduction measures, being watched for trouble. Jamie gives a list of items lost to a few close friends so they can keep a look for anyone seen busting (wearing) their bits. Anyway, the matter sort of blows over for five weeks and a new drug dealer with pages of power spice paper by the name of Junior appears on the wing and the twins build a rapport with him. With spice, Junior buys some clothes and not wanting to lose them in a cell spin he offloads them to someone else to look after and the person in question is a friend of the twins. The friend, having the list, notices that some of the clothes look like those described so calls Jamie down and says:

"Is this your tracksuit mate", holding up the pieces.

"Yeah man, where the fuck ya get that"?

"Junior asked me to look after it, he got it off of Jay", (brother of Jack). Immediately the twins set about seeing the brothers, well, it was Jay initially and ask:

"You sold some of my shit for spice to Junior mate, how the fuck is that and where did you get it"?

"I got it from another spur", (wing) says Jay.

"Did you get anymore"?

"Naa man honestly lads I didn't".

"Ok 'cause we're gonna go find out", and the lads go to Junior and ask if he's anymore items and he proceeds to pull out the best part of all the bits they lost confirming they'd indeed come from the brothers. Junior, being a good sort, gives the bits back and Jamie starts taking their clothes back to the cell when someone tells him:

"Your brother's smashing someone up in Matty Green's cell", and when he goes down he sees Jay deservedly smashed up and in a puddle of his own blood, inflicted by Kev's righteous hand. That one dealt with, when Jack, the other brother returns to the wing Jamie wastes no time telling the cunt:

"You've got to have it ya mug: me or me brother"?

"Please don't do me", the cunt says, "I'm sorry man I really am", and the slag actually starts crying the prick junky no moral cunt and even as I write that here in Oxford I acknowledge that on drugs I too am capable of this sort of behaviour and more. I am only ever one pipe or hit or drink away from insanity. Anyway, the boys leave the thief for now as screws are noticing the accumulation of nosey interested prisoners outside the cell. Another friend of the twins, John O'Shea says to them:

"Come on, I know someone else who was involved, that little mug called Squirrel upstairs".

"Come on then", say the twins and the three of them go up the stairs and bump into a fella called Sticks on the way.

"Where you lot goin'? What you up to"?

"Tryna find Squirrel the little mug 'cause he was the cunt who tricked the screws into opening our door so the brothers could rob us when we were at work".

"Ahhh lads, please, look, the little cunt is my dosser, my joey like, ya know, me fragal who cleans my cell and does my dirty work and that. Can we just go and give him a little slap so he don't go off the wing"? and the boys agree. The now four go find the fragal and corner him in a cell.

"Right", says one of the twins, "we know what you fuckin' did, stealing our shit bro so you've got to take a slap from me and me brother but first say thanks to Sticks for stopping you getting proper smashed up you muggy little cunt".

"Thanks Sticks, sorry Kev, sorry Jamie", says the wheedling weakling. Kev tells him to:

"Stand still and don't fuckin' move or cover up ya little mug", but the wrongen does, flinches until Jamie says:

"If you move again we're both gonna proper do ya", and Kev lands a slap on him but Jamie, not satisfied, punched him in the face splitting his eye open. Kev then says to Squirrel, whose lip was literally quivering:

"Say thanks to Sticks again Squirrel", and I have to confess that as I type from the handwritten I feel for Squirrel right now. Once he does as asked Jamie says:

"Now fuck off ya little prick". John then says:

"Let's go get that other cunt now; Jack", and they make their way down the stairs but on route bump into Junior who tells them:

"No need lads, I put a page on his and Malia's (another co conspirator in the theft) head".

"Bless mate", said the boys and the next they knew two people came and told them:

"It's done", and indeed it transpired both were at that very moment nursing serious head injuries inflicted by a couple lunatic spiceheads who, when using, like me, will do anything for a fix. And that, dear reader, is that.

29-03-2019 1900hrs. Didn't put pen to paper yesterday; no particular reason bar laziness and despondency. Phoned J----, my sister today and she informed me that our lovely mum, as I requested, would be buried not cremated and that the funeral is to be the 18th of next month. I'm pleased J---- opted and agreed with me that burial is best for I will have somewhere to sit and talk to me mum when I need to. I suspect, should God decide to see to it that I get out of jail alive, that I'll be spending a lot of time at her graveside in contemplation and conversation. Anyway, when I phoned my sis for a second time she was crying her eyes out in the vets because now mum's gone her cat has gotten ill very quickly with what I suspect is a broken heart and has to be put down. She wants to be with me mum. Me? Well, I spent an hour down the ATB Unit then did a mental circuit with 'H' and Smartyn. Marcus didn't come; his girlfriend Lauren leaving him has left him bereft of spirit and energy. Anyway, I returned to the wing for lunchtime bang up, napped, got unlocked, got canteen for it is Friday and then went and played volleyball down the gym where I'd set up my bed if I could. I get great relief and release in exercise. I can't be fucked to write so that's it for the night. Love people. Oh, and I'm 74 or 75 days clean.

30-03-2019 0830hrs. Saturday morning and me and Smartyn are getting some washing together for Sat-Nam to do because Mart got given some spice so we can get some perks in like coffee and milk and sweets and hair cuts and extra washes without spending canteen funds. Also, I'll give my pal Marcus his due, bless him, for he said that if I need spice for stuff I only need come ask him. I love that fuckin' guy. The poor fucker is really struggling coming to terms with the fact his lovely lady, stolen from the landings, has gone and got herself a new fella. Marcus told me that what concerns him most is whether or not the new guy is someone we all know. Were it the case then Marcus could well end up resorting to acts of extreme violence; I know him well enough to know this could well be the outcome should he feel betrayed by a friend. When Lauren told him on the phone that she'd moved on, Marcus immediately set about smashing fuck out his cell. He also told Lauren that should it be the case Marcus knows the fella she can count on him letting loose with a carving knife. Anyway, Lizzo is singing her pisstake 'Juice' on 4Music and me and the one like the Smartyn love it. Martyn turns off the TV and puts a Giggs CD on and we rap along to deep dark rap. I'm struggling to enjoy writing today, forgive me.

02-04-2019 1700hrs. As you can see from the date, it's three days since I put pen to paper. I'm struggling to want to write. But I owe you a brief synopsis of events these three days passed. First, bully Craig D again let loose with his fists, smashing up his cellmate Reece, yes, little Manc hyper Reece, poor little cunt. The bully slag broke three of his ribs, splut a cut over the right eye and broke a cheekbone. This infuriates me. I am disappointed with Craig. He can be ok but I would never, ever bang up with him because I'd kill the cunt. I've always been a good bully leveller. Marcus is finding things very hard since the loss of Lauren. Smells Like Teen Spirit comes on the radio and I muse on the fact I have to write a speech for me mum's funeral. I digress. Peter Lanes had a proper spice seizure last night; Kempy, his cellmate, had to smash him up for Pete was attacking Kemps and after Kempy calmed him down Peter suddenly flopped on the floor and after having some sort of fit he suddenly stopped breathing so Kempy had no choice but to get on the cell bell. He omitted telling the health care team that attended that Pete had smoked spice through fear of both of them facing punative action. Steve Lanes, Rick's son and Pete's nephew has done himself a mischief in the gym and rolls round the wing in a wheelchair presently. Paul Stone has been caught stealing from his cellmate, little blond Frank and upon returning to the cell they shared tonight found his stuff thrown outside by a fuming, justifiably so, Frank. Tony Giles, my moody beloved friend has moved in with Jay Beany and both have been absolutely out their cannisters on spice ever since. Me, Martyn and 'H' have been smashing the gym. And, finally, I have been talking to Tan on Marcus's mobile most days. That's all I have dear reader.

04-04-2019. 1815hrs. My dreams are full of death at the moment. Twice last night I awoke, hyperventilating and lathered in sweat. The first dream was of a lion that had run down a gazelle. Once the gazelle was on the floor the lion took a chunk from just beneath its eye and I awoke when jets of blood started squirting rhythmically from the arterial wound. I was so scared but can't quite fathom why this would frighten me so much as it did in my dream state. The second dream causing me such deep dark terror is a little easier to understand with its ability to incite fear in me for it was indeed horrific. So, I'm in some sort of prison yard in the dream bouncing a ball from the back wall. I know it is a prison yard because there's netting across the top and razor wire everywhere. So, I'm bouncing this like clown coloured ball off the wall when a pretty late twenties early thirties blonde comes onto the yard through a door with frosted glass in it. She comes on and sits in a large leather chair. She takes absolutely no notice of me but I am utterly transfixed with her. From a bag on her lap she removes a scalpel and plunges it straight into her neck. Somehow she works it round, up, round and down again, cutting off her face which literally slides off of the bone but she catches it. Then she turns to me, whom she'd hitherto completely ignored and looks into my soul with the most malevolent eyes I'd ever seen and I feel a rush of pure terror run right through me. I know she's coming for me so I set my step toward the frosted panel door and hear her steps behind me, tap tap getting quicker tap tap tap but I get through the door and slam it closed, thinking I'm safe. I stand a few feet from the door and see her form approaching the glass so I run to the door to try hold up the handle and I'm screaming 'nooooo' but she's stronger and the handle is moving inexorably downward and I wake, actually, literally, crying. As I sit here now I wonder if my mother's death has brought about these dreams. But then I ruminate I've been having the likes of these for like ever. As I write, right now, Martyn, from the top bunk, passes down a leather wristband with a steel plate on it and engraved on that are the words 'together we make a difference'.

"What's this"? I ask, fingering the not unpleasant thing.

"Mum gave it to me today on the visit".

"Bless ya", I say, "were they both in good spirits and glad to see you looking so well"?

"Yeah", he says, "last time they see me I was proper fucked up still coming off the crack and smoking loads of spice so all I wanted from them was money and it really upset them".

"So I bet they weren't only surprised at how healthy you look but also at the way you were with them too".

"Yeah man, they said that. That I not only look different but sound different too. They were proper glad to see me man".

"How did your fit sexy sister look"? I can't help but ask.

"After the visit", Martyn says, "a screw, a young black haired geezer, came up to me and said 'is that your bird' and I said 'naa man that's my mum and my sister'". Martyn's half sibling is an absolutely stunning light skinned nineteen year old sort. Martyn says the screw looked a bit stumped, sheepish I dare say.

"If you'd have said 'yep, me bird guv' you can bet your bottom dollar he'd've said 'done well for yourself there mate'", and Martyn laughs.

"Yeah, probably", he says and he tells me that on the visit his sister was weasring the newest I Watch and that he asked her for it, in the hope of being in the same situation as Marcus with his illicit mobile.

"What did she say"?

"You can't have it 'cause it comes on the contract with my phone".

"What", I say, "can you use 'em without the phone being near 'em then"?

"Yeah man, course ya can".

"If she'd've give you it you could've ended up with another two years if you got caught with it".

"I know", he says, looking out our window onto the yard, "quick, quick, come and have a look at the size of this rat", and I go to the window and indeed there is a fuck off fat rat the size of a small fuckin' cat.

"No fuckin' way", I say, "the size a that cunt"!

"Never seen anything like it", says Mart.

376

"Oh my days", I say spotting another one, "did you see that cunt come up out the drain in the middle Mart"?

"Look over there, look, look toward the gate", and under the small gap beneath the gate a skinny fox has slipped into the yard.

"Oh my days", I say, "he's actually following that fat fuck off rat with his eyes", and we are both watching as the skinny but handsome fox looks forlornly at the rat he's no chance of catching and making a meal of. This is the first time I've seen these critters. The last cell, the one I occupied for the best part of a year, looked out over E wing whereas this one looks out over our very own A wing yard. I love the handsome fox but not the rats so much though I'd still like the chance to grab one for Brad, who'd no doubt love and nurture such a prize the weirdo. Mart is still at the window and I ask:

"What ya waitin' for"?

"The fox has gone but the rats just slipped down the big drain in the middle"!

"You know that cunt in the wheelchair who everyone says is a rapist"? I say now.

"Yeah", says Martyn, "I've heard that too". Now remember dear reader that though rats are ok on the yard, we don't like 'em on the fuckin' landing.

"Well, that cunt, so I've heard, puts food under the door at the end of the landin', ya know the door by cell 116 right at the end 'cause it's got a massive gap underneath it".

"He does, there's always like food all lined up under it before bang up", says Mart, now playing Mario on a little electronic device as we listen to deep dark rap on the big new stereo Martyn brought for eight cans of mackeral from another wing. The fella he got it off is his friend, selling it so cheaply because he is to be imminently released. The thing proper pumps and has the beds vibrating with bass. Mart was able to get it by taking the food trolley down to the kitchens (servery worker job) to collect the food and stuffing the stereo into one of the roomy compartments then happily wheeling his prize back to the wing. I now stand and read the last page to him and watch as his handsome young face creases into a smile of pure pleasure and he actually laughs out loud before saying:

"That's fuckin' sick man"! and I can't describe the satisfaction I get from seeing the approval and enjoyment in him and he continues, "you couldn't describe it better man", and I say:

"See, it's all very normal to me and you Mart but the public will fuckin' love it mate".

"It's like the little mad things we get up to init"?

"Like you casually bowling down with a trolley and secretely stuffing a fuckin' humungous stereo in it along with the dinner you funny cunt"!

"It's wicked though the stereo in it"?

"It's the nuts"!

"Game a cards"?

"Why not"? and so I'll sign off dear reader.

2045hrs. Just phoned J----. She sounded really tired but is holding up.

05-04-2019 1700hrs. Just been banged up on a Black Eye Friday. No beatings I know of to be fair but I've not been around much today. I was at work at ATB from 0830 to 1000hrs, then I did a circuit before going back to the unit. After lunch I get my own canteen then trot back to the gym for volleyball with Marcus, Kempy, 'H', Gibbo and Ricky Lanes, bashing the ball about for an hour. Now me and Mart are sitting listening to Radio 1 Extra and Steflon Don's Got A New Girlfriend. Now Rhianna is Work Work Working and I'm thinking she's a sexy fucker. Oh, other news, sexy CM Ms Harding has now gone to be CM of the Segregation Unit and has been replaced by Ms Saunders who is already filling the wing with terror with her proactive approach to her new role. Her enthusiasm will somewhat wane I dare say as she comes to accept that the only way that the problems inherent on 'A' wing can only be solutioned is if there are fundamental changes to the allocation of funds at an operational level. Putting prisoners on 'Basic Regime', running around the wing complaining to veteran 'A' wing staff that she can smell spice everywhere and noticing people collecting vapes in with ideas of actioning punative measures against them is all well and good but moving people off the wing will not solve the issue. Maybe I'll be pleasantly surprised but Ms Harding is a bloody good CM and she did her best on here. She saw many people get into active recovery and I reckon Ms Saunders would do well if she could replicate her efforts. I mean, both me and Martyn, both hardcore addicts were both caught up heavily in the spice culture yet I'm 80 days clean and Mart has 116 under his belt. And I mean, we are proper clean, not like some who think they are yet still use pregabs and mirtazapine yet claim recovery. We use nothing. And that is no mean feat in this environment.

"This is Amber's dog", says Martyn now, showing me a photo. He shows me other pictures, one of a pretty little thing.

"Who's that"? I ask, giving the girl a thorough perusal.

"Her name's Sarah", says Mart, "mate of mine, proper little hottie ain't she"?

"How old is she"?

"Seventeen", he says, and I avert my eyes in mock disgust!

"Take it away, I can't look at that bro"!

"She fucks bare forty year old geezers man"!

"Still", I say, "I feel noncy looking at her", and Martyn laughs.

"I've known her since she was a kid, thinks she's proper bad she does".

"What, is she your girl's best mate"? I say this for she is in other pictures with Amber.

"Yeah, they're going on holiday together".

"Where they goin'""?

"Turkey", he says, "when I spoke to her on the phone today she said she's just bought a new swimsuit and I told her I want a picture of her wearing it".

"You really miss her don't ya mate"?

"I do", he says, "she said when she comes back off holiday she's gonna come up and see me".

"What you've got to understand Mart is that to a 24 year old bird the sentence you got seems like a fuckin' long time bro".

"When I got back to jail from court after getting sentenced I phoned her and when I told her how long I got and that I wouldn't be getting out for a fuckin' long time she proper broke down". Martyn got weighed off in 2018 and has to serve half of the eight years. As I say, four years is a lifetime to a young girl. Saying that, she clearly loves him for I hear them talk on the phone. In other news, my sister managed to get hold of my brother who is currently holidaying in Argentina to tell him the tragic news. I spoke to my niece S---- on the phone last night; she's a funny pretty little thing of eleven years.

"I'm sorry I haven't seen you for so long S---- and I'm sorry I've been so selfish".

"You've been very selfish and very naughty", she said.

"I know, but I won't be selfish any more I promise".

"Yeah, I hope so", she says, "you need to be good now".

"I know", I say, somewhat sheepishly, "do you remember", I said, changing the subject, "when I used to babysit for you and as soon as your mum left the house you and your brother C---- would proper play me up"?

"Hahaha", she laughs, "we used to proper beat you up didn't we"?

"You did", I say, "as soon as your mum left you used to attack me straight away".

"You used to be naughty too", she says.

"Only to try and be fun but I remember one time your mum said 'don't let 'em in my room' and soon as she went you shot straight

379

upstairs and started spraying her expensive perfumes and using her make up and when she got back the room was like a bomb had hit it".

"It was good fun though and you are a rubbish adult"!

"I used to have to blackmail you both with money just to get you to go to bed but you took my money and still didn't go to bed! I do miss you though".

"I miss you too; do you promise to be good when you get out"?

"I do S----, I do. Do you promise to still be a pretty little princess"?

"Yeah".

"Deal then, put your mum on and I'll see you soon".

"Bye Andrew".

"Bye Sienna", and J---- comes back on the line.

"Fuckin' heartbreakin'", I say.

"Long as you do the right thing now Andrew you'll have us all back in your life".

"I know, and for that I thank God J----".

"We all love you Andy".

"I love you too". Difficult this stuff, families. Me and Martyn play cards for sit ups.

1930hrs and we end up doing 200 sit ups each.

"That circuit was sick this morning weren't it Smartyn"?

"It was", he replies in this cell this evening, "did you see me run to the toilet about five minutes after we stopped"?

"No, why"?

"Had to throw up in it, proper like acid reflux, I couldn't breathe".

"It fucked me up too; I think the hardest bit was after doing the reps, runnin' around the hall three times with that fifteen kilo weight on ya back man, that was a fuckin' killer bro".

"Yeah, and them ball slams were bollox weren't they"?

"Ahhh mate, they were making me feel fuckin' sick too, for real", and as I write 'for real' I think of an ex of mine called Emma W, a girl I fell in love with and whom I knew from school. She is still a hottie and we are still friends. She used to use 'for real' as a question.

"Fuck me, you're a sexy fucker", I would say and she would respond:

"What, for real"? Ahh, Emma, wouldn't mind bouncing about with you right about now. The pumping music in the cell has the bed frame vibrating and the circuit has my muscles aching; particularly those at the small of my back. It was mental with burpees, curls, press ups, squat thrusts, tuck jumps, and many more testing terrors. Between sets we'd run round the gym as usual. I fuckin' love it to be fair.

"I'm going to do cardio tomorrow, proper sweat it out", says Mart as he peruses a victim empathy in cell work pack which his Offender Manager gave him.

"If you need help doing that Mart, don't be afraid to ask", I say and if I haven't told you the last exercise in the pack listed crimes from shoplifting to graffiti to burglary and asked Mart to specify who he thought would be affected by such crimes. Obviously with burglary it's the victims but also taxpayers because the police are of course publicly funded as are the courts and probation etc. And graffiti, a thing many of us would view as victimless is of course also a crime for which the local authority are responsible for cleaning and that is of course also publicly funded. Shoplifting, well, the shops have to put up prices to cover their losses affecting the public and of course enforcement here, again, is paid for publicly. There really is no such thing as a victimless crime. The part now is about 'self disclosure' and is asking him how he feels about his crimes, how he thinks his crimes affected his victims, how he felt about his behaviour then and how he feels now. Before he saw this pack I dare say, being so young, he'd never really given it much thought. Me either for that matter though I have known right from wrong for many years but, as with him, when I do drugs I turn, literally, insane. The pack really forces the respondent to look deeply into the feelings of the victims of crime. It is along the same lines as 'restorative justice' which brings offenders and victims together and has proven extremely effective in impacting the perpetrator. A friend of ours recently went through the process. He'd burgled a small, privately owned shop.

"I thought nothing of it Sloaney", he'd said, "but when the old couple who owned the shop visited me and told me they had no insurance and that they didn't even feel, after the burglary, that it was worth getting out of bed in the morning I was so gutted for 'em and it still makes me feel sick to this day when I think about them, the poor cunts", and I tell you dear reader the pain was written all over his face. He'd had a profound, almost spiritual experience meeting this poor old couple. Anyway, I have just phoned my sister again. Today she said she has been cleaning and packing all the stuff from my mum's little flat. She said she found like fifty hats, all with various broaches and pins in and it brought my sister to tears. She also said she found the five or six cards I'd gotten my mum beneath the bed and I can't expain how heart wrenchingly sad this is to me. How I wish I had never missed a mother's day. How I wish I had not presumed I'd all the time in the world.

"You know alcohol has much of the blame in this sad story don't you J----"? I said tonight.

"Oh, without a doubt", she said, "I'm a little bit upset with V---- (the boyfriend) 'cause she was tryna stop Andy".

"Oh J----, it ain't his fault", I say, "even though I never particularly liked the geezer he, even if he could of stopped himself, wouldn't have been able to stop her drinking. She was an alcoholic".

"I know, I'm just absolutely gutted Andy".

"I know right. I feel absolutely sick as a pig man. I still expect you to phone the jail saying there's been a mistake".

"I wish I could". And, dear reader, so do I.

07-04-2019 1730hrs. I put an application in today but wrote Kempy's name and number and cell location stating, obviously as if the app were from Kempy himself: 'me and my cellmate Peter Lanes have been having a relationship but want to take it to the next level. We want to be safe so was wondering if we could have some prison issue condoms please. Also, I have piles which could be painful during sex so if possible could I also have some Anusol cream as well please. I have severe anal bleeding so would be very grateful, signed, Steve Kemp'. Even as I was filling the application in I was sniggering and laughing to myself at the idea of Kempy getting the app back but when I sneakily chucked it into the office, ya know, putting me arm round the door it wasn't long before the lovely Ms Hulbert was calling over the intercom 'Sloane, Andrew Sloane to the office please' and when I went down the pukka little officer was chuckling, mirth written all over her face.

"We know this is you Sloaney".

"What'd'ya mean"?

"This app for, what is it, Anusol cream and condoms for Kempy-I know your handwriting Sloaney".

"Please help me with it though Miss", I implore her.

"What d'ya want me to do"?

"Just write in the reply bit 'will put you down to see healthcare ASAP' and I'll just put a moody signature on it Ms so he thinks it's a genuine reply".

"Ok, but can you promise me I won't get in trouble"?

"Ms, Kempy's good as gold and neither of us, any of us Thanet boys would let you get in trouble".

"Ok then", and she fills it in. I run the app upstairs where Kempy and Peter are sitting watching Breaking Bad and just slip it under the door. I wait five minutes before going in to sit with them but the pair of cunts are on me.

"We know it's you Sloaney ya cunt", says Pete.

"What you on about"? but Kempy is laughing his nut off.

"You fuckin' knob", he says, "have the staff actually seen it"?

"What the fuck you on about bro"?

"Fuckin' condoms and Anusol; what the fuck even is that"?

"It's for piles and that", I say, "let's have a look at that app", but even as I read it out I can't help laughing at my own humour and these two cunts are creasing too.

"Who filled in the bottom"? Kempy asks.

"Ms H", I say.

"I'm gonna go see her and ask her how long 'till healthcare see me for my Anusol an that".

"She's a proper laugh she is that lovely little thing", says Pete.

"She is man she's cool", says Kempy, "I'm going down there now".

"Make sure she's alone though Kempy 'cause she worries don't she".

"I will", and he does. He comes back.

"She just laughed man but she said she wanted the app back 'cause it had her handwriting on and she didn't want to get in trouble so I gave it to her".

"She's quality", I say, "you can proper tell she's been brought up in a loving home man, there ain't a bad bone in her body".

"You sound like ya fallin' in love ya cunt", says Pete.

"If I was thirty two not forty two I probably would tell her that she's a bit of me but she's twenty six so I'm behaving. Anyway, she's got every cunt on the wing thinking that they've got feelings for her. She's pretty professional now though. She ain't no mug".

"I know, I saw her telling that Stuart the other day, 'cause he brushed her hair, like playing with her hair and she told him to keep his fuckin' hands off of her", says Pete.

"Fuckin' right an' all", I say, "cunts thinking they can put their fuckin' hands on her; looking is one thing but no one has the right to put hands on the women who work here".

"If I'd've seen that", says Just For Men, "I'd've fuckin' told him too, banter is one thing, but touching the women another, they need to feel safe".

"Don't get me wrong", I have to say, "if she asked me to touch her that'd be a whole different ball game".

"She is fuckin' fit", says Kempy, "lovely little bum on her".

"You two are a proper pesty pair a cunts", says Pete.

"What, so you wouldn't then"? asks Kempster.

"Well, yeah, course I would yeah"!

"Shut up then", says Kempy, "we're just saying what you think".

"What everyone thinks", I say. And, dear reader, it isn't just the sex we miss but the intimacy of human touch. Surrounded by people we are nonetheless lonely in here.

08-04-2019 1720hrs. Fredo on radio. Gangster shit. Today has been pleasant enough. Smashed the gym. I'm looking and feeling buff right now. I'm currently playing Black Jack with Mart and after regaling my day down the ATB Unit with Jason, Naomi and the gorgeous Lucy I say to him that:
"I've got feelings for every beautiful female in the prison man".
"Yeah yeah", he replies.
"What d'ya mean"?
"You've only got feelings for their vaginas", says he.
"I'm not that shallow"! I say in mock outrage.
"That's what you say", he says, "but that one you work with is fuckin' fit though don't ya think"?
"Who, Lucy"?
"Yeah man, she's sexy".
"Proper", I say, "ready for more cards"? We play and Martyn brings it back to 3-3. Then 4-3 to me. I end up winning five three.
"You hate it, you can't get near me"!
"It's all a learning curve", he says.
"Can't believe I've got 83 clean days under me belt Mart man; just a few months ago I was smoking that spice. How many days are you clean now"?
"119 man and I can't believe it either".
"What films we got on tonight Smartyn"?
"Dunno", he says, "ain't looked".
"We'll check film four at nine bells in it", I say, "hopefully there'll be a good one on".
"Maybe the late one after that will be a good horror".
"Hope so", I say, "I fuckin' love horrors-what's your favourite horror film Mart"?
"Easy", he says, "The Conjuring".
"What's it about"?
"Like proper paranormal stuff, people getting possessed and stuff".
"Is it freaky"?
"When I watched it I was on my own, in my girlfriend's room and I was absolutely shitting myself man, proper scary".
"What, a big hairy arsed man like you"? I say, "is it that scary"?

"Yeah, it's proper freaky believe me, my girlfriend just couldn't watch it, she didn't like it, wouldn't watch it, said it'd give her nightmares for life"!

"I fuckin' love being scared do you"?

"Yeah", he says, "I love horror films man".

"You've got to watch The Ring one day Martyn man, can't actually believe you ain't seen it". Now Martyn has a black baseball cap on and is walking, posing in shorts and vest playing gangster.

"Proper bad boy. Hat's bangin' man", I say.

"Is in it"? he says.

"You know if the screws find it they'll take it off of you", I say, "how the fuck did you get it out your box in reception"?

"When the screw was marking off the clothes I'd got sent up and what I was down there to pick up, like when he turned his back I just swiped it out the box in it", he says, "anyway", he continues, "why ain't we allowed 'em"?

"I think you can have 'em but not like black ones like the screws wear", I say, "'cause the security teams wear 'em, like black caps, don't they".

"Oh yeah, they do, I forgot about that", says Mart, "they wouldn't let me have some of my nice tracksuits today either 'cause they're black".

"You having a coffee this time of night"? I ask as I see him putting on the kettle.

"Yeah, d'ya want one"?

"Naaa, I'll have a hot chocolate", I say, "it's mad, I used to be able to sleep on mental base amphetamine but coffee has me pinging off the walls if I drink too much of late".

"Coffee don't affect me", says Mart, blowing his nose now, "I can drink it all day and in the night and still sleep like a baby".

"That one you brought this week", I say, referring to the Kenco, "that one in particular keeps me up all fuckin' night if I drink it later than three PM". So, dear reader, he makes the drinks and is now making a new curtain for the window out of a bed sheet. I'm gonna settle down to Brian Cox's book which I'm half way through. Reading about the most recent test of Einstein's General Relativity: the gravitational waves detected by the LIGO detectors. Magnificent!

09-04-2019 0815hrs. Dotty is, as usual, mouthing off on Radio 1Extra. I wish she'd shut up and play some music. I took umbrage to her one morning when she, in her daily 'trashbag' room 101 take off, placed Stone Henge in there calling the wonder a 'pile of stones' and basically showing an incredible amount of ignorance. Anyway, the music is pumping and 'H' has just come in the cell.

"What did you have for dinner last night Sloaney"? he asks, "did you have the hotpot"?

"Yeah", I tell him, "why"?

"What about you Martyn"?

"I had it too".

"Have any of you been sick"?

"Naa, why"? I ask.

"'Cause about five people are saying they had the hotpot last night and reckon they've been up all night sick".

"Were they all spiceheads"? asks Martyn.

"Thinking about it", says 'H', "yeah, actually, all of 'em are proper spiceheads".

"And they reckon it's the food and not the K2 cockroach killer they're smoking"? I say.

"Or the alloy wheel cleaner"? says Martyn.

"Or the fuckin' fish tranq"! says 'H'!

"Yep", I say, my voice sarcastic, "wouldn't be the stuff they're all smoking; must be the food", and we all have a little chuckle that these people are smoking mental chemicals and actually surprised to find themselves vomiting, as I used to, profusely. Anyway, outside the open cell door, as I wait for freeflow to be called so I can get to my Healthy Living course with the sexy 50 year old Vicky, it is fuckin' noisy. Yesterday the wing was crazy as I told you. Three alarm bells on here, two for fights and one for a psycho smashing windows with his fists. Frosted wire reinforced windows which fucked his hands right up. Off to my course, adios.

1715hrs. Fredo is rapping 'Mmm Mmm Mmm' talking the truth of the towns and cities for the youth of Britain today. 'Outside the betting shop selling twenty shots' meaning selling crack and heroin of course. Before becoming famous and doing what he does best, rapping, Fredo was undoubtably shotting hard food to cats like me. Someone had to! As much as I can understand the argument that this type of music glamorises thug street life there is also the fact that art has always reflected reality. And can we really argue a point about when this reflection should be disallowed? I think not, for should such be given credence history becomes even more warped than it already is by the media and rich and powerful. Art such as that of Dave and Fredo, talking of shootings, drug dealing, stabbings, womanizing and the reality of life in Britain today is only telling the truth and no matter how distasteful to the bourgeois, it is just that, objective truth. Imperative, immutable and undeniable. The biggest artists in the world at present, Drake, Travis Scott, Stormzy, Giggs, Dave, Fredo, Andy Mill and myriad more all talk of life before music being cutthroat. And the streets, both here and in the western hemisphere in general are deep, dark and at night down right dangerous at present. And it is not just restricted to our cities either. People are being stabbed and shot and bludgeoned to death all over the UK right now. Inner city estates to villages and seaside towns. The youth are unsafe on our streets today. I mean, it was only about sixteen, seventeen months ago at the time of writing that I myself was holding a samurai sword to two young men telling them 'if you make me I swear I'll run this fuckin' thing right through you pair a cunts' in such a menacing voice you'd of believed me man! These two young shotters, kids, thankfully did believe me and handed big Damo what we came for. I can't help but wonder, as I write, what you, dear reader, will think of me! Burgling, knife wielding, angry psychotic quick to violence madman that I have been! Truth is, without drugs in me I would never behave these ways! Ever! Am I a monster? I mean, I've been violent all my life and assaulted women too. Of all my crimes, and they are many, punching partners shames me most. Again, without drink and drugs I'd manage my feelings less destructively but I am only one pipe, one drink away from insanity. I have the disease of addiction. Release the beast and a beast I become. Anyway, I have digressed. We have problems in Britain at present.

10-04-2019 2030hrs. Not planned to write anything today. However, there is one thing worthy of note which happened earlier. Well, a couple if you count Marcus picking up ten pages of power paper to distribute on the wing. So, dear reader, the person now banged up with Craig D, who's an angry man at the best of times, is a psycho from Thanet named Kirk. Now Kirk was recently, I think I told you, at the hospital wing in Elmley after being carted out of here with a serious psychotic episode induced, of course, by spice. After regaining, to a certain degree at least, his sanity, Elmley saw fit to send him back here and yesterday, when he landed here on Alpha, he swore he'd finished with the demon drug. Now, Kirk is a nutter himself, a stand up guy with no history of gayness or anything, not that it would be bad if he were, I'm just telling you the facts, for a reason. No sooner had he swore he'd finished with the spice he was smoking hard and it rapidly became evident his sanity was hanging by a very thin thread indeed. Anyway, today when we came out after lunch time bang up Craig D pokes his head into our cell and says:
"Alright boys", then begins to leave.

"Craig", I say, and he comes back.

"What's up"? he says.

"Why you running round looking all Speedy Gonzales"?

"I need to find a cellmate, need to get Kirk out, he's got to go Sloaney".

"Why, why"? I ask, ever the nosy parker.

"Naaa man, I don't want to say, he just has to go".

"Come on man, you can trust us", and Craig comes into our cell, pushing the door to behind him.

"Boys", he says to me and Martyn, "he's fucked in the head; for the whole hour over lunchtime bang up he's been up and down off his bed with his cock in his hand trying to touch me sexually".

"No fuckin' way"! says Martyn.

"Whaaaaaa", is all I can say.

"So that's why I'm running around checkin' every cell on the wing for another person to move in with. Please don't tell anyone though lads 'cause the cunt ain't well".

"We won't mate, don't worry", I say and no sooner has he pulled the door to behind him I turn to Martyn who looks at me and says:

"No fuckin' way"!

"Whaaaaa", I say again, "'had his cock out the whole time and was tryna touch me sexually'"!

"Oh shit"! says Martyn and we laugh out loud then I go to the door, pull it open and call:

"'H', 'H'".

"Yeah, what's up"? he says poking his head out from a cell a few doors from ours.

"Come 'ere man", and he does.

"Kirk has been up there with Craig with his cock in his hand tryna touch Craig up out his nut on spice"!

"No fuckin' way, what, Kirk's got his cock out tryna grab Craig up and that"?

"Yeah man", says Martyn.

"Sheeeiiiit", says 'H'.

"Don't tell anyone though, I promised I wouldn't but simply couldn't help myself".

"He's truly fucked Kirk though ain't he"? says 'H'.

"Defo", I say, "pickled bro". When I get to the ATB Unit I tell Jason and Lucy. They laugh but at the same time are clearly pained at the tradegy inherent here. Seeing such I, too, reflect, feeling for poor Kirk. Anyway, at 3p.m I go to the gym and fuck myself up with Martyn and

'H'. Upon returning to the wing I learn Craig couldn't find a cell mate so I guess he'll have to keep his bum to the wall tonight.

11-04-2019 1810hrs and my sleep is still very fractured. When I think of my little mum I get an oppressive, sickening feeling like someone is pushing down with heavy hands upon my chest and abdomen. I miss her more than words can say and carry great shame for the way I have treated her and my sister. I have robbed, manipulated, embarrassed and terrorised them when in active addiction, turning my mum's houses into crack dens at times. She has had two boyfriends since my dad and both I've punched, knocking them clean out for trying to stop me manipulating my mum for money. And remember, though my mum drank, she was a binger who would have months and months off the sauce and was a normal, functioning and beautiful member of society trying to get by. I have to tell you that other than when a boy, boxing and bashing kids at school oh, and in prison I suppose for there's been much violence for me in these places, I have never, ever assaulted anybody when clean and sober. Drugs make me insane. Actually, most of the violence in prisons, too, has been drug related. But I digress. At an NA meeting today in the prison I shared of the grief I'm currently experiencing and I could hear my own pain loading my words. Oh mother, mother, I am so so so sorry. Anyway, in other news, the fake doesn't really need a wheelchair suspected nonce kiddy fiddler, got out his wheelchair today rather rapid when he decided to break the nose of me mate Martin D with a sneaky sly punch. Martin has been helping the suspected sex offender. The suspected nonce is so called because there are rumours, even from his fellow travellers, gypsys, that he attacked a fourteen year old girl and if his own are disowning him well, that speaks volumes. We can't prove it so no one has weighed him in. But there you go. My shoulders hurt from gym yesterday and I enjoy the pain. Looking forward to a circuit tomorrow. Martyn is making hot chocolate. Jay Beany got ten days CC today, Cellular Confinement down the block, the segregation unit. Marcus, God love him, was out his nut this evening at dinner time wanting to play fight with me and he let me use the illicit mobile to call Tan. Bye for now dear reader.

13-04-2019 1800hrs. Radio 1Extra are pumping out rap as me and the Martyn finish a round of cards in which I beat him 5-1.
"You're fuckin' shit lately bro", I tell him.
"I know", he says and creases his face up to squeeze out a savage fart, "I dunno what's happening lately with me man, I need to take a shit", and he disappears behind the curtain to noisily empty his bowels with

much straining and farting and gasps of relief. The smell of shit pervades the cell like a thick wet fog. Anyway, the reason I put pen to paper is because Martyn said I should write about what we heard last night.

"What d'ya mean"?

"The geezer screaming", he says.

"Oh my God", I say, "how could I forget about that poor cunt? Patmore wasn't it"? I ask, making sure I've the right prisoner.

"Yeah, Patmore man, thought he was dying", and we both laugh remembering. To us it's quite common and I suppose it's really not funny but me and Martyn, and the rest of the wing going by the howling to be heard coming from the cracks in the doors, found it fuckin' hilarious. It started with an emergency buzzer four cells down then the door to the same cell being kicked. After prolonged booting on the steel Patmore started screaming out the side of his door:

"Guv, guv, please guv, help, help me oh help me please I'm gonna die", now he's in a single cell so me and Smartyn knew straight away.

"Spice attack", said Mart.

"Defo, turn the TV down", I say, "so we can hear properly", and it ain't long.

"Help, guv, heeeeellllllppppp, guv, guv, pleeeeeeaaasssee, oh God I'm gonna fuckin' die guv", and me and Martyn and the rest of the wing are mocking, crying with laughter out the side of the cell doors.

"Sheeeeiiiitt boy"! says Martyn as we hear Oscar One come on the wing, loads of screws and they're at his cell door now.

"What's the matter mate"? a screw asks the fella from the other side of the door.

"Guv, guv, you better go and get the resuscitation staff 'cause I'm having a heart attack man please please guv I'm gonna die if you don't"! and he actually starts proper screaming.

"Have you been smoking spice"? asks the officer talking to him.

"Yeah, but I didn't smoke it, I think someone put it in my food at the servery", and this is just too much, me and Martyn in stitches now.

"Did you fuckin' hear that Mart"?

"Yeah", says Mart through tears of laughter, "he must think they're fuckin' stupid, 'spiked at the servery'"!

"So you've had spice"? asks the screw.

"I think so, but it ain't the spice can you open the door please else I'm gonna die guv please man help me I'm gonna fuckin' die guv"!

"It's just the spice mate", says the screw, "have a hot sugary drink", and I can't be bothered to labour this but the cunt had the screws at his door for two hours and when he continued that if they didn't do something he would take his own life they eventually marched him up to the safe cell upstairs which is suicide proof and sort of like a padded cell. They'd've stripped him of his clothes and placed him into unrippable nylon tee shirt and shorts so he can't fashion them into hanging or strangling apparatus. Also, his bedding would be of the same material and there would be a screw sitting outside the cell all night which instead of having a door has a big metal prison gate so the prisoner inside can be seen at all times. He'd also have no TV because of the sharp stuff he could use to slash his wrists. Reader, you must understand that these spice attacks, these terrifying trips are frequent here. I myself used to fear them but love them at the same time. They take you to a place, sometimes, where one believes that death is indisputably imminent. I found the more I faced this terror the more I grew in a way. I mean, I've died on heroin but that's different. There's no real fear involved. One minute you're awake, then you fade to the other place peacefully and then you wake up if you're lucky, or unlucky, depending on where your life is at that point in time. Of course there was that one special overdose where my heart stopped for ninety seconds and I was gifted with a vision but such as that is once in a lifetime. But acid or mushrooms or spice or hallucinogens in general, well, they cause a man to breakthrough to that realm otherwise invisible, that place we have forgotten as a species, the place where God is tangible. And since then I have had more for, as I say, I wrote another book in prison. Over ten months I spent there. Though clean and sober today, (here in Oxford typing up the handwritten manuscript) by the grace of God, I had, though I knew it not then, more pain to come. And the offence was a domestic, with a girl I am still extremely close to to this day. For though she suffered at my hands, she knows my soul. Indeed, the next book is again a prison memoir but I thread the tale of her and I throughout, chapter on her, prison, her, prison, until in the end I tell of the fateful day in that hotel room where I assaulted her. The book will have her name on the cover. Anyway, enough. In this cell now it is 88 days since last I used any mind altering substance. And make no mistake, though I have enjoyed tripping for the insights revealed me, me, on drugs, equals absolute insanity. Thursday coming we lay my lovely little mum to rest.

15-04-2019 1020hrs. My prayers this morning were of gratitude for simply being given the grace to face another day. For I like breathing and don't want to be leaving this Earth, this bounteous, beautiful, golden green garden anytime soon. Anyway, I ache satisfyingly from yesterday's workout. Marcus is getting fat from the antipsychotic pills he pilfers and the spice munchies which make a pig of the man. He has again been picking up thousands of pounds worth of A4 spice soaked paper and is undoubtably raking it in yet only to use the profits to fund his predilection for opioids, benzos, pregabs and potions galore. The other day he spent £100 on distilled liquor brewed expertly by someone from another wing and purchased by Marcus in the meds que. He is so out his nut of late he doesn't know who owes him what. Yesterday, to Kempy:

"You do know you still owe me six packs of vapes", he said to him.

"What the fuck you on about ya mug"? says Just For Men, "I paid you the three I owed you on Friday".

"Yeah", says El Chubbs, "but you still owed me for that other ID card I gave you on Wednesday".

"What the fuck", says Kemps, "what other fuckin' ID card? I ain't had no other spice off of you Marcus, you need to slow down on the drugs mate", and inside I'm sniggering at their bickering so say:

"Kempy man I thought more of you bro".

"Fuck off Sloaney this is serious", he says.

"I'm just saying though", and Kempy knows what I'm doing, "I'm just saying I think I was there when he gave you the other ID card bro".

"Oh don't fuckin' put ideas in his head please"!

"Was you really there Sloaney"? says Marcus.

"No you silly cunt and furthermore Marcus you're so out ya fuckin' nut of late, giving so much away to the mugs on the wing you ain't got a clue who owes you what let alone what pittance ya pals owe ya".

"I ain't been out my nut I've been sorting myself out lately".

"Oh my God", says Steve Just For Men Kemp, "is that what you call it, laying on Bradder's bed dribbling like a retard; yeah, proper sorting yaself out int ya"?

"In it Steve"? I say, then, turning to Marcus, "who the fuck you kiddin' mate? You're only kiddin' yourself and what's more, look at the state of you lately ya fat fucker, you're fallin' apart Marcus man and I ain't tellin' ya to hurt you, I'm saying it because I fuckin' love you mate". Anyway, door's just opened for lunch.

Ok, so it's 1200hrs and I eat my lunch upstairs in Brad's with Kempster, Ricky Lanes, Jake, Reece, Pete Lanes, Gibbo and Marcus who's buying peoples chicken, cake and custard for spice the fat fuck. Of course he's also purchasing all the drugs he can get his grubby hands on. The cell was so packed, heaving with people and hot with the heat of all the bodies but me and Kempy are just laughing our heads off at Smarcus.

"What you two laughing at"? drawls El Fat One, "what's the matter with ya you pair a cunts"?

"Laughing at you ya mess, look at the state of ya, like a fat stoned walrus", Kempster says.

"What", says El Chubbs, "d'ya like the way I'm Pablo-ing it yeah"? and he buys another piece of chicken from lifer Steve Bennett, our pal, "hold that", he says to Steve B, passing him a bowl filled with cake and custard, "whilst I eat this chicken".

"Wow, you're an animal Marcus", I say above the din of the chatter.

"Gis a joint then", says Steve Bennett still holding the bowl before Marcus with two hands like a servant waiting for his master's orders.

"Hold up a minute, El Chappo's got to eat first", says Marcus with hooded spice shot eyes.

"Look at you Bennett", says Kempster to lifer Steve whom we all love, "standin' there like a fuckin' slave with that bowl".

"No way man", I laugh, "Marcus, this poor cunt scuttles about for you every day, cleaning your cell and look at the poor cunt, waiting for you like an Egyptian slave whilst you stuff your fat face, and all for a scrap of that shit".

"Pablo El Chappo's got to eat man"!

"Come on Marcus, sort me out a joint please mate", says lifer Steve.

"I will man I will", he says, throwing bones in the bin, wiping grease from his mouth with his sleeve before taking the bowl from Steve B's outstretched arms and stuffing his face with the cake and custard.

"Sort him out Marcus man for fuck sake", says Kempy pointing to Bennett who's looking forlornly at Marcus like a dog waiting for a petting from its owner, "look at the poor cunt".

"Please Marcus man, I do everything for you", says Steve B.

"Alright alright", says Pablo, putting down the pudding and pulling an ID card out his pocket. He tears off a one and a half inch by quarter inch strip, "eeeyar", and gives it to poor Steve.

"Thanks Marcus man", and the lovable lifer fucks off out the cell to smoke his prize.

"You're fuckin' ruthless Marcus man", says Kempy, "he cleans for you, gets your meals from the servery, does your washing and everything man".

"And Pablo pays him well".

"Don't you feel sorry for him"? I ask.

"Do I fuck, I pay him loads".

"You do proper treat him like a cunt", says Kemps.

1700hrs. Went gym at 1400hrs and did a chest workout with Martyn where I did my best bench press ever, 110kg, completely on my own. As I pushed it up I said to Mart who was spotting me:

"Don't touch the fuckin' bar", and heaved the fucker up. Did some cable work after, some flies and dumbell press. Then one of the gym orderlies, a big gangster lifer named Mark R, who is literally, literally, the fittest bloke in the nick said:

"Sloaney, fancy a go of this", and he's pointing to a mini circuit he's putting his panting pal through.

"Really"? I ask, looking at the state of his mate and thinking fuck that.

"Ok", he says, shrugging his shoulders, "just thought you of all people was man enough, that's all", and Mark's smart and knows this will get my tiny little brain thinking.

"Fuck it", I say, "come on then, what we doing"?

"Right, see those dumbells"? and he's pointing to a 20kg set.

"Yeah".

"One squat, deep squat holding them to your chest then over to the bar", and he's pointing at a bar loaded with 50kg.

"Yep".

"So, this side of the bar, one burpee where your chest touches the floor then two footed jump to the other side of the bar and back to the dumbells for two squats, then two burpees but you do one at a time so one, two footed jump over then the other then the squat ya get me? So, your last set will be ten squats with the bells, ten burpees with the chest touch with the jump between each one ya got that"?

"Ok", I say thinking that don't seem that bad, "easy", and here one of the other lunatic gym orderlies, Jimmy, Kev the gym screw and Mark all chuckle deviously.

"You reckon"? says Kev.

"I'm not so sure now seeing you lot grinning"!

"Come on then", says Mark, setting his watch to time me, "ready"?

"Yep".

"Go", and I do.

"When you squat, make sure your elbows touch your thighs", says Mark and remember I've these dumbells to my chest dear reader. Anyway, let me tell you, I did finish. Pure stubborn pig headedness got me through but oh my God I wanted to stop at four reps of each. At four squats and four burpees with the jump I was fucked. No excuses but I was written off from yesterdays circuit and had just done a workout but I finished the thing in eleven minutes sixteen seconds. Afterwards I lay on the rubber flooring panting, ignoring the calls to get up and walk it off on the treadmill. No, I lay there fucked but wholly satisfied with my perseverance and determination. Now for some cards. Mart beats me 5-4, his first win for a while. 1Extra is pumping Bruno Mars this Sunday night, musical G that he is. Then Prof Green raps about 'out here in this jungle, ain't nothing nice round here' talking the truth of the murderous streets of London today where an epidemic of stabbings is currently in full flow. Anyway, Lord Of The Rings is on so bye for now.

15-04-2019 0730hrs and I say my prayers, have a wash and eat me breakfast. I put some gel on my hair and mess it up, opting for the untidy look rather than the usual side parting.

"What d'ya think Smartyn"? I ask, turning to him and posing, "of the hairdo"?

"Yeah man, it's cool, better than the normal combover anyway"!

"Combover? Fuckin' combover! You're ruthless ya cunt"!

"Ain't that what they call it when people like comb hair over the patches where they ain't got none and that"?

"Yes Martyn, that's exactly what they call it bro. It's just I'm tryna come to terms with my thinning hair gradually, gently mate and you're hammering the point home ruthlessly bro"!

"You've just got to 'accept the things you cannot change'" he says, quoting the serenity prayer we say in Narcotics Anonymous.

"You're such a cunt"! I laugh, "I have still got some hair ya know"!

"I know", he says, "some, but you could do with some caffeine shampoo to be fair"! The door opens and Jake and Brad pop in.

"Mornin' boys; what's happening"?

"I just wanna get out now Sloaney", says Jake, "I need to dip my cock into some pussy".

"Who ya thinkin' of"? I say, and remember that Jake is also from Thanet.

"I was thinking that sexy blonde slut Jamie Lee".

"Oh my days, she's a proper tool bro", I say.

"Int she"? he agrees, "fit as fuck mate".

"Someone told me yesterday she's on the gear", I say, "but I'll bet she's still well sexy".

"She used to well wanna fuck me", says Jake, "she was always showing me her little G-strings and thongs and that. She used to like, pull her trousers down a bit and rub her arse up my leg going 'you know you wanna fuck me Jake' and I can't believe I never did to be fair"!

"Ahhhh Jake don't man", I say, feeling sexy even thinking about Jamie Lee, "she is a proper little sort"! Anyway, after exchanging pleasantries with Bradders both these boys fuck off. In brief news, yesterday J.T and Kirk the loon of the sexual touching broke into the staff office . Don't know what they stole but there'll be murders over this today I'm sure. Oh, and I'm 90 days clean this morning.

1220hrs, lunchtime bang up. Just before we got locked up I was upstairs in Kempy and Pete Lanes' cell. With me: Kemps, Pete, Kirk and Marcus. Kirk of the psychotic episode and Craig D touching fiasco the other day. Now Kirk is a big, burly, handsome funny fucker and, as I say, also from Thanet. However, he is proper losing it on the spice lately, again. He now asks Marcus:

"Gis a pipe please Marcus mate, I've run out of spice".

"Alright", says Marcus, "I'll give you a pipe but you have to do it all in one go".

"Yeah man, I'm up for that", says silly cunt Kirk.

"Eeee yar then", says Marcus passing him a piece of paper four by one inch, "fold that up and pipe it in one go".

"Naaa Marcus man, ya can't do that", says Pete, "Kirk man, don't be an idiot bro, that's gonna fuck you up mate".

"Naaa, I'll do it, watch", and he fashions a foil lined milk carton pipe.

"My God", says sonorous Kempy as Kirk licks off the whole lot in one go, holding the poison deep in his lungs.

"Sheeeiiiit boy", I laugh, "watch this cunt now, watch", I say to the cell.

"I'm alright man", says Kirk, but his eyes are now bright red, the colour is draining from his face and his arms and legs are starting to shake. Soon his head is back, mouth open as he sits and his hands are locked into claw like resemblances with rigour mortis.

"Oh-my-God", says Kempy, "well, at least we know he's still alive 'cause his hands keep twitching".

"Pass that hair gel", says Marcus and Kempy does and Marcus wipes copious amounts of it, followed by toothpaste all around Kirk's face and in his ears and nose and mouth and hair. He also puts the same all over his clawed, locked up hands.

"Gis that shower gel", he says to Pete and Pete passes it. Marcus proceeds to squirt it into Kirk's open mouth.

"Come on Marcus man, that's too much", I say.

"He loves it man, don't worry, he likes it honestly trust me man". This cunt, I fuckin' love him but he's savage.

"That's what you look like Marcus when you're out ya nut", I say.

"I never get that bad".

"You fuckin' do", says Kempy.

"You do Marcus", echoes Pete.

"I've seen you like a proper mong many a time Marcus mate", I say, "shit man, what we gonna do with him"? I ask, meaning Kirk of course.

"One more thing", says Marcus, who now bends down and ties Kirk's shoelaces together.

"Marcus man, you're fuckin' ruthless", says Pete.

"Watch this", says Marcus, who then stands back and shouts 'Kirk, Kirk, quick man screws are coming' and Kirk jumps up like a startled cat, trips and falls face first and I swear there's bubbles coming out his mouth and he's a fuckin' mess man. Through the shower gel he is trying to say 'cunts' from the floor but he is incoherent, a state. We carry him home to his own cell before the staff come round to close the doors and we are all in fits of hysterical laughter at the state he is in. I know I'm a bad bastard for finding it funny but I just can't help it for in his own cell he's writhing like a fish on the floor, twitching and making all sorts of strangling sounds and he's covered in all the shit Marcus did to him. Kirk is dribbling out his tiny little mind God bless him. Marcus and Kempy, the biggest and strongest, get him onto his bed and clean him up a bit. We all go sit back in Pete and Kempy's cell and Kempy says to Marcus:

"Marcus man, you always have to take it too far".

"Fuckin' funny though".

"Yeah, it is, but he's on the edge as it is".

"He'll be alright", says Marcus.

"Marcus", I say, "that's exactly what you look like when out ya nut bro, all that rigour mortis, that limb locking and the palsy shaking mate. Not a good look is it"?

"Naaa man, Pablo never gets that bad bro".

"You fuckin' do bro, worse sometimes to be honest", and before I could press the point home it was time for bang up where I sit and reflect on the danger of what we just did to poor Kirk, for being there I'm responsible too.

1720hrs. Whole wing wasted. Can't be fucked to write. One good thing, Martyn has a 'D' cat review tomorrow where he will be considered for open conditions. Before I do put down my pen let me tell you that on the stereo is a track by Kalashnikov which raps: 'it's murder, when man test the terra firma, man's shotting rocks to make an earner, it's murder, murder, murder, murder.........you'll find your body buried in suburbia, it's murder'..........As I listen I'm reminded of the time my Invicta House tower block flat in Margate had had the door kicked off by the police on a bust, making it insecure and leaving me unable to lock it at all. I was dealing drugs at the time and suspect it was about 2002-2003. I had put an A4 piece of paper on the door which told any punk looking to rob or hurt me that: 'if you come through my door and are not police I will stab you with a carving knife before asking questions' and in brackets I'd put: 'stab you 'till the knife comes out your back'. PC Choo, a local police officer, knocked my door one day.

"You have to take this down Andrew, it's madness mate", and old PC Choo was alright to be fair.

"Why PC Choo? This, my home, is the only place I can murder people and get away with it man".

"Sloaney", he says with an exasperated sigh, "you can't murder people and get away with it mate".

"PC Choo, I'm just saying to people that if they enter without permission and I'm home well, they're fucked. It's a deterent". I did take it down as asked though. Thing is, at the time, I meant what it said on that sign. I was so paranoid with all the drugs I was taking and am grateful no one ever forced my hand for I'd be in here for a fuck load longer! I stress again though, put a drug in me and there is always potential for extreme violence, yet without drugs I'm a different guy.

17-04-2019 0745hrs. Tomorrow I go to say goodbye to my poor long suffering mum. God love her. Yesterday I received a lovely sympathy card from a lady I've known for many, many years. Sarah L was once an occasional lover but she always let me know she wasn't interested in a boyfriend. But she has always, always been my friend. She has never turned her back on me and has helped me multitudinous times when I have been extremely desperate. She is the only person, bar Jason, Lucy, Naomi and Paul Highm here to give me a card. I can't quite express my gratitude here. The card reads: 'To Sloaney, so sorry to hear about your mum, give me a call if you want my number is…….much love, will write you a letter soon and I'd love to hear from you, you have my address, thinking of you, love you, Sarah'. In other news, Jeff 'H' McCarthy went home yesterday. He is a real loss to the wing; big and influential, he helped to keep peace on here. Indeed, yesterday found Alpha with a funny atmosphere though this could be caused by the spice stocks having been depleted. Also, Craig D kicked Kirk out and there was very nearly violence between the two of them. And finally, yesterday, a nasty bully cunt called Dan M------, a piece of shit if ever I knew one and about whom I've never heard a good word, nearly drew me to acts of violence. So, I came off of A wing yesterday to go to work and as I go along my way he stops me:

"Oi, go back on the wing and get Marcus for me, I need to see him for spice", but I had done this for him last week, leaving me hating myself for people pleasing.

"No mate, I've just come off the wing and ain't going back on there" and as I walk off I hear the cunt mutter something to someone and I stop, turn, but, seeing two screws close by I simply turn and go upon my way. Had they not been there my intention was to say 'what ya saying ya fat

398

spastic'? but I turned the other cheek for it'd not have ended well and with officers present it's pointless. When I got to work Jason, who knows me very well by now says:

"You alright mate"?

"Well, J, what it is"......and I explain what happened, for he will tell no one so I can let this stuff out here. I continue that, "were it not for the staff there J I'd've smashed that fat bully cunt's head in. What troubles me J is that there is still this aggressive animal in me and were it not for consequences I'd've let the cunt have it".

"Sloaney", says J, "that's the thing see, now you think of consequences. Think about what would have happened if you'd of attacked him; you'd've lost your 'D' cat, your 'enhanced', and gone down the block and what for? An horrible bully. And you did the right thing being assertive. Also mate", continues the worthy man, "we all get these thoughts. When I'm riding me bike to work in the morning and some fucker cuts me up in a car, I'd love to jump off and smash their heads in. But I think of the consequences, I'd lose my job, lose the house 'cause we have a mortgage, and for what? Nothing when you really reflect. So we all get these thoughts mate; it's what you do with them that counts. The difference is now you stop and think. Anyway, wanna coffee"?

"Love one man, and thanks J, I appreciate you I really do", I say, "I'm a little bit worried at the awkwardness walking past him now".

"Don't worry about it mate, it's done now and you know better than anyone else to keep it in the moment, don't worry about what might happen, forget about it mate, you've let him know now and he won't ask you again", and dear reader, later that day I had a class to go to for a pre release interview and guess who walks in the door? Yes, the bully fat fuck and guess what he said? Nothing, apart from 'you alright Sloaney'?! God gifts me the likes of Jason. I'm very blessed to be fair. Remember I told you Jason is a thirty year vet of Rochester? And he's also ex forces.......that's by the by but just wanted to tell you! We also, in one of the offices down here, have another old school thirty year vet of Rochy called Mr Gibb. Another very nice fella. Again, this officer is so supportive. Remember also that I told you that long term officers either go one way or the other? They become extremely cynical or go completely the other way, brimming with love and looking to help anyone they spot with potential to turn their lives around. When I regaled the tale of the bully cunt to Rob Gibb yesterday he said:

"In the good old days people like him would have a trip and fall in the shower and no one would say a dicky bird about it".

"I know right", I say, "in those days, as soon as someone was marked as a bully the staff'd even turn their backs whilst the cunt got what was coming".

"These days", says Gibby, "we have to approach it differently, those days are long gone Sloaney".

"Thing is Gibby, bullies understand only one language and that language, violence, in my experience, is the most effective tool in changing their behaviour".

"I know, I get it", he replies, "if they get their head smashed in for bullying they think twice about doing it but it is a different place, prison today. What people need to know is, and I've seen some suicides in here in my time, is that bullies can cause people to take their own lives and that is the worst possible outcome of their behaviour but it happens".

"When I was in Chelmsford nick two years ago Gibby we had a youngster, not yet in his twenties if I recall correctly, and he was getting bullied. He lived two doors up from me and me cellmate. One night, we could hear activity so turned the TV down in time to hear one officer say to another 'it was just too late, I tried, but he'd gone' and the next three hours or so there were paramedics outside his cell whilst they dealt with the body and stuff. And a year prior to that, in the same jail, just before I got there another inmate famously, for it was all over the news as he had severe mental health problems, had managed to electrocute himself to death", and dear reader should you want to you can look this up on line. There was a great furore about it because the fella was supposed to be on continuous suicide watch. What makes it worse is that he was a first time offender who would not even of been in jail were it not for a shortage of mental health beds. He should never have been in jail in the first place. Chelmsford, I must say, is a filthy, archaic, depressing and rat infested place with a dangerous staff team who don't give a fuck for their wards. There is a culture of bullying amongst the staff there. I saw much uneccessary heavy handed manhandling of prisoners there and one officer in particular, a heavy smoking tall lanky motorbike riding bully cunt screw who's name I wish I could remember was brutal to all and sundry. One time, I was stoned on B wing, and he hated prisoners being stoned. So I'm sitting getting my hair cut and this cunt comes, looks at my eyes, grabs me by the lapels and literally drags me to my cell, with half a haircut the horrible cunt. People were terrified of him. And screw cunts like him, bully fuckers whether in uniform or prisoners, cause people to despair and, in extreme circumstances, take their own lives.

1800hrs. Just beat young Martyn at cards, 5-3.

"What is there to write about today Mart"?

"Ricky Lanes on the servery".

"Oh yeah", I say, "that was funny", and dear reader, firstly I should tell you Ricky has, somehow, bagged himself a job on the servery. However, as you know by now, he has a predilection for drugs and spice whilst in prison in particular. Since he has been working on the servery things, milks, cakes, cereal packs and baguettes and other items like the pack of biscuits we get on a Friday have been going missing. Milk alone is highly sought after by gym bods who'll pay good spice for extra cartons. I love Ricky and always get my stuff because Martyn is the Number 1 on servery so I couldn't really give a fuck what Rick gets up to. But he is undoubtably nicking shit to get spice. Now Rick, bless him, when he is serving food gets in a right old tiz and the sweat shines on his bald pate the more stressed he gets. When people are holding up the line, like earlier on this evening, he starts proper losing the plot.

"For fuck sake", he could be heard saying in fluster, "stop holding the line up and fuckin' move will ya"? and I go to Kempy, who's in the que behind me:

"Look Kempster, he's proper losin' it again mate", then I raise my voice, "Ricky, stop stressing mate or your hair'll fall out", which illicits a laugh from the que as he's not a hair on his head of course.

"And you can shut the fuck up Sloaney", and his head is going red but it is Kempy's next jibe that proper gets the cunt blowing out the ears:

"Ricky, oi Ricky", goes the deep bass voice of Kemps, "you wanna take all those milks and cakes out ya pockets and you'd be able to move about a bit quicker you fat thieving fucker", and the whole que erupts into raucous laughter at this.

"You can shut up Kempy ya fuckin' mug", says Ricky.

"What, truth hurt"? says Kempy, and I'm in stitches.

"You're a cunt Kempy, ya know that", and Ricky's temper has me crying all the more as he squirms uncomfortably under the scrutiny and Rick says to me, "and you Sloaney ya prick".

"What the fuck did I do"?

"Fuckin' like a spoon ya cunt, encouraging him".

"You know we love you Rick", says Kempy now.

"It's true Rick, we do", I echo.

"Fuckin' hurry up Rick ya prick", says his brother Peter now, also with us in the line.

"Shut up Peter ya fuckin' mongrel", says Rick, "don't you fuckin' start". Anyway, me and Kemps, in the gym today, were clean and pressing 70kg which is a personal best for me. I couldn't believe that I managed to snatch the bar from the floor, flick it to my chest before pressing it above my head with that weight. Progress. Funeral tomorrow.

1815hrs 18-04-2019. I went to a wonderful send off for me mum today. There were about 50 people I think and had we had the funeral on social media it'd have been a fuck load more. We tried to keep it as quiet as possible, restricted to family and close personal friends. I don't really feel like writing about it to be honest. Rest in peace dear mum.

19-04-2019 0821hrs. A republican gunmen shot dead a journalist in Derry last night. Though my mum was catholic, this stuff used to upset her greatly. Anyway, in other news, when I came back yesterday I was sitting in Kempy and Peter's cell and suddenly we could hear raised voices outside on the landing and Kirk is going:
"Yeah, but I can sell 'em mate", and his cellmate, literally just moved on the wing, goes:
"Mate, I've just walked on the wing five minutes ago and you're walking out the cell with my trainers in ya hand".
"Yeah", mumbles Kirk looking dishevelled and out his nut, "but I can sell 'em like now in it".
"I don't wanna sell 'em ya mug", goes his new cellmate, "put 'em back before I weigh you in ya cunt".
"Alright mate, no need for that is there"? says Kirk. Moving on, in my final piece of news this morning, the scouser next door, a spice cat who literally sells his food every day, set the fire alarm off four times in his cell last night. Fuck knows what he was doing but the final time Oscar One came out to him they took half an hour reviving the cunt after another spice attack, for he is a regular, flopping on the floor and foaming at the mouth. Most people put socks over the smoke detectors so I'll go in there and clue him up tomorrow. Oh, and wheelchair suspect nonce was literally dragged by his feet by the staff to his cell last night after refusing to bang up at lock up time. More later.

10am. Bless El Fatto. He gave me the illicit mobile this morning so that I could phone my sister. After all the preperations for the funeral etc she is drained and feeling poorly.
"It's all the stress you've been under J----, that's all mate", I told her, not very helpful but true nonetheless. Also, Marcus bought a load of Golden Virginia rolling tobacco so I've been treated to a roll up or two this morning, much needed I must say. Sat in Pete and Kempy's cell now with these couple a cunts I love and Drake's 'Gods' Plan' is playing and I'm thinking that I hope God has a plan for me. And in other news I've had using dreams, drug using dreams, two nights in a row. The new CM

walks past the cell now and nods her head in our direction for the cell door is open and I ask Peter:

"D'ya think she's sexy Pete"?

"Yeah", he says laconically, "she's alright for a lettuce licker".

"What d'ya mean 'lettuce licker' bro"? I say.

"She's a proper lesbo int she, like a proper into birds man", he says.

"Really"? I say, "what a shame, she's got something very sexy about her".

"Yeah", says Pete, "she's fit but she definitely eats minge 'cause she's married to a bird".

"How the fuck d'ya know that"? I ask.

"Everyone knows she's a carpet muncher", says Pete, "likes a bit of furry rug".

"I didn't know that", I say.

"I promise ya Sloaney", he reiterates, "she loves to lick lettuce mate and no man's ever got a chance of getting up that, trust me".

"Look at that on telly Pete", I say, pointing to the sexy songstress Normani, a fuckin' fit black beauty on 4Music who's doing a duet with Khalid, "I'd fuckin' marry her man, stunning".

"Sloaney man you know I'm not into niggers".

"Peter man, what's the matter with you bro"?

"I had a really weird dream last night that me and Ron Senior (Thanet friend of many years) were out in Spain and I murdered someone but when I got nicked they nicked me for noncing as well", he says, ignoring my question.

"No way man you're fucked".

"Yeah", he goes on, "I'd slept with this like spastic bird in a wheelchair, there was like wing mirrors on it and fluffy dice and in the dream I slept with her but they were saying I'd nonced her up and then I was in prison and Arge and Broomy the screws were going round the wing going 'yeah, there's no way he's guilty of that, he wouldn't nonce a spastic up'".

"Oh my days man", I say, chuckling nonetheless, "you can't help your dreams bro".

"Proper weird dreams lately but don't tell anyone will ya"?

"Pete, I'm writing right now in front of you bro as you can see, it's only a dream mate. I didn't think you was into shagging disabled people though bro".

"Shut up Sloaney ya mug, it was well disturbing man, I woke up proper sweating thinking I'm on a nonce charge".

"My God Pete", I say, "you're gold dust ya cunt".

"What d'ya mean"?

"The things you come out with; you have to admit you're not exactly politically correct are ya? Half of it's bollox though, 'cause you talk as if you're a racist but I know you don't really hate people for the colour of their skin".

"Course I don't, but I still wouldn't shag one though".

"Pete", I say, "if that Normani came in this cell now in stockings and suspenders you'd be up her like a rat up a drainpipe ya lying cunt".

"I wouldn't Sloaney honestly, but I know you would".

"Whaaaaa", I say, "I'd marry her in a heartbeat bro, absolutely beautiful she is".

"You'd fuck anything though mate, you've always been the same".

"Yeah, but she's marriage material".

"It's just the way I've been brought up", says Pete, "none of my family like niggers".

"That word Pete man, it's an awful word bro", I say, "my grandad was the same, like your family but they didn't know any better Pete".

"I just wouldn't bring black into my family".

"Well, I could love that bird", I say, "and Pete, me personally, I love that creamy caramel skin and I'm so vain I imagine the most beautiful kids being brought forth by me and her". And I'm gonna put down me pen and mingle.

1715hrs. Just came into the wing after being on the yard for an hour where I eat my dinner. The sun was shining directly above me and his rays still now finger their way through the bars outside the perspex window, highlighting tendrils of dust dancing around the cell as Smartyn bustles about putting canteen goods away, clearing off the side so there's room to make a cup of the new Millicano coffee we purchased and received today. It must be at least 22 degrees this Good Friday, absolutely beautiful for an April day. I don't like to think too much of the reasons for the steady rise in global temperatures year on year, especially after watching a climate change highlighting documentary with Sir David Attenborough. Anyway, my beloved, moody, skinny arse friend Tony Giles has put the canvas I commissioned onto our wall. It is a Banksy-esq depiction of a baby holding a machine gun and we love it. In other news, me, Martyn, Kempy, Smarcus and Steve Lanes did a mental circuit earlier. 1Extra are playing deep, dark rap, Giggs at present with Baka Not Nice rapping 'Mr gunman, put your gun down, Mr gunman, this is my town'. Dale Pearson today, for some reason, had the raving hump. We all really like him, us little lot but since he has started smoking spice again we don't see so much of him. He literally smokes from the moment he wakes up to the time he gets off to sleep, usually absolutely spangled I'm guessing. Screws are regularly finding him unconscious on his cell floor. Yesterday, after kicking fuck out of the platic bins on the wing, sending shit and detritus all up the landing, he went into his cell and slashed his own arm savagely with a razor blade.

"What the fuck is that Dale"? I asked today, upon seeing the open, gaping wound on his arm for he refused to let any medical team near him.

"I cut myself yesterday in it".

"Why"?

"The screws pissed me off so much so it's either draw blood from them or from myself. Drawing blood, one way or the other, is the only way of calming me down".

"Mate", I say, "I don't know what to say to you. But Dale, you were alright when you weren't smoking that spice, it ain't good for your mental health, you know that don't ya"?

"Yeah course", he says, "but if I don't have it now I proper get the sweats and my stomach, wow, my stomach man, I get proper sick in it".

"I know mate, I went through it myself but I promise you, if you can lay off it for five days or so that passes".

"I know", he replies, "I've done it myself before but I kinda like smoking it ya know"?

"But when you ain't got it, you get proper aggressive of late; you're a big lad, and when you kick off you scare people".

"I don't mean to", he says and I think sincerely, "I just have to let my anger out though Sloaney", and, having had enough of my attempt at a poor therapeutic intervention he goes upon his way.

22-04-2019 1740hrs and it's the end of the bank holiday weekend. It is Monday evening. I wrote nothing yesterday and am unsure if I did the day before because I ran out of paper. I don't feel like writing right now to be honest; however, there has been some serious violence on the wing and Marcus is in hospital. I will write more details tomorrow. Currently, officer 'Arge', the Senior Officer, is taking people out of cells trying to get information. He'll get nothing from me and Martyn. Before I down my pen know this: Marcus had gone in on someone first, three handed the twat. The three of them attacked someone then the victim of the attack got three people together and found Marcus, doing the same to him. It's all madness, I'll get more info from Brad tomorrow but know this: Marcus was pissed up and running in on people who owed him money with a couple of 'yes' men, all his real friends were out on the yard sunbathing. Poor old Brad was caught in the crossfire. Me, Kempy, Pete, Ricky, Steve Lanes and Tony Giles lay in the sun whilst all this took place. First we knew of an incident was an alarm going off and a firm of security screws running onto the wing. More tomorrow.

23-04-2019. After the bank holiday weekend it is refreshing to be down the ATB with Jason, Lucy and Robb Gibb who I'm becoming increasingly fond of. Rob has one of those faces that looks like it's about to burst into mirth at any given moment and when he does laugh his eyes alight with the sheer joy of it. Anyway, so, this morning when the door opened I shot straight up to Brad's cell and noticed all the people involved in the fracas were banged up, marking how seriously they are taking the whole thing. I asked Brad for the full SP on what had happened.

"It left me feeling sick Sloaney", says poor Bradders, running a hand through his substantial head of hair as he always does when perplexed, "Marcus, I don't know if you noticed, was absolutely out his nut yesterday".......and I interject:

"What on"?

"Fuckin' everything, you name it, all the usual but what did it were him, Dale and that little Paul all got hold of a load of MDMA and two litres of proper distilled hooch".

"Never a good mix", I say.

"Anyway", says Bradders, "they're all sitting here fuckin' out of it and Marcus starts talkin' about all the people who owe him money and you know what Dale's like, he started saying 'well, let's go and smash some cunts up then' and Marcus starts going through his debt list and you know that Stuart opposite you on the ones"?

"Yeah, he's been left banged up this morning too".

"Well, the three of them decide to go down there and put it on him for money he owes Marcus and Dale, who was supposed to just stand there whilst Marcus gave Stuart a slap, proper clumps Stuart after Marcus had just clouted him".

"Well, I love Marcus but mate, three people going in on a geezer, well, that's bullying bro".

"Yeah I know right", says my worthy interlocutor, "anyway, so Marcus, Dale and that Paul think it's all done and as usual Marcus is sat up here, just me and him and he's proper monged out on the bed and suddenly the door gets kicked open and there's Noel (spoke of him earlier in narrative, big Medway lunatic), that Stuart and Jonesy from downstairs and Noel goes 'move Brad' and thinking nothing of it I move and Noel pulls out a pool ball in a sock and smashes Marcus round the head with it a few times then that Stuart and Jonesy also have a go then

406

Dale walks in and smashes that Stuart with a mental punch but before it could go any further someone shouts 'screws' and everyone disperses".

"Fuck me", I say, "and we were all out on the yard sunbathing"!

"Honestly man it was horrible and then the screw, seeing everyone flying out the cell and then seeing Marcus with gashes all over his head and face presses the alarm bell and as you know they've all been locked up ever since".

"Fuck me Brad, that leaves all us Thanet boys in a bit of a position".

"Well, not really mate", says Brad, putting the kettle on, "if they'd've done it for nothing then yeah, we'd have to do something about it but Marcus is a mug behaving like that but I'll tell you what, Noel and Dale are itching to get at each other and Dale has sharpened a right shiv up and is saying to me he's gonna stab Noel up".

"Fuck me", I say quite concerned to be honest, "and that cunt is a genuine lunatic, take a train to stop that cunt".

"But so is Noel", says Brad, "I've known him for years and he doesn't give a fuck man trust me".

"I know that too".

"You know what the best possible outcome would be"?

"What"?

"That they move 'em all off the wing 'cause if they don't there's gonna be a fuckin' war on here mate believe me".

"That's what I'm scared of Brad; I've got ten or eleven weeks left and don't wanna get involved in this shit man".

"Same as me Andy", says Brad, passing me a welcome cup of coffee, "and I've spoke to Kempy, he says the same. Like I said, if they'd've done it for nothing something would have to be done but what those three done, going down there to that Stuart was wrong ya know"?

"I agree mate", say I, blowing on my drink to cool it, "could fuckin' do without this shit", and that dear reader is the rundown.

1040am and I'm covered in paint for I am decorating the ATB Unit. Sitting down for a break I pull out me pad and paper. Last night, me and little Martyn had some cross words but they brought us closer together to be fair. I can't even remember what I'd said to him but I do remember he'd responded by making fart noises and this annoyed me greatly.

"What the fuck does that mean Martyn"? I'd asked. He doesn't respond.

"Martyn", I continue, "what the fuck does that mean, them stupid fart noises"?

"Whatever you want it to mean".

"And what the fuck does that mean you sarcastic little cunt"?

"Whoooaaa", he says now, "no need to fly off the handle".

"Fly off the handle"? I say, "mate, you're a fuckin' 27 year old man and you think it's appropriate to respond to people with fuckin' fart noises? Let me tell you Mart, you've been moody for days mate. I try to talk to you lately and you just mug me off. I can see you bottling stuff up. If I piss you off, just tell me man. And let me tell you something else, if you keep bottling stuff up and don't let off the valve by expressing resentments, eventually it leads to relapse mate".

"Whatever you say mate", he says, again, sarcastically.

"What the fuck d'ya mean by that"?

"Well, you know everything don't ya"?

"No, I don't, but I do have some experience you cheeky cunt. You rarely go to the NA meetings lately, when you do you never talk; I never know how you feel. All I'm saying is it's not a good long term recipe for sobriety and I have some experience man".

"Whatever man".

"You're driving me mad Martyn, I never know what you're thinking. I'd rather you tell me to shut up, stop talking or tell me your feelings than keep mugging me off bro".

"I don't mean to mug you off", he says, "I just ain't been feeling right lately".

"Well", I say, "fuckin' talk to me mate 'cause, like you, I've a lot on me plate right now. All the shit on this wing; in my head every day I'm seeing my mum buried in a fuck off great hole in the ground and thinking how cold my little mum is under all that earth and I'm worried sick about my family because the anniversary of my dad's death is fast approaching and at the same time I'm having to second guess how you're feeling bro. We are now the only two really clean people on the wing, What you're doing is brave Martyn. But you never talk. And I know you've got issues. The way your stepdad treated you. Your own dad abandoning you. Amber. You've never talked about this shit have you"?

"Naa man", he says, and I can see he's getting emotional, "I never have; never had anyone who wants to listen".

"Well, I do", I say, "and Claire from Goals Group can arrange counselling for you and I give you my word, you'd grow from it man".

"I've always been taught that men don't show feelings ya know, like it's weak or something", says the poor little sod.

"Well, people like me and you Mart, it's absolutely critical we talk about feelings.. And the more you talk of them the easier it becomes and the better you feel, I promise mate".

"Sometimes", he says, "when I'm in those big NA meetings and you talk and other people talk the whole time I'm thinking 'I'll talk in a minute I'll talk in a minute' but I get really nervous and never do".

"You know what I used to do when I felt like that? 'Cause I used to find it hard talking in front of loads of people too. I started by just saying 'I'm Andy and I'm an addict, I don't have much to say but just wanted to connect to the meeting and say thankyou for bringing the meeting into the jail' and that's it. And the more I did it, the easier it got for me to open my mouth. Now, as you've seen, I can just open my mouth and ramble on and on and on about what's bothering me, what I'm feeling or what I'm exited about. Anything Mart, so, mate, just connect with the meeting in little ways at first ya know"?

"I like that, yeah man I will".

"And Mart", I say, "the reason NA works is because these issues, like your dad or girlfriend or whatever, you'll hear other people talking about the same struggles. And when we relate, we grow, learning of the ways others dealt with trauma. Identifying, realizing we are not alone in the things we've experienced and the way we feel about them".

"Yeah man thanks I know I need to talk".

"I don't have the answers mate really I don't mucca".

"I appreciate you telling me things man I do", and dear reader he is genuine here and a thoroughy nice guy to be true. Nobody else is clean on here to speak of right now and we feel pretty isolated. But we persevere.

1510hrs.

"I've had some funny old using dreams since me mum's funeral", I say to Jason and Lucy down the unit when they both get a minute for a quick break.

"Lucy gets some weird dreams don't ya Lucy"? says J.

"Have you been having strange dreams of late too Luce"? I ask.

"Yeah", she says, "last night I had one about a 9 pence honeymoon to India, Lady Gaga and a stray cat".

"I think the weird dream fairy must be sprinkling dust of late", I say, and continue, "I really wanna tell you about a dream Peter Lanes told me about the other day but it's really un PC.....fuck it, I'm gonna tell ya", and I relate that tale with all the awful language about disabled people included and Jason and Lucy can't help but laugh though this could be at my head growing red as I try to contain my own hilarity in the telling.

"Well", says J, "at least it's only a dream. When I was in the forces three lads I knew told me they'd been out in another country on the piss and they'd all come across this disabled girl and all three of them had sex

409

with her, all consensual of course. Afterward they realized that her wheelchair had been stolen from the dock so they hung her up on a hook and left her there and told some randomer about her so they could get her another one, yeah, I mean, I said to them 'how fuckin' low can you go as human beings' but they just laughed".

"God"! I say, and I look at Lucy trying not to laugh, "I know it's fuckin' savage but it is funny Jason you have to admit", and he too, against his will, can't help but acknowledge that it is. You be the judge dear reader.

1715hrs and upon returning to the wing I find that all involved in yesterday's palava are unlocked apart from Dale who is still banged behind his door. I reckon the staff know that it is too dangerous, at present, and too early, to have him and Noel out together at the same time. I go to Brad's and find Marcus, bandage around his head and gashed above the eyebrow, laying on Brad's bed as per usual and definitely more than a little inebriated.

"What the fuck were you playing at yesterday, going in three handed on that Stuart"?

"We didn't go three handed", he says, "yeah, there were three of us there but I didn't expect Dale to smack Stuart after I'd already given him a dig".

"But he did", I say, "and you clearly were three handed".

"Yeah, there was three of us there but it weren't like that Sloaney".

"What was it like then because I've heard from multiple sources that you all went down, pissed and dizzled up, looking for blood; look, all I want to know is are you gonna forget it 'cause you're as much to blame as Noel, Stuart and Jonesy".

"I'll forget it for now, but I have to get revenge Sloaney".

"Marcus mate", I say, "I'd fuckin' leave it if I were you. Have you all got nicking sheets coming? You down the block tomorrow? I'm surprised you're all out, well, except Dale; why's he banged up"?

"Fuck knows but we'll all know if we're nicked tonight at bang up. That's when they'll give 'em out", and though Marcus talks of revenge and tries to refute he was in the wrong I feel if Dale is not around him he'll swallow his pride. I tell Marcus that the response from Noel was perhaps a little disproportionate but Noel was only angry 'cause he thought his pal was getting bullied and to me that's, well, commendable. Oh dear reader, I am tired of all this petty but undoubtably dangerous shit.

24-04-2019. 1Extra is on the radio and Martyn just gave me a lovely new Pentel Energel liquid gel ink pen with which I write right now. Dale was moved to E wing today but came straight back because someone went to the E wing office and said Dale had threatened to kill him so he was brought straight back to Alpha for there's no space on any of the other wings. Upon reurning to the wing for lunch I went upstairs and said to Kempy:

"Why are Marcus and Dale loitering around downstairs right near where Noel and Stuart and that are sitting"?

"Well", says this deep bass voiced Adonis, "both of 'em are saying that they ain't leaving it".

"Marcus won't do anything", says Peter.

"He fuckin' will", says Kempster, "him and Dale are both proper burning and stewing over what happened".

"I know what Marcus is like", I say, "he really does ruminate, like stew on shit and both him and Dale feel like their pride is wounded".

"Trust me", says Kempy, "I can see it going right off on here believe you me and Marcus and Dale are dangerous with a tool in their hand".

"Oh, Dale's definitely a psycho", I say, "and we all know Marcus has carved a few people up in his time". Dear reader, let us hope it does not go off on here but note this: I shall not be getting involved if I can help it. The whole situation is predicated on bollox. Like I've said before, had El Chubbs been attacked for no reason then, well, I think it likely I'd be in the middle of this. However, you wanna go round the wing, out ya canister weighing people in then you must expect the consequences. I didn't take two geezers into a cell and beat and bully a fella. No, this is Marcus's problem although, saying that, I wouldn't were I present, stand and watch him get beat either. But he can leave this now, done, dusted, and as I say, I hope to God he does.

1720hrs and I painted more of the ATB Unit today and as well as being a workout in itself seeing the thing coming to fruition is aesthetically pleasing to my tiny little mind. At two p.m I went to the gym where I met Kempy and Smartyn. We did five sets of clean and press going up to seventy kilo with which I could only do two reps at a time. After that we put 90kg on and did five sets of deadlifts. In between sets of these, like whilst another person went to the bar, we did sets with the roll out thing to strengthen the core. Not sure if I've explained this: it's a small single wheel with handles each side. One gets to the knees with wheel in hand and rolls out to a plank position 'till the body is flat to the floor, before coming up again and repeating. Sounds easy and looks so when observing others but believe me it is a cunt. Anyway, after that we went to the squat rack doing five sets with 70kg, sets of ten. Then it was to the leg press with 150kg for five times ten sets then we worked the calves until the lactic acid burned those difficult to work muscles, causing my face to contort in agony which of course is the very idea! To finish, the same super fit gym orderly, Mark who killed me the other day, got me on the bike saying:

"One kilometre at level 20".

"Easy", I said but my Lord, wow, it fucked me causing that metal taste and my heart and lungs to feel as though they were about to burst.

"Fuck me, my mouth tastes like iron", I say to Mark, puffing and panting.

"That's 'cause you're working at 90% of your aerobic capacity. That's how you actually increase your fitness levels", and I know he is right though I wish there were an easier way than making oneself sick!

"How old are you Sloaney"? asks Ryan, the gym screw who has a trainee prison gym officer beside him whom I've never seen before.

"Forty-two", I say, "forty-three next month. Why"? But he has turned to this new guy saying 'see'?

"Why Ry"? I ask again.

"He thought you was about thirty", he says.

"Ahhh mate, you're a fuckin' legend", I say, turning to the new fella. I'll take that all day long. I return to the wing with the lads and go to Brad's.

"I can't wait to get out of here Sloaney ya know? I'm sick to death of jail, I really am", says my pal of old, Bradders.

"I feel the same Brad, but I need to be here you know"?

"Oh, don't get me wrong", says Brad, "I always pull the positives but I've just fuckin' had enough now mate; I've spent twenty years in these gaffs now and it's a fuckin' drain".

"Me too, fifteen in these places and it's boring man. I look at it like the Lord is reinforcing my recovery. Helping me get some clean time under me belt and showing me, as I get tired of prison, why I don't want to come back to these places".

"This is it for me, I ain't coming back", and dear reader I can tell you that as I type this up in this lovely house in Oxford in what is now March 2022 that Brad is, in fact, in jail. But I digress, and he is talking now in 2019: "after that bollox the other day with Noel and Marcus, all that violence, since then I've been thinking 'fuck this shit' ya know"?

"Yeah, fuck that shit. But we don't have to get involved Brad", and you can see dear reader this was a worrying time looking back.

1840hrs and Martyn, the little fucker, just beat me 5-2 at cards.

"You've cheated somehow mate, done something to the cards like marked 'em or something".

"Nope", he says with a satisfied smirk, "you just didn't play your cards right man".

"Fuckin' on form tonight ain't ya"!?

"Yeah man, and it's been a good day today".

"I can see you've been feeling better of late", I say and it's true, as I said earlier, since we cleared the air the other day his spirits have been lifted. Sometimes conversations that are difficult to be had have to be countenanced in order to build better relationships.

0820hrs 25-04-2019. Everyone on the wing is kicking off. Even before the door was opened me and Martyn could hear someone shouting out the corner of their door:

"It's a fuckin' liberty Ms Slane-I like to watch the TV, the news in the morning", so I grabbed my remote and turned the TV on to find that the screen is just white noise.

"Glad we got a stereo", I say to Mart, " least we can catch up with the news".

"Yeah man", says Mart, "let me just find the remote". Once the door had opened I went out to empty our bin and saw, literally, a line ten deep of people waiting to get in the office and complain about the lack of TV. As if the staff, like the normal screws, can do anything about it. Last time this happened it was three days before anything was done. You must understand, it isn't like an ordinary system; there are scores of TVs on the wing all running from an integrated bespoke sophisticated system that is prone to fail occasionally.

"Loads of people going down the block this morning", says Martyn now, sitting and preparing porridge.

"Really"? I say, "what, have all those lot, Marcus and Noel and co been nicked for the other day then"? and remember dear reader there were six involved in that bollox.

"Yeah", says Mart over the din of the noise on the landing outside the open cell door and the blaring stereo, "I just heard Marcus saying to Kempy upstairs 'like how the fuck can we be getting nicked three days later' 'cause apparently", continues Mart, "the nickin' has to be issued within 48hrs don't it"?

"That's what I thought", I say.

"Did you see that little punch up a minute ago by the door to health care"? says Martyn now.

"What the fuck, when? What, like literally this morning"?

413

"Yeah", says Martyn, "loads of screws just ran on; that Jonesy was fighting with someone from 'B' wing who was over here getting his meds".

"Fuck me", I say, "he's always fighting that cunt".

"The other geezer got restrained and got carried off", says he, "can you hear Reece? Listen", and I do and we can hear little hyper Reece running up and down the landing shouting at the top of his lungs, not giving a fuck, saying:

"Who's got spice, who's got the spice? I need fuckin' spice", in his high pitched Manchester dialect.

"He is a funny cunt", I say.

"He's fuckin' nuts in 'e"? says Martyn who's known him since they were kids, "he's always been a clown, like proper loud".

"I wish he'd sort himself out the cunt", I say, "I mean yeah, it's comical watching him at times but I feel sorry for the poor fucker. Especially after being on Bridge with him and getting to know him and that".

"He just don't wanna stop", says Martyn.

"I dunno. Sometimes I think he wants to but I just don't think he knows how".

1030hrs. My hands are covered in paint as I stop, retiring from the walls for fifteen minutes for a nice cup of tea. I have done all of the bits that can be done with a roller and am now cutting around the edges; the fire extinguisher box, the various signs and skirting and door frames with a small brush. I love admiring the transformation of the surface as the work approaches fruition.

"Told you it'd turn out alright that colour didn't I"? said Jason upon my arrival at the unit this morning. As I drink my tea I marvel that exactly one hundred days ago today I could be found smoking tea bags! And Bible paper with strips of spice soaked paper.

1750hrs. Smartyn just beat me at cards. We had an NA meeting come into the jail today, first one for the best part of two weeks. Narcotics Anonymous has a thing called Hospitals and Institutions which is a committee of NA members who kindly bring the message of hope into places where people can't get out to a meeting and this committee, these meetings brought into these places is sometimes the first place people hear that there is a way out. I spoke at length today of my fears and struggles and hopes for the future. The fella who came in to do the share had been clean eight years and was entertaining with his message. He, like his audience, had once been a prisoner himself and of course this endeared him to all the lads listening for if he could do it then, it follows, so could they. He explained about going to meetings and building a network of friends who are clean and also spoke at length on the twelve steps, the real work, where the transformative power of the fellowship is at its mightiest. The steps are where we learn of what it is we suffer; a malady of more, a sickness that disallows us from using any form of mind altering sunstance for we are wired differently, addicts, and cannot moderate or stop when started, to the death, literally. In the steps we look at ourselves in a way others don't; we learn things about ourselves that empower us and, most of all, we learn acceptance. We look hard at our defects of character and learn to recognise when they rear their head in our lives. We learn to behave as productive and decent human beings and this, for the mental, chaotic and suicidal addict is a miracle in itself. The only way for me to keep a check on me is through working a program for the rest of my life, allowing me to have a life. Anyway, when I came back to the wing I was eating my dinner in Brad's when Marcus came in, followed by J.T and psycho Dale the big handsome nutjob. J.T says to Marcus:

"I can't believe what Sloaney told us the other day; you going into Sloaney and Martyn's cell and looking at photos of Martyn's sister Melissa on the wall with five people in the cell then pulling your pants down and wanking yourself off"!

"I weren't seriously wanking", says Marcus, "just having a little shuffle", and we all laugh.

"It was fuckin' funny", I say, "and have you seen her J.T"?

"Oh my God", says J.T, "she's a proper little sort int she"?

"Fuckin' proper tool", says Marcus.

"When we banged up that night", I say, "I felt I had to reassure Martyn that that's just your sense of humour Marcus; but you had me in stitches you funny cunt".

"Was Martyn alright though"? asks Marcus.

"Yeah, course he was", I say truthfully, "he knows you're a joker by now", and I continue, "why's everyone got the hump on here right now"?

"Why d'ya think"? says Dale, "no cunt's got any spice on the wing", and right now, banged up for the night with Mart, I say:

"Did you notice that everyone had the hump on here tonight"?

"Yeah man no spice in it"!

"Yeah man, did you really notice? Like, everyone was proper edgy".

"Yeah man", he says, "everyone proper going on like they were ready to kick off, like fly off the handle at any minute".

"Thank fuck we're out of it all", I say.

0808hrs. Door's open 26-04-2019. Outside on the landing it is very noisy; voices raised talking of, predominantly, violence either past or yet to be perpetrated.

"You shoulda seen it", a lad called 'Salman' is saying, "Scouse punched him and the geezer flopped like a tree falling, proper outcold", and now Stuart, who was involved in all that violence the other day is saying:

"The geezer just stabbed him bruv, it was savage and well over the top, proper unnecessary", and someone whose voice I do not know is saying:

"If he thinks it's all over he's got another thing coming". Reece's voice now, the young arse fucker is bringing laughter though which ripples out from his small audience up the landing somewhere. Me? Well, I had weird dreams last night, one involving Adam W, who is a genuinely nice bloke in conscious life but in my dream was running the wing and we came to an altercation in which I was telling him 'I'll cut you you cunt'! Another dream had Dracula having me in a headlock telling me ' I am Dracule' and I was thinking 'fuck me your breath smells' but I suppose the breath of a bloodsucker would. In another dream I was on Ramsgate beach. Oh, and in other news, I have had another outbreak of herpes which usually only breaks once a year but due to stress and worry and such is attacking me once every quarter at present. I felt the unmistakable blisters on me cock last night. Anyway, the sun is shining through the bars of the window and the forecast is for warm sunny weather and though only fifteen degrees today they predict, tomorrow is set to tip the mercury at twenty five Celsius. In other news again, Nicola Sturgeon is promising another Scottish independence referendum though we had the 'once in a lifetime' vote five years ago which failed and kept the Scots in the Union. What with Brexit this is shit I dare say we could do without right about now though being half Celt I can symathise with those wanting independence.

"Can you smell that fuckin'' burning tea bag out on the landing"? says Craig D now, wandering into the cell.

"That'll be him next door mate", says Martyn, "he fuckin' loves it, pure raw tea bag", and it is true that the fat funny scouser next door smokes tea bags on their own, even if it hasn't been rolled in a nicotine patch and without spice which would be, were there drugs in it, somewhat understandable. He simply opens a tea bag, pours the contents into Bible paper and away he goes.

"Martyn man did you hear all that talk of violence on the landing ten minutes ago"? I say once Craig leaves the cell.

"Yeah", says Mart, "whenever there's no spice people get proper hyperactive. You watch, it'll be a proper spice hunt on here today 'cause the weekend's coming up and people will be trying to get it off of other wings and at work and that 'cause there's none on here at the moment".

"Well, I hope someone gets some to be fair Mart", I say, "least it keeps the fuckin' wing quiet".

1400hrs 26-07-2019. Black Eye Friday. Jason was off today; not sick, he never takes a sick day and is a workaholic. So, I was alone with the luscious and lovely Lucy who wore a yellow headband halfway through her lustrous youthful hair and soon as I saw her I thought of the sun. So, yesterday, I finished the border areas and cutting in of the fucking great wall I painted and upon removing the masking tape I nearly had an orgasm as I gazed upon the finished product. How satisfying! The lines are so clean and correct! All around the skirting, fire extinguisher box and signs is perfectly done. Considering I've never before done any painting for I've been a reprobate all my life this was extremely pleasing to me. Anyway, after the unit today I went and did a heart popping circuit with Mark the gym orderly shouting at me all the way through saying things like:

"Come on Sloaney, don't let it beat ya, you're fuckin' slackin'", which of course drives one on all the harder. Anyway, volleyball in a bit so more later.

1700hrs. Thoroughtly enjoyed a buzzing and closely fought game of volleyball. On our team were Smarcus with his head bandaged up, Kempy, Rick Lines and a new addition to the wing named Matty Butler who, according to all who know the guy, has a good moral compass but is a complete fuckin' lunatic when he goes. However, he is clean and sober so is a welcome addition to a wing struggling to get any real recovery at present. Before I rest my pen for the evening let me inform you that I had a great chat with Jay Nevin tonight who's eased up on his alcoholism and is therefore not running around the wing terrorising all and sundry. He can be a pleasure at times but, like me in active addiction, he's fuckin' batshit when he's at it. Fundamentally, like many of us, he's a good guy and I've never had any real trouble with him myself. Interestingly, let me tell you what one of the questions in the Narcotics Anonymous Step Working Guide asks in Step 1. It asks: 'what did you do in your active addiction that goes against all your core values and principles'? Now that question is monumental for me for it gave insight into my true nature. I have not got a moral deficiency, rather, I am sick and need a program in my life on a daily basis to arrest that sickness which when let loose in the worst way, in active addiction, causes me to do things I would not do under any other circumstances, ever. Just saying. One more thing, when doing a circuit earlier 'Valerie' by Amy Winehouse played on the radio and this was my mum's favourite song. Breaks my fuckin' heart man.

27-04-2019 0820hrs. It is wild, wet and windy outside the cell window this morning as the remnants of storm Hannah pass over the British Isles. Smartyn is still sleeping in his sack above me. I'm writing by the light of the TV-BBC News, for I don't want to pull open the curtain and disturb the little fucker. I have eaten, coffeed and prayed and washed and filled my water bottle with creatine. I was planning on working legs today but the circuit yesterday has put paid to that. Oh, and I phoned Tan yesterday; sometimes I still feel like I'm very much in love with her.

"I love you Sloaney".

"And I love you Tan", were words that were very definitely spoken. I also sent a birthday card to my sister though it is two weeks late but since the death of my mum I am thinking that to presume there will always be time to appreciate people in the future is dangerous and can leave one feeling that one did not do enough for a loved one whilst they were still here, like I feel re my mum. Anyway, yesterday I saw Tony Giles who seemed to be in agony.

"You alright Tony"? I had asked.

"Not really Sloaney", he'd replied, "these fuckin' cunts here, I've been telling them for months I've got abcesses in my mouth and that I need antibiotics but the pricks just don't fuckin' listen so today I went to the nurse for an appointment and she said she can't prescribe anything so I pulled eight razor blades out my pocket and stuffed them into my mouth then wrote on a piece of paper 'now get me a fuckin' doctor' and the next thing you know I had all these nurses and screws around me trying to calm me down but they got me a doctor and finally gave me some creams and shit".

"Fuckin' hell mate, is that what it takes to get some proper healthcare here at the moment? I've had to ask my boss Jason to help me by bringing me in Corsodyl Tony 'cause I know it takes six weeks to see a doctor here. It's fuckin' disgusting mate. I love the prison but health care is one area that the system really does need to address".

"Sloaney", says Tony, "last night I actually used a razor blade to cut open one of these sores in my mouth 'cause I was in so much pain I was nearly crying with it in frustration; I just don't know what the fuck else to do ya know"?

"Ahhh Tony man, bless ya you cunt, anyway", I say, looking at a mural of Marlon Brando in The Godfather that he's painting, "that's the bollox; who commissioned this one"?

"I've had about ten people asking me if it's for sale but it's already sold to a geezer on 'D' wing", and as I write dear reader I can hear stirrings from the bed above me as Smartyn stretches and yawns to wake to the world of steel and bars and screws and madness.

"Morning you little fuckin' punk you", I say as his legs dangle over the bed before me.

"Sounds well windy out there this morning don't it"? is the first thing he says today.

"Shit in it"? I say, "and I thought it was gonna be warm this weekend. Hey, Smartyn, I thought I was gonna be doing squats today but that circuit fucked me up bro. My quads and calves are killing me", and it's true, they are, "it's mad, we go heavy doing legs but I don't get the rip I've got today from that circuit. It's those fuckin' squat jumps I reckon and all the reps we do".

"Look man", he says, jumping off the bed, "can you see my six pack? I reckon I've lost a kilo or two in bodyfat".

"You are actually getting a six pack ya little benny", I say to my little pal. Stocky and strong as fuck not so little little pal. Anyway, in other news, Marcus and co seem to have gotten away with the violence last weekend. And it has, for now at least, died a death it would seem.

"Wow look Sloaney", says Martyn now, "those two little sluts on the TV".

"Ahhh man", I say, looking at this set of twins, "sexy cunts".

"I'd bum 'em both", says Martyn.

"Don't", I say, "it's actually painful. Ms H is looking proper fit with her holiday tan int she though"?

"Yesterday", replies Martyn, "she was like leaning over doing paperwork in the office and I could like proper see down her cleavage man, fuckin' hell she's sexy".

"Banging pair a tits on her to be fair bro", I say truthfully.

"Have you seen the way like everyone just hovers around her? Like, when she's in the office there's loads of heads loitering around her"?

"And that goes for wherever she is", I say, "I feel like doing the same but don't 'cause I just start dreaming I'm gonna marry her and that she's being especially nice to me 'cause she likes me! But I know I've got no chance and besides bro it ain't attractive, pesting around the female staff".

"Yeah, but I think she loves it", says Martyn.

"I dunno", I say, "I just think she's a genuinely nice person who tries to be decent with everyone".

"Yeah, but she must know the effect she has on everyone, I mean, she is a bit flirty", says Mart.

"I honestly think that's just her being nice", I say, just as the cell door is opened this Saturday morning. I'm now sitting in Kempy's cell and Brian Cox is on TV talking of the Andromeada galaxy 2.5 million light years away. Usually mass is redshifted as it speeds away from us with the expansion of the universe discovered by Edwin Hubble but Andromeda is blueshifted and on a trajectory to collide with us one day!

In Brad's cell now. Tony Giles just poked his head in looking like he has a snooker ball in his mouth the poor cunt.

"Do you want one a these Brad"? says Gibbo now pulling some tablets from his pocket.

"What are they"? asks Brad.

"Them 'Es' that fucked Marcus up yesterday. He only had one and he was proper fucked", says Gibbo.

"Oh", says Brad, "I wondered why he was so out his nut yesterday. His pupils were fuckin' massive and he was proper gurning man".

"Yeah man, I've got one for me, one for you and one for Marcus but I told him to save it as he's still looking fucked now. You know what he's like though, he can't wait".

"Go on then Gibbo", say Brad, "and I'll give you a pregab".

"Ahhh sweet man", says Gibbo passing Brad the pill, "ready"? and they both hold up their ecstacy tablets, "go", says Gibbo and they pop them at the same time.

"So, what have you had today Gibbo"? Brad asks now.

"Well, I've had two 400mg tramadols, two pregabs with the one you just gave me, half a litre of distilled and a couple of gabbies", he says.

"Pretty much the same as me then", says Brad. I look on and feel kinda left out.

"This is the only fun I get with the drugs now", I say, "watching you lot getting out ya nuts. Is it bad that I laugh when people are having savage spice attacks and are screaming in terror"?

"Well, it's a bit bad that you get off on other people's misfortunes", says Brad.

"But Brad", says Gibbo, "it's human nature to watch people fuckin' up and laugh though in it"?

"Coarse it is", I say, "other wise Harry Hill would be out of a job bro".

"Yeah", says Brad, "but there's got to be limits. I mean, you wouldn't laugh at somebody getting run over by a bus or a train would ya"?

"Depends who it was", I say.

"I know it's bad Brad", says Gibbo, "but you have to admit that spice attacks are funny".

"They are, but they kill people and nut people off for life. I do worry but yeah sometimes it is fuckin' funny to be fair".

"When they start proper screaming like the geezer who ended up in the safe cell recently me and Martyn were in fuckin' stitches", I say.

"But you're evil Sloaney", says Brad, laughing at me. Tony Giles walks back in the cell and has a mouth full of blood soaked toilet roll.

"What the fuck you done Tone"? asks Brad.

"I just stuck a pin in it but there's no puss coming out, just blood", and he places a sowing needle he borrowed from Brad to perform the operation back on Brad's side before walking out the cell looking very pale, very skinny and very sick to be honest. I'm worried about the moody cunt right now.

1210 hrs. I had half hour with the new guy Matt Butler who, it turns out, knows one of my best mates, Dougy Dance, very well. You may remember me telling you dear reader that I attended Dougie's funeral not long ago in October 2021. Only spoke to his brother Scott yesterday with whom I'm also very close.

1300hrs. As I sit in Oxford typing now I ask myself 'should I include my dreams' but I'm going to for it is important, I think, to share myself wholly. So, back to the manuscript. Very strange dreams last night. In one I watched God, like Zeus, turn over a ship that had capsized in the ocean, refloating it and I felt I was the vessel. Then, during the same dream, still on the ocean with other smaller vessels beside and around me I felt like I was being downloaded information from above with the same sounds we used to get when loading a programme onto an old ZX Spectrum computer from a cassette tape years ago when I.T was in its relative infancy. The screeching, squeeling sounds I dare say many of you won't remember. Finally, somewhere between sleeping and waking I was scribing, writing as I slept. A very, very odd thing and I've not the skill to describe it with my poor penmanship. It felt like this writing was stopping me sleeping yet I must have been sleeping to be dreaming!

1800hrs. Went to the gym at 3pm 'till 4 and spent my time trundling along on the cycle. I'm doing a proper timed circuit called 'ultrafit' next Friday so until then my sessions are gonna be purely cardio so that my muscles will be unripped and ready. Anyway, upon return to the wing I went and sat with Peter Lanes, my pal of old, and told him of the dream about the ship and he said:

"Well, that ship thing, I'd look at it like this: your life was upside down and you were drowning. God came down and turned you the right way up", and dear reader I like that interpretation.

28-04-2019 1045hrs. Though the weather outside isn't howling like yesterday it isn't particularly warm either and the cell is chilly. Though it is our bang up this Sunday morning our door is open as Martyn is a servery worker so gets out to spruce the serving area up. Paul Stone, Stoney, is out getting his meds and pops his head into our cell.

"Got any sugar sachets Sloaney"?

"Yeah mate, hold on".

"Sorry to ponce off you first thing on a Sunday morning", he says apologetically.

"That's ok mate, how you been anyway"?

"I'm alright Sloaney man, but I ain't been too well of late as you know".

"You're very thin Paul", I say, looking at his emaciated form and thinking it's definitely, 100% the spice, "if ever I can do anything for you mate don't be frightened to ask will ya"?

"Nice one mate, I appreciate that man", and the thin fella who once rolled around in a cell fighting with me ambles off to make himself a cup of coffee bless him. Now Stuart, from across the road and who was involved in 'Marcusgate' and who's actually alright shouts out the corner of his door:

"Sloaney, can I have a couple of sugar sachets please mate", and I go and stick a few under the door through the small gap. Now Martyn walks in the cell and goes with a crinkled nose:

"Fuckin' hell, that stinks", and I laugh.

"I think it's all those dates I eat last night and this morning, oh, and the protein of course".

"Like a wall of fart when I walked in; a wall of fart"! and on 4music Dua Lipa is warning us not to 'pick up the phone' and I marvel at her olive skin and perfectly turned calves. The whole wing has been opened now for lunch and outside the cell door I can hear many voices raised in laughter which is always a good sign. Now Mr Russell the good looking and decent screw pokes his head in and asks upon seeing my pen on the move:

"Still writing then Sloaney"?

"Yep, the day I leave here is the day I wrap it up Mr Russell".

"Fair enough", he says, "can you see yourself writing anymore"?

"Reckon there's at least ten books in me guv, God willing".

"I wish you luck, speak to you later, I've got to open the rest of the landing".

"Cheers guv", and just as he leaves the fat tea bag smoking scouser who has a spice attack everyday and sells all his food for it comes and pokes his head in and says:

"D'ya wanna buy my chicken today Sloaney"?

"Scouse mate, why ask me bro 'cause I ain't got what you need man".

"D'ya know who has got any spice though"? and he couldn't look and sound more scouse if he was wearing a shell suit.

"You might wanna try Marcus mate, he's the go-to guy ain't he? Sorry mate, but I'm just not in tune with it anymore bro".

"Cheers Sloaney. Could I nick a couple of sugar sachets off of you mate"? and trying not to look exasperated I pass him a handful.

"Nice one Sloaney, cheers mate", says the poor cunt before shuffling along on his way. Pharrell Williams is singing about being happy on the box and the sights and sounds of the video and music make me realize how happy, how grateful I feel today and even as I think it I remind myself not to get carried away because of the old mood swingometer. I try more and more these days to keep myself grounded. Martyn comes in:

"Fuck me, behind that servery it proper stinks".

"Why"? I ask, "usually it's alright, nice and clean behind there ain't it"?

"Yeah", he says, "but whenever I have a day off it doesn't get cleaned properly 'cause most of 'em on there are lazy cunts and all they care about is finishing and getting the next spice spliff ain't it"?

"Well, yeah, I can see that", I say, "you've got to put your foot down Martyn and not let them take the piss mate. You've been on there the longest".

"I know, I'm gonna tell 'em this morning. What about Kirk last night in the showers", says Martyn now, "that was mad weren't it"?

"What a fuckin' weirdo"! I say, widening my eyes in the remembering, "he ain't all there at the moment is he"? And remember dear reader that Kirk isn't gay but by God he's losing the plot of late.

"Naaa man", says Mart, "did he actually touch you"?

"Yeah", I say, "just drying myself off and he comes in and cups my nuts and says 'that ain't bad in it' and I said to him 'I've had an outbreak of herpes' and that if he touched it his hand would fall off but he just laughed", and now Martyn, who was there so knows very well what happened is laughing, his cute face creased in mirth.

"You little cunt", I smile, "he had a good look at you though too didn't he? I saw him look over the cubicle door at you"!

"Yeah", he says, pulling himself together, "but thank fuck I had me boxer shorts on. I dunno what's wrong with him man; is he like a proper gaylord or something"?

"Naaa, I've known him a while and never heard anything, think it's just the spice. Did make me feel a bit uncomfortable though, big hairy arsed man cupping me tings bro", and Martyn, again, finds this proper funny! "You little fucker", I say but I too of course can see the funny side. It is hilarious, the stoned zombie like way Kirk came in the shower and like without preamble cupped my parcel. Wow! Anyway, just been and got my dinner. I sit back down and on 4Music Billie Eilish is singing 'Bury A Friend' and this young girl with her macabre style is sort of growing on me and is very popular at the moment. Ricky Lanes was serving the cake and custard and even before I'd gotten to the que I could hear him shouting to someone:

"Just move along ya fuckin' div, come back at the end to see if there's any left over", and I thought to myself, as I smiled, how much I love this family. They're all fuckin' nuts, including Rick's son Steve who along with his hilarious cellmate Sam Hodges is slightly unhinged like most of us here. Sam has immaced every hair from his body including his sack and crack. He came out on the yard yesterday and flashed us all. Funny, furry faced little fucker was completely hairless down there.

"No fuckin' way", I'd said.

"Sloaney", he'd said, "it puts at least another inch and a half on me cock mate; got to be done", and his handsome face with designer stubble topped with slightly psychotic looking eyes splits with laughter showing straight white teeth the young arse fucker.

"No, I get that", I say, laughing with him, "standard procedure outside-I always make sure the stalk is hairless, looks bigger definitely"!

1400hrs. 'Same time teachers were giving out tests, man was giving out testers' raps 'Dave' on the stereo right now. This is basically saying that when he was at school and the teachers were distributing learning, he had started distributing class A drugs to cats for I have had many a tester off of people wanting to tempt me with the quality of their crack and heroin. The door has just opened, Martyn had shot out straight away but I had stayed put, laying prostrate on me bed with the remote control.

"Close the door please mate", I say to him and he does so, leaving me in peace. I can't be doing with all the madness on the landing right about now. The herpes, along with Tan being on my mind is trying to push my hand to a five knuckle shuffle but I have not masturbated for well over a month and am loathe to squirt my life force into the toilet bowl for though I do not believe in sin I have an inherent feeling that giving away my prana like that is wasteful.

"I wanna use the mobile but Marcus says the battery is dead", says Martyn, coming back into the cell now.

"I thought you said that it was Stevey Lanes' day with it today", and Marcus and Steve have sort of gone into business together.

"I thought it was", says Smartyn, "I wanted to call Amber to wish her a happy birthday", and I want to tell Mart that constant contact with this chick is causing him unnecessary pain on a long arse sentence but don't have the heart to do so. Like me with Tan, who used to visit regularly, I learned that letting go was easier. When I do call her, like once a month or so on the mobile I struggle with constant thoughts of the sexy little fucker for some days afterward. Thoughts of who might be touching her are painful. I never ask her those sorts of questions.

"You gonna let me in your bed when I get out Tan"? I had asked her a couple of days ago.

"Course I am", she'd said "I need you to put your cock in me; it's been too long".

"I've fuckin' missed you in all seriousness to be honest Tan".

"I've missed you too; I think about you every day and have done since you went away".

"Ditto babe", I'd replied, "no matter, not too long to wait now".

"Do you know where you're gonna be living yet? You can always come and stay at my flat in Broadstairs if you want, the offer's still there if you need it".

"Bless you Tan", I reply, "I might need to take you up on that offer. They are trying to get me a place though. You'd be ok with that wouldn't ya"?

"Yeah", she says, "long as you're not with another woman I don't care where you are", and she's no worries there. I think.

1700hrs.

"I love that Billie Eilish", I say to Martyn now, "her music is well interesting although I think it's sort of aimed at the, like, strange suicide bunch ya know"?

"What, like all the little girls looking at pictures on line of people cutting 'emselves an' that"? asks Martyn.

"Exactly", I say, "there's been a bit on the news lately about the government trying to pressure social media companies to remove self harm content and suicide stuff ain't there"? And it's true because recently a youngster killed herself and it was discovered through investigating her browsing history that she'd been looking at disturbing content. Sexy macabre too-young-for-me Billie Eilish's music definitely centres on this suicide sentiment endemic in the young today which is fuelled by the digital era we currently occupy which is, let's not forget, a relatively new phenomena. Anyway, I am 103 days clean today. It is the 28th of April 2019. My father took his own life on May 1st 1998. I'm determined not to let myself slip into a state of sadness. Poor orphan me! Naaa, only joking! Sort of. Enough of that. At the gym today I did 30 minutes on the treadmill and 30 on the bike. Light exercise until the event to really test my fitness levels Friday with Mark the orderly down the gym who is sadistically looking forward to pushing me to my limits. He does get the best out of me. Upon returning to the wing earlier I had a quick shower with Kempy then went and sat in his cell with him and Peter.

"I love the way you interpreted my dream Pete", I say.

"Did ya like that Sloaney yeah"? he replies puffing on a spice spliff.

"I did".

"What dream"? asks Kempy and I describe it and what Pete said about it.

"And", I say, "I honestly believe that the screeching and downloading sounds was my Higher Power sending information to me".

"You an 'alf talk some shit", says Kempy.

"That's the drugs where they've fucked you up making you think shit like that Sloaney", says Peter.

"It ain't shit ya cunts", say I, "even as we speak I have a constant ringing in my ears, a frequency that increases and decreases, like, constantly fluctuating".

"'Fluctuating'", scoffs Kempy, smiling.

"You are mad Sloaney mate", says Peter laughing.

"What", I say, "d'ya really believe I'm going mad"? I ask, genuinely interested.

"Well you've never exactly been the full ticket mate have ya, come on mate", says Pete.

"You're fucked ya cunt", says Kempster, "you've always been shot away".

"I honestly don't think so lads", I say, "I feel pretty sane right about now".

"Well, you keep telling yourself that", laughs Kempy, but it's all in good humour and I love these couple of cunts. Me and Martyn are gonna read some NA literature right now so more later perhaps.

1900hrs and I find it fascinating that all the 'stuff' in the universe cannot sufficiently account for the movement of it. Physics has shown us that the universe is flat, the stuff we can see is 5% of its content, dark matter accounts for 25% of the stuff we can't see and don't yet know of and dark energy, which seems to be driving the accelerating expansion of our universe, accounts for 70% of the stuff contained within its boundaries, if indeed it has boundaries. We have absolutely no idea whatsoever about 95% of what the universe contains. Matter accounts for just five percent and I find this incredible. I wish I had the time and money and knowledge to study maths to a level where I could comprehend just that little bit more.

29-04-2019 1620hrs. I have, thus far, been blessed to've had a wonderful day today. Upon entering the ATB Unit this morning for work Jason said to me:

"There's some chicken and chips and onion rings that Gibby brought in for you in the staff room Sloaney".

"Really"? I say, straight away struck again by the kindness of these people.

"Yeah", continues J, "there's two bits of lovely chicken breast, I've had some, it's lovely".

"What, two bits for me"?

"Yeah, it's just in there in that box look", says J, pointing, "just stick it in the microwave and away ya go".

"Ahhh man", I say, opening the box and eyeing the two succulent lumps of breaded breast, onion rings and proper French fries, "I dunno what to say J", and I go to Gibby's office, "thanks Mr Gibb man that's really nice of you", and the fact that even at home he thought of me is incredibly touching.

"What's that? The chicken? Me and the wife couldn't eat it all last night and I thought 'I know someone who'll appreciate that'", and he laughs heartily knowing I love me food.

"I'm truly grateful guv, cheers mate, proper bit of protein".

"Well, we don't want you getting skinny do we", he says. I go to the microwave and heat me prize, then polish it off in record time. Dear reader, I can't explain, after eating jail fare for a year, how tasty this spicy chicken, these juicy lumps were. I sat and savoured for ten minutes, ten delicious minutes, something which before, at other times in my life, I would truly take forgranted.

30-04-2019. 1115hrs. As I sit in Oxford I think on the repetitive nature of the narrative yet this reflects prison life! I'm currently bored typing and only get excited when something is kicking off, someone is behaving off key or some drama or other is being played out. Back to jail. I'm glad Marcusgate, the potentially very violent situation of late seems to have died a death. The edge of war, like an ill sheathed knife and all that. Still, thinking on those immortal lines, I'm sure Marcus will stir more broils in strands afar remote........the other end of the prison perhaps for he is owed money on every wing right now due to the fact he has been going to education of late, in the afternoons, building his empire of distribution. Again, how he fuckin' manages to sleep I do not know. Not because of the ethical questions inherent here, rather because of the juggling of so much money, the debts and responsibilitly to the lifer nutter he deals with, who supplies him. I can't mention his name but the guy is a lunatic of the highest order and make no mistake. Anyway, I'm at work. From the room I'm decorating at the end of the corridor in this unit I hear Gibby's radio burst into life with the third alarm bell of the morning.

"Fuck me Gibby", I shout, in between brush strokes, "it's been proper going off this morning ain't it"?

"I know", says he, "did you hear that last one? It sounded like there was a female screaming in the background", now dear reader you need to know that when an alarm bell is pushed either via the radio or one of the emergency buttons on the wall all staff get it over the radio followed by the controller telling all staff where the bell came from so that all available staff can urgently attend.

"I thought I heard that too", I say, "where was it"?

"Delta (D) wing", he replies, "if you look out the window you may see one being dragged off to the seg", and sure enough I do and I do. An inmate, surrounded by screws and in locks is marched past the unit toward the block, head held down so he can't spit and headbutt and he's shouting:

"You fuckin' mugs, you fuckin' cunts, wait 'till I get hold of one of you I'm gonna bite ya fuckin' nose off". Not a happy chappy clearly. After the sight of all these blokes, Claudia, the red head and very pretty head of education walks past the unit in a black flower print knee length skirt and I watch the way in which her buttocks undulate beneath the thin material.

"You're a fuckin' lech", I say to myself and smile as I jump off the chair and get back to work feeling incredibly gracious for simply being alive today.

1800hrs. The 1st of May tomorrow. Usually the approach to this day is filled with dread but I have had a wonderful week thus far though, as I told you before, I try to keep my moods as close to the neutral zone as possible. Never allowing myself to become too elated, instead just savouring with gratitude the pure peaceful pleasure I find in simply being alive at present for God knows I should be dead. I told Gibby how good I've been feeling earlier and he said:

"It seems to be all coming together for you Sloaney. If you can find pleasure in the simple things you won't need to do drugs or commit crimes anymore".

"And Gibby", I say, "I really believe I had to go to those dark places so I could appreciate my life today".

"It's no diferent from me", he says, "although I didn't obviously take the path you took, I learnt to appreciate my life through seeing the awful states people could get themselves into. It used to get to me. I mean, when I used to work in Brixton they had a whole wing, where I worked, full of Cat A prisoners with serious mental health problems. There were some seriously sick people there and I used to say to myself 'things could always be worse' but it was bloody hard working with those lot".

"I can imagine mate", I say, "I worked as a support worker in a mental hospital and I found it so fuckin' hard; it depressed the fuck outta me and was a contributor to my relapse after being clean for four years".

"What", says Gibby, and already I can hear the mirth in his voice, "you worked in a mental hospital"?

"Yeah", I say, a smile creeping on my own face for I can see where this is going, "why"?

"Oh, no, nothing", he says, but his eyes are crinkling up at the corners; twinkling, the devil.

"You cheeky cunt", I say, laughing now, "I see you Gibby"!

"What"? he laughs outright now, "I didn't say a word Sloaney"!

"You didn't need to", I smile back at him, "truth is, I couldn't believe they give me the fuckin' job. I had to go through every offence on my criminal record but I knew I'd won them over to be fair. But the job was fuckin' hard work. Especially when I realized I couldn't help these seriously sick people past making their lives as comfortable as I could in my small capacity. I went into the job thinking I could change their lives because I was naïve to be fair. I was deluded and the job fucked me up".

"Where was it you worked"?

"Littlemore Hospital in Oxford. I became very depressed very quickly".

"Yeah, it's bloody sad", says Gibby, "still, another reason to thank God for what you have got".

"For real man", and I am grateful dear reader. I'm also grateful for the lovely gel pen Jason gave me today. Peace out.

1st of May 2019. 1820hrs. Me Dad's day. But I'm not gonna talk on that. Other than to say God rest him.

"What you up to Sloaney"? asked Ms H when I got back from the gym today.

"Not a lot Ms really; how're you anyway? Still enjoying the job"?

"Yeah, I love my job man", she said, "how long you got left now anyway, can't be long now can it"?

"July tenth Ms H", I said, all the while thinking 'my days you're fuckin' beautiful'.

"Bloody hell", she says, "all the old lot, the lot that were on here when I first started the job are gone. When you go there'll be no one left".

"How long you been here now then Ms"?

"Exactly a year this month; it's gone well quick".

"Is it stressful Ms H"?

"Sometimes", she says, "I don't know why, but when people like chat shit about me it really upsets me ya know"?

"What d'ya mean? I hope you leave your job at the gate when you go home"?

"It's hard sometimes Sloaney. Like, do you remember that Ben? The one you used to call 'Cutyoucutme'? He used to slash himself with razor blades, that one"?

"Yeah, why"?

"Well, I had to like, not try and help him so much 'cause I think he was getting the wrong idea. I heard he was telling people, like, me and him were getting close and that 'cause that's my career on the line when prisoners start chatting that sort of shit".

"Ms H", I say, "listen man, you're an attractive and caring young woman. Many of the men here, and I perhaps include myself in this, are emotional retards and can't differentiate between someone being nice, like you trying to help them, and someone fancying them ya know? I really empathize with the female staff here because so many of us have never been shown any real care and we mix it up with amorous intent. You're always gonna get it Ms and when you realize it and pull away from an individual as you did with 'Cutyoucutme', some like him will get resentful and try to spread gossip. No one would believe him so chill man, don't worry about it".

"But I do Sloaney 'cause people talking like that could get me in trouble; it makes me insecure about even being nice to people".

"Don't change the way you do your job because some silly cunt gets the hump when you draw away and does a bit of gossiping to any

430

gullible enough to listen. Give your fuckin' head a wobble Ms 'cause I don't wanna leave you thinking you're driving yourself mad over bollox"!

"No, look, Bradley said exactly the same thing as you so I'll take it on board".

"Good, 'cause the system needs officers like you who actually care".

"Thanks Sloaney".

"No probs Ms; I'm gonna get me dinner, see ya later", and I remember just before 'Cutyoucutme' left, due to the cunt continuously monopolizing staff time to the detriment of the rest of us, thinking, 'will no one rid me of this troublesome cunt' and marvel at my own lack of compassion when being affected by someone else's despair. The poor fucker.

06-05-2019. Not written for a few days. Strange dreams last night in which I was in a bath with Tan. I had used, relapsed, but thought, in my dream, that I still looked as healthy as I do right now but upon looking into a mirror after getting out the water I screamed at my junkie esq appearance, pale and skinny and drawn and I awoke with a scream from my sleep, sweating and trembling with horror. By now you'll know that my dreams mean much to me as I try to interpret them. And this one, indeed, came to actual fruition I can impart from here in Oxford right now. I did end up at Tan's out my nut with a raging crack and smack habit.

07-09-2019. 11am. The future is worrying me greatly as my release date approaches. I think of the words of Marcus Aurelius: "you will meet it, if you have to, with the same weapons of reason which today arm you against the present", and though the passage rings true I think now that if I relapsed all rational principle and power to reason leaves me and anything is possible. I am truly ever but one pipe, one crack pipe from absolute insanity. There is nothing I am not capable of in active addiction. Knifepoint robbery, burglary, robbing my family, beating my friends and even assaulting girlfriends. I become a monster, a heathen, feral and frightening. God protect me from me.

Yesterday one of the new fellas on the wing came to get his food at the servery as of course we have to here. Martyn is the man that ticks off the names as we go past with our plates. He looks to the sheet to see what meal we have ordered, shouts 'pasta bake' for example and the fella behind the jump on the main part of the meal, Craig D at present, dishes out the allocated meal. Well, the new fella is a white guy moody muslim and because me and Martyn do not know his real name we have decided to call him 'Flake'. We gave him this nickname due to the fact that because of his penchant for the spice Flake has picked the fuck out his hands and neck and face leaving fuck off great scabs all over himself, including upon and all over his very bald head. So, Flake had rocked up to the servery yesterday:

"What cell mate"? asks Smartyn of Flake as the menu list is done by cell, and I'm thinking: 'I hope none of those scabs fall into the food'!

"104", says Flake.

"There ain't a meal here for you mate", says Martyn.

"Why not"? asks Flake.

"Says here you're on Ramadan bro so you'll get a box of food tonight".

"Oh, shit, oh, yeah, I like forgot man in it", says Flake, and he scuttles off, dropping a few scabs along the way I dare say. People pretend to be Muslims to get a better diet but also to fit in in jails with large Islamic communities. Flake can't be a very good Muslim if he forgot he was in Ramadan. Later on Martyn says to me:

"Flake looks proper out his nut, look, look, he's in his doorway doing the palsy wobble like El Chubbo was doing yesterday", and sure enough I look over and all I can see is Flake bent over almost double, arms hanging loosely and his bald bescabbed head bobbing up and down in the typical spiced up way.

"Fuck me", I say, "cunt's a proper mess in 'e"?

"Whaaaaattt"! says Mart, "the state of his head though, and the back of his hands and arms and look at his neck bro"!

"Fuck me, he must be proper picking the fuck out himself man; savage"!

"Ahhh man", says Martyn, "disgusting"!

"Poor cunt though ay"? I say, "he musta come on the wing with the spice though 'cause apparently there ain't any on here". We go into our cell and I see a load of tiny spice joint sized strips of paper on the side and ask Martyn:

"What's that"?

"I'm gonna, like, walk around the wing and drop 'em on the floor and watch people like scuttle about pickin' 'em up thinkin' they've had a right touch findin' a free bit of spice", and he laughs at his own idea.

"Hahahahaha", I laugh too, "that's a fuckin' wicked idea Mart. You'll have to drop some outside Flake's cell and Scouse's next door".

"I've sprayed 'em all in odour neutraliser, like, that spray air freshener stuff too", says Martyn.

432

"You're fuckin' ruthless ya cunt; drop a couple now, go on". Martyn does and though Scouse is nowhere to be seen and Flake is out his nut already fucked we creased up in laughter as cat after cat thought they'd hit the jackpot. I have to say that Mart makes me cry sometimes with mirth; spraying these strips with product is genius!

"Smoking odour neutraliser won't fuck 'em up too much will it"? asks Martyn now.

"Well", I say, "no more than the cockroach killer bro, I wouldn't worry too much".

"Fuck 'em in it", says Mart. Anyway, at another point this weekend I was sat in Kempy and Peter's cell with them two, Craig D, Marcus and lifer Steve Bennett.

"Who's that"? says Marcus, looking toward the open cell door.

"Who"? asks Kempy.

"That tall blonde screw on the landing", says Marcus.

"Behave yourself", says Craig D, "she's well into her sixties man".

"Naaa, not that old", says Pete, "fifty-two I reckon and I'd still bang her".

"Me too", I say, "banging bum".

"Spose I would too", says Craig, "she's not English though ya know".

"Where's she from"? asks lifer Steve before raising his voice to this, to me, never before seen screwess standing outside the cell now by the dining table, "oi, Miss, Miss, come 'ere a second please", goes lifer Steve, and she does, filling the doorway and he continues to her, "where you from Miss"?

"I am from Itaaaalllliiiiaaa", she says.

"Oh, Italy", says Steve.

"What's good in Italy Miss"? asks Kempy.

"Well now", she says in her accented English, putting an index finger to her lip in thought, "there are lots of good things in Italy".

"Like what though"? asks lifer Steve.

"We make a the Lamborghini, the Ferrari and the motorbike you know"?

"I must admit", says Steve, the lanky grey haired skinny fucker whom I love, the lifer, "they do make a good engine".

"And ah the pasta", she says now, "and the ice cream and lots of other things".

"Yeah", says Steve, and 'cause I know the cunt I can sense something is coming, "banging cheese too".

"Banging"? says the screw.

"Yeah, like good cheese", says Steve.

"Ahhh yes, we make ah the very good cheese, the best cheese", and she seems to be genuinely enjoying chatting to us.

"I've heard they make the best smegma too", says this cunt, this incorrigible lifer.

"Smegma"? says the screwess looking confused.

"Yeah", says he to the poor hapless woman, "you know, it's like a real posh expensive cheese, smegma", and the whole cell, all of us, have red heads where we are trying not to laugh at the nonchalant way the sarcastic cunt drops his lines.

"Ahhh", she says, oblivious, "I never knew this smegma but I will definitely try the smegma soon", and she happily pulls the door to and ambles on her way, clueless, and as soon as she is out the way I say to Bennett:

"Smegma, fuckin' smegma"!

"You're a cunt Steve", says Marcus but we are all crying in laughter.

"Bennett", I say between guffaws, "you are truly a cunt of the highest order.......fuckin' smegma", and I mimic her: "I must try this smegma", and we all crease up again, "you're a prick Steve", I tell him. And, dear reader, just in case you've lived in a cave I can tell you that 'smegma' is the cheese like accumulation which builds up behind the foreskin of men who don't wash for lengthy periods and is stronger than stilton, I know, for I've been homeless.

"I wonder if she'll go home and do a google search on smegma", says Bennett.

"You are a funny cunt", says Craig, whose head is red from laughing, "it's the way you say things with a proper straight face".

"I don't know how you do that", says Pete, "soon as you said it I had to put me head down".

"We all did", says Kempy, "how the fuck you kept a straight face then I do not know". As I type now from the document, taken back, clean and sober for eight months (14 now as I edit) out here in the real world, I revisit this cell in 2019 and chuckle as my fingers dance across the keyboard. If I hadn't of been able to clean up, this never would've gotten out there to you dear reader and I must say, I'm not displeased with much of the narrative to be fair. Hope you're enjoying it too. Anyway, back to the manuscript and another day this weekend I was once again in the same cell with Kempy and Pete and Bennett again walks in.

"Cor Sloaney", he says, "I just been having proper banter with Ms Slane; she's fit as fuck man and I get a hard on just talking to her sometimes".

"She is sexy", I say, "she's another one like Ms H, a genuinely nice person".

434

"I'd fuckin' love to get up that", says he, lifer Steve now.

"No one's got no chance with her man", says Kempy, "she is fit though".

"Sexy for a nigger", says Peter Lanes.

"Fuck sake Pete", says Kempy.

"Pete man she's lovely, don't be like that man", I say.

"Oh shut up Sloaney", says he.

"Anyway Bennett", I say to lifer Steve, "she genuinely believes you're a raving iron".

"Why? What d'ya mean"? he says, "why would she think I'm gay? I ain't gay"!

"'Cause the other day", I say, "me and her were talking and I said to her as you went past 'I fuckin' love Bennett and I think he's proper brave like coming out in prison Ms'".

"Ya didn't say that did ya Sloaney"? he asks, aghast.

"Yeah man", I say, "I explained that you'd been in jail for twelve years and that you've had boyfriends in here and that".

"Naaa man Sloaney you didn't, please say you didn't, I'm gonna go down there and tell her I'm not gay", and he scuttles out the cell, returning and standing at the doorway five minutes later saying:

"Did you really say that Sloaney"?

"Yes bro, she proper believes you're a raving iron Steve", I say, "she promised me she wouldn't say anything though; it's no biggy man", but Steve, smiling, moves out the way and the gorgeous (and she is) figure of Ms Slane appears in the doorway too.

"Sloaney", she says, smiling, "you had him proper worried", and she laughs.

"I went straight down", says Steve, "and said 'Ms Slane, I dunno what you've heard but I'm not gay'", and Ms Slane says:

"And I said to him 'what the fuck you on about I don't think you're gay, why d'ya say that'? and he goes 'that fuckin' Sloaney told me he'd like proper convinced you I'm gay 'cause I've been in jail for years'! You're a little bugger Sloaney", she laughs.

"You cunt Sloaney", says Bennett.

"Got ya though didn't I"?!

08-05-2019 10am.

"Why didn't you go to 'H' wing yesterday"? asks Gary, one of the prisoners on the Thinking Skills Programme at the unit where I work. He is a stocky fella of five feet eight or so who's having a difficult time of it at present. Remember, 'H' wing is for enhanced, well behaved prisoners and I was offered a place on there yesterday.

"Well", I say, "I'm happy where I am ya know? I've been on there for a year and I'm comfortable; I know everyone, all the boys and staff and I've got a blinding cell mate. Also, I've only got eight week left so moving is pointless really. Anyway Gary, what's happening with you"?

"I'm still not able to leave my cell", says Gary, "the geezer, the mug I had a fight with has put £500 on my head. All his mates are looking to get a hold of me. And it's not like I can't fight, I can handle myself Sloaney"!

"I gather that", I say, "but what do you think would happen if you just said 'fuck it' and came out your cell onto the landing"?

"I know what would happen", he replies, "if I go out on that landing it's gonna go off. Because the fella feels I got the better of him he is looking to have it again with me", and what you need to know basically is that Gary had a fight with a fella on his wing, 'G' wing. Since the fight and because the fella sells a lot of spice and has put pages on Gary's head Gary does not leave the cell unless escorted by a screw. He is accompanied absolutely everywhere including to and from the ATB Unit where I talk to him today.

"What possible outcomes do you see Gary? Is there no way you'll go out on the landing"?

"Sloaney, it ain't gonna be no one to one thing if I go out on that landing bro. If it was I'd go and have it with the cunt. He's got all his mates involved and the whole situation is bollox. What I find really unfair is that all I did was defend myself but it's like I'm the one being punished ya know"?

"I feel for you mate", I say, "if it was me though I'd front it. Saying that, I had a situation twenty five years ago in young offenders where I was so outnumbered after ripping a geezer off I simply refused to leave the cell 'till they moved me prisons; that was in an 'A' stroke 'B' cat nick though and I'd've got carved right up. Never had to do it again though thank fuck".

"That's one of the options I'm thinking of. Or maybe H wing. But this cunt's got people everywhere and the thing is I'm out soon, possibly July", he says, "and if I get caught fighting with the cunt again I know I'm gonna lose days. If I had my way I'd go down the block, stay behind the door on bang up for the rest of my sentence". Thing is dear reader, now, aged though I am, I would, were I Gary, go out and simply attack the cunt kamikaze style, frenzied psychotic attack. But I feel for Gary but am also aware that I only have his side of the story. Like myself though Gary has a relative degree of intelligence and I can imagine he is overthinking this situation. Anyway, all conditioned things are impermanent and when one sees this with wisdom, one turns away from suffering. He has but weeks left to serve and all will be well soon enough. He can use this as motivation not to return. No yesterdays are ever wasted for those that give themselves to today and at least he's doing this excellent course down here at this unit. I wish him luck.

10-05-2019 1800hrs. Haven't written for a couple of days (funnily enough, typing three years later I've not been at the PC for a couple days either....anyway, back to jail) but just to catch up with literally a couple of lines: Lucy, Jason and Mr Highm got me a card and some lovely gifts including a beautiful pen for my birthday which is tomorrow. They also brought in a lovely cake and lots of love which I again find quite overwhelming. Martyn has also touched my heart by getting me a card and chocolate and I knew not what to do but squeeze the little fucker in thankyou. Anyway, there has been lots of heroin on the wing of late; Marcus El Chubbs has been selling lots of it and due to the nature of the drug a boy from Brighton named Elliot, small little fella, has two black eyes and Briggsy from Thanet also sports wounds. Reece has also been smashed up and all these injuries on these three boys are directly related to the heroin influx on the wing right now. Heroin breeds violence, always has, always will. In other news, I have been smashing the gym and took a minute twenty one seconds off of my ultra fit time. Buzzing with that. Martyn, due to the current heroin influx has been grinding coffee smooth and mixing it with coffee mate to imitate the drug before wrapping little amounts in cling film wraps and dropping them on the floor round the wing so he can then watch as hapless fucks pick them up gleefully thinking they've had a right touch. Bad, I know, but I do chuckle!

12-05-2019. Not written a lot of late and don't feel like doing so now. My excuse is I'm reading David Icke's Tales From The Time Loop and thoroughly enjoying some of the historical information contained therein. This guy knows some secret shit. And much of what he says, though I can feel your ridicule dear reader, rings closer to the truth than much of the bollox fed to you and I through a biased and ulterior motive driven media. Anyway, it was my birthday yesterday and Brad made me a card which many of the boys on the wing signed. Bradley put on the front 'toe be or not toe be' in reference to my comedic feet. It was a lovely gesture and so many signatories wishing me well means the world. In other news, Kev, the gym officer who's time on the ultra fit I am just not quite able to pip pushed me proper yesterday and I squatted the most weight I've ever managed with 165kg on my back. Today I did chest and arms but I took it easy for my legs are ripped and I know from experience that

437

having every muscle in the body broken at once can bring down one's mood. Let me describe the Ultra Fit challenge: 1.5km bike ride at resistance setting 16, 500 metre row, 40 reps lat pull down plate 6, 60 reps hip flexes, 50 press ups, 60 crunches, 100 step ups with 10kg in each hand, 40 reps shoulder press 25kg, 800 metre run 10% incline and finally forty reps bench press with 40kg; I have the sheet I borrowed from the gym before me. Those gym boys, the staff, Kev, Ryan and Mr Butler have been an integral part in me getting and staying clean in an environment not suited for such. The lifer orderlies Jimmy and Mark have also given much of their time to me. The latter in particular proper puts me through my paces and each time I train to his tune I leave the gym proper fucked up. Jimmy puts the circuits together and does so sadistically to make sure we are tested and each time I finish, and I always manage to, I feel an immense satisfaction and sense of achievement. In general I feel incredibly grateful for my circumstances at present. Anyway, in other news, El Chubbo, Bradders, Kempy and Dale have been amongst others booting hard (smoking heroin) and have habits which will cause them significant discomfort when the opiates run out. Chubbo is going right downhill again and Dale is terrorising the wing shaking people up to feed his own desire for ever more drugs. Anyway, I love the banter I have with Tony Giles who is doing me another picture. When I walked past him with my dinner earlier he's at the dining table painting and I say to him:

"Alright ya skinny mug".

"Who the fuck ya talking to"? comes the inevitable response.

"You ya prick, get in the cell and I'll smash the cunt outta ya"!

"Really? You reckon yeah"?

"I'd kick the granny outta you Tony I tell ya"!

"Only with a snide punch like you got me with as a kid", he jokes now, reminding me of the time I did in fact snake him many years before.

"Ahhhh Tone, had to go there with that didn't ya"!

"Oh shut up, you know I love ya", he says, "when you out Sloaney"?

"July tenth".

"Not long then. I can't fuckin' wait 'till December to see the back of this place", and I can tell you from here in Oxford dear reader that Tony is now living homeless in Canterbury, struggling to find help and support from the powers that be.

21-05-2019 1300hrs. And I can tell you that Brad got out today God bless him.

438

1735hrs. So, the wing without Bradders. He gave his mouse away but within hours the fella he gave it to learned of the cleaning, the feeding and instead of taking on such responsibility he freed the poor cute little thing. Anyway, Marcus came down to the ATB Unit today for a coffee with me, Gibby, Lucy and Jason and, remembering Lucy is very beautiful dear reader, Marcus says:

"Show Lucy why you've got a foot fetish Sloaney; show us your feet".

"What you on about ya mug", say I, smiling but horrified, "I ain't got a foot fetish Marcus man".

"Why, what's wrong with your feet Andy"? asks Lucy.

"Nothing Luce", I say, "he's just being a weirdo".

"Have you got a foot fetish though"? asks Lucy.

"Of course not", say I.

"Show us ya feet then, come on, show Lucy Sloaney", says Marcus the cunt.

"What's actually wrong with them Andy"? asks Lucy again, clearly interested now.

"I've got a bit of a bunion Luce that's all".

"Oh, that's no big deal", she says.

"You ain't fuckin' seen 'em"! says Marcus.

"What, you got 'em on both feet then"? asks Lucy.

"Come on, just get 'em out", says Marcus, the smiling assassin, and he turns to Lucy, "these are, like, super bunions though Lucy, honestly, it's like he's got a thumb stickin' out the side of his feet they're so fuckin' massive Luce you've never seen anything like it I promise you"!

"You're such a knob Marcus", I say, but, realizing he ain't gonna give up I remove a shoe and sock.

"Ahhhh", says Lucy, "they are some trotters those though ain't they. How'd'ya get 'em? I thought only women got bunions".

"Wearing trainers too small as a kid when I was running away from kid's homes and that I think", I say, pulling on my footwear once more.

"Do they hurt"? she asks.

"Only when I get new shoes or when it's cold".

"Fuckin' ugly though ain't they Lucy"? says Marcus.

"Don't be horrible", says Lucy but she's laughing, "they ain't that bad really".

"He's fuckin' horrible to me Lucy", I say.

"I'm only messin' Sloaney", says Marcus and to be fair we had a good laugh down there today. Anyway, I don't know if I told you me and Martyn's idea about the A wing recovery BBQ? If I didn't then this is the basics: there's a notice board on the wing where people check lists put up

439

every day about where each person is allocated work for the morning and then afternoon periods. Also, all general notifications go on here too. Well, we had the idea using a bit of clip art I did down the Unit to advertise an upcoming A wing BBQ with space for people to place their names for me and Martyn just wanted to see how many gullible fools would fall for it. There are already at least fifty names on there! I had put on it 'come to the A wing recovery BBQ on Bank Holiday, 27th of May. Burgers, sausages and fizzy pop. Limited space so be quick'! Anyway, in other news, Flake was thrown to the floor today by staff after refusing to bang up for some reason. Tony Giles is on hunger strike because after the operation to remove seven nodules from his mouth and throat he can't eat solid food and no contingency has been made to feed him. He showed me inside his mouth earlier and there is awful inflammation which would clearly cause significant discomfort were he to eat solid matter. Finally, this afternoon, Marcus was swagged off of the wing by security for a piss test.

"I can't believe it Sloaney", he said upon his return, "I'm fucked"!

"Well, what you gonna fail it for? What's in your system"?

"Spice, benzos, crack and heroin man. That's gonna be another month I'll have to serve in jail now the cunts".

26-05-2019 10am. It is Sunday morning on a bank holiday weekend in May. Martyn has just gone down to the kitchens to get the food trolley accompanied by Craig D who has but four weeks left to serve. Last night Craig stuck it on the fella I have introduced to you as Flake. Well, Flake is on Ramadan though the skinny white northerner has never seen the inside of a mosque in his life. Anyway, each day, those on Ramadan receive an orange box which keeps their food, to be consumed once the fast is over in the evening, warm. Well, Flake never washes his box up as he's supposed to so the kitchen have refused to do it, leaving him without a meal. He started kicking off at the servery and threatening the boys behind the jump which, of course, includes mental Craig D. Craig, upon hearing Flake saying:

"Whichever of you servery lot have grassed me up for not washing my box up watch-no one can tell me anything on this wing", he said in his northern drawl, "I'll smash any cunt on this wing", the warlike Craig immediately said:

"Who the fuck you talking to you mug"? Craig says, continuing, "it was me who told the kitchen that you're the dirty cunt who don't wash your box; who the fuck do you think you are? Why do you assume someone else will do it for you"?

"But, but, Craig"….starts Flake.

"No, go on, get the fuck away from the servery before I smash your fuckin' head in you fuckin' mug cunt", and the guy, who but minutes before was willing to fight anyone slinks away from the servery with his tail between his cowardly legs. Anyway, right now I am sitting writing this for you on the yard with Pete Lanes beside me and he is saying:

"We was out in the meds que this morning and that bully cunt Darren S was mugging everyone off on 'A' wing 'cause he got kicked off here".

"Why was he mouthing off"?

"Because he was tryna push in the que and I stuck it on him. I told him: 'you're a fat fuckin' bully mate' and the cunt shut up".

"He is a fuckin' bully man", I say, "horrible cunt". Out here on this yard right as I write me and Pete sun ourselves and Dale Pearson is punching pads held by barbarian 'tryna touch me sexually' Kirk H. Steve Lanes is doing deals with Marcus who has pages and pages of power paper round him at the moment and who is owed over a thousand pounds. Some youngsters like James, a big handsome lunatic, are doing a circuit. Paul Stone just skulked out here looking like Smeagle but no sooner had the sun touched his face he retreated, as if allergic to it. Craig D is now doing pull ups on the rooted in the concrete equipment and young Lenny, a twenty something kid with dark hair dark eyes and slight build who is, we surmise, probably homosexual, is telling Craig as Craig sweats, bare chested and showing considerable muscle, that:

"You're looking proper fit now Craig mate".

"Trying mate, trying", says irascible Craig and Pete Lanes next to me pipes up to Lenny:

"Where you from Lenny? Brighton"?

"No, I'm originally from Kingston, Surrey, but I live in Hastings now".

"You're defiantely a benny though ain't ya Lenny"?

""I ain't no benny", says Lenny to Pete.

"Half a benny then", says incorrigible Peter and now Lenny has walked to the other end of the yard doubtless to get away from the bigot sitting beside me. Peter shouts as he walks:

"Wiggle it, just a little bit.....come on Lenny, you are a bit gay though ain't ya"?

"I'm about twenty percent gay", says Lenny.

"I knew you was a bit of an iron", says Pete to him before turning conspiratorially to me and and saying:

"See, I knew he was a shit stabber", and now Moody Matchstick Model Cabinet Maker Trevor has come out on the yard and I say:

"Fuck me Trev, ain't the bright light hurting ya, like burning your eyes"? and he coughs and splutters a bit before saying:

"Fuck off Sloaney ya pisstakin' cunt", but he's smiling and asks;

"How long ya got left mate"?

"July tenth", I tell him.

"Oh yeah, two days before me", and he shuffles back into the wing. Now another youngster called Charlie, dark hair, blue eyes and cute 19 year old face comes out and asks me:

"What ya doin' Sloaney? What ya writing? I've heard you're writing a book"?

"That's what I'm doin' now. Who told you"?

"You know that big tall northern screw? I think they call him 'Scouse', he told me".

"Oh", I say, quite surprised, "didn't know he knew 'cause he's new on here really".

"Yeah", continues Charlie, "he told me 'Sloaney's written a book in the year he's been here, he's proper got something about him", and I'm loving hearing this, shallow fuck that I am. Anyway, Pete Lanes has gotten hold of today's Sun On Sunday and is showing me a picture of the new Honda Goldwing being reviewed in the back of the paper.

"If your book sells Sloaney you can buy me one of these; d'ya like it"?

"Fuckin' beautiful bike", I say honestly, "look at the engine popping out the sides, like proper space age ain't it"?

"Gorgeous in it", says Pete, "I'd love a bike like that".

"Me too", I say, "you might wanna get yourself a license first".

"Fuck that", he says, "I don't need a license, not on one a them anyway, I bet it goes like a rocket. Have you got a license"?

"Yeah, not a bike one though", and now Peter gets up.

"Where ya goin' ya cunt"?

"Goin' in ta get me meds man", he says, "and they're feeding, look", and we see another prisoner, Chris Brown, real name, wander out on the yard eating his roast dinner and now Marcus walks out with Kempy, both with chicken legs in hand and I say to Kemps:

"Watch my paperwork bro while I go get my dinner". I get my meal and eat it in the sun on the yard. What a lovely, lovely morning. I sit outside until I hear the 'ding dong ding' of the tannoy, exactly like a supermarket, calling us all in for bang up. I'm now in the cell, the door is banged and I pick up Russell Brand's 'Recovery' which I'm thoroughly enjoying reading. Little Mix are on the box singing 'Touch' and I am reminded of my time in Essex where I first heard it, and the pace of my drug use then, homeless and destitute. I marvel that I am 131 days clean and sober. How very lucky I feel today.

442

1700hrs. As you know dear reader it is Bank Holiday weekend, Sunday of the same. Yesterday in the gym with Kempy and Marcus I did chest and the cunts worked me to absolute failure. When with these pair a cunts it's not just the workout I enjoy but the pisstaking banter also. Anyway, I am ruminating, musing on shit today. I was just thinking that in my experience if you take away one thing in a relationship with a lovely lady you gain something else. You get sublime beauty to look at in one but not so much upstairs but get a plain Jane and you get brains too. Very rare for extreme physical beauty to be juxtaposed with a sharp intellect. Saying that, A---- is an exception here, she of the airplane arrest fiasco. And, now, Tan. In the context of jail though I realise sacrifices and gains are also inherent. I left Marcus's cell where I did, it must be said, find myself exposed to constant drug use up close and personal necessitating the wearing of a dust mask to protect me from the fumes of the crack smack and spice but I was regularly to be found creasing up in hysterics with his banter and insane behaviour. At present, and do forgive me, I am struggling to get a fucking conversation out of Martyn and I find it incredibly frustrating at times. I feel I'm turning into an Epsilon Minus Semi Moron. I struggle to get more than one word answers out of Mart and have to constantly remind myself the poor fucker has just had the best part of ten years stuffed up him so I cannot expect him to be the life and soul of the party. I feel I'm really mean in my thinking, judging him as different from me. Not as clever! How dare I? Who the fuck do I think I am? I have been asking the infinite to protect me from myself for if I do let loose with language hurtful to Martyn it isn't just him who suffers, no, I do too for I beat myself up no end with shame these days and already have enough of that to deal with after what I have become in life. Thief, junkie, robber, woman beater. Make no mistake though, despite all my attempts at self control I sometimes let the poor fucker have it and three days ago I called him a moron because of his lack of interest in anything else but his musculature in the most visceral of tones. And, predictably, a few hours later, after ruminating on my cruelty I apologised profusely asking him for forgiveness which he freely gives the good natured cunt. Right this instant Mart is watching Godzilla with a moronic smile on his cute face. I told him, when he asked if I was going to watch it:

"I'm not a fuckin' moron mate and can't enjoy watching a big plastic fuckin' dinosaur puppet bro". I beg you dear reader, do not judge me on this alone. I am just learning what it means to be good, kind, compassionate and for the most part I am. It is incredibly frustrating here, in prison. I have to remember that I am the anomaly here, that Martyn is amongst his equals for sadly the majority of the prison

443

demographic is lacking in even the basics of reading, writing and numeracy levels, as was I when entering these walls as a kid. And compounding this fact is the truth that people like Martyn fear education because they believe, erroneously I reckon, that any attempt at academic pursuit will invariably end in failure. And of course this is not how education works in these places. I have watched people become enthused who hitherto thought they could never achieve. Fear is a massive obstacle to overcome. I mean, look at me with maths! I was also embarrassed, compounding the problem further. Yet I achieved and quickly at that! I am an old man and have known many troubles, but most of them never happened. It was just fear. And fear is a liar. We never grow if we stay forever in our familiar patterns, never straying from the beaten track. This is why I continuously fight my addiction. People often ask me why I keep going through awful opioid withdrawels and it is because I refuse to give up, to settle for that shit. I want more, yet even now I fear I am not good enough. But these spectres fade with every day I get clean. And the clean time I have had in the past proves I can do it with every day reinforcing it. Even with drugs wrapped all around me I can do it. I'll never forget the fear, though, going back to education, that I felt when first I walked into AddemupAde's class. It was right in the gut. Embarrassed, uncomfortable but as I learned I can learn my burgeoning belief gave me feelings of awe and wonder; the realization that my fear was false. A lie. Even as I write I feel awash with gratitude for the serendipity of circumstance that brought me here at this time. Meant to be. God shot. Ade, A wing, the ATB Unit. God does, indeed, work in mysterious ways and I need to remember, every minute of every day, to be grateful when lamenting the lack of intellectual stimulas or when wanting to be horrid to my peers who for the best part are extremely damaged people who I should be trying to help, not hinder. I can, dear reader, be a horrid fucker at times. I am aware of this and can therefore do something about it. Anyway, as I am writing I am suddenly aware of the short duration I have left to serve. It is Monday the 27th of May tomorrow. June is upon us and on July ten I exit the gate. Again, I remind myself to be grateful for I do not wish to become a lamenting energy vampire. I know better. I have been blessed. Be thankful Sloane. Oh, and by the way, I watched the dinosaur puppet film and thoroughly enjoyed it. And there is a lesson there indeed.

0900hrs 27-05-2019. Morning dear reader. Bank holiday Monday. I wish to quickly update you about a recent regime change here at HMP Rochester. As I described to you earlier in the book, on the weekends we have been subject to an association/bang up/bang up/association rolling rota. So, if we are out Saturday morning we would be banged up in the afternoon and vice cersa on the Sunday. Reversed the following weekend. Well, now we get out both morning and afternoon. And in the core week, Monday to Thursday anyway for Friday we will bang up after the evening meal, we are now banged up at 7pm as opposed to 5pm. However, though this seems like a shift it is really but a return to the normal regime here that was in place before Rochester was put into 'special measures' by the Home Office due to high levels of violence, drug abuse, self harm and suicide some years ago. Another point of note is that there has been policy put in place that we are now no longer to be called 'prisoners' or 'offenders' but 'residents' instead! I can see the lovely liberal logic in this but, me personally, well, I did wrong and was jailed for doing so and feel 'prisoner' to be an apt decription of what I am right now. Resident implies I've a choice to check out whenever I wish which of course I do not. Anyway, I'm currently sitting in my cell listening to Absolute 80s radio and outside the open door Jonesy, a short arsed Chatham based bod is shouting at Satnam, our wing washer. Now Satnam is the only person of ethnicity on our wing which seems crazy I know. His heritage is Pakistani I think.

"What's your problem mate"? asks Sat of Jonesy now, "I told you, your washing was in the machine last night and I've just put it in the dryer now".

"I've been waiting two days you paki cunt", says Jonesy.

"Alright mate", says the pretty decent and always placid Satnam, "you'll have it this afternoon".

"Fuckin' make sure I do 'cause I ain't got no clean underwear".

"No worries man I'll have it for you", and now Martyn walks in the cell and I ask:

"Did you just hear what that fuckin' Jonesy was saying to Satnam"?

"No", he says, "what did he say"?

"Fuckin' shouting at him and calling the poor cunt a paki bro".

"No way man, that's fuckin' out of order; I like Satnam".

"Me too", I say, "I'd love to bite chunks out that horrible little cunt Mart. I'd love to see Sat switch on the prick".

"What did Satnam say to him"? asks Mart.

"Nothing mate, that's the worst thing about it bro. Poor cunt didn't even retaliate. Satnam ain't like that is he? I've never once seen him get angry man". And it is true; Sat is a prolific shoplifter outside but non violent.

"Why you putting your work boots on"? I ask Mart.

"Just going down the kitchen to take the trolley back from last night. See you in a bit".

"I'll put the kettle on for a coffee when you get back bro".

"Cheers mate", and just for the record dear reader know it is lucky there are laws for if not I'd let loose on cunts like Jonesy on a regular basis. Horrid little cunt.

1800hrs. Not gonna write much. Kempy is now banged up with Marcus because Pete Lanes goes home in three weeks and both Kemps and El Chubbo have a little while yet to serve. Had a great workout with the pair of cunts today and upon returning to the wing I was sure to get Marcus's prison number from his door so I could write an application in his name so I can put it beneath the office door before I go to work in the morning. This is the app: 'Guv, yesterday when I was doing weights I felt something slip out of my anus. Upon further inspection I felt a plethora of piles which I can only describe as a bunch of grapes hanging out my bumhole. My cellmate Steve Kemp has rubbed some soothing cream into the affected area but it hasn't helped despite his kindness. Please could you contact healthcare for an emergency appointment in order for me to get some Anusol cream for Kempy to rub into my anus. He is really helping me out and has been extremely understanding. Signed, Marcus T'. I know I'm immature and keep doing this stuff but I get great pleasure at the idea of Marcus trying to explain this app to a doctor or nurse. Definitely putting that bad boy in in the morning. Oh, one more thing, Tony Giles, who is looking very ill of late due to smoking so much spice and not eating, told the screws he'd swallowed a razor blade which prompted the prison to have him taken out to hospital. Tony told me that should he not get the medical care he thinks he needs he is going to get on the roof via our exercise yard. In fact, he has been buying and saving up drugs, predominantly gabapentin and pregablin and spice to make his sojourn to said roof a little more comfortable should the need to get up there arise.

28-05-2019. Been glossing doors all day at the unit whilst whistfully wondering on the beauty of Lucy. At one point Lucy had her back to me in her office and I couldn't resist going 'oi' extremely loudly which nearly caused her to shit herself. I've never seen someone so startled!

"Fuckin' hell Sloaney I nearly had a heart attack"!

"Not at the tender age of twenty-four Lucy; impossible". I had the DAB on whilst I brushed and a new tune which has me pursing my lips in pleasure by Offset and 21 Savage called 'Enzo' comes on which is so deep and dark it had the hairs on my body atremble. Behind the booming beat and bass is a murderous melody which feels as if it's almost gonna come and get ya. Anyway, it is now evening and we are banged up and

Drake's 'Gods' Plan' is on Radio 1Xtra whilst Martyn cleans his teeth with 'miswak', a natural 'toothbrush', really a stick which comes from the root of the Peelu tree. Martyn is telling me of it's marvellous abilities but to me it's basically a bit of fuckin' wood. I don't tell him that and instead just go 'yeah man, sounds good'. Martyn is constantly going on and off of various products. Creatine and whey protein for training were the best thing since sliced bread a little while ago, then, for a few weeks, he went off of them but now is once again using them. Then he got the whole spectrum of vitamin tablets only to decide after a few days that they were causing his skin to erupt in spots. I don't know how many times I have told him that mid twenties such outbreaks are to be expected and that it is possible that just twelve months into a hefty bit of porridge they could be related to stress. Sometimes, when I get up from my bunk and look at him laying on his bed I see a very forlorn and fearful look upon his cute face which makes me feel so sad. I know that the poor wretch is suffering. Every day, without fail, he talks of Amber who is currently holidaying in Turkey. And he is down in the dumps because when Steve Lanes had Marcus's mobile the other day the screws spun the cell and found it so Martyn has had little contact with her, restricted now to the prison pin phone system which is expensive. By the by, Steve Lanes paid someone to take the rap for the phone, the person saying they left it in there by accident and that it wasn't Steve's. Jake my little mate from Thanet got a punch tonight for money he owes for drugs and we can't be wrong and strong so he had to take it. J.T has lost lots of weight of late and I am worried about him. He is still smoking spice and buscopan hard on top of the massive methadone script and pregablin the prison give him. Kempy and Marcus haven't got 'their' app back yet and I am hoping it gets returned from healthcare tomorrow but reckon the wing staff are probably on to me and know it is my humour and nothing more. Oh, Marcus spoke on the phone to Bradders yesterday and apparently he is flat out on the crack and smack already bless him.

"Amber", Martyn says right now which causes me to look up and he has in his hand a photo of him and her together in a photo both in happier times, "look at our chins, they're the same shape ain't they"? and indeed that area of their face is shaped remarkably similarly.

"They are ain't they", I say, "except the fact yours has a load of hair stickin' out of it mate. You really are missing her ain't ya"?

"I am man and I ain't gonna be able to talk to her for two weeks whilst she's on holiday. Do you know if I can still call her whilst she's there"?

"I'm really not sure to be fair mate. I know in the old days it used to cost bundles to call people abroad but I don't know about now in the modern era".

"I'll just try and call her on Friday in it. Otherwise it's going to be shit not talking to her for two whole weeks man".

"It'll fly by Martyn mate", I say, "Tan is on holiday too, in Spain", and this is indeed true. Again I spoke to her on the dog and bone at the weekend and she is a little disappointed that I don't feel it is a good idea moving in with her straight from jail.

"But if you come to me you don't even have to work. I'm in a lovely flat in Broadstairs, I've got a two year old BMW now and I'll put you on as named driver. All you have to do is look after the little dogs. And you'll have sexy me all to yourself".

"But Tan", I said, "I have to work for my own sanity. And I need to empower myself. We have to be on an equal footing and I can't be dependent on you".

"But I don't mind. I've got plenty of money and we won't want for anything".

"I mind though babe. I have to have my own place".

"Where you gonna be then"?

"It's looking like I'll get a place, like supported housing in Folkstone. How long is that to drive Tan"?

"About forty minutes", she says, "will I be alright coming over to see you where you're going"?

"Of course you will. I really do love you Tan".

"I love you too" she says bless her, "I'm well looking forward to you getting out 'cause I've really missed you".

"Fuck me Tan I've missed you too", I say truthfully, "anyway", I continue, "what you wearing you sexy cunt"?

"You don't want to know, I'm proper slobbing it in my nighty looking very un-sexy".

"Just a nighty? Ahhh Tan, I'd love to be pulling the back of it over your bum and pulling your knickers to the side"!

"Knickers"? she scoffs, "I'm not wearing any".

"Oh my days babe stop right there this is too much", and dear reader indeed it is!

"Would you like to be bending me over right now"? she asks in her sexy scratchy tones.

"You'd be getting fucked hard Tan. I remember now, I can see you in my mind's eye walking around in just a T-shirt with your sexy bum just visible below the bottom of it; you've really got the best arse ever"!

"I know", she says, "banging in it"?

"It is".

"You can fuck me in the car when I pick you up if you want to when I get you from the gates. I'll wear a sexy little slut skirt without underwear so you can stick your cock straight in me".

"Fuck sake, stop now, I'm starting to pant like a dog".

"Ahhhh, bless ya, well it ain't long now".

"Are we like gonna be boyfriend and girlfriend Tan"?

"Do you want to be"?

"Well, yeah, I think so", I tell her, "I don't see myself with anybody else to be fair".

"Cool then. Do you want me to come and see you before you get out"?

"No point really babe and anyway you're always fuckin' workin'. Look babe, money's running out. I fuckin' love you Tan. Be good and look after yourself will ya"?

"Love you too and you be good too. Phone me soon please".

"I will, bye babe".

1700hrs. 30-05-2019. Catherine, my Forward Trust straight talking key worker amazed me today. Like I told you, I have been preparing to be released to a hostel in Folkstone which undoubtably has its merits but Catherine came to see me at my work with another option, a place at a twelve step recovery project in Stoke Newington, London. The woman, behind the scenes, has been working so hard to insure I do not find myself homeless upon release. She gave me some paperwork to fill out and whilst she talked my hair stood on end as my intuition told me this is the way I must go; London. Tan won't be too happy but this has to be about me right now.

1-06-2019. 1100hrs. So, this morning I can say the sentence 'I'm going home next month' which isn't entirely true for 'home' would be the deadbeat district of Thanet in Kent. Instead it looks like I shall be going to our glorious capital, bustling, buzzing, London town. Anyway, I have a bit of a zig on this morning because last night Mr Kirk said, over the tannoy 'lads it's early bang up tonight because of the new regime' and we were behind our doors by half past four. Now, on all other days, under the new regime which was, according to Kirky's announcement, instituted yesterday, on Monday, Tuesday, Wednesday and Thursday we would be open until 7pm. Fridays, canteen day, it is now to be half four. And weekends it is open all day 'till five with both sessions as opposed to the one on one off I have told you of. Yet it is Saturday morning and eleven a.m and we are banged up when under the new regime we should be out. By now dear reader you should know that doing a bit of bang up does not bother me; I can do it. But it is the hottest day of the year so far and glorious sunshine is streaming through the bars in the window. If the regime change started yesterday, why the fuck are we banged up? Anyway, who knows is the answer. Yesterday I did a triathlon down the gym. I may have explained the format but if not it's this: 3000 metre row at level ten on the machine followed by a ten kilometre cycle at level ten on the static bike. Then a 3000 metre run at 3% gradient on the treadmill. Look, dear reader, you must remember I am 13.5 stone and packing plenty of muscle. I do a lot of heavy weightlifting though cardio is where my heart is at. However, I still managed to complete in 50 minutes. That ain't bad at 43 years old and to be fair I could do it quicker for my heart and lungs had more and it was the sides of my calfs that slowed me with pain on the final obstacle, the run. Still, very few prisoners have the stamina, heart and psychological resilience to even attempt the feat. Anyway, onto other matters. A friend of mine on here named Groggsy, a blond haired blue eyed Medway nutter of five feet seven or so has given me a poem he wants me to put in the book. It is about his ex girlfriend and titled 'Had Enough Of Sue'. Here goes. Take it away Groggsy:

Sue, I've had enough of you.
I'm sick and tired of not having nothing to do.
The life we've had has fallen through.
When we first met, I was confused, sad and lonely.
My brain was screaming 'she's the one and only'.
Please baby, don't get upset; you showed me some good times, I learnt to love and am forever in your debt.
The good times were great, the bad times were many.
Do I still have love for you? No, not any.
I think we were doomed from the start.
Not only 'cause of the drugs and booze. I don't think I ever really had your heart.
Your love was the drugs, the smack, the crack and laying on your back.
Living from hit to hit, it would drive me mad but you didn't give a shit.
We've been together eight years.
Struggling to get by, struggling to get high.
Smack and crack Sue cut me some slack.
If I had to pay for this life I'd take it back.
I never asked for this, I wasn't born this way.
If all women are like you I would wish to be gay.

Talk about hold me back, life can't only be about smack.

Boy, how we were living. Think about the flat, I've stepped in cleaner dog shit than that.

We even struggled to feed a cat.

No gas or electric, no hot water, no food in the fridge, just think baby, wasn't it hectic?

Life was so much stress, money so tight anyone who came round I wanted to fight.

The tag people or bailiffs would want to come in but we would bever let them in to our house of sin.

So, Sue, I've had enough of you. I wish you luck with your life and may it be free of strife.

The last twelve months have changed me for the best. I just can't do all the unrest.

I want something new and Sue it ain't you.

I want a girl who cares for my health and makes me better myself.

I'm sick of having low self opinions and I'm sick of smack head minions.

No good will come of you being my wife unless I want to continue ending my life.

Yes Sue I'm sad but finally realize I'm not fucking mad.

I want to concentrate on my babies not staying with you and catching rabies.

I want a girl that will help me do great, not some slag that drops me out then meets me at the HMP Rochy gate.

I feel I got good things to come, not some slag who's had a dealer in her bum.

I'm finally thinking about myself and putting me before your health.

If you don't care, why should I? If you don't change you're gonna die.

Sad and alone, only you at home, dirty and damp, a scag head tramp.

Things could have been different, things could have been great.

Not now though, it's too late.

You'll never change but really your life isn't mine to arrange.

I hope and pray that off the good path I won't stray.

And I wish you health and happiness some day.

I'm sad to say that our life together is no more.

It's not really you, I'm just sick of being a skag head and poor.

The End.

Dear reader, that is Ian 'Groggsy's' poem. Sad and tragic all at the same time. I myself particularly like the bit about rabies and her having a

451

dealer in her bum and by now I dare say you've worked out that I love a bit of gutter humour. Anyway, yesterday Marcus and Kemps managed to acquire lots of Golden Virginia tobacco so me and Martyn have been indulging luxuriously in the rarity of a roll up. For the record, I am 137 days clean and sober. Absolute 80s is playing Fleetwood Mac 'Looking Out For Love' and Martyn is sitting looking at old photos of him and Amber together in happier times. Yesterday, a sexy 21 year old screwess who usually works D wing came to do a shift on here and said to me:

"You're the one writing the book aren't you"?

"I am", I said, "pretty much wrapped up now Miss as I'm off soon".

"Do you mind if I read a few pages"? and she's at the cell door and I feel sheepish but grab the document, part it like a deck of cards and hand her a few random pages.

"Don't watch me as I read it though", she says, parting her pretty face in smile.

"Ok", I say and I saunter out onto the yard with Russell Brand's book in hand. She comes out ten minutes later with a smile.

"That was well funny Sloaney, I enjoyed that", and once she has gone I read what I'd given her and immediately feel a wave of horror run through me as I see it was the part about the prostitute hanging smalls from the tree and me lasciviously planting sloppy kisses on her bum! I quickly run into the wing and find the fit young fucker.

"Miss man I'm sorry, that was a bit crude wasn't it? I haven't offended you have I"?

"Noooo", she says quite candidly, "like I say I thought it was well funny and besides, I'll bet there's worse than that in there"!

"There is that's true", I reply and I shuffle along my way before I get lost in her dreamy eyes.

12 noon. Just returned to the cell after being out for an hour for lunch. I sat outside with my chicken burger and chips, on the yard, basking bare chested in blazing sunlight with a skimpy pair of chequered shorts on. The day wears the sun's glory like a golden gown.

"It's so fuckin' hot man", says Martyn now, drawing water from the tap.

"Sweltering in it mate"? I say, "oh yeah, roll this up bro", passing him a roll up I pull from my pocket.

"Oh sweet man, where'd'ya get that"?

"Marcus and Kempy gave me it on the yard".

"Did you have to pay for it"?

"Naaa man, course not; if they've got it and can afford it those boys are good as gold. I love that pair a cunts to be fair".

452

"Do you notice", says Mart, "that Marcus has always got like people following him around and that"?

"Yeah", I say, "ya know why that is don't ya"?

"Spice in it", says Martyn.

"Of course", I say, "Marcus makes out like he don't like it but he loves all the attention really. And Kempy for that matter now he's banged up with him. They both love lording it over everyone". We are chugging away at a fag now as rosy fingers wave through the window, illuminating the cell. I'm out next month and muse on how quickly time has passed. This time last year I was so despondent, depressed and derelict in the throes of active addiction. This month, from last years perspective, seemed a very long way off indeed. The world seemed an awful and despairing place for me at the time yet here I am, once again clean, and still fighting.

1700hrs. From 2pm until 3pm I bathed in the sun on the yard, my skin enjoying our blazing star's caress. After that me, Kemps and Smarcus went to the gym where we worked chest and traps to exhaustion. On the bench press, once we'd all pushed our maximum: Marcus 130kg, Kempy 120kg and me 110kg we went down the weight to sixty kilos to rep out more times with the lighter weight.

"You two reprobates gonna give me a roll up for tonight"? I asked.

"Sloaney", says Marcus, "you've had £25 worth of burn off us already for fuck all: I'll tell you what, if you can rep out thirty with the 60kg then we'll see you alright".

"Thirty"! I say, "fuck off man, twenty".

"Nope", says Kempy the helpful cunt, "if you can do thirty we'll give you two".

"Alright then, but no making me laugh or tryna put me off you pair of pricks".

"Sweet then, go on", says Marcus. I do. Halfway through Kempy goes:

"Look at him, going proper boss eyed and that", and I laugh 'cause I can feel things happening to my face as I struggle.

"Shut up Kempy man", I splutter trying not to laugh at the languid prick. He knows all he has to do is open his mouth to make me laugh. I complete the set.

"Fuck me", goes Kempy, "amazing what you can do when you want something in it"?

"That was good though", says Marcus.

"I can feel a proper rip in my chest man, I love that feeling", I say. It's true, and I am amazed at how fit I have gotten in such a relatively short period of time. I mean it is but a matter of months ago I was lifting nothing but a joint of deadly spice to my lips. I couldn't run for a bus without having a heart attack. I consider myself very, very lucky.

02-06-2019. 12 noon. Had me hair cut this morning by J.T's cellmate, Stuart. He did a bloody good job too and I am looking fresh, clean cut and handsome with two days sexy stubble upon my chiselled features. I also have the lobster red glow of sunburnt skin on my face, body and legs and the shower slaughtered me this morning, feeling like my nerves were on fire. First thing this morning I shot up to Marcus and Kempy's cell to get a roll up. Though it was but nine bells the cell stunk of crack cocaine.

"Fuck me, it's like a crack house in here", and just as I say it Kemps puts a pipe to his lips and licks off a fuckin' great lungful.

"Just bought £200 worth", says Marcus. I get the fag I wanted and say my goodbyes.

"Oh", says Kempy, exhaling thick creamy crack smoke, "got what you want and straight out the door ay"?

"Come off it Kemps", I say, "you know it ain't like that; just don't want to be smelling that shit bro", and I go on my way, knowing they both understand. Marcus, Kempy and crazy Kirk had massive bulging eyes, cracked out their heads. I, of course, have smoked and injected crack for years but today I can't make the maths work in favour of using. Nice for a minute but then all the shit that comes with it. Anyway, again this morning Ms B---- was on duty and Martyn has given her the nickname 'brows' because of the thick black brows below the fringe of her lovely blonde Barnett. Martyn is talking now:

"Ahhh man, "Brows is well sexy ain't she? She came down to take the trolley with us to the kitchen and I couldn't stop looking at her bum man".

"She's just got that dirty sexy look", I say, "like she can proper fuck. Some brows though, like two slugs man".

"I'd fuckin' love to smash her", says Mart.

"Me too", I say honestly, "right now I'd settle for a pair of her knickers to smell whilst I knocked one out".

"She's only about 25 I reckon", says Martyn.

"27 I would say. Perfect age".

03-06-2019. Morning. All down the ATB Unit are happy with my paintwork. Jason pulled me into his office and said:

"Sloaney, at home last night I noticed in my cupboard this big tub of whey protein. I forgot I had it. I bought it but couldn't stand the taste of it. I was gonna throw it out but was wondering if you could do anything with it"?

"Really"? I say, "'course I could man; it's costing me a fortune in here buying that stuff every week so that would really help man".

"I'll bring it in Wednesday for you", he says, the worthy fucker, "'cause I'm gonna drive in Wednesday 'cause me bike will be in the shop".

"Ahhh mate, thankyou man. I appreciate that I really do". So bloody good to me down here it is sometimes hard to take. Jason is consistently kind to me. He has also seen fit to get me an assistant down here to help me with the decorating in the form of Alfie Rossiter, a proper Romany gypsy and much loved character I have known many years in the system who currently resides on 'H' wing.

"What d'ya want me doing Sloaney boy"? he asked in typical traveller dialect that must be heard to be believed; I love it. Some of my own words come out with the same inflections through having been around it for so long over the years.

"Well Alf, thing is mate I've been so busy painting I've been neglecting the cleaning so if you can carry on glossing I'll do the corridor and toilets and offices and stuff if that's alright with you"?

"Naaa that's cushty chavvy", he says, "point me in the right direction and orf I go boy, you just watch me", and I smile at his big toothy genuine grin.

"Bless Alfie, I appreciate it man".

"No problem at all cuz. Which door am I at boy"? and I show him and we both get so stuck into our work we forget the time and miss freeflow, getting back to our respective wings fifteen minutes late. Gibby phones the wing to let them know we are not wandering about the nick selling drugs and such to insure we don't get a negative entry. Life is good.

1700hrs and guess what? The new regime is fully in place. We have had an extra half hour at our places of work (1630 finish), we returned to the wing to be fed by 1700 and now we are banged up but will be let out for and extra hour and a half at 1730hrs. Being as it is lovely outside right now this is glorious for I can soak myself in wonderful ultra violet rays. In other news the screws have got the right hump with Kempy for, dear reader, they had to pick him up from the floor earlier so inebriated was he. He has literally been unconscious since noon on the usual concoction of drugs: opioids, benzos, pregablin, spice and hooch. He is barely breathing the silly cunt; silly because he knows better than to behave like this blatantly for he is rubbing it in the face of the staff and remember that despite the truth on here it is supposed to be a recovery wing and to be so careless could cause him to lose his place on here with his mates.

1900hrs and Kempy has now been taken to hospital in a bad and potentially critical condition. Marcus was also out his nut; I always know when he is proper smashed for he gets well gay, only in a pisstaking way of course but he came out on the yard and was touching me up and tryna kiss me slobberingly to my horror. Still, seriously, him running around like a mong, Kempy, his cell mate, in hospital means I can feel a storm coming for the two of them for they are taking the piss really.

04-06-2019. 0800hrs and first thing I do upon the door swinging open is fly upstairs to check on the whereabouts and state of Just For Men Kemps. He is, thankfully, out the hospital and in the cell and though looking a little ropy , wan, drawn and shaky he is ok it would seem. Steve Bennett, lifer Steve, comes into mine and Martyn's cell once I return from upstairs.

"What you writing so early mate"?

"Well, I just shot up to check on that cunt Kempy so I'm writing it up now".

"Is he ok though"?

"Well, he's back and breathing which is all we can ask I suppose. What really pissed me off Steve was last night when me and Steve Lanes, Pete Lanes and Sam Hodges were outside the cell with all the paramedics in we found out that they didn't know what Kempy had taken 'cause Marcus was too scared of getting in trouble so Sam told 'em and I shouted so the whole landing could hear that if anyone had a problem with what Sam bravely done they could come see me. It ain't grassing to let medical professionals know what's been taken so they can save a fuckin' life man"!

"Fuck me no", says Steve, "you have to tell paramedics what someone has taken when they overdose else how the fuck they gonna deal with it"?

"Exactly Steve, exactly. Bless Sam though, he bowled straight into the cell and told the ambulance people exactly what Kempy had had and that's when they decided to take him to hospital. I think that where he'd had so many different drugs they realized he was in real danger".

"Did you see him though? With the oxygen mask on his face? I thought he was dead", says Steve.

"I was worrying about the cunt all night man. I had an argument with him the other day about his drug use and he got the raving hump with me".

"Well, at least he's ok".

"Amen to that".

1700hrs and we'd've been on the new regime tonight but on 'H' wing someone slashed themselves up so the staff who'd've been covering the extra time on 'A' wing had to go out on escort to the hospital. Me and Martyn are cool with that and besides, it's raining outside. In other news let me briefly tell you what Kempy did last night. In the hospital, he jumps from the bed, takes down his trousers and pisses all over the floor in his delirium. I know he was obviously not with it which is exacerbated by the fact that in the process, he tells me, his 'parcel', a zippy bag containing paper spice and dihydrocodeine tatrate tablets, or DF118s (one of my old favourites, quite different and much stronger than regular codeine and known colloquially as 'DFs') fell to the floor and one of the two prison officers with him picked it up, waiting for today where they gleefully inform him he is now nicked and to face the governor for consequences. Anyway, tonight I go up to see Marcus and Kemps and the two of them, with Dale and Kirk, were all smoking smack, chasing the dragon or 'having a boot' to put it in more modern parlance. Regardless of what you call it, they were all smoking heroin, diamorphine hydrochloride and absolutely out their respective cannisters. Right now Martyn is dealing cards so I'm a put me pen down. Brian Cox is on TV later with The Planets which takes precedence over Love Island. I only watch that to perv at flesh anyway. Materialistic thick people who nonetheless make for amusing telly. Perhaps, this year, with one of the poncy men a biomedical degree holder the conversation will not be so banal like last year when one of the contestants thought Brexit was some sort of cereal!

06-06-2019. D Day. Lest we forget. That's all.

07-06-2019. Midday. Writing of late isn't coming easy to me. When I do feel the muse is with me, putting eloquent sentences together in my mind it is usually in the early hours and to get up and turn on the light to write would be an extremely selfish thing to do considering that blessed repose is the only escape young Martyn gets from his lengthy sentence. Anyway, today saw a massive turn out down the gym for the cicuit including Martyn of course but, for the first time, Craig D and Tony Giles also came down and with a bit of encouragement both did splendidly. The format was the Dirty Dozen which we went through thrice and even I was left panting, gasping and greedily grasping at the oxygen in the air at the end. A thoroughly enjoyable fifty minutes or so.

After that I went to the Unit where I found Marcus, feet up, trying to chat up the lovely Lucy. This afternoon we have volleyball; can't wait. The only other thing to share is that I had deep dark dreams last night involving my parents who I miss terribly. My pain, at times, is palpable.

1700hrs. Banged up for the night. After I got my canteen me, Gibbo, Kirk the lunatic and sex pest pal of mine Sam Hodges all went down the gym for volleyball. Now, remember Kempy O.D'd and went to hospital the other day and of course the gym staff know of this because all depts get round robin emails about any serious incidents in the nick. Well, going into the gym hall Ryan the gym screw, great guy, pulls him at the gate:

"Hold up Kempy, I want a word with you", and 'cause I can guess what's coming I hang about.

"Why"? says Kempster, "what's up"?

"Well", says Ryan, "got to say Kempy, I expect more from you".

"Yeah Kempy, he's right mate", I say.

"Shut up Sloaney", says Kemps.

"What the fuck you doing Kempy, taking all them drugs? What's up with you"? says Ryan and all the while I'm shaking my head and tut tut tutting in the background.

"Yeah Kempy, I'm not angry with you bro, I'm just disappointed really", I say, and inside I'm loving his discomfort; he gives me a scathing look.

"I didn't think you was like that Kempy", says Ryan, "you just don't seem the type".

"I think he's crumbling under the pressure Ryan to be fair; just not himself lately", I stir.

"Shut up for fuck sake Sloaney", says Kempy.

"Well", says Ryan, "if you ever need to talk you can always come to us down here you know that don't you"?

"I appreciate that, thanks man", says Kempster to Ryan and Kempy walks into the sports hall where we play volleyball and he turns to me straight away smiling saying:

"You're such a fuckin' tool Sloaney", and I say:

"Do you like the way I was tutting and shaking my head all ruefully though"?

"You fuckin' knob, you're lucky I love ya you cunt".

"I'll smash you up ya mug", I say.

"Yeah right", says the lazy laconic prick as we stride onto the court. We pick teams with the gym staff and gym orderlies and bounce the ball about for an hour. Best day of the week. Circuit then volleyball. Boom.

458

08-06-2019 1700hrs. Though the new regime has been instituted and said regime says we should be out morning and afternoon weekends, it hasn't come to pass today due to staff shortages. We were out in the morning and let out again at three for the gym. Marcus, Kempy and Craig failed to show for all were absolutely fucked up on drugs today. Craig has been doing so well lately, the warlike fuck, so I was surprised to see him in such a state.

15-06-2019. 0900hrs. Haven't written for a while. It is Saturday morning. I dreampt of yet to be invented technologically advanced aircraft last night. Second time I have seen the same machines in my dreams. Anyway, these last few days my insecurities and anxieties have manifested in me being overly jokey and overcompensating, me being cutting and horrid and moody, being overly flirty with female staff and, most distasteful, in me seeking reassurance which is an ugly trait indeed. I ruminated last night and reflected on my state at present. I thank the Ley Community for teaching me to recognise these things. Moving on, as I say, it is Saturday and we are out both periods today with the new regime. The door is open. Scouse from next door comes in.

"Got any coffee whiteners lads please"?

"Nope", says Smartyn, angry because Scouse and his cellmate had their radio blasting all night next door making it even more difficult than it already is for me and Smart to get off to repose. I myself had to stuff balled up toilet paper in my ears. Scouse goes to leave the cell.

"Scouse", I call, bringing him back, "Martyn and I look after you all the time, we will give you some milk but mate, your radio is blasting all night, can you at least sort of turn it down at midnight bro"?

"Is it keeping you up lads yeah? I sleep through it myself like", says Scouse.

"No offence Scouse", I say, "you would wouldn't you because you're out ya fuckin' nut every night mate whereas me and Martyn are clean and sober so sleeping is a bit more of a natural process ya know, necessitating a relative degree of quiet mate".

"Ok lads", says Scouse amicably enough, "I'll make sure it ain't on loud too late for ya".

"Cheers mate", I say, I give him what he wants and he goes on his way. Martyn has now left the cell to bounce about the wing but I myself stay put, listening to summer bangers on 4Music. Outside the door it is noisy and I marvel at the cacophony of different dialects, making for colourful listening. I love being round such an eclectic bunch but regularly slate anybody not speaking with a southern accent. We have people on here from Leeds, Warrington, Liverpool and Manchester amongst us, a crop of southerners, Kent and London and Sussex predominantly. I suppose here I should examine why it is that when I have the hump with someone I go for the most obvious different thing about that person. So, if a fat person pisses me off I'll immediately think 'fat cunt', if the person is not that pretty it'd be 'ugly cunt' but, and this is painful to admit for it goes against all my true core values, if the person is black it'd be 'black cunt' and this makes me cringe inside admitting this to you. I have no inherent dislike of northerners but I think we all, if we examine ourselves honestly, go for the first reference point of difference in anger. I mean, I wouldn't tell Cheryl Cole no to the request of a date simply because she asked me in a northern dialect would I? Anyway, I am now 154 days clean. And though as I say I have been struggling of late, the thought of picking up has not entered my mind. And these testing times, like last week, strengthen and enlighten me. The fact I can reflect and recognise my patterns is a gift in itself.

1430hrs. Open. Alarm bell rings on the wing. Someone tried to punch Ms Slane. Staff pile on from other wings and an officer comes and bangs our door shut along with everyone else's so the fella can be dragged to the block in locks. Steve Bennett comes to my cell door.

"Still banged up"?

"Clearly Steve".

"I'll get a screw", and little Ms H comes and opens our door. I am struggling to concentrate with all this activity. People are hyper on the wing. Sat here watching Katie Perry on 4Music. Peace out. Oh, how could I forget? My lovable friend El Chubbo has been kicked off the wing for suspected drug dealing, so no more Marcus.

16-06-2019. 0900hrs. Morning people. Just want to share a poem with you from my pal James Hynd. It's called 'Growing Up':

Locked in prison I cannot do much.

I must endeavour to stay in touch.

With family and friends and people who will be there to the bitter ends.

So I write my letters and speak on the phone never in my life have I felt so alone.

Years gone by years left to do, when will this torture ever be through.

I have a release date but will that be the end.

License conditions drive me round the bend.

You cannot go there and you must not do that.

I wish this probation officer would shut his trap.

But if I break it all down and think it through, the responsibility is on me, not you.

So I hold it down and do the best I can.

I went to prison a boy, and left a man.

The End.

Now James, or Jay as he is known, is a hard man for sure. Solidly built and not one to suffer fools lightly he has been a pain in the arse of the system for years. However, he has had something of a spiritual awakening of late and spends much of his time in the prison chapel where he works. Certainly seems to have caused a shift in him and very much for the better. He was kicked off of 'A' wing some months ago and is now on 'D' wing but has now stopped using drugs and is far less aggressive which is a massive turnaround. When I first arrived back in jail, in Elmley on the Isle Of Sheppey, this man I've known in these places many years saw to it that I did not want for anything. And that was a comfort in that rotten to the core prison where the staff are corrupt from the top down. Savage place and this is in stark contrast to its highly esteemed reputation as a modern penal flagship when it first opened. Staff shrotages, cutbacks and lack of morale have seen it plummet. Horrid, horrid jail. Dark, gloomy and frightening even for the initiated. So much violence and a terribly foreboding atmosphere. Anyway, moving on. Now my pal, El Chubbs has gone there has been a massive reduction in the amount of spice on the wing. Just thought I'd mention that. It is still very much here of course but his leaving has left a hole that will undoubtably be filled sooner rather than later. Though I am clean, I still at times get tempted to do a little dealing and thing is I know I could got to Marcus where he is now on 'G' wing and he'd load me up with pages which I could use to inflate my empty bank balance but, to be honest, I can't square it with myself when clean. It would be a betrayal I feel to the likes of Jason and Lucy and AddemupAde and Catherine my drug worker and Jan and Steve and Woody from Bridge. And the staff on here too. As I say, I'd never help them to weed out dealers, not my job, but I won't take the piss and deal myself. Amazing my true core values. Yet these go out the window soon as I pick up and I do things I would not do under any other circumstances. Moving on, Craig D, my warlike pal was just in the cell and upon seeing me writing said:

"Sloaney, you are putting the bad things about the prison in there as well mate ain't ya"?

"Of course, there genuinely are lots of things need fixing here bro. But, to be fair, my experience here has been a positive one too so I can't do anything more than reflect that but, as I say, there is much to be desired here man".

"Some of the little things", says Craig, "like screws losing applications and digging people out and that".

"Craig man, losing an app or two in this chaotic environment can be forgiven. And as for digging people out, to be honest, they only do that if people are flat out at it, taking the piss and on the spice or dealing or being a cunt. They don't dig me out. And Craig, think about it, we have some of the rudest, most obnoxious and ungrateful cunts in the country on here bro. I try to see it from the screws perspective: being spat at, punched and that. One having his arm broken the other day. Don't get me wrong, there are some shit cunt screws as you and me both know and I get why some of them get a bucket of shit and piss thrown over them. But on here the staff are generally really decent in my opinion", and what I don't add, because Craig is my friend is that you , Craig, sometimes lose your temper over the slightest bit of bollocks because you are one of the angriest people I know. Just the other day you were threatening to spit in Ms H's face. And the only real reason for this is because you didn't have any spice. Craig is out in twelve days and I am worried for him. He will, I know, be back. If he can't stay clean here how can he do it out there? I put this to him the other day and he said:

"I'm gonna be alright because out there it ain't in my face all the time. I can get away from it", and though he has a point, when one really wants to get clean one can do it anywhere. Anyway, Kemps just came in for a coffee looking decidedly more perky now our friend El Fat One has gone. Christine And The Queens excellent track 'Tilted' is on 4Music and I sit and sip with me lovely pal.

17-06-2021. 1010hrs. At the Unit. Alfie is rubbing down doors with sandpaper in preparation for painting. Lucy, Gibby, Jason and Naomi are in a staff meeting. Radio One is blaring bangers and I'm sat in the group room writing for you. Again, I slept very well last night after a decent day. The weekends are the worst part of the prison week for apart from the gym we're confined to the wing and banged up at 1630hrs on the Friday, Saturday and Sunday which leaves multiple boring hours to kill. The pressing problem when banged up so early is not sleeping between the hours of sort of five to eight p.m because to do so detracts from sleep at more appropriate hours causing restless sleeplessness which anyone who's done a bit of bird will tell you is the worst. Anyway, before coming into the Unit, when on Freeflow I hung about a bit as all the wings went to work in the hope of bumping into me old mate Marcus. Soon as we see each other we both bust out big toothy grins. The wing

462

without him just ain't quite the same. Anyway, Alfie has just returned to the Unit after popping to Waste Management with our rubbish.

"'Ere", he says, "come 'ere mush, right, listen cuz yeah, me cousin's just come off 'B' wing, he's just told me the boys 'ave got fighting on there and me cousin's walked past the cell, see the 'geery', (traveller for man) on the floor holding his ear'ole in his hand and me cousin says to the geery 'you better go to the hospital with that boy, go on, go tell the screws your ear'ole's off boy'", and I say to Alfie:

"What's it all over bro"?

"All over poxy 'cams' (traveller for money) mush, all over money boy", says Alfie.

"What", I say, "was his ear literally in his hand Alf"?

"Mother dies boy his ear was in his hand and five people 'ave bin dragged down the block over it boy".

"Fuck me", I say, "it's all going off. Two people were thrown to the floor by screws on 'A' wing over the weekend too".

"Must be that time of the year mush", says Alfie philosophically whilst pulling on his vape, "it's been goin' off all over the prison Sloaney".

"I appreciate you letting me write you up Alfie".

"Wha'd'ya mean chavvy"?

"Like write stuff down as you talk ya know"?

"Ahhh bless ya boy", he says, "I'm gonna bring a photo down of me ol' trailer boy so you can put it in ya book".

"I will too Alf; thankyou".

"You're cushty boy ya know that chavvy"?

"Cheers Alf"!

1150hrs and I've just returned to the wing but been banged up along with everybody else due to an alarm bell incident.

"What's gone on Mart"? I ask my little cellmate.

"That geezer, the young tall skinny fella with the cast on his arm tried to hang himself".

"Shit man, is he alright"?

"Dunno, seemed pretty serious though".

"Fuck it", I say, "I've got to know if he's alright man", and I get on the bell and Ms H comes to the door.

"What's up Sloaney"? asks the lovely lady.

"Miss", I say, "please, can you just tell me that the fella ain't dead, so I can relax? He's only young Ms H".

"Oh no, he's alright, he's not dead, so don't worry", and I really appreciate this.

"Thanks Ms H, I am grateful you have the balls to share that information, thankyou", and I am grateful because I heard other prisoners asking the same question of other staff and getting the stock response:

"We can't talk about ongoing incidents; we're dealing with it". I suppose with cons like me and Martyn they are willing to be a little more forthcoming.

1700hrs. Bang up for half an hour then out until 7PM. The sun, though intermittently obscured by clouds is out so when the door opens I shall shoot out to let it stroke and caress my skin. I just eat a massive curry and am on tons of protein and creatine which feeds the muscles I ripped on the weekend. I just said to Martyn that I can feel, in the strangest of ways, the stretching of my skin as the muscle beneath expands. There's also the fact I cannot get into my jeans because of the width of my thighs and my T-shirts are ever tighter though a short while ago they hung off of my emaciated frame as though from a coathanger such was the situation of my shoulders. I must say, I'm one lyrical fucker if I do say so myself!

1930hrs. Final entry today. I love Craig, warlike Craig, but when he is stoned he's a fuckin' mong like everyone else who indulges in spice, including, when using, me. So, we were on the yard earlier and with his fat belly out, whilst stuffing cake into his spice hungry face he decides he wants to playfight and puts one, two, three punches on my arm until I flash him an unmistakable look whilst my mouth told him:

"I don't fuckin' playfight Craig", and he mumbled:

"Alright alright", and I said:

"I'm forty- fuckin'-three mate, not three", and I walked away from his space, not wanting to be near him when he's doing the palsy shuffle and looking like a complete retard or special person or neurologically diverse person or whatever the fuck the current snowflake PC terminology is today. Out.

2130hrs. I miss my mum and dad. Period.

0755hrs 18-06-2019. One thing I forgot to mention yesterday is that Dale, my handsome psycho mate who was so involved in Marcusgate has slashed his leg with a razor blade down to the very bone in a self harming episode. He is in a really bad place and upon hearing about this I went up to see my mate Kempy.

"Why'd he do it Steve, what's up with him"?

"It's every fuckin' time he takes pregabs Sloaney. So, he takes a load on Saturday and Sunday and then crashes into depression when he wakes up without any yesterday", says Steve. And, indeed, when users of this relatively new drug don't have them they can find themselves in very dark places. Anyway, nothing more to report apart from the fact Craig, bless him, came down and apologised to me first thing this morning. I'm now going to type a poem written by a geezer, a rough hard looking type from Crawley named Stuart Batchelor. Here goes, take it away Stu:

Prison Life.
Coming through the prison gate
I did this crime, I sealed my fate
This long dark road to living hell
This tiny dirty prison cell
Broken windows, graffiti'd walls
Angry villains packing tools
Prison slang and burning stares
I'm feeling strained but no-one cares
I'm here alone, confused depressed
I'm feeling broken feeling stressed
The door bangs shut the lock engaged
I feel the anger internal rage
Clouded thoughts of life ahead
Body's here but mind is dead
Voices shout from cell to cell
Another fight "ALARM BELL"
Musty smells of crack and spice
Dirty beds all filled with lice
Broken tables bent up chairs
Stale bread and rotten pears
I wish that I could turn back time
I swear I would undo this crime
I close my eyes and try to sleep
My inner demon "YOU WENT TOO DEEP"
Long dark nights alone no wife
This is HMP Lewes life.
The End.

I think you'll agree it's rather good! Written when Stu was on remand in HMP Lewis prior to coming to Rochy.

19-06-2019. 1900hrs. Peter Lanes gets out in the morning. I gave him a big hug for I love the miserable bigot dearly. During the squeeze I implored him:

"Please Pete, please don't inject a snowball tomorrow bro. If you use, smoke it for fuck sake".

"I swear Sloaney, I promise I won't do anything stupid". The reason I worry is because, as I think I have elucidated before, prisoners are particularly vulnerable and prone to overdose upon release due to tolerance having decreased during incarceration. Although, as you have seen, prison is full of drugs it is predominantly spice and pharmaceuticals. Yes, occasionally smack and crack appear but not in steady and prolonged patterns enough to build resistance. Many a man has gone out and whacked a fuck off great snowball only to be found in the spot they took their last shot. Be safe Pete.

20-06-2019. 0819hrs. So, Pete has gone bless him. I received a letter off of my friend, ex lover Sarah today, the lovely lady who so kindly sent me a card when she heard about the death of my mother. In the letter she told me that nothing changes in Thanet and that I'd do well to stay away from Invicta House as everything is exactly as I left it. Riddled with the socio-economic problems which plague most seaside towns in this country currently. Anyway, I shall write back to Sarah later. As I have said before, I really struggle with kindness being shown to me and this worthy woman has always been there for me, even when I have been at my worst.

1700hrs. No staff to facilitate an unlock at 1730hrs so that's us for the night. Gladiator is on the telly tonight and this epic is always worthy of a watch despite many previous viewings. I have been ruminating on on the fact that though I love HMP Rochester many may see this as a damning indictment of the modern penal estate. There is much good here and any lack stems from underfunding and government. The prison does the best with what it has.

24-06-2019. 1200hrs. Just checking in with you dear reader. On the other side of a recent herpes outbreak now and my energy levels are returning to normal and my sleep too. I had some great workouts in the gym over the weekend which is now thankfully over-they fucking drag man. Even more so now what with my release date bearing down upon me. Nothing out of the ordinary to report. There are three people on here seriously self harming at the moment including Dale who again this weekend slashed an arm so badly he had to go to hospital to have it

466

stitched. Another lad on Saturday had his head smashed in but all this is pretty normal to me though to you I dare say this behaviour is quite the contrary of what you consider ordinary. Oh, one other thing, the fella on 'B' wing who had his ear bitten off is unable to have it stitched back on. He went to some specialist unit but they told him that they will have to make him a plastic one. Alfie was telling me this this morning and Lucy, having access to all systems, confirmed that this is indeed the case. Crazy that a few months ago on the same wing, I think it was 'B' wing, could have been 'D', nonetheless, crazy that another fella lost an eye. Again through violence.

26-06-2019. 1930hrs. Me and Martyn are in the cell listening to a classic hip hop album with Grandmaster Flash and Rob Base and Easy Rock, bopping our heads back and forth. Anyway, my mate 'Groggsy' who wrote the poem about a 'dealer in her bum' has been writing for me. So here goes a little from him about his life and in his own words, unmolested by me. He's 38 by the way:

I remember being at home in Rainham, Kent. I have two brothers, one three years older and one five years younger. The feelings that spring to mind from my younger, more innocent years are of being in our family home when I was approximately ten years old, me and my brothers would fuck around as young boys do, being loud, naughty, fighting as boys being boys. My father used to work away from home quite a lot. I didn't understand at the time but we couldn't of been very well off. My mum being at home out of work looking after us boys. If dad was at home it was because he was working nights. This is when I started to feel the wrath of dad. If we woke him up he would go sick. The more tired he was the more sick he'd go, mostly on me. Maybe cause I'm the middle one or because I was the loudest, fuck knows. In the end dad must have gave up with the night work or maybe he decided he'd be better off staying in digs cause the more pissed off he got with us the more I enjoyed it, once my arse stopped stinging from the slaps I should add! From what I remember I would always hold my hands up, take the blame so Simon my older brother was left pretty much alone. When dad would come home from working away I remember being happy, excited even. Forgetting how fucking miserable he is or was. I was probably thinking we'd be going fishing or judo. You could tell what mood he was in by the way he pulled up in his car or how he shut the front door even. If we had played mum up through the week and I heard dad skid up against the kerb where he couldn't wait to slap the fuck outta me I'd be upstairs and under the bed like a ferrit. I don't know why kids run upstairs cause

467

there's nowhere to go after that is there? I soon stopped after I was repeatedly dragged out by my feet and thrown down the stairs to apologise for something I probably hadn't done then kicked back up them again and told don't bother coming down till the morning with no dinner. Oh yeah, this will make you chuckle. I remember he come home with the hump one time me and Simon must have come up with a plan and were a bit older now coz I knew what was coming. If I remember correctly we had pelted one of the neighbours kids with blackberries fucked his clothes up along with the stuff on the washing line. Anyway I stuffed loads of magazines down the back of my trousers. Dad was so enraged the stupid old cunt that he forgot to take my trousers down and when he let rip he screamed he was so angry and you could almost see his hand pulsating. I never did that again coz that did make him go nuts but when it all died down me and my brothers laughed about it and it made me mum laugh as well. Mum was never like dad, I'm not sure if she even liked him. He was or is just our dad. As I got older and even more resentful I went from being kicked and slapped to being driven off in the car and getting my head kicked in big time and being made to sleep in the garage or in the garden so mum wouldn't see my fat lips or bruises or black eyes. Did I deserve any of it? I don't think so and these days the doctors would say I had ADHD or autism or maybe I was just really naughty. All I can tell you is that I would never ever subject my kids to anything like that and I'm an addict or addict in recovery. Well, that's a little bit of my life, maybe I shall write some more up it's up to Sloaney, all the best, Ian Miles AKA 'Groggsy'. PS if you've just read that you can probably understand why I am writing it from a prison cell and not sat down with my family. I was hardly ever home from around 15-16 years old and was using drugs at 13. Man, I felt unloved and unwanted.

And dear reader I did indeed want to hear a bit more about this interesting fella and thought you might too so back to you Groggsy:

During the first year at senior school I started smoking cannabis with friends that had followed me to the same school-The Howard School in Rainham, Kent. I was soon to learn that my older brother was a recreational drug user, cannabis, speed and LSD. He was using these drugs with his pals who became the older hippy lot to me and I and some of my pals thought they were cool as fuck. My dad was into all the old school music like Pink Floyd, Led Zepplin, Jimi Hendrix, Cream and Fleetwood Mac to name a few. To a naïve and easily led hippy kid like me and my bro these drugged up hippy trippy missions were awesome and we wanted some of that hippy awesomeness and strangely we were magnets for the kids that also thought it would be the bollox to be a trippy hippy-I was smoking bongs and eating speed before I smoked a fag. I remember being about fifteen years old and completely bolloxed walking round Rainham shopping pavilion wearing my dads' wedding trousers that were pin striped flares with a flowery shirt on with fuck off great collars and listening to a song called 'Strange Brew' by Cream. What a knob. I knew everyone was looking and laughing but did I give a shit? No! Obviously not. Oh yeah, I was listening to my tunes on a Sony Walkman! At school I was only tiny but I was a popular kid because I became pals with a lot of my older brothers friends, and they thought I was funny coz I was small, I could fight and most of all cause I smoked puff and stuff. Eventually my only friends were the druggy ones and all my pals were older so I became intolerant of younger kids that were my age or younger and this attitude has stuck with me for as long as I can remember. Well, my life in and out of school was getting more and more chaotic. I was, it seems, always fucking grounded coz letters kept coming through the door from school saying they were worried about me and looking back I bet they were especially when I weighed in one of the bullies who puched my one and only non drug using pal and I went full on psycho and beat the shit out of him on the foot bridge and when he hit the floor I smashed him up with the rear end of my push bike. It went from cheers and 'fight fight fight' to stunned silence coz I was only foor foot and about six stone but no one ever touched me or my mate again after that and the bully never bullied again, not around me anyway ha ha! My non drug using friend was necessary because his mum worked with my mum and the Howard is a massive school that is spread about a bit. Well, from one day to the next I never saw what lessons I had or where the lessons were but lucky for me my non drug using friend always had the same lessons so I would follow him like a homing pigeon and this even went on till I was sixteen and we picked the same classes for GCSEs. Obviously he was aware I was always smashed. I picked art, drama and history, all the hippy stuff. I didn't think things were going too bad until one day I went home and mum suggested I have a home tutor, obviously suggested by the school letters. I was fuming to start with but the fella was shit hot. To me this meant I could fuck about more at school dick head that I am. The last couple years at school I was hardly there. Me and the boys used to turn up wearing black Reebok Classics, black Armani jeans and white Ralphy shirts with school tie! We met at the gates only to walk to the shops and ask someone to buy us some bottles of White Lightening and some fags as the speed made me want to smoke. Then we would jump the train, get off once kicked off for having no tickets then go and find some gangs of lads to pick a fight with. We assumed we were representing our school-again, dickheads! I was rapidly spiralling out of control. I was stealing all the booze from my house like whiskey gin and vodka even bottles of wine to drink in the park near our school. I never thought me and my pals were doing anything that outrageous but come on, that's totally fuckin crazy ain't it!? Luckily enough, with hardly any coursework other than art I passed all my GCSEs in well under an hour for each exam-I told you-cool as fuck!

And that, dear reader, is a snapshot of Groggsy! He's a gruff, hard little fella with a good heart. Well loved on the wing.

27th of June 2019. It is 1630hrs and upon returning from the Unit to the wing I, a seasoned vet of such scenes, am shocked at the amount of writ off spiceheads on the landing doing the palsy shuffle with glowing red glassy eyes. I talk to Stevey Lanes and Sam Hodges who I know are doing most of the dealing on here at present:

"What the fuck's going on? Everyone is spasticated on here man"!

"Fuck knows what this shit is I've been given but it's knocking people over left right and centre", says Steve, continuing, turning to Sam, "tell him what we done to Jonesy earlier Sam".

"Ahhh you shoulda seen it Sloaney", says Sam, eyes alight with mischief, "Jonesy was begging us for some spice so we took him in a cell and told him we'd give him some but only if he smoked the whole lot in one go straight away in front of us", then Steve takes up the thread:

"So I ripped him off a fuckin' great strip and he roared it on the pipe in one go".

"He held it for a second", chips in Sam.

"He did", continues Steve, "but then he slowly starts wobbling and then pukes the biggest pile of puke you've ever seen", and here Sam comes in again:

"Then the next thing you know he's fuckin' proper screaming, screaming as if he's being murdered but trying to brush his skin as if there were things all over him".

"And all the time me and Sam were crying in stitches of laughter", says Steve.

"You rotten bastards", I say, smiling, "he's alright now though ain't he"?

"Yeah", says Steve, "we waited like fifteen minutes 'till he stopped screaming then locked the cunt in the cell to keep him out of sight of the screws". And this, dear reader, is my environment. However, if God continues to smile upon me this should cease to be the case on July tenth

470

which is but a hair's breadth away. Martyn has just come into the cell now and I say:

"Have you seen the state of the wing? Everyone is absolutely spangled"!

"In it"! he says, "almost everyone who came to the servery collecting their meals looked proper writ off, must be some strong shit. Oh", says Mart, "do you know if Stevey Lanes got his tobacco or not"?

"Yeah", I say, "he told me soon as they let us out again at half five he's gonna come see us".

"He's got a quarter ounce for me", says Mart.

"Sweet", I say, "so we can sit and watch Insidious tonight chugging on fat roll ups boy"!

28-06-2019. 1400hrs. Friday. On the circuit this morning I, out of the ten participants, was four exercises ahead of my nearest competitor. I think I enlightened you to the rigours of the dirty dozen a while back. If not, and besides the narrative can match the repetitive nature of prison, then here it is again: we start with five laps of the massive sports hall to warm up. Then to our individual stations-a mat and bar weighted with 20kg where we are to do our exercises. In between each set of twelve reps we do a lap before returning to our station for the next exercise. Inclusive in the dozen exercises are power cleans, curls, press from chest, press behind neck, bent over row, squats, upright rows all with the bar then squat thrusts, press ups, sit ups, dorsal raises and finally burpees. I went through the list three times and Simon, a cage fighting psychopath was four exercises behind me. I'm a fuckin' machine at present. Anyway, door's just opened. Actually, I just shot out and got my canteen. As I passed the office I see Ms H up on the desk doing something to the roll boards and go in and tell her:

"My God Ms, you look absolutely bangin' up there like that".

"Fuck me Sloaney, what's happening to you lately"?

"Sorry Ms", I say, already regretting my outburst, feeling sheepish and immature and not a little silly, "I told you that the closer I get to release the less the filter between brain and mouth is effective".

"You're cool Sloaney, I don't mind and I don't mind a compliment to be honest", says the worthy lady. And now as I sit here with Absolute 90s banging out the tunes with the cell door open I look up and see Ms Slane's banging pert bum and realize how very pesty I am feeling. It's definitely breeding season for all I can think about is fucking! I'm right now making a mental note to try draw my thinking away from the more base urges. Outside the cell door people are running back and forth as debts are paid and drugs are accrued and the activity makes for a noisy landing. Dealers are literally running around with pen and paper collecting debts. Literally. I again feel gratitude that I am no longer involved in this activity. Not long ago I myself was in debt up to my eyeballs and in fact I never paid half of what I owed for once I got clean I no longer wanted the drugs I owed these people so paying them became less of a priority; unethical perhaps but, hey, these are dealers we are talking about here. The look on the faces of people running about can only be described as intent. Jake Harvey comes into my cell now.

"How long you got left now Sloaney"?

"Eleven days and a breakfast bro".

"Good on ya man", and he goes along his way. Now I am sitting outside the cell door at the dining table and Groggsy is next to me and Lenny who the other day told martyn he'd had an erotic dream about him and who is '20% gay' walks past and young four foot nothing but very bright Elliot is jabbing him playfully and Groggsy says to Lenny:

"Hit him back Lenny, go on, don't have it bro", but we all know it's only playful. I turn to the left and still Ms H is on a chair doing the boards in the office, sticking out her pert butt and unconsciously driving all us sex starved cons radio rental. In the cell behind the office in the doorway I briefly catch a glimpse of J.T and his cellmate Stuart doing the palsy shuffle, absolutely wankered.

"Fuck me Staurt", I say and both of them grin like Cheshire cats. Gibbo now appears before me:

"You going volleyball Sloaney"?

"Yeah mate, defo", I say.

1645hrs. Bang up. Went to volleyball and played the same team as last week. So, on my side was Kempy, me of course, Gibbo and Kirk. Now Kirk, the cunt, was spastically spangled on spice the soppy cunt and really did manage to truly infuriate the fuck out of us other three.

"For fuck sake Kirk man",I would say as Kirk served the ball like a fuckin' Zombie. Then he'd miss an easy shot and I'd go:

"For fuck sake Kirk, you're a true fuckin' retard ya know that"? and Kirk would mumble some muggy apology through lips wet with spittle, turning bright bloodshot eyes upon me:

"Shloaney man I'm shorry bro pleashe bro".

"What's the point in coming down"? Gibbo said at one point but Kirk's debilitated lacklustre demeanor depressed Gibbo so much he too started sulking which left just me and Kempster with any real gusto and energy on our side. Kev, Alan and Ryan, the gym staff found the whole sorry fiasco hilarious and I confess myself to a mirthful moment or ten observing the sight of Kirk attempting to play. Anyway, Radio 1Xtra are now playing bangers and Martyn and I are bopping along to the beats as Skepta raps sick shit through the speakers. With the closing of the door comes a lowering of my libido for I haven't got the lovely ladies engaging me in conversation; and they do as I'm not such a bad bloke after all but they don't know the depth of the effect their lovely scent, heady perfume and pretty faces have upon me. Just prior to bang up I was on the yard sunning myself with Ms H plotted up beside me talking on politics between the staff in the prison. I dare say if she could see the images flashing across my frontal lobe between my 'yeahs'? and 'oh, whys'? and delibaretly nonchalant responses she'd be shocked! In my mind she sits chatting beside me in pristine white underwear and her voluminous lustrous raven black hair is loose and flowing over her shoulders. Anyway. Martyn got another quarter ounce of tobacco yesterday and is now rolling a fat fag each for us. Love.

Burn smoked. When I'm not able to get myself a smoke I'm constantly sucking on nicotine mints to alleviate any withdrawel symptoms and moodiness stemming from such. It could be a whole lot worse; I could be clucking, climbing the walls in heroin or other opioid/opiate withdrawel. Truly I don't feel like I could do it again, I really don't. I may have another use up in me but I'm not sure I've another recovery. As I sit here now, banged up with the sunlight gloriously winking through the window, watching dust eddies playfully whipping this way and that in the barely perceptible breeze blowing through the grill I pray this is the last time my freedom is forfeit. I must not get carried away by the oncoming of the real world and would do well to remember that recovery is not a destination but a journey and I must be grateful for every grace given day. If I start getting ideas I'm fixed and don't need to practice the NA principles and work a programme I'll soon be fucked and robbing and stealing and hurting people once more for to use is for me to invite insanity into my life. In active addiction I become a monster and all my core values and morals go out the window. I would never under any other circumstances burgle, rob at knifepoint, hurt my family, assault partners or beg on the streets from a cardboard box. Complacency is the enemy of the addict in recovery. Anyway, Catherine, my brilliant Forward Trust drug worker came to see me to tell me I have a telephone interview with the place in London that I am hoping to go to. I live in hope.

29-06-2019. 1700hrs. Martyn is listening to the same song on the same CD over and over again and though this irks me somewhat I am learning to not let loose with my tongue on the poor young lovely fucker.

473

We were let out the cell with the rest of the wing at 1400hrs and immediately I got out onto the yard in thirty degree heat. I've really caught the sun out there today and that's with but an hour in the morning and an hour this afternoon for at 1500hrs me and the Kemps flew down the gym where we worked our chests and abdominals. We did light weights with high reps, fifteens and twenties which has caused a rip in my muscles I can feel already. When I got back to the wing Ms H stopped me:

"Wait Sloaney, I wanna talk to you".

"Go for it", I say.

"Did you see the alarm bell earlier or had you gone off the wing"?

"I didn't hear it Ms, I must have been down the gym; why, what happened"?

"You know that geezer, (yes, Ms H talks this way) Ross, in the cell at the end of the landing on the ones opposite Steve Bennett"?

"Yeah, the fella who tied a rope round his neck and pressed the alarm bell (this isn't the young guy who had a serious go the other day) so you'd all find him 'trying' to hang himself", I say.

"Yeah, well, he's obviously on Basic Regime but somehow he's got out, an officer accidentally let him out for association when as you know on Basic he should be behind the door right"?

"Ok, go on".

"Anyway, so Ms Slane clocks him on the yard and tells him he's got to bang up but he ain't having none of it".

"Ms H, it does beg the question though; what idiot let him out? I guess you're gonna tell me there's been trouble"?

"Yeah, well", continues Ms H, "he starts proper kicking off on the yard saying 'fuck you I ain't banging up' so Mr Mads pressed the alarm bell 'cause he was proper going for it and getting like well aggressive and that and all the staff that flew on the wing, like about twenty of 'em, wouldn't go near him but, well, Ms Slane, my God Sloaney"!

"What did she do"? I ask.

"Fuck me right, she proper like launched herself at him and he was going sick, threatening to smash screws up but she just went for it, threw him to the ground making all the big blokes look stupid; I must admit, I was well impressed".

"She's a fuckin' legend ain't she"? I say, "she actually don't give a fuck. You know what that Ross will do now though don't ya"?

"No" says Ms, "what"?

"Well, he'll start doing those stupid scratches on his arm with a razor blade or once again he'll wrap a sheet round his neck and press the bell the twat so you can all see him 'trying' (and I do air inverted commas) to hang himself". No one truly trying to end their life would alert someone to the fact via the cell bell. I mean, my father took his own life and kept the preperations and the act itself very secret. Serious suiciders will not wish to be disturbed. However, saying that I do know these types can go on to have a serious go at it and I need to take away my own angst at the drain on resources these people are and not think about my suffering (like more bang up when they are being dealt with) and recognise the geezer is disturbed and extremely unhappy. There are many on these landings would be better served in hospitals but there isn't the provision to see to it they get proper psychiatric care and that is very, very sad. Anyway, Martyn has thankfully turned off the repetitive CD which I've heard like a trillion times and Radio One are blaring bangers, house anthems. Tonight at 9pm we have a treat in the form of the film Anchorman 2. I haven't seen the fist one but know that anything with Will Ferrell is going to be good. I've nothing really to report of any note. I mean, as usual there's the threats, punches about the prison, bells, spice zombies palsy shuffling, people pounding boxing pads showing off pugilistic skills on the yard in much the same way a peacock shows off its feathers. There's the normal conversations on crime and anecdotes of prison life, talk of crack houses and whores and smashing back doors in etc. All very boring to me I must say. Peace out.

30-06-2019. 1430hrs. Banged up at present this Sunday afternoon but waiting with baited breath for the door to open at three where I'll meet the Kempster and head down the gym. Sitting on the yard this morning with Kemps and he said as we sat sunning ourselves:

"Who the fuck am I gonna talk to when you're gone Sloaney? Can't believe you're leaving me with all these morons man it's hard enough as it is".

"Fuck me Steve, you ain't fuckin' far behind me are ya to be fair, what is it, October"?

"Yeah man, still, it's four months off mate".

"Less than that by my maths mate and it honestly seems like yesterday I was saying I had a few months left bro; it'll fly by as you well know Steve".

"I even miss Marcus", says Just For Men, "never thought I'd be saying that about that reprobate. And Bradders, and even that moody cunt Peter to be fair"!

"I know right! Never though I'd feel that way either. But I feel like I got close to Pete again after so many years apart. And Brad. And you and Marcus as well".

"And Tony Giles and Rick Lanes", says Kemps.

"It's been good to get to know Ricky's lad Steve too. And his cellmate Sam: he's one funny cunt that fucker", I say.

"Yeah", says Kemps, sucking at his vape, "I like Sam man. Mad though in it? All these youngsters from our manor we've never met before".

"Old cunts now Steve bro. Shows our age".

"Don't feel old though", says Steve, "still going strong".

"I have to admit that last time I was flat out in Oxford I felt fuckin' old at times Steve. Especially during those times I was struggling to get the drugs to anaesthetise myself with. The old aches and pains which were bearable when young became anything but man. Honestly Steve, I don't think I'd be long for this world if I went back at it".

"That's why I'm finding it so hard to get off this last bit of methadone Sloaney. It ain't easy to go through that like it was when we were kids. And the fuckin' sleeping bit man, that's the pits bro", says Just For Men.

"And the limb thing, ya know, that thing where you can't lay still, like that horrible restless leg and arm shit where ya just wanna cut the cunts off".

"I fuckin' hate that man. And like even though you feel absolutely drained you can't rest one bit. I swear I was once awake for three weeks with literally not a wink", says Steve.

"I know, and when you tell people that who have never been through it they don't believe ya"!

"How the fuck did you do it"? says Steve.

"I dunno Steve to be fair. I don't know why I keep fighting. But it was shit mate. I was literally in psychosis with the not sleeping thing. Banging up every day knowing I'd be staring at the walls, sweating but freezing cold was savage. It's been some journey and I just hope to God I never have to do it again". Anyway people, Martyn's just got up from a snooze. He must intuitively know the door's about to be bust for the gym. Mart has been training with Stevey Lanes of late for he, like many others, can't quite keep up at the frenetic rate me and Kempy train at. Anyway, Bethan Ledley is playing bangers on 4Music. Cleaners are outside the cell door mopping the landings. Cell bells can be heard going off intermittently. And in about five minutes the door will open for gym as I say. Ten days time the door will open for me and I will not be returning to the cell. Roll on July tenth.

1645hrs. I'm back. Kempster never made it to the gym as he chose to smoke heroin instead. Upon returning I of course took the piss.

"Oh, got some smack instead bro? Winning Kempy, what a touch".

"Well, you're going home soon anyway ya cunt".

"What the fuck's that got to do with anything bro"?

"Look, I feel bad enough as it is. Least I told you the truth".

"You've got to start thinking seriously about change Steve. I know better than to lecture but something has to give, I'm just saying". Anyway, Groggsy has peened some more for you dear reader so let's have a little look see. Take it away Groggsy:

After I left school things started going downhill fast and it turned out that it was only me and my constantly smashed pals that couldn't see it. Please understand that though I was and am a very mixed up fella at 15 to 16 I wasn't as streetwise as I thought and hoped which I suppose was to do with the fact that I was into judo in a big way from 6 years old until I was 16 and from a 12 year old somethimes training three or four times a week travelling for hours to Kent training schools and other clubs that wanted me there to fight in their team competitions and shit like that. As you can probably understand this wore very, very thin with my dad continually pushing, always angry. We were being sent faxes, telephone calls and letters all wanting me to fight here, show up there and there was even talk of me fighting in the national team and fucking Olympics once I put on weight and grew. Shit man, all this when my pals were getting high, out with girls and partying. Well, my teenage hormones made the decision for me. I was done with the judo. Dad went sick but fuck him. So, if you do the maths I already only knew the judo stuff for ten years solid then at 16 I was gone out the door staying with pals most of which were ten years older than me even the girls coz girls my age used to do my head in as did the boys. With no involvement from my parents my addict brain took over my life so fast that by the time I stopped for breath I was drinking anything with over 5% alcohol and consuming anything that was illegal including a daily quantity of heroin and I was only going home when I knew no one was there around once a month sometimes seeing mum to let her know I was alive. Just writing this has made me feel so sad coz all them times I dismissed my mums' concerns as being old and miserable moaning. Now I know that mums are always right. I wish I had listened to the many warnings. But why was I never pushed in the direction of help? Anyway, once the diet of smack and crack had taken hold as it does all the other drugs that I assumed were fun became dull and boring, probably pre planned by pals as they were already heavy drug users. Our days became full and busy with the chores of funding and supporting and finding this new nightmare. Shoplifting through the day and drumming (burgling) throught the night. Strangely I enjoyed all this. Sixteen, maybe a bit older I was surrounded by all the new cool as fuck lot. Drug dealers, hard nuts and pots of money-most of the time. But

I hadn't yet experienced properly the perils of a smack drought or a bad cluck but that seems to be normal at the beginning because people don't mind sharing when they see you up and coming through the ranks of addiction. Well, that's how my life started. If you add to all that several prison sentences, the deaths through drugs of about fifty friends, the death of my first born daughter and her mum losing several places of residence you'll get why I'm writing this in a jail cell. Today though there's one huge difference. I have been banged up for nearly two years. I have stopped taking the drugs and am filled with a new confidence that I can now live a meaningful life and contribute to the community that I have helped tear apart. Yes it will be hard as I have been an addict for half my life but I'm very willing to try and with the right help from the right people I will conquer my addiction and live a happy fulfilling life. Chase some dreams that I haven't been able to chase. Peace out. Groggsy.

1-07-2019. Home this month. Boom! Anyway, last night the fella in the 'safe cell' I spoke of earlier in the narrative, or 'suicide cell', on constant 24hr watch decided, at three in the morning, to start screaming and shouting, waking the whole wing with his antics.

"Help, help, fuckin' heeelllllllpppp me", etc etc. Screaming that people were coming to kill him. This was followed by banging and crashing as he put paid to anything not screwed down. This morning after I'd prayed and washed I shot up to see him, fella I've spoken of before, named Patmore.

"Patmore", I said, "look mate, I know you're going through a hard time at present but please have some consideration for the rest of us on the wing will ya"? Now, dear reader, he was sitting on his bed with a plastic prison bowl sat on his head and he looked at me with wild eyes:

"Why the fuck do you think I'm sitting here with a bowl on my head"? he asks me looking very deranged.

"Why"? I say.

"'Cause I'm stopping the transmissions. They've implanted chips in my head bro. They think I'm fuckin' stupid, they're trying to fuckin' kill me and reading my thoughts the cunts". Dear reader, he is very sick indeed and this is a direct result of smoking spice. How very very sad I'll think you'll agree.

1210hrs. Just returned to the wing and as soon as I do I traipse to the safe cell to see if Mr Patmore, the poor cunt, is ok, only to discover the safe cell empty. Fuck knows where they've taken the lad; possibly a secure hospital, who knows? Selfishly though I do think to myself 'thank fuck for that' because we'll all be able to sleep tonight but I can't help but feel true pity for the demented, deranged and tormented fucker. He's only small, slight and now very bald as he shaved all his hair off to rid himself of any thought reading devices hidden in his hair. To say he has lost the plot is euphemism indeed; he's possibly fucked for life. And all this through spice. The spice, as me and Kempy discussed with Pony Piles (Tony Giles) earlier is just as powerful as any double dipped LSD tab and, just like LSD can land users in mental institutions for the rest of their natural lives. Coming from me, a seasoned vet of most if not all mind altering substances, the fact that I myself respect spice and fear it more than any other should warn you well away from it. At least heroin, in overdose, will only kill you. Spice, as a powerful hallucinogen can torment you with terror for years after the last dose so potent are its effects on the human psyche. As well as causing vivid hullucinations and visits to the spirit realm it also exacerbates any deep rooted fears and insecurities you may have, bringing them very much to life. Deep rooted things like, for me, the fear I may die in jail used to come on me hard at times. As did my secret terror of spectres and demons in the dark. As you know, in the end, I found some enjoyment, some twisted fun being gleaned from such but make no mistake I truly, at a cellular level, thought, no, knew I was going to die at times. Luckily enough, my previous experience with other drugs of this nature cushioned my shock somewhat and I'm away relatively unscathed but some of the experiences will stay with me for life, as will some of my trips on acid from when I was but a boy. But nonetheless I could well of found myself, like Patmore, in a very precarious predicament with my sanity on a thin thread indeed. It could easily have happened, experience or not. Be wary before partaking of such poison people, heed me I beg you. If you must have a go, curiosity killing the cat and all that, then don't be a big man and go at it hard first time. Take a tentative puff and put the thing down. One puff. If you don't heed me you'll regret it believe me. And never, ever have a bong of this gear before you've come to know this stuff. It could well kill you. I have seen big arse grown men screaming in terror, taken from the wings, never to be seen again. Your call.

1745. We're out 'till 7pm. The sun is hidden behind an ominous looking grey sky portending rain but as of yet no water falls so I'm on the yard on a blanket writing for you. Martyn just skipped out excitedly to tell me that 'Brows' the sexy screwess is on the landing the horny little fucker. Kempy has just plotted up next to me.

"Look at me Steve", I say and when he does I immediately clock his tiny pupils.

"How the fuck are you able to afford smoking smack every day Kempster"?

"Been getting treated for a couple of days", he says languidly, "I couldn't afford to pay for it". We are watching people walking round and round the yard as the sun briefly makes an appearance, the day pulling on a golden gown.

"Look at that Charlie's T-shirt", Kemps says now, "it's that new label called 'Trapstar'".

"Thinks he's a proper trapper (drug dealer) don't he"? I say.

"Can you imagine that cunt coming to serve you up? Have to rob the poor cunt wouldn't ya"? and I laugh at the truth of this.

"Ya fuckin' know that don't ya Steve. The only thing I'd be thinking if that cunt came to sell me drugs is 'bingo'"!

"I'd have a serrated bread knife straight to his throat the poor soppy wet cunt", says Kemps.

"Yep", I say, "he'd a defo seen the business end of my samurai sword to be fair".

"He is actually in for shotting", says Steve. Now young Sam Hodges plots up next to us and says, upon hearing what we're talking of:

"You'd feel sorry for the poor cunt though wouldn't ya? He actually looks like a girl with those silly pony tails either side of his head". Now Sam starts a conversation about robbing cash machines:

"I'm telling ya", he says, "that shop at the bottom of Millmead, TNS, and The Wheatsheaf pub, they're asking for it. You could literally just pop the doors on the Wheatsheaf, like the patio doors piece of piss, amd take the cash machine. They hold ten, fifteen grand and there are lots of fruit machines too with five hundred pound jackpots".

"Yeah", says Stevey Lanes who's also joined us now, "me and Sam have been talking about this for weeks. And the good thing is that if you did get nicked for it it's only commercial burglary so worst ways it's only a couple years tops".

"It's so fuckin' easy", says Kempy and now Sam says:

"It's only commercial burglary if you don't have to rip them out the floor. If you do have to it counts as a ram raid".

"What", says Kemps, "even if you don't smash a car into the gaff? It doesn't, it's still only theft".

"Ramsgate train station has two cash machines", says Stevey Lanes now, "they could be taken piece of piss too. Not even in the wall, just like those silly little shop ones. Even when the station is empty it's possible to do it, when the doors are open. But even when the doors are locked it'd be a piece of piss to break 'em open". Charlie has sat down now. He's only a kid and I think he was being bullied on the wing he was on before and even though I would rob him if he were selling drugs to me I try to be kind to him and watch out for him on here because, of course, like every other wing there are bullies on here too always looking for victims. Now Steve and Kempy are discussing 'Stoneshoe', a new fella fresh on the wing who walks with the black gangster bowl, you know, the one sided shuffle that looks quite cool on some guys but not on this geezer.

"What a clown", says Stevey L.

"I know", says Kemps, "he's like a big fuckin' stupid kid man".

"Oh come on lads", I say, "he is a knob but he's probably just scared chaps. He's only young and likely been around black culture all his life". Around us some lads are playing catch with a tennis ball pillaged from fuck knows where. Hep C boy, Yellow Paul comes out and kindly gives me a Golden Virginia roll up for later on bless him. He has the same hue as Homer Simpson. Now Stoneshoe comes out and asks Stevey Lanes for spice but Sam tells him:

"You already owe us £30 ya cunt. Come see us when you've cleared ya debt".

"I'm getting sick of the old man now", says Stevey L, talking of his dad, Ricky, "all I do is sort the cunt out and he's so fuckin' ungrateful".

"I lent him a box of vapes last week to get him out of trouble", says Sam, "we're always helping him". Now Gibbo comes out and creeps up behind Stevey L who's lying front down on the duvet I brought out and pulls his cock out and actually places it on Stevey L's head and we all burst out laughing. Stevey goes:

"Get off me you dirty cunt; you're sick Gibbo man", but he too finds it funny. Gibbo is now reuptaking the discussion on robbing drug dealers saying:

"Don't think you won't get nicked for robbing drug dealers 'cause I got ten years for robbing one with a crossbow".

"I know", says Stevey Lanes "I know people who've been put away for holding dealers up".

"I'd never rob a dealer again", says Gibbo, "too fuckin' dangerous man".

"Do you know what I see when I look in your eyes Gibbo"? I say now.

"No, what".

"Absolute insanity ya mental cunt", and he laughs at this along with the rest of us. Kempster and Stevey L shoot into the wing followed by Stoneshoe and young Charlie. Time has fuckin' flown. Ms Slane comes out and says:

"Fifteen minutes lads if you want to get showers", and I pick myself up, say my goodbyes and head in for a much needed shower. Love.

02-07-2019. 0800hrs. Martyn has a stinking cold fucking him up for two days now whilst I myself seem to've swerved the nasty virus. My sleep these last couple days has been blissful. I even slept, truth be told, through most of the Patmore stuff the other day. The sun is shining this morning and I feel light, hopeful, happy. I have the telephone interview with the place in London today at 1030hrs so wish me luck if you like me, if not, well, fuck you really. The Lionesses are playing America in the World Cup tonight and I am hoping we beat them if only to stuff it up the arse of Meghan Rapinoe the sportsperson stroke activist who probably wants to be called gender neutral. I bet she's a carpet munching man hating gender fluidity promoting whinger of the highest magnitude. Not that I dislike lesbians. I'm one myself. I just can't stand man hating whiners. In Wimbeldon Serena Williams has been knocked out by a fifteen year old. Apart from that I've nothing juicy to report. I miss my mum every day. People keep coming in the cell for milk, sugar etc and I try to be kind and patient and it helps when I remember I too used to spend every penny on drugs and ponce necessities off others who didn't. There for the grace of God go I.

1930hrs. Dear reader, I bagged the place in London and so happy was my drug worker Catherine that I saw her shed a tear of joy at the prospect of me going somewhere which could be the start of a better life, away from drugs and crime and pain and fear and misery. Bless her.

03-06-2019. 0812hrs. Just to briefly regale the tale of a dream I had last night. So, in my dream, I was living in this community of people in days of yore for the place was like a hamlet described in Flora Thompson's Lark Rise To Candleford. We had come under attack from some sort of dark force that lived, unseen, in the forest. Whilst out doing chores, two men had been killed by boulders that came from the forest at ferocious velocity and the other occupants, struck with grave terror, tasked me, as their leader, to lead them from the Hamlet to a place of safety, away from the malevolence which threatened our previously idyllic little part of England. So, I led them out, losing two more men on the way but insuring the safe arrival of everyone else including of course all the women and children. Then some sort of message comes to me telling me that for some reason I must return to the hamlet on urgent business and I have to go back through these dark woods alone where, along the way, I dodge massive missiles which manifest from nowhere from the treetops. I feel grave terror but continue bravely and make it back. When indoors my front door suddenly bursts open and the dark force stands before me. And the personification of this is a friend of mine from real life who was in the forces and we simply hugged. Then I woke and wrote for you. What it means I do not know.

0915hrs. So I am now sitting at work. After yesterday's news I still find myself floating on a pink fluffy cloud. I feel incredibly grounded, grateful and very very lucky. Lucy is in today looking lovely as usual; yesterday she had to go for a training day at HMP Pentonville which she tells me she enjoyed. Jason is, as he did with Mr McCauley yesterday, interviewing new, prospective facilitators to fill the position which would bring the staff team to capacity needed to be able to meet targets; I.E run as many courses as the powers that be stipulate should be running each year in the prison. Resolve and Thinking Skills Programme that is. As I've said before, Resolve is for violent offenders and TSP for all else. Marcus came to the gate to the Unit earlier.

"Sloaney, what you up to? I spoke to Tan on the mobile last night". Marcus has acquired another illicit phone.

"Oh", I say, "what did she have to say"?

"She told me her little chihuahua got attacked by a fuck off great seagull down the beach. We just shot the breeze really".

"What else did ya talk about"?

"Well", he says, "it was all going well 'till I mentioned your name".

"What'd'ya mean"?

"Well, I said, like, Andy's going to London but he said he'll come and see you once he's settled in and that and as soon as, like, I said your name she just clammed up. I think you've upset her man".

"Ahhh man. Bless her. I do fuckin' care about her. There's no two ways about that. What else did you talk about"?

"Not much really. She said she's been working seven days a week and is a bit run down. I think she's really hurt you're not goin' home to her".

"I feel bad as it is Marcus I do but if I go back to Thanet I'd be no good to man or beast. Please tell her I do care about her. No, tell her I love her 'cause I do. I just have to be selfish right now 'cause if I'm not I'll end up right back where I came from. The thought of the deadbeat streets of Thanet fills me with dread. Same deadbeat people, same boarded up High Streets. Same idiots driving around thinking like they're Pablo fuckin' Escobar with a kiss me quick hat and a stick of rock selling shit drugs. I'd rather open my fuckin' viens than go back there man. The place is a breeding ground for Benefits Britain and the Jeremy Kyle show Marcus".

"Fuck me Sloaney, you make it sound awful. It ain't that bad".

"Fuckin' is to me mate. I can, like, sense mood and atmosphere and there I can feel the depression, the hopelessness. If I went back there I'd be self medicating, back on the drugs in no time I know it".

"No", says Marcus, looking thoughtful, "it is a fuckin' shithole. I don't blame you for wanting to get away ya know. I've got less than five months left and I'm already starting to worry about where I'm gonna go when I get out. Love you Sloaney man", and my friend is gone.

1730hrs. We'll be let out to bask in the sun in a minute. After lunch earlier on I had to go to the resettlement centre for an interview with a very pretty probation officer named Bethany. She wore one of those criss cross tops which exposed her copious bra and breasts each time she leaned forwards. I feel like throughout the whole half hour I gazed out the window so as to not get lost or caught looking at the glorious globules of flesh. I only looked at her when I saw in the periphery of my vision that she'd raised her head from the paperwork so acutely anxious am I not to appear an uncouth barbarian. I could of got lost in her baby blues, let alone that chest!

1930hrs. I laid in the glorious sun for an hour and a half. Kempy lay beside me the handsome Greek looking golden prick. Tonight we were talking about body parts we feel insecure about.

"If you could change a part of your body Kempy, what would it be"?

"Well, I think I'm quite handsome but my nose is a bit big, so yeah. I'm happy enough with it though. Oh, and I'd sort my hair out 'cause it's proper greying now".

"I'd sort my feet", I say, and Kempy laughs to the point of crying, "what's so funny ya cunt"?

"I'm just remembering the size of the bunion you showed me".

"You horrible cunt", I laugh, "they ain't that bad".

"They ain't that fuckin' good though are they"? says the languid prick before lazily pulling on his vape, "anyway", he continues, "please show me 'em again Sloaney".

"Fuck off, what, so you can take the piss ya cunt"?

"I won't, honestly Sloaney, I won't, honest, please, just show me again. I'm interested. Honest. Do they hurt"?

"They're proper fuckin' painful in the winter Kempy man. And if I bang 'em on something it's excruciating".

"Show me again man, I promise I won't laugh". I take off my shoe then peel off a sock and hold up the worst of the pair for perusal. No sooner has the cunt laid eyes on it he's pointing going:

484

"What the fuck"? and laughing so much there are literally tears falling down his face.

"What Steve you horrible cunt"? I say, but he just laughs harder before saying, "you could get a job at the circus ya cunt with them, ya know, in a cage next to the bearded lady or the elephant man or something", and I can't help but laugh myself.

"You're savage ya cunt", I tell him but he's in bits, in hysterics at his own humour.

"I'm just imagining what sort of reaction you'd get at the circus like when you reveal 'em an' that".

"Same reaction I get from you ya prick", and this makes him laugh all the more.

"Stop it man I'm crying. Sheeit man, wow, Sloaney, ya wanna get them sorted bruv", and he's wiping water from his face. I put my sock and shoe on and lay down. Kempster keeps chuckling intermittently mumbling stuff like 'shit man' and 'wow' the prick but I laugh with him. In all fairness, my bunions are bloody big and clown like. Anyway, I'm 168 days clean today.

06-07-2019. Dear reader, remember my mate who I used to get my spice off, Phil The Face? Well, he was released maybe three months ago but lo and behold, upon exiting the wing today I hear a shout from 'E' wing, Echo wing and I recognise his voice immediately. I go to the window of his cell, old stlye with no grill.

"Sloaney man, look at you, you look well big man"!

"The fuck you doing back Phil? You've lost loads of weight man".

"Thanks man, fuckin' hell, I hit the crack and smack hard didn't I. They've given me a full recall".

"How long you got to serve then"?

"Another eighteen months man".

"Fuck me Phil", I go, not knowing what else to say.

"Fuckin' gutted Sloaney man".

"Mate, I'm gutted for you. Look, I've got to go but we'll talk before I leave man".

"See ya soon bro", he says and I feel so sad for him. Not a bad one to be fair. As I walk to the gym I think to myself that that cannot be me! Anyway, last thing to tell today. Last night I dreampt I was on the Old Kent Road in London. At the end of the big, wide and dark street was a massive, massive pile of human skulls. Thousands of them. Fuck knows what it portends. My path is set regardless. But I found the dream ominous to say the least.

07-07-2019. 0935hrs. Last night I dreamed again. In this dream I'd been released from jail and had moved into a property with my old friend Pete Lanes. In my dream he had relapsed for the first time and he gave me the pipe which I put to my lips, the crack pipe, but didn't smoke, instead giving it back to him saying 'no thanks mate'. Weird.

1245hrs. Went to Kempster's cell when the door was opened but found him in deep conversation with Dale who has bandages over his forearms.

"What the fuck"? I say to Dale, "ahhh Dale man, what the fuck ya done now"? Kempy looks upset but Dale flashes his brilliant smile in his handsome face before pulling up one bandage revealing a long line of big arse stitches and I wince:

"For fuck sake", I say.

"I know man, horrible in it"? says Kemps.

"Why Dale? Shit man it ain't funny bro", I say to him.

"I know it ain't. You could actually see the tendons in my arms when I done it. I've been in hospital all night".

"Dale man", I say, "you're so good looking bro. Why keep fuckin' yourself up like this"?

"It's these cunts Sloaney", he says, "they came to me last night and said they're coming in to take my telly because I refused to go for a piss test. I told 'em if they do that I'm gonna hurt myself. They came in proper firm handed and took it so I waited 'till they'd shut the door then ripped a razor blade right up both arms boy", and now he laughs maniacally before saying, "that'll fuckin' learn 'em, that'll show the cunts".

"But Dale", says Kemps, "you're hurting yourself more than anyone else mate. I mean, for fuck sake, they don't care. You're hurting all the people that love you, and your pals, like me and Sloaney".

"He's right Dale", I say honestly, "I feel so fuckin' helpless", and, dear reader, I do. You'll know from the narrative that Dale, at times, drives me mad. But I love the poor psycho nonetheless. He has no true evil in him and is just very, very mixed up. And that makes him dangerous. To himself and, when frustrated and raging, to others too. He needs real help in a safe environment. This place, with the dangerous psychosis inducing drug spice so readily available and Dale willing to sell his prescribed meds, given to level his mental health extremes, is not, ever, going to be conducive to any kind of recovery for Dale. No matter how much the likes of me and Kempy inculcate, beg, plead and support him, here, he is lost. And Dale is but one of the many self harming here in Rochester right now. There are at least ten on here. There was a significant lull a while ago but like the violence here it peaks and troughs. I don't have answers dear reader. But I'll tell you this for nothing, the spice is the biggest driver of violence and self harm and psychotic episodes in prisons across the country at the moment. Elmley was exactly the same. We must get this drug away from what are, essentially, some of the most vulnerable people in our society. There'll undoubtably be those that think we deserve all we get and that we shouldn't come to jail in the first place. Well, remember, no one grows up thinking 'I want to go to jail and be a junkie when I get older' do they? There are some tragic tales within these walls. I myself am very damaged and have been frightened and confused my whole life. It is only now I see hope on the horizon. Hold On Pain Ends. Hope.

08-07-2019. 1000hrs. So, today, tomorrow, gone. I have no work this morning because Jason and Lucy are both, along with Naomi and the new lady Kim, a proper dragon, off today for training. Miss Slane, bless her, let me off the wing anyway so I could have a wander on Freeflow where I bumped into Kirk and Marcus. Kirk got kicked off 'A' wing for smashing his cell up and is now on 'E' wing where he will doubtless do the same and be moved again. Marcus is on 'R' or Ridley wing and has gotten himself into £400 of debt for crack which he can't pay. His business, which he usually runs so well despite his own predilection for drugs has collapsed under the weight of his own greed. Despite this he was upbeat this morning. I've just now returned to the wing where I find Martyn laying on his bed in the dark looking forlorn and I think to myself I should've stayed out in the sun, wandering from one end of the prison to the other. As you can probably imagine dear reader I am getting a little excited but I am also fraught with anxiety to be honest. I mean, I was convinced I would die here not long ago. It seems that recently I have learned the fragility of life.

1210hrs. I'm getting excited and must keep myself grounded. I have a gym session this afternoon gifted by Kev, the gym instructor, who told me just to turn up at the gym gate if I wanted a couple extra gym sessions prior to my release. Pump myself up a little. In other news I really miss my poor mum. God love her. As I say, she loved Lord Jesus and I've no doubt he'll have her safe.

09-07-2019. 1100hrs. Me and Kempy spent two hours in the gym yesterday. We worked chest extensively and intensely for the first hour and spent an hour on the treadmill thereafter. I thoroughly enjoy Kempy's company. Right now I am back at the Unit with Alfie.
"What a journey", I say out loud, to no one in particular.
"Where ya gotta go then boy", asks my illustrious Romany companion.

"Not that sort of journey Alf", I say, "I mean, like, what a journey it's been here. It's been scary, beautiful and enlightening. Didn't start off too good but I'm in a better place than I was when I got here".

"Done it now int ya chavvy. You're out now boy. Finished"!

"I can't fuckin' wait Alf", I say, just as lovely Lucy walks into the room.

"You must be getting excited now", she says musically. God she's a sort!

"I am Luce. Just tryna stay grounded and not get carried away".

"You'll be fine", she says and I think 'God you're a fantastic example of woman'.

"I feel very lucky Lucy to be honest. And grateful", and Jason comes in now. Over the weekend he rode a stage of the Tour De France. Ten gruelling hours in the sadle.

"Was it hard J"? I ask.

"That last climb", he says, "ten kilometres up a mountain after being on the bike for over nine hours. That was the only time I thought 'I can't do this' but I kept going and finished with a reasonably good time".

"Did your mate, the fella who went with you, finish"?

"I didn't think he was gonna do it but he did. He finshed an hour and a half after I did. It was definitely one of the hardest ones I've ever done. It was forty degrees which didn't help".

"Forty degrees"! says Alfie, "cor boy, I bet you were sweating buckets weren't ya"?

"It was pouring off me Alfie", says J. We sit and have a coffee and I bask here, feeling very privileged to've spent these months amongst these wonderful lot. Jason goes out and returns with a lovely fountain pen from the whole team down here. I don't quite know what to say. I am moved to my core and hug it out with all before returning to the wing. What a gorgeous bunch they are.

1210hrs. Just had my last lunch. Banged up now with my little mate Martyn whose nose is covered to alleviate the smell of the super shit I just let loose. This is prison life. On my return to the wing the Amazonian goddess Ms Slane said:

"Sloaney, oh no, I can't believe I'm not gonna see you again, come here", and this great, very brave and very bright young officer actually gives me a squeeze. It makes me once more feel emotional. Despite all its woes, Rochester has much good within its walls and the staff on this wing are brilliant. Full stop. Every one of them. Some morons will say 'all screws are cunts' by sheer point of fact they work in the field but that is ignorant tripe. If you want help and are willing there are, in every jail, good caring decent officers there for those wishing to truly change their ways. They have gone above and beyond for me, both on the landings, at the unit and, oh, also at the gym. And in the services trying to help addicts like me. Give more investment and the problems highlighted in this document can be rectified.

1915hrs. I must sign this off. I have tried my best to give my truth and perception of prison life and I hope you have enjoyed it. I could only have done more had I been in possession of a dictaphone but, alas, this is my experience and it is what it is. Goodbye for now dear reader.

The End.

Epilogue.

21-01-2022. I returned to jail. I relapsed. I assaulted a friend of mine with whom I am still close and who I truly respect and love. Drugs make me a monster. Turn me insane. I was released nine months ago. The last time I used was the day before I was released from jail. I am therefore nine months clean and sober. I am in a good place, with good friends and attend regular NA meetings and work the steps daily to insure I stay clean. I am not hurting anyone, robbing anyone, manipulating or assaulting anyone. But that stuff is one crack pipe away. I pray each day that God keeps me safe and ask Him to let me rebalance my karmic debt by helping others and being of service to the world. I go by grace. Let's love each other. One more thing, I wrote, of course, another manuscript in a 'B' cat jail where I spent ten months. If this is well received I shall type it up for your perusal. Humbly yours.

At the final edit, for this is self published, I am 13 months and 16 days clean, typing this from a beautiful property on a sunny July day in Oxford. Many people I have used with are now dying. I work a programme daily with NA to stay clean and go at my recovery in the same way I did my using. I wish to thank the charity Adapt, and it's CEO Edwina Cobb for giving me the opportunity to return to this wonderful city. If you are a junkie and in need of help, look Adapt up for you need no local connection, will be housed indefinitely and have access to a six month treatment programme for free with highly trained specialists who can start you off on a new journey. I must also thank St Aldates church for the love and welcome they have given me. And finally, I thank God for grace I do not deserve.

Printed in Great Britain
by Amazon

86345917R00281